COMPARATIVE ECONOMICS

Second Edition

JAMES ANGRESANO

John Brandt Professor in Economics
Albertson College of Idaho

PRENTICE HALL, Upper Saddle River, NJ   07458

Library of Congress Cataloging-in-Publication Data

Angresano, James
    Comparative economics / James Angresano. -- 2nd ed.
        p.   cm.
    Includes bibliographical references and index.
    ISBN 0-13-381633-8
    1. Comparative economics.   I. Title.
HB90.A54   1995
330--dc20   95-24833
                                                                CIP

Cover art: John Martin, The Image Bank

Acquisitions editor   *Leah Jewell*
Production manager   *Maureen Wilson*
Buyer   *Marie McNamara*
Marketing manager   *Susan McLaughlin*
Assistant editor   *Teresa Cohan*

© 1996, 1992 by Prentice-Hall, Inc.
A Division of Simon & Schuster
Upper Saddle River, New Jersey 07458

Printed in the United States of America
10   9   8   7   6   5   4   3   2   1

ISBN 0-13-381633-8

Prentice-Hall International (UK) Limited, *London*
Prentice-Hall of Australia Pty. Limited, *Sydney*
Prentice-Hall Canada Inc., *Toronto*
Prentice-Hall Hispanoamericana, S.A., *Mexico*
Prentice-Hall of India Private Limited, *New Delhi*
Prentice-Hall of Japan, Inc., *Tokyo*
Simon & Schuster Asia Pte. Ltd., *Singapore*
Editora Prentice Hall do Brasil, Ltda., *Rio de Janeiro*

For my wife and children,
whose unending love and support
have provided the inspiration for me to prepare this edition of the book.

CONTENTS

PREFACE   **XV**

Section One
Introduction

1 AN INTRODUCTION TO THE STUDY OF COMPARATIVE ECONOMICS   1

Introduction   1

The Evolutionary-Institutional Approach to the Study of Economies   7

Outline of the Book   19

Key Terms and Concepts   21

Questions for Discussion   21

References   22

2 EVALUATING AND COMPARING ECONOMIES   23

Introduction   23

Some Basic Issues   24

Evaluating the Performance of an Economy   27

Comparing Economies: Some Issues   32

Evaluating and Comparing Economies: Examples   32

Concluding Remarks   37
Key Terms and Concepts   37
Questions for Discussion   37
References   38

Section Two
Premodern Economies

3   ANCIENT ROME
50 B.C.–A.D. 150   39

Introduction to the Premodern Economy   39
Rome: 50 B.C.–A.D. 150: Profile of the Empire   41
Historical Legacy and Context   42
Philosophical Basis   43
Social and Political Structures   44
Principal Institutions   46
Behavior of the Economy   49
Institutional Change   58
Performance of the Economy   58
How Rome Illustrates the Evolutionary-Institutional Theory   59
Concluding Remarks   59
Key Terms and Concepts   60
Questions for Discussion   60
References   60

4   THE MEDIEVAL ECONOMY
England, A.D. 1000–1400   62

Medieval England   62
Attitudes Towards Economic Activity and Working Rules
    –Pervasive Church Influence   63
Rigid, Hierarchical Social and Political Structures   66
Medieval Institutions   69
Behavior of the Economy   72
Irregular, Modest Institutional Change   80
The Economy's Performance: Increased Benefits for Relatively Few   82
Medieval England and the Process of Evolutionary-Institutional Development   84
Looking Ahead   85
Key Terms and Concepts   85

Questions for Discussion   85

References   86

Section Three
The Evolution of the Laissez-Faire Market Economy

5   **THE LAISSEZ-FAIRE MARKET ECONOMY**
     Historical Context and Philosophical Basis   **87**

The Mercantile Era: 1500–1750   88

The Enclosure Movement   90

Change in Religious Attitude   91

The Poor Laws   93

The Industrial Revolution   94

The Philosophy of a Market Economy   95

Adam Smith—Model of a Market Economy   96

Thomas Robert Malthus—Population Issue and Reform of the Poor Laws   102

Jean-Baptiste Say—Macroeconomic Stability, Laissez-Faire, and
     Competitive Markets   104

David Ricardo—Free Trade and the Theory of Comparative Advantage   107

Summary   109

Key Terms and Concepts   109

Questions for Discussion   109

References   110

6   **ENGLAND'S LAISSEZ-FAIRE MARKET ECONOMY**
     1830-1870   **111**

Historical Legacy and Context   111

A Laissez-Faire Philosophy   112

Social Class Structure   114

Political Structure: Parliamentary Power   115

Institutions Promoting Laissez-Faire Market Conditions   116

Behavior of the Economy   119

Institutional Change: Expansion of Market Activity and Freer Trade   124

An Unprecedented Performance by the Economy   125

Key Elements Affecting the Evolution of England's LFME Institutions   128

Looking Ahead   128

Key Terms and Concepts   129

Questions for Discussion   129

References   129

Section Four
Command Over a Market Economy

7 COMMAND OVER A MARKET ECONOMY
Germany, 1933-1945   131

Introduction   131

Post-World War I European Recession   132

National Socialist German Workers' Philosophy   135

German Social Classes and Political Ranks   139

CME Institutions   141

Behavior of the Economy   143

The Evolution of Nazi Economic Institutions   147

Performance of the Economy: Rapid Recovery from Depression and
    Wartime Destruction   148

Evolution of the German Economy: The Rise and Fall of Nazi Institutions   151

Looking Ahead   152

Key Terms and Concepts   152

Questions for Discussion   152

References   152

Section Five
Guided Market Economies

8 THE PHILOSOPHICAL BASIS FOR A GUIDED MARKET
ECONOMY   154

Introduction   154

John Maynard Keynes   155

Keynes's Interpretation of Economic History   156

Keynes's Model   159

Keynes's Conclusions and Policy Prescriptions   163

Summary: The Impact of Keynes's Philosophy   164

Key Terms and Concepts   165

Questions for Discussion   165

References   165

9   THE JAPANESE ECONOMY
1946-Present: Historical Legacy and Context, Philosophical Basis,
Social and Political Structures, Principal Institutions   167

Introduction   167

*A Legacy of a Feudal Economy, Isolation, and Active State Intervention in
     Economic Matters   168*

A Pragmatic Philosophy for Reconstructing the Economy   174

Social Uniqueness and Concentrated Political Power   176

Principal Institutions—Many Originating from Japan's Historical Legacy   180

Summary   193

Key Terms and Concepts   194

Questions for Discussion   195

References   195

10   BEHAVIOR OF THE JAPANESE ECONOMY
1946-Present   197

Leadership, Cooperation, and Persuasion in Resource Allocation Decisions   198

Extensive Private Ownership With Tempered State Control Over Resources   201

*Markets, Tradition, and State Guidance As Social Processes for Coordinating
     Economic Activity   204*

Institutional Change Driven By Foreign Authorities and New Technology   212

*Performance of the Economy: Rising from a Poverty Level to Become One of
     the World's Richest Nations   215*

*The Japanese Economy and the Evolutionary-Institutional
     Process of Development   228*

A Final Observation   229

Key Terms and Concepts   229

Questions for Discussion   229

References   230

11   THE FRENCH ECONOMY
1946-Present   233

Introduction   233

A Long History of State Intervention   234

A Philosophy for Guiding Macroeconomic Activity   236

Social and Political Structures: Meritocracy and a Presidential Republic   240

Public Institutions on the National and Supranational Level   243

*Behavior of the Economy: Transformation at the National and
     Supranational Level   245*

Privatization, the European Union, and Reduced Planning: Factors
    Promoting Institutional Change   254
Performance : A Long Period of Favorable Growth, but Unemployment Persists   255
A Summary of the Evolutionary-Institutional Process of Development in France   257
Looking Ahead   259
Key Terms and Concepts   259
Questions for Discussion   259
References   259

Section Six
Social Economies—Democratically Controlled

12 **THE PHILOSOPHICAL BASIS FOR A DEMOCRATICALLY**
    CONTROLLED SOCIAL ECONOMY   261
Introduction   261
The Early Reformers   263
The Fabian Society   270
The Beveridge Report   273
Looking Ahead   276
Key Terms and Concepts   277
Questions for Discussion   277
References   277

13 **THE SWEDISH ECONOMY**
    1932-Present   279
Introduction   280
The Roots of Welfare Reform   280
The Evolution of Social Democratic Philosophy   282
An Egalitarian Society with a Parliamentary Democracy   287
Principal Institutions: Important Role for Organized Labor, Management,
    and Cooperatives   294
An Economy Influenced by Collective Bargaining   297
Institutional Stability Until the 1990s   314
Performance of the Economy: Alleviation of Poverty, But
    New Problems Have Arisen   316
Development of Sweden's Economy as an Illustration of the
    Evolutionary-Institutional Theory   323
Looking Ahead   325

Key Terms and Concepts   325

Questions for Discussion   325

References   326

14   THE EUROPEAN UNION
Fifteen Economies or One, or Will It Be Both?   329

Introduction   330

Historical Legacy: Integration as a Means for Maintaining Peace   331

A Philosophy for Integrating Economies   335

Promoting Social and Political Harmony   339

Supranational Institutions   342

Working Rules and the Behavior of the EU   344

Institutional Change: A Trial-and-Error Process   362

EU Economic Performance: Benefits from Integration   371

Concluding Remarks   376

Appendix: Levels of Economic Integration   377

Key Terms and Concepts   380

Questions for Discussion   380

References   381

Section Seven
Social Economies—State Controlled,
But In the Process of Transforming

15   THE PHILOSOPHICAL BASIS FOR COMMAND OVER A SOCIAL
ECONOMY AND THE SOVIET UNION: 1928-1989   384

Introduction to Chapters 15-18   384

Karl Marx   385

Marx's Conception of Society   387

Marx's Theory of History   388

Marx's Model of Capitalism's Demise   390

Marx's Model of Socialism   394

Marx's Vision of True Communism   396

Concluding Remarks   397

The Soviet Economy: 1928-1989   398

Introduction   398

Historical Legacy and Context: 1917-1928   399

A Marxist-Leninist-Stalinist Philosophy   403

Congruent Social and Political Structures   404

State-Controlled Principal Institutions   407

Communist Party Control of the Economy   409

Modest Institutional Change Until the 1989 Political and
    Economic Revolution   414

Performance of the Economy: Assessment Difficulties Due to
    Politicization of Data   419

The Rise and Fall of a State-Commanded Economy as an Illustration of the
    Evolutionary-Institutional Theory   425

Looking Ahead   426

Key Terms and Concepts   426

Questions for Discussion   426

References   427

16   TRANSFORMATION ISSUES   430

Introduction   430

In the Aftermath of the 1989 Revolutions   431

The Philosophy of the New Ruling Class and Their Western Advisors   439

Emerging Social Classes and Shifting Political Structures   442

Coexistence of Old Institutions with Evolving Institutions   445

The New Economies   447

Rapid, Widespread Institutional Change   463

Performance of the New Economies   464

CEE Transformation and the Evolutionary-Institutional Theory   476

Looking Ahead   477

Key Terms and Concepts   477

Questions for Discussion   477

References   478

17   THE HUNGARIAN ECONOMY SINCE 1946   483

Introduction   483

Historical Legacy: From Soviet Domination to Transformation   484

Development of an Eclectic Philosophical Basis   487

Nonegalitarian Social and Political Structures   490

Transformation of State-Dominated Institutions   494

Behavior of the Economy   496

Evolution of Alternative Institutions   513

Performance of the Hungarian Economy   515

Evolutionary-Institutional Change in the Hungarian Economy   519
Concluding Remarks   521
Key Terms and Concepts   522
Questions for Discussion   523
References   523

18   THE CHINESE ECONOMY SINCE 1976   526

Introduction   526
A History Shaped by Foreign Influence and Maoist Ideology   527
A Pragmatic Philosophy for Development   530
Efforts to Establish an Egalitarian Social Structure While Maintaining
    Centralized Political Power   534
Evolution of Private and Semiprivate Institutions that Coexist
    with State Institutions   537
Behavior of the New "Socialist Market Economy"   539
Institutional Change: Economic Reform without Political Reform   558
Performance: The World's Fastest Growing Economy   560
China's Complex and Unpredictable Development as an Illustration of
    the Evolutionary-Institutional Theory   568
Some Thoughts Regarding China's Future   569
Key Terms and Concepts   569
Questions for Discussion   569
References   570

Section Eight
Summary

**19   SUMMARY AND CONCLUSIONS: LESSONS FROM
AN EVOLUTIONARY-INSTITUTIONAL ANALYSIS
OF ECONOMIES   574**

The Evolutionary-Institutional Nature of Economies Restated   575
Historical Legacy: Learning from the Past to Understand the
    Present Economy and to Avoid Policy Mistakes for the Future   576
Philosophical Basis: The Need to Understand Societal Values and Identify
    the Consensus View   576
Social Structure: A Widening Gap Creates Social and Political Unrest   578
Political Structure: Is Democracy a Prerequisite for Successful Performance
    by an Economy   579

Principal Institutions and their Working Rules   580
Institutional Change: The Outcome of an Evolutionary Process   580
Behavior and Performance of the Economy   581
Concluding Remarks—Transforming an Economy   582
References   584

GLOSSARY OF KEY TERMS AND CONCEPTS   585

INDEX   597

PREFACE TO THE SECOND EDITION

This book is intended to serve as the primary text for comparative economics, world economic history, and European economic development courses, and as a supplemental text for area studies courses. The book's evolutionary-institutional perspective has been developed to provide an analytical framework that explicitly identifies an economy's historical, philosophical, social, political, and economic characteristics and how they interact to establish and modify the economy's principal institutions.

The first edition was published in 1992. At that time the European Community was moving toward full implementation of the working rules for a common market, Central and Eastern Europe were introducing rules designed to rapidly transform their economies, Japan seemingly was destined to become the world's wealthiest economy, and the impact of China's eclectic transformation policies was uncertain. As the second edition is completed in early 1995, we see a different picture for each of these economies, which the evolutionary-institutional theory, upon which the book is based, predicts.

The second edition is consistent with the first in that both examine the evolution of economies over the past two millennia. Representative economies are evaluated according to the type of working rules introduced by society's authorities to resolve production and distribution matters. In each case these rules reflect the philosophical basis of the authorities as well as the historical context within which the rules were introduced. The scope of the book is primarily European, since the philosophical bases and most principal institutions of contemporary economies have roots in Europe. There is, however, considerable coverage devoted to both Japan and China in recognition of their economic power, worldwide influence, and rapid growth and transformation of their respective economies.

All contemporary examples contained in the first edition are included in the new edition, with the evolutionary path of contemporary economies analyzed being updated. It also features an in-depth analysis of transformation issues in Central and Eastern Europe, with an entire chapter devoted to this topic. Lessons to be drawn from early transformation policies are emphasized, including the problems which have ensued from the implementation of orthodox policies that failed to consider the historical legacy of these societies.

The evolutionary-institutional theory is the most distinctive feature the book offers. This theory is novel and gives the book a sound theoretical foundation. The theory is quite useful as an analytical device with which to understand and explain the path of all economies. It emphasizes that economies are fluid, as working rules and principal institutions are constantly subject to modification.

Basing an analysis of economies on this theory shifts the reader away from the "capitalism-socialism" dichotomy of the orthodox approach to comparative economics, which treats economic "systems" in a taxonomic manner (i.e., each type classified according to selected criteria). The orthodox approach places too much emphasis upon theoretical performance of such "systems" and too little upon the unique cultural and historical factors which shape a particular economy. This new edition explains in depth the problems that policies based upon such an approach have introduced in the transforming Central and Eastern European economies.

Another unique feature of the book is the number of topics not generally contained in similar books. These include ancient Rome, medieval England, the European Union, and an analysis of transformation policies. In addition, an entire chapter is devoted to theoretical issues regarding evaluating and comparing economies, along with some examples. The issues of selecting criteria, measuring them, and compiling an index of an economy's performance are analyzed, with emphasis placed upon the potential for an analyst to adopt a subjective approach to evaluation in a particular (ideological) direction.

Finally, chapters devoted to the history of economic thought are provided to identify the theoretical philosophical basis for the broad types of economies included. These chapters provide the reader with an appreciation of the ideological basis that underpins the real-world economies being investigated. The chapters also provide an important bridge to student understanding of economics by reinforcing and elaborating issues of economic thought, thereby allowing students and instructors to make connections between abstract economic theories and their relevance to the actual, concrete economies presented.

Overall, the purpose of the book is to provide a fresh, realistic perspective for anyone interested in studying economies. It should be attractive to those seeking an innovative approach to the study of economies and societies, especially to anyone willing to recognize the contribution of relevant political, social, philosophical, and historical factors to the nature and evolution of economies.

ACKNOWLEDGMENTS

The Center for Post-Soviet and East European Studies, and the libraries of the University of Texas at Austin and Central European University in Prague provided invaluable assistance. I am also very grateful to Jerik Hausner, Chief of Advisors to the Deputy Prime Minister for Economic Affairs—Poland, and Klaus Nielsen from Roskilde University, Denmark, for inviting me to work with them on a European Union funded international research project analyzing the Central and Eastern European transformation. I am also indebted to the following people for their comments and insights: Jan S. Prybyla, Pennsylvania State University; Michael Pisani, Colorado Northwestern Community College; Brent McClintock, Carthage College; and Menakshi N. Dalal, Wayne State University.

My family has been the primary source of inspiration in this and my other research endeavors. My wife, Elizabeth, offered many creative suggestions and constructive criticisms, which improved the quality of the book beyond what I am capable of doing.

As always, the full responsibility for any errors rests with the author.

1

AN INTRODUCTION TO THE STUDY OF COMPARATIVE ECONOMICS

OBJECTIVES

1. Discuss issues involved with reforming a society.
2. Define key terms and concepts, including *institution, economy,* and *philosophical basis.*
3. Specify the focus of the book, namely to study comparative economies from an evolutionary-institutional perspective.
4. Explain the evolutionary-institutional approach to the study of economies, including its five themes, components of its framework, and unique features.

INTRODUCTION

Assume that a revolution has occurred in a foreign nation. The leaders of the victorious forces meet to establish a new society, having become disenchanted with the effects of the previous political regime and economy on the majority of the population. The meeting might proceed as follows.

A list of issues which need to be addressed is presented.

1. What rules are to govern the new society?
2. How will the rulers (authorities) be chosen?
3. Who will make the rules?
4. To what principles or philosophy should rules for political and economic matters be related?

5. How will the physiological needs of the society be met?
6. What should be produced?
7. How much of each particular good or service should be produced?
8. How should resources be combined to produce the desired quantities of goods and services?
9. How will the goods and services produced be distributed among the members of the society?
10. What rights will individuals have concerning acquisition, disposition, and utilization of goods and services?
11. Should the same economic responsibilities and opportunities be available to all persons regardless of their gender, age, creed, or ethnic group, among other characteristics?
12. How should someone who is incapable of performing any productive tasks be treated?
13. Which code of morals and ethics should guide society's behavior?
14. Which religion, if any, should members of society be permitted to practice?
15. Should any holidays be observed? If so, which ones?

These questions have confronted the numerous political parties that developed in Central and Eastern Europe (CEE) since 1989. One hypothetical party, the New Democratic Party (NDP), might have answered some of the questions in the following manner. The nation will be governed by a parliament whose members are elected by popular vote. Any group is free to form a party and nominate candidates to run for a seat in Parliament. Rules will be established according to the will of a majority of Parliament.

The NDP philosophy for developing the economy includes its conception of the current social and economic realities and its vision of the ideal economy in the year 2010. The NDP's conception is that the nation's historical legacy, which included a monopoly over political power by one party, state ownership of natural resources and most means of production, and reliance upon an unworkable centralized scheme to plan nearly all economic activities, led to a poor, stagnant economy relative to those countries which enjoy greater political and economic freedoms. Part of the NDP vision is the realization of a standard of living, which includes a per capita income equivalent to at least $3,000 in 1990 U.S. dollars; higher average life expectancy; lower incidence of crime; no less than 200 square feet of housing space per person for each family; continuous availability of a selected market basket of food costing the typical family no more than 30 percent of its net monthly income; 100 percent literacy for persons over 12 years of age; less than 3 percent unemployment; and an average workweek of 30 hours. In addition, the NDP vision includes a national commitment by which families with above-average incomes would be willing to redistribute some of their income and wealth to less affluent members of the society.

The NDP's next task is more difficult—answering more specific economic questions. Fortunately, there are examples of countries that have experienced economic development from which the NDP can learn: England (1830–1870) relied upon free markets with little government interference (Chapter 6); Japan (post 1946) has both a very competitive economy and a strong guidance role played by public institutions (Chapters 9 and 10); Sweden (post 1932) has combined public guidance of the economy with private ownership and extensive social insurance and welfare schemes (Chapter 13); and China (post 1979) has experienced rapid economic growth without relying on extensive privatization of state-owned enterprises (Chapter 18). While these cases also offer the NDP insight concerning the social, religious, and cultural questions, the NDP would be likelier to draw from its own nation's historical legacy when resolving such matters. For example, if the nation had a long history of Catholicism prior to becoming a communist state (which is the case for Poland), then a greater role for the Catholic Church in social, economic, as well as cultural and religious matters might be proposed.

It may have appeared at first that the questions on the list at the beginning of this chapter could be classified in discrete categories, i.e., political, economic, social, cultural. The NDP example illustrates that economic questions cannot be dealt with separately from the others. Problems inherent in the transformation of an economy are not simply economic, or political, or social. Rather, they are complex combinations of these and other factors—including philosophical, cultural, and historical. The NDP's economic decisions about property rights are guided by the society's code of ethics and are arrived at politically through parliamentary procedure rather than a mandated centralized scheme.

Assume you belong to a committee assigned to draft a proposal for the economy of a Central American nation whose corrupt dictator was deposed by U.S. military forces. A majority of the nation's population is poor, ownership of land is highly skewed, the industrial sector is backward and of modest size, the two major crops produced are bananas and coca leaves, there is a small elite class of very wealthy landowners, and the distribution of land ownership, wealth, and income is highly skewed. How should your committee approach this task?

Before you begin to discuss what the rules for economic behavior should be and how economic decisions will be related to one another in a coherent, coordinated manner, you should recognize the need to define some terms and concepts. These terms are *institution, economy,* and *philosophical basis for an economy.* You propose the following definitions:

> *Institution*[1] Institutions are normative patterns of social organization and behavior. They are normative in the sense that they define modes of

---

[1]Three extensive discussions of institutions are provided by Walter C. Neale, "Institutions," *Journal of Economic Issues,* 21, 3 (September, 1987), 1177–1206; Frederic L. Pryor, *A Guidebook to the Comparative Study of Economic Systems* (Englewood Cliffs, NJ: Prentice-Hall, 1985), pp. 12–50; and Geoffrey M. Hodgson, *Economics and Institutions* (Cambridge, England: Polity Press, 1988), pp. 10, 62–66, 116–144, 267–272.

action or social relationships that society believes are expected and proper in particular situations (e.g., people exchanging gifts at Christmas time). Institutions have a tendency to create patterns of behavior which are durable and routine due to traditions and customs or legal constraints. The patterns of these and other institutions are regularized by common rules. The pattern of behavior will invariably be "shaped by the values of the participants (the beliefs legitimizing such interactions), norms regularizing the interaction [e.g., property laws, customs and class mores, values], sanctions and rewards, and the motives of the individuals involved."[2] Institutions which perform economic functions incorporate methods, organizations, actions, and traditions that coordinate production and distribution decisions. Examples include the Organization of Petroleum Exporting Countries (OPEC) cartel, labor unions, a central bank, a fast-food restaurant, a manufacturer of computers, and the U.S. Social Security Administration.

Institutions can be identified operationally, for they have three characteristics:[3] There are people engaged in activities, the activities are governed by common working rules (see below), and there is a philosophical basis or justification for the actions and rules. The U.S. Defense Department illustrates these characteristics. There are some people involved with gathering and disseminating information and others who formulate a global, strategic plan. Once the plan is approved, rules exist concerning implementation and compliance—all of which are subject to review as international political events unfold. Finally, there is justification for the strategic planning activity. While this institution is highly structured, such is not the case for all institutions (e.g., India's caste system).

Economy   An economy is not a static entity but an ongoing process comprised of the aggregate of institutions which perform economic functions and determine economic conditions. These institutions behave according to working rules,[4] many of which are established by authorities who allocate scarce resources while answering questions pertaining to production and distribution of goods and services. Working rules establish rights and duties of the economy's participants and serve to establish order among conflicting interests and to strengthen the social process for coordinating economic (as well as social, political, and cultural) matters by outlining the boundaries of behavior for economic activity. Working rules are both formal and informal, and are imposed for institutions at different

---

[2]Pryor, *A Guidebook to the Comparative Study of Economic Systems,* p. 14.

[3]Neale, "Institutions," *Journal of Economic Issues,* p. 1182.

[4]John R. Commons focused on the importance of working rules in his analysis of capitalism. He argued that "In every transaction there is a Conflict of Interest because each participant is trying to get as much and give as little as possible. Yet nobody can live or prosper except by Dependence on what others do in managerial, bargaining, and rationing transactions. Hence, they must come to a working agreement . . . . To the entire process we give the name, Working Rules of Going Concerns, the purpose of which is to bring "Order out of Conflict." See Commons, *Institutional Economics,* vol. 1 (Madison, WS: The University of Wisconsin Press, 1959), p. 118.

levels (e.g., household, firm, nationwide) either with or without sovereign power exercised by the state. The formal regulations (e.g., minimum wage laws) recognized and sanctioned by society establish every member's rights, duties, and liberties and what members can expect the state to perform in the collective interest. Formal rules establish a legal structure within which property rights are defined and transactions can be undertaken. Transactions are patterns of integration entered into by participants to ensure order in production and distribution activities. They involve an exchange of goods or services at an agreed-upon price. Participants face a choice of opportunities and exercise their economic power within the working rules established by authorities. Arbiters may become necessary to settle any dispute between transacting parties.

The informal rules (opinions or attitudes regularly held by a majority of the society such as the belief that the state should provide assistance to its poorest citizens) provide some basis for the establishment of working rules. Informal rules are contained in public opinion, which identifies society's important problems and what should be done to alleviate them.[5]

The institutions which comprise an economy are interrelated such that they "define the choice sets of independent economic sectors, . . . define the relationships among individuals, and . . . indicate who may do what to whom—and how much it will cost."[6] Societies attempt to establish institutions and working rules to achieve order to the extent that there is "predictability without rigidity and flexibility without chaos."[7] Taken together, these institutions "provide rules and folkviews [attitudes] for all the activities in which members of the society engage."[8] Attitudes are views regarding what economic, social, political, and cultural conditions should prevail along with a conception of the same types of conditions as they actually exist in that society. Technological changes stimulate changes in attitudes (informal rules), which can lead to subsequent changes in (formal) working rules. Change also could ensue from a revolution, which establishes different authorities in power, or from the spread of popular attitudes (as people become dissatisfied with the existing conditions and rules perpetuating those conditions), which subsequently influences authorities to establish new formal rules. Such has been the case of rising health care costs in the United States, which have stimulated voters to seek alternatives to private health care. Many have been encouraging their congressional representatives to pass legislation establishing a health care service that covers all citizens and is funded, at least in part, by the government.

[5]Roger Troub, "Economics, Public Opinion, and the Culture of Technical Control," *Journal of Economic Issues*, XXVIII, 1 (March 1994), 243. Public opinion is defined as "the sum of all the public's opinions, attitudes, and values."

[6]Daniel W. Bromley, "Reconstituting Economic Systems: Institutions in National Economic Development," *Development Policy Review*, 11 (1993), 131–151.

[7]Ibid., p. 150.

[8]Neale, "Institutions," *Journal of Economic Issues*, pp. 1196, 1197.

Philosophical Basis for an Economy   A viewpoint which specifies the place of an individual within society, an ideal state of political, social, and economic reality to serve as a set of ultimate goals for society, and a general program suggesting broad policy measures that will guide society from its actual conditions toward the ideal reality. This economic philosophy will be multidimensional in the sense that social, political, and cultural as well as economic elements are contained therein. An example of such a viewpoint is contained in Adam Smith's *An Inquiry Into the Nature and Causes of the Wealth of Nations,* which provides the philosophical basis for a market economy (see Chapter 5).

Assume your committee accepts these definitions. You now begin to discuss questions pertaining to the philosophical basis for the economy and the primary production and distribution issues. There are two particular concerns. First, what should be the philosophical basis upon which the new economy will be established? Second, what mechanisms and institutions should be adopted for resolving production and distribution matters? Note that throughout history these issues have been debated and settled in societies no matter how dissimilar these societies have been (e.g., a primitive island economy such as that of Robinson Crusoe versus an industrialized economy such as contemporary Russia).

How would you respond to these last two questions? What type of economy would you recommend be implemented: free enterprise with a modest role for the state in economic decision making; the assumption of political control and command over economic decisions by a select group of leaders; democratic control of the economy with a commitment to redistribute resources according to need; or some other economy with different rules for production and distribution? Before offering any views, you might decide you need to broaden your awareness and understanding of how societies throughout history have addressed the questions mentioned earlier in this chapter. Using the definitions already provided and the themes and framework discussed next, Chapters 2–18 will provide that awareness and understanding. Chapter 19 returns to the scenario of the postrevolution meeting and reconsiders the list of questions.

Objective of This Book

The objective of this book is to study comparative economies through a summary of selected economies' history, describing each economy from an evolutionary-institutional perspective. To achieve this objective examples of economies and economic philosophies from different periods of history will be presented. The discussion of each economy will focus on its evolution and behavior, especially the importance of historical conditions and attitudinal changes in the establishment and modification of working rules for institutions. Consequently, political, social, and cultural factors will be included where relevant.

THE EVOLUTIONARY-INSTITUTIONAL APPROACH TO THE STUDY OF ECONOMIES

The evolutionary-institutional perspective is based upon five themes.

Theme 1

Economies are best understood within an historical context, for contemporary institutions and working rules are the result of an evolutionary process. A study of history enables an analyst to appreciate the evolutionary process and avoid perceiving different economies as being part of a system of economic taxonomy (e.g., "capitalist" or "socialist"), as well as to refrain from believing that people over time and in different societies respond in a consistent, uniform manner to changes in economic variables.[9] An historical study demonstrates that the combination of factors shaping the economy of a particular nation is unique. Therefore, understanding an economy requires "a familiarity with the history of [that] economic society, a sense of how . . . dominant institutions came into being in the first place. Only from the standpoint of history can we see . . . institutions, and the problems they create, as part of the ongoing process of . . . economic life."[10] In tracing the evolution of the principal institutions that shape particular economies, one arrives at a better understanding of different economies and the field of comparative economies as well. After World War II the imposition of the Occupational Authority in Japan and the establishment of the Soviet Union as the authority over East Germany significantly influenced the postwar development of both economies. Post-1989 CEE economic reformers inherited industrial sectors characterized by obsolete technology, energy-intensive means of production, and overstaffed labor forces that have inhibited efforts to transform industrial institutions and make their products competitively priced and appealing to potential customers.

Theme 2

Studying both economic and noneconomic factors is necessary. For example, a nation's economy is affected by its social and political structures as well as the means by which rank and status within those structures are determined and changed. Rank is defined as an official position and is used to refer to political designations (e.g., Roman Emperor, U.S. Senator). Status is defined as a relative position in the social structure (e.g., members of the aristocracy in England, multimillionaires in the United States, patron-client relationships in

---

[9]Joseph Schumpeter argued that of the three fundamental fields that comprise economic analysis—history, statistics, and theory—economic history is the most important.

[10]Robert L. Heilbroner, *The Making of Economic Society*, 7th ed. (Englewood Cliffs, NJ: Prentice-Hall, 1985), p. xiv.

underdeveloped countries). Since ranking orders in social and political structures frequently mirror one another, changes in the social and political structures often lead to changes in authorities. Such changes will have a subsequent effect upon the establishment, interpretation, and enforcement of the economy's working rules. For example, the rise to political power of Sweden's Social Democratic Party led to subsequent changes in the economy's working rules—especially those pertaining to publicly funded and administered insurance and welfare programs. The increasing number of women and minorities in upper levels of the U.S. social structure has coincided with greater proportional representation of members in these groups in the political structure as well as new working rules (particularly regarding hiring practices) which favor both women and minority job applicants.

Theme 3

The evolutionary-institutional perspective embodies the view that economies are characterized by ongoing processes of dynamic transformation. That is, economies are fluid over time, not static, for their working rules and institutions are subject to modification. Institutions maintain order through working rules. New technological conditions (such as the Internet) may modify the working rules under which order is maintained, necessitating efforts to establish new working rules. Changes in working rules create new institutions, so that institutions are part of the evolving process which characterizes an economy. Seeking an alternative to state-owned enterprises, many Chinese villages have developed township-village enterprises characterized by a unique combination of (collective) village and semiprivate ownership and control (Chapter 18). The agreement among European nations to pursue economic and political integration through common policies designed to integrate economic activity among member nations has spawned institutions such as the European Commission and the European Parliament (Chapter 14).

The analysis focuses broadly on principal institutions, especially their working rules, and the social and political structures as they influence economic activity both at particular points in time and over time. While habits and routines (both the outcome of historical development) account for regularized activity within institutions, history indicates that viable economies are fluid so as to respond to changes in endogenous and exogenous factors such as technology, relative scarcities, trade agreements, and environmental problems. Fluidity is manifested by changes in working rules, which modify the legal foundation within which institutions exist. Permitting private individuals to engage in import and export activities has altered dramatically retail trade activity throughout CEE since 1989. Legalized gambling has transformed the economies of Atlantic City, New Jersey and Las Vegas, Nevada.

Institutional change may be gradual, following a period of economic stability and general societal satisfaction with the economy's performance. An example would be Japan throughout the 1980s during which, due to rapid economic growth and political stability enjoyed the previous three decades, few changes in principal institutions and working rules were introduced. Rapid institutional change is likelier to occur during an apparent crisis, such as a great depression or political revolution. The five-year periods after 1932 and 1989 illustrate radical transformation efforts of economies throughout the world, particularly in Europe. In each case perceived failure of the economy to satisfy national goals led to changes in attitudes, political unrest, a new philosophy toward the economy, and introduction of new institutions and working rules (e.g., The New Deal in the United States and the elimination of state planning commissions throughout CEE).

Typically, within an economy there are prevailing habits and actions within institutions that are repeated, particularly if the outcome is deemed successful. Over time, however, the economy may experience growing disorder among institutional components which cease to be in harmony with other components and consequently initiate conflict. This can stimulate the dynamic process whereby chaos breeds discontinuity within institutions and new institutions are adopted. The 1994 U.S. health care and welfare reform debates are examples of this process.

The evolutionary-institutional perspective presents societal change as a dialectic process of circular causation and cumulative change within and between principal institutions, which can be either in a positive or negative direction. Expectations and evaluations play an important role with lags between political policies, the economy's performance, and the public's response. For example, there was a four-year euphoria in Bulgaria following the 1989 political revolution before the persistent recession fueled discontent, despair, and growing demand for an alternative to the "free market economy" policy proposals advocated by World Bank and International Monetary Fund advisors (Chapter 16).

Within institutions comprehensive (versus cosmetic) change is a long-run process, since members must adapt while resistance to change is overcome. There are cognitive constraints which limit the speed of behavioral change, which is itself the result of a learning process. People require time to absorb new information, technology, and forms of organization. Institutional change will be resisted by those affected if (1) such change is forced upon them before they are fully informed and trust that there will be rewards for adhering to the new working rules; (2) participants' attitudes include a learned helplessness due to decades of being discouraged from taking any initiative (a common CEE problem); and (3) an entrenched bureaucracy exists whose members fear that they will lose their social position, income, or privileges as a result of institutional change. On the government level, bureaucratic inertia can delay implementation of an adequate body of working rules (legal framework), infrastructure, financial institutions, and other prerequisites for transformation of the economy. Such resistance is widespread throughout CEE, thereby inhibiting effective transformation of poorly performing economies. Similar resistance is common throughout the U.S. public school system or the agricultural sector of the European Union.

The ongoing process by which society identifies values consistent with the prevailing philosophical basis determines its needs and the means to satisfy them, and also modifies its institutional arrangements serving to reallocate economic opportunities (another reason those who benefit from existing principal institutions resist institutional change). The process has two aspects. First, domains in which rules apply are negotiated whereby societal needs will be articulated, clarified, evaluated, and prioritized by political authorities. For example, the United States, European Union, and Japan each impose import restrictions upon agricultural goods, ostensibly to protect the lifestyle and income of members of their respective agricultural sectors. Second, the decision-making process is a "confluence of self-interest and other forces, including passions . . . moral judgments, and interpersonal bonds" such as commitment, obligation, and trust.[11] Authorities often respond to constituents with considerable economic and political power (such as a labor union or association of insurance firms) when making their final decision. For example, many members of the U.S. Congress who voted against the North American Free Trade Agreement between Canada, Mexico, and the United States claimed to be acting in the interests of workers rather than consumers.

Theme 4

The study of comparative economies should place emphasis upon the philosophical underpinnings which shape the participants' values in the particular economy being analyzed. Today's institutions, attitudes, and values shape future institutions through a "selective, coercive process"[12] whereby the conventional perspective is altered. New economic philosophies foster attitudes (informal rules), which subsequently influence authorities to alter (formal) working rules, thereby reshaping or establishing institutions. Health concerns in many nations are changing rules for production of nuclear energy or tobacco products.

The process begins when the public becomes aware of a problem, manifested by a deviation between actual and expected performance of a particular social or economic indicator (such as distribution of income, crime, or average life expectancy). If the problem persists, a sense of urgency may develop, and people may begin seeking alternative means for alleviating the problem. When the benefits and costs of alternative solutions are identified, informed individuals weigh the advantages and disadvantages of each alternative. They may look to social scientists to be eclectic while identifying alternative choices and explaining the costs and benefits of each alternative. Eventually people take a position which may not only reflect narrow, selfish interests but might also contain an ethical dimension as well.[13] The contributions of Adam Smith, John Stuart Mill, Karl Marx, and John Maynard Keynes, among others, influenced the attitudes of citizens and the authorities who have developed the rules for ninteenth- and twentieth-century economies. Many U.S. social scientists are occupied determining costs and benefits of alternative solutions to pressing social problems such as health care, welfare, and crime.

[11]Paul C. Stern, "The Socio-Economic Perspective and Its Institutional Prospects," *The Journal of Socio-Economics*, 22, 1 (Spring 1993), 3.

[12]Geoffrey M. Hodgson, *Economics and Institutions* (Cambridge, England: Polity Press, 1988), p. 139.

[13]Troub, "Economics, Public Opinion, and the Culture of Technical Control," pp. 244–249. A problem with the orthodox, neoclassical perspective toward comparative economics is that it depicts people's participation in an economic system as limited to their roles as consumers, producers, and suppliers of resources and not as active participants in the modification of their economy's institutions and rules.

Theme 5

One cannot conclude that an advanced level of economic development in a particular nation suggests that its working rules and institutions will generate the same favorable performance if adopted or imposed in another nation. Nor can one assume that favorable performance of a particular economy will continue over time. One of the most common fallacies in social science is to assume that "a trend once established is likely to persist indefinitely."[14] For example, while many economic historians would agree that entrepreneurial activity within a laissez-faire economic environment contributed to the rapid economic growth and development experienced by the U.S. economy between 1865 and 1930, few would argue that continued reliance should have been placed upon laissez-faire policies (versus Keynesian-type guided market policies—see Chapter 8) following the financial panic and macroeconomic instability of the early 1930s.[15] Unfortunately, many advisors of CEE nations have made the mistake of assuming that since Western European and North American nations have achieved relative economic prosperity by establishing economies in which privately owned and controlled firms have been the dominant institution, a "free market economy" could be (and should be) implemented throughout CEE. The attempt to do so rapidly has contributed to considerable economic and social costs throughout the CEE region.[16]

The Evolutionary-Institutional Theory

Emphasizing the importance of history, social and political structures, and fluidity is not revolutionary in comparative economic studies. The contributions of an evolutionary-institutional approach are the theory and framework which explicitly identify these factors, place them at the center of the analysis, and describe how they interact. Economic relations are considered part of a broader social context, inseparable from the political and social sphere. The economy is not considered to be a separate entity but is viewed as comprising only "part of a complex network of socio-cultural relationships."[17] Presenting economies within an historical context illustrates there has been a plurality of combinations of institutions and rules adopted by societies to resolve their production and distribution problems. Compared to Cuba, North Korea, and the CEE nations, China has introduced some unique institutions and rules since 1979, which have transformed much of its

---

[14]G. C. Allen, *The Japanese Economy* (London: Weidenfeld and Nicolson, 1981), p. 165.

[15]John Maynard Keynes was once chided for shifting his policy stance from favoring free trade to proposing a protective tariff. Keynes's retort was, "When the facts change, I change my mind. What do you do, sir?" Alfred L. Malabre, Jr. and Lindley H. Clark, Jr., "Changes in Economy Cause Much Confusion Among Economists," *The Wall Street Journal*, March 27, 1989, p. 1.

[16]The lack of knowledge of economic history and history of economic thought contributed to faulty policy reocomendations, such as assuming entrepreneurs would emerge and establish manufacturing firms following widespread privatization and reduction of subsidies to state-owned enterprises. This problem is discussed further in Chapter 16.

[17]Wallace C. Peterson, "Institutionalism, Keynes, and the Real World," *Journal of Economic Issues*, XI, 2 (June 1977), 203.

economy while contributing favorably to rapid economic growth and rising standards of living. The historical view indicates that society's principal institutions are "highly complex, interactive, and always in a state of adjustment to changing conditions,"[18] which include people's ideas and perceptions as well as actions.

Less emphasis is placed on identifying a few key variables or specifying a finite number of relationships, which can be used to construct a simple model of social change or to serve as the basis for classifying and comparing economies. While the evolutionary-institutional framework provides a formal structure for understanding economies, less emphasis is placed on precision and forecasting outcomes if particular institutional arrangements and working rules are adopted.[19]

The framework embodies the view that behavior of individuals is partly influenced by noneconomic factors and, therefore, is only partly predictable since it is neither always foreseeable nor uniform within or among economies. Also it is believed that the behavior of economies does not conform to any "empirical regularity" because of the complex interaction of principal institutions, social and political structures, and working rules. Along with technology and exogenous influences to economic performance such as the international economic environment, principal institutions, social and political structures, and working rules are "juxtaposed and [at times] counteracting"[20] features of an economy. Precise, accurate forecasts of economic activity or an economy's path are highly unlikely because economic events are determined by these counteracting features and are not fully synchronized with mechanisms influencing them. This perspective opposes the conventional view of economies held by recent advisors to CEE governments. They believed that certain stimuli, consisting of such available tools as stringent monetary and fiscal policy and liberalized prices, would induce desired changes throughout CEE economies. It was assumed that using the proposed stabilization measures and widespread privatization as stimuli, the desired induction to changes in economic behavior virtually was guaranteed, as a chemist's combining of particular elements is certain to produce a specific reaction. Chapter 16 will evaluate the outcome of transformation efforts based upon this perspective.

The evolutionary-institutional approach provides an alternative to the orthodox treatment of comparative "economic systems," or "isms," which tends to utilize classification schemes categorizing economies in simplistic terms such as "capitalist" or "socialist," and focuses on comparing the performance of supposed

---

[18]Alan Randall, "Property Institutions and Economic Behavior," *Journal of Economic Issues,* XII, 2 (March 1978), 3.

[19]One critic chides academic macroeconomists for assuming that by manipulating variables such as the money supply or aggregate demand, they can "homogenize the behavior of millions of individuals." The same critic opposes the growing emphasis on mathematics in economics curricula for becoming "as mathematical as the physics department . . . [which is because] [t]he further away economics strays from reality, the better it can be sold as 'scientifically precise.'" Jude Wanniski, "Macroeconomics: The Enemy Within," *The Wall Street Journal,* June 27, 1991, p. A14.

[20]Tony Lawson, "Why Are So Many Economists So Opposed to Methodology?" Paper presented at the European Association for Evolutionary Political Economy Conference, Barcelona (October 1993), p. 11.

examples of such systems. The "economic system" and the process of change are generally conceived in mechanistic terms characterized by the specification of a set of economic relations. These relations are fragmented and reduced to include primarily economic variables. The focus is on movements toward or attainment of equilibrium rather than on an evolutionary process of societal change, with the belief that general equilibrium theory is the only starting point for explaining how "economic systems" that are not centrally planned behave.

Those adhering to an orthodox perspective toward "economic systems" tend toward the view that competitive markets operate effectively in most societies, or would operate effectively in the absence of state intervention. They identify mechanistic patterns of behavior when, in fact, no such patterns may exist. The purported behavior of individuals is based upon a deterministic view in which, through unrealistic assumptions and illegitimate generalizations, individuals are believed to respond in a predictable, mechanical manner to changing economic variables (particularly relative prices) according to invariable preferences and beliefs. General propositions are arrived at and postulated as valid for every time, place, and culture. Economic forces are perceived as having an inevitable tendency toward a competitive equilibrium that constitutes an optimal outcome. Among the problems encountered when adopting such a market-centered approach is that analysis will lack a sense of culture and history and will all but ignore the evolutionary nature of institutions.

In place of the orthodox approach and its emphasis on a specified set of economic relations, the evolutionary-institutional theory is based upon the interrelationship between a society's beliefs (philosophical basis), power structures (social and political structures), and working rules for institutions. The theory explains the nature and evolution of economies by specifying that:

1. Most production and distribution activities are coordinated through principal institutions. Japanese firms often form *keiretsu* for the purpose of engaging in bilaterally negotiated (versus free market) transactions (Chapter 9).

2. The origin of these institutions, their activities, and the rules governing them stem from the interrelationships between the society's historical legacy and context, philosophical basis, and decisions made by authorities who emerge from the social and political structures. England's Parliament introduced a gold standard during the early nineteenth century to increase confidence and liquidity in the nation's banking system and to link international markets by coordinating the flow of trade and payments for goods (Chapter 6).

3. Authorities retain, modify, or define new working rules according to which the society resolves its economic problem. International trade agreements (such as granting a particular nation most favored nation status) must be approved by the U.S. Congress before becoming a formal working rule.

4. Changes in working rules can modify institutions or create new ones, with the economy evolving in the process. (Remember that the economy is defined as the institutions which perform economic functions.) Privatization laws passed in the Czech Republic have led to the establishment of privately owned and controlled manufacturing, trade, and service enterprises, which compete in some sectors with remaining state-owned enterprises.

5. The philosophical basis accepted by authorities and the economy's performance determine whether the working rules are retained, modified, or replaced. Authorities can choose to ignore poor performance indicators (e.g., Romania between 1945 and 1989), which postpone changes in the working rules. Authorities can recognize poor performance and modify or replace existing working rules (e.g., repeated, prolonged attempts by the U.S. Congress to reduce the federal budget deficit). Authorities can be replaced through peaceful means (e.g., an election or succession of a monarch), or following a revolution, in which case the new authorities who usually accept a different philosophy for developing the economy are likely to introduce different working rules.

The evolutionary-institutional framework, which illustrates this theory, is outlined in Figure 1-1.

Six interrelated factors will be included in the discussion of each economy.

1. *Historical Legacy and Context.* The society's institutions and philosophy toward economic life will be influenced by what has survived in the nation's consciousness from its history. Joseph Schumpeter argues that

> . . . the subject matter of economics is essentially a unique process in historic time. Nobody can hope to understand the economic phenomena of any, including the present epoch, who has not adequate command of historical facts and an adequate amount of historical sense. . . . [Moreover] the historical report cannot be purely economic but must inevitably reflect also institutional facts that are not purely economic: therefore, it affords the best method for understanding how economic and noneconomic facts are related to one another.[21]

The reluctance to introduce free markets in the contemporary Soviet economy can be traced to the 1920s. The authorities' evaluation of the New Economic Policy's provisions to permit some free market activity in industry and agriculture was that such activity threatened the state's

[21]Robert L. Darcy, *The Economic Process: A Structured Approach* (Columbus, OH: Publishing Horizons, 1986), p. 54.

industrialization drive. The state wanted to limit prices and either was unable to control prices or, having set prices, was unable to induce peasants and selected industry managers to produce sufficient levels of output consistent with the goal of rapid industrialization (see Chapter 16). Another example is the desire within Europe following World War II to integrate so as to supervise jointly atomic energy, coal, and steel production—the main implements of war.

2. *Philosophical Basis.* The attitudes held by participants in economic activities and the economy's working rules are related to a philosophy for economic behavior. The Church provided a philosophy for medieval

Figure1-1   Evolutionary-Institutional Framework

Historical Legacy and Context:

Institutions and economic, political, and social conditions at the beginning of the period being analyzed.

Philosophical Basis:

Influences the attitudes (informal rules) of participants upon which the (formal) working rules are based.

Social and Political Structures:

Explain which authorities have the power to establish and interpret the working rules.

Often introduce or perpetuate rules which enhance their rank and status.

Working Rules:

Economy is comprised of a number of interrelated institutions whose boundaries for permissible and forbidden activity are established by working rules.

Principal Institutions:

Origin—institutions are socially determined, prescribed by tradition, or evolve from interaction of history and philosophy with authorities who establish new working rules.

Characterized by *activities* (of participants), *working rules* (governing institutions), and *attitudes* (toward activities and rules).

Institutions establish and coordinate production and distribution patterns and give durability and meaning to routine activities.

Behavior of the Economy:

1. Criteria for illustrating how society is organized to resolve its economic problem:

a. Organization of resource allocation decision making: centralized, decentralized, cooperative.

b. Working rules governing ownership and control of resources: public, private, cooperative.
    i. Importance of right to possess, use, dispose, or make use of the output of the good or service owned and/or controlled.

c. Social process for coordinating information, and for making production and distribution decisions: markets, tradition, economic planning.

2. Institutional change

a. Institutions can be fluid, adapting to the changing needs of society.

b. Change in a principal institution (e.g., the political party in power) can lead to changes in other institutions.

3. Performance

a. Changes in social and economic indicators which influence the attitudes of the economy's participants, especially the authorities.

---

society by prescribing moral axioms for proper conduct when individuals engaged in commercial activities, in which avarice and usury were considered sinful. Such a philosophy provides symbols and ideals in the minds of both the economy's participants and outside observers. Resistance to changing the health care system to a one-payer (government-funded) scheme in the United States reflects the nation's preference for free enterprise and adverse attitudes toward institutions funded and managed by the government.

3. *Social and Political Structures.*   These explain which authorities will have the power to establish and interpret the working rules which coordinate economic activities. Without a recognized authority to enforce the rules, chaos will prevail throughout the economy. Authorities often prescribe rules designed to maintain their lofty rank and status. The ability of Ferdinand and Imelda Marcos to accumulate vast wealth is an egregious example of this process. Authorities in societies where considerable resources are controlled by the state have an interest in resisting reforms in favor of free markets, for this would result in their losing economic and political power. Such has been the case with CEE and Chinese authorities concerning reforms governing their respective agricultural sectors, and with members of the U.S. Congress who are reluctant to relinquish control over resources by decreasing federal government expenditures.

4. *Working Rules.*   The economy is depicted as comprised of interrelated institutions for which the working rules establish the boundaries for activity. In the United States a license must be obtained from the government before a firm can be established in particular industries,

including communications and transportation. Changes in working rules can lead to the establishment of new institutions. There are about 300 working rules contained in the Single European Act of 1986, which taken together created a single European market in 1992. As a result, there is harmonization throughout the member nations of a broad range of activities pertaining to agriculture, transportation, product standards, and working conditions, among other areas.

5. *Principal Institutions.* These are socially determined, not inherent in any type of economy. Economies differ according to their institutions and the relative importance of particular types of institutions (e.g., large or small private firms, cooperatives, state-owned enterprises). Their creation is affected by the historical legacy, philosophical basis, social and political structures, and the working rules. They have an important impact on the economy, being instrumental in establishing and coordinating most production and distribution patterns of behavior, and giving meaning and durability to routine activities. Significant features include their origin, the activities participants perform, working rules governing them, their impact on the economy, and the philosophical basis for these activities and rules. Recent experience in CEE transformation indicates that Ronald Coase, a recent winner of the Nobel Prize in economics, was correct in arguing that prices are not all that is important regarding coordination of economic activity. Rather, institutional mechanisms which provide information and perform additional functions concerning working rules are necessary in order for market forces to operate and be regulated.

6. *Behavior of the Economy.* The economy's behavior will be presented as consisting of three components: how it is organized to resolve the economic problem; institutional change; and performance.

In describing how each society is organized to resolve its economic problem, three questions will be addressed. First, how is resource allocation decision making organized? (1) The organization can be centralized, to varying degrees, with some higher authority such as the state, a ministry official, or feudal baron making the major production and distribution decisions; (2) decentralized, with many individuals such as producers or consumers making the key decisions; or (3) cooperative, where producers of a similar good or service jointly make decisions. In each case the rest of society may influence the decision makers through purchasing particular goods and services (thereby increasing the profitability of producing those goods and services), making or withholding contributions which serve to maintain the authorities in power, or voting for authorities or specific policies. In most societies the organization of decision making includes centralized, decentralized, and cooperative decision making, with the relative importance of each type of organization subject to change. During the past few years East German agricultural cooperatives have been transformed into private farms.

Second, what are the rules regarding ownership and control over productive resources? Economies will differ according to the degree of public, private, or cooperative ownership and control and the corresponding working rules. In each economy rules differ concerning the right of any organization to possess, use, dispose (e.g., sell, bequeath), or make use of what is produced by the good or service owned. For example, ownership of humans (i.e., slavery) is not permitted in most societies. Ownership of land may or may not entitle the owner to construct any type of building, to remove and sell resources on the land (e.g., dirt and trees), to raise livestock, to transfer ownership and control to someone else through sale or inheritance, or to sell any goods produced on the land, depending upon the rules governing such a resource.

Third, what type of social process has been adopted for coordinating information and for making production and distribution decisions? Alternative types of processes which coordinate production and distribution decisions include markets, a traditional mechanism, or some form of economic planning. These processes influence not only economic performance indicators but also attitudes and values, the social and political structures, and principal institutions adopted.

Planning is a process which identifies goals (e.g., rates of economic growth) and proposes policy measures designed to achieve the goals. The broad forms of planning are: (1) centralized (common to East European economies before 1990), where one authority had the ultimate power and responsibility for making the production and distribution rules which become laws for the society; (2) indicative (adopted by France after World War II—Chapter 11), where state officials seek private-sector cooperation in the pursuit of broadly defined goals; and (3) active, where the state intervenes through discretionary fiscal and monetary policies for the purpose of guiding the performance of the economy. Each of these processes can be identified in nearly all societies (markets and formal planning usually do not exist in primitive societies), with the relative importance of each process varying over time. For example, CEE nations have begun to introduce market processes to replace planned activities deemed to have produced inefficient results (Chapter 16).

Focusing on institutional change reinforces the fact that economies are evolutionary in nature. Institutional change will be illustrated by identifying the institutions that change during the time period within which each economy is analyzed. Change can be gradual, such as the growth of towns during the medieval period, or sudden, following a revolution or a war. In this case a change in a principal institution (e.g., the political authority) generally leads to dramatic institutional changes. This occurred in Japan in 1946 after the Occupation Authority assumed control of the economy. Also, the emergence of the Communist Party in China led to the sudden establishment of people's communes in the 1950s.

There are many factors which can be included in evaluating the performance of an economy (see Chapter 2). The significance of each economy's performance is its impact upon the attitudes of those who influence the establishment and modification of working rules. For example, the adverse performance of the agricultural sector of the Soviet Union stimulated the chief authority, Premier Mikhail Gorbachev, to propose reforms which lessened the degree of state control over production and distribution decisions in the farm sector. Throughout Eastern Europe in 1989, shortages of basic goods and services led to widespread demonstrations demanding economic and political reforms.

China's economy since 1978 (Chapter 18) illustrates that adverse economic and social performance indicators for the previous two decades stimulated authorities to introduce widespread reforms while maintaining a totalitarian political structure. New working rules permitted greater economic freedoms to individuals as pragmatism began to replace the doctrinal Maoist ideology. Decollectivization in agriculture was initiated and farmers were provided opportunities to increase their income by selling excess produce in open markets. New principal institutions were permitted, and township and village enterprises emerged to provide a new base for industrial production. State-owned enterprises continued to be subsidized, but their relative importance was gradually reduced while some are being transformed into limited-liability companies responsible for their own profits and losses. Meanwhile many private, cooperative, and township and village enterprises have flourished. The prolonged, dramatic improvement in the economy's performance indicators continues to stimulate the introduction of additional reforms designed to reduce state control over economic activity.

Another illustration of the evolutionary-institutional theory is the European Union (Chapter 14). The historical legacy was centuries of warfare between neighboring countries, culminating in World War II. Stimulated by the desire to avoid military conflict and by the view that public-private cooperation was efficacious for steadier and more rapid economic growth and development, authorities from six European nations agreed to relinquish some national authority to a supranational institution, the European Coal and Steel Community. The working rules of this organization were designed to coordinate production and distribution of the two key resources necessary for waging war: coal and steel. Other institutions were introduced for the purpose of supervising economic activity, including a High Authority and a Court of Justice. The organization of resource allocation decision making was centralized. There was private ownership with public control over output and distribution, while markets and some indicative planning coordinated production and distribution. The favorable performance of this community created positive attitudes among member nations' citizens and authorities toward further economic and political integration. This ultimately resulted in working rules establishing the European Community.

OUTLINE OF THE BOOK

Although comparing the performance of economies is not a principal objective of this book, the issue of evaluation and comparison of economies' performances is significant. Chapter 2 addresses the conceptual issues with particular emphasis placed on the importance of the analyst's viewpoint.

Chapters 3–18 are divided into seven sections, each focusing on examples of economies with similarities in their historical background, philosophical basis, and working rules for economic behavior. Pretwentieth-century examples are included to enhance understanding of the roots of our cultural heritage (and the roots of certain working rules), and to illustrate economies where neither markets nor planning mechanisms were significant. Part II contains two premodern economies, ancient Rome (Chapter 3) and medieval England (Chapter 4). In each society markets were present, but the rules and philosophical basis for economic behavior differed significantly from those of modern economies.

Part III focuses on the evolution of England's economy from the medieval period through the mercantile era and into the modern (i.e., post-1830) period, when self-regulating markets began to assume greater significance in resolving the production and distribution questions. Chapter 5 presents an outline of pertinent historical events during the 1500–1830 period, a brief discussion of the mercantile economy, and the philosophical basis (classical economics) of the laissez-faire market economy. An example of such an economy, England during the 1830–1879 period, is contained in Chapter 6.

The period between World Wars I and II witnessed the emergence of four broad types of economies, each based upon a philosophy which differed from that of the classical economists. The political and economic turmoil following the end of World War I, especially the worldwide economic depression, stimulated the emergence of political regimes which preferred working rules for their society's economy that differed significantly from those of the pre-World War I economies. Part IV (Chapter 7) focuses on the historical context, philosophical basis, and working rules for the economy of a society (Germany), whose authorities sought to establish state command over an economy with extensive private ownership of the means of production.

Other societies which adopted a more democratic, gradual approach to economic reform are discussed in Part V. In the wake of the Great Depression, John Maynard Keynes proposed a new economic philosophy (Chapter 8). This view aimed to preserve democratic political institutions and private enterprise while extending the state's responsibility for the economy's performance. Chapters 9–11 provide three examples of societies where rules for the economy and institutions were consistent with the Keynesian paradigm: Japan (Chapters 9 and 10) and France (Chapter 11).

An alternative view toward the degree of state involvement in economic matters developed in the early 1930s (Part VI). This view emphasized the importance of democratic political institutions and private ownership of production facilities. However, it also advocated an extension of publicly funded and distributed social insurance and welfare measures, redistributive policies, and broader regulation of a society's economy. Chapter 12 presents the historical context and philosophical basis for such an economy, while Chapter 13 provides an example (Sweden). Chapter 14, The European Community, illustrates a supranational economy whose member nations' collective aims are consistent with the philosophical basis discussed in Chapter 12.

Part VII focuses on economies whose political authorities, to varying degrees—particularly before 1989—have sought to maintain command over production and distribution activities. Chapter 15 contains the philosophical basis of this movement, as contained in the contributions of Karl Marx, and an example of a pre-1989 economy where such a philosophy was introduced (former Soviet Union). Chapter 16 evaluates the transformation throughout CEE, focusing on macroeconomic and transformation policies and the performance of selected economies (Bulgaria, the Czech Republic, Hungary, and Poland). Chapter 17 presents the example of Hungary, focusing on the changes in political structure and transformation policies introduced since 1989. An analysis of China as the fastest growing economy over the past 15 years is contained in Chapter 18. Key aspects of transformation policies are identified and compared to those adopted in CEE. Finally, Part VIII (Chapter 19) summarizes the main themes of the book, returns to the issues posed at the beginning of this chapter, and draws conclusions concerning a perspective for understanding and comparing economies.

KEY TERMS AND CONCEPTS[22]

Economy	Philosophical Basis
Historical Legacy	Social and Political Structures
Institution	Working Rules

QUESTIONS FOR DISCUSSION

1. Why are economies best understood within an historical context?
2. How have the historical legacy, philosophical basis for the economy, and social and political structures in the United States influenced the health care reform debate and new working rules?
3. Why have the working rules of the Japanese economy remained relatively unchanged over the past decade, while those of China have changed considerably?
4. For the baby-boom generation minimum wage laws, an all-volunteer army, affirmative action programs, and trade agreements affected our economic and social activities. Identify and discuss some changes in working rules introduced during the past few years that have affected your personal economic activity, while modifying the nation's economy as well.

[22]Definitions of key terms and concepts are provided in the glossary at the end of the book.

REFERENCES

Allen, G. C., *The Japanese Economy*. London: Weidenfeld and Nicolson, 1981.

Bromley, Daniel W., "Reconstituting Economic Systems: Institutions in National Economic Development," *Development Policy Review*, 11 (1993), 131–151.

Commons, John R., *Institutional Economics*, vols. 1 and 2. Madison: University of Wisconsin Press, 1959.

Dalton, George, *Economic Systems and Society: Capitalism, Communism and the Third World*. Middlesex, England: Penguin Books, 1977.

Darcy, Robert L., *The Economic Process: A Structured Approach*. Columbus, OH: Publishing Horizons, 1986.

Elliott, John E., *Comparative Economic Systems.*, 2nd ed. Belmont, CA: Wadsworth, 1985.

Gregory, Paul R., and Robert C. Stuart, *Comparative Economic Systems*, 2nd ed. Boston: Houghton Mifflin, 1985.

Heilbroner, Robert L., *The Making of Economic Society*, 7th ed. Englewood Cliffs, NJ: Prentice-Hall, 1985.

Hodgson, Geoffrey M., *Economics and Institutions.*, Cambridge, England: Polity Press, 1988.

Lawson, Tony, "Why Are So Many Economists So Opposed to Methodology?" Paper presented at the European Association for Evolutionary Political Economy Conference, Barcelona (October 1993).

Malabre, Alfred L., Jr., and Lindley Clark, Jr., "Changes in Economy Cause Much Confusion Among Economists," *The Wall Street Journal*, March 27, 1989, p. 1.

Neale, Walter C., "Institutions," *Journal of Economic Issues*, XXI, 3 (September 1987), 1177–1206.

Nove, Alec, "Economics of the Transition Period," *Forum*, 5, 11–12 (July–August 1992), 1–15.

Peterson, Wallace C., "Institutionalism, Keynes, and the Real World," *Journal of Economic Issues*, XI, 2 (June 1977), 203.

Pickersgill, Gary M., and Joyce E. Pickersgill, *Contemporary Economic Systems: A Comparative View*, 2nd ed. St. Paul, MN: West, 1985.

Polanyi, Karl, *The Great Transformation*. Boston: Beacon Press, 1957.

Pryor, Frederic L., *A Guidebook to the Comparative Study of Economic Systems*. Englewood Cliffs, NJ: Prentice-Hall, 1985.

Randall, Alan, "Property Institutions and Economic Behavior," *Journal of Economic Issues*, XII, 1 (March 1978), 3.

Stern, Paul C., "The Socio-Economic Perspective and Its Institutional Prospects," *The Journal of Socio-Economics*, 22, 1 (Spring 1993), 1–11.

Troub, Roger, "Economics, Public Opinion, and the Culture of Technical Control," *Journal of Economic Issues*, XXVIII, 1 (March 1994), 240–256.

Wanniski, Jude, "Macroeconomics: The Enemy Within," *The Wall Street Journal*, June 27, 1991, p. A14.

2

EVALUATING AND COMPARING ECONOMIES

OBJECTIVES

1. Emphasize the objective and subjective aspects of evaluating an economy's performance.
2. Explain that the factors which influence the performance of an economy include not only the institutions and working rules, but also the goals and priorities established by authorities and environmental factors such as international economic and political conditions.
3. Identify and explain the steps to follow when evaluating an economy's performance.
4. Identify and explain some standard performance indicators.

INTRODUCTION

When journalists or political leaders evaluate the performance of a particular economy or compare the relative merits of one type of economy to another, the conclusions they draw inevitably reflect unstated values. Numerous errors in critical reasoning can often be identified when such evaluations are reported in national magazines or newspapers. Although it is appropriate for political leaders to promote the type of economy they think best, it is important for economists to evaluate and compare different economies as objectively as possible.

Consider the image of Sweden as reported in the U.S. press. Tax rates in Sweden are compared to rates in the United States or Japan. Information is presented indicating the relative freedom enjoyed by citizens of these "capitalist" nations compared to Sweden's "socialist" economy. More recently, Sweden's rising unemployment and low rate of economic growth are emphasized. The conclusion drawn by analysts is that this information demonstrates the superiority of "capitalism" over "socialism."

There is no doubt that according to particular indicators of economic freedoms (e.g., tax rates, influence of the state over living and working conditions), the average resident of the United States or Japan enjoys more economic freedoms than do Swedish citizens. However, the argument that this information provides the basis for concluding that "capitalism" is superior to "socialism," while politically appealing to those who favor free enterprise, is not critically sound. Certain indicators, which may be selected as criteria for performance, are often ignored by the U.S. press when evaluations of Sweden are made. For example, improvements in the average Swedish family's standard of living since the 1930s as compared to changes in the same economic and social indicators for other nations whose economic conditions were similar to those of Sweden as of 1930 generally are not cited. Nor are data included for Sweden's higher life expectancy at birth or significantly lower murder rate. A more objective analysis would recognize that Sweden's economic conditions were not nearly as conducive to rapid economic development in the 1930s as these conditions were in the United States or Japan. In particular, Sweden's incidence of poverty, available technology suitable for industrialization, and ability to attract foreign investment were less favorable.

The reader should not think that a defense of the Swedish economy or of "socialism" is being offered. Indeed, the treatment of the U.S. economy in East European, Middle Eastern, or Latin American presses is far from being unbiased. Rather, the point is that an understanding of the complexities of evaluating and comparing economies is a prerequisite for making any analytical evaluations or comparisons. The purpose of this chapter is not to alter the values of the reader. Rather, the objective is to introduce a perspective and methodology with which to evaluate and compare economies.

The complex issues pertaining to the evaluation and comparison of economies will be discussed first, followed by an outline for evaluating the performance of an economy. Some issues pertaining to comparison follow, with emphasis being placed on various bases for comparison and on the many areas in which economies differ. The chapter will conclude with sample evaluations, one of which includes a comparison of some contemporary economies.

SOME BASIC ISSUES

A few key points should be kept in mind when evaluating or comparing economies. First, you must distinguish between theoretical models of an economy (e.g., laissez-faire market economy—see Chapter 5) and real-world, or actual, economies. Models of economies are built around a philosophical basis and are simplified to the extent that many principal institutions, especially those of a social and political nature, are not incorporated. In reality all economies are mixed (i.e., combinations of "models"). In each economy one can generally identify combinations of elements found in each model, such as free markets and planned economic activities; private, cooperative, and public ownership; and privately and publicly provided goods and services. For example, there are no contemporary examples of economies which conform to a laissez-faire market model (although some would argue that Hong Kong is the exception). In addition, no economy (including Cuba and North Korea) conforms strictly to any centrally planned model, for there are free markets (albeit some illegal ones) in all nations in which there is command over a social economy. One needs to avoid labeling an actual economy according to a stereotype term such as "market economy." The classifications used in this book (e.g., *guided market economy*) are intended to provide a broad heading under which actual economies with some similar characteristics are included. These economies have less in common than some theoretical classification schemes suggest.

Second, the performance of an economy is influenced by goals and priorities established by authorities and by environmental factors such as technology, natural resources, a political revolution, war, natural disaster, and international economic factors as well as luck (e.g., beginning to transform an economy during a worldwide period of prosperity such as Japan did in the 1950s versus CEE nations' attempts at transformation during a period of European recession).[1] Goals and priorities are both political and economic, and the two aspects are interrelated. The performance of two identical economies (i.e., economies with the same rules and institutions, at the same stage of economic development, and with the same resource endowment) could easily differ if priorities and the amount of resources allocated differed between them. Assume there are two nations with identical economies. Country A could emphasize improving its environment, while Country B could focus on rapid economic growth. The overall performance of each economy will reflect the priorities established as well as the impact of the working rules for the economy. Country B will more likely grow faster, but Country A will have cleaner air and water. Drawing any conclusions regarding which economy performed better will depend upon the analyst's values regarding the importance of the environment relative to economic growth.

An example where performance has been influenced heavily by goals and priorities would include the postrevolutionary (1949 to mid-1970s) drive in the People's Republic of China to achieve self-sufficiency through a policy of self-reliance in lieu of trading with Western nations or inviting foreign investment and technical expertise. (Each of these would have contributed to economic efficiency

---

[1]For further discussion of the influence which policy and environmental factors have on the performance of an economy, see Alexander Eckstein, ed., *Comparison of Economic Systems: Theoretical and Methodological Approaches* (Berkeley: University of California Press, 1971).

but would also have increased China's dependence on foreign authorities and economic forces.) Another example is the single-minded pursuit of rapid economic growth in Japan after 1946, the political objective being to spare the nation further humiliation from Western powers.

Third, an economy's performance is affected by its behavior under laissez-faire policies as well as by active policies and policy instruments.[2] In addition, how the economy performs will determine which other economic, social, or political policies are necessary. Rapid growth which creates low unemployment but exacerbates expectations of inflation and environmental quality will stimulate the introduction of anti-inflation, antipollution measures. Unfortunately, it is difficult to isolate the effect of either the autonomous economy or active policies when measuring economic performance, or to determine in advance how effective policies are under *ceteris paribus* conditions.

Fourth, evaluating and comparing economies cannot be purely objective. Quantitative measures of an economy's performance do not organize themselves in a systematic manner. Some analyst has to organize them. The particular features measured, the method of measurement, and the relative importance attached to each feature will be influenced by the analysts' point of view (i.e., their preferred philosophical basis for an economy, especially its goals; what the analysts wish to see happen; and their conception of how economies actually behave). Analysts may purport to be engaging in positive analysis, but their hidden values (e.g., a preference for free trade) generally lead to conclusions which are biased.[3] The degree to which an analyst is objective will be easier for a reader to evaluate if the analyst's values (e.g., preference for free markets, desire for state-induced redistribution of income and opportunities) are explicitly stated, for people hold different values and weight them differently regarding their relative importance when evaluating and comparing economies. For example, advisors to underdeveloped or CEE nations are likely to select any positive trend in performance when evaluating the effect of the policies they recommend, while those whose interest is academic are more likely to select performance criteria in a more objective manner. In addition, World Bank and International Monetary Fund advisors to countries such as Bulgaria or Poland are quick to emphasize the explosion in private-sector economic activity, while ignoring the adverse social effects of macroeconomic stabilization and privatization policies they have recommended.

If a society's values are relatively homogeneous, well defined, and stable, then empirical observations of that economy's performance by a like-minded analyst will tend to be more objective and realistic. Such might be the case for an

---

[2]See Frederic L. Pryor, *A Guidebook to the Comparative Study of Economic Systems* (Englewood Cliffs, NJ: Prentice-Hall, 1985), pp. 60–66.

[3]For a detailed discussion of the objectivity issue, see Gunnar Myrdal, *Value in Social Theory*, Paul Streeten, ed. (London: Routledge and Kegan Paul, 1958). According to Myrdal, biased conclusions will result from analysis which is "systematically twisted in the one direction which fits them best for purposes of rationalization." (Ibid., pp. 76, 77).

analysis of the Japanese economy over the 1951–1970 period by a Japanese analyst. Throughout Japanese history there has been a consensus to accept the goals established by the authorities, especially those established by the Ministry of International Trade and Industry over the past 40 years. As a result, there has been overriding national support for the postwar pursuit of rapid economic growth, with all other goals being subverted in the process. For most societies, such as the United States, values are more heterogeneous than in Japan, unstable (especially as the relative political power of different interest groups shifts), and contradictory (e.g., the goal of reducing the size of the public sector while increasing expenditures on national defense, day care for children, care for the elderly, and health care for all citizens). There is no simple solution to the objectivity question. Awareness of this issue will enable analysts and readers to be more critical of evaluations and comparisons of economies, and will reduce their likelihood of blindly accepting evaluations and comparisons which claim to be objective scientific research.[4]

One final note—when evaluating and comparing economies it is necessary to distinguish between forces which explain development and change of an economy's principal institutions and those which explain the performance of an economy. Chapters 3–20 will emphasize institutional development and change of an economy's principal institutions and those which explain the performance of an economy. The remainder of this chapter will address the evaluation and comparison issue.

EVALUATING
THE PERFORMANCE
OF AN ECONOMY

Appraising the performance of an economy should be undertaken with the following points in mind. First, an economy's performance can be defined in many ways, depending upon the performance criteria, methods of measurement, and weights attached to each criterion when overall performance (in the form of an index) is calculated. The choice of criteria is up to the analyst, and there is not unanimity regarding how most economic variables (e.g., economic growth, inflation, unemployment) should be measured. Second, the performance of an economy is influenced not only by institutions and rules, but by the national and political environment within which an economy exists. External factors such as favorable weather, availability of natural resources, and either avoiding involvement in a major

---

[4]An example of objective research is "quality of life" analysis. Periodically there are published studies which rank the 100 largest cities in the United States according to a measure of quality of life. One study concluded that two cities in a particular midwestern state had the highest quality of life among all major U.S. cities evaluated. Upon further reading it turned out that the study was carried out by two analysts who were members of the faculty of the major university in that same state, both of whom undoubtedly claimed that the results of their study were determined in an objective, scientific manner.

war or profiting from war-time participation of allies will, of course, positively affect an economy's performance regardless of its institutions and rules.

The definition of an economy (see Chapter 1) includes institutions and rules (including policies), since they are interrelated and because changes in rules establish new institutions. The *ceteris paribus* problem of separating the economy's impact on performance from that of the environment is easier to appreciate if one understands how broad the range of environmental factors can be. These factors include the availability and quality of natural resources; normal climatic conditions; size (e.g., value of total output) of an economy; level of economic development; size and quality of labor and capital; level of technology; relations with the external economy (e.g., trade policies, degree of economic integration); and random events, including war, internal revolution, and adverse climatic conditions. All of these factors affect an economy's performance, and few, if any, are identical between economies. While this does not prevent evaluations and comparisons of economies from being made, the strength of an analyst's conclusions will depend upon the degree to which *ceteris paribus* conditions are accounted for.

Evaluation Procedure

There are four steps to follow when evaluating an economy's performance. The first three steps are the selection of criteria which, taken together, will comprise the analyst's definition of performance; the identification of performance indicators for each criterion; and the measurement of these performance indicators. (It is desirable to quantify the behavior of each indicator when possible.) The final step is the compilation of an index consisting of the quantitative performance measure of each criterion weighted according to its relative importance.

The following list of performance indicators includes those generally found in standard evaluations of economies. Since the selection of criteria is up to the analyst, any analyst would be free to include other criteria or exclude any of the following criteria when evaluating and comparing economies. Problems concerning identification, measurement of performance, and interpretation will be discussed for each criterion where necessary. Because evaluation is not purely objective, what follows is viewed as one approach to the evaluation of economies. This chapter is intended to expand awareness of the evaluation and comparison issue, not to offer a definitive method of measurement.

ECONOMIC GROWTH.   Changes in the rate of economic output serve to demonstrate the extent to which goods and services are available in an economy. Many assume that greater availability is preferable, especially if no one has less of any goods or services or if the quality of the environment does not deteriorate as a result of growth. One indicator of growth is the increase in real gross national product per capita, which focuses on the real value of goods produced and consumed while taking account of population growth. Measurement would involve determining the total value of currently produced goods and services, the rate of inflation, and the rate of population growth. Problems arise which make evaluations and comparisons of economies more difficult. One problem, which will apply to every criterion selected for each economy, is the quality of the data and the means by which the data were gathered. The gathering and compilation of data are subject to human error and (for political purposes) falsification. Another problem concerns which goods or services to measure. Standard gross national product indicators do not include measurement of leisure time lost or gained due to economic growth; household or yard work performed by residents; the negative costs due to growth (e.g., externalities and regrettables); or illegally produced goods and services. A third problem concerns how meaningful value indicators such as prices are established, especially in economies where prices are established for control purposes as compared to prices established by fluctuating demand and supply factors. Still another problem (known as the "index number" problem[5]) concerns the comparison of two different baskets of goods or services over time. When computing an index for the volume of goods in each basket, which prices should be the basis for measurement? The earlier period, later period, or some average of the two periods? Measurements of growth rates will differ depending upon the period chosen.

ECONOMIC STABILITY.   The extent, duration, and regularity of fluctuations in employment levels, prices, the value of an economy's currency on the international money market, and the level of output are other criteria of performance. Variables used to indicate performance include the rates of employment, unemployment, and underemployment; changes in consumer price index or the value of the GNP deflator; deviations of a currency vis-à-vis major trading parties; and deviations of gross domestic product from some historical average. A "misery index" consisting of the sum of inflation rates and the rate of unemployment can be selected as a performance indicator. Institutions such as those controlled by monetary authorities and enterprise management and labor unions influence the strength and longevity of both inflation and unemployment. One problem that arises concerns policies toward unemployment, which differ between economies. Some nations (e.g., Sweden) will devote more public resources to providing employment or retraining for certain individuals temporarily out of work, while persons in the same predicament might be classified as unemployed in another economy. Another problem is the identification of acceptable levels of performance before negative performance is assumed. Is a 5 percent rate of inflation a good or bad performance? How do you compare inflation between economies where prices are set in a relatively free market versus an economy where prices are established by authorities? In determining an overall measure of stability, it is necessary to decide which indicator is more (or less) important. Do stable prices offset high unemployment and periodic low growth?

[5]For further discussion, see Robert W. Campbell, *The Soviet-Type Economies*, 3rd ed. (Boston: Houghton Mifflin, 1974), pp. 89–96.

STATIC AND DYNAMIC EFFICIENCY.   How effectively an economy uses its resources is another standard indicator of performance. Static efficiency pertains to the effectiveness of using resources at a point in time. The level of efficiency is indicated by the economy's capital-output ratio, or by how closely an economy operates relative to its production possibilities frontier. Dynamic efficiency pertains to how effectively an economy utilizes its resources over time, and can be measured according to the growth of output per unit of capital, per unit of labor input, or according to total factor productivity. Dynamic efficiency concerns that growth (as indicated by the outward shift of an economy's production possibilities frontier) not attributable to increases in the quantities of labor, capital, and raw materials. One difficulty in measuring static and dynamic efficiency is how precisely to identify an economy's production possibilities were it to operate at maximum production efficiency. This difficulty typifies the complex task facing analysts of economies, since good measures of performance for most criteria are especially difficult to define and to implement (i.e., actually measure the behavior of the criteria).

INTERNATIONAL BALANCE OF TRADE, PAYMENTS, AND CURRENCY VALUE. The performance of an economy in the international arena is reflected by its balance of payments, balance of trade, and exchange rate. Absolute values and trends for all three are measured for each country by national and international institutions (e.g., International Monetary Fund, World Bank). One evaluation problem concerns how to interpret positive or negative balances or a declining currency value. Deficits in a country's balance of payments could be attributable to its providing military and nonmilitary aid abroad, while a trade deficit could be traced to the effect of rapid domestic growth fueling a demand for imports. In each case the deficit could be considered as a positive contribution to the economy's performance. Declining currency values, while potentially contributing to domestic inflation, will benefit an economy's export industry. Another problem with interpreting the relationship between an economy and the international economy is that the rules for payments and trade as well as currency values are heavily influenced by domestic and foreign authority decisions, as well as by the economy's behavior.

INCOME DISTRIBUTION.   The nature of income distribution is another performance criterion often cited. Standard indicators are the Lorenz curve, Gini coefficient,[6] or a ratio of the percentage of income received by the lowest 40 percent of the households to that received by the upper 20 percent. One problem

---

[6]A Lorenz curve plots the percentage of income received by specific segments of the population, such as each decile or quintile. It is plotted against a line of perfect equality, whereby each segment would receive an equal proportion of income. For example, the upper 20 percent of the population would receive 20 percent of the income, and so on. A Gini coefficient is the ratio of the area between the Lorenz curve and the line of equality to the entire area under the line of equality. It ranges in value from slightly greater than 0 to 1.0. Coefficients greater than 0.5 indicate relatively high degrees of income inequality.

associated with these performance indicators is that they only measure income inequality, failing to account for the extent to which income is redistributed through measures such as payments in kind, welfare programs, "free" social services, or services where the user cost is determined on a sliding scale according to ability to pay. The standard performance indicators also do not indicate the degree of income differentiation between a nation's geographic regions. In addition, neither indicator reflects the distribution of wealth. There is disagreement regarding whether a highly or moderately skewed distribution of income or wealth is desirable, for some believe wider income and wealth differentials are necessary to stimulate laborers and entrepreneurs, avoiding the complacency that often ensues from guaranteed incomes.

QUALITY OF LIFE.   This broad criterion can be comprised of numerous performance indicators, including the degree of air, water, or noise pollution; housing space per person; the quality and variety of a typical citizen's diet; the health of the population; the incidence of crime and public corruption; the availability and cost (as a percentage of a typical family income) of a certain market basket of consumer goods and services; the amount of leisure time enjoyed; access to and quality of education and health care; and the availability and cost of cultural amenities such as concerts, movies, newspapers, television, and other forms of entertainment. Among the many specific means to measure the quality of life are pollution indices, crime rates, average life expectancy at birth, and infant mortality rates.

Summary.   This list of criteria, with their corresponding performance indicators, methods of measurement, and problems concerning measurement, could be easily extended. The major point is that the choice of criteria is up to the analyst. By explicitly stating your value premises and selecting criteria consistent with your values, you can begin to evaluate an economy in a manner relatively free from the hidden biases that characterize many analysts purporting to offer an objective evaluation of an economy or economies. Analysts will, however, always face the difficulty of quantifying and measuring the behavior of performance criteria.

PERFORMANCE INDEX.   Once the first three evaluation steps have been completed, an index of overall performance must be compiled before comparisons between economies can be made. Relative weights of each criterion's performance must be selected. The weighting step is especially important in determining the final "value" of performance because it determines the degree to which particular criteria matter. In an extreme case, for example, eight criteria can be selected and measured, with criterion 8 (say, economic growth) being assigned a weight of 0.75 (where the weights for all criteria will add to 1.0). Economy A could outperform economy B in terms of criteria 1 through 7, but economy B could be deemed the overall performance winner on the basis of a much higher rate of economic growth than economy A's rate of growth. As with most decisions in the evaluation procedure, the selection of weights is up to the analyst. Any change in the value of weights assigned will result in a change in the value of the performance index. In addition, identical outcomes (e.g., similar rates of growth, inflation) will produce different indices depending upon the relative importance assigned to each criterion by different analysts.

COMPARING ECONOMIES: SOME ISSUES

Economies, real or theoretical, can be compared according to many categories. Among the many comparisons one can make between economies are those between their overall performance, as measured by indices derived by the previously discussed method; between the principal institutions, social and political structures, and rules of actual or theoretical economies; and between the overall performance of economies as compared to the goals established by the authorities. Comparing two or more economies which are at a different level of economic development may provide a misleading assessment of how those economies differ concerning their respective effects upon economic performance. Better comparisons are those between alternative economies' performance during comparable periods of development (e.g., when two or more nations were experiencing an industrial revolution).

Another factor which complicates the comparison of economies is that each nation has its own history and culture which affect the nature of the social and political structures, and which contribute to different economic and political goals. Each of these features will affect the behavior of the economy in question. For example, as of late 1989 Hungarian authorities were more pragmatic and not as strongly tied to Marxist-Leninist principles as were their Soviet counterparts. This difference helps to explain the more extensive and rapid pace of economic growth in Hungary relative to Romania and Bulgaria since the early 1980s.

Since it is so difficult to define performance criteria precisely and to isolate the performance of an autonomous economy, meaningful comparisons of economies are difficult to make. In particular, it is troublesome to establish which forces have influenced an observed outcome. However, since the relative merits of alternative types of economies play such a central role in domestic political campaigns and international relations, comparisons are not only inevitable but necessary. Illustrations of the evaluation procedure follow.

EVALUATING AND COMPARING ECONOMIES: EXAMPLES

Some examples illustrate the evaluation process. In the first case assume that analyst A favors illiteracy, short average life expectancy, a skewed distribution of income, political instability, a high incidence of poverty, and high unemployment. Using these criteria and data provided by the World Bank to evaluate the performance of all economies in the Western Hemisphere, it would probably be concluded that the economy of Haiti outperformed all the rest.

In the second example, the values of analyst B are more traditional. They include a bias toward income equality; high life expectancy at birth; high literacy rates; a healthy natural environment (e.g., low air, water, and noise pollution); and economic stability. The definition of performance, and the evaluation and comparison that follow, reflect these preferences. This example includes data for actual economies over the 1965–88 period.

Performance of the sample economies is defined to consist of five criteria.

1. *Average annual rate of real economic growth.* This is measured by computing changes in gross national product per capita. There may be measurement problems encountered when measuring either GNP or population.

2. *Per capita GNP.* Since each economy's official GNP figures are expressed in its own national currency, the specific exchange rate chosen for converting them into a common *numerare,* namely dollars, will influence the results. In the case of the data in Table 2-1, the value of the dollar over the 1984–1986 period was used, a period during which the dollar was relatively strong. As a result, the GNP per capita figures are biased upwards. However, this upward bias does not affect the ranking of the relative performance of the economies in the following example.

3. *Average annual rate of inflation.* This indicator of economic stability will be indicated by the growth rate of the gross domestic product implicit deflator.

4. *Distribution of income.* The indicator of performance is the ratio of the income earned by the lowest 40 percent of the households to that of the upper 20 percent. Given a number of measurement problems, these figures should be interpreted more cautiously than the other figures presented.

TABLE 2-1 Performance of Selected Economies, 1965–1988 Average

CRITERIA	UNITED STATES	JAPAN	SWEDEN	CHINA
Growth[1]	1.6%	4.3%	1.6%	5.1%
Per Capita GNP[2]	$16,690	$11,300	$11,890	$310
Inflation[3]	5.9%	6.1%	8.3%	1.2%
Income Distribution[4]	0.43	0.58	0.49	0.47
Quality of Life[5]	98	99	99	80

[1]Average annual growth of GNP, 1965–1986.
[2]For 1985, using the average exchange rate for the dollar over the 1984–1986 period.
[3]Average annual rate of inflation, measured according to the growth rate of the gross domestic product implicit deflator.
[4]Figures shown are the ratio of the income earned by the lowest 40 percent of the households to that earned by the upper 20 percent.
[5]Physical Quality of Life Index,

Sources: World Bank, *World Development Report, 1988,* and Michael P. Todaro, *Economic Development in the Third World,* 4th ed. (New York: Longman, 1989).

TABLE 2-2   Ranking of Criteria Among Economies

CRITERIA	UNITED STATES	JAPAN	SWEDEN	CHINA
Growth	3	2	3	1
GNP Per Capita	1	3	2	4
Inflation	2	3	4	1
Income Distribution	4	1	2	3
Quality of Life	3	1	1	4
Index	13	10	12	13

5. *Physical quality of life.* This index is based upon three indicators: life expectancy at age 1, infant mortality, and literacy. For each indicator, a scale was developed with 1 representing the poorest performance of any nation evaluated and 100 representing the best performance. All samplecountries were assigned a score for each indicator depending upon how their indicator (e.g., life expectancy at age 1) compared to the most favorable indicator of any nation analyzed. Since Sweden had the highest average life expectancy during the years for which the data were compiled (1973), it was assigned a score of 100. The figure in Table 2-1 is the average of the three scores.[7]

To compare these performances, an overall index of performance must be compiled for each economy. One easy way to construct an index is to assign a value of 1 through 5 to each nation's performance in a particular area, depending upon how it compares to the other economies. For example, Japan's economic growth rate of 4.3 percent is second highest, so it would receive two points. Meanwhile, the U.S. per capita GNP is highest ($16,690), so for this criteria it would receive one point. Table 2-2 lists the comparative performance of each economy based upon this method of compiling an index. Note that the index is compiled by weighting each criterion equally and then adding each nation's relative performance. This method, of course, does not distinguish between good and bad within categories. For example, the relatively high rate of inflation in Sweden is given the same weight as if it had been 5 percent lower. Overall, Japan's economy performs the best based upon the choice of criteria, measurement procedure, weights assigned, and method of compiling the index.

A third example defines performance as consisting of the unemployment rate and the percentage change in gross domestic product, consumer prices, and earnings—all for 1993. The analyst prefers low unemployment and change in consumer prices as well as high growth of GDP and earnings. The countries being

---

[7]For further discussion of the Physical Quality of Life Index, see Michael P. Todaro, *Economic Development in the Third World,* 4th ed. (New York: Longman, 1989), pp. 108–112.

compared include Britain, Denmark, France, Japan, Sweden, Switzerland, and the United States. Unemployment and growth in earnings are given twice as much weight as the other two criteria. The index is computed as stated previously, except for the difference in weights. The results, included in Tables 2-3 and 2-4, indicate that for 1993 Switzerland's economy performed the best, while that of France's economy performed the worst.

TABLE 2-3 Performance of Selected Economies, 1993[1]

COUNTRY	CRITERIA			
	GDP	UNEMPLOYMENT	CONSUMER PRICES	EARNINGS
Britain	+2.5%	9.9%	+2.5	+3.0
Denmark	-1.2	11.6	+1.8	+2.7
France	-1.2	12.2	+1.9	+2.6
Japan	+0.5	2.7	+1.2	-2.5
Sweden	-0.7	8.8	+1.7	+2.7
Switzerland	+0.2	5.2	+1.8	+5.3
United States	+3.2	6.5	+2.5	+2.8

[1]GDP, consumer prices, and earnings are rates for all of 1993; unemployment is the rate for January or February 1994.

Source: *The Economist,* March 12, 1994.

TABLE 2-4 Ranking of Criteria Among Economies

COUNTRY	CRITERIA				
	GDP	UNEMPLOYMENT	CONSUMER PRICES	EARNINGS	INDEX[1]
Britain	2	5	6	2	22
Denmark	6	6	3	4	29
France	6	7	5	6	37
Japan	3	1	1	7	20
Sweden	5	4	2	4	23
Switzerland	4	2	3	1	13
United States	1	3	6	3	19

[1]The scores for unemployment and earnings are doubled, since they have been assigned greater weight than growth of GDP or consumer prices. Thus, the U.S. index is 19 (1 + 3 x 2 + 6 + 3 x 2).

The last example selects a broad range of economic, social, cultural, and political indicators to compute a quality of life for six selected nations. The ten performance indicators, each of which is given equal weight, include GDP growth, inflation, unemployment, taxes, pollution, life expectancy at birth, murder rate, daily newspapers, military expenditure, and gender equity in politics. For this example, high growth of GDP, low rates of inflation and unemployment, low tax rates, low pollution levels, high life expectancy, low birth rates, high number of newspapers, low military expenditure, and high gender equity are considered "good" performance. Tables 2-5 and 2-6 show the values of quality of life indicators and relative ranking for the selected nations. Based upon criteria and weights selected, South Korea ranks highest while Hungary ranks as having the lowest quality of life among the selected nations.

TABLE 2-5 Quality of Life in Selected Nations, 1983–present

CRITERIA	UNITED STATES	KOREA	JAPAN	MEXICO	HUNGARY	CHINA
Growth[1]	2.7%	4.1%	9.2%	1.4%	-0.6%	9.4%
Inflation[2]	3.8	1.8	5.1	59.2	15.2	8.2
Unemployment[3]	7.4	2.2	2.4	3.2	12.2	2.3
Taxes[4]	27	30	16	18	50	45
Pollution[5]	19.7	8.5	5.2	3.7	6.1	2.2
Life Expectancy[6]	76	79	70	70	70	69
Murder[7]	13.3	0.7	1.3	30.7	3.7	1.0
News[8]	250	587	280	127	261	30
Military[9]	5.6	1.0	4.0	0.4	2.1	5.0
Gender[10]	6	2	2	12	7	21

[1]GDP growth, annual average percentage 1983–1993.
[2]Annual average percentage, 1983–1992.
[3]Unemployment as a percentage of the labor force, 1992.
[4]Total taxes as a percentage of GDP, 1991. These are estimates for Hungary and China.
[5]CO_2 emissions, tons per capita, 1989 or latest estimate.
[6]Life expectancy (years) at birth, 1991.
[7]Murders per 100,000 men, 1990 or latest estimate.
[8]Daily newspapers per 1,000 people, 1988–1990. The figure for China is an estimate.
[9]Military expenditure as a percentage of GDP, 1991 or latest estimate. The figure for China is an estimate.
[10]Women members of congressional body as a percentage of all members, 1991 or latest estimate.

Source: *The Economist*, December 25, 1993–January 7, 1994.

TABLE 2-6 Ranking of Criteria Among Economies

CRITERIA	UNITED STATES	SOUTH KOREA	JAPAN	MEXICO	HUNGARY	CHINA
Growth	4	3	2	5	6	1
Inflation	2	1	3	6	5	4
Unemployment	5	1	3	4	6	2
Taxes	3	4	1	2	6	5
Pollution	6	5	3	2	4	1
Life Expectancy	2	1	3	3	3	6
Murder	5	1	3	6	4	2
News	4	1	2	5	3	6
Military	5	1	4	1	3	6
Gender	4	5	5	2	3	1
Index	40	23	29	36	43	34

CONCLUDING REMARKS

If the results of the examples are neither intuitively nor politically appealing, remember the following points that have been stressed throughout this chapter. First, the evaluation and comparison of economies are not purely objective, with the values of the analyst influential in the definition of performance, choice of criteria, measurement of criteria, relative weights assigned to each criterion, and the compilation of an index.[8] Second, it is difficult to separate the influence of the environment and policies from the autonomous performance of an economy. Finally, evaluation and comparison of economies should and will be made. Keep the limitations discussed throughout this chapter in mind when studying conclusions from such exercises, or when evaluating or comparing economies.

KEY TERMS AND CONCEPTS

Biased Conclusions   Lorenz Curve
Economy's Performance   Performance Criteria
Gini Coefficient   Performance Index

QUESTIONS FOR DISCUSSION

1. Using the examples included in the chapter, can you change the weight assigned to the criteria so that relative rankings change?
2. Explain the steps one should follow when evaluating the performance of an economy. Then use these steps to evaluate each of the following: five local restaurants, any four television programs, and each class you are taking this semester.
3. Explain three ways a performance index can be computed.
4. Are an economy's principal institutions and working rules the only factors which influence its performance? Explain.
5. Explain why five analysts would likely arrive at different conclusions if they addressed this question: "Which of the following economies has performed the best since 1989: China, Germany, Mexico, Poland, and France?"

---

[8]Readers may feel that this chapter justifies the "my opinion is as good as yours" syndrome. However, the ability to defend a position requires that opinions drawn be based upon sound critical reasoning. One step toward a more reasoned approach is to spell out criteria for evaluation, and this will contribute to the quality of intellectual debate. For example, if a person takes the position that greater wealth differentials and little government involvement in the economy are important value premises, other students could challenge the efficacy of holding such values by demonstrating that economies with such conditions experience high unemployment and crime rates.

REFERENCES

Campbell, Robert W., *The Soviet-Type Economies,* 3rd ed. Boston: Houghton Mifflin, 1974.

Eckstein, Alexander, ed., *Comparison of Economic Systems: Theoretical and Methodological Approaches.* Berkeley: University of California Press, 1971.

"Economic Indicators," *The Economist,* March 12, 1994, p. 124.

Myrdal, Gunnar, *Against the Stream.* New York: Vintage Books, 1975.

————, *Value in Social Theory.*, Paul Streeten, ed. London: Routledge and Kegan Paul, 1958.

————, *An American Dilemma,* vol. 1. New York: Pantheon Books, 1972.

Pryor, Frederic L., *A Guidebook to the Comparative Study of Economic Systems.* Englewood Cliffs, NJ: Prentice-Hall, 1985.

Todaro, Michael P., *Economic Development in the Third World,* 4th ed. New York: Longman, 1989.

Vining, Rutledge, *On Appraising the Performance of an Economic System.* Cambridge: Cambridge University Press, 1984.

"Where to Live: Nirvana by Numbers," *The Economist,* December 25, 1993–January 7, 1994, pp 39–42.

Wiles, P.J.D., *Economic Institutions Compared.* New York: John Wiley, Sons, 1977.

3

ANCIENT ROME

50 B.C.–A.D. 150

OBJECTIVES

1. Introduce the premodern economy, explaining how it is distinctive from the post-1750 "modern" economy.
2. Emphasize the significance of the philosophical basis on the acquisition and distribution of wealth throughout the Roman Empire.
3. Examine the link between the social and political structures, and how working rules for the economy were influenced by those at the top of these structures.
4. Explain the nature and extent of state regulations in coordinating the economy's production and distribution activities.

INTRODUCTION TO THE PREMODERN ECONOMY

For the purposes of this book, the era of "modern" economies is considered to begin during the late eighteenth century in England when many of the institutions of that country were assuming the character of a market society. A majority of the means of production was privately owned, markets for land, labor, and money were becoming increasingly important to the economy, and the incentive structure promoted the pursuit of individual profit and greater possibility of upward social mobility. While evidence of these features can be identified in nearly every preeighteenth-century society, it is not clear whether any particular market feature was a significant factor in the economies of those societies.

What was the nature of the premodern economy? Any attempt to answer this question must be circumspect. Hundreds of diverse societies prevailed throughout the three to ten millennia that constitute the premodern period. Any narrow categorization purporting to capture the essence of the premodern economy would be simplistic and more misleading than helpful. Such a case occurs when premodern economies are depicted as being organized on the basis of "tradition." This is generally interpreted to mean that the roles of the various participants are inherited from their ancestors, the goods produced and the technology used are "what always was," and the means and ratios of distributing goods are based on custom. It is usually held that such economies rely on some system of barter and are static, at least internally (i.e., changes in working rules or institutions are initiated by external forces).[1]

Numerous questions must be addressed if one attempts to describe the characteristics of any premodern economy. Did prices fluctuate? Was the quantity supplied dependent upon the relative prices of goods and services for sale and the relative prices of inputs necessary to produce the goods and services? Were daily needs such as basic food, clothing, and shelter of inhabitants in the economy dependent upon prices they received for contributing their property or labor to the production of goods and services? In other words, were markets central or peripheral to the standard of living of most people?

The following propositions represent the author's view concerning the nature of the premodern economy:[2]

1. There simultaneously existed economies at very different stages of development. There were some societies at relatively primitive stages in which the principal institution was the tribe which migrated in search of game. More developed societies featured considerable division of labor (including professions), more hierarchical social and political structures, and cities in which manufacturing and commerce emerged, along with local and long-distance trade.

2. The premodern economy was heavily influenced by the social and political structures of the society. Examples would be the impact of Roman aristocracy on the redistribution of wealth extracted from inhabitants of the empire, and the impact of the monarch and barons on the manorial organization of production and distribution in feudal societies.

---

[1]There is no evidence that any economy ever relied upon barter (i.e., moneyless market exchange) as the primary mechanism for coordinating economic activity. For further discussion, see George Dalton, "Barter," *Journal of Economic Issues*, 16, 1 (March 1982), 181–190.

[2]These propositions have been drawn from contributions contained in selected works of classicists, economic historians, and archeologists. These scholars include Rondo Cameron, M. I. Finley, Kevin Greene, Karl Polanyi, Nicholas Purcell, and Aaron Wildavsky. Their works were selected because of their diversity of positions regarding the importance of markets in the premodern world.

3. The state's influence over the economy's working rules could be extensive in the case of the Egyptian and Roman Empires given the strength of the central government. However, for most societies, especially during A.D 500–1500 central governments lacked the power to exercise effective control over economic activity due to transportation and communication constraints.

4. The extent of private market activity is still undetermined. Some historians believe the volume of trade was not sufficiently widespread to create an economy characterized by "an enormous conglomeration of interdependent markets"[3] in which peasants relied upon trade for their well-being. These same scholars accept that merchant activity and money lending both existed, but that these activities were considered dishonorable and were not a vital means by which most individuals provided for their daily needs. Money lending, while primarily carried out within the aristocracy, was neither a principal source of income nor an activity for the purpose of stimulating production and economic growth. The profit motive and rules of profit maximizing generally were not the basis for typical economic activity. Instead, mechanisms such as redistribution (see Roman grain dole) and reciprocity (in which goods and services flow between two parties who desire to establish or maintain cooperation and social relationships rather than gaining in the exchange) were primary social processes for coordinating economic activity.

5. Religion played an important role in defining the philosophical basis toward economic activity. The profit motive and social sanction of gain in exchange generally were not condoned.

Other scholars argue that the volume and extent of goods traded in markets that were not state regulated were considerable. In particular, they cite evidence of long-term trade by private merchants. They also believe that peasants were not self-sufficient subsistence farmers, arguing that peasants did rely upon markets to satisfy a number of their daily needs.

Given the ongoing controversy concerning the relative importance of market activity and that evidence supporting either view is inconclusive, no firm position will be taken regarding the extent of market activity in either ancient Rome or medieval England. With this in mind, the economies of these societies are presented within the analytical framework outlined in Chapter 1.

ROME, 50 B.C.–A.D. 150: PROFILE OF THE EMPIRE[4]

During the second century A.D., the Roman Empire encompassed most of Western

---

[3]M. I. Finley, *The Ancient Economy*, 2nd ed. (London: Hogarth Press, 1985), p. 22.

[4]Information contained in profile is taken from Peter Garnsey and Richard Saller, *The Roman Empire* (London: Duckworth, 1987), pp. 1–9; and Rondo Cameron, *A Concise Economic History of the World* (New York: Oxford University Press, 1989).

Europe as far north as southern Scotland and all lands west of the Rhine and Danube, all peninsulas and islands of the Mediterranean Sea plus the coastal land around the Black Sea, the northern strip of Africa (to the Sahara Desert) and most of Egypt, and much of the near Middle East (parts of contemporary Armenia, Turkey, Israel, Iran, Iraq, Jordan, and Syria). At its height the population of the empire was roughly 80–100 million people, with about 7 million living in Italy, of whom about 1 million resided in Rome. Italy's absolute population and population density, combined with the agricultural productivity potential of the peninsula, meant that it could not be self-sufficient in terms of feeding itself. Thus, conquest to establish a redistribution system for grain, olive oil, and (at times) meat was undertaken. The population in the conquered lands encompassed numerous cultures, languages, climates, and diets. Residents included nomads and sedentary farmers, primitive tribes and cultivated urbanites, bandits, and well-educated individuals.

The remainder of this chapter will describe the economy of the Roman Empire during the period 50 B.C. to A.D. 150. These specific beginning and ending dates have been selected in lieu of politically significant dates, such as 27 B.C. when Augustus assumed the role of emperor. This is done to avoid implying that the assumption of power by a new emperor had a major impact on the principal institutions and the behavior of the Roman economy, as it generally did not between 50 B.C. and A.D. 150. Institutional changes were quite modest compared to changes experienced by modern societies over the past two centuries.

HISTORICAL LEGACY AND CONTEXT

The years of conquest and civil strife preceding the rise to power and death of Julius Caesar created unique economic and political conditions within the Roman Empire. The empire expanded to include territories bordering the Mediterranean Sea and much of northern Europe (e.g., contemporary France, West Germany, Austria, England, and Wales). It was inhabited by over 50 million people, with between 1 and 2 million living in the city of Rome. Conquest of new territories served to solidify the empire's border while lessening the threat of attack in existing provinces. Broad military power and sophisticated, effective communications and transportation networks enabled Rome to generate a vast, steady flow of wealth from the empire. (Since it was the political and economic center of the empire, every road in Italy led to Rome, as did all the routes navigated in the Mediterranean.)

The finest products from all over the empire and beyond were brought into Rome. These riches included valuable foodstuffs such as fruit, grain, honey, wine, and olive oil; metals such as gold, silver, copper, tin, iron, and lead; a variety of other products including marble, ivory, pottery, linen, wool, and livestock; and perhaps the two most valuable assets in a world where most wealth came from manual labor working to produce primary products—land and slaves. Rome was not able to acquire these goods because of wealth generated from local manufacturing, for the value of such goods produced was negligible. Rather, it could afford such riches due to income received through ownership of land, and from rents, taxes, tribute, and gifts collected from inhabitants of conquered provinces and from citizens. The burden of supporting Rome was spread throughout the empire. Some areas provided food and other supplies required for the army. Others provided money to pay for government administrators and military salaries or supported the city of Rome by providing slaves and paying their taxes in kind, especially with grain. Most of the wealth collected accrued to the emperor and the few Roman families who controlled the senate. The working rules for the redistribution of the amassed wealth were made by this select group of Roman aristocracy.

PHILOSOPHICAL BASIS

Three attitudes were important in shaping the working rules of the economy: the perception regarding the role of the city of Rome within the empire; the belief that members of the aristocracy should receive a major portion of the wealth produced, albeit with an obligation to redistribute their wealth to constituents in time of need; and the belief that certain occupations were honorable while others were dishonorable. As the supreme economic and political power, Rome "arrogated to herself the financing and direction of the world's activities and claimed the right to consume the world's riches."[5] The city of Rome was a parasite, for little was produced while resources were systematically extracted from the labor and wealth of Italy and provinces throughout the Roman Empire. The administration of the empire reflected the authorities' objective to raise revenue to support the army, government administration, needs of the city of Rome, and to maintain the aristocracy in their accustomed lifestyle.

Most of the wealth acquired was distributed to members of the aristocracy. This class, however, was expected (and at times obligated) to engage in civic patrimony through redistributing some of their wealth to the needy in cities when food shortages arose or when public finance was insufficient for other purposes. In Rome the primary responsibility for assuring a steady supply of food, contributing to the maintenance and construction of public buildings and temples, and financing some of the expenses associated with the military fell upon the emperor, while members of council and magistrates bore a similar burden in other cities.

The outstanding example of civic patrimony is provided by "The Accomplishments of Augustus."[6] Among the activities financed from the Emperor Augustus's personal wealth on behalf of the state and the people of Rome were:

[5]Jerome Carcopino, translated by E. O. Lorimer, *Daily Life in Ancient Rome* (Middlesex, England: Penguin Books, 1986), p. 194.

[6]Naphtili Lewis and Meyer Reinhold, eds., *Roman Civilization Sourcebook II: The Empire* (New York: Harper & Row, 1966), pp. 9–19.

1. Administration and distribution of grain to inhabitants of Rome.
2. A gift to every citizen of Rome, and to some soldiers settled in the provinces a share of the "spoils of war."[7]
3. The transfer of money from the emperor's own wealth to the city treasury.
4. The building and repairing of public structures such as a senate house, temples, theaters, aqueducts, and forums.
5. The provision of entertainment to the city's inhabitants in the form of gladiatorial, theater, and circus shows as well as an exhibition of a naval battle.

The attitudes toward the honorableness of occupations influenced participation in economic endeavors by members of each strata within the social and political structures. In general, the upper classes faced a moral and legal restraint on their active participation in commercial activities. Certain occupations were considered "beneath the dignity of the truly wealthy and the respectable."[8] The view toward the dishonor of participating in trade and other commercial activities was articulated by Cicero. He argued it would lower a person's moral and social status to be engaged full time in the pursuit of private profit, whether through manufacture, lending money, or trading. Cicero identified as undignified such occupations as collector of harbor taxes, moneylender, retailer, wage earner, and craftsman. He condoned large-scale trading if the organizer was involved with the redistribution of the goods acquired, and if that person devoted most of his time to an agricultural estate. Cicero did not argue that less honorable occupations were unnecessary. Instead, he offered the landed aristocratic view in defining respectability of occupations for members of the aristocracy, freeborn men, foreigners, freedmen (former slaves who purchased their freedom), and slaves—and there is evidence that this philosophy was influential.

SOCIAL AND POLITICAL STRUCTURES

Social Structure

Roman society was highly stratified, divided into two broad social classes—the upper class (*honestiores* or patricians) and the lower class (*humiliores* or plebeians). Class is used in the generic sense, and was determined by status and rank. Romans were "obsessed with status and rank; a Roman's place in the social hierarchy was advertised in the clothes he wore, the seat he occupied at public entertainments, the number and social position of his clients and followers, and

---

[7]Ibid., p. 14.
[8]Henry C. Boren, *Roman Society* (Lexington, MA: D. C. Heath, 1977), p. 211.

his private expenditures on slaves, housing and banquets."[9] The social structure featured extreme differentials in wealth and status between classes. Status was based upon a Roman's "social estimation of his honour, [and] the perception of those around him as to his prestige."[10] Rank, however, was established by legal regulations. Property qualifications controlled entry into the ranks of the aristocracy. The formal structure of civilian wealth qualifications represented ratios of about 1: 2.5: 10 (i.e., the senator must have roughly 2.5 times the wealth of an equestrian and 10 times the wealth of a decurion).[11]

Many of the rules which established and perpetuated "explicit and active domination of the Roman social structure by wealth and by wealth requirements"[12] pertained to property, redistribution of wealth accumulated from the empire, and political appointment. By having the power to establish working rules and to control the army, the aristocracy, especially the emperor, could maintain their control over their assets and the power to receive the largest share of the wealth extracted from the provinces. Since wealth requirements existed for the attainment of different rank, and since the distribution of wealth was heavily dependent upon one's rank, members of the aristocracy were able to maintain their eminent position in Roman society throughout (and beyond) the 50 B.C.–A.D. 150 period.

The social structure remained stratified and relatively stable over most of the 50 B.C.–A.D. 150 period. A Roman emperor's ability to amass enormous wealth was assured by rules, or lack thereof, concerning allocation of provincial riches. An emperor would inherit the wealth of his predecessors, which included large estates (*latifundia*) in Italy and other provinces, as well as the right to all wealth generated in certain provinces (e.g., Egypt). In addition, there were no rules preventing an emperor from "replenishing his private purse from the resources of the imperial Exchequer, into which passed the taxes levied for the maintenance of his soldiers, and none dared to suggest an audit of his accounts."[13] In addition, status and occupation were to a large extent hereditary. Offspring of the aristocracy, soldiers, merchants, craftsmen, peasants, and slaves were likely to marry those of similar status. Given the limited market there was little likelihood of an industrial class acquiring social and economic power to challenge the Roman aristocracy. Working rules were designed to perpetuate stability (in terms of wealth and status differentials between ranks) throughout the social structure. As Cicero argued, "[r]ank must be preserved."[14]

[9]Garnsey and Saller, *The Roman Empire: Economy, Society and Culture*, p. 199.

[10]Ibid., p. 118.

[11]R. P. Duncan-Jones,*The Economy of the Roman Empire*, 2nd ed. (Cambridge: Cambridge University Press, 1982), pp. 3–5. The wealth requirement for a senator was roughly 1,000,000 sesterces (about ($40,000), while for an equestrian and decurion it was 400,000 sesterces ($16,000) and 100,000 sesterces $4,000), respectively.

[12]Ibid., p. 3.

[13]Carcopino, *Daily Life in Ancient Rome*, p. 81.

[14]Ramsay MacMullen, *Roman Social Relations* (New Haven: Yale University Press, 1974), p. 105.

Political Structure

Wealth followed power in ancient Rome, for the opportunity to amass considerable wealth usually depended upon one's place in the highly centralized political structure. For a brief time (50–31 B.C.) during the period under consideration, Rome was a republic. Power was shared between two consuls, a city assembly (the authority for the city of Rome's laws), and the council (the senate, responsible for finance and foreign policy). After the Imperial Order was established, power became more concentrated. Emperors could exercise virtually unlimited authority over the economy's working rules. The degree to which this power was used depended upon the strength and personality of each emperor. Some would rely upon (or be led to follow) the advice of the council, an advisory group of friends who held the rank of senator or equestrian. Below the council was the full Senate, normally responsible for the financial management of the Empire.

In an empire without a large bureaucracy or trained civil servants, the emperor's staff (which included freedmen and slaves) carried out important financial and judicial duties. This staff worked with a procurator (of equestrian rank) to manage the revenue and expenditures of the emperor. Provincial authorities, whether in a province controlled by the emperor or the senate, were responsible for maintaining law and order and collecting taxes in order to enrich the aristocracy in Rome, fund the city of Rome's expenses, and contribute to the cost of entertainment, military presence, and the construction and maintenance of public buildings and infrastructure throughout the empire, especially in Rome.

PRINCIPAL INSTITUTIONS

Four institutions were instrumental in the establishment and coordination of the major production and distribution patterns in the Roman economy: the emperor, the nonimperial aristocracy, slavery, and the army.

The Emperor

Emperors possessed virtually unlimited power to establish or modify working rules. Therefore, they could exert significant control over many of the empire's resources, the redistribution of wealth, and the treasury in Rome. Since Egypt was the richest province by virtue of its ability to produce an abundance of agricultural products, it came under the emperors' special supervision. To protect their interests, emperors prohibited members of senatorial rank from even visiting Egypt without permission, entrusting administration of this rich province to appointed officials from the equestrian rank. Emperors' military decisions affected the economy in the provinces—especially those on the frontier. Emperors usually made the allocation decisions concerning who would be granted lucrative shipping contracts. Finally, emperors could influence an individual's social status. Some fortunate Romans were able to realize a rise in social status when, as a result of the emperor's generosity, they were able to meet the wealth requirement for the next highest rank (e.g., equestrian to senator).

Nonimperial Aristocracy: Senators, Equestrians, and Decurions

The ranks of the aristocracy included about 1 percent of the population. By virtue of their status, Roman aristocrats were under social pressure to spend heavily.[15] Their influence on Roman production and distribution patterns followed from using their wealth and political influence to import luxury goods and slaves to Rome, support public works, provide supplies to the army, provide for the indigent, purchase landed estates, mines, fisheries, and forests, engage in money lending or shipping, and extract funds from taxpayers should these aristocrats hold a high political position in a province. They could make loans to communities and local authorities ("client kings") who were not able to pay taxes. Through corruption and extortion (e.g., overestimating the amount of grain owed for taxes to the empire), they could collect interest in excess of the legal limit established at 12 percent.[16]

Although greater wealth could be accumulated from land than commerce, senators and equestrians engaged in commerce to the extent permitted by informal or working rules. Senators were prohibited from engaging directly in merchant activity. A working rule existed which forbade senators from owning a ship capable of transporting large quantities of goods. Members of the Senate, however, could engage in merchant and money-lending activity through an agent. Equestrians had the means and social sanction to bid and receive state contracts. They served as superintendents of imperial properties and large-scale traders and shippers holding contracts from the state of supplies necessary to support the city of Rome as well as provincial cities. In a society which featured only modest civil services, reliance upon contracts between Rome and private individuals was widespread.

Slavery

While it is not possible to estimate accurately the size of the slave population throughout the empire for the 50 B.C.–A.D.150 period, the presence of slaves contributed to the preservation of the Roman social and political structures and to economic production. One significant contribution of slaves was as a conspicuous symbol of status and wealth for their owners. The extent of an aristocrat's wealth and status was indicated by the number of slaves used as personal servants. One estimate shows that Augustus's household had thousands of slaves, with a few hundred serving the personal needs of his wife, Livia. The concentration of wealth

---

[15]Duncan-Jones, *The Economy of the Roman Empire*, p. 32.

[16]A. H. M. Jones, *The Roman Economy: Studies in Ancient Economic and Administrative History*, P. A. Brunt, ed. (Oxford: Basil Blackwell, 1974), p. 118. Jones argues that "[t]here is no evidence to estimate how much of the profits of the provinces went to the treasury and how much into the products of the Roman upper class, but there are a number of figures which suggest that private profits greatly exceeded public revenue." Ibid., p. 119.

and status within the upper class was perpetuated by the manner in which slaves were allocated and retained. Slaves were either purchased in an open market, received as a gift from another member of the aristocracy, or born into a household through natural reproduction. Thus, wealthy families, especially those who already owned slaves, could easily acquire or maintain a staff of slaves.

Slave labor was ubiquitous throughout the empire. In addition to providing household services, slaves contributed to the steady production of essential goods and services by working in skilled and unskilled occupations. These included public administrator (keeping financial accounts for the emperor or other ranking officials throughout the provinces); physician and teacher; builder and maintenance worker for public structures, public baths, streets, sewers; manager of agricultural estates, shipping operations, warehouses, and brickyards; self-employed craftsman, shopkeeper, pawnbroker, and moneylender; and mine worker and galley oarsman. To the extent that slaves dominated some of these occupations, free men were denied work opportunities while wages for day workers (especially in agriculture) would be lower. Slavery also affected anyone who sought to enter commerce through petty trade by limiting the demand for goods and services offered in marketplaces. Since slaves were numerous in aristocratic households, wealthy families were able to provide for their own food, clothing, and other essential household needs. Consequently, the size of markets was limited as these families were less likely to patronize petty craftsmen and merchants.

Slaves belonging to those aristocratic families may have been provided with the type of education and training with which they could work in lucrative, albeit dishonorable, occupations (e.g., manager of a commercial enterprise). Some slaves were able to accumulate sufficient wealth (through commercial activity or an inheritance from their master who had no natural heirs) to purchase their freedom, the cost of which was set by their owner and generally approximated the prevailing market price for slaves. Although these former slaves became citizens, many would still be obligated to perform economic duties for their owner, such as being required to pay a percentage of their future earnings to their former master or master's household. A few freedmen became as wealthy as any member of the aristocracy, save the emperor. Evidence indicates that of the ten wealthiest members of Roman society who lived between 27 B.C. and A.D. 150, four were freedmen.

The Army

The Roman army, usually 300,000 to 400,000 strong, was charged with transmitting the Roman way of life throughout the provinces, gathering tribute (e.g., wheat, olive oil, barley, vegetables, fruits, wine), maintaining order, protecting the frontiers from invasion, building roads and fortifications, and occasionally conquering new territories. The army effectively protected the empire from outside invaders, native rebellion, or pirates. The economy benefited from the lack of disturbance to commercial activity. Joining the army offered upward social mobility as well as higher income to young peasant men. In addition to sharing in the booty following a conquest, members of the army received incomes which exceeded those of typical peasants and petty craftsmen. Upon completion of 25 years of military service, a generous retirement benefit was granted as well as citizenship for anyone not already enjoying that privilege.

BEHAVIOR OF THE ECONOMY

The behavior of the Roman economy includes how the economy was organized to resolve its economic problem (organization of resource allocation decision making, rules governing ownership and control of resources, and social process for economic coordination); institutional change throughout the period; and the economy's performance.

Organization of Resource Allocation Decision Making

Because the extensive empire was controlled by an imperial administration based in Rome, resource allocation decision making which affected taxes, coinage, government expenditures, and the working rules for state trading and private commercial activities was highly centralized. This was partly due to the responsibility which fell upon the emperor to disburse funds for public purposes, a situation created "by the force of circumstances, and by the weight of the enormous personal wealth accumulated [by the Emperor]."[17] As the emperor allocated funds for purposes ranging from feeding the inhabitants of Rome to constructing roads throughout the empire, it became increasingly difficult to distinguish between the state's income and the emperor's personal wealth.

Since Rome viewed its provinces as estates of the Roman citizens, a source of exploitation, and an extension of its empire through conquest, the services offered to most provinces were rudimentary, and the number of Roman officials present was low. It has been estimated that to govern a provincial population of over 50 million people there were fewer than 200 administrators of senate or equestrian rank residing in the provinces. There was, however, an efficient system of tax collection, which combined with the productivity of the provinces to generate sufficient income for the central government.

TAXES AND EXPENDITURES.   The majority of the expenditures of the central government were to maintain the aristocracy and for military purposes (e.g., salaries, equipment and supplies, ships), with public works, buildings, entertainment, the city of Rome's grain supply, and salaries of civil service and other government officials comprising most remaining expenditures. To finance these expenditures, Rome relied upon tribute and booty, proceeds from state-owned resources such as mines, and a system of taxation.

---

[17]M. Rostovtzeff, *The Social and Economic History of the Roman Empire, Vols. 1 & 2,* 2nd ed. (Oxford: Clarendon Press, 1957), p. 55.

The Roman system of tax collection was efficient. Property taxes provided the largest single source of revenue. These were a fixed amount (about 1 percent assessed on property including arable land, vineyards, olive groves, slaves, and ships), which did not vary according to the size of a harvest. A poll tax on adults between the ages of 12 and 65 was assessed either on males or on all adults, depending upon the province. The harbor taxes (i.e., customs duties) were set between 2 percent and 2.5 percent of the value of goods imported throughout the empire with the notable exception of luxury goods imported from the eastern provinces which faced a 25 percent import duty. This rate was established for two purposes: to discourage the outflow of currency from Rome and to acquire revenue from wealthy Romans whose demand for the luxury imports was highly inelastic.

Among the effects of Roman tax and expenditures policies was that Romans residing in Italy naturally benefited. They were responsible for paying only miscellaneous taxes while they enjoyed the benefits of protection, public services, and (in Rome) free grain—all financed primarily by the provinces. In addition, there was a multiplier effect as income shared among the aristocracy, including salaries of administrative officials, was spent in Italy. There was also an uneven pattern of expenditures throughout the provinces which generated a redistribution of wealth. A majority of revenue collected came from Mediterranean provinces, while a high proportion of total state expenditures was allocated to the army, which was generally stationed along the frontiers in poorer provinces (e.g., Britain).[18] The less developed areas consequently benefited from the inflow of funds and from the merchant activity established in towns which grew up adjacent to Roman forts and affected the surrounding province.

The taxation system also exacerbated the dual nature of Roman society, especially in Italy. It promoted the growth of tax-exempt estates while diminishing the well-being of peasant proprietors.[19] Dualism served to limit trade for nonluxury goods and services. Markets for most goods and services were small due to the impoverished standard of living most peasant families experienced. In the long run (i.e., post A.D.150) the combined effects of no booty from additional conquests, rising military costs to maintain existing frontiers, and the declining ability of those being taxed to meet their obligations led to debasement of the currency as the empire attempted to resolve growing fiscal and monetary problems.

Ownership and Control of Resources

Ownership and control of resources in the Roman economy were concentrated within the aristocracy. If the emperor's wealth is considered "public" while that of the remaining members of the Roman Empire "private," then the economy was characterized by modest public ownership and extensive public control of labor, land, mines, and the rights to use and dispose of the products of certain resources

---

[18]A. H. M. Jones, *The Roman Economy: Studies in Ancient Economic and Administrative History*, pp. 127, 128.
[19]Ibid., p. 129.

(e.g., right to fish and sell the catch). There was extensive private ownership and modest private control of key resources (e.g., land), with ownership and control highly concentrated among members of the aristocracy.

LABOR.   In the Roman Empire there were few people who would be considered wage laborers, the counterpart to salaried and hourly workers in contemporary economies. Workers were generally not "hired" in the Roman economy. There were craftsmen and merchants who sold their products and peasants who provided for themselves and engaged in petty trading activities. In addition, there were dependent laborers—clients and those in debt bondage—who performed many duties, especially as tenant farmers in Italy and the provinces. Persons in debt bondage were compelled to work not only in agriculture, but in mining or in the construction or repairing of infrastructure. Finally, there were slaves.

In Rome and throughout Italy aristocratic control over those engaged in a craft, the peasantry, and slaves enabled the wealthy class to maintain their social status without facing the threat of a rising commercial class. Freeborn craftsmen and peasants, however, competed with slave labor. All engaged in a craft whether freeborn, freedmen, or slaves faced strict control by the imperial government.[20] Those engaged in agriculture were subject to working rules by which "Romans never permitted the development of a peasantry with powerful property rights either in Italy or in the provinces."[21] The effect of the empire on rural labor in the provinces was not as dramatic. While Roman presence in the provinces led to new institutions at the apex of social and political structures, the rules pertaining to native workers changed very little after Roman conquest (except for the taxes imposed).

LAND.   The emperor controlled a considerable portion of the best arable land, including the entire province of Egypt. Control over the output of land in the provinces was essential to the empire. Much of the food which fed the Roman army and citizens of the city of Rome was collected from the provinces, especially those in Africa. The aristocracy's investments in land generally took the form of a *latifundia*. These great estates were not the dominant institution in the rural economy. They did, however, signify the extent of their owners' status and wealth as they were large plantations with facilities not unlike those found in a small village, and many were capable of being self-sufficient by producing their own food, clothes, tools, carts, and pottery. Work was performed either by slaves and day-wage laborers (hired during plowing and harvesting seasons) managed by a slave-bailiff, or by free tenants permitted to farm on estate property. Craftsmen (either freeborn, freedmen, or slaves) were employed as millers, bakers, potters, iron workers and blacksmiths, and butchers, among other occupations. Other workers toiled in the fields producing

[20]Boren, *Roman Society*, p. 210.

[21]Peter Garnsey, ed., *Non-Slave Labour in the Graeco-Roman World* (Cambridge: Cambridge Philological Society, 1980), p. 2.

foodstuffs destined to be traded, generally in nearby towns or city markets.

OTHER RESOURCES.   In addition to labor and land, gold, silver and tin mines, marble and granite quarries, and ships were key resources in the Roman economy. All were subject to state control. However, private traders and *negotiatores* could engage in trade if granted a state contract. This would give them the right to acquire and dispose of goods (e.g., grain, marble) owned by the state. The activities of traders and *negotiatores* are discussed later in this chapter.

Social Process for Economic Coordination

The relative importance of markets versus state regulation of economic activity as processes to coordinate production and distribution decisions throughout the Roman Empire remains an unresolved issue. This section discusses both means, especially regarding production and distribution of widely exchanged goods and services such as grain, olive oil, wine, marble, and slaves, as well as luxury goods such as incense, ivory, spices, silk, and jewelry made from precious metals.

TRADE VIA MARKETS WITH PRIVATE BUYERS AND SELLERS.   A majority of the empire's inhabitants lived off land they either owned or rented, or subsisted with earnings as day-wage laborers. Locally most output was consumed by peasant producers, while some was sold in local markets as a means to pay rent and taxes (where these payments were not made in kind) and to provide income for purchases of goods and services peasant farmers were unable to produce. The primary items traded were wheat, barley, olive oil, and wine. Local markets were generally periodic, for it was difficult to sustain a number of producers without an organized system of distribution or a large number of customers. Relatively easy means to distribute their produce only existed for peasants located near a city, an army fort, or a supply route.

Trade also occurred on the regional and long-distance level. Trade within and between regions was inhibited by transport costs, relatively small markets, and uniform production conditions (which led to homogeneity of goods produced). Due to poor roads and the need for considerable labor and livestock, transport costs by land, in particular, were especially high, perhaps more than 5 and 20 times the cost of river and sea transport, respectively. Merchant activity occurred on the regional level, especially as such trade coincided with military activities. Merchants traded with soldiers and nonmilitary inhabitants along the supply routes and around frontier forts. The army and forts of the empire attracted those seeking to trade. Merchants became involved with transporting supplies for the army and in the process carried other goods to be sold along the supply route or at the fort.

Regarding long-distance trade the risk, transport costs, and relatively small markets led such trade to be restricted to luxury goods in addition to military and other state needs. Cities, especially Rome and provincial urban areas such as Alexandria, Egypt, were major centers of commercial activity. Growth of market activity for nonluxury goods coincided with growth of the cities, especially provincial cities, as mass markets slowly developed for products such as textiles, pottery, and wine.

Because of the size and wealth of its population, Rome was by far the largest and wealthiest single market, and was a magnet for trade all over the empire. Rome was a "consumer city on a large scale"[22] (whose inhabitants' income was derived from their place in the social and political structures, from rents earned as absentee landlords, or from providing services while catering to the needs of the aristocracy. The state's role in requisitioning goods and the high incidence of impoverished inhabitants, many of whom were provided with grain and entertainment, limited the effective size of the mass market. A thriving trade in luxury goods existed, however, for the aristocracy (including absentee landlords residing in the city) indulged their lavish lifestyles by consuming many imported luxury goods. Goods such as perfume, jewelry, ivory, and mirrors were brought to Rome mainly from the Far East, and were paid for in precious metals.

Very few people earned their living as producers. The role of manufacture and trade in the empire was limited because of the agrarian nature of the economy, primitive technology, high transport costs, and the state's redistribution activities. Those engaged in nonagricultural production were primarily specialty craftsmen (e.g., tanners, furriers, carpenters, metal workers). Inhabitants of Rome engaged in private commercial activity included aristocracy (who financed ship owners, invested in the cargo traded, and lent money), rich merchants, financiers and other merchants, and retailers. In addition, an increasing number of city bourgeoisie owned more than 100 "corporations," which produced cloth, furniture, and poultry. These organizations were managed by plebeians and slaves

There were private bankers, many of whom were freedmen, who became wealthy following their receiving manumission. Their banks accepted deposits, extended short-term loans to nobility in need of cash, provided mortgages, and issued credit for nautical ventures—the only type of commercial loan. In this case "a lender advanced money on the security of a merchant's ship or cargo, or both, on condition that if the voyage was successful he got his money back with high interest, but if his ship were sunk he lost his money."[23] More sophisticated financial or other types of business institutions did not develop in the Roman economy. The primary reason was that Roman law did not provide for limited liability, so all joint ventures had to be partnerships. The joint-stock company or the modern corporation was simply inconceivable to Roman attitudes toward commercial activity.

STATE REGULATION OF TRADE.   In broad terms the state regulated trade through public expenditures, operating a redistribution scheme, and establishing working rules for commerce. Public expenditures which promoted trade included

---

[22]Keith Hopkins, "Models, Ships and Staples," *Trade and Famine in Classical Antiquity*, Garnsey and Whittaker, eds., p. 88.

[23]A. H. M. Jones, *The Roman Economy*, p. 188.

military activities, which made water transport safer (through suppression of pirates) and required that supplies be purchased and distributed to the army stationed throughout the empire; construction of public buildings and maintenance of infrastructure (waterways, ports, aqueducts, roads, warehouses, public buildings, marketplaces); regulation of the supply of money; provision of a uniform currency system; and charging modest customs duties and tolls. In addition, merchant trade occurred along official supply routes and ensued from suppliers of grain and marble to the state selling any excess goods transported. On the other hand, redistribution schemes such as the grain dole, contracts with shippers to provide marble and other supplies for cities and the army, and receiving taxes in kind generally involved civil servants and slaves rather than merchants. Private trade in terms of consumer goods which traveled long distances suffered as a consequence, assuming an important role in major urban centers.

The state introduced large-scale redistribution schemes because it needed assurance of a steady supply of goods (e.g., grain, cloth, marble). Such schemes included control of transport, import centers and prices; state subsidies to some of those commissioned to produce, transport, distribute and keep records of certain goods shipped, stored and transported; state-financed import centers (with warehouses) and marketplaces; and state-established maximum prices for which certain goods could be traded after the state had redistributed its supply. Public officials were concerned that sufficient supplies of foodstuffs be available and sold at reasonable prices. City magistrates were hired to sell goods at less than prevailing market prices if such prices exceeded the state-established maximum prices. In addition, it was the duty of magistrates to "prevent abuses in the market place of Rome . . . [They] checked weights and measures in the open market, watched prices . . . and tried to prevent sharp practices of all kinds in commercial dealings."[24] The state financed its regulation of trade activities with precious metals and through funds acquired from taxes, tribute, and tolls, which were imposed at a modest rate of 2.5 percent of the value of the transported goods. Labor for construction and maintenance of infrastructure and buildings was organized by the state, drawing from the pool of free citizens and inhabitants, soldiers, convicts, and slaves. Cities often supported some slaves who would be responsible for maintaining civic property, stocking public baths, repairing streets, and cleaning sewers.

State trading of marble and grain involved open bidding for contracts to ship those goods. Merchants would charter all or part of a ship, respectively, with which to meet the contractual terms with the state and to transport goods for private trade. Shippers with whom merchants worked also fell into classes depending upon the degree of responsibility assumed for the financing, purchasing, and sale of cargo. There were agents of a ship owner in charge of a sale, and financiers. Some prominent Roman citizens were commissioned by the state as shippers in return for grants of privileges (e.g., immunity from the civic requirement that wealthy citizens

[24]Geoffrey Rickman, *The Corn Supply of Ancient Rome* (Oxford: Clarendon Press, 1980), pp. 34–35.

contribute to civic needs out of their own personal wealth). Two examples illustrate the activities and rules of state trading: the marble trade and the grain dole.

MARBLE TRADE.   Marble trade included a considerable level of imperial involvement, since it was part of the state redistribution scheme. The state-owned mines and quarries, many of which were managed by private contractors under a franchise agreement, in Greece, Gaul, northern Africa, Egypt, and throughout the eastern empire. Marble was mined and transported on ships by contractors commissioned by the state. The marble was taken to importing centers, usually Rome, to provide material for building purposes. While private individuals could purchase marble at these centers at prices set by the state, most of the marble was imperial property and was either stockpiled in state-controlled marble yards or designated for public buildings, some of which were quite elaborate. If contractors transported a supply of marble in excess of the amount commissioned, they were free to sell it throughout the empire. Archeological evidence of marble discovered throughout the empire indicates a widespread trade in marble.

GRAIN DOLE.   The grain dole was the largest redistribution scheme in pretwentieth-century economies. Cities throughout the empire, especially Rome, often were unable to produce enough grain to feed themselves due to the uncertain arid climate combined with other water and land constraints. Prior to 50 B.C. there had been reliance upon private grain supplies, but the uncertainty of supply, slowness of land transport, and irregularity of foreign shipments (pirates exacerbated the problem) led to periodic grain shortages, rising grain prices, and occasional famine—bringing about great social unrest.

The state became involved with subsidizing grain during the second century B.C. Within Rome and its rural surroundings, civil strife and economic hardship were rampant when Caesar was named dictator. Periodic crop failures due to uncertain weather encouraged migrants into Rome where the state provided them with free grain. By the time Augustus assumed power, the public expected the emperor to protect them from food shortages and rising food prices. Augustus astutely perceived the potential consequences of food shortages amidst the wealth enjoyed by the aristocracy in a city (Rome) whose inhabitants believed they were entitled to a guaranteed supply of food. In response, the state institutionalized a redistribution scheme for grain. Officials were appointed and state funds allocated to secure and distribute grain to citizens of Rome and other major cities, and to ensure low prices for the grain which the public had to purchase (since consumption of grain was roughly double the amount of grain distributed to the typical family by the state).

The redistribution scheme required acquisition, transport and storage, and distribution of grain to urban citizens and members of the army. Grain generally was acquired as tribute from provinces, from rent on public land or imperial estates, from the private stocks of the aristocracy, and through state purchases from merchants or landowners. The state set target quotas at high levels to hedge against poor harvests and significant losses incurred during shipping and transport. Private owners of a ship capable of transporting about 70 tons of wheat, and willing to do so for six years, were commissioned under state contract to carry out the task of acquiring and transporting grain for Rome and other provincial cities.[25]

Grain was transported to the port city of Ostia where the state had financed construction of improved harbor facilities. From there grain was transferred to boats capable of traveling up the Tiber River to Rome, where it was unloaded and stored in state granaries until being distributed, usually on a monthly basis. The entire redistribution process was supervised by a public official who could directly oversee the final distribution of grain to Rome's citizens. Evidence concerning the working rules for final distribution is not clear, but generally the procedure was as follows.

In Rome, eligibility for receipt of grain was extended to resident soldiers plus about 250,000 male citizens at least 14 years of age who resided within the city.[26] Given their average family size the amount of grain distributed was destined to feed over 700,000 persons. The amount distributed, however, was not sufficient to feed a family of four, nor was it the objective of the grain dole to do so. Rather, it was intended to placate the population by mitigating their suffering from inadequate supplies of food. Families had to purchase the rest of their grain on the open market. To prevent abuses in the marketplace, public officials monitored prices. Should prices rise above acceptable levels, they could either sell state grain at below-market prices or fine any offending merchants who sought to push up market prices by hoarding grain. While merchants' profits from grain sales were tempered by state regulation, no such regulations were faced by millers and bakers. They profited from the grain dole, for Roman citizens had little choice but to have their grain ground by the miller and baked into bread by the baker. For the state to have performed these services would have been an expensive distribution nightmare.

ROMANIZATION.   The state influenced economic activity throughout the provinces. Romanization meant the promotion of urban life, which helped Roman authorities to collect taxes, administer Roman laws, and recruit provincial inhabitants to join the army or become local civil officials. To assure a constant flow of daily needs such as grain, meat, wine, salt, weapons, and uniforms for the army and civil servants, supplies were requisitioned by the state. This state-financed activity influenced patterns of demand and supply throughout the empire as well as the flow of goods along military supply routes. The demand for bulk supplies enabled shippers to overcome high land transport costs by attaching goods meant for the civilian market to army shipments.

Roman presence throughout nonurban areas in the provinces had a modest and perhaps temporary effect on the local economies. Money received by Roman authorities, civil employees, and members of the army spread monetization and commercialization. This provided an opportunity for subjects to

[25]Ibid., p. 123.
[26]Garnsey and Saller, *The Roman Empire: Economy, Society, and Culture,* p. 83.

sell goods for coins, which would enable them to pay their taxes, if payment in kind was not possible. Towns grew up around forts, while the demand for goods and services encouraged artisan and merchant activity. This was especially true in more primitive regions of the empire such as Britain compared with more developed Middle Eastern provinces where urbanization and long distance trade existed well before Roman conquest. However, if the army was transferred, local civilian trade generally decreased near forts and along supply routes.

MONEY SUPPLY.[27]　All state payments were on a cash basis and all currency was in the form of coins, so ownership and close supervision of gold, silver, and copper mines and the mints were deemed essential by the state to maintain control over the economy. In general, the Romans seemed to have understood, through common sense, the relationship between the quantity of money, interest rates, and prices, especially the price of land. The state attempted to promote a favorable inflow of booty and taxes so as to maintain adequate levels of liquidity and price stability without excessive minting and circulation of additional coins.

Shortages of liquidity in the face of growing demand for money was a state concern, for normally it did not borrow funds. If taxes collected were not sufficient to meet its obligations, alternative sources of finances available included largess from the aristocracy, the sale of property (e.g., houses, jewelry), issuance of new coins, establishment of rules forbidding coins from being exported out of Italy, or the debasement of the currency.[28] Debasement was accomplished either by mixing a base metal with the metals used for the coins (gold, silver, bronze, copper, zinc) or reducing the weight of coins.

SUMMARY OF STATE IMPACT ON TRADE.　The state's financial needs were modest and the flow of taxes was generally sufficient to meet public needs. As a result, economic planning or widespread state ownership did not characterize the production and distribution of most goods and services. The administered trade for grain and marble, among other goods, was carried out by contractors whose bids were accepted. The redistribution schemes of the state, particularly the tributary trade in grain, were strategic transactions through which the social and economic spheres of the Roman Empire were integrated. Financing of the venture or sale of excess goods transported in the process was subject to very few, if any, state working rules. Rules existed which limited the extent of commercial activity by aristocracy. Economic activity was enhanced by uniform Roman laws, which created a coherent legal framework to facilitate strict enforcement of contracts and protect property owners throughout the empire.

[27]For a complete discussion of the monetary activities by the state, see E. LoCascio, "State and Coinage in the Late Republic and Early Empire," *The Journal of Roman Studies,* 71 (1980), 76–86.
[28]For further discussion, see LoCascio, "State and Coinage in the Late Republic and Early Empire," p. 85; and Garnsey and Saller, *The Roman Empire: Economy, Society and Culture,* p. 21.

INSTITUTIONAL CHANGE

Between 50 B.C. and A.D. 150 there was continuity in the working rules for the economy, although the senate's degree of power waned vis-à-vis autocratic emperors following the establishment of the imperial order in 27 B.C. Otherwise the social and political structures remained stable and enduring, as did the philosophical basis for economic activity. Regulations of the centralized redistribution system preserved the highly stratified society, inhibiting mobility into the aristocracy during the period. Urbanization and an expansion of trade did, however, lead to a growing number of city merchants, some of whom accumulated enough wealth to join the ranks of the decurion, equestrian, and sometimes even the senatorial class.

Due to the peaceful conditions within the empire after 27 B.C., new conquests or internal rebellions rarely occurred. One result was that the number of prisoners captured (the primary source of slaves) and sold on the slave market slowly declined. Meanwhile the demand for slaves increased faster than the natural growth of the slave population. This created higher prices for slaves, making the employment of slave labor on estates or in mines unprofitable. In response, some estates were divided into small holdings to be worked by tenant farmers. At the same time working rules were imposed to restrict peasant mobility. Greater reliance on dependent free labor was not confined to estates, for some of those peasants unable to find work in agriculture might have had no alternative than to become indentured laborers, replacing slaves in the mines.

PERFORMANCE OF THE ECONOMY

There was an expansion in trade, stable prices, and economic growth during most of the 50 B.C.–A.D. 150 period. Growth of trade in luxuries and everyday items partly was due to improved transportation, more sophisticated banking practices, and an extended use of coinage. Crude evidence that prices were stable comes from the basic rate of military pay for a member of the legion, which remained constant from 27 B.C. to A.D. 85, increased 25 percent at that time, and remained constant until after A.D. 150.[29]

Economic growth, primarily in agriculture, was due to rising agricultural productivity, more land brought under cultivation, a growing population (and therefore work force), and greater division of labor which increased labor productivity.[30] Concerning relative profitability of agricultural products, wine may have offered considerable potential for profit, although evidence of price

[29]The rate of pay was 900 sesterces until A.D. 85, and 1,200 sesterces thereafter. The average annual rate of increase was less than 0.5 percent. See R. P. Duncan-Jones, *The Economy of the Roman Empire,* 2nd ed., p. 10.
[30]Kevin Greene, *The Archeology of the Roman Empire* (London: B. T. Batsford, 1986), pp. 14–15.

fluctuations indicates that the potential for considerable loss existed as well. This would have been likely if a large expansion in the number of acres cultivated to produce wine (in anticipation of high profits) coincided with abundant harvests. Another profitable venture was livestock, for raising poultry, lambs, and pigs was profitable if the producer was located near a large town or city. For the other staples, cereals and olive oil, profit rates seem to have been lower but steadier than wine. Olives, due to the greater time for trees to mature, offered less return but did have the advantage of not being as labor intensive as cereal production.

HOW ROME ILLUSTRATES THE EVOLUTIONARY-INSTITUTIONAL THEORY

The economy of Rome is a premodern society which illustrates the evolutionary-institutional theory. Coordination of most of the empire's production and distribution activities can be traced to activities and discussions by the principal institutions—the emperor and other members of the aristocracy, slavery, and the army. A lesser role was played by peasants and those merchants involved with transporting goods for state and private consumption.

The origin, activities, and working rules for these principal institutions evolved from Rome's unique history, the philosophical basis for the economy, and decisions of authorities who introduced and enforced working rules. The attitudes of Roman society justified a highly skewed distribution of wealth and power as well as exploitation of the empire for the city of Rome's benefit. Heavy reliance was placed upon a system of taxation and extraction of booty, tribute, and slaves to maintain the aristocracy, the military, and certain citizens and inhabitants. Some important production and distribution activities were part of a centralized redistribution system. The relatively favorable performance of the economy, monopoly over political power, control of the army by the aristocracy, and rules inhibiting the development of a powerful commercial class or peasantry meant that the activities and rules governing the principal institutions remained relatively stable between 50 B.C. and A.D. 150.

CONCLUDING REMARKS

Centralization of decision making and the highly skewed distribution of wealth contributed to stability in the Roman economy throughout 50 B.C.–A.D. 150. After A.D. 150 the combination of Roman aristocratic values, exploitation of most laborers, a shrinking tax base, and the debasing of the currency acted to promote economic decline. Greater centralization of Rome's power (especially regarding tax collection) occurred because exploitation of the empire became less profitable, thereby requiring that more onerous taxes be collected. The greatest burden fell upon taxpayers from the lower class, especially poorer landowners. During periods when bad weather adversely affected harvests, some peasants were unable to meet their financial obligations and lost their holdings. Land ownership became further concentrated as wealthy landowners purchased the land which thereby became available.

Over time Italy began to decline as the center of the empire. This trend was stimulated by the decreasing number of slaves and rising production costs, and coincided with a greater role for Spanish imports into Italy. Eventually the fall of Rome in A.D. 476 created the political and economic conditions for a new set of economic institutions, namely those of a feudal economy. An example of such an economy is presented in Chapter 4.

KEY TERMS AND CONCEPTS

Barter   Market Economy
Grain Dole   Premodern Economy

QUESTIONS FOR DISCUSSION

1. In what respect did the Roman political structure mirror the social structure?
2. What was the role of the *latifundia* in the Roman economy?
3. What were the working rules governing the grain dole?
4. What measures were adopted by the state for the purpose of regulating trade?
5. Explain how and why the Roman aristocracy had such extensive influence throughout the economy.
6. Why do you believe the state regulated trade?
7. Using the information provided in this chapter, evaluate the following statement: "The existence of markets in an economy does not necessarily mean that there was a market economy."

REFERENCES

Cameron, Rondo, *A Concise Economic History of the World.* New York: Oxford University Press, 1989.

Dalton, George, "Barter," *Journal of Economic Issues,* 16, 1 (March 1982), 181–190.

Davisson, William I., and James E. Harper, *European Economic History*, Vol. I. New York: Appleton-Century-Crofts, 1972.

Duncan-Jones, R. P., *The Economy of the Roman Empire*, 2nd ed. Cambridge: Cambridge University Press, 1982.

Finley, M. I., *The Ancient Economy,* 2nd ed. London: Hogarth Press, 1985.

Garnsey, Peter, ed., *Non-Slave Labour in the Graeco-Roman World.* Cambridge: Cambridge Philological Society, 1980.

————, Keith Hopkins, and C. R. Whittaker, eds., *Trade in the Ancient Economy.* London: Hogarth, 1983.

————, and C. R. Whittaker, eds., *Trade and Famine in Classical Antiquity.* Cambridge: Cambridge Philological Society, 1983.

————, and Richard Saller, *The Roman Empire: Economy, Society and Culture.* London: Duckworth, 1987.

Greene, Kevin, *The Archeology of the Roman Empire.* London: Batsford, 1986.

Hopkins, Keith, "Taxes and Trade in the Roman Empire (200 B.C.–A.D. 400)," *The Journal of Roman Studies,* 70 (1980).

Jones, A. H. M., *The Roman Economy: Studies in Ancient Economic and Administrative History,* P. A. Brunt, ed. Oxford: Basil Blackwell, 1974.

————, "Inflation Under the Roman Empire," *The Economic History Review,* 5, 3 (1953), 293–318.

Lewis, Naphtali, and Meyer Reinhold, eds., *Roman Civilization Sourcebook II: The Empire.* New York: Harper & Row, 1966.

Mayhew, Anne, Walter C. Neale, and David W. Tandy, "Markets in the Ancient Near East: A Challenge to Silver's Argument and Use of Evidence," *Journal of Economic History,* 45, 1 (March 1985), 127–137.

Polanyi, Karl, Conrad M. Arensberg, and Harry W. Pearson, *Trade and Markets in Early Empires.* Chicago: Henry Regnery, 1957.

Rickman, Geoffrey, *The Corn Supply in Ancient Rome.* Oxford: Clarendon Press, 1980.

Rostovtzeff, M., *The Social and Economic History of the Roman Empire,* Vols. 1 & 2, 2nd ed., Oxford: Clarendon Press, 1957.

Webber, Carolyn, and Aaron Wildavsky, *A History of Taxation and Expenditure in the Western World.* New York: Simon and Schuster, 1986.

4

THE MEDIEVAL ECONOMY

England, A.D. 1000–1400

OBJECTIVES

1. Introduce the factors that contributed to the slow evolution of market activity on a national scale.
2. Link the philosophical basis, especially the teachings of the Church, to the working rules and behavior of the economy.
3. Distinguish between the working rules for economic activity of the manor and those of the town.
4. Describe the working rules pertaining to state regulation of the national economy and guild regulation of the town economy.

MEDIEVAL ENGLAND

The population of medieval England was about 2 million in 1066, and it grew to between 5 and 6 million by 1348. In A.D. 1000 England's monarchy exercised only modest control over the economy. Barons (usually dukes or earls), their vassals, and the Church directed most economic activities of the predominantly rural society, although scattered, semiautonomous towns were beginning to develop their own working rules for economic, political, and social conduct. The pervasive nature of social, political, and economic activities was that of a feudal society. The organization of these activities was localized and protective. The noble and peasant classes formed communities almost completely isolated from external economic and political forces, with the major exception being their common spiritual ties to the Church. Beginning in the eleventh century, this isolation would slowly erode as markets gradually developed on a local, regional, and international level.

When the Anglo-Saxons and Danes conquered England, they introduced political and economic institutions and working rules similar to those of their Germanic feudal societies. Another factor in the origin of the feudal society was the bankruptcy of civil order following the fall of Rome, which led to a void in the provision of protection, justice, infrastructure, and rules for economic activities. There also was a general absence of efficient means for communication and travel beyond one's immediate environment. The maintenance of the social and political structures and the economy in such societies required the efforts of a large number of servile agricultural workers and craftsmen to support the ruling class.

ATTITUDES TOWARD ECONOMIC ACTIVITY AND WORKING RULES—PERVASIVE CHURCH INFLUENCE

Three views were central to the philosophical basis toward the medieval economy: the teachings of the Church concerning a proper code of behavior in economic activities, the traditional belief that society should be structured in a feudal manner, and the townspeople's view toward commercial activity. The influence of the Church was most significant while the economy was static and agrarian (roughly A.D. 1000–1200). While the Church maintained a considerable influence over behavior of the peasantry, the growth of towns after 1200 (with a concurrent growth in commerce and trade), combined with greater monarchical needs for revenue, led the lay authorities to modify their views concerning behavior the Church had deemed improper. In particular, "[r]oyal legislation was often motivated not by high principles, but by the exigencies of the moment, the need to placate powerful pressure groups or to raise money."[1]

The feudal viewpoint that influenced the working rules of England's medieval economy was that society should be "pyramidal . . . with the many supporting the few."[2] Although distinctions between groups (e.g., nobles, peasants) were strict and rigid, groups were "organically interrelated,"[3] that is, mutually supportive. The concomitantly adversarial yet supportive nature of the feudal order can be summarized as follows:

> The superior individual granted his protection and diverse material advantages that assured a subsistence to the dependent directly or indirectly; the inferior pledged various protestations or various services and was under a general obligation to render aid. These relations were not always freely assumed nor did they imply a universally satisfactory equilibrium between the two parties. Built upon authority, the feudal regime never ceased to contain a great number of constraints, violences and abuses.

[1]J. L. Bolton, *The Medieval English Economy: 1150–1500* (London: J. M. Dent & Sons, 1980), pp. 328, 329.
[2]Ibid., p. 321.
[3]R. H. Hilton, *A Medieval Society* (Cambridge: Cambridge University Press, 1983), p. 10.

However, this idea of the personal bond, hierarchic and synallagmatic [reciprocally binding] in character, dominated European feudalism.[4]

In the rural areas peasants supported the landlords, for it was believed that "the landowners were a 'feudal' class entitled to the non-agricultural revenues and bearing the non-agricultural charges inherent in the contracts of tenure and in the public functions they perform."[5] In the towns merchants and craftsmen benefited from the labor of other town residents who were lower in the social and political structures. All members of society, especially nobles, owed allegiance to the monarchy and were required to provide their monarch with economic and military support. Monarchs were not interested in proposing fiscal and monetary policies for the purpose of affecting economic growth, employment, or price levels. Rather, they focused on regulating specific aspects of the economy, primarily for two purposes: to acquire revenue to finance administrative, regal, or military activities; and to appease members of the land-owning and mercantile classes who sought protection of their special interests.

Attitudes in towns regarding trade and manufacturing were different from those held by the monarchy, landowners, or the Church. The prevailing code for commercial conduct reflected the attitude that industry and trade should be strictly regulated and monopolized. This view has been stated as follows:

> A jealous and rigid commercial monopoly isolated every locality from its neighbor, and sought to set up an impenetrable barrier of protective tariffs and stringent regulations. . . . Every town strove with varying degrees of success to become a self-dependent unit with the active powers of aggression and defences; and the exclusion of strangers, the imposition of tolls, the right of reprisals, the restriction of "foreign" competition, were all economic weapons in their municipal armoury.[6]

The Church prescribed rules for economic conduct that were compatible with its religious doctrines. The philosophy of the Church toward economic life consisted of moral axioms for economic behavior to which all members of medieval society were morally bound. The axioms covered matters such as private property, profit, price, and credit. In a predominantly agrarian society the Church held the view that only God owned land, but that custody of land in medieval England rested with the Church or the monarch, whose role was assumed by divine right. In addition, as the largest landowner in England (by the early fifteenth century the Church—especially the monasteries—owned about 25

[4]Marc Bloch, "Feudalism-European," in Edwin R. D. Schuman, ed., *Encyclopedia of the Social Sciences,* 6 (New York: Macmillan Publishing Company, 1937), p. 203.

[5]M. M. Postan, *The Medieval Economy and Society* (Middlesex, England: Penguin Books, 1986), p. 178.

[6]E. Lipson, *The Economic History of England, Vol. I: The Middle Ages,* 10th ed. (London: Adam and Charles Black, 1949), pp. 264, 265.

percent of the land compared to 6 percent ownership by the monarch),[7] the Church had to reflect an implicit acceptance of the feudal order and the property rights inherent therein. Concerning other property (e.g., livestock, tools), the Church recognized and endorsed individual (versus communal) possessions.

The ecclesiastical view toward profit making was against the pursuit of profit in trade. The Church also preached to lend money for interest was to commit the mortal sin of usury. Essentially, the Church held it to be immoral to trade or lend money if the intention was to gain a material surplus beyond what was necessary to maintain one's present status or to contribute to charity. Trade was justifiable according to the use to which goods and services exchanged were to be put. The Church's doctrine of just price, "that [price] which would yield the makers of goods and their sellers sufficient income to maintain them in their respective social ranks,"[8] served as a guide for moral behavior in trade. In contemporary terms, a just price would be a competitive market equilibrium price which yielded a normal return to the seller, while a just price for labor (just wage) would be no less than the legally regulated minimum wage in the United States. To sell a good for more than its just price was to commit the mortal sin of avarice. This doctrine led the Church, well in anticipation of Adam Smith, to condemn impediments to the free interplay of market forces (see Chapter 5). While the economy was heavily agrarian, preachings against the pursuit of profit in merchant and financial activities had little impact. However, expanding commercial activity required the Church to modify its view toward commercial activity to coincide with changes in the business community's behavior.

For most inhabitants of medieval England, the Church was effective as the purveyor of proper economic behavior. By holding out promises of eternal salvation for its obedient followers, the Church was in a position to influence every aspect of village life. The clergy hurled graphic threats of eternal damnation for behavior it deemed unacceptable at a largely illiterate and superstitious population. For instance, persons who failed to pay their tithes were subject to excommunication. The Church was active in secular matters, especially those of a social and economic nature. By scheduling religious celebrations to coincide with the calendar of agrarian activities (e.g., the feast of St. Michael coincided with the end of the fall harvest—Michaelmas, September 29), the Church enhanced the cohesion of the community and contrived a relationship between the supernatural and everyday activities.

---

[7]Carlo M. Cipolla, *Before the Industrial Revolution*, 2nd ed. (New York: W.W. Norton & Co., 1980), p. 57.
[8]Postan, *The Medieval Economy and Society*, p. 255.

RIGID, HIERARCHICAL SOCIAL, AND POLITICAL STRUCTURES

Social Structure

The social structure in medieval England was comprised of the nobility, the clergy, the middle class (those who managed the affairs of the royal court or the manor, town burgesses and other town inhabitants including guild members who were not burgesses, and members of the military), and the peasantry. The social structure was based upon personal allegiance pledged between superior(s) and inferiors. Allegiances were freely entered into, contractual, and personal, since an individual, not the entire family, pledged support. Since respectability lay chiefly in control over land, the ability to secure access to land affected one's status quite profoundly. Due to the relatively static nature of the distribution of land between social classes there was little social mobility.

NOBILITY.   The nobility consisted of the monarch, the barons, and the vassals. The monarch had overwhelming status as well as economic and political power. Each baron (of whom there were approximately 200) was obligated to serve the monarch through personal service, including the provision of a fighting force in time of need, and by paying dues or taxes. Vassals (knights), in turn, were bound to serve their barons by providing military and advisory services upon request, as well as certain dues. In return the baron provided the vassal with land and, initially, the other means to establish a manor.

CLERGY.   In addition to enjoying a relatively high status the clergy also participated in strengthening the feudal social structure. The Church validated and sanctioned oaths of allegiance and loyalty sworn between barons and their vassals and between the monarchs and their barons. The oath was made in the name of God. As a result, the personal bond between nobles was strengthened and made permanent. Any violation of the oath during their lifetime would subject a noble to possible excommunication from the Church. The Church also condoned and thereby perpetuated the feudal status of the peasantry. There is evidence that the obligations imposed on its tenants by the clergy were anything but lenient and were in some cases more burdensome than the duties peasants of the lay manorial lords (i.e., barons and vassals) had to endure.

MIDDLE CLASS.   Towns were comprised of associations which featured some degree of egalitarianism among members. Those likeliest to comprise the upper level of the town social structure would be its citizens, known as burgesses, who were the "formal members of the community."[9] Typically, the burgesses

---

[9]Susan Reynolds, *An Introduction to the History of English Medieval Towns* (Oxford: Clarendon Press, 1977), pp. ix, x.

would include merchants, some master craftsmen, and even landowners who did not reside in the town. Every other inhabitant of the town was technically free from servile status. The degree to which these persons were free is exemplified by the structure and behavior of the craft guild, an association of skilled members of the same occupation (e.g., tailors, cobblers) residing in a town. Although it might be argued that apprentices were denied most liberties, the working rules governing urban areas recognized the freedom of this group. That is, apprentices and other town residents were not relegated to the servile status of the peasantry.

PEASANTRY.   Although some peasants were free (*freemen*), the principal social characteristic of medieval England's society was the servile, unfree peasant (often referred to as *serf*, or *villein*). The villeins willingly commended themselves to a baron who was capable of providing physical protection in a brutal era. There were gradations of social status within the peasantry that can be distinguished by the nature of dependency and servility toward their baron or vassal. In addition, there were variations within each gradation, especially in regard to rights to land. It should be emphasized that the social structure of the peasantry was fluid (i.e., the nature of each gradation, including rights and burdens, varied over time and between manors during the medieval period).

At the end of the eleventh century, the composition of the peasantry as a percentage of the rural population was as follows: freemen (14 percent), villeins (41 percent), cottars (32 percent), and landless servants (slaves) (10 percent).[10] In terms of the distribution of land, the peasantry had access to over three fifths, since barons and vassals cultivated only about 40 percent of the arable land. The land to which the peasant had access comprised the village, while the land reserved for the lord of the manor was known as the demesne. Within the village, villeins held about 45 percent, freemen 20 percent, and cottars 5 percent.[11] Peasants of free status paid rent to the baron for their land holding and provided a few days of labor service to the demesne, generally during the harvest period. The two subdivisions of this group included freemen and sokemen. The former were subject (after the twelfth century) to the rules of the royal courts concerning their tenure rights and rights to dispose of their property. Consequently, they were independent of the baron's jurisdiction in these matters. Sokemen, on the other hand, were subject to the baron's jurisdiction and were restrained from selling rights to their land or from pledging allegiance to another baron. They were free, however, to leave their land and migrate to another manor.

The unfree status of villeins relegated them to dependence upon their baron. The villeins theoretically had few property rights. However, the customs of the village and manor (working rules perpetuated by tradition) protected villeins

---

[10]Edward Miller and John Hatcher, *Medieval England: Rural Society and Economic Change 1086–1348* (New York: Longman, 1985), p. 22.
[11]Ibid.

from arbitrary attempts by the baron to reallocate resources (e.g., access to certain areas of land), the rights to which had been assigned customarily to the villeins. Villein status did contain elements of legal uncertainty, however, since the labor services required by the baron might not generally be fixed or defined in advance of the time they were required. Thus, while the villein's tenure rights to land were relatively clear, their obligations (the quantity of labor services and fines) were subject to change and could be imposed on short notice.

Political Structure

The relationship of the political structure to the medieval economy of England parallels that of the social structure. In terms of political authority after 1066 the nobles organized England into a series of estates (land holdings consisting of one or more manors, with the monarch, a baron, or a vassal as lord over a particular manor) on which tenure principles became more orderly and more uniform. Both the monarch and the barons held a preeminent position over their respective manors in most decisions pertaining to property rights, resource allocation, and the interpretation and modification of working rules. Within the village there was some communal authority, while the towns developed their own, nonfeudal political structure.

MONARCH.   Monarchs were concerned with receiving income to finance military ventures, constructing walls and castles, storing food for the royal court and for public feasts, and paying interest on borrowed money. There was a royal court which supervised a system of justice that applied throughout the kingdom. In addition, there was a parliament and "central departments of state" through which the monarch defined working rules for the economy and interfered when expedient (e.g., to raise revenue for war) in economic matters.[12] The Parliament consisted of a House of Lords and a House of Commons.

BARONS AND VASSALS.   Monarchs generally were not interested in governing the everyday affairs of the manors, villages, or towns. Nobles had rights of jurisdiction on their personal manors, where they served as the chief military, administrative, and judicial officer. The manor was the primary administrative (and fiscal) unit for the village. In political terms the manor had jurisdictional powers over nearly all property rights, resource allocation, and criminal matters, with the baron (or vassal) or an agent (e.g., the shire reeve) assuming the duties of judge and police chief. Consequently, nobles were in a position to interpret and enforce rules pertaining to the peasantry's rights in marriage, inheritance, legal disputes, indebtedness, and transactions for the exchange of rights to land.

[12]Bolton, *The Medieval English Economy: 1150–1500*, p. 322.

Those accused of breaching any rules of the manor would be subject to appear in the manor court. The court served as the means for establishing and enforcing rules pertaining to rents, fines, labor services, and acceptable behavior. This institution gave barons broad powers to make arbitrary decisions in their own interest. This political control of the manor maintained the status of peasants, forcing them to meet their feudal obligations. Labor service conditions and other peasant duties were imposed to support the manorial economy to the extent deemed necessary by the baron.

COMMUNAL AUTHORITY.   The village normally served as both an organ of the manorial political structure and as an authority regarding communal activities. Acting communally, the peasants performed the political and administrative functions of the village such as the issuance and administration of rules pertaining to agrarian activities (e.g., tenure rights to the fields, animal husbandry, plowing), rights of inheritance, assessment of royal taxes, and military service. Although the village generally behaved in a supportive, complementary fashion toward the manor, community action in opposition to manorial edicts was not uncommon. This became especially true in the thirteenth century when manorial attempts to renew the exacting of labor services from village residents met with widespread resentment and collective opposition.

TOWN.   The town political structure was vertical to the extent that certain associations or classes were dominant over other groups and were in a better position to influence political and economic matters. The governing and administrative body which defined rights and had jurisdiction over urban matters was the town court, which was independent from the Crown and manorial courts. The court had the power to supervise and control commercial matters and regulations, such as contract disputes, weights, measures, prices, and quality of food sold, as well as criminal matters. The authority to establish many of the town's rules concerning the production and sale of goods was assumed either by the town court or merchant and craft guilds. Craft guild authorities not only owned and controlled the means of production, but through the guild they established the rules for the two lower classes of members: journeymen and apprentices.

MEDIEVAL INSTITUTIONS

The principal institutions which established and coordinated the major production and distribution patterns of England's medieval economy were the manor, village, Church, town, and monarchy. Before describing them, the point must be stressed that "the variety of the medieval scene is its dominant characteristic."[13] There was a broad variety of manors, villages, and towns, so one

[13]Miller and Hatcher, *Medieval England: Rural Society and Economic Change 1086–1348*, p. 110.

must be careful not to overgeneralize from representative models or examples. In addition, it is important to note that the economy in A.D. 1000 did not contain a network capable of linking economic activity over a wide area. Rather, the economy was comprised of isolated regional economies and local economies so that the relative importance of particular institutions may have differed within and between local or regional areas.

Manor

The manor was the predominant institution of medieval England. Nearly the entire kingdom was characterized by these rural communities of roughly fifty to a few hundred people. In terms of size there were three categories of estates: *large* estates of over 20,000 acres on which there were 20 or more manors, each with a demesne exceeding 500 acres; *medium* estates of 2,500–20,000 acres with 5–20 manors whose demesnes ranged from 200–500 acres; and *small* estates with less than 2,500 acres with 1–5 manors whose demesnes were less than 20 acres.

The lord of a manor could have been the monarch, a clergyman, baron, or a vassal. The manor consisted of the lord's house, his demesne, buildings for agricultural and light craft purposes, and a village where there was land upon which the tenant peasant population depended for their livelihood. The lord derived income from the demesne and the peasant holdings. Most work was performed by dependent peasants who were obligated in varying degrees to their lord. Peasant labor was utilized to grow crops and to raise livestock on the demesne. Peasants also owed their lord a portion of what was produced on the strips of land allocated to them in the village (discussed later). Peasants could keep the remaining produce for their family needs, and could perhaps further provide for themselves through part-time labor outside of the demesne.

Village

Adjacent to the demesne was the village, over which the lord was the authority regarding peasant access to land for cultivation and grazing purposes. As part of the manor many of the village's social, political, and economic activities were carried out according to traditional rules and working rules prescribed by the lord. Villages ranged in size from hamlets with a few families to nucleated communities with large common fields for cultivation and grazing. The economy of villages differed according to relative emphasis on farming, pastoral husbandry, industry, and commercial (market) activity. Even farming villages were not oriented solely toward agriculture, for light industrial activities often were performed. These included milling, ale brewing, smithing, mining (of tin, lead, coal), cloth making, and production of forest crafts.

The heart of the village was the church, around which peasant homes were clustered. The land surrounding each house was the croft, an enclosed area the peasant family could utilize at its own discretion for cultivation or grazing purposes. There were common fields of arable land upon which the peasants raised most of their food. The common field might be about 400 acres irregularly divided into fields called furlongs, which were further divided into strips that constituted the basic unit of a peasant's holding. Each peasant might have the right to between 5 and 30 acres scattered in strips among the common fields. This area was also used as communal pasture following the fall harvest.

Church

Upon entering almost any medieval village, a visitor would immediately be aware of the influence of the Catholic Church in the community. Undoubtedly the largest building in the village, the church's central location "symbolized the place of the Church in medieval life."[14] As a partial return for faithful service and contributions, the community might use the church and churchyard for village meetings and court, for storing goods, as a marketplace, or even for entertainment purposes. In addition, the Church held its own manors, whose working rules were similar to those on lay manors.

Town

Medieval towns were permanent settlements in which a large proportion of the population was occupied in nonagricultural pursuits with social, political, and economic activities and rules distinct from feudal institutions. Town autonomy was achieved only after centuries of struggle with neighboring barons, the Church, and the monarch. Such a struggle tended to promote common interests and the emergence of a fraternal spirit within each town.

Towns varied from one another in terms of their size, focus of economic activity, location, impetus for origin, or constitution. Towns of various sizes and locations focused on producing a single product (e.g., cloth, tin), shipping (port towns), serving inhabitants of an abbey, monastery, or castle, or being the center of commerce and government (e.g., London). The population of the town was normally greater in numbers, older, and denser than its village counterpart. The inhabitants had different legal status, ranging from free citizens who owed allegiance to the monarch (but not to any baron, vassal, or to the Church) to runaway peasants. The occupations of the townspeople were divided among manufacturing, service, and agricultural activities. Work did not follow the rhythm and routine of manorial life, for the urban areas had their own economic and social working rules organized around handicraft production and trade activities. A few towns were founded by barons and, consequently, were dependent upon and subject to the authority of the baron.

There was an economic link between towns and the surrounding countryside, for the urban and rural economies complemented and depended upon each other. Many activities in the towns revolved around commercial matters—namely, the weekly market, which was frequented by villagers. Towns

[14]Ibid., p. 29.

depended upon rural areas to supply their food (and perhaps their raw materials), to purchase goods and services towns produced, and to provide labor for urban industries. Cultural amenities offered in towns may also have attracted villagers to the urban setting. Since towns had higher death rates and lower fertility rates than the countryside due to the crowded, unhealthy conditions and higher average age of town members, rural to urban migration was necessary to sustain the growth of towns.

Monarchy

As owner of all land and the ultimate and unquestioned authority, the monarch potentially could influence the economy, especially through establishing working rules designed to regulate trade or protect noble land holders. However, manors and towns were scattered without an efficient transportation or communication network linking them. In addition, monarchs were often involved with military matters. As a result, the role of the monarch, while significant concerning macroeconomic matters (e.g., royal taxes) was not extensive in the everyday activities of the economy.

BEHAVIOR OF THE ECONOMY

The Dominance of Centralized Decision Making

Centralization of decision making within the manor and town dominated the medieval economy. The monarch was the main authority concerning taxes and expenditure decisions, with Parliament beginning to assume some importance during the fifteenth century. The monarch also established working rules for international trade and was instrumental in granting permission for towns to incorporate. On the manor, decision making concerning most working rules was centralized. Manorial lords were the ultimate authorities. In villages cooperative decision making existed in terms of allocating plots of land and the use of capital equipment. Concentration of decision making in towns varied. In some towns it was centralized within elected civic authorities, while in others it was decentralized among merchant and craft guild authorities.

Both the monarch and the barons held a preeminent position over their respective demesnes for decisions pertaining to property rights, resource allocation, and interpretation and modification of working rules, especially obligations of the peasantry. Monarchical control over the working rules could be exercised through any of the following options: increase the size of the royal demesne (land reserved solely for the monarch's pleasure); demand higher inheritance duties; sell the control of land held by the monarch for a minor; accept payment from nobles in place of their military obligations; sell charters to towns (granting them autonomy from the neighboring manors); and (from the thirteenth century) raise taxes on the agricultural production of peasants.[15]

The weight of monarchical control fell most heavily on the peasants for several reasons. First, any expansion of the royal demesne would ultimately reallocate use of scarce land away from the village. Next, the peasant was typically subject to conscription, which became increasingly likely in the thirteenth century as rules changed regarding eligibility for military service. The monarchy served to protect the landed monopoly, especially through its military power to guard against peasant revolts and its sanctioning of manorial courts.

On the manor lords were able to require and exact many forms of payment from the villeins. These regular and unavoidable payments included money rents on land customarily held, and fees collected for milling and baking (processes over which the baron held a monopoly); marriage of a daughter (and occasionally a son); and "recognition" when a new lord assumed control of the manor. Peasants were sometimes required to have their livestock graze on the demesne, thereby contributing vital manure to the lord's land, while depriving their own land of this vital resource.

Informal rules pertaining to use of ploughs and division of fields illustrate the cooperation required in feudal agricultural production typified by transactions of reciprocity and communal management of the commons. The heavy ploughs introduced in England by the Anglo-Saxons required a team of horses or oxen ranging from two to eight in number. Since few peasants owned two, let alone eight, beasts of burden, a cooperative, mobilized effort for ploughing and land reclamation became necessary in the village. The method of ploughing adopted led to further developments "in the dimensions and shapes of fields, in the general routine of agricultural operations and in the ways in which land was occupied and managed."[16]

Fields were divided into long, narrow strips the dimensions of which were determined cooperatively by the amount the plough team could work in a day—approximately 1 acre. The number of strips allocated to each tenant was determined by the tenant's contribution to the plough team. Tenants would hold these strips in severalty while sharing the use of the meadow, commons, and waste with the baron and the rest of the peasantry. Strips from all over the arable fields of the village were dispensed to each tenant in an egalitarian attempt to give everyone a share of different grades of land. Crop rotation patterns, while variable between villages, had to be coordinated according to the cooperative system of ploughing, distribution of land holdings, and scheme for livestock grazing. By the middle of the 1000–1400 period the three-field system was widely used. During a given year one third of the land would lie fallow, another third—generally the land which had been fallow the previous fall—would be sown with a winter crop

---

[15]Bolton, *The Medieval English Economy*, p. 324. Note that minors of noble families might be placed under the monarch's protection following the death of both parents. Consequently, rights to the land bequeathed to the minor were held by the monarch.

[16]Postan, *The Medieval Economy and Society*, p. 52.

(e.g., wheat or rye), and the other third would be utilized in the spring for growing barley and oats.[17]

The organization of decision making in the towns was shared between town authorities and leaders of merchant and craft guilds. In some towns, civic authorities maintained central control by denying guilds the "right to coercive jurisdiction over its matters of trade,"[18] while in others major economic decisions were decentralized within the merchant and craft guilds. In either case, the scope of matters subject to consideration depended upon the extent of liberties a town received from the monarch.

Ownership and Control of Land, Labor, and Other Productive Resources

In medieval England land was either publicly owned (i.e., by the monarch) or owned by the Church, with control over certain areas exercised by the monarch, private individuals (e.g., barons, vassals, peasants, and town residents) or by a group acting cooperatively (in the case of the village). Ownership and control of capital were both private on the manor and in the towns, and cooperative in the case of the village. There was extensive private control over labor on the manors, and cooperative control by the guilds in towns.

The social and political structures of medieval England serve as the basis for understanding the distribution of wealth and the resolution of competing claims for scarce resources. The interrelatedness of these structures and the economy is exemplified by the nature of ownership and control over the principal resource—land. This is summarized as follows:

> At every [feudal] level, there is a fusion of the economic and political components of feudalism, which is realised in the hierarchy of *juridical-conditional ownership*, i.e., parcellised sovereignty. This hierarchy was comprised of complex sets of vertically defined rights and obligations based both on political and military power and on land. Within it there was an inevitable parcellisation of power linked to a coincident parcellisation of land—the distribution of political power was isomorphic with the distribution of economic power.[19]

The degree of feudalization pertains to the extent of manorial obligations owed by villagers to the lord. There was a consistent relationship between the size of manors and the proportion of the land held by villeins, as demesne, or by freemen (see Table 4-1). Lords on large manors could exert greater political power over tenants, thereby perpetuating a higher degree of villein tenure and status. The greater the size of the manor, the greater the degree of feudalization and, therefore, the larger the proportion of the lord's income in the form of labor

---

[17]Lipson, *The Economic History of England,* Vol. 1, pp. 264, 265.
[18]Ibid., p. 375.
[19]Miller and Hatcher, *Medieval England: Rural Society and Economic Change 1086–1348,* pp. 221, 222.

services, fines, and taxes (versus money rents).

TABLE 4-1 Manorial Size and the Degree of Feudalization (percentage of land held)

LARGE MANORS			MEDIUM MANORS			SMALL MANORS		
DEMESNE	VILLEIN	FREEMAN	DEMESNE	VILLEIN	FREEMAN	DEMESNE	VILLEIN	FREEMAN
25%	52%	23%	35%	39%	26%	41%	32%	27%

Source: E. A. Kosminsky, *Studies in the Agrarian History of England*, translated by R. Kisch, introduction by R. Hilton (Oxford: Blackwell, 1956), in John E. Martin, *Feudalism to Capitalism* (London: Macmillan Press, 1986), p. 32.

The comparative economic value to the lord of villeins versus freeman tenants depended upon the value of rents received from free peasants compared to the value received from villeins in the form of agricultural output from their labor services, taxes, and numerous fines and assessments. Rents were generally low and customarily rigid. The primary value to the lord of villeinage, especially before the development of market networks, was the fact that it provided a reserve source of labor which could be mobilized at the manorial administrator's discretion to perform the plowing, planting, cultivating, and harvesting tasks, among others. Villeinage provided " . . . the safety factor in the labor organization of the manor, supplementing regular manorial workers and casually hired hands at those times when the demand for labor was at its highest in the medieval countryside."[20] The extent of labor services was variable, to a degree, providing manorial administrators with greater flexibility in calling forth a supply of this resource as needs arose on the lord's demesne.

Three aspects of villeinage characterize its political, social, and economic status: conditions of land tenure, payments exacted by the lord—including those in excess of rent for the use of land, and personal servitude. Villeins did not own land, but they had customary rights to the land for their own use and to pass along to their survivors. By virtue of these rights villeins had various degrees of control over different types of land. They could possess their homestead and use the croft immediately around it to produce anything they were capable of producing.

Working rules established cooperatively within the village and "custom of the manor" (i.e., traditional rules which had prevailed for decades and, perhaps, centuries) determined how and when villeins could utilize holdings within the village allocated to them by the lord (or acquired through purchasing the rights for use from another peasant, subject to the baron's permission). Such types of land included the meadow, open fields, commons, and waste. Upon a villein's death the beneficiary (primogeniture was customary) would inherit the same rights as those previously held by the deceased. The heir would, however, first be required to pay an inheritance tax and an entry fine to the lord, subject to

[20]Ibid.

the custom of the manor. The tax generally was the choicest head of livestock. The village church usually took the next best head. Neither the villeins nor their offspring had the right to leave the manor permanently without the lord's permission, which was seldom granted without the assurance that another villein of like status would become available to perform the same labor services and pay the same fines. In addition, any villein leaving the manor was required to pay an annual tax. As a result of these rules, villeins were basically tied to the lord's land.

The final and most distinctive aspect of villeinage was the labor servitude required of each villein. Villeins were obligated to work on the lord's demesne a fixed number of days per week, contributing their own beasts of burden and perhaps a carriage. Villeins also owed their labor services for an extra number of "boon" days during the harvest season. The work included plowing, planting, cultivating, shearing sheep, and transporting goods to mills, other manors, and perhaps to a market. The labor services, like the specific payments, were unavoidable and burdensome. It was not uncommon for the villein to be forced to hire someone to work his own land so that he could discharge his feudal obligation of labor service on the demesne.

Town inhabitants were subject to a different, nonfeudal set of rules. In particular, town residents (with the exception of apprentices) were not subject to servile status, although their "real liberties" were limited.[21] Each town could appoint its own authorities to establish, interpret, and enforce rules concerning ownership and control of economic activity, or strict control over commerce and industry could be exercised by merchant and craft guilds. The merchant guild was the more prominent institution, for its members were burgesses from whom the members of the town court were usually drawn (although nearby landowners might also be guild members). The merchant guild regulated many aspects of trade (see p. 77).

Craft guilds controlled industry, for guild rules governed the quantity and quality of goods produced, wages and prices, and entry into the craft. Although guilds had the power to limit outside competition while setting wages and price levels favorable to themselves, they typically set "just" prices. Strict rules regulating production standards protected the customer from the purchase of defective or low-quality merchandise. The master craftsmen not only owned and controlled the means of production, but through the guild established the rules for the two lower classes of members: journeymen and apprentices. The term *journeyman* should not be construed to mean that all guilds were exclusively male. There is evidence that many women worked in the brewing, woolen, and silk-weaving industries.

The apprentice was a live-in servant residing with the craftsman. During this time the apprentice was basically in a servile status, although this condition was temporary and necessary to provide an apprentice with the proper technical

[21]Reynolds, *An Introduction to the History of English Medieval Towns*, p. 75.

training as determined by the craft guild. The contractual relationship between master and apprentice furthered the interests of both parties without permanently bonding either side. Masters provided room, board, and technical training, the quality of which was regulated by the craft guild authorities. In return apprentices generally served their masters for up to seven years, but not beyond the age of 24.

At the end of the apprenticeship, an individual rose to the rank of journeyman. Now the former apprentice would receive a wage and, after about a year of customary service to the craftsman under whom training had been given, was free to seek employment from anyone in the trade. The guild limited the number of craftsmen, so journeyman status was dependent on more than time served in the occupation, demonstration of competency, or ability to acquire sufficient capital to establish a shop of one's own. Consequently, many individuals never rose in status above the journeyman level.

Tradition Coinciding with Regulated
and Unregulated Markets as Social
Processes for Economic Coordination

There were three types of markets through which trade occurred: international, regional (in which cloth was the main product traded), and local (which served an area of a few square miles). The economy of medieval England featured state (i.e., monarch) and local (i.e., guild) regulation over commercial activities, especially international trade and trade within a town. Unregulated market activity gradually increased during the thirteenth and fourteenth centuries, especially trade between manor and towns, and trade between towns. On the manor and within the guild there were also traditional means for producing and distributing goods and services.

STATE REGULATION. Throughout the medieval period there was a "spirit of regulation and monopoly."[22] One example of a regulated institution was the wool staple. It was endorsed by the monarch in the fourteenth century and was located in Calais, France. This institution held a monopoly over the purchase of English wool which was destined for export. Only merchants who belonged to the wool staple could legally export wool. Growers and other merchants who sought to export wool had to channel their goods through the staple. Merchants who belonged to the staple advanced customs receipts to the monarch and, in turn, had the responsibility of subsequently collecting customs duties themselves from sellers of wool.

By the fourteenth century the extent of state regulation was considerable. Rules were passed regulating rights to produce and standards of production (e.g., size and quality) for products such as cloth, tin, and lead. The extent of these rules is exemplified by the statute which prescribed "the capacity of barrels for eels and butts

---

[22]Postan, *The Medieval Economy and Society,* p. 251.

for salmon."[23] Navigation acts were established in an effort to confine transporting of English exports to English ships. Overall, there was a clear trend toward government attempts to regulate aspects of the economy by the fifteenth century.

GUILD REGULATION.   Institutions involved with manufacture and trade "tended toward association,"[24] as the authorities in such institutions sought to protect their status through regulation of all aspects of production and exchange. In particular, town authorities sought to protect local producers, traders, and consumers from "outside competition and extortionate tools."[25] Rules governing a wide range of merchant and craft activities, especially eligibility for guild membership, and rules controlling the activities of their members were established. Such rules included standards concerning size and quality of product, method of production, price of product, and wages of producers (craftsmen and hired laborers).

There were positive and negative features of these rules. Consumers of merchant guild products benefited from quality standards guaranteeing them a fixed weight or measure as established by the guild and standards that prices be reasonable and "just." Craft guilds maintained control over quantity and quality of goods produced, so that consumers were protected from defective goods. Producers were well trained and could not participate in production until they had completed a lengthy, supervised training program. Laborers received a wage consistent with their status. There were also rules prohibiting work when the light was poor or on Sunday. Local supplies were assured, for craftsmen were prohibited from selling their goods outside of the town for higher prices without an adequate local supply being assured. On the negative side the monopoly power of the guild and fear of outside competition inhibited technological change and may have kept craftsmen's wages and prices above a "competitive" level. There were towns in which this problem was somewhat alleviated when the monarch established local rules which granted outsiders the opportunity to sell their products in the town market. Overall, the economic effect of guild rules throughout the medieval economy is uncertain, for evidence is not available pertaining to the net effect of guild activities in representative towns.

UNREGULATED MARKET ACTIVITY.   Medieval peasants were not merely self-sufficient subsistence farmers whose only contact with markets was at the traveling fairs. It is most likely that the primary purpose of a typical peasant's enterprise was to meet household needs and feudal obligations through work on land holdings and the demesne. However, there is considerable evidence that by the twelfth century market activity was on the verge of becoming an important feature of peasants' lives, and that by the fourteenth century nearly all peasants

[23]Bolton, *The Medieval English Economy: 1150–1500*, p. 328.
[24]Cipolla, *Before the Industrial Revolution*, p. 94.
[25]Reynolds, *An Introduction to the History of English Medieval Towns*, p. 127.

lived within 10 miles of a local market. Meanwhile networks creating regional markets were developing.[26]

Peasants increasingly came to rely on market activity both to supplement their income and to secure provisions (e.g., salt ale, fuel, clothing materials) they were unable to produce within their households. In order to satisfy the need for such provisions, light industrial activities developed. In many villages one might find mining, fishing, and the production of wool, iron, cloth, and wooden craft products. Peasants had the opportunity to supplement their income beyond what their land holding would yield. In addition to selling their agrarian labor services to other peasants, peasants could earn income through working in small-scale industries, such as ale brewing, food processing, or carpentry. Enterprising individuals from a nearby town might hire peasants for semiskilled or unskilled tasks, such as carting or spinning wool, if the peasants would work for lower wages than town residents.

Peasants could sell any surplus they produced (such as eggs, milk, or grain) within the village or in local markets. A further potential source of income was the sale of their rights to strips of land. Evidence indicates that peasants who could afford to do so tended to purchase strips of land as their family size increased, and they tended to decrease the size of their land holdings through the sale of land rights, as their household size diminished. Besides the market for land rights, there was a market network for wheat, especially for surplus produced on the demesne.

One basic difference between trade within the town economy and market activity in the village was the emphasis within towns upon commercial activities on a regular (e.g., weekly, monthly) basis. This reliance increased throughout the 1000–1400 period as trade activity expanded. Although towns were often involved with trade on the regional and international level, most of the demand for local goods and services came from within the town and the surrounding countryside. The towns were linked economically to the surrounding countryside, for the urban and rural economies complemented and depended upon each other. Many activities in the towns revolved around commercial matters, especially the weekly market which was frequented by villagers. Towns depended upon rural areas to supply their food (and perhaps their raw materials), to demand goods and services produced in the town, and to provide labor for urban industries. Cultural amenities offered in towns may also have attracted villagers to the urban setting. The largest source of effective demand was the lord's household, which

---

[26]The expansion of a money economy is reflected by the evidence of money loans extended within the peasantry. This evidence included "inter-peasant pleas of debt, detention of chattels, and broken agreements [which] are sufficiently numerous in court records . . . to indicate that the buying and selling of commodities between inhabitants of the same village or group of hamlets within the same manor was an important feature of the peasant's economy." See Hilton, *The English Peasantry in the Later Middle Ages*, p. 46. For further discussion of the extent to which market activity was important in medieval England, see Kathleen Biddick, "Medieval English and Market Involvement," *Journal of Economic History*, XLV, 4 (December 1985), 823–831; and R. H. Britnell, "The Proliferation of Markets in England, 1200–1349," *The Economic History Review*, XXXIV, 2 (May 1981), 209–221.

increasingly relied upon towns for providing basic goods and services as well as for being the conduit for imported luxury commodities.

External trade had a greater impact on those towns which were specialized, particularly in the production of wool, corn (i.e., wheat), tin, and animal hides. These items were England's principal exports, while imports were mainly luxuries such as wine, dyes for cloth, sugar, rice, spices, and furs. The multiplier effect on the local and entire economy was limited, however, by the modest volume of trade and the modest size of England's relatively underdeveloped commercial sector

Production and distribution activities were affected by the Church. Part of the Church's justification for its vast accumulation of wealth was its responsibility to provide for the sick and poor. The Church served as a conduit for income transfers to the destitute, although the proportion of aid allocated was generally very modest relative to the total income the Church received. Establishment of almshouses and hospitals was financed by the Church out of surplus income created on its manors and payments received through contributions of parishioners from tithes and pennies collected during mass. This humane support for those suffering from sickness and abject poverty was necessary in a society whose other principal institutions did not make such provisions.

The economic power of the Church also contributed to the growth of market activity in the village and town. As a partial return for faithful service and contributions, the villagers could use the church and churchyard for storing goods and as a marketplace. The Church was also a source of demand for urban products, raw materials, and labor. This was especially true in particular urban markets which were stimulated by the construction of a church or cathedral. During the building of Salisbury Cathedral, for example, more than 2,000 workers, some of whom were hired from beyond the town limits, labored on the project. The construction of these magnificent religious structures drained resources from other needs of society, especially improved housing for the peasantry.

IRREGULAR, MODEST INSTITUTIONAL CHANGE

Institutional change was irregular rather than a slow, gradual process over the 1000–1400 period. Dynamic interaction among a number of forces stimulated change. The primary force was demographic change. Population growth created pressure within the villages, given the relatively low carrying capacity of the land. The growth of the population until 1348 and the drastic decline in population which ensued from the plague of 1348 (which killed between 30 percent and 40 percent of the population) affected manors, villages, and towns through its influence upon prices, availability of land, and labor and the expansion of trade. Shifts in political power and the growth of industry and trade were secondary forces influencing institutional change.

Included among the institutional changes occurring during the 1200–1400 period on the manor were the end of traditional vassalage (knightly service to the manorial lord), greater opportunities for middle-class people to become landlords, and most important of all, the transformation of peasant status, manifested by the wide-scale commutation of traditional villein obligations. The power of the monarch and relative economic and political importance of the town both increased. These changes followed no discernible pattern over the medieval period. Rather, for much of the 1200–1400 period (and beyond) the dynamic interaction between external (e.g., growth of trade, demand for wool) and internal (e.g., growth and decline of population) factors led to the breakdown of the feudal order and the emergence of a society whose economic and social relations were more commercial. Markets for land became more prevalent, assisted by the sale of land by the monarch (who needed to raise revenue) and sale of monastic land.

Monarchy

Political power gradually became centralized as subjects began to owe more taxes to the monarch and fewer labor services or dues to their lord. The extension of monarchical authority meant the monarch relied less upon revenue produced from the royal manors, claiming a greater portion of tax revenue and military power (i.e., proportion of England's armed forces) directly from subjects whose obedience was transferred from lord to monarch. The change in relative power and scope of the monarchy "caused transformations in the fiscal, military and administrative aspects of the feudal state."[27]

Towns

The political structure of England was affected as the growing influence of townspeople enabled them to place representatives in the parliament. This ultimately led to an expansion of the burgesses' influence over the working rules of the economy. In addition, state policies and the growth in urban population stimulated an expansion of trade and market activity. The impact of the wool staple in Calais was a boon for London, for working rules required English exporters to ship their wool through London, where it was exported to Calais. The wool trade also was a stimulus to the entire economy, since the foreign trade multiplier increased due to the decrease in remittances abroad of profits earned in England, primarily by Italian and Flemish merchants. Improved trade relations with Gascony and Flanders stimulated growth in urban areas which produced cloth. Towns grew as manor households and villages came to rely more on trade. This growth had implications for the labor market and the feudal order, especially in the fourteenth century.

[27]John E. Martin, *Feudalism to Capitalism* (London: Macmillan, 1986), p. 110.

Manor

The effect of urban growth was felt in the countryside. An expanding commercial network, in which there was "increasing sophistication of the institutional framework facilitating exchanges,"[28] led to greater reliance on markets (in lieu of fairs) within the village and the manor. Beginning in the thirteenth century, growing demand for wool coupled with rising demand for imported luxury goods stimulated manorial estates to be reorganized in terms of administration and purpose. Rising emphasis on efficiency ensued, with emphasis placed upon pastoral farming. By the late fourteenth century new rules pertaining to rights to use land replaced customary tenure. Continued growth of the wool industry brought an expansion of pastoral farming, and areas of land that had previously been used for common pasture by peasants began to be enclosed.

The gradual decline of villeinage was due to the combined effect of demographic changes with changing attitudes within the peasantry. Following the drastic reduction in population after the plague of 1348, the economic climate for peasants was more favorable. There was less labor available for landlords, land values had declined, wages rose, and nobles faced higher royal taxes. Growing unwillingness to accept servile labor status and the alternative of moving to an urban area exacerbated the peasant depopulation problem initiated by the plague. The Peasant Revolt of 1381 was the culmination of a long period of discontent. This revolt was not so much a reaction against poverty or villeinage as "a demonstration that men were now so far advanced on their road to freedom and prosperity as to resent more than ever the surviving vestiges of old oppressions."[29] As landlords competed for scarce labor and sought to retain the peasants on their land, servile obligations were reduced, rents lowered, and wages increased.

THE ECONOMY'S PERFORMANCE: INCREASED BENEFITS FOR RELATIVELY FEW

Overall, a modest proportion of peasant families could satisfy their basic needs, while perhaps half of them lived on the brink of starvation. The typical diet was deficient in vitamins and protein, and contributed to the vicious circle of poverty most peasants experienced. Lack of nutrition led to low productivity of labor, which resulted in low per capita output and, therefore, low household income. Peasants were poorly clothed, since woolen cloth was very expensive. Housing was small, poorly insulated, and meagerly furnished. It should not be surprising that the health of the peasant population was generally substandard. Inadequate nutrition and disease caused by filth, rats, and mosquitoes contributed to high

---

[28]Miller and Hatcher, *Medieval England: Rural Society and Economic Change 1086–1348*, p. 64.
[29]Postan, *The Medieval Economy and Society*, p. 172.

death rates, as did the incidence of violent acts committed by peasants against one another or inflicted upon peasants by nonresidents of the village.

The greater the degree of obligatory labor services and payments owed to a baron the worse off the peasants would be. These obligations were essentially a fixed cost, inescapable even when the peasant needed to work his own land or engage in market activity to supplement his income. Peasants without secure land tenure or sizable land holdings (i.e., more than about 10 to 15 fairly productive acres) and a steady wage suffered. Unfortunately, about half of the peasantry had land holdings smaller than this subsistence level, while only about one fifth had sufficient land to be able to produce a surplus for the market. The poor productivity of the soil was a key factor, as were the scarcity of land available for grazing and the resources available to the peasant from the village waste.

The 1200–1320 era saw some prosperity enjoyed by estate owners due to expanding market opportunities, rising prices, falling wages, and greater efficiency in estate management. The result in terms of economic growth, however, was not favorable. Low levels of investment were one reason for the meager growth rates of the demesne's output. The pace of technological change was slow, mostly consisting of different methods for managing the demesne and of different patterns of crop rotation. Little change occurred in tools or in agricultural processes. Despite the crop rotation system, extensive exploitation of land on which there were insufficient applications of fertilizer resulted in low, and even declining, productivity. Another factor contributing to low growth rates was the overt compulsion (in the form of villeinage obligations) which provided disincentives for productive effort.

The economic impact of town activity on the economy of medieval England was modest prior to 1400 in terms of output, but was important in that towns facilitated the expansion of market activity and thereby hastened the end of the feudal society. Low levels of commercial activities kept output levels and, consequently, potential gains from economies of scale at a minimum. Evidence indicates that only a small proportion of profits was reinvested in town commerce. Merchants and craftsmen preferred to use their surplus to enhance their status by purchasing land. Given the size of the town market, some potential for profit from raising sheep, and the social tenor of the medieval society which gave respectability and status to landowners, gentrification of the prominent townspeople was a logical course of development. Overall, despite increases in English exports (especially wool, tin, and corn), some growth in the productivity of land (leading to more production for the market), and an "increasing sophistication of the institutional framework facilitating [market] exchanges,"[30] expansion in trade did not improve appreciably the standard of living of most inhabitants of England until after the fifteenth century.

---

[30]Miller and Hatcher, *Medieval England*, p. 64.

MEDIEVAL ENGLAND AND THE PROCESS OF EVOLUTIONARY-INSTITUTIONAL DEVELOPMENT

The principal institutions of medieval England, especially the manor, coordinated most of the feudal society's production and distribution activities. The monarch was the ultimate authority regarding transaction disputes and working rules, while the Church was purveyor of a moral code of behavior for economic matters. The influence of the town was modest, although town activities provided the basis for an expansion of commercial activity during the fifteenth century and thereafter.

The origin of medieval England's principal institutions can be traced to the fall of Rome. The absence of an authority capable of maintaining working rules for an economy and protecting inhabitants from outside military forces led to the emergence of isolated, protected units to which peasants without masters went for protection. Peasants had little alternative but to assume villein status in return for physical protection and access to the means of production. Thus evolved the feudal society based upon a pyramidal social and political structure with reciprocal bonds pledged between superior and inferior members. The society was organized into manors, and the views of the Church provided stability to this order by justifying the strict hierarchy. In addition, the teachings of the Church were not consistent with the development of a commercial class capable of improving its status and standard of living through earning profits in the marketplace.

The tribes which conquered England introduced the feudal institutions characteristic of their homeland, and the authorities who established and maintained working rules (e.g., Norman nobility) perpetuated the feudal order. In particular, the status of the nobility was preserved through rules governing rights to the land. In towns guild members adopted rules which, although offering some protection to consumers of the goods and services, perpetuated their own status by limiting entry into the guild and strictly limiting opportunities for merchants and producers not residing within the town limits.

The organization of the medieval economy was consistent with the philosophical basis for economic activities. For most of England (i.e., the rural society) decision making and ownership and control over the means of production were highly concentrated within the noble class, with an important role for the Church. Towns, while characterized by a strict social and political hierarchy, were organized differently from the rest of the feudal society. In particular, laborers were not subject to the type of villeinage obligations required of the peasantry.

The philosophical basis accepted by the authorities changed slowly, especially since the performance of the economy did not adversely affect the monarch, the rest of the nobility, and the Church prior to the fourteenth century. Perpetuation of feudal working rules was also due to there being little social mobility and only modest influence of members from the middle and lower classes over the working rules. As a result, institutional change was gradual. The extension of commercial activity was accepted by the monarch and Church, primarily because both needed additional sources of revenue.

Demographic changes, changes in the attitudes of peasants, and the gradual increase of market activity began to stimulate institutional changes in the fourteenth century. Changes in nobles' attitudes favored production of wool through more efficient estate management and enclosures of land which peasants had relied upon for producing crops and for their animals to graze. These new attitudes recognized the growing potential to earn profit through trade. At the same time villeinage duties were gradually removed, partly in response to growing opposition within the impoverished peasant class, culminating in a series of peasant revolts. The end of labor services and the expansion of trade were important factors contributing to the evolution of the laissez-faire market economy.

LOOKING AHEAD

After 1400 the expansion of trade and concentration of political and economic power in the monarchy led to the emergence of a mercantile economy in the sixteenth century. Mercantile policies and other factors contributed to further evolution of England's economy, leading to the emergence of the laissez-faire market economy in the 1830s. These factors as well as the philosophical basis for coordinating most economic activity through unregulated markets are discussed in Chapter 5.

KEY TERMS AND CONCEPTS

Church	Monarch
Feudal Attitudes	Town
Guild	Villeinage
Manor	

QUESTIONS FOR DISCUSSION

1. What was the doctrine of just price?
2. Explain why institutional change in the medieval economy was irregular, and at times widespread.
3. What economic and social purposes did guilds serve?
4. What were the working rules of the manor concerning economic activity?
5. How did the teachings of the Church maintain the feudal society?
6. Since they held a monopoly, why did guild members refrain from charging as much as their customers could pay?
7. In what respects did the economic, political, and social features of the medieval economy inhibit entrepreneurial activity (in the modern sense of an entrepreneur)?

REFERENCES

Bennett, H. S., *Life on the English Manor*. Cambridge: Cambridge University Press, 1971.

Biddick, Kathleen, "Medieval English Peasants and Market Involvement," *Journal of Economic History*, 45, 4 (December 1985), 823–831.

Bloch, Marc, "Feudalism-European," *Encyclopedia of the Social Sciences*, 6, Edwin R. D. Schuman, ed. New York: Macmillan, 1931, pp. 203–210.

Bolton, J. L., *The Medieval English Economy: 1150–1500*. London: J.M. Dent & Sons, 1980.

Britnell, R. H. "The Proliferation of Markets in England, 1200–1349," *The Economic History Review* 34, 2 (May 1981), 209–221.

Cipolla, Carlo M., *Before the Industrial Revolution: European Society and Economy 1000–1700*, 2nd ed. New York: W. W. Norton, 1980.

Douglas, David C., and George W. Greenaway, eds. "The Domesday Survey," *English Historical Documents, 1042–1189*. London: Eyre and Spottis Woode, 1953, pp. 847–851.

Hilton, R.H., *A Medieval Society*. Cambridge: Cambridge University Press, 1983.

————, *The English Peasantry in the Later Middle Ages*. Oxford: Clarendon Press, 1975.

Landreth, Harry, *History of Economic Theory: Scope, Method and Content*. Boston: Houghton Mifflin, 1976.

Lipson, E., *The Economic History of England, Volume I: The Middle Ages*, 10th ed. London: Adam and Charles Black, 1949.

Martin, John E., *Feudalism to Capitalism*. London: Macmillan Press, 1986.

Miller, Edward, and Hatcher, John, *Medieval England: Medieval Society and Economic Change: 1086–1348*. New York: Longman, 1985.

Pirenne, Henri, *Economic and Social History of Medieval Europe*. New York: Harcourt, Brace and World, 1937.

Postan, M. M., *The Medieval Economy and Society*. Middlesex, England: Penguin, 1986.

Pryor, Frederic L., "Feudalism as an Economic System," *Journal of Comparative Economics*, 4, 4 (December 1980), 56–77.

Reynolds, Susan, *An Introduction to the History of Medieval Towns*. Oxford: Clarendon Press, 1977.

5

THE LAISSEZ-FAIRE MARKET ECONOMY

Historical Context and Philosophical Basis

OBJECTIVES

1. Identify and explain six primary factors that contributed to the evolution of the market economy over the 1400–1830 period: mercantile policies, enclosure movement, change in religious attitudes, poor laws, industrial revolution, and contributions of philosophers such as Adam Smith, Jean-Baptiste Say, Thomas Malthus, and David Ricardo.

2. Explain the basic tenets of the philosophical basis of a laissez-faire market economy (LFME).

A number of interrelated factors contributed to transform England's feudal economic, social, political, and cultural institutions over the 1400–1830 period. By the early nineteenth century a different type of society had evolved, namely a market society which adopted rules that established a laissez-faire market economy (LFME).[1] Factors which contributed to the transformation included mercantile policies, the enclosure movement, the change in religious attitudes, changing rules pertaining to income support for the poor, the industrial revolution, and the philosophical contributions of the classical economists. Each will be discussed in turn.

---

[1]For further discussion of the features of a market society, see Karl Polanyi, *The Great Transformation* (Boston: Beacon Press, 1957).

THE MERCANTILE ERA: 1500–1750

Throughout the 1500–1750 period, political and economic institutions changed in response to the bitter competition among European powers who discovered that enormous wealth could be derived from colonial trade and plunder of new territories. England, for example, was involved in a heated rivalry with France and the Netherlands for control of international trade and foreign territory. This rivalry, coupled with the centralization of state power when Henry VIII split with the Roman Catholic Church and confiscated its lands throughout England, contributed to the emerging power of the monarch vis-à-vis feudal barons. A nation-state was emerging. In order to enhance its political power, the state needed to increase its wealth, and it sought to do so through regulation of economic activity.

The growth of centralized political institutions within a nation-state coincided with a commercial revolution in the sixteenth century which affected the social and political structures. During this period relative gains in social, political, and economic power were made by merchants, manufacturers, and shippers while the power of the barons and local craftsmen began to decline. In response to new technology (e.g., the telescope and sextant) which improved navigation, exploration expanded to the Far East and North America. The volume of output, trade, and transport increased. Tea, spices, sugar, dyes, cotton, and woolen textiles were among the products English traders carried to and from international ports. The monarch and Parliament began to regulate economic activity in order to achieve a favorable balance of trade while assuring the nation's access to supplies, raw materials, and precious metals. The formal rules and measures of this regulation are generally referred to as mercantile policies.

Mercantile Policies

These policies emphasized an increasingly active role for state regulation in economic matters. The ultimate goal was to enhance national (i.e., monarch) power and wealth through conquest and accumulation of precious metals. Mercantile beliefs held that the wealthiest nation was that which accumulated the most precious metals. National rivalries required a strong army and navy, and to finance these military needs the state regulated selected areas of the economy. British shipbuilding was subsidized for the purpose of increasing the size of the monarch's navy and the merchant fleet. Rules promoting the transport of British exports and imports (discussed later) led to an expanded shipbuilding industry, better seamanship, greater profits for the commercial classes throughout the empire, and increased state revenue—much of which came from differential duties applied to goods traded.

The policies, or instrumental goals, of the mercantilists were protective in nature, as the state regulated economic activity for its own objectives. Tariffs and subsidies were applied selectively for a variety of purposes. The state sought to acquire precious metals, stimulate domestic agricultural production, and encourage the manufacture of a wide variety of goods. The state simultaneously sought to prohibit the export of raw materials, discourage imports of finished goods, stimulate the expansion of shipbuilding for merchant and military purposes, and promote colonialization. The colonies were deemed valuable because they provided a means to increase the availability of raw materials (e.g., timber, cotton, sugar) and to serve as a market for the nation-state's exports. Realizing a favorable balance of trade was a vital aspect of mercantile policies, as was the buildup of military strength in the form of a large army and navy. It is noteworthy that Japan adopted similar trade policies after World War II (see Chapters 9 and 10).

Colonialization, as a mercantile policy, served the purpose of promoting the balance of trade. Rules were passed to promote a prosperous and productive agricultural sector, create a variety of domestically manufactured goods, and further the exploitation of colonial resources. For example, charters were granted by the monarch to joint-stock companies (e.g., the East India Company, the Virginia Company of London) giving these companies a monopoly over the right to trade and settlement in a colony. Colonies were a ready export market, coerced into purchasing manufactured goods from the home country (i.e., England). Colonies were regulated as to the nature of the goods they sold and were permitted to export goods only to England. As a result, its colonies supplied England with vital raw materials and some processed goods. England designated certain commodities as "enumerated," giving it the sole right within its empire to regulate trade of such goods. Regulations such as the Woolen Act of 1699 prohibited any colony from exporting goods that could compete with England's manufactured goods, especially cloth.[2]

Some mercantile policies were directed toward internal needs, such as unifying the economy by removing barriers to internal trade (e.g., eliminating tolls while improving transportation and communication facilities); and providing a uniform standard of currency, weights, and measures. In addition, a large loyal population was desired to provide military manpower and to stimulate domestic output. Other regulations of trade existed for the purpose of promoting output and exports while making England more self-sufficient. There were subsidies to encourage domestic industries likely to manufacture exports, including a monopoly to individuals or groups who started new industries; embargoes and tariffs on imports which competed directly with English manufactures (e.g., woolens); and subsidies to farmers to sell wheat abroad and import duties against foreign grain.[3]

---

[2]These policies can be compared to those of Japan as it has sought to internationalize its economy through penetrating the Asian region to develop offshore production facilities to export with wealthy Western nations.

[3]These subsidies were on a sliding scale so that if domestic prices rose too high the subsidies would cease. This served to limit the inflationary effect of rising grain prices on real wages.

The Effect of Mercantile Policies

How did mercantile policies contribute to the emergence of the LFME and the demise of the feudal economy? Overall, they reflected and provided new informal and formal rules, which served to stimulate institutional change away from feudal institutions. The political authority played a central role. Medieval towns were transformed by the extension of monarchical economic regulations. Relatively isolated local markets, previously controlled by guild members, were linked to other markets as a national market subject to state regulations was created. Noncompetitive guild practices were gradually replaced by rules designed to enhance national wealth.

Realization of the monarch's goal of extending royal power required regulation of the economy, partly for the purpose of providing additional sources of revenue. Paradoxically, these regulations stimulated the evolution of the LFME. In particular, mercantile regulations prompted the economic liberals (e.g., Adam Smith, David Ricardo) to argue for the adoption of free trade rules. It should not be construed, however, that the state's activities created free markets prior to the late eighteenth century. Generally, economic regulations gave some parties monopoly rights with which they realized economic profits. Landed interests benefited from rules prohibiting the import of grain or wool. The Navigation Acts led to an expanded role for British shipping companies, whose expanded revenue improved the nation's balance of payments.

THE ENCLOSURE MOVEMENT

Enclosures of land, which included the demesne, commons, arable open fields, and the waste, transformed English agriculture throughout the late fifteenth to the early nineteenth centuries. Enclosure basically involved absorbing small, scattered plots worked by a number of tenant farmers (who had tenure of land by right, having been recorded in the manor court) into a larger agricultural unit generally owned by landlords and frequently enclosed by hedges or ditches. The movement lasted for more than two centuries, and by the early nineteenth century roughly two thirds of England's agricultural land was enclosed. In the process common rights to the land, a main feature of the feudal economy, gradually were abolished.

The enclosure movement increased the productivity of the land and profitability of landowners, affected farm labor, and resulted in the evolution of a commercial rather than agrarian sector. Use of land became more specialized, land was farmed more intensively, and landowners increased their investment in response to the rising demand for food. These improvements were aided by technological advances in agricultural machinery and horticulture during the eighteenth and nineteenth centuries. The higher productivity kept the price of food within an affordable range for most families, as evidenced by the growth in population during the latter half of the eighteenth century. Landlords benefited from enclosures. Not only did the value of their land increase, but their profits increased from raising woolen products and food (especially grain and meat).

Effect of Enclosures

Whether the net effect on the majority of the agricultural population was positive or negative depends upon one's intertemporal perspective and focus. According to those who accept the economic efficiency inherent in an LFME, agricultural employment did not decrease following the expansion of enclosures in the eighteenth century.[4] When enclosures placed more land under cultivation, the demand for farm labor increased. Where enclosures were for the purpose of raising sheep, there would be demand for cottage industry labor to process the wool. Those marginal laborers forced out of agriculture may have found employment in the higher-paying industrial sector. From a different perspective which focuses on the short-run effect enclosures had on subsistence farmers, such a favorable conclusion is not reached. This view emphasizes that the absence of a smoothly functioning labor and goods market in the eighteenth century prevented those who were displaced from finding urban employment. Displacement would be likely if pasture was put in place of converted arable land, while agricultural wages declined, since more workers were available for the land being tilled. The social costs, which are well documented, included the gradual breakup of the peasant class and the feudal way of life as the commercial, market-oriented agriculture increased in prominence. Without the waste and commons, peasants were denied ability to raise their own dairy and poultry products. The numbers displaced, however, were relatively small during the eighteenth century.

CHANGE IN RELIGIOUS ATTITUDE

Religion played an important role in shaping the informal rules and influencing the entire fabric of England's social and political structures throughout the 1000–1870 period. During the medieval period the teachings of the Catholic Church influenced economic behavior. In particular, the view prevailed that salvation of the soul was achieved through adhering to the superior moral authority (i.e., the Church), an authority which considered the accumulation of wealth and lending money for interest as sinful. During the sixteenth and seventeenth centuries a new religious ethic emerged which changed the informal rules toward economic behavior and shaped the nature of Adam Smith's LFME philosophy. The new ethic was conducive to the spread of the existing commercial society. Ultimately, the change in religious attitudes contributed to the adoption of different formal rules for England's economy.

---

[4]W. H. B. Court, *A Concise Economic History of Britain* (Cambridge: Cambridge University Press, 1958), p. 39.

The new religious doctrine with its revolutionary ethic toward economic behavior emerged from the Protestant Reformation. The teachings of Martin Luther and John Calvin (collectively referred to as Calvinism) included a new scale of moral values and ideas for economic and social conduct more closely attuned to an English economy that was becoming increasingly commercialized throughout the sixteenth and seventeenth centuries. This doctrine provided a resolution to the moral dilemmas posed by Catholic rules against profit making and money lending. The Protestant ethic included the view that not only sanctioned but actually glorified the accumulation of wealth if achieved through hard work and thrift.

A central tenet of the Protestant ethic was that faithful Christians should answer their calling. It was believed that individuals were placed on earth to fulfill a God-given task, and that to win God's grace one should live by fulfilling ". . . the obligations imposed upon the individual by their position in the world."[5] In terms of economic behavior, accumulating wealth from hard work was not only condoned but was considered a sign of being virtuous. According to the new ethic, " . . . practical success is at once the sign and the reward of ethical superiority."[6] Where profitable opportunities presented themselves, the faithful Calvinist was expected to pursue profits with a divine purpose. However, wealth was not to be used for consuming luxury goods or for enabling one to enjoy greater leisure. Instead, the Protestant ethic instilled in the faithful that proper behavior included ". . . scorning delights, [being] punctual in labor, constant in prayer, thrifty and thriving, filled with a decent pride in themselves and their calling."[7] Overall, the new ethic toward economic behavior encouraged economically efficient business practices, and provided a justification to anyone who questioned why income and wealth were not equally distributed. The Protestant ethic held that ". . . the unequal distribution of the goods of this world was a special dispensation of Divine Providence, which in these differences, as in particular grace, pursued secret ends unknown to men."[8]

Effect of the New Religious Beliefs

According to some historians, the effect of changes in religious attitudes upon the evolution of the LFME was significant.[9] Calvinism gave divine sanction to the rules by which the institutions of a market economy would operate in a manner not considered sinful. The accumulation of wealth became the informal rule for

[5]Max Weber, *The Protestant Ethic and the Spirit of Capitalism* (New York: Charles Scribner's Sons, 1958), p. 80.
[6]R. H. Tawney, *Religion and the Rise of Capitalism* (Gloucester, MA: Peter Smith, 1962), pp. 266–267.
[7]Ibid., p. 211.
[8]Weber, *Protestant Ethic*, p. 177.
[9]Not all historians accept the Weber-Tawney thesis. For a different view, one which focuses on the role of trade through kinship ties fostered by a common religion, see Peter Mathias, *The First Industrial Nation*, 2nd ed. (New York: Methuen, 1983), pp. 142–148.

man's ultimate purpose in life. Material success became a Christian virtue, and people were driven to accumulate wealth through enterprise, energy, personal thrift, and abstention. Calvinist churches effectively induced such behavior, believing it to be their mission ". . . to exercise a collective responsibility for the moral conduct of their members in all various relations of life, . . . [especially] in the sphere of economic transactions."[10]

The significance of the Protestant ethic in the evolution of the LFME is that it overlapped with other interrelated factors (e.g., enclosures) to shape the rules which established the LFME. The new ethic stimulated new informal rules, especially those concerning investment and savings and the treatment of the poor, which subsequently led to changes in formal rules.[11] The Protestant ethic stressed the importance of a disciplined labor force and the regularized savings of profit to be reinvested. Shunning the feudal way of life, seventeenth- and eighteenth-century English entrepreneurs increasingly pursued wealth by investing more heavily in capital rather than land.

The dilemma posed by the existence of poverty among affluence was resolved by the Protestant ethic. There was little pity for the poor, while emphasis was placed on inducing people to secure gainful employment rather than providing charity. This informal rule contributed to the passage of the Poor Law Reform Act of 1834.

THE POOR LAWS

Informal and formal rules concerning the organization and financial support of England's common people began to appear in the early sixteenth century. These rules were modified over the next three centuries in response to changing social and economic problems and the central government's views about its social and political responsibility toward the poor (i.e., persons unable to support themselves by their own earnings). Common people considered poor fell into one of the following categories: the working poor, many of whom were underemployed, whose earnings were not sufficient to provide for themselves or their family; the impotent who were physically unable to work due to age or health reasons; the able-bodied not able to find work; and those who were not willing to work (e.g., vagrants referred to as "rogues" and "vagabonds"). All of the persons considered poor depended upon charity or public payments to survive, and they comprised about half of England's total population in the late

---

[10]Tawney, *Religion and the Rise of Capitalism*, p. 125.

[11]Adam Smith's philosophy (discussed later) was imbued with the new ethic. His conception of entrepreneurial behavior was that of a good Calvinist who, after accumulating profits, would save and reinvest in capital to promote greater economic growth and additional profits. The coordinator of economic activity in Smith's LFME was the invisible hand, the religious significance being that Smith ". . . saw in economic self-interest the operation of a providential plan." Ibid., p. 192.

seventeenth century. Most of them were poor due to underemployment.

Rules governing the organization of labor consisted of a number of Poor Law Acts passed over the 1500–1834 period, which applied to the unemployed and unemployable; the Statute of Artificers (1563), which applied to employed persons; and the Act of Settlement (1662), which concerned the mobility of people, often restricting their legal place of residence. The Poor Laws were designed to provide those deemed deserving with some relief from poverty while deterring vagrants from roaming the English countryside.

The unemployment problem and the desire to restrict vagrants from roaming the countryside and committing crimes led to the Act of Settlement in 1662. This act contained rules which, in effect, created a condition of villeinage between the poor and their parish. The poor were restricted from freely seeking employment beyond their parish, and were not permitted to settle in a new community unless they were able to prove they were capable of supporting themselves without the assistance of public funds. The overseers of the poor were concerned with conserving parish funds, and discouraging vagrant outsiders from settling in a new parish was often accomplished through oppressive measures. At the parish discretion vagrants could be forcibly removed and returned to their place of origin.

By the late eighteenth century artificial restrictions (contained in the Poor Laws, Statute of Artificers, and the Act of Settlement) against the free mobility of labor as well as the infringement against persons' natural liberties came under severe criticism, especially from Adam Smith. His criticism was rendered during a period of rapidly changing social, economic, and political conditions. Frequent wars disrupted the flow of food imports, leading to higher domestic food prices. This inflation occurred while the English population was rising and as enclosures were contributing to a larger number of seasonally unemployed workers. These trends led to an increased number of poor, causing public costs of poor relief to increase dramatically.[12]

The effects of the new Poor Law will be examined later. These effects must be analyzed within the context of England's post-1834 industrial society. The world's first industrial country was created by an industrial revolution.

THE INDUSTRIAL REVOLUTION

This section will briefly outline the nature of the industrial revolution and focus on its contribution to the emergence of the LFME in the 1830s. Throughout the period from 1000 to the early 1700s, relatively modest changes can be identified in the mode of production, with the major technological changes occurring in the military

---

[12]Between 1792 and 1818 the cost of poor relief roughly trebled. See Ursula R. Henriques, *Before the Welfare State* (New York: Longman, 1979), p. 19.

area. Beginning around 1750, however, a major historical transformation began within which many people (especially those in agrarian areas) could not fit into the changing economy without a radical change in interpersonal relationships, especially as they came to reside in urban industrial areas. Eventually different working rules were adopted to manage the industrializing economy.

Basically, the industrial revolution was a combination of three separate but interrelated revolutions: technological, social, and economic. The technological revolution consisted of the change in industrial techniques and the concentration of capital and labor, resulting in the factory's becoming the center of nonagricultural economic activity. This revolution began during the first half of the eighteenth century with inventions that enabled inanimate energy to be harnessed and concentrated in one area, namely, a factory. The center of the industrial growth was within the coal, iron, and textile industries where technological changes (e.g., steam engine) made factory production profitable. It became necessary for producers to adopt the new technology to remain competitive. Therefore, it became inevitable that work and housing had to be concentrated, leading to a social revolution as urbanization replaced the rural way of life.

The emergence of urban centers initiated a number of social changes. The need for public services arose, and the roles played by the new authorities and laborers (e.g., police, firefighters, sanitation workers, local bureaucrats) had no counterparts in rural England in the eighteenth century. Family life changed dramatically, for children as well as adults were confined to the repetitive and often dangerous tasks within factories for work shifts of 12 to 16 hours daily. The authorities were faced with the task of managing this changing society with its expanding factory production and urban working class.

The method for managing the society was contained in the economic revolution as the formal rules for establishing a LFME were introduced. The most fundamental change was the organization of the factors of production according to self-regulating markets. The enclosure movement and the associated rules created a market for land. The adoption of a gold standard established an international money market. A competitive labor market was created by the 1834 Poor Law Reform Act. The philosophical basis which stimulated first new informal, then formal working rules for the economy was provided by the merchants and pamphleteers directly involved in the newly emerging markets and by the classical economists.[13]

THE PHILOSOPHY OF A MARKET ECONOMY

Adam Smith, Thomas Malthus, Jean-Baptiste Say, and David Ricardo provided the philosophy upon which the formal working rules of a laissez-faire market

---

[13]For a discussion of the contributions of merchants and pamphleteers, see Joyce Oldham Appleby, *Economic Thought and Ideology in Seventeenth-Century England* (Princeton: Princeton University Press, 1978).

economy are based. Their ideas were initially considered radical and as such were not put into practice until decades after they were first published. The sequence of events is consistent with the model of institutional change. The economy's performance and the views of philosophers provided the basis for altering informal rules, and authorities, often in response to interest groups, subsequently introduced new formal working rules through the political process. The essential point is that state intervention is necessary to establish the institutions and working rules of a market economy, as well as to sanction the informal rules which maintain the social and political structures.

ADAM SMITH—MODEL OF A MARKET ECONOMY

Adam Smith was perhaps the greatest and most influential writer in the field of economics. He is referred to as a writer and philosopher of economics rather than as an economist. Smith's education was in moral philosophy and theology, but his inquisitiveness, extensive travel, and desire to provide the means by which society could alleviate poverty led him to provide a philosophy and suggestions for changes in the working rules.

Before focusing on the rules by which Smith's proposed market economy would behave, one must recognize that economic philosophies are culturally and historically determined. As a result the proposed rules for governing an economy contain a philosophical basis and a set of working rules appropriate to that point in history. The same attitude and rules will perhaps not be appropriate for another society at that period or for any society during another period. The main point is that the model of a laissez-faire market economy is based upon the views of a Scotsman influenced by the philosophy of the Enlightenment, especially the belief in natural law (laws of nature which govern the operation of the economy), and by a desire to provide an alternative to mercantile policies for those nations experiencing industrialization during the late eighteenth century.

Smith's writings, especially *An Inquiry Into the Nature and Causes of the Wealth of Nations,* contain four ingredients necessary for an economic philosophy.[14] These ingredients are a vision of the qualities which would characterize an ideal society; a conception of the socioeconomic reality of the society for which change is being suggested; a model of the new economic institutions being proposed, including a suggested role for the state; and theories and principles (laws) by which the economy should behave.

Smith's Vision

Adam Smith's primary vision was of a society which was affluent and just, distributed wealth equitably, and had liberal trade policies. This society would

---

[14]Hans E. Jensen, "Sources and Contours of Adam Smith's Conceptualized Reality in *The Wealth of Nations*," *Review of Social Economy,* 35, 3 (December 1976), 259–274.

increase the nation's wealth through economic growth. Such a notion was unprecedented in economic history. To Smith, wealth consisted of the goods which all the people in society consume. The necessary economic growth was to be achieved by a nation which adopted working rules necessary for a competitive market economy. The primary justification for Smith's market economy deserves repetition: The market economy is a model for stimulating economic growth. The purpose of economic growth is to improve the material well-being of the poorest members of the society. The nature of this process will be discussed later in the chapter.

The Conceptualized Reality of
an Eighteenth-Century Scottish
Scholar Sympathetic to the
Teachings of Calvin

Smith was generally optimistic regarding mankind's ability to realize economic growth using his model of a market economy. This optimism stemmed from his education in moral philosophy and his belief that the world behaved according to a universal natural order. He felt the Great Creator had imputed behavioral propensities in man which, if permitted to operate within the proper institutions (i.e., an unfettered market economy), would promote economic growth, thereby alleviating poverty.

Smith believed that people were basically benevolent, empathetic toward those poorer than themselves, inclined to "truck" (i.e., have dealings), and driven by their own self-interests. He also felt that within the economy there were three classes of people: landlords, laborers, and entrepreneurs. He argued that entrepreneurs would be the "undertakers" of society. That is, being good Calvinists, these owners of enterprises who accumulated a profit would tend to reinvest the surplus rather than squander it on luxury goods for their own consumption. This behavior could be expected partly because of their own self-interest and partly because they would be empathetic toward the poor. Since the entrepreneurs would derive pleasure from the improved well-being of the poor, they would reinvest their profits, eventually leading to higher wages. Smith thereby condoned the entrepreneurs' high profits, believing that these profits would be returned as investment funds to the income stream.

The behavior of entrepreneurs and laborers within the proposed market economy would be predictable, almost mechanistic. The foundation for this belief (held by Smith and almost every economist who followed) is the view that a universal natural order prevails. Smith adopted this view from earlier scholars, some of whom were his mentors, who themselves were influenced by the Enlightenment philosophy. These eighteenth-century philosophers, including Isaac Newton, held that the universe was mechanical and ordered, with its components behaving according to the natural laws of science (e.g., Newton's laws of physics).

By relying upon this conception of reality, some eighteenth-century philosophers sought to apply natural laws to the social sciences. Smith's model of a market economy, with its behavioral assumptions and emphasis upon tendencies toward order (i.e., equilibrium) stems from his conception that a natural order characterizes the behavior of economic forces. He set out to identify those natural laws and subsequently to propose the proper attitude and working rules within which society could harness those laws and apply them to pursue his vision of an ideal nation.

Smith's interpretation of history influenced his economic philosophy. He believed that mercantilist policies, which had been in effect since the midsixteenth century, had created a static economy in which the distribution of income and wealth was highly skewed. He objected to the monopolistic control exerted by the state in both economic and judicial affairs, arguing in favor of a system of "natural liberty." Under such a system individuals would be left free to engage in economic activity for the sake of their own best interests. Smith therefore proposed a model that was in contrast to the extensive regulations and controls inherent under mercantilist policies.

Smith proposed a model of an economy which would promote economic growth. He wanted to permit people to be free to make decisions such as what to produce, how to produce, and how much to produce, according to what they believed to be in their own self-interest. He wanted individuals' incomes to reflect their contributions to the economic well-being of others. The distribution of income would be determined by purchases made freely in a competitive marketplace. People would not enjoy higher incomes due to their receiving preferential treatment from the state (e.g., domestic producers profiting from a tariff imposed on the good they are producing), as they had under mercantile policies.

The Model of a Market Economy

The problem facing Smith, given his vision and conception of the socioeconomic reality, was how to create institutions from which social order, natural liberty, and economic growth would ensue in an individualistic society. His solution was his model of a market economy. Four aspects of this model merit discussion: (1) the role of behavior; (2) the laws of the market; (3) the dynamics by which economic growth and rising wages would be realized; and (4) the proper role for the state.

BEHAVIOR.   According to Smith, the pursuit of self-interest would stimulate the economically productive actors (e.g., laborers and entrepreneurs) in the market economy. When private individuals act independently to improve their own interests, the net effect would benefit the entire society in the most efficient way. In an unfettered economy where entrepreneurs are not inhibited from realizing high profits and laborers are permitted to seek the highest wage someone would offer them, more goods would be produced and consumed than under alternative ethical-moral attitudes and working rules.

LAWS OF THE MARKET.   What would be the informal working rules of the market economy? Smith identified four laws that would guide the individual production and consumption decisions as if the economic activity was being coordinated by an "invisible hand."

Law 1:   People perform the work that society wants (and will pay for) because self-interest induces them to do so. Will the workers be forced to accept relatively low wages while the entrepreneurs retain high profits? No, argued Smith, because competition among employers for labor will establish wages at competitive market levels.

What did he mean by competition? Basically, there is competition in a market if the economic power of all units (e.g., producers, consumers, or laborers) is so small relative to the entire market that the actions of one or a few are insignificant in their effect upon prices or wages. Due to competition, the essential ingredient in a competitive market economy, the motives of entrepreneurs (to maximize profits), laborers (to maximize wages), landlords (to maximize rents), and consumers (to purchase goods and services at the lowest prices) are blended together to create social harmony.

Even if selfishness and greed underlie these motives, Smith believed his market model would work for the benefit of the entire society if competition prevailed. To Smith, any form of monopoly was an enemy of the people. In his view, anything that would inhibit the behavior of competitive market forces would lessen social welfare.

Law 2:   Higher prices are a self-curing disease. In a market economy there will be no need for any rules by which authorities would regulate prices. Within competitive markets prices would tend to gravitate continually toward their "natural" level. This would be the price at which producers would be earning a return on their financial investment and effort sufficient to induce them to continue to produce some particular good or service. If a product's price exceeds its natural price, Smith argued, then profits would be higher than necessary to retain producers in that market. Existing entrepreneurs would subsequently expand output of the product. Meanwhile other entrepreneurs, lured by the possibility of earning high profits, would enter the same market. The result would be an increase in supply, which would depress the initial price toward its "natural" level.

Law 3:   Producers in society will manufacture the quantities of goods the society desires. Driven by the profit motive, entrepreneurs must respond to changing consumer demand. Purchases of goods and services communicate to producers what people are able and willing to pay. An example should illustrate this law.

Assume an entrepreneur produces and sells two substitute items of clothing (*A* and *B*). Let the natural price of *A* be $20 and that of *B* be $15. Now suppose the demand for *A* rises. This will drive up its price, for quantity demanded will exceed quantity supplied at $20, creating a shortage. The entrepreneur will respond by increasing the price and then by producing more of *A*. Other entrepreneurs capable of producing *A* will note the higher price. Attracted by the potential to earn above-average profits they will enter the market and produce more of good *A*. Subsequently, the price of *A* will gravitate toward its natural price

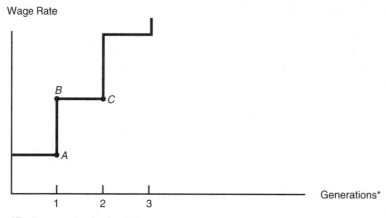

Wage Rate

Generations*

1   2   3

*Each generation is about 15 years.

Figure 5-1   Long-Term Wage Trend

of $20, with more of *A* being produced and sold. Meanwhile, the demand for *B* declines, driving down the price and quantity produced. Thus, the influence of consumer demand and competition among producers leads entrepreneurs to provide the quantities of goods and services that the society desires.

Law 4:   The market regulates the incomes of those who cooperate to produce the goods and services. Entrepreneurs and laborers working in a particular industry with rising profits should share in the prosperity. Entrepreneurs will seek to expand their output, thereby demanding more laborers. Since they will have to attract laborers from competing firms (once full employment prevails), wages will be bid up and all workers in the more profitable industry will benefit. Meanwhile, industries for which the demand for their goods and services is falling will experience lower profit rates for its entrepreneurs. This will mean that the demand for labor in this industry will decline and laborers' incomes will decline.

The Process of Economic Growth

How would Smith's market economy generate economic growth? How could output and profits increase along with wage levels? His answer is provided by his two dynamic "laws of behavior": the law of accumulation and the law of population.[15]

LAW OF ACCUMULATION.   In Smith's economy the role of the entrepreneurs was the key. They would be responsible for increasing output levels while enabling laborers to enjoy higher wages. Figure 5-1 illustrates an essential point about Smith's market model: that it is a long-run growth model with perhaps 15- to 25-year lags between rising output and rising wages.

[15]Robert L. Heilbroner, *The Worldly Philosophers,* 5th ed. (New York: Simon and Schuster, 1980), pp. 61–66.

As mentioned earlier, Smith referred to entrepreneurs as the "undertakers" of society. He believed that their sympathetic, parsimonious nature, combined with their desire to pursue their own self-interest, would lead them to behave like good Calvinists. That is, most profits would be reinvested, contributing to capital accumulation and the hiring of more laborers. Free trade was significant here, for the elimination of trade barriers was crucial to the wide (i.e., international) market Smith claimed was essential. He stressed that the large market enabled labor to become more specialized, arguing that the extent of the market would limit the division of labor. Greater specialization of labor would lead to higher productivity per worker. Smith's extensive travels throughout Europe had taken him to a pin factory where he recognized the tremendous potential for higher productivity from having laborers specialize in a particular task. As he observed in *The Wealth of Nations:*

> One man draws out the wire, another straights it, a third cuts it, a fourth points it, a fifth grinds it at the top for receiving the head; to make the head requires two or three distinct operations; to put it on is a peculiar business; to whiten it is another; it is even a trade by itself to put them into paper. . . . I have seen a small manufactory of this kind where ten men only were employed and where some of them consequently performed two or three distinct operations. But though they were. . . . indifferently accommodated with the necessary machinery, they could, when they exerted themselves, make among them about twelve pounds of pins in a day. There are in a pound upwards of four thousand pins of a middling size. Those ten persons, therefore, could make among them upwards of forty-eight thousand pins in a day. . . . But if they had all wrought separately and independently . . . they certainly could not each of them make twenty, perhaps not one pin a day.

Smith identified three benefits or gains from specialization: improved dexterity, more efficient use of workers' time, and greater likelihood of invention. Workers performing the same repetitive task would become more adept at doing their job, would save time by not moving about to perform different tasks, and would be likelier to invent a more efficient method for performing their particular task. Entrepreneurs, recognizing the benefits from the existence of a wider market and from specialization of labor, would increase their demand for labor while continuing to reinvest their profits in capital. Once full employment had been reached at the initial level of wages (Figure 5-1, point A) this increased demand for labor would lead to higher wages as employers competed for the relatively scarce workers (Figure 5-1, segment A-B). Would the rising wages curtail the rate of profit, thereby inhibiting future economic growth?

LAW OF POPULATION.   Smith's conception of a mechanically ordered world led him to argue that other natural forces prevailed that would contribute to the continuation of economic growth. The level of population (and therefore the number of laborers) would be regulated in a natural manner. The rate of population growth would be a function of the wage level. As wages rise, the death rate would decline, since families could afford better food, clothing, shelter, and other life-sustaining needs. Eventually (about 15 years later) there would be a greater supply of labor. Since higher wages have meant lower profits, capital accumulation and the demand for labor would have declined. The interaction of these forces would result in a leveling off of wages, rising profits, greater accumulation of capital, and lower rates of population growth (Figure 5-1, segment *B-C*).

Smith believed that over generations the effect of rising profits, capital accumulation, and specialization of labor would more than offset the mitigating effect of population growth upon wages. The long-run outcome would be economic growth combined with a gradual rise in wage levels, thereby alleviating poverty. Smith argued that in order for the natural laws to generate this outcome the state must assume a radically new role in economic affairs—it must adopt the policy of laissez-faire.

Role of the State

Smith believed that the state, employing its mercantilist policies, was "spendthrift [and] irresponsible." He proposed a laissez-faire ideology in which the state would perform only three legitimate functions that would supplement the otherwise unregulated market economy. These functions were establishing and maintaining a system of justice; financing and administering the means for national defense; and providing any goods or services the market could not or should not provide (e.g., roads, bridges).

Changes in the formal working rules that would complete the emergence of a self-regulating market economy were not approved by the British Parliament until the 1830s, almost 60 years after Smith proposed his model. While he had provided a new ethical-moral attitude and a new set of formal working rules for the economy, three issues required further articulation: (1) How would society provide for the poor? (2) Would a market economy create full employment? (3) Should trade barriers be removed? The answers to these issues were subsequently provided by three economic philosophers: Thomas Malthus, Jean-Baptiste Say, and David Ricardo.

THOMAS ROBERT MALTHUS— POPULATION ISSUE AND REFORM OF THE POOR LAWS

During the late eighteenth century debate arose over the growing number of paupers and the rules by which they should be treated. The impact of the number of poor on economic growth was becoming a popular debate. Population estimates for England had indicated a rise in the number of English citizens from 5 million in 1750 to about 9 million in 1800. Some scholars at that time argued that a growing population was beneficial to society, since it provided a natural source of wealth.

Using these same figures, a minister named Thomas Robert Malthus developed a theory of population. His conclusions would stand in sharp contrast to the optimistic forecasts of Adam Smith and his followers. Whereas Smith had predicted that in a market economy natural laws would foster economic progress and social harmony, Malthus believed that certain natural forces threatened humankind's existence. His conception of these forces led him to conclude that in nature the fittest will survive and that the size of the human population will be regulated by the quantity of food.

Malthus's population theory, articulated in *An Essay on the Principle of Population*, lends considerable weight to these conclusions. He begins by making two basic postulates: "That food is necessary to the existence of man," and "[that] the passion between the sexes is necessary and will remain nearly in its present state." He went on to state a logical position concerning the relationship between the size of population and food per capita, namely that "the power of population is infinitely greater than the power in the earth to produce subsistence for man." This would lead to natural checks on the population, first through sickness, epidemics, and perhaps infanticide. Ultimately famine would bring an end to population growth should the other checks not sufficiently raise the death rate.

He believed the rate of population growth would be geometric, meaning that it would grow by a constant percentage of the whole population over a fixed time period. He was intrigued by the notion of doubling time, recognizing that anything which continues to grow geometrically will increase by greater and greater absolute amounts in subsequent equal time periods. Malthus argued that the output of food would grow at an arithmetic rate. He defended this contention by noting that land does not breed, and that as more labor and other inputs are applied as productive inputs to fixed amounts of land, diminishing returns to both the labor and land would eventually ensue.

This population theory is significant for the study of economics not only for its emphasis on the nature of diminishing returns and an economy's carrying capacity (i.e., the size of the population it can support), but also for its policy implications. Malthus's theory was influential in the debates between members of Parliament, which stimulated changing attitudes regarding treatment of the poor. A majority of the members of Parliament interpreted Malthus as follows: There were too many people in England; charity was cruelty in disguise, for it hastened the inevitable famine by fostering the growth of the poor segment of society; and the Poor Laws allocated scarce resources away from the means to promote economic growth while increasing the number of poor who, in turn, demanded greater relief payments to pay for ever costlier food.

Sympathy for paupers began to wane, especially as the cost of maintaining them rose. The informal rules during the early nineteenth century shifted toward laissez-faire policies influenced by attitudes in favor of survival of the fittest and scornful of the improvident and lazy. Gradually, Parliament came to believe that the poor should assume responsibility for their own fate. Reflecting upon the implications, Parliament concluded that:

> Paying relief would not solve the problem of poverty but would merely increase the income of the poor and enable them to raise more children. Poverty would continue because there would be no increase in food supplies for the larger population. It was not necessary, therefore, to look to economic or social causes to explain the problems of the poor. They were caused by the old system of poor relief, which had continuously generated more poverty until the crisis had finally come. The solution was obviously to eliminate the relief system.[16]

The new formal rules, embodied in the Poor Law Reform Act of 1834, contained a different basis for poor relief—one based upon the laissez-faire views of philosophers, members of Parliament, and upper middle class industrialists. The act provided for an expanded role for the central government regarding the supervision of the poor. Relief would continue for those physically helpless, unable to work due to age or health reasons, but relief was abolished for those able to work.[17] The passage of the Poor Law Reform ended the outdoor relief payment system in England. An unfettered labor market was established, and its consequences will be discussed in Chapter 6.

JEAN-BAPTISTE SAY—MACROECONOMIC STABILITY, LAISSEZ-FAIRE, AND COMPETITIVE MARKETS

During the first two decades of the nineteenth century England experienced economic instability. Mounting foreign competition and easy money policies during and after the Napoleonic Wars led to domestic unemployment and inflation. There was public criticism of the new industrial economic order, especially of the view that industrialization and economic growth were beneficial to society. One issue under debate was whether an economy organized according to Smith's market model could achieve and maintain full employment of workers and capital.

By the early nineteenth century a number of people had addressed the issue of macroeconomic stability. They can be distinguished according to their emphasis upon demand or supply as the principal factor determining the level of economic

---

[16]Daniel R. Fusfeld, *The Age of the Economist*, 4th ed. (Glenview, IL: Scott, Foresman, 1982), p. 36.

[17]Those drafting the law erroneously assumed that unemployment was voluntary in nature, but most unemployment in England was involuntary during the early nineteenth century. Two main intentions of the new Poor Law were to stigmatize relief while disciplining the poor, and to facilitate the transition from agrarian to industrial employment throughout the nation. Only through entering a workhouse could an able-bodied person receive relief in return for performing public works projects or even meaningless tasks. The living and working conditions in workhouses were now intended to be undesirable, but not materially harsh. Families were broken up, as people were segregated according to sex and age.

activity. On the demand side stood the mercantilists and Malthus, who anticipated John Maynard Keynes's argument that economic growth was a function of effective demand. Supply-side advocates included Smith and a Frenchman who articulated Smith's macroeconomic views so persuasively that his doctrine would become the conventional wisdom among economists for over a century.

The central theme of Jean-Baptiste Say's "law of markets" was that supply creates its own demand. This theme supported the policy of laissez-faire, stressing that the inherent stability of market forces would automatically lead the level of aggregate supply to equal aggregate demand at a full-employment level of output. Say assumed that the consumers' desire for goods and services was unlimited, and that their ability to purchase was assured by market forces. During the production process incomes would be generated that would be sufficient to take the goods and services produced off the market. Gluts or shortages of goods or services would only be temporary—no long-run deficiency in demand was possible. Income received in the form of wages, profits, rents, or interest represented potential demand. Say assumed that all income would be returned to the income stream, transformed into effective demand without any leakages.

Unemployment and inflation would exist in a market economy, but they were only due to noneconomic factors such as war and adverse weather. In the long run unregulated economic forces would alleviate these problems. Say's faith in a laissez-faire market economy is contained in his conception of reality, which is based upon two assumptions.

First, his conception of behavior included the view that money is useful only as a means of exchange for commodities. Hoarding money yields no satisfaction. People are inclined to return all their earnings to the income stream through purchasing or investing. All savings would be invested, and entrepreneurs would prefer to lower prices rather than keeping a good in stock for which a surplus existed at the initial price. Thus, there would be a prompt sale of the goods and services produced and money would circulate rapidly throughout the economy.

Say's other assumption concerned the speed and completeness of market adjustments. Wages, prices, and interest rates were assumed to be flexible. Consequently, any disequilibrium in the labor, goods, or money markets would be temporary, and market adjustments (i.e., changes in demand and/or supply) would quickly restore equilibrium.

The following example is meant to demonstrate the market adjustment process. Assume an equilibrium wage, price, and interest rate exist in the labor, goods, and money markets, respectively (see Figure 5-2).

1. Suppose people seek to save more. Consequently, the average propensity to save (planned savings/disposable personal income) increases while the average propensity to consume (planned consumption/disposable personal income) falls.
    a. In the money market the supply of savings shifts right to $S\$_1$.
    b. The demand for goods shifts from D_0 to D_1.

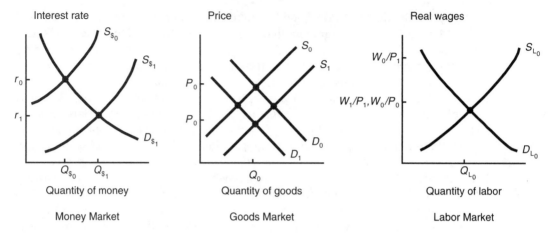

Figure 5-2   Competitive Adjustments: Money, Goods, and Labor Markets

 c. At r_0 the quantity supplied of savings supplied exceeds the quantity of savings demanded for loanable funds, and interest rates decline from r_0 to r_1 (the surplus savings will be eliminated by the fall in interest rates).

 d. At the initial price, P_0, the quantity demanded is less than the quantity supplied. Therefore, producers reduce prices to eliminate the surplus.

2. Now there is a movement of price toward P_1. At P_1 people will be able to afford the same quantity of goods and services as they originally could since the decrease in price is proportional to the decline in spending (assume they both fall by 5 percent).

 a. In the long run, the quantity demanded will exceed the quantity supplied (S_0) at P_1. (To restore equilibrium requires further adjustment, which is discussed shortly).

 b. Therefore, the output level will not decrease even though prices fall.

3. What about wages? Will not the decline in prices result in some workers becoming unemployed?

 a. As the price falls to P_1, real wages increase to W_0/P_1.

  i. At W_0/P_1, the quantity of labor supplied exceeds the quantity of labor demanded.

  ii. Therefore, entrepreneurs will reduces wages to W_1, and eventually all previously employed workers will find a job at W_1/P_1. Note that workers' real wages have been restored to their initial level.

4. Given that interest rates have declined from r_0 to r_1, an increase in investment occurs, and the supply shifts in the goods market to S_1.

 a. This creates full employment (QL_0) and no loss in output (production remains at the initial level of Q_0). In addition, the quantity of labor demanded will equal the quantity of labor supplied, the quantity of goods demanded will equal the quantity of goods supplied at lower prices, and the level of investment will equal the level of savings at a lower rate of interest.

In summary, Say had faith that the market economy would automatically tend toward a full-employment level of output. Involuntary unemployment would not be possible. Students should note that this is a long-run view and that competitive adjustments might take months or perhaps years to restore the market to equilibrium. Support for establishing the working rules for a competitive market model was almost complete. All that remained was a convincing argument that a policy of free trade would enhance a nation's economic well-being more than a system of trade which included protectionist measures.

DAVID RICARDO—FREE TRADE AND THE THEORY OF COMPARATIVE ADVANTAGE

State-imposed trade restrictions had been part of mercantilist policies in England for centuries. During the early decades of the nineteenth century, a debate arose between powerful landlords and entrepreneurs over tariffs against foreign-produced wheat, stimulating a former stockholder, landlord, and member of Parliament to propose a classic economic theory that has influenced trade policies for over a century.

David Ricardo's conception of the economy included a powerful landed gentry, urban poverty, and vestiges of mercantilism in the form of the Corn Laws. The purpose of these laws was to regulate the price of corn (i.e., wheat) so as to maintain a minimum price for domestically produced grain. A sliding scale of import duties was central to the working rules. If the domestic price of corn rose, the import duties would be lowered. Should the domestic price decline, then the import duties would be raised.

Landlords argued that they continually needed protection from foreign competition, emphasizing their view that agriculture was the primary source of wealth for a nation. Entrepreneurs and laborers objected to the tariffs. They argued that higher prices of food meant higher money (but lower real) wages, thereby curtailing economic profits, reinvestment for capital, and economic growth.

Ricardo sought to propose working rules that would enhance economic growth. He believed in a policy of laissez-faire in a competitive economy where free domestic and international trade was the rule. Such an economy would be characterized by entrepreneurs earning profits which would be reinvested in capital, thus stimulating growth. Ricardo's free trade position was defined in his classic theory of comparative advantage.

This theory, although developed according to some restrictive assumptions, is applicable to a world in which many countries trade multiple goods. Basically, Ricardo distinguishes between a competitive advantage enjoyed by one nation (where it can produce a particular good at a lower absolute cost than another nation) and a comparative advantage held by one nation in the production of a particular good. Such an advantage is depicted by the relationship among competitive advantages. The following example will illustrate this theory. Assume there are two countries, England and Sweden, that can produce wheat and cloth. Assume further that the capability to produce each good is represented by Table 5-1. The numbers represent output per 50 units of labor.

TABLE 5-1   The Basis for Trade

PRETRADE	WHEAT	CLOTH
England	400	200
Sweden	800	100
Total output	1,200	300

The price of cloth in England would be 2 units of wheat, while the price of cloth in Sweden would be 8 units of wheat. Ricardo argued that in such a situation there is a basis for trade, for there is a difference in the relative cost (or efficiencies) of producing each good. England has a comparative advantage in the production of cloth since 1 unit costs only 2 units of wheat (the amount of wheat England would have to forgo producing if it chose to manufacture one more unit of cloth). Sweden has a comparative advantage in the production of wheat since 1 unit costs only 1/8 unit of cloth versus costing 1/2 unit of cloth in England.

Ricardo argued that both nations would benefit if each specialized in the production of that good for which it had a comparative advantage, and engaged in trade with each other (or other nations in the multiple-nation case). Thus, England would produce only cloth and Sweden would specialize in the production of wheat. "World" output of cloth would be 400 units, and that of wheat 1,600 units. England would sell cloth to Sweden at a per unit price greater than 2 units of wheat but less than 8 units of wheat. Sweden would likewise sell wheat to England for a price which exceeded the pretrade domestic price in Sweden, but was lower than the pretrade domestic price in England.

Gains from such a free trade policy are numerous. The lowest-cost producers will be the only enterprises able to survive in a competitive economy. The market, not state policies, will regulate the incomes of producers and workers. Free trade also liberates resources while increasing total output, lowering prices, and raising real wages. Therefore, free trade generates greater consumer demand, higher profits, expanded investment in capital, and more jobs. The wider market also permits a greater division of labor, resulting in more gains from specialization.

Ricardo's theory, published in 1817, slowly changed the attitude in Parliament toward trade restrictions. Not until 1846, however, were the Corn Laws repealed.

SUMMARY

The change in the formal working rules for an unfettered market economy were completed before the middle of the nineteenth century. Smith's model, with its corresponding attitude and working rules, was established by changes in the formal working rules adopted by the British Parliament. Society would thereafter be organized according to new informal and formal working rules for the economy. The roles played by entrepreneurs, landlords, laborers, and the state had been redefined. Policies for promoting wealth, for dealing with poverty, and for handling trade had been altered radically. The behavior of this new economy and its impact on British society will be presented in Chapter 6.

KEY TERMS AND CONCEPTS

Conceptualized Reality	Poor Laws
Corn Laws	Religious Attitude
Enclosure Movement	Ricardo's Theory of Comparative
Industrial Revolution	Advantage
Laissez-faire	Say's Law of Markets
Malthus's Population Theory	Smith's Laws of the Market
Mercantile Policies	Vision

QUESTIONS FOR DISCUSSION

1. What effects did mercantile policies have on the British economy?
2. What was the purpose of the Poor Laws?
3. What were the basic tenets of Calvinism?
4. List Smith's four laws of the market.
5. Under a laissez-faire policy, what is the role of the state regarding economic matters?
6. What is meant by "supply creates its own demand"?
7. How did Malthus's population theory contribute to the reform of the Poor Laws?
8. Why did Ricardo believe the Corn Laws should be repealed?
9. How did the Protestant Reformation contribute to the evolution of the LFME?
10. How does the philosophical basis of an LFME as proposed by Smith, Malthus, Say, and Ricardo differ from the philosophical bases of premodern economies?

REFERENCES

Appleman, Philip, ed., *An Essay on the Principle of Population*. New York: W. W. Norton, 1976.

Boyer, George R., "An Economic Model of the English Poor Law Circa 1780–1834," *Explorations in Economic History* 22, 2 (April 1985), 129–167.

Court, W. H. B., *A Concise Economic History of Britain*. Cambridge: Cambridge University Press, 1958.

Crafts, N. F. R. *British Economic Growth During the Industrial Revolution*. Oxford: Clarendon Press, 1985.

Dillard, Dudley, *Economic Development of the North Atlantic Community*. Englewood Cliffs, N.J.: Prentice-Hall, 1967.

Ekelund, Robert, Jr., and Robert D. Tollison, *Mercantilism as a Rent-Seeking Society*. College Station, TX: Texas A & M University Press, 1981.

Fusfeld, Daniel R., *The Age of the Economist*, 4th ed. Glenview, IL: Scott Foresman, 1982.

Heilbroner, Robert L., *The Worldly Philosophers*, 5th ed. New York: Simon and Schuster, 1980.

————, *The Making of Economic Society*, 7th ed. Englewood Cliffs, NJ: Prentice-Hall, 1985.

Henriques, Ursula R., *Before the Welfare State*. New York: Longman, 1979.

Hill, Christopher, *Reformation to Industrial Revolution, Volume 1, 1530–1780*. New York: Pantheon Books, 1967.

Jensen, Hans E., "Sources and Contours of Adam Smith's Conceptualized Reality in *The Wealth of Nations*." *Review of Social Economy*, 35, 3 (December 1976), 259–274.

Landreth, Harry, *History of Economic Theory*. Boston: Houghton Mifflin, 1981.

Mathias, Peter, *The First Industrial Nation*, 2nd ed. New York: Methuen, 1983.

Mokyr, Joel, ed., *The Economics of the Industrial Revolution*. Totowa, NJ: Rowman and Allanheld, 1985.

Needy, Charles W., ed., *Classics of Economics*. Oak Park, IL: Moore, 1980.

Polanyi, Karl, *The Great Transformation*. Boston: Beacon Press, 1957.

Smith, Adam, *The Theory of Moral Sentiments.*, D. D. Raphel and A. L. Macfie, eds. Oxford, England: Clarendon Press, 1976.

————, *An Inquiry Into the Nature and Causes of the Wealth of Nations*, Edwin Cannon, ed., Chicago: University of Chicago Press, 1976.

Tawney, R. H., *Religion and the Rise of Capitalism*. Gloucester, MA: Peter Smith, 1962.

Weber, Max, *The Protestant Ethic and the Spirit of Capitalism*. New York: Charles Scribner's Sons, 1958.

Youings, Joyce, *Sixteenth-Century England*. London: Allen Lane, 1984.

6

ENGLAND'S LAISSEZ-FAIRE MARKET ECONOMY

1830–1870

OBJECTIVES

1. Distinguish the laissez-faire market economy (LFME) of England from premodern economies.
2. Link the contributions of the classical economists and the attitudes of business leaders to the adoption by Parliament of working rules that established an LFME.
3. Identify specific changes in working rules that established an LFME.
4. Explain the role of self-regulating markets in England's economy.
5. Examine the controversy regarding the LFME as a model for economic growth and as an unregulated process against which people sought protection.

HISTORICAL LEGACY AND CONTEXT

Between 1400 and the mid-1830s England evolved from a feudal to a mercantile to a commercial society. Factories and competitive markets became dominant institutions, as Parliament established working rules which created a laissez-faire market economy (LFME). The most fundamental change was the organization of the factors of production according to self-regulating markets.[1] The enclosure movement and associated working rules (see "Social Process for Economic

---

[1]Everything needed for the production and distribution processes (i.e., all inputs) is placed on sale. All output is disposed of through free markets. Laborers rely upon wages, the rate being established in a labor market, for most of their personal income.

Coordination," p. 120) created a market for land. The adoption of a gold standard established an international monetary mechanism by means of which the flow of trade regulated the nation's money supply and, in the process, the price level. A competitive labor market was created by working rules such as the 1834 Poor Law Reform Act. The industrial revolution brought increased productivity in the industrial sector. There was an exodus from rural cottage industries to industrial urban areas. Consequently, labor was available to satisfy the entrepreneurs' demands for factory workers. The working rules by which "free" trade was established were introduced between 1842 and 1860. There was a considerable time lag between the philosophies introduced by intellectuals such as Adam Smith and other classical economists (between 1776 and 1820), the consensus of business support for laissez-faire policies, and changes in the formal working rules pertaining to free trade—especially the repeal (in 1846) of the Corn Laws. This is consistent with the evolutionary-institutional theory. Change in the economy's working rules "remains very dependent on institutional processes, and political sequences, which have a rhythm and a logic of their own to some degree."[2]

A LAISSEZ-FAIRE PHILOSOPHY

There were two generally accepted informal rules which were consistent with the implementation of an LFME. To begin with, after 1815 intellectuals and government and business leaders—particularly the powerful export and import lobbies—recognized that population growth created a need to import more food, and that the English economy was dependent upon exports, especially textiles. Second, there was a general attitude toward managing the society which contained the "conviction that good results only could be obtained by making each man dependent on himself alone."[3] A major objective of LFME proponents was the establishment of free, competitive markets—especially for international trade.

The free trade argument as put forth by the intellectuals was persuasive. They argued that free trade would mean lower prices, lower wages (since wages were tied to the cost of essential goods—especially the price of grain), and economic growth. Some of these intellectuals, however, offered arguments in favor of selected protectionist measures. Smith was in favor of the Navigation Acts in the interest of promoting English shipping, and he also favored publicly funded education. Reverend Malthus saw some benefits from the Corn Laws, while David Ricardo was not opposed to some subsidization of landlords. Other economists spoke out for factory acts to establish safer and healthier working conditions, especially for children. Taken together these views provided some basis for arguments against free trade.

---

[2]Peter Mathias, *The First Industrial Nation,* 2nd ed. (New York: Methuen, 1983), p. 273.
[3]Edward P. Cheyney, *An Introduction to the Industrial and Social History of England,* revised ed. (New York: The Macmillan Co., 1927), p. 227.

In reality many of the views of the classical economists did not coincide with the interests of merchants and capitalists. Smith felt that these individuals would engage in rent-seeking behavior, and thus the state needed to establish rules (e.g., abolish or drastically reduce tariffs and import quotas) to enable the "invisible hand" of competitive markets to regulate this behavior. Some businesspeople feared that free trade would mean lower profits due to greater competition. While merchants and entrepreneurs admitted that free trade would maximize benefits (e.g., greater output, lower prices) for the international economy, they were uncertain how free trade would affect England. Some landlords, merchants, and producers had come to expect protection of their investments. Others (e.g., producers of finished silk products) liked the prospect of importing cheaper raw materials, but still wanted protection against finished products. Overall, businesspeople's attitudes toward free trade depended upon their calculations of the likely changes in their own profits. Merchants and entrepreneurs who were anxious for a free trade policy to be implemented put forth influential arguments in the 1840s. In particular, they argued that the combination of population growth and trade restrictions contributed to higher food prices, with a concurrent rise in wages. By late 1841, during "the trough of the worst trade depression of the century,"[4] producer and merchant arguments in favor of free trade working rules intensified.

During the 1840s Parliament was swayed by a number of ideological and economic factors. Parliament acknowledged the contributions of the classical economists, especially the coherent logic of the theory of comparative advantage. Many members were influenced by the attitude that individuals, not the state, should be responsible for their own well-being. Evidence that the value of England's exports was declining, while that of imports had risen during the late 1830s, stimulated fears of lower rates of economic growth. Members of Parliament agreed that population growth meant upward pressure on food prices, which would lead to increased wages. The depression of 1839–1842 occurred while the Corn Laws and Navigation Acts were still in effect, undermining faith that protectionist working rules were consistent with economic prosperity.

Ultimately it was the performance of the English economy while protective measures were in effect that swayed Parliament to repeal the Corn Laws. In light of the 1839–1842 depression, Parliament reasoned that a free trade policy could not be any worse than protectionist measures. In 1842 tariffs were reduced on wheat, and the ensuing positive trends of economic growth and inflation created attitudes in favor of more rules promoting free trade. By 1846 Parliament decided to ignore the efforts of those rent-seeking commercial interests still demanding protection from competition. The state was prepared to repeal the Corn Laws and abolish or reduce many other import duties, and to reduce its responsibility for control over the economy. Parliament also committed

---

[4]Mathias, *The First Industrial Nation*, p. 272.

to balance the state's budget, expenditures being reduced to the lowest level "compatible with the provision of defence [sic] and police."[5] They had faith that private interests, especially entrepreneurial activity, would stimulate output, exports, and employment levels, all for the good of England. The Navigation Acts were abolished in 1849. Between 1853 and 1860 Parliament reduced the state's budget, abolished income taxes, and reduced nearly all import duties, the tariff on tea being an exception. Since tariffs were reduced but not abolished for all products, "free" trade in post-1860 England actually meant freer trade.

SOCIAL CLASS STRUCTURE

England's social structure during the 1830–1870 period was characterized by relatively clear distinctions between social classes. These distinctions were essentially self-defined by members of each class, most of whom believed it was important to identify with a particular social group.[6] Class antagonisms between the upper (e.g., aristocracy, middle) classes and those lower in the social structure were considerable. Most working class members and paupers were deemed "nonrespectable," especially if they were dependent upon charity to survive, frequently drunk, or unable either to live in one place or to hold the same job. Factors which served to delineate classes included heredity, "respectability," and occupation.

The upper class consisted primarily of aristocracy, many of whom were landowners who had inherited their estates and titles. Though accounting for less than 2 percent of all English families, their annual earnings amounted to over half the total national income.[7] Wealth and status were closely linked. Members of the English upper class not only were at the top of the political structure but also were part of the " 'gentrification' of the commercial and industrial class . . . [which] tended to slam the door shut to further [middle and lower class] entrants."[8]

The middle class comprised about 20 percent of the population and covered a wide spectrum of occupations, income levels, and extent of wealth. What members of the middle class had in common was acceptance of the bourgeois ethic—the Puritan belief in hard work, thrift, sobriety, competition, and religious observance; the desire to attain respectability, which "consisted in earning a degree of independence by one's own efforts, in self-discipline (especially in sexual and bibulous matters), . . . in veneration for home and family as the basic social organism from which all other virtues flowed,"[9] and in not engaging in the

[5]W. H. B. Court, *A Concise Economic History of Britain* (Cambridge: Cambridge University Press, 1958), p. 192. This view is consistent with Adam Smith's philosophy concerning the state's proper role under a laissez-faire policy.

[6]For a concise discussion of the English class system, see Walter C. Neale, *The British Economy: Towards a Decent Society* (Columbus, OH: Grid, 1970), pp. 3–12.

[7]Eric J. Evans, *The Forging of the Modern State* (London: Longman, 1983), p. 277.

[8]Joel Mokyr, ed., *The Economics of the Industrial Revolution* (Totowa, NJ: Rowan and Allanheld, 1985), p. 19.

[9]Evans, *The Forging of the Modern State*, p. 280.

drudgery of manual labor. Members of this class were able to influence working rules in the urban areas, and after 1830 gradually made their influence felt in Parliament when rules in favor of laissez-faire policies were being debated.

The common people, roughly 70 percent of the population, belonged to the working class. Below them were the paupers, whose numbers often exceeded 10 percent of the population before 1850. The working class consisted of skilled workers and artisans, urban wage earners, casual laborers, street vendors, and prostitutes, among others. The working class was essentially "wage earning, propertyless, and voteless, [whose members felt they were] victims of callous, greedy, privileged and rich-without-reason upper classes."[10] The standard of living realized by the working class and paupers was generally poor prior to 1850, especially in terms of working and living conditions. These conditions were exacerbated by economic recessions which caused tenure of employment to be irregular.

POLITICAL STRUCTURE: PARLIAMENTARY POWER

Since property ownership was the basis of power in the political structure throughout the 1830–1870 period, the views of most authorities were those of the bourgeois. The upper class stood at the apex of England's political structure, and from this relatively small class of landed aristocracy came the nation's highest authorities. The monarch's powers were relatively modest. The political power of the manufacturers and merchants increased throughout the period, while that of local government authorities declined. Most power over working rules for the economy was exercised by Parliament. This body consisted of two houses—the House of Commons, whose members were elected, and the House of Lords, an hereditary aristocracy comprised of all titled gentlemen throughout England.

The working class stood at the bottom of the political structure. Prior to 1830 few working class members were permitted to vote. Consequently, hardships they experienced due to poor performance of the economy could not be translated into peaceful replacement of authorities with individuals sympathetic to working class needs. At the beginning of the 1830–1870 period, middle class manufacturers and merchants as well as working-class members began to demand some political power. Although the middle class did not identify with the working class, they formed a union for the purpose of receiving greater recognition. Both groups opposed the aristocratic stranglehold of a Parliament that was not representative of England's population, and which established working rules for the economy consistent with narrow aristocratic interests. The Reformist movement sparked riots throughout England, and eventually stimulated Parliament to pass rules (see "Social Process," p. 120), which improved working conditions for many factory

---

[10]Neale, *The British Economy: Towards a Decent Society*, p. 9.

and mine workers as well as those who toiled in agricultural "gangs."

INSTITUTIONS PROMOTING
LAISSEZ-FAIRE MARKET CONDITIONS

Over the 1830–1870 period four institutions were instrumental in establishing and coordinating the major production and distribution patterns in England's LFME. These institutions were the factory; financial institutions, especially the Bank of England, joint-stock finance companies, and the gold standard; Parliament; and self-regulating domestic and international markets.

The Factory

The factory and the factory town were symbols of nineteenth-century England, replacing the handicraft workshop or the village located near the land which tenants had rented. From the outside, factories resembled workhouses, and may have been patterned after them. Inside, the factory functioned "as an engine, the parts of which [were] men . . ." who were not required to think.[11] Relations between management and workers in the factory differed considerably from relations within the workshop or the manor. No longer were workers (e.g., former artisans) their own masters. Unlike lord-peasant relations, there was "none of the traditional sense of responsibility"[12] toward workers. Some historians argue that employers held a condescending attitude toward their working class employees. Absolute control over factory workers was exercised by the employer. Labor was placed on the same footing as the other factors of production (land, capital equipment, and money)—treated as commodities rather than as human beings. When demand for the factory product declined, workers were relieved of their jobs. Since most workers had meager (if any) savings, able-bodied individuals who became unemployed could only survive through charity, since they were ineligible for public assistance according to the provisions of the 1834 Poor Law.

Working conditions subjected laborers to the strict discipline and rhythm of the factory. The typical work schedule was 12 to 15 hours per day (or perhaps during the night), six days per week. While working conditions in the factory may not have been worse than conditions in some workshops, there was a significant difference concerning child labor in workshops versus the factory. In the workshop children could learn a skill with hope of advancement, while in the factories children (some of whom were seven years of age) had little opportunity to acquire skills for

[11]From Adam Ferguson, "An Essay on the History of Civil Society" (1765) in Christopher Hill, *Reformation to Industrial Revolution* (New York: Pantheon Books, 1967), p. 214.
[12]Ibid., p. 218.

advancement.[13] Living conditions in factory towns were dreadful, although they improved slowly throughout the nineteenth century.[14] The anomie which characterized villages was missing. Due to the sudden demand for workers and subsequent migration to urban industrial areas, towns grew rapidly. The population in one industrial area, Liverpool, rose from about 138,000 to 299,000 between 1821 and 1841 and to over 500,000 by 1870.[15] Meanwhile public administrators were inexperienced in managing such towns. Consequently, urban industrial areas tended to be overcrowded, polluted, unhealthy places in which to reside.

    In terms of economic efficiency the factory system was superior to the handicraft form of production. Productivity of all factors of production increased, especially that of labor, due to gains from specialization. Mass production led to reduced output costs and lower prices. Through such efficiency, factories contributed to changing attitudes toward free trade. Authorities became convinced that an industrial society should be managed according to laissez-faire policies, and that the result would be greater economic growth and benefits derived by all members of society.

Financial Institutions: The Bank of England, Joint-Stock Finance Companies, and the Gold Standard

The Bank of England was founded as a private concern in 1694 to finance the monarch's needs. In return, the bank had a monopoly over joint-stock banking until 1826. It viewed itself as a large commercial institution, while serving as the government's banker. The bank was the repository for most of England's gold stock, and it was empowered to issue notes at a rate which depended upon the quantity of gold it held. It did not become a central bank in the modern sense until after 1870.

---

[13]A vivid description of factory life in the first half of the nineteenth century is provided by Friedrich Engels. (From E. P. Thompson, "The Making of the English Working Class," p. 804) in Trevor May, *An Economic and Social History of Britain 1760–1970* (New York: Longman, 1987), pp. 57, 58. "The supervision of machinery, the joining of broken threads, [there] is no activity which claims the operative's thinking powers, yet it is of a sort which prevents him from occupying his mind with other things. We have seen . . . that this work affords the muscles no opportunity for physical activity. Thus it is, properly speaking, not work, but tedium, the most deadening, wearing process conceivable. The operative . . . must not take a moment's rest; the engine moves unceasingly; the wheels, the straps, the spindles hum and rattle in his ears without a pause, and if he tried to snatch one instant, there is the overlooker at his back with the book of fines."

[14]One historian provides the following account of factory towns. "They contained huge ramshackle tenements and long rows of miserable cottages in which the families of the working class crowded four and even more persons per room. Sanitary facilities were generally nonexistent, and refuse of all kinds was disposed of by being thrown into the street. Drainage facilities, where they existed, usually took the form of open ditches in the middle of the streets, but more often than not rain, wastewater, and refuse were left to stand in stagnant pools and rotting piles that filled the air with vile odors and served as breeding ground for cholera and other epidemic diseases. The streets were mostly narrow, crooked, unlighted, and unpaved." See Rondo Cameron, *A Concise Economic History of the World* (New York: Oxford University Press, 1989), p. 187.

[15]Taken from Francois Crouzet, *The Victorian Economy* (New York: Columbia University Press, 1982), p. 97; and Mathias, *The First Industrial Nation*, p. 417.

Public confidence and liquidity are the key to every banking system. England's frequent monetary crises reflected problems with a monetary system in which the Bank of England was the only joint-stock company permitted to extend investment credit. When demand for money increased considerably, the bank experienced a liquidity shortage. It was forced to contract credit, generally leading to a recession. Two working rules introduced new financial institutions before 1830, and by 1870 confidence and liquidity within England's banking system were generally high.

In 1826 Parliament sought to strengthen the banking system by permitting joint-stock companies to extend credit for capital investment. The success and growth of joint-stock financial companies thereafter were due to their managerial talent and their willingness to offer more favorable loan terms than their competitors. These companies not only served to make the banking system more competitive, but they changed the nature of investment. By extending the availability of credit, they helped to lessen the importance of the entrepreneur-investor-manager who relied on internal funds for finance. In place of individual entrepreneurs rose investors who could allocate their funds through joint-stock finance companies to different ventures without concern for managing them.

The gold standard was introduced in England after 1819 following a working rule by which Parliament required that Bank of England notes would be convertible into gold by 1821, thereby making the British pound equivalent to a fixed amount of gold sterling. The bank would hold large quantities of gold to cover its note issue and banking operations. Other banks did not hold their reserves in gold, but instead held their main reserves in the form of Bank of England notes. The gold standard not only served to increase confidence and liquidity in England's banking system, but it linked international markets while coordinating the flow of free trade (see "Social Process" section for further discussion, p. 120).

Parliament

The LFME did not emerge "naturally," but was the conscious result of changes in formal working rules for the economy. The primary authority in England for economic matters was Parliament, whose members were ultimately swayed by economic philosophers and commercial interests advocating laissez-faire policies in the name of maximizing England's wealth while reducing the cost of regulation. During the first six decades of the nineteenth century, Parliament repealed trade protectionist rules and introduced other rules (e.g., the Poor Law Reform Act of 1834), which served to create self-regulating markets.

Self-Regulating Domestic and
International Markets

A market can be defined a number of ways. It is a place where buyers and sellers meet to exchange goods and services for an agreed-upon price. It is also a mechanism which produces prices. If it is self-regulating, then the prices will be established through the interaction of supply and demand. In an economy characterized by self-regulating markets, the quantities and prices of goods, services, and factors of production will be determined by these markets. Some have referred to an LFME as a "market system," by which they mean that nearly all production and distribution decisions are coordinated through the interplay of supply and demand forces within unregulated markets. For the first time in history markets became the dominant institution of an economy, and markets were bound together through price signaling in the allocation of resources.

Examples of domestic and international markets can be cited for both ancient Rome and medieval England. The significance of the nineteenth-century English economy is the overwhelming extent to which unregulated markets influenced decisions concerning what to produce, how much of each good or service to produce, how to combine resources to produce these goods and services, and how the revenue generated by production should be distributed. The behavior of an economy characterized by self-regulating markets is discussed next.

BEHAVIOR OF THE ECONOMY

Organization of Resource Allocation Decisions

Decision making concerning allocation of resources for production and distribution purposes in the LFME of England was primarily decentralized. That is, private manufacturers and merchants, operating under minimal government interference, made decisions on an individual basis. Centralization of decision making was confined primarily to Parliament's actions concerning trade regulations, factory legislation, and care of the poor.

Since labor, land, and money (to purchase capital) were organized according to self-regulating markets, which meant that these inputs could be purchased as needed, decisions regarding the allocation of these inputs were decentralized. The degree of decentralization depended upon the competitive nature of each market. In markets where the producers were highly concentrated (i.e., relatively few producers accounting for a high proportion of an industry's output), organization of decision making was more centralized. This would be the case, of course, whenever decision makers colluded. Evidence from the 1830–1870 period indicates that in most industries there was considerable competition (i.e., decentralization of economic decisions. Consistent with the rent-seeking theory of behavior, there were attempts by decision makers in some industries to collude. Overall, however, attempts to collude did not seem to have any "significant economic effect."[16] Based upon the absence of collusive agreements among producers, little organization among labor, and laissez-faire policies of the state

---

[16]Mathias, *The First Industrial Nation*, p. 354.

toward regulating production and distribution activities, the period from 1830 to 1870 can be considered "as the hey-day of the competitive economy in Britain."[17]

Ownership and Control of the Means of Production

Throughout the period private, individual ownership and control of the means of production predominated. In addition, there were many owners, so that decision-making power was diffused. The extent of state control over the means of production was modest, but not absent. It is noteworthy that despite the philosophical basis favoring laissez-faire policies, the number of government workers increased between 1830 and 1870.

One reason for a larger bureaucracy was the growing need for administrators and other civil servants for purposes such as collecting customs and excise duties; inspecting factory conditions and enforcing provisions such as the minimum safety and health standards contained in factory acts; supervising those unable to work who qualified for assistance under provisions specified by the Poor Law; and gathering certain data for Parliament (e.g., census).[18] The cost of such public measures relative to total spending throughout England was quite modest. As of 1870 public authority expenditures were less than 5 percent of England's gross national product, with over 80 percent of these expenditures allocated for servicing the national debt and for military expenditures.[19] The rate of growth of government expenditures was less than that of national income. As a percentage of national income, public expenditures decreased from 20 percent in 1820 to 11 percent in 1850, and to about 7 percent in 1870.[20] Government purchases of goods and services as a percentage of gross national product declined slightly from an average of 5.5 percent over the 1860–1864 period to about 4.4 percent by 1870.[21]

Periodic financial crises throughout the 1830–1870 period stimulated debates concerning rules governing control of credit, the ratio of bank notes to gold, and entry into the banking system. In general, laissez-faire policies applied to the state's regulation of the banking system. Concerning its own financial matters the state focused its attention on "rigorous balancing of the public budget, and the reduction of public expenditure to the least amount compatible with the provision of defense and police."[22]

Social Process for Economic Coordination

Coordination of most production and distribution activities was through self-

---

[17]Ibid., p. 355.
[18]Evans, *The Forging of the Modern State*, p. 285.
[19]Mathias, *The First Industrial Nation*, pp. 39, 428.
[20]Ibid., pp. 39, 423, 429.
[21]Ibid., p. 424.
[22]Court, *A Concise Economic History of Britain*, p. 191.

regulating markets. Entrepreneurial activity was instrumental in goods and services markets, while gold played an important role in financial markets. Laissez-faire was not always the rule, for Parliament introduced a few measures to protect certain groups from the potentially harmful effects of unregulated markets.

ENTREPRENEURIAL ACTIVITY. The nineteenth-century English entrepreneurs were more dynamic than the artisans who dominated handicraft production until the industrial revolution. Entrepreneurs initiated or closely supervised inventions and / or industrial innovations, which they applied to production, and sales activities of the companies they founded. Laborers were hired at wage rates established in a competitive labor market (i.e., no working rules established minimum wages in any industry). Entrepreneurs worked long hours, bore financial risks by borrowing or using their own capital for productive investment, took the initiative, and resourcefully managed their factories to provide high quality and greatly varied goods and services to England and the nation's trading partners. Entrepreneurial activity was induced by the Puritan work ethic, the potential for realizing greater social status through exploiting profit opportunities, and supply-side factors such as technological progress.

Entrepreneurs took advantage of free trade opportunities, some of which they helped to create as some of these businessmen were elected to Parliament. They used their influence to limit the extent of publicly provided education. Entrepreneurs' disdain for the working class was manifested by their fear that educating England's "lower orders [was a] . . . dangerous indulgence since it might nurture ideas above people's station [in life]."[23] Entrepreneurs were not bashful, however, about lobbying for working rules designed to promote their particular interest. Their rent-seeking efforts were "largely ineffective in the long run in economic terms," however.[24]

FINANCIAL MARKETS. In financial markets capital was perfectly mobile throughout England. Savers were free to deposit funds into this market, while investors could receive credit at a market-determined rate of interest. A majority of funds for industrial investment came from business profits rather than from the extension of credit. The stock exchange was not a major source of capital for long-term industrial purposes until after 1870.

Faith in the LFME meant faith in the gold standard. This automatic mechanism was independent of central banks or governments. Proponents of the gold standard believed in the gold standard's ability to stabilize the monetary system and automatically coordinate international trade and finance transactions. Under a gold standard each nation agreed to convert paper currency and bank credit into gold coins on demand, and permitted gold coins to be freely exported.

---

[23]Evans, *The Forging of the Modern State*, p. 30.
[24]Mathias, *The First Industrial Nation*, p. 35.

The currency of each nation was fixed relative to a certain quantity of gold (e.g., 1 British pound sterling = 4 ounces of gold). In order to enable the gold standard to guide the international economy effectively, nations had to subordinate their domestic economies to the international economy. That is, discretionary monetary and fiscal policies were not considered efficacious means for regulating an economy. Instead, nations faithfully permitted market forces to correct any imbalance in economic activity. Faith in the self-correcting nature of the gold standard, which restored stability between nations with different rates of economic growth, labor productivity, and trade flows was essential to the smooth functioning of the international economy.

Consider the following example. Assume England's exports of goods and services to the rest of the world were lower in value than its imports. The result would be an outflow of English gold rather than a depreciation of currency (and a decline in terms of trade) vis-à-vis England's trading partners. As a result, the money supply in England, which was tied to the nation's gold supply, would decrease. Rather than depreciate the value of the pound sterling, prices, interest rates, and money (but not real) wages were expected to decline so as to maintain a level of domestic spending consistent with a full employment level of output. There might be temporary shortages in spending, but in the long run output and employment would tend toward a full-employment level.

PARLIAMENT AND THE *DOUBLE MOVEMENT*.   The *double movement* which occurred throughout the 1830–1870 period, was the clash between economic liberalism advocating that society be managed according to self-regulating markets, and the reaction by people who lobbied for working rules to protect themselves from potentially adverse effects of unregulated supply and demand forces.[25] Overall, the state's role over production and distribution activities was limited, especially in terms of acquiring raw materials, facilitating investment, or training labor. The few state enterprises which existed prior to 1870 were involved with producing items for military purposes. The attitude prevailed that there was no need for state involvement as long as the economy under laissez-faire policies performed favorably, which it did (as never before) between 1846 and 1870 (see "Performance," p. 125). The authorities' belief in the efficacy of the LFME's working rules was exemplified by "their faith in the ability of the private capitalist to maintain investment and employment at any level which might be required by the national interest."[26]

The cries for protection were responded to, albeit unwillingly, only when the authorities were convinced that the net effect of laissez-faire was not only harmful to certain English citizens, but also threatened the future performance of the economy. For example, publicly funded health measures were introduced

---

[25]The term *double movement* was introduced by Karl Polanyi. For further reading see Polanyi, *The Great Transformation* (Boston: Beacon Press), 1957, especially pp. 40, 76, 83, 175–177, 182–184, 188–192.
[26]Court, *A Concise Economic History of Britain*, p. 192.

partly to assure a steady, healthy supply of labor. However, despite the strong philosophical basis in favor of laissez-faire, once protectionist measures were introduced they not only remained in place, but expanded (especially after 1870). This same pattern, of course, was also followed by the state bureaucracy. Similar patterns will be identified for economies discussed in later chapters.

Protection was sought by groups from all levels within the social structure, including some landowners, middle-class merchants, and factory and agricultural laborers as well as the poor. Various groups felt their status and income were threatened by the working rules (e.g., repeal of the Corn Laws) of an LFME. In particular, there was concern over the working conditions in factories, availability of credit, and public health and education. Parliament responded by introducing working rules consisting of a "network of measures and policies . . . designed to check the action of the market relative to labor, land, and money."[27]

The extent of protectionism was not widespread in terms of affecting most production and distribution decisions. That protectionist measures were introduced is significant, however. It illustrates that while the laissez-faire philosophy is logical and appealing from an economic efficiency viewpoint, those who may be affected by forces beyond their control tend to seek some form of protection. This attitude is not confined to nineteenth-century England. In contemporary societies where unregulated markets are principal institutions for coordinating economic activity, similar patterns of behavior can be identified. Even in Hong Kong, the bastion of free enterprise, ardent supporters of laissez-faire were not opposed to government intervention (by temporarily suspending trading in the colony's stock market) during the stock market crash in October 1987.

Among the protective measures retained or introduced by Parliament after 1830 were tariffs, legislation protecting factory and mine workers, public health programs, more assistance for those unable to work, and public education. All tariffs were not abolished, although they were reduced after the mid-1840s. In particular, tariffs were imposed on "land-intensive raw materials and food" such as coffee, wheat, cotton, tobacco, wine, sugar, tea, and rum.[28] One could argue that the retention of tariffs was not for the purpose of protection, but to provide revenue for the state. Overall, the reduction of tariffs, which served to narrow the difference between domestic prices in England and the world prices by about 21 percent,[29] served as a revenue enhancing measure, since the volume of imports increased enough to offset the tariff reductions.

[27]Polanyi, *The Great Transformation*, p. 76.

[28]Donald N. McCloskey, *Enterprise and Trade in Victorian Britain* (London: George Allen & Unwin, 1981), pp. 159–162.

[29]Ibid., p. 160.

INSTITUTIONAL CHANGE:
EXPANSION OF MARKET
ACTIVITY AND FREER TRADE

Throughout the 1830–1870 period, there was only modest change in the principal institutions, although the relative performance of factories, the Bank of England, and markets (especially international) increased. Within Parliament the relative influence of the middle and working classes grew. Favorable performance of England's economy (see p. 125) meant there was relatively little pressure on Parliament to alter dramatically the working rules, save the protective measures discussed earlier. The philosophical basis for the LFME and the four principal institutions would change very little until the effects of the Great Depression were felt in the 1930s.

With the exception of the factory acts regulating working conditions and specifying rules concerning the employment of children, the factory not only remained an important institution but expanded in importance. Domestic and international markets also grew in importance throughout the period, as indicated by the rapid growth of international trade (see p. 126). While competitive domestic markets were the rule by the early 1830s, changes in the working rules between 1846 and 1860 gradually established freer competition in international markets. One of the reasons for these changes was the growing influence of merchant and manufacturing (as opposed to land-owning) interests in Parliament. This influence, in turn, followed the extension of voting rights in the early 1830s.

One important institutional change occurred in the financial sector following the introduction of Peel's Act of 1844, which addressed the problem of the availability of credit. Under a gold standard a deficit in the balance of payments meant an outflow of gold and, thus, a decrease in the money supply. Equilibrium could be restored either through a decline in prices or through the depreciation of the pound vis-à-vis other currencies, each of which would induce exports. Maintenance of stable exchange rates was necessary, since London was the financial center of world trade. Therefore, credit was restricted and due to decrease in the money supply, prices were expected to decline. Industrialists and merchants objected to this restriction and influenced the introduction of rules permitting the Bank of England to issue notes that were not backed by gold. This dramatic change enabled the bank, not the automatic regulation of the gold standard, to control the flow of domestic credit. Such a role represented a departure from an unregulated market for money. In effect, this type of banking "was essentially a device developed for the purpose of offering protection" to business enterprises in need of credit.[30]

---

[30]Polanyi, *The Great Transformation*, p. 192.

AN UNPRECEDENTED PERFORMANCE
BY THE ECONOMY

Using criteria such as economic growth, price stability, and international trade, shipping, and finance activities, the economic performance of England's LFME between 1830 and 1870 was "astonishing"[31] in absolute terms and in relation to other nineteenth-century European economies.[32] Never before, nor since, has a single nation exercised such a degree of control over the world economy.

Economic Growth and Price Stability

While internally consistent data are not available for the overall growth rate of the economy prior to 1856, the 1856–1870 annual growth rate of gross domestic product was about 2.2 percent.[33] Average annual growth of manufactured exports was more impressive at 5.6 percent between 1830–1857 and about 3.0 percent for the rest of the period.[34] One estimate of price stability using an index accounting for prices of agricultural and "principal" industrial goods indicates that prices increased less than 10 percent between 1830 and 1870.[35] There were a number of factors contributing to the favorable growth and price stability. These included the rate of savings and capital accumulation, entrepreneurial activity, and cheap imports due to reduced trade barriers. In terms of economic efficiency, the factory system was superior to the handicraft form of production. Productivity of all factors of production increased, especially that of labor, due to new technology and gains from specialization. Mass production led to reduced output costs and lower prices.

International Finance and Trade

Two other factors which enhanced the economy's performance were the services offered by England's financial institutions, and the expansion of exports following reductions of trade barriers. England was the hub of world trade, with London serving as the financial center. Not only bills of exchange but funds in search of short-term returns were attracted to London. The 1860s were the "apogee of the London discount market—the most remarkable example of international finance operating under purely private institutions, responsive only to the price mechanism and the laws of the international gold standard."[36]

English shipping dominated marine transport as no other nation ever has. As a result, the nation reaped considerable income from "invisible" exports

---

[31]McCloskey, *Enterprise and Trade in Victorian Britain*, p. 139.

[32]See N. F. R. Crafts, "Economic Growth in France and Britain, 1830–1910: A Review of the Evidence," *The Journal of Economic History*, XLIV, 1 (March 1984), 49–68.

[33]R. C. O. Matthews, C. H. Feinstein, and J. C. Odling-Smee, *British Economic Growth 1856–1973* (Stanford, CA: Stanford University Press, 1982), p. 22.

[34]Matthews et al., *British Economic Growth 1856–1973*, p. 448.

[35]Mathias, *The First Industrial Nation*, p. 421.

[36]Ibid., p. 329.

(services such as shipping, insurance, or finance) and returns (e.g., profits, interest) on foreign investments. In fact, these earnings were so extensive that England experienced a favorable balance of payments despite having a rising balance of trade deficit over the 1830–1870 period.

International trade had a significant effect upon the major sectors of the English economy and the nation's economic power vis-à-vis the rest of the world. While historians disagree over the contribution of foreign markets to England's economic growth prior to the middle of the nineteenth century, most agree that trade was instrumental in establishing England as the undisputed world economic power by 1870. There are a number of reasons why trade was so important.

Free trade enabled England to import cheaper raw materials than could be produced domestically, if they could be manufactured at all (e.g., raw cotton, sugar). Rising levels of imports sent more English pounds abroad, fueling foreign demand for England's industrial output. The formal rules creating free trade contributed to the volume of England's exports and imports, with both increasing over 240 percent between 1841 and 1870.[37] Overall, exports as a percentage of England's gross national product increased from 10 percent to about 25 percent between 1831 and 1870, while during the same period the value of imports rose from 14 percent of gross national product to about 30 percent.[38] Three principal sources of exports were the large, low-cost iron industry, the modernized engineering industry (which produced capital equipment), and the textile industry.

Between 1830 and 1870 textiles contribution to total export earnings declined from about two thirds to less than one half, while the combined value of iron, steel, machinery, and coal exports grew from less than one twentieth to almost one fourth.[39] High volumes of exports enabled economies of scale to be achieved in those industries, and created external economies—especially in the textile industry. The degree of international specialization between England and the rest of the world has never been duplicated. By 1870 about 90 percent of England's exports were industrial products, while England became the world's largest importer of primary products.

Summary of the Economy's Performance: 1830–1870

The trend toward industrialization which began in the early eighteenth century continued throughout the 1830–1870 period. The value of manufactured goods rose from about 37 percent to 42 percent, while the combined value of agriculture, forestry, and fishing declined to 15 percent from the 1830 level of 28 percent.[40] The degree to which authorities accepted the laissez-faire philosophy is indicated by

---

[37]Mathias, *The First Industrial Nation*, p. 279.
[38]Brian Murphy, *A History of the British Economy 1086–1970* (London: Longman, 1973), p. 631.
[39]Ibid., p. 635.
[40]Ibid., p. 222.

the low percentage of gross national product accounted for by government expenditures, including defense. This percentage generally remained about 5 percent throughout the period. The English government provided little direct assistance either to the industrialization process or toward mitigating the hardships endured by paupers and some members of the working class. Production efficiency and high rates of economic growth contributed to changing attitudes towards free trade. Authorities became convinced that an industrial society should be managed according to laissez-faire policies, and that the result would be greater economic growth and benefits derived by all members of society.

There is disagreement among economic historians concerning the extent to which industrialization affected the standard of living experienced by members of each social class between 1830 and 1870. In light of the difficulties encountered when evaluating an economy, controversy over a precise evaluation of an economy's performance in terms of changes in the standard of living are inevitable. This is especially true for the pre-1850 period for which reliable data generally are not available. In particular, accurate measures of alienation or health and living conditions for most households do not exist.

Available evidence does permit some inferences to be drawn. The standard of living as indicated by consumption of meat and wheat products and by average life expectancy did not appear to improve for most English citizens between 1830 and 1850.[41] There is evidence that income inequality increased during this period. One analyst argues that in terms of male earnings, the Gini coefficient for the entire economy was 0.293 in 1827, and rose to 0.358 in 1851.[42] However, after 1850 the standard of living, especially for the working class, "increased indisputably."[43] Real wages rose after 1850, especially during periods when favorable harvests coincided with expanding trade (i.e., during a harvest-trade cycle). Evidence indicates that the Gini coefficient for the economy declined after 1850.[44]

The state's tax system and pattern of expenditures adversely affected the lower classes' standard of living. Indirect taxes were regressive, especially excise taxes on goods such as beer, spirits, and bricks, which together accounted for about two thirds of public revenue. Meanwhile, more than half of public expenditures were payments to holders of bonds for the national debt. Nearly all bondholders were members of the upper class. The redistribution of income on the local level through the parish was progressive, but the amount of assistance provided was not of sufficient magnitude to offset the regressive indirect taxes imposed by Parliament.

[41]Joel Mokyr, "Is There Still Life in the Pessimist Case? Consumption during the Industrial Revolution, *The Journal of Economic History*, XLVIII, 1 (March 1988), 90.

[42]Jeffrey G. Williamson, "Earnings Inequality in Nineteenth-Century Britain," *The Journal of Economic History*, XL, 3 (September 1980), p. 467.

[43]Mokyr, "Is There Still Life in the Pessimist Case?" p. 90.

[44]Williamson, "Earnings Inequality in Nineteenth-Century Britain," p. 467.

KEY ELEMENTS AFFECTING THE
EVOLUTION OF ENGLAND'S
LFME INSTITUTIONS

Four principal institutions, whose origins were discussed in Chapter 5, were central to the coordination of most production and distribution activities between 1830 and 1870. *Domestic and international markets* grew in importance as trade restrictions were relaxed by *Parliament.* Free (i.e., freer) international trade not only linked world commodity markets and stimulated specialization of labor and production, but also enabled England to become the undisputed world economic power. *Factories* expanded, especially in the textile and iron industries. Foreign demand for textiles and capital goods was satisfied by English manufacturers. The stability of the pound and availability of credit were ensured by *financial institutions* whose activities were shaping not only the domestic, but the world economy.

The relative political influence of social classes was altered after 1830 as some merchants and producers, whose status increased with their wealth, were able to influence authorities in Parliament. In addition, the arguments of philosophers and the performance of the economy (e.g., the depression of 1839–1842) shaped Parliament's attitudes. Parliament introduced rules establishing free trade, benefiting manufacturers and traders (versus landowners). The continued favorable performance of the economy after 1846 in terms of economic growth, price stability, expansion of exports, and availability of cheaper imports enhanced the desire to retain laissez-faire policies with a few exceptions. When a threat to the economy was perceived, as in the case of public health and factory conditions, which threatened to reduce the supply of labor, Parliament introduced protective measures.

Favorable performance of the economy, especially after 1850, meant that there were few changes in working rules that significantly modified principal institutions. One such change was Peel's Act of 1944. This rule made credit easier to obtain than it had been under the automatic functioning of the gold standard. Overall, however, favorable performance of the economy meant that the working rules of the LFME were retained.

LOOKING AHEAD

Working rules similar to those which characterized England's LFME between 1830 and 1870 prevailed until the 1930s, albeit in modified form, as the government gradually extended protective measures. The dominance of laissez-faire economic policies in other Western industrial economies began to wane after the end of World War I. Thereafter, macroeconomic instability and political revolutions led to the emergence of alternative economies. One type, the command over market economy established in Germany, is presented in Chapter 7.

KEY TERMS AND CONCEPTS

Double Movement	**Gold Standard**
Factory	**Laissez-faire Policy**
Free Trade	**Self-regulating Markets**
Freer Trade	

QUESTIONS FOR DISCUSSION

1. Distinguish between free trade and freer trade.
2. What were the arguments against the establishment of free trade?
3. In what respects was England the undisputed world economic power in 1870?
4. How did the English entrepreneur of the 1830–1870 period differ from the guild merchant of the medieval period?
5. Identify and explain an example of the double-movement concept in the United States over the past decade.
6. Does the performance of the English economy during 1830–1870 justify Say's law of markets? Explain.
7. Explain how the gold standard was expected to act automatically to regulate the English economy.
8. Using available data and the material in this chapter, can you find any laissez-faire market economies in the world today?

REFERENCES

Boyer, George R., "An Economic Model of the English Poor Law Circa 1780–1834," *Explorations in Economic History*, 22, 2 (April 1985), 129–167.

Cameron, Rondo, *A Concise Economic History of the World*. New York: Oxford University Press, 1989.

Court, W. H. B., *A Concise Economic History of Britain*. Cambridge: Cambridge University Press, 1958.

Crafts, N. F. R., "Economic Growth in France and Britain, 1830–1910: A Review of the Evidence," *The Journal of Economic History*, XLIV, 1,(March 1984), 49–68.

Crouzet, Francois, *The Victorian Economy*. New York: Columbia University Press, 1982.

Dillard, Dudley, *Economic Development of the North Atlantic Community*. Englewood Cliffs, NJ: Prentice-Hall, 1967.

Evans, Eric J., *The Forging of the Modern State*. London: Longman, 1983.

Mathias, Peter, *The First Industrial Nation*, 2nd ed., New York: Methuen, 1983.

Matthews, R. C. O., C. H. Feinstein, and J. C. Odling-Smee, *British Economic Growth 1856–1973*. Stanford, CA: Stanford University Press, 1982.

May, Trevor, *An Economic and Social History of Britain 1760–1970*. New York: Longman, 1987.

McCloskey, Donald N., *Enterprise and Trade in Victorian Britain*. London: George

Allen & Unwin, 1981.

Mokyr, Joel, "Is There Still Life in the Pessimist Case? Consumption during the Industrial Revolution, *The Journal of Economic History,* XLVIII, 1 (March 1988), 69–92.

Murphy, Brian, *A History of the British Economy 1086–1970.* London: Longman, 1973.

Neale, Walter C., *The British Economy.* Columbus, OH: Grid, 1980.

Needy, Charles W., ed., *Classics of Economics.* Oak Park, IL: Moore, 1980.

Polanyi, Karl, *The Great Transformation.* Boston: Beacon Press, 1957.

Williamson, Jeffrey G., "Earnings Inequality in Nineteenth-Century Britain," *The Journal of Economic History,* XL, 3 (September 1980), 457–476.

7

COMMAND OVER A MARKET ECONOMY

Germany, 1933–1945

OBJECTIVES

1. Explain how the breakdown of the laissez-faire market economy (LFME) created a climate within which a command over a market economy (CME) emerged.
2. Identify the new political movements that would provide the philosophical basis for the CME, both throughout Europe and within Germany.
3. Examine the distinguishing features of the German economy, especially how it is a reaction against unregulated markets, laissez-faire policies, and liberal democracy.

INTRODUCTION

Those western nations which were industrializing during the century following the Napoleonic Wars adopted rules for their economies which closely conformed to those of a laissez-faire market economy (LFME). Although instances of state intervention meant that not all markets were self-regulating, as of 1914 the authorities in most Western nations believed that a self-regulating market economy would promote economic growth efficiently, and that macroeconomic stability, especially full employment, would occur automatically.

Due to favorable performance of most LFMEs during the late nineteenth and early twentieth centuries, the informal and formal working rules of an LFME were prevalent, especially throughout Europe, until 1914. Two major events shattered the stability of the international economy and the universal faith in the

LFME—the First World War and the Great Depression. The war not only led to loss of life and assets, but also to social instability, class conflicts, and a distrust of "economic liberalism"[1] and LFME institutions. Interventionist efforts by national governments during the war, including temporary abandonment of the gold standard by most European nations,[2] demonstrated that state-directed measures to supplement the market could be effective. Public demands for state intervention were intensified by postwar inflation and the shrinking volume of world trade, which exacerbated unemployment.

Beginning in 1917 European nations, facing declining exports, rising unemployment, and high rates of inflation, began to introduce rules which effectively ended laissez-faire as a domestic and international policy for macroeconomic stabilization. As societies began to lose faith in the ability of a self-regulating market economy to guarantee prosperity, negative attitudes developed concerning the type of liberal society a market economy tended to create. In Russia, Germany, and Sweden, among other nations, adverse economic conditions, especially high unemployment and low levels of investment, facilitated the acceptance of doctrines which included economic philosophies that were hostile, in varying degrees, to the LFME. Each of the doctrines, as well as the new working rules for the corresponding economies, will be presented in this and subsequent chapters. In the command over market economy (CME) case of Germany, a predominantly LFME was reformed "at the price of the extirpation of all democratic institutions"[3]—especially those concerned with political and economic matters.

POST-WORLD WAR I
EUROPEAN RECESSION

During World War I state guidance of economic activity in the form of regulating production and distribution activities (e.g., prices, production levels, distribution of consumer goods and services) was necessary throughout Europe. When the war ended political authorities across the continent inherited nations with macroeconomic instability, and there was widespread uncertainty over the future of the gold standard. Many authorities believed that the working rules for economies which prevailed until World War I could be reintroduced, with prewar rates of economic development ensuing. This was a classic example of the mistaken assumption that the performance of an economy in one context would

---

[1]Economic liberalism, in this context, refers to the liberal (and in the opinion of some, radical) views of the classical economists who advocated a laissez-faire philosophy with a self-regulating market economy in lieu of mercantile policies.

[2]There were two basic reasons for this decision. Nations sought to prevent an outflow of gold to rival countries, and the rapid increase of currency in circulation following the outset of the war precluded nations from honoring a commitment to convert bank notes into gold. By the mid-1920s most European countries returned to the gold standard.

[3]Karl Polanyi, *The Great Transformation* (Boston: Beacon Press, 1957), p. 237.

be duplicated if the same working rules were reintroduced in a different context.

   After 1920 neither London nor New York was able to function effectively as the center of the world's financial activities, for neither was able to meet the demand for credit. The United States needed to increase its level of imports to give foreigners sufficient dollars to enable them to repay loans owed to the United States, which had been incurred during the war. By 1930, excess production capacity and falling demand led to rising unemployment in Western industrialized nations, stimulating protectionist policies designed to curtail unemployment. The Smoot-Hawley Tariff was an ill-advised formal rule introduced by the U.S. government in 1930. As a result of this rule and subsequent retaliatory measures introduced by European nations, the volume of international trade declined considerably. Economic instability and continued unfavorable performance of European economies throughout the 1920s would result in the abandonment by the mid-1930s of the gold standard—a principal institution of the LFME—throughout Europe as well as in the United States.

   During the late nineteenth and early twentieth centuries, small political groups in Western Europe began developing attitudes that rejected democratic liberalism (i.e., a system with freely elected authorities from competing parties) and sought alternatives to an LFME. The new political groups believed that existing democratic governments were responsible for the perceived poor performance of the economy. Some groups began to advocate the doctrine of communism (see Chapter 15). Other opposing groups rose on the ground swell of popular support for a disciplined, authoritarian society.

   Between 1917 and 1930 economic, social, and political conditions created a climate that was conducive to widespread acceptance of these political groups. Many nations experienced serious recessions, followed by the Great Depression. Working-class people feared that they would be relegated to lower-class status as a result. In addition, strong nationalist feelings developed in the countries which lost the war and resented the harsh settlement terms. In Germany new authorities promised a political structure and philosophical basis for organizing society, including the economy, that appealed to the fears and emotions of the population. Subsequently, new working rules were introduced consistent with the nationalistic, imperialistic views held by the new authorities.

Germany

Between the end of World War I and 1932 the German economy experienced hyperinflation (1921–1923), followed by five years of relatively favorable performance, followed by a depression in 1929. The severity of the depression was such that the hardships of increased unemployment, lower national income, and declining real wages were greater in Germany than in other Western industrialized nations. High tariffs on German exports exacerbated domestic economic problems, as the economy was very dependent upon foreign trade.

   In 1930 the economy was characterized by concentrated power within the industrial sector, a dual economy (i.e., a modern industrial sector paying high wages and a traditional, less productive agricultural sector with lower wages), and a strong role for the state. Germany had a history of cooperation between the state and private financial and industrial enterprises, including state intervention in economic activities through subsidies, tariffs (especially against coal and steel), and aid to private firms in selected industries. Cartels with concentrated private ownership and public supervision had been established under state guidance in the coal and steel industries. This concentration of private ownership was encouraged so that both industries could be rationalized (i.e., become more technically efficient through realizing economies of scale while cooperating so as to avoid excess capacity throughout the industry).

Fear of another hyperinflation prevented the state from abandoning the gold standard. Instead, payments to all foreigners were suspended and strict exchange controls were imposed. These controls violated Ricardo's theory of comparative advantage and precluded significant gains from free trade. The German state regulated bilateral trade agreements requiring its trading partners to use the German marks earned from their own exports to purchase German goods or services. The net effect of these policy measures was to lower trade volumes, decrease the availability of credit, increase unemployment, and decrease output. State involvement in the German economy had expanded to such an extent by 1932 that some analysts described the economy as "state socialism," since the volume of state expenditures was over 30 percent of Germany's national income.[4] If state influence (e.g., receipt of revenue, price controls) over public enterprises such as railroads and public utilities is included, then the percentage of income under state control was over 50 percent.[5]

By early 1932 propertied classes had lost faith that the Weimar Republic, a popularly elected national assembly under President Paul von Hindenburg, could promote economic policies consistent with prosperity. These classes were unified in their determination to introduce an autocratic political structure whose authorities they would be able to control. Such a structure was promised by the National Socialist German Workers (Nazi) Party. In addition to offering an alternative to the LFME, the Nazis' appeal to the bourgeois and other groups lay in their concentrated leadership, mass appeal for unity (to end the internal disunity Nazis claimed was plaguing the country), and emphasis upon discipline. Prevailing attitudes of the German people were receptive to the Nazi message. Germans were "anticapitalist," especially regarding liberal rules toward trade and organized labor activities. State intervention was accepted.

A weak democratic tradition was exploited by the Nazis as they spoke out

[4]Gustav Stolper, *The German Economy* (London: George Allen & Unwin, 1940), p. 219.
[5]Ibid.

against individualism and liberalism.[6] Nazi philosophy appealed to industrial leaders, bankers, landowners, members of the military, and bureaucrats—all of whom feared the type of "socialism" which had been introduced in Russia. The Nazis capitalized on this fear, arguing that *their* economic program would retain private ownership with the state directing the economy toward the pursuit of national goals as defined by the nation's leader. In 1933 Hindenburg was persuaded by influential Germans to appoint the leader of the Nazi Party, Adolph Hitler, chancellor. By 1934 Nazi Party representatives had been elected to a majority of the seats in the national assembly. After Hindenburg's death in the same year, Hitler became president of Germany.

NATIONAL SOCIALIST GERMAN WORKERS' PHILOSOPHY

Three aspects of the philosophical basis will be discussed: the contributions of intellectuals, the views of the leading authority (i.e., Hitler) after he assumed power, and some specific features of the philosophy which served as the basis for the working rules of the CME.

Intellectuals

The philosophical basis for the CME proposed by the Nazis before assuming power was comprised of selected views taken from the writings of intellectuals and activists, many of whom were part of political movements that developed throughout Europe during the late nineteenth century. These movements were stimulated by the poor performance of some economies characterized by an LFME and democratic governments.[7] The intellectuals and activists expressed concern over what they believed to be the inherent political and economic instability of the LFME. They argued that this instability was manifested by a breakdown in discipline throughout society, macroeconomic problems (e.g., high unemployment and inflation), and weak, corrupt leadership which they believed was the inevitable result of a democratic political structure. Intellectuals rejected the democratic view against elitism, arguing that a select, elite group should provide vision and define what was in the national interest.

Economic crises throughout Europe during the early 1920s and 1930s

---

[6]According to Thorstein Veblen, "the dynastic spirit of the Prussian State had permeated the federated people." See Dudley Dillard, *Economic Development of the North Atlantic Community* (Englewood Cliffs, NJ: Prentice-Hall, 1967), p. 509. Dillard states that "warlike aspirations of the Prussian leaders found support in the romantic loyalty, militant patriotism, and overwhelming sense of pride of the whole German people in their recent achievements." Ibid. Thus, the German people were willing to mobilize for World War I, and these attitudes carried over into the 1930s.

[7]Polanyi argues that "Fascism, like socialism, was rooted in a market society that refused to function." Polanyi, *The Great Transformation*, p. 239.

stimulated some intellectuals (e.g., Gioacchino Volpe) to propose that the LFMEs be replaced with an alternative economy. They advocated reforms such as participatory forms of management with significant labor involvement, and redistribution of wealth through high income and profits taxes assessed against the bourgeois. Few specific working rules for the economy were proposed, however. The intellectuals believed that once the political structure consistent with their views was established, effective working rules for production and distribution would follow "by [the] miraculous generating power of action."[8]

The overriding theme of nationalism was present in intellectuals' writings. They called for "a state which pulled together into one spiritual unity the creative souls of its citizens . . . a state whose very nature was identical with that cultural expression for which these men yearned."[9] Intellectuals argued that people could only be creative if they acted harmoniously according to the interests of their national authorities. A "corporative state" would be established, which would discourage pursuit of profits for individual gain. All members of the labor force, including owners of private property and laborers, would accept the "state's disciplinary intervention . . . in the productive process."[10] These "corporative men," abiding by a new set of informal rules, would willingly serve the public interest as defined by the authorities. The main symbol of the corporative state would be an authoritarian political structure with a strong and wise leader.

Authorities

German authorities essentially "borrowed whatever suited them from other political doctrines."[11] The authorities were able to assume power without proposing a coherent, consistent economic policy.[12] Instead, their views were mostly negative, condemning alternatives to the CME (e.g., communism, the LFME) as well as democracy.

The views of the intellectuals served Hitler's government well. They used the writings of intellectuals to justify political revolution. Despite describing the intellectuals' program (i.e., the National Socialist German Workers' Party basic program) as being "unalterable," Hitler did not hesitate to deviate from the

---

[8]P. Vita-Finzi, "Italian Fascism and the Intellectuals," in S. J. Woolf, ed., *The Nature of Fascism* (New York: Vintage Books, 1969), p. 229.

[9]George L. Mosse, "Fascism and the Intellectuals," in S. J. Woolf, ed., *The Nature of Fascism*, p. 209.

[10]Edward R. Tannenbaum, *The Fascist Experience: Italian Culture and Society 1922–1945* (New York: Basic Books, 1972).

[11]Otto-Ernst Schuddekopf, *Revolutions of Our Time: Fascism* (New York: Praeger Publishers, 1973), pp. 16, 17.

[12]In 1920 the Nazis published a social and economic program, which "read like a letter to Santa Claus" in terms of what it promised. Karl Hardach, *The Political Economy of Germany in the Twentieth Century* (Berkeley, CA: The University of California Press, 1980), p. 53. Included in the list were general promises such as the guarantee of employment to all Germans, land reform, and antiusury declarations—all of which stressed the primacy of the national interest over individual self-interest.

economic components when it suited his interests.[13] His government's economic philosophy could be described as opportunistic, for German authorities admitted that their program was not based upon any economic theory. Authorities appealed to the masses through a charismatic leader who promulgated myths and aroused fears and other emotions, especially by focusing on scapegoats (see "Social Structure," p. 139). Rational thought was scorned. In its place were substituted emotion, passion, and impulses. Authorities gathered support by using lower-ranking political hacks to spread propaganda that was based upon material borrowed selectively and opportunistically from the writings of intellectuals. Members of the society were "educated" to feel part of a glorious, strong, superior state that was "deified . . . as the supreme embodiment of the human spirit."[14] As part of a common culture (i.e., a "Nazi" society), they were expected to accept the philosophy and policy measures proposed by their leader.

After Hitler assumed power he broke with the intellectuals in favor of pragmatic alliances with industrial leaders, among others, in order to solidify his political support. As a result, the philosophy of intellectuals did not coincide with the practice of CME authorities. Intellectuals opposed the property owners, the establishment, and elite authorities in favor of workers and the poor. After assuming power, the CME authorities rejected the creative, educated views of intellectuals while taking pragmatic measures (e.g., aligning with the property-owning class) to solidify their political power. Authorities also introduced working rules which reduced or eliminated the power of organized labor. Thus, one of the ironies of the CME is that while its intellectual philosophical basis was antiestablishment (particularly against the upper class), the actions of its authorities enhanced the interests of the property-owning class—especially owners of industrial capital. Except for the rank and file within the political structure, the allocation of resources was in favor of the elite after the CME was established in Germany.

Specific Features of Nazi Philosophy

Three features of this philosophy are noteworthy: the anti-LFME and liberal democracy sentiments, the lack of a coherent economic program, and the belief in the primacy of politics.

ANTI-LFME AND LIBERAL DEMOCRACY. There was considerable "anticapitalist" sentiment in Germany during the 1920s and early 1930s. The poor performance of the economy after World War I, exemplified by the hyperinflation of 1921–1923, led to a general mistrust of private ownership and control of financial institutions as well as of all individuals or institutions able to accumulate

---

[13]Roy C. Macridis, *Contemporary Political Ideologies* (Boston: Little, Brown, & Co., 1983), p. 54.
[14]Rondo Cameron, *A Concise Economic History of the World* (New York: Oxford University Press, 1989), p. 361.

large amounts of financial capital. In particular there were fears that persons would become rich through obtaining credit, making profitable business investments, and then repaying their loans with money whose value had depreciated due to inflation (a pattern common during the hyperinflation period). Ultimately, such attitudes led to state control and some ownership over financial enterprises.

Another CME position was opposition to trade unions. The CME philosophy stressed order and unity for all citizens, and sought to discourage antagonism between labor and management. The economic goals were to be defined by the leader, not result from the pursuit of self-interest by individual producers, sovereign consumers, or organized laborers interacting in unregulated markets. Acceptance of the CME philosophy required individuals to subordinate themselves completely to the "exigencies of the state."[15] The state would define what was in the national interest, and had the right to change the definition at will.

ABSENCE OF A COHERENT ECONOMIC PROGRAM.   Neither intellectuals nor the Nazi authorities who eventually assumed power had "any cohesive economic theory."[16] One reason was the idealistic belief held by intellectuals and political activists that the intuition of the leading authority would solve all problems. There was also faith in state regulation (but not ownership) of the means of production. The concentration of private economic power was retained in recognition of large industrial complexes. To promote efficiency and avoid "harmful" effects of competition (e.g., duplication of production capacity), cartels were encouraged in major industries.

There were a number of "pledges" to particular interest groups, publicized clear, simple slogans and propaganda themes that appealed to the particular emotions felt by each group. Farmers were promised protection from competitive market forces, subsidies, and "pure communitarian values"[17] (i.e., individuals would obey the party leaders who, in turn, would establish goals and policy measures for the entire German community). Workers were promised employment. They were very receptive to such a promise, for unemployment had increased from about 1 million to 6 million between 1928 and 1932. Members of the military were promised that the armed forces would be rebuilt and that the provisions of the Treaty of Versailles would be ignored. The middle class was promised employment security and stable income, and that the threat of communism would be eliminated.

PRIMACY OF POLITICS.   The philosophy for the CME held that the working rules for the economy were secondary to political goals. Emphasis was placed on a new culture in which the importance of the group would be stressed,

---

[15]Stolper, *The German Economy,* p. 233.

[16]Edward R. Zilbert, *Albert Speer and the Nazi Ministry of Arms* (London: Associated University Press, 1981), p. 47.

[17]Macridis, *Contemporary Political Ideologies,* p. 187.

with conformity and respect for authority expected of everyone. The "leadership principle" would be in effect. According to this principle, "[t]he leader decides everything and everybody must obey. . . . He is the law, and hence above the law. . . . His will is arbitrary, absolute, and superior."[18] The Nazis claimed that their leader had superior intuition and, therefore, was able to distinguish right from wrong and identify what means should be employed to satisfy national objectives. In these respects the power of the CME leading authority was similar to that of a Roman emperor or a medieval monarch.

The type of society consistent with CME philosophy appealed to those seeking order, discipline, and elitist authorities to whom they were willing to submit. Attitudes held by those attracted to a CME included lack of faith in, or experience with, democracy; respect for authority to the point of unquestioned obedience; and strong feelings of nationalism—including belief in the superiority of their society vis-à-vis the world community. Proponents of a CME had faith that the creative, pragmatic mind of the leader could solve economic and political problems, so they willingly submitted to the leader who had the superior insight to define what was in the nation's best interest. This leader was to be selected by a few elite, for it was believed that a majority of the population was not capable of self-government. Conformity was preferred over individualism, although individualism was tolerated as long as it was consistent with the achievement of authority-defined national goals.

GERMAN SOCIAL CLASSES AND POLITICAL RANKS

In Germany the political structure was strict and hierarchical, with a top-down flow of authority. Efforts to regiment society (i.e., establish a rigid, well-defined social structure according to the authorities' vision) were successful, consistent with the philosophical basis which favored formation of a corporative state and corporative citizens (see p. 142).

Social Structure

The Nazi authorities sought to create a corporative state in which the energies of all citizens would be unified and their nationalistic feelings strengthened. This would require a revolutionary reorganization of the social structure. Authorities adopted a "preceptorial vision of social organization,"[19] whereby education was utilized to channel the enthusiasm, energy, and creativeness of the masses toward behavior that complied with the state's wishes. For example, to increase mass enthusiasm and arouse mass (but perhaps not majority) support, the state

[18]Ibid., p. 194.
[19]Charles E. Lindbloom, *Politics and Markets* (New York: Basic Books, 1977), p. 62.

regimented many German youths and laborers into mass organizations, such as Hitler Youth. There they were indoctrinated to become corporative persons who sacrificed personal gain for the good of the nation.

A perverse form of social Darwinism was practiced as CME authorities reorganized their society's social structure according to their attitudes. Authorities believed in survival of the fittest, with the state defining which groups were most fit (i.e., superior). Discrimination and persecution were the unfortunate results of such a view. The society was divided into insiders and outsiders according to criteria established by authorities. Three types of overlapping outsiders (or outcasts) were identified:

> ideological enemies—those who propagated or even simply held beliefs and values regarded as a threat to national morale; . . . so called "asocials"—the socially inefficient and those whose behavior offended the social norms of the "national community;" . . . [and] biological outsiders [e.g., members of the Jewish community] who were regarded as a threat because of their race or because they were suffering from a hereditary defect.[20]

In Germany, the racist view that Aryans were superior, and thus insiders, was preached to the population. Among the Aryans, those with highest status were the political authorities, with the leaders of industry, large landowners, and military officers also enjoying high status. Below them were managers (white-collar workers), labor leaders, journalists, teachers and civil servants—all of whom taught and supervised the masses (e.g., blue-collar workers, independent small businesspersons, farmers).

Political Structure

CME authorities believed that the party was the true source of authority in the state. All other political parties were eliminated. The party leader was deemed infallible, while other party members were subject to dismissal without notice if they were not fully obedient or efficient. Such a political structure, with absolute power concentrated within the highest authorities, was referred to as "genuine leadership" by the Nazis. The pervasive attitude was that rule by the elite was essential, with little faith placed in individual freedom or popular government. Although the leader and his party had absolute political power, the term *totalitarianism* was not used to describe the political structure. Instead, the nation was described as a strong, nationalistic, and militaristic leader-state whose citizens adhered to the leadership principle. The appeal of the CME was not in any economic philosophy with internally consistent working rules, but in promises to restore and maintain solidarity, unity, order, and obedience in everyday life.

---

[20]W. F. Bruck, *Social and Economic History of Germany from William II to Hitler* (New York: Russell and Russell, Inc., 1962), p. 84.

The CME authorities did not rise to power from a mass, grass-roots revolution, but through a convenient alliance between party authorities and the bourgeois following the election of 1933. Therefore, power was shared between the party and "traditional sociopolitical and economic elites"[21] (i.e., industrialists and landowners) whose support the authorities had needed to acquire power. Since both state and private authorities had disdain for liberal democracy and the LFME, state intervention became pervasive in all aspects of life.

In order to secure compliance from the population, the authorities favored a preceptorial system over a bureaucracy. Under the preceptorial system, education served as a mechanism for social control, for it offered a means to mobilize support throughout society for centrally determined goals. "[A] small enlightened governmental elite instructed the masses in much the same way that [the philosopher] Rousseau . . . imagined a 'superior intelligence' transforming each individual."[22] Such a system was accepted by the masses in Germany, for the people readily preferred strict hierarchical social and political structures from which solutions to social and economic problems emanated in an authoritarian manner. The people believed in "communitarianism" where one freedom (that of an authority who spoke for all people) replaced individual freedoms. In Germany freedom meant "obeying the party that represented the . . . community, and the leader of that party . . . [so that] [t]he individual and the community would become one."[23]

CME INSTITUTIONS

The German economy featured three institutions which coordinated the major production and distribution patterns: the leader of the ruling party (the *Fuhrer*), the ruling party, and the corporative state. The distinction between party rhetoric and reality is important to note, for the publicized purpose of the corporative state and the manner in which it functioned differed according to the will of the authorities, especially the party leaders.

Party Leader and the Party

The Fuhrer (i.e., Hitler) spoke for the state and party. The role of the Fuhrer and party were not, however, referred to as that of a dictatorship in a totalitarian state. Rather, the official working rule was that the leadership principle should apply throughout a corporative state. According to this principle, the party leader

---

[21]Stien Ugeluik Larsen, B. Hagtuet, and J. P. Myklebust, *Who Were the Fascists: Social Roots of European Fascism* (Bergen: Universitet Forgalet, 1980), p. 37.

[22]Lindbloom, *Politics and Markets*, pp. 54–56.

[23]Macridis, *Contemporary Political Ideologies*, p. 196.

combines in his person the highest offices of the state and of the party. The party represents the movement that speaks for the leader and the State and acts on their behalf. Party officials occupy virtually all the important posts in the state. . . . Finally, the leader, with top party officials, controls the economy, which, like everything else, was supposed to be subordinate to the state and to its ideology."[24]

Corporative State

The corporative state represented the authorities' view concerning how society should be organized. It was believed that in order to protect citizens and the state from the adverse effects of an LFME and liberal democracy a system of corporations should be established to control various economic activities. Corporations were economic groups organized along functional lines into associations. Employers and workers were first asked and then required to reorganize into confederations, with all confederations united into one national federation.

There were a number of reasons provided by the party for the establishment of the corporative state. It would enable the authorities to defend society against the LFME and socialism. It would restore social cohesion, uniting a fragmented society by entwining employers and employees. The intent was to change attitudes so that in place of employers and workers the people would recognize leaders (party officials and leaders of industry) and followers (workers). As a result, cooperation and consultation rather than antagonism would ensue under the supervision of the state authorities. The corporations would promote harmony throughout society by enabling all groups to understand and contribute collectively to the common good. Conflicts between producers and laborers could be resolved more easily. For example, rules regarding technical training, levels of employment, prices, wages, working conditions, and freedom for labor (e.g., strikes were not permitted) would be regulated by the corporation. Each major branch of industry was regulated by one corporation.

A hierarchy of state-industry-worker organizations existed. Below Hitler and the Nazi Party officials was the Estate of Industry and Trade. Activities were coordinated by the National Economic Chamber under the supervision of the Minister of Economics. Six Reichsgroups were formed which, taken together, encompassed industry, trade, handicraft, banks, and insurance firms, and other types of enterprises. In addition, "German industry [was] divided into fourteen economic districts . . . [which created] a wide network of centralized and decentralized groups, committees and boards embrac[ing] all branches of [the] economy."[25] Thus, German producers and laborers were part of a united network designed to enable the state to exercise complete authoritarian control over them while eliminating duplication or overlap of functions, thereby avoiding problems ensuing from rivalry between

---

[24]Ibid., p. 203.
[25]Bruck, *Social and Economic History of Germany*, p. 214.

competing enterprises or between management and labor.

The German corporative state was a fraud in terms of what authorities promised employers and workers and what transpired after the corporative state was firmly established. All citizens were bound to the state through the corporations, with workers coming under more stringent control than the elite industrialists. The corporative state served to control wage settlements, the flow of international trade, and the allocation of raw materials and credit, and it supervised the investment decisions of the major industrial enterprises. Essentially, establishment of the corporative state was a means to subjugate the means of production for the achievement of political objectives. State control, not harmony and cooperation between employers and workers, was the overriding activity throughout the corporative state.

BEHAVIOR OF THE ECONOMY

Organization of Resource Allocation Decision Making

In the highly centralized corporative state that characterized the German economy, party authorities would make most major production and distribution decisions, with elite industrialists having some influence. Economic choices (regarding what to produce, what prices to set, and what the level of wages and use of profits should be) were forced from above. Such a scheme of decision making reflected the philosophical basis that favored the primacy of politics under the leadership principle. The establishment of new social and political structures, with power concentrated within the leader, and general acceptance of a new philosophical basis enabled the party to control decisions pertaining to production and distribution activities.

As with the case of an LFME, in which a market economy could exist only in a market society (i.e., a society willing to let itself be controlled by free-market forces), a CME could exist only in a society willing to accept the new social and political structures as well as a philosophy which stressed the leadership principle. The state had the final word concerning labor-management relations (e.g., the length of the workweek, wages) as the influence of trade union leaders was eliminated. In addition, the state could set prices and dictate the composition of output and the purpose for which profits would be used.

Primacy of politics exemplified the organization of decision making in Germany, for political decisions determined the economy's needs. The influence of interest groups declined continually after 1933, although large industrial firms recognized that their fate (i.e., profits) was tied to the ability of the state to achieve its aims. The justification for centralized resource allocation decision making by the state was first, the need for Germany to recover from the effects of the depression, and, later, the need to ensure unity as the nation prepared for war.

Hitler was the supreme authority, for he personally approved all state-sponsored working rules pertaining to production and distribution decisions. Such a decision-making scheme was not in the best interests of microeconomic efficiency or macroeconomic coordination. While he seemed to grasp production figures, Hitler did not comprehend basic macroeconomic or microeconomic principles, nor did he seem concerned about the consequences of his political decisions, especially those pertaining to foreign policy, on the German economy.[26] Some power was delegated to lower party authorities between 1933 and 1936. During this period Hjalmar Schacht, Minister of Economics, was free to establish economic policy. After 1936 Hitler made decisions more frequently as he wished to control the forced rearmament drive.

Ownership and Control of the Means of Production

Ownership of enterprises was predominantly private, but state control over the economy through the corporative state was pervasive. The corporative state regulated industry according to what was deemed in the nation's best interest (including subsidizing selected producers to guarantee that they would not suffer debilitating losses). According to the CME philosophical basis, the elite were the only ones capable of managing the economy. The power of the state prevailed over individual welfare. The state mistrusted big capital and unregulated market forces. The power of trade unions was destroyed. The state strictly controlled enterprises' right to use and dispose of private property.

Control over capital markets was especially important to German authorities, for they wished to ensure that an ample supply of credit would be available to finance industrial growth. Consequently, controls were imposed to check capital flight abroad; to require financial institutions to absorb public debt; to limit the ability of firms to raise capital through private market activity; and to encourage firms to reinvest their profits in a direction deemed consistent with the national interest. Sometimes investment was directed to stimulate industrial expansion for the purpose of promoting rearmament or other important areas where the private investors were not willing to risk an investment. In addition, through destruction of trade unions—by brute force—wages, and thereby consumption, were curbed in the interest of boosting private profits and, subsequently, investment.

Overall, the German Estate of Industry and Trade was designed to enable the party to control economic institutions that were privately owned. Private

[26]Lack of coordination of economic decisions throughout the German economy would stimulate John Maynard Keynes to argue that "[t]he ideas of economists and political philosophers, both when they are right and when they are wrong, are more powerful than is commonly understood. Indeed the world is ruled by little else. . . . Madmen in authority [e.g., Hitler], who hear voices in the air, are distilling their frenzy from some academic scribbler of a few years back." Daniel R. Fusfeld, *The Age of the Economist*, 4th ed. (Glenview, IL: Scott, Foresman and Company, 1982), p. 1.

property, in principle, was justifiable as long as it was used to further the common good, but the ability of private individuals to amass wealth had to be controlled. Therefore, the state controlled the use to which such property could be put. As long as industrialists behaved in a manner that promoted industrial growth (and later the war effort), they were given freedom to manage the microeconomic aspects of their organizations.

Belief in private property was so strong in Germany that some enterprises which had been socialized in the 1920s were converted to private ownership after 1933. This was consistent with the CME philosophy which was against "state socialism." While ownership of financial institutions passed into private hands, strict control was retained by the state. After 1931 there was a trend to privatize publicly owned enterprises. In this regard a 1935 working rule repealed a previously adopted rule (in 1919) by which enterprise engaged in energy production had been socialized.[27]

Social Process for Economic Coordination

Unregulated markets were relatively unimportant means for coordinating the major production and distribution decisions in Germany. Instead, the economy was closed as the state attempted to impose bureaucratic control through state-organized cartels while passing working rules to increase the economic power of such organizations. Among the factors subjected to direct state control were prices, wages, lending activities of financial institutions, investments, production levels, and foreign trade. The ability to control trade was significant to Nazi authorities, for one of their objectives was for Germany to become self-sufficient. Industrial profits were promoted by keeping wages low, prohibiting foreign competition, and encouraging cartels.

Primacy of politics rather than a coherent economic policy (with a blueprint for the economy—however broad) or philosophical basis upon which an effective planning scheme could be based was the primary means for coordinating production and distribution activities. The state sought to subordinate the means of production to pursue its goals. The extent of centralized state control over the economy intensified directly with the expansion of rearmament and war activities. In part, this was due to Hitler's obsession with military matters and his inability to grasp basic economic principles. A lack of macroeconomic coordination was the result, and management of the economy became mismanagement under a scheme of chaotic economic controls. These controls included planning activities (e.g., formation of cartels, fixing prices,

---

[27]As the war deepened, the state passed working rules giving it the power to exert even greater control over the economy. One analyst described the German economy as "a monopolistical economy— *and* a command economy. It is a private capitalistic economy, regimented by the totalitarian state." Dillard, *Economic Development of the North Atlantic Community*, p. 558.

working rules affecting laborers and bankers), along with "regimentation, coercion, outright thievery, and espionage."[28] The degree to which controls were applied intensified as Germany first mobilized, then waged war.

State coordination activities were effective during the recovery period between 1933 and 1936. Introduction of Keynesian-type fiscal policy measures (see Chapter 8) financed through deficit spending enabled Germany to recover from the effects of the Great Depression faster than any other western industrialized nation. Authorities believed that considerable state intervention was necessary to protect the economy from international market forces and to direct income so that high profits were earned by industrialists. These profits then could be taxed by the state or guided into investment projects consistent with the state's goals (e.g., rearmament).

An economic plan which outlined state goals and policy measures for the next four years was established in 1933. Its primary emphasis was on work creation as the state sought to lower unemployment. Three measures were taken. The first was to boost employment and stimulate aggregate demand through ambitious public works programs, which led to the construction of an extensive highway (*Autobahn*) network and improved rail and waterway transportation facilities. These projects were carried out by private firms under government supervision, with the state providing credit. To guarantee the necessary credit, a second measure introduced was state control over the banking system. Assumption of control was followed by an unprecedented expansion of credit, for the public works projects were financed by short-run government loans, with little money raised through private financial markets. The third measure was state control over production, distribution, and consumption, with severe restrictions placed upon the mobility of agricultural and industrial laborers.

A second economic plan, which was in effect from 1937 to 1941, was directed through the Armed Forces' War Economy and Armament Office created in 1934 to serve as the economic planning staff of the Ministry of War. This agency would determine military needs, coordinate the procurement of supplies for the armed forces, and maintain control over raw materials. The overall purpose of the second plan was to enable Germany to produce sufficient quantities of raw materials and foodstuffs for the armed forces.

Some specific features of state control over labor, prices, banks, volume and composition of output, foreign trade, industry structure, and investment are noteworthy. Regarding state regulation of labor activities, collective bargaining and strikes were abolished. In addition, real wages were kept low through state control over wages and prices. After 1936, prices were frozen and could only be increased with the permission of the state-appointed authority, the Price Commissioner. These state controls, along with import and foreign exchange

---

[28]Kurt London, *Backgrounds of Conflict: Ideas and Forms in World Politics* (New York: The Macmillan Company, 1947), p. 91.

controls, had the effect of curtailing consumption and limiting the variety and quantity of consumer goods produced.

The volume and direction of investment as well as the volume of output in selected industries were also state controlled. All large bank loans were subject to state review before approval. The supply of raw materials and other inputs required by industries were guided by the state. The state regulated foreign trade through establishing bilateral trade agreements with Germany's trading partners to secure raw materials and foodstuffs Germany was not capable of producing in sufficient quantities.

There was little direct state subsidization of industry. Instead, the high profits earned by industrialists, which resulted from state-supervised low wages, high fixed prices by state-established cartels for the purpose of eliminating wasteful competition, and state controls which eliminated foreign competition, were guided into productive investments. Dividends were limited to no more than 6 percent of profits in order to encourage firms to reinvest in projects deemed by state authorities to be in the national interest. The state also provided credit and some subsidies and tax rebates as incentives for selected firms to boost output. Nearly all business enterprises receiving assistance were large corporations. To increase its control and to promote industrial efficiency a working rule, the Corporation Law of 1937, was introduced. This rule required smaller firms to give up the corporate form of organization, forcing them to merge with larger firms.

THE EVOLUTION OF NAZI ECONOMIC INSTITUTIONS

The major institutional changes in Germany occurred within the corporative state. Hitler and the Nazi Party remained in control until the end of World War II. There were no major innovations in economic policy, primarily due to the concentration of decision making within the party leader and party elite, who had neither training as economists nor the desire to seek and accept the advice of trained economists. They sought to control the economy through their strong will and ignored basic rules of efficient resource allocation and incentives.

Regarding the corporative state, the principal change occurred during the mid-1930s after Nazi authorities were in power. There was a shift away from the antiestablishment, pro-working class policies to a tightly controlled economy under which workers were subdued, the interests of industrialists and large landowners were promoted, and less voluntary and more compulsive measures were imposed on employers and workers that required them to engage in activities deemed by authorities to be in the state's best interest. In the process the traditional role of entrepreneurs was curtailed.

Under the new corporative state entrepreneurs were supposed to manage (i.e., focus on how goods and services were produced at the microeconomic level) but not to initiate production of new goods and services, or to establish new enterprises without explicit state permission. Allocation of raw materials, pricing decisions, and the competitive structure of each industry were determined by the state. Risk of loss from investing in new capital was assumed by the state. In addition, the state provided protection from foreign competition, supervised formation of cartels (thereby protecting selected German firms from any potentially adverse effects of domestic competition), curtailed wages, and allowed prices to be fixed. The corporative state evolved so that the size of firms increased, and there was closer contact between state authorities (particularly those representing the military) and industrial leaders—especially regarding allocation of resources to produce implements for war. Ultimately, German authorities were responsible for the behavior and performance of the economy. This responsibility followed from Hitler's belief that the economy was "merely a means for attaining certain vaguely outlined yet, in principle, quite unattainable political goals— goals which, though certainly of great incidental benefit to German industry, were not determined by economic considerations."[29] The performance of the German economy reflected this type of leadership.

PERFORMANCE OF THE ECONOMY: RAPID RECOVERY FROM DEPRESSION AND WARTIME DESTRUCTION

Some indicators of economic performance in particular years are included in Table 7-1. There are two factors affecting the years included and the reliability of the data. First, the war wreaked havoc with the ability of national and international organizations to gather accurate data for the German economy. Second, German authorities have been accused of reporting data that indicated a more positive performance of the economy than actually was the case.

The German economy experienced rapid recovery compared to other western nations from the adverse economic conditions created by World War I and the Great Depression after Nazi authorities assumed power. In terms of increasing growth of output and lowering unemployment, the German recovery was impressive and can be attributed to a combination of deficit spending, rapid expansion of credit, and huge public works projects. Ultimately, however, the economy failed not only according to the authorities' standards (i.e., that a new society would be established which would last for a millennium; and that a corporative state would reduce class antagonisms), but in terms of poor performance of certain economic indicators. Reasons for the collapse of the economy include the heavy dependence upon foreign raw materials, Germany's inability to wage a rapid, successful war effort to secure such supplies, and

---

[29]T. W. Mason, "The Primacy of Politics—Politics and Economics in National Socialist Germany," in Woolf, ed., *The Nature of Fascism*, p. 185.

incoherent economic policies. Among the problems created by state policies was the relatively modest multiplier effect from state and private investments due to the suppression of wages and high rates of savings.

Beginning with the change in political structure in 1932 until the nation was heavily involved with war in 1939, the performance of the German economy was mixed. In terms of declining unemployment and growth of gross national product there was rapid recovery from the Great Depression. However, growth rates varied considerably among sectors. When making resource allocation decisions, authorities emphasized growth of heavy industry while demonstrating little concern for the living standards of most people. The positive features of such decisions included growth of national output in excess of 200 percent and even more rapid growth of national savings (over 300 percent) between 1932 and 1938.[30] Net national product, which had fallen almost 20 percent between 1929 and 1932, increased almost 100 percent during the next six years (see Table 7-1).

TABLE 7-1 Economic Growth, Unemployment, and Cost-of-Living Data for Germany in Selected Years, 1929–1945

NET NATIONAL PRODUCT[1]		UNEMPLOYMENT[2]		COST OF LIVING INDEX	
1929	51.7	1930	15.3%	1929	100
1932	41.8	1932	30.1	1932	70
1936	66.2	1934	14.9	1936	76
1938	81.3	1937	4.6	1939	78
1945	—	1938	2.1	1944	85

[1]Million marks, in constant prices.
[2]As a percentage of the work force.

Source: B. R. Mitchell, *European Historical Statistics: 1750–1970* (New York: Columbia University Press, 1975), pp. 170, 738, 785, 787.

Part of this rapid increase was due to the high rates of savings and investment. National savings rates increased from 11.5 percent of national income in 1932 to 18.0 percent in 1938.[31] Gross investment, which had declined from 18 percent of national income in 1928 to 9 percent in 1932, rose to 23 percent in 1937.[32] Meanwhile, unemployment fell and prices, which were subject to state control, remained stable (see Table 7-1). Unemployment stood at 5.6 million people in 1932 and declined to about 2.5 million by May 1934, to less than 1.5 million by December 1936, and to less than 1 million by December 1937.[33]

The imbalance in the growth rate between sectors was due to the

[30]Arthur Schweitzer, *Big Business in the Third Reich* (Bloomington, IN: Indiana University Press, 1977), p. 334.

[31]Jurgen Kuczynski, *Germany: Economic and Labor Conditions Under Fascism* (New York: Greenwood Press, 1968), p. 82.

[32]S. J. Woolf, "Did a Fascist Economic System Exist?" in Woolf, ed., *The Nature of Fascism*, p. 134.

[33]Kuczynski, *Germany: Economic and Labor Conditions*, pp. 96–98.

authorities' emphasis on armament production. The percentage of national income devoted to armament expenditures increased from 2 percent in 1932 to 34 percent by 1938, to 70 percent by 1942.[34] Overall, industrial output doubled between 1932 and 1938, while agricultural output increased less than 10 percent. Consumer goods production lagged behind, increasing only 4 percent between 1928 and 1937.[35] Labor productivity reflected these trends. Production per employed worker grew 11 percent between 1932 and 1937, and for production goods it increased 24 percent, rising 44 percent and 87 percent for workers employed in the iron and steel, and vehicle industries, respectively.[36] However, labor productivity remained stagnant for consumer goods industries, including those producing foodstuffs.

Industrialists fared much better than laborers, for after 1932 income distribution became more unequal.[37] The percentage of national income going to industrialists increased from about 19 percent in 1932 to 28 percent in 1938, while over the same period the percentage going to the rest of the population who were not employed by the state declined from 59.8 percent to 52.2 percent.[38] The percentage of national income which went to industrialists was due to rising profit rates. Profit rates for all industries, which had fallen from about 6 percent in 1928 to -4 percent in 1932, increased to 6 percent by 1938.[39] For light industry the pattern was similar, but not as dramatic as that for heavy industry. Industries experiencing rapid increases in profit rates after 1932 included iron, steel, and metal manufacturers (4 percent in 1928, -6 percent in 1932, and 5 percent in 1938); machinery (4 percent in 1928, -7 percent in 1932, and 8 percent in 1938); and electrical (7 percent in 1928, -14 percent in 1932, and 10 percent in 1938).[40]

Since a high percentage of income went to war implements and profits for industrialists, while wages were held down by the state, the standard of living of most Germans declined after 1932. Net weekly real earnings of employed workers grew only 9 percent from 1932 to 1937, while consumption levels decreased.[41] For example, from 1932 to 1938, per capita consumption of fats (e.g., meat, eggs, fish, cheese, milk, and other dairy products), starches, and fruits and vegetables declined. As a percentage of total national product, private consumption had risen from 73 percent in 1929 to 79 percent in 1932 (but this would be expected during a depression), but fell to 60 percent by 1936, and fell again to 52 percent by 1938.[42]

[34]Ibid., p. 85.

[35]Woolf, *The Nature of Fascism*, p. 134.

[36]Kuczynski, *Economic and Labor Conditions*, p. 117.

[37]Maxine Y. Woolston, *The Structure of the Nazi Economy* (New York: Russell and Russell, 1968), p. 218.

[38]Kuczynski, *Economic and Labor Conditions*, p. 86.

[39]Woolston, *The Structure of the Nazi Economy*, p. 76.

[40]Ibid.

[41]Kuczynski, *Economic and Labor Conditions*, p. 5.

[42]Schweitzer, *Big Business in the Third Reich*, p. 336.

Overall, consumption levels were lower in 1938 than in 1932, as output of consumption goods decreased 10 percent between 1928 and 1935.[43] The standard of living declined much further after 1938 due to the impact of the war. One indication of the extent of decline was the drastic loss of output, for German industrial output in 1945 was only one fourth of the 1941 level.

EVOLUTION OF THE GERMAN ECONOMY: THE RISE AND FALL OF NAZI INSTITUTIONS

Poor economic performance, compounded by the aftermath of World War I and the Great Depression, led to the emergence of attitudes sharply opposed to the principles of an LFME as well as to democracy. There was a growing desire to establish a society which was nationalistic and militaristic, capable of establishing order and discipline through authoritarian methods. Within the German population there was a willingness both to follow a strong, charismatic leader as well as to accept considerable state control over economic activity.

The Nazi philosophy for the type of economy they introduced reflected Germany's historical legacy. The views of intellectuals and authorities favored establishment of strict social and political structures under the leadership of an elite group. From that group emerged a leader whom other party authorities and supporters believed possessed a vision, inspiration, and power—someone capable of establishing discipline and order in a new society. A coherent economic policy with consistent working rules was not deemed essential. Instead, a leadership principle was advocated with only a few authorities making decisions. This, of course, was the case with the absolute party rule of the Nazis. As Fuhrer, Hitler possessed unlimited power, and was declared and widely believed to be infallible.

The principal institutions reflected the views of the authorities as well as the social and political structures more so than in most twentieth-century western economies. Establishment of the corporative state, in particular, was consistent with the desire to concentrate coordination of production and distribution patterns under state authorities. Consequently, the organization of resource allocation decision making, working rules governing ownership and control of resources, and the social process for coordinating production and distribution decisions reflected the top-down flow of authority from the party leaders who emphasized the achievement of political goals through waging war. However, authorities ignored the potentially adverse effects of a closed economy which was not permitted to take advantage of the benefits provided by competition between firms, entrepreneurial talent, incentives to stimulate workers, or potential gains from foreign trade. The closed, centrally controlled CME, by insulating itself from

[43]Ibid.

foreign competition and by setting prices that were not sensitive to demand and supply, created an economy with an "irrational system of costs and prices."[44] Such management (or mismanagement) by Nazi authorities was reflected in the performance of the German economy.

LOOKING AHEAD

Another alternative to the LFME that emerged in the 1930s was the guided market economy. Its historical context and philosophical basis are discussed in Chapter 8.

KEY TERMS AND CONCEPTS

Corporative State   Preceptorial System
Leadership Principle   Primacy of Politics

QUESTIONS FOR DISCUSSION

1. What were the main features of the corporative state?
2. What were the major tenets of the CME philosophy?
3. Why did Germany and other European nations seek an alternative to laissez-faire economic policies?
4. In what respects can the German economy during the 1933–1938 period be considered to illustrate the double movement, that is, a reaction against the adverse effects upon society of unregulated market forces?
5. Why is the primacy of politics inconsistent with a coherent economic policy for an economy?
6. From an economic point of view, evaluate the positive and negative aspects of the CME in Germany.

REFERENCES

Bruck, W. F., *Social and Economic History of Germany from William II to Hitler.* New York: Russell and Russell, Inc., 1962.

Cameron, Rondo, *A Concise Economic History of the World.* New York: Oxford University Press, 1989.

Cassels, Alan, *Fascist Italy.* New York: Thomas Y. Crowell, 1968.

Dillard, Dudley, *Economic Development of the North Atlantic Community.* Englewood Cliffs, NJ: Prentice-Hall, 1967.

Fusfeld, Daniel R., *The Age of the Economist*, 4th ed. Glenview, IL: Scott, Foresman, 1982.

[44]Woolf, "Did a Fascist Economic System Exist?" *The Nature of Fascism*, p. 143.

Hardach, Karl, *The Political Economy of Germany in the Twentieth Century.* Berkeley, CA: The University of California Press, 1980.

Hayes, Paul M., *Fascism.* New York: The Free Press, 1973.

Klein, Burton H., *Germany's Economic Preparations for War.* Cambridge: Harvard University Press, 1968.

Kuczynski, Jurgen, *Germany: Economic and Labor Conditions Under Fascism.* New York: Greenwood Press, 1968.

Laquer, Walter, ed., *Fascism: A Reader's Guide.* Berkeley, CA: University of California Press, 1976.

Larsen, Stien Ugeluik, B. Hagtuet, and J. P. Myklebust, *Who Were the Fascists: Social Roots of European Fascism.* Bergen: Universitet Forlaget, 1980.

Ledeen, Michael Arthur, *Universal Fascism: The Theory and Practice of the Fascist International, 1928–1936.* New York: Howard Fertig, 1972.

Lindbloom, Charles E., *Politics and Markets.* New York: Basic Books, 1977.

London, Kurt, *Backgrounds of Conflict: Ideas and Forms in World Politics.* New York: The Macmillan Company, 1947.

Macridis, Roy C., *Contemporary Political Ideologies.* Boston: Little, Brown, & Co., 1983.

Mitchell, B. R., *European Historical Statistics: 1750–1970.* New York: Columbia University Press, 1975.

Polanyi, Karl, *The Great Transformation.* Boston: Beacon Press, 1957.

Schuddekopf, Otto-Ernst, *Revolutions of Our Time: Fascism.* New York: Praeger Publishers, 1973.

Schweitzer, Arthur, *Big Business in the Third Reich.* Bloomington, IN: Indiana University Press, 1977.

Stolper, Gustav, *The German Economy.* London: George Allen & Unwin, 1940.

Tannenbaum, Edward R., *The Fascist Experience: Italian Culture and Society, 1922–1945.* New York: Basic Books, 1972.

Woolf, S.J., ed., *The Nature of Fascism.* New York: Vintage Books, 1969.

Woolston, Maxine Y., *The Structure of the Nazi Economy.* New York: Russell and Russell, 1968.

Zilbert, Edward R., *Albert Speer and the Nazi Ministry of Arms.* London: Associated University Press, 1981.

8

THE PHILOSOPHICAL BASIS
FOR A GUIDED
MARKET ECONOMY

OBJECTIVES

1. Explain the historical context with which John Maynard Keynes introduced this philosophy.
2. Examine the extent to which Keynes's philosophy was revolutionary.
3. Discuss the components of the Keynesian paradigm, including his interpretation of economic history, model of a 1930s' laissez-faire market economy (LFME), theories explaining his model, and conclusions and policy prescriptions.

INTRODUCTION

The ability of the political regime in Germany, as well as in the Soviet Union (see Chapter 15), to control their economies to the extent that high unemployment was not a problem by the early 1930s stood in sharp contrast to the experience of other western industrialized societies. Some feared that growing unrest among the working class could lead to the emergence of less democratic regimes that would introduce authoritarian working rules for the economy at the expense of the free enterprise way of life, especially individual freedom. These fears stimulated the development of still another alternative, the guided market economy, for which the philosophical basis was provided by John Maynard Keynes.

JOHN MAYNARD KEYNES

Keynes is considered by many to be the twentieth century's leading intellectual in the field of political economy, although much of his life was not spent as an academic economist. He was a public servant, investor in the financial markets, mathematician, historian, and government advisor. During the 1920s and early 1930s he was fearful that fascism and bolshevism (i.e., communism) would appeal to those nations suffering from unemployment and poverty but still clinging to the self-regulating market philosophy. In his view, the political and economic turmoil following World War I upset the stability, economic efficiency, and freedoms which Europe had enjoyed since the early nineteenth century. The Bolshevik revolution in Russia and the effect of heavy reparations imposed on Germany and Italy at the Treaty of Versailles contributed to the poor material conditions, poverty, social decay, radical redistribution of wealth due to rapid inflation, and high unemployment which plagued each of these nations in the postwar period. What faith these nations had in the rules and virtues of "capitalism," especially liberalism, individualism, and equity concerning the distribution of wealth, was destroyed. Keynes observed that Germany and Italy adopted alternative economies under authoritarian political regimes which were prepared "to sacrifice the political liberties of individuals in order to change the existing economic order."[1]

The appeal of authoritarian economies, especially their ability to satisfy citizens desperate for social, political, and economic security, was recognized by Keynes. These economies were able to reestablish full employment more easily than their "capitalist" counterparts. Savings were likelier to equal investment at a full-employment level of output, since investment decisions could be made by decree from the state authority without reliance upon the decisions of many private investors. Keynes lamented, however, that the price of immediate political and economic efficiency of the macroeconomic policies of "fascist" and "bolshevik" economies was the "diminution of individual liberty, enforced in part by governmental sanctions, but mainly by economic sanctions through concerted action . . ."[2] He was convinced that " . . . the world will not much longer tolerate the unemployment which . . . is associated . . . with present-day capitalistic individualism."[3] However, he was equally confident that the features of "capitalism" that he valued so highly, namely freedom, individualism and macroeconomic efficiency, could be preserved by revolutionizing the manner in which "capitalist" nations dealt with economic issues. Keynes developed a theory

---

[1]John Maynard Keynes, "Social, Political and Literary Writings," in Donald Moggridge, ed., *The Collected Writings of John Maynard Keynes*, 28 (London and Basingstoke: The Macmillan Press, 1982), p. 28.

[2]John Maynard Keynes, "Essays in Persuasion," in *The Collected Writings of John Maynard Keynes*, 9 (London and Basingstoke: The Macmillan Press, 1972), p. 304.

[3]John Maynard Keynes, *The General Theory of Employment, Interest and Money* (New York: Harcourt, Brace and World, 1964), p. 381.

designed to convince political economists and state authorities that a self-regulating market economy was inherently unstable, and that an alternative guided market philosophy with its corresponding working rules could preserve the democratic character of the political and economic institutions that had created prosperity in many nations.

The analytical framework employed by Keynes consisted of a model and theories which he used to refute Say's Law, with its basic tenet that a self-regulating market economy would automatically achieve a full employment level of output. To be successful required that he convince a community of economists and political leaders heavily committed to classical and neoclassical doctrines of economic thought that while such an economy eventually would achieve full employment in the long run, it would persistently fail in the short run to sustain full employment within the socioeconomic conditions of the 1930s. Keynes was interested in the short run, arguing that "we are all dead" in the long run.

Keynes's success in overcoming what had been the conventional wisdom for over a century can be attributed to the economic crisis of the 1930s and his revolutionary approach. This approach depicted the changing nature of the socioeconomic factors in contrast to the assumptions inherent in classical economic theory. Keynes did not refute the deductive reasoning of Say. Rather, he demonstrated that twentieth-century changes in economic actors, corresponding motivations, principal institutional arrangements, and economic processes led to the creation of new problems: unemployment, and an arbitrary and inequitable distribution of wealth and income. Keynes's model reflected this new socioeconomic reality, and he manipulated the variables of his model, which behaved according to his theories, to demonstrate the inherent instability of the twentieth-century laissez-faire market economy.

KEYNES'S INTERPRETATION
OF ECONOMIC HISTORY

Classical economic theory was based on the belief that economic progress could be realized through the ability of an unregulated market economy to generate economic growth. It was essential that a significant portion of the profits created in this process be saved and reinvested in capital equipment. Adam Smith had argued that the distribution of wealth and income should be skewed in favor of the entrepreneurs who owned and managed the firms. This socioeconomic class was far likelier to abstain from consuming goods and services than either the landlord or laboring classes. As Keynes observed, the justification for the "capitalist" system rested upon a "double bluff."[4] The "capitalist class" would

---

[4]John Maynard Keynes, "The Economic Consequences of the Peace," in *The Collected Writings of John Maynard Keynes,* 2 (London and Basingstoke: Macmillan and Co., 1971), pp. 11, 12.

receive the largest portion of the incomes generated by the production process but were duty bound to invest in capital equipment while refraining from consumption. Meanwhile the laboring class had to accept a modest return for its efforts so as to provide sufficient profit, and thus investment levels, to stimulate favorable rates of economic growth.

Keynes observed that by the middle of the 1920s neither class was willing to accept its designated station in life any longer. Those receiving profits were unwilling to continue to forgo consumption of the greater variety of personal goods and services available. Laborers were no longer willing to temper their wage demands and curb their appetite for consumer goods. Keynes argued that

> the principle of accumulation based on inequality was a vital part of the prewar order of society and of progress as we then understood it . . . this principle depended on unstable psychological conditions, which it may be impossible to re-create. It was not natural for a population, of whom so few enjoyed the comforts of life, to accumulate so hugely. The war had disclosed the possibility of consumption to all and the vanity of abstinence to many. Thus the bluff is discovered; the labouring classes may be no longer willing to forgo so largely, and the capitalist classes, no longer confident of the future, may seek to enjoy more fully their liberties of consumption so long as they last, and thus precipitate the hour of their confiscation.[5]

Keynes's interpretation of history led him to conclude that the economic progress of the 1815–1914 period had created new economic institutions and socioeconomic classes whose views regarding the working rules of economic society differed from the behavior classical economists had assumed characterized the entrepreneurial, landlord, and labor classes. Whereas nineteenth-century progress was led by the great entrepreneurs who owned and managed their companies, the twentieth century witnessed the emergence of the modern corporation within which ownership and management became separate functions. Industrial relations between management and labor also changed, as solidarity among workers and changes in working rules led to the growing importance of labor unions. Keynes divided the new society into three socioeconomic classes, emphasizing that the behavior of each group differed from classical assumptions and was conditioned by new informal rules (i.e., psychological laws).

RENTIER CLASS. Keynes refers to those who own but do not manage businesses as rentiers (persons who receive a fixed income from investments, such as bonds). This was a class of speculative investors willing to supply (i.e., part with) their savings to entrepreneurs only when these investors projected that they would receive a sufficient reward (e.g., interest from bonds).

[5]Ibid., p. 13.

ENTREPRENEURS.   This class managed but did not own business enterprises. They borrowed from rentiers to invest in production facilities. Their behavior was guided by the psychological expectation of a future yield in capital assets. Keynes believed that "animal spirits" characterized their behavior, arguing that entrepreneurs, as investors, were not simply rational calculating individuals but responded impulsively to anticipated profits.

One of the central factors which would determine whether or not a market economy would grow prosperously or suffer from recession was the rate of capital formation. The savings-investment market, in which the rentiers and entrepreneurs met, was fraught with uncertainty. There was no guarantee that savings and investment would be sufficient to provide a full-employment level of output, especially with the uncertain, unstable behavior of investors. Savings might equal investment, Keynes argued, at a low level of output where the economy could become mired for an extended period. This issue will be articulated further in "Keynes's Model."

LABORERS.   It was assumed by Keynes that people would prefer working to unemployment, even if it meant accepting a job at below the prevailing wage. In general, however, workers would resist a cut in their money wages even as prices were declining. Keynes observed that in England between 1924 and 1934 real wages actually rose despite the deep recession plaguing the economy. Changes in prices and money wages no longer would eliminate an excess supply of labor, so persistent unemployment would ensue.

Keynes also focused on another class whose behavior significantly affected the level of economic activity—consumers. All members of the three classes and their family members comprised this class. Keynes argued that the market for consumer goods was becoming more important during the first third of the twentieth century due to economic progress, which enabled manufacturers to offer a wider variety of goods, higher incomes especially to the rentier class, and greater availability of consumer credit.

According to Keynes, aggregate demand was likely to fall periodically over the long run. He demonstrated that given an inequitable distribution of income, a constant marginal propensity to consume, and a declining average propensity to consume, total consumption would tend to decline relative to rising incomes in a growing economy. Consequently, the gap between actual aggregate demand and the full-employment level of aggregate demand would tend to increase.

His conception of the effect of history on the social and economic order influenced Keynes's conclusion that the savings-investment process no longer would automatically function to create full employment. In order to demonstrate this conviction, he developed his model of income and employment determination. His analysis of the model demonstrated the need for an alternative philosophy with a corresponding set of modified working rules.

KEYNES'S MODEL[6]

A list of the principal elements which constitute Keynes's model, including his theories, is presented in Figure 8-1. A brief discussion of each element will provide a better understanding of the basis for the policy prescriptions for a guided market economy.

Figure 8-1 Keynes's Model and Theories

1. Output (Y) and employment (N) = dependent variables.
2. $Y, N = f$ (aggregate demand).
3. Aggregate demand = consumption (C) + investment (I).
4. $C = f$ (propensity to consume and disposable income).
5. Propensity to consume refers to average propensity to consume (APC) and marginal propensity to consume (MPC).
6. MPC is used to derive the autonomous spending multiplier.
7. $I = f$ [interest rates (r) and the marginal efficiency of capital (MEC)].
8. r is influenced by the liquidity preference and the quantity of money.
9. MEC is an expected rate of net return on a potential investment in a (real) capital asset.

Since Keynes believed that a laissez-faire market economy was not capable of maintaining a full employment level of output, he developed a model which he could use to explain how income and employment levels were determined in such an economy. He took a position held by only a few before him (including Thomas Malthus)—that the values of his dependent variables would be determined by the level of aggregate demand. Aggregate (or effective) demand would determine employment levels which, in turn, would determine the level of output. Whereas Say had assumed potential demand would automatically be transformed into effective demand, Keynes's analysis of his model led him to believe otherwise.

He began by identifying the two components of aggregate demand for a closed economy in which the government played a neutral role, namely, consumption and investment. Keynes's theory of consumption emphasized the importance of what he referred to as the propensity to consume. He used the marginal propensity to consume to derive the spending multiplier with which he demonstrated the downward cumulative spending-responding process induced by a decrease in autonomous spending (that portion of consumption and investment which is independent of the prevailing level of income). Keynes

[6]The model presented is a basic reduced version of a Keynesian model. Its primary purpose is to illustrate the theoretical justification Keynes believed he had for the conclusions he drew and policy prescriptions he offered—particularly his case for deficit spending and expansion of the state's agenda to include guidance of key macroeconomic activities.

argued that income and employment levels tend to increase or decrease in a cumulative manner. The importance of the average propensity to consume was contained in his belief that this parameter tends to decline as incomes rise. In what later became known as Keynes's absolute income hypothesis, he argued that spending gaps (i.e., when aggregate demand is less than aggregate supply) were likely in a growing economy, since wealthier individuals would consume relatively less as their incomes increased. He used his theory of investment to explain why the increase in total savings would not all be returned to the income stream through investment spending.

Investment was determined not only by the rate of interest, but also by what Keynes referred to as the marginal efficiency of capital. He identified the relationship between these factors using an investment-demand curve. This curve depicted an inverse relationship between the interest rate and the amount of investment for an economy "relating the rate of aggregate investment to the corresponding marginal efficiency of capital in general which that rate of investment will establish."[7] Interest rates were determined by the quantity of money (regulated by the monetary authorities) and the preference of the rentier class to hold their assets in the form of cash, referred to as their liquidity preference. As a historian, Keynes saw the rentier class receiving less satisfaction from material rewards achieved "[not through] production, but from speculative placement of liquid funds."[8]

Combining these elements in his model, Keynes focused his theoretical analysis on the interaction of the goods, money, and labor markets. He was especially interested in the interrelationship between the money market and the demand for investment goods. He concluded that a "casino" atmosphere prevailed in which rentiers and entrepreneurs, responding instinctively to uncertainty and different psychological motives, made impulsive decisions that were unlikely to generate (equal) levels of savings and investment sufficient to create a full-employment level of aggregate demand, especially during a period of recession (i.e., low spending levels, pessimistic attitudes toward business).[9] Keynes feared that when the combined level of investment and consumption was inadequate to keep pace with increases in output, the results would be declining profits and lower investment. This would lead to involuntary unemployment (see Figure 8-2) and, in the worst-case scenario, a liquidity trap where the demand to hold cash balances was infinite (see Figure 8-3).

---

[7]Hans Jensen, "Some Aspects of the Social Economics of John Maynard Keynes," *International Journal of Social Economics*, 11, 3/4 (1984), 79.

[8]Keynes, *The General Theory*, p. 136.

[9]Keynes, *The General Theory*, p. 161. He referred to "instability [of expectations] due to the characteristic of human nature that a large proportion of our positive activities depends on spontaneous optimism rather than on a mathematical expectation . . . Most, probably, of our decisions to do something positive, . . . can only be taken as a result of animal spirits—of a spontaneous urge to action rather than inaction, and not as the outcome of a weighted average of quantitative benefits multiplied by quantitative probabilities." Ibid.

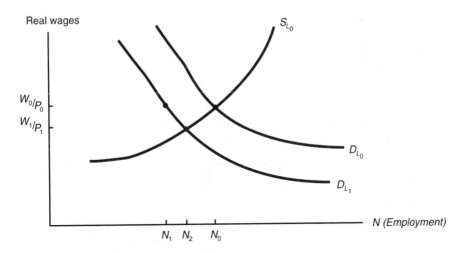

Note: If real wages declined to W_1/P_1, the labor market would clear. N_2 workers would be hired, and what unemployment prevailed would be voluntary in nature.

Figure 8-2 Involuntary Unemployment

Prior to Keynes the conventional wisdom held that anyone willing to work at the prevailing wage could secure employment, and that potential demand would equal effective demand so that only those who chose to be unemployed would be without a job. Keynes, however, claimed that Say's Law was no longer valid. Citing the importance of the propensity to consume and the rate of capital formation (i.e., new investment), Keynes argued that the key factor upon which the levels of employment and unemployment depended was aggregate demand. When there was a level of spending which was below that necessary for full employment to be maintained, involuntary unemployment would result (see Figure 8-2). That is, the deficiency in aggregate demand corresponded to a lower demand for labor (DL_1) so that the actual level of employment (N_1) would be less than the supply of labor willing to work at the prevailing wage.[10] Note that involuntary unemployment would persist if a decline in prices, but not money wages, accompanies the deficiency in aggregate demand.

Rising levels of involuntary unemployment would ensue during a period when pessimism among entrepreneurs inhibited their desire to borrow and invest despite falling interest rates, while the rentier class preferred to hold cash, speculating that the price of bonds would decline (i.e., yields increased). The extreme case is illustrated in Figure 8-3. Here a very low interest rate (r_0), with a corresponding low rate of return on bonds, leads rentiers to hold their assets as cash, speculating that bond prices will decline. Monetary authorities will be

[10]For further discussion see Keynes, *The General Theory*, pp. 30, 173.

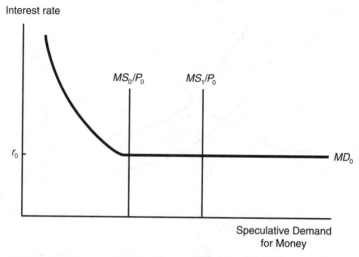

1. Given low interest rates, the short-run return on bonds after
   accounting for the risk factor is low, perhaps even negative.
2. Therefore, everyone sells bonds, speculating that the price of bonds
   will increase in the future.
3. However, open market operations could not increase the price of bonds
   (interest rates rise, bond prices fall, bond yields increase) nor would
   a decrease in the rate of interest be helpful.
4. Therefore, a perfectly elastic demand to hold money exists (Md_0).
5. If this occurs when investment is stagnant and the economy is at a
   less than full-employment level of output equilibrium, then monetary
   authorities would be impotent to cure the economic disease of serious
   recession/depression by increasing the money supply from MS_0 to MS_1.

Figure 8-3   Liquidity Trap

impotent in this case to stimulate investment. Expanding the real money supply
to MS_1/P_0 will leave the interest rate unaffected without a corresponding increase
in investment levels. Keynes argued that even if monetary policy could push
interest rates lower, greater investment might not be forthcoming if
entrepreneurial expectations were such that "the schedule of the marginal
efficiency of capital is falling more rapidly than the rate of interest."[11] The most
dismal of all economic scenarios would ensue, with the economy settling at a low
level of equilibrium where high unemployment and pessimism among savers and
investors were widespread.

[11]Ibid., p. 173.

KEYNES'S CONCLUSIONS AND
POLICY PRESCRIPTIONS

Keynes's analysis led him to draw a number of conclusions from which he offered the policy recommendations that would serve as the basic tenets for a guided market economy. He placed the blame for macroeconomic instability on economic society, especially the forces which determine the investment function. Basically, there was too much uncertainty surrounding the determination of investment, with no assurance that savings and investment would be sufficient to produce a level of aggregate demand consistent with a full employment level of output. Keynes called into question the belief that society needed high levels of savings from the rich, noting that there was a paradox of thrift (i.e., lower levels of savings ensue after households plan to increase savings) if savings were excessive. The animal spirits of entrepreneurs and the possibility that few investment opportunities would be deemed attractive based upon the prevailing marginal efficiency of capital led him to conclude that a self-regulating market economy's ability to generate stability and prosperity was, indeed, precarious.

His major policy recommendation, which has since been the cornerstone for guided market economies, was that the state's agenda had to be modified so as to achieve "institutional complementarity" with the private sector.[12] Each sector was to focus on the economic function it was best suited to provide. Keynes accepted the basic tenets of neoclassical economic theory that decentralization of economic units and the interplay of self-interest were not only necessary to preserve the individual freedom and liberty he valued so highly, but would lead to a more efficient allocation of resources at the levels of industry, firm, and household. In particular, he allowed that material incentives and some income and wealth differentials were necessary to stimulate entrepreneurial activity.

The state's agenda, as promised by Keynes, would differ significantly from its neutral economic role under a laissez-faire philosophy. No authoritarian state was proposed. Rather, the state was to assume the responsibility for achieving a full-employment level of aggregate demand without inflation, while lessening income inequalities. The government's goal was to promote macroeconomic stability by guiding the economy toward achieving a full-employment level of aggregate demand. The state's task was "to determine the aggregate amount of resources devoted to augmenting the instruments [of production] and the basic rate of reward to those who own the means of production."[13] Keynes called upon the state to assume "central controls," three of which were to guide the propensity to consume through progressive income taxation, to control the rate of interest, and to engage in what he referred to as "public works" (actually government spending programs financed by deficit

[12]John E. Elliott, *Comparative Economic Systems*, 2nd ed. (Belmont, CA: Wadsworth, 1985), p. 149.
[13]Hans E. Jensen, "J. M. Keynes as a Marshallian," *Journal of Economic Issues*, 17,1 (March 1983), 72–73.

spending).[14] The state also needed to take control of the investment function. Keynes believed that neither monetary measures to influence the interest rate nor the decisions of rentiers and entrepreneurs would be sufficient to guarantee prosperity.[15] He called for a "somewhat comprehensive socialization of investment," whereby the state would supply investment funds from communal savings during depressed economic periods and effectively would lessen reliance upon the rentier class and the casino environment or organized securities markets.[16] By socialization of investment, Keynes was not advocating authoritarian measures to control the economy. Instead he "urged that the government 'assume an ever greater responsibility for directly organizing investment' by means of indicative planning,[17] 'communal savings through the agency of the state,' and other controls, including managing the monetary system"[18] in lieu of the gold standard.

SUMMARY: THE IMPACT OF KEYNES'S PHILOSOPHY

Keynes's proposals for reforming a laissez-faire market economy were broad, for he had to devote most of his efforts toward changing the informal rules (i.e., the authorities' and economists' way of thinking about macroeconomic theory and policy). He needed to provide a theoretical framework from which one could conclude that a departure from the classical faith in the inherent stability of self-regulating market economies was necessary in the 1930s. Once attitudes were changed, Keynes believed new formal working rules would be adopted through an expansion of the state's agenda and the reform of key institutions.

The economic theory, policy measures, and social philosophy contained in Keynes's work could be used by state authorities to change the working rules of a laissez-faire market economy. Subsequent chapters focus on the Keynesian-type formal working rules (often referred to as "administrative guidance") introduced in economies such as Japan (Chapters 9 and 10) and France (Chapter 11), and on the establishment of democratic social economies through the virtually complete adoption with further extensions of Keynes's proposals in Sweden (Chapter 13) and in many member nations of the European Union (Chapter 14).

---

[14]For a complete presentation of Keynes's conclusions, see Keynes, *The General Theory*, pp. 372–384.

[15]Ibid., p. 376. Keynes advocated ". . . the euthanasia of the rentier, and, consequently, the euthanasia of the cumulative oppressive power of the capitalist to exploit the scarcity-value of capital." Ibid.

[16]Jensen, "J. M. Keynes as Marshallian," pp. 72–73.

[17]Indicative planning is discussed in Chapter 11.

[18]Jensen, "J. M. Keynes as a Marshallian," p. 73. The gold standard was the monetary system nearly all nations were on from the early nineteenth to the early twentieth century. One of its key features was a working rule that fixed a nation's unit of currency in terms of a specified quantity of gold (e.g., $35 for an ounce of gold).

KEY TERMS AND CONCEPTS

Double Bluff	Liquidity Trap
Involuntary Unemployment	Propensity to Consume
Keynes's Model of an LFME	State's Agenda
Keynesian Revolution	

QUESTIONS FOR DISCUSSION

1. What is the difference between voluntary and involuntary unemployment, and how is this difference significant for the philosophical basis of a guided market economy?
2. Why did Keynes fear "fascism" and "bolshevism?"
3. What was the double bluff? How does it relate to Keynes's interpretation of economic history?
4. To what extent did the historical context within which Keynes lived influence his policy prescriptions?
5. Explain the relationship between Keynes's model and Say's Law.
6. Why did Keynes believe that an LFME was inherently unstable (i.e., likely to tend toward unemployment)?
7. How does the philosophical basis for a guided market economy differ from that of an LFME?

REFERENCES

Bleaney, Michael, *The Rise and Fall of Keynesian Economics*. New York: St. Martin's Press, 1985.

Chick, Victoria, *Macroeconomics After Keynes: A Reconsideration of the General Theory*. Cambridge, MA: The MIT Press, 1983.

Dillard, Dudley, *Economic Development of the North Atlantic Community*. Englewood Cliffs, NJ: Prentice-Hall, 1967.

Elliott, John E., *Comparative Economic Systems*. 2nd ed. Belmont, CA: Wadsworth, 1985.

Jensen, Hans E., "Some Aspects of the Social Economics of John Maynard Keynes," *International Journal of Social Economics* 11, 3/4 (1984) 72–91.

————,"J. M. Keynes as a Marshallian," *Journal of Economic Issues*, 17, 1 (March 1983), 67–94.

Keynes, John Maynard, *The General Theory of Employment, Interest, and Money*. New York: Harcourt, Brace & World, 1964.

————, "The Economic Consequences of the Peace," in *The Collected Writings of John Maynard Keynes*, 2. London and Basingstoke: Macmillan and Co., 1971.

————, "Essays in Persuasion," in *The Collected Writings of John Maynard Keynes*, 9. London and Basingstoke: The Macmillan Press, 1972.

————, "Social, Political and Literary Writings," in Donald Moggridge, ed., *The Collected Writings of John Maynard Keynes*, 28. London and Basingstoke: The

Macmillan Press, 1982.

Oser, Jacob, and Stanley L. Brue, *The Evolution of Economic Thought*, 4th ed., San Diego: Harcourt Brace Jovanovich, 1988.

9

THE JAPANESE ECONOMY

1946–Present:
Historical Legacy and Context,
Philosophical Basis,
Social and Political Structures,
Principal Institutions

OBJECTIVES

1. Examine the historical roots of Japan's social and political structures and principal institutions.
2. Explain how Western influence, primarily the Occupation Authority, put Japan on the path toward becoming a world economic power with political and economic institutions not unlike those in most OECD nations.
3. Introduce the important role played by the Japanese state in establishing the working rules and guiding the economy.
4. Explain some unique characteristics of Japanese institutions.
5. Demonstrate how relationships within *keiretsu* and individual firms reflect Japan's social structure.

INTRODUCTION

The post-World War II Japanese economy represents the quintessence of a Keynesian-type guided market economy. Initiatives from the private sector, complemented by state-sponsored activities and working rules, have effectively promoted economic growth and development. Since 1950, Japan's rate of economic growth has been greater than that of any nation belonging to the Organization for Economic Cooperation and Development (OECD). Average life expectancy has increased steadily and has been among the highest in the world since 1981.[1] Before evaluating the behavior of the Japanese economy, especially its

---

[1] As of 1991, the average life expectancy at birth in Japan was 79 years—higher than for any other nation.

performance (see Chapter 10), the nation's historical legacy, philosophical basis, social and political structures, and principal institutions will be presented.

A LEGACY OF A FEUDAL ECONOMY, ISOLATION, AND ACTIVE STATE INTERVENTION IN ECONOMIC MATTERS

Japan's principal institutions and social structure differ considerably from the other economies described in this book. This is partly because of Japan's nearly total isolation from the rest of the world throughout 1600–1867. The racial homogeneity and cultural cohesiveness that developed in the island nation, as well as the contributions of the state and private sector, form a powerful legacy that must be examined in order to understand the economy's institutions and behavior since 1946. This legacy emerged from two periods, circa 1600–1867 and 1868–1946, which will be discussed in turn.

Pre-1868: A Feudal Economy

The Japanese economy during the 1600–1867 period was similar to that of medieval England. Strict social and political structures prevailed, with many poor peasants supporting a ruling warrior class. This authority's ability to preserve such a social structure was aided by the absence of foreign influence and by the philosophy of Confucius. A particularly influential Confucian teaching was the belief that society should be divided into strata of differing status and authority. Through preaching this ideology, the ruling class was able to create a stable social structure and secure widespread acceptance of the political structure.

Within this highly regimental social structure respect for authority (i.e., anyone with greater status) was expected of everyone. Younger family members, for instance, showed deference toward their elders and everyone in the family obeyed the father. In relations outside the family, strict obedience was expected from heads of household toward village and government authorities, and so forth up the social structure. In commercial institutions such as merchant houses, the employment scheme contained the same regimented, hierarchical, and paternalistic traits characteristic of the social and political structures.

By 1868 a number of economic conditions existed that would facilitate the subsequent modernization efforts under the Meiji regime (see p. 169). One condition was rising agricultural productivity, which was attributable to working rules promoting land tenure, reorganization of the village political structure, and more efficient farming practices. Other conditions were an expansion of commercial activity with a concomitant development of financial organizations, and the emergence of skilled artisans capable of producing fine textiles (especially silk), metal wares, and pottery.

1868 —1946

Although one single event did not transform Japan from a feudal to a modern society, a strong impetus came in 1868. The overthrow of the House of Tokugawa and the restoration of Emperor Meiji meant the end of *shogun* authorities and the centralization of economic and political power. Under the new authority Japan ended its isolation, recognizing that such a policy placed the nation at a competitive disadvantage vis-à-vis the rest of the world. The introduction of rules conducive to expanding commercialization enabled the business-oriented social classes to contribute to the modernization of Japan's economy. With a unified effort from the state and leaders of major business enterprises, Japan pursued modernization of its economy and armed forces with a patriotic sense of purpose.

ROLE OF THE STATE.   The state provided a major impetus for the modernization drive throughout the late nineteenth and early twentieth centuries. In 1868 Japan lacked the infrastructure, technology, and managerial expertise required for industrialization, the commercial know-how necessary for trading with Western nations, and entrepreneurs with sufficient working capital necessary to develop industrial and commercial enterprises according to late nineteenth-century Western standards. After 1868, the state assumed the burden of promoting development. Relying on public funds and models of Western institutions, the state provided the financial support for the modernization of Japan's infrastructure and industries, including their managerial and commercial practices.

The state funded the introduction or modernization of postal and telegraph services, education (a national system of comprehensive education was established in 1872), railways, and steamships for the merchant marine fleet. For industries deemed vital to the national purpose, the state provided support such as government ownership and control of certain industries, subsidies for others, funding for citizens to travel abroad to learn Western techniques, and the purchase of Western machinery for Japanese technicians to study and attempt to imitate. These state-sponsored efforts were instrumental in successful technology transfer from the West. In turn, the new technology spurred Japan's economic modernization and stimulated institutional changes.

State ownership and control of industry was limited to a few industries. The state recognized the private sector's lack of industrial linkages and economies of scale in heavy industry. There also were shortages of trained technicians, scientific knowledge, and working capital. Consequently, the state owned and operated the key support industries for those heavy industries which were unlikely to achieve scale economies if left under private control. These industries included railways, iron, and steel. The state also provided financial support to manufacturing and mining concerns involved with electricity generation, cement, chemicals, munitions, and petroleum and coal mining, among other industries. For fiscal revenue purposes, the salt and tobacco industries remained in government hands.

The state directed development of other industries such as silk, banking, shipping, agriculture, and fishing. The success of these transformations, such as the regulation of the silk industry, was dependent upon cooperation between the state and the private sector. Toward this end, the Japanese government complemented and coordinated both ancient and modern methods. Silk as well as tea and cotton textile exports provided a vital source of foreign exchange throughout the late nineteenth and early twentiethth centuries. The state sponsored the introduction of producer associations in a number of industries, including fishing, to promote guidance and supervision of all persons and enterprises engaged in a particular trade. It provided the agricultural sector, especially rice and silk producers, with low-interest loans for production, funds for projects to improve land (e.g., drainage and irrigation systems) and to purchase land, plus assistance in time of distress.

Such distress was felt throughout the entire economy after 1929, especially when silk exports fell dramatically during the Great Depression. Administrative guidance of the economy ensued through government-directed depreciation of the yen, curtailment of interest rates, and deficit spending (with credit supplied by the Bank of Japan). As a result, unemployment levels remained relatively low and the potentially damaging long-term effects of the depression were mitigated. Expenditures for the development of military capabilities throughout the 1930s stimulated the economy's macroeconomic performance in terms of economic growth and low unemployment as well.

ROLE OF MAJOR BUSINESS ENTERPRISES.   Throughout much of the Meiji era, Japan's economy was similar to that of many Third World nations today in terms of its dual structure—the coexistence of a modern, commercial sector and traditional peasant enterprises. In Japan this dualism was especially pronounced because the modern business enterprises were organized within large, conglomerate-type groups known as *zaibatsu*. There were four *zaibatsu*: Mitsui, Mitsubishi, Sumitomo, and Yasuda. Each was a family owned and rigidly controlled (through a holding company linkage) house of business. A *zaibatsu* was comprised of a variety of industrial concerns involved with activities such as manufacturing, construction, mining, domestic and international trade, finance, and insurance. The *zaibatsu* also controlled subsidiary enterprises, further concentrating their great economic power. Despite the extent of their business interests and reliance upon modern technology and western management practices, *zaibatsu* retained traditional elements of Japanese culture in their internal relationships with employees. Building upon the institutional foundations of the nation's feudal era, *zaibatsu* were organized on the basis of "familial principles of hierarchy, loyalty and dependency [as their industrial relations within the firm reflected the] hierarchical familism of traditional Japan."[2]

The positive impact of the major *zaibatsu* on Japanese economic growth and development over the 1868–1946 period was pervasive. In a relatively

[2]Kanji Haitani, *The Japanese Economic System* (Lexington, MA: D.C. Heath & Co., 1976), p. 118).

traditional society *zaibatsu* contributed vital entrepreneurial talent. They were able to accumulate capital and realize economies of scale through efficient production methods in what was a developing nation. Their diversification led to investment in complementary industries, thereby promoting linkages between and within industries. Although examples of cartel agreements among *zaibatsu* existed, competition between their respective enterprises for greater market share was not uncommon. Overall, the great business houses were the backbone of their nation's modernization drive, loyally executing the state's economic policy through what has been the hallmark of the Japanese economy: state-private sector cooperation.

JAPAN'S INDUSTRIAL REVOLUTION.   At the beginning of Japan's modern period (i.e., 1868), the nation's economy was predominantly feudal. The social and economic conditions present in most Western nations on the eve of their respective industrialization periods were absent in Japan. The nation lacked many natural resources, engaged in very little overseas trade, possessed few of the scientific skills necessary for industrial modernization, and held the attitudes of a traditional, feudal society. Yet by 1940 Japan had become the first non-Western nation to experience an industrial revolution. The per capita rate of real economic growth for roughly the same period (circa 1880–1940) exceeded that of every other industrial nation except Sweden.[3] Japan's economy was comparable to that of the advanced, industrialized Western nations. It possessed the resources necessary to manufacture capital and consumer goods efficiently. Its financial institutions, methods of communications, shipping industry, technicians, entrepreneurs, laborers, and government officials were on a par with contemporary skilled standards. A unique combination of social, political, and economic factors blended together between 1868 and 1940 to facilitate Japan's industrial revolution.

Isolation prior to 1868 fostered attitudes within the Japanese that the uniqueness and homogeneity of their language and race reflected superior values and qualities. Doctrines promoting this consciousness were periodically communicated to the population. An example of the universal preaching of axioms for behavior was the Imperial Rescript on Education. Passed in 1890, it

> was read on the Emperor's birthday [every year until 1946] before the assembly of members of all schools and colleges . . . [It was] an enunciation of ethical principles which [were] to govern the thoughts and actions . . . of the whole nation. The Rescript reasserted the doctrines of "ancestor worship, filial piety, loyalty to superiors and duty to the State," doctrines that were valid for all times and in all places.[4]

[3]Ryoshin Minami, *The Economic Development of Japan: A Quantitative Study* (London: Macmillan Press, 1986), pp. 36–43. Also refer to G. C. Allen, *The Japanese Economy* (London: Weidenfeld and Nicolson, 1981), p. 12. Allen points out that Japan's real national income grew at a rate of 4.5 percent over the 1900–1940 period, a rate "unmatched" by any other nation.

[4]Allen, *The Japanese Economy*, p. 15.

Such attitudes, which are still held by the Japanese today, were conducive to the modernization of their economy.

There has been a noticeable absence in Japan of hostility toward large conglomerate business institutions. The exercising of authority by groups rather than individuals, the view that their duty to promote the national purpose superseded their individual rights, and the discipline instilled during the long feudal period, when people were taught to accept a vertical social structure, combined to instill within the Japanese a selfless, team-oriented, almost ascetic view toward their individual roles in their nation's economy. Such attitudes were as conducive to an industrial revolution and its concurrent institutional change as those attitudes which resulted from the Protestant Reformation in Great Britain and Holland during the eighteenth and early nineteenth centuries. Throughout the modernization drive, the Japanese preserved their unique cultural heritage. They were capable of assimilating Western technology, labor-management relations, and management techniques into their manufacturing and commercial enterprises without substituting Western values for their own. Although foreign producers were able to offer a wide variety of lower-priced goods to the Japanese, these producers did not gain a large share of the Japanese market. This can be attributed to the Japanese people's high propensity to maintain their traditional consumption pattern in the face of the demonstration effect of lower-priced foreign products.

Japan's low rate of population growth, universal system of education, abundant and skilled labor force, and ability to unify, harness, and channel the collective energy of the nation toward achieving the nationally defined purpose (i.e., modernization to achieve parity with foreign powers) all contributed to rapid growth. The *zaibatsu* role was significant, as was a certain degree of good fortune. Japan's industrial revolution coincided with a period of rising economic growth and development abroad. The expanding world market welcomed Japanese exports, especially raw silk, for which the income elasticity of demand was relatively high. Rising levels of farm and fishery production enabled the nation to feed itself without having to rely upon imports, thereby avoiding a drain on foreign reserves. Farmers' skills extended beyond their agricultural pursuits, and their ability as artisans enabled those who migrated to urban areas to become productive workers in the growing industrial enterprises. Higher productivity also meant rising farm incomes, providing a market for the industrial sector's output. It should be noted that all institutions in Japan were not transformed during the modernization period. As a result a dual economy existed in some areas of the nation and still persists today with the superstructure of modern enterprises coexisting alongside the traditional institutions such as peasant agricultural units and small-scale enterprises producing pottery, fans, paper lanterns, textiles, and silk.

State of the Economy—1946

Japan naturally encountered numerous economic problems immediately after World War II. The extent of destruction of homes, factories, and merchant marine vessels was pronounced. The nation faced not only the loss of all its foreign assets, but also claims for war reparations by the Allied nations, and domestic shortages of food, clothing, health care, raw materials for manufacturing, energy supplies (especially coal), and foreign exchange. Domestic income, which had accumulated from private savings during the war and from public bonds, combined with spending for scarce goods to create inflationary pressure. Following the cessation of military forces, closing down of armament production facilities, and the return of 6 million repatriates who had been living abroad in Japanese controlled territories, unemployment and underemployment levels rose dramatically. Production levels were less than those of 1930, while estimated national wealth in 1945 was approximately equal to the 1935 level. Ten years of economic growth had been lost.

Despite these unfavorable conditions, there were certain productive resources, plus traditional industrial practices and government programs which not only survived, but developed further during the war and eventually spearheaded the nation's economic recovery. Among these were manufacturing capacity in certain industries (e.g., pig iron, rolled steel, aluminum, and machine tools) and trained engineers and skilled laborers previously employed in armaments factories. Industrial organization and industrial relations (each of which is discussed later) that would contribute significantly to reconstruction involved the practice of subcontracting out work to smaller firms, the enhancement of the seniority wage system and lifetime employment practices, and labor-management relations where industrywide trade unions were gradually replaced by company unions. The lifetime employment policies were not enshrined in most labor contracts but were the product of informal rules with strong expectations on the part of both labor and management about the outcomes. Workers expect to be retained by their firm, while management expects workers to remain loyal and refrain from seeking more favorable wage and working conditions from other firms. Social programs, including national health insurance and old-age survivors' benefits, and a state-sponsored program to promote farmers' interests, which included price supports (for rice) and land reform, were retained. In summary, the postwar economy contains many industries and institutions which had been introduced or modified during the war.

Perhaps the most essential of the favorable qualities which was not only preserved, but even strengthened by the war experience was "[t]he unique character of her [Japan's] culture [which] conferred on her a social cohesion that defeat did not impair. In fact, the discomfiture of those who had been responsible for her ruin removed a source of internal dissension and left her more completely unified in purpose than before."[5] The concerted, organized, adaptable response to the challenge of rebuilding the economy was characteristically Japanese. The same sense of nationalism during a time of perceived crisis that unified the nation in 1868 would enable Japan to focus its national energy effectively toward rapid economic growth following defeat and humiliation in World War II.

---

[5]Allen, *The Japanese Economy,* p. 26.

A PRAGMATIC PHILOSOPHY FOR
RECONSTRUCTING THE ECONOMY

Immediately after World War II Japan, for the first time in centuries, was under the control of foreign leadership, namely, the Supreme Commander for the Allied Powers (Occupation Authority). From 1946 until the return of independence in l952, the Occupation Authority imposed fundamental institutional reforms that Japan was powerless to resist. The philosophical basis for the new working rules was the goal of bringing Japan into conformity with Western methods of dealing with political and economic issues. Immediate emphasis was placed upon demilitarization and democratization. To prevent Japan from waging war, strict limits were placed on the nature and size of its military capabilities. The demobilization and disbandment of the armed forces eliminated any threat of Japanese foreign aggression. Such reforms did serve Japan's interests, however, for the nation was able to redirect all productive resources toward economic recovery.

Before the war-torn economy could be stabilized, there were three major reforms designed to democratize the economic order: breaking down the four family-owned *zaibatsu* whose economic power had inhibited competition in many production and financial areas; sanctioning organized labor activities; and introducing land reform, replacing absentee landlords with 6 million owner-cultivators whose average holding was about two acres. This final reform has been evaluated by outsiders and Japanese alike as being significant due to its magnitude, its decentralization of ownership and control, and its role in promoting economic growth.

The Occupation Authority was also instrumental in stabilizing the economy, which was suffering from high inflation. A central Occupation Authority figure in planning the economic recovery was an American banker named Joseph Dodge. His views toward economic policy were similar to those of the classical economists (i.e., balanced budget, stringent monetary control, and stimulation of the economy through supply-side measures). His program of deflationary fiscal and monetary policies brought inflation under control and served to create a favorable climate for expansion of manufacturing.

Since the end of foreign occupation, the Japanese government's philosophy toward managing the economy has been a curious blend of tradition, regulation, protection, growth promotion, and free market policies. The policymakers, many of them government bureaucrats and entrepreneurs with technical training, have demonstrated pragmatism, patriotism, and discipline. There has been a willingness to employ state-private enterprise cooperation while pursuing rapid economic growth and the benefits from economies of scale. Social welfare spending and taxes have been curtailed in pursuit of a balanced budget and high levels of private investment. In addition, Japan's policymakers have been able and willing to adapt policies to changes in the world economic climate.

Japan embarked on its path to economic recovery by concentrating the nation's attention on a single goal: rapid industrialization, especially of heavy industries such as chemicals and steel. Due to Japan's cultural homogeneity, patriotic and industrious entrepreneurial and labor classes, and a national consensus that the good of the country took priority over individual gain, it was socially, politically, and economically feasible that "all other ends were subordinated to the rapid development of her manufacturing industry. . . . Japan embarked on [a] whole-hearted pursuit of a single, overriding purpose, a purpose that commanded the assent of the mass of the people."[6] Available resources would be measured and allocated carefully so that waste would be minimized.

Whereas the Protestant ethic was significant in shaping the spirit of entrepreneurs in a laissez-faire market economy, the teachings of Confucius provided the basis for the informal rules which constitute the Japanese ethic regarding social, political, and economic behavior. This ethic, some argue, has contributed favorably toward the development of Japan's guided market economy.[7] In particular, this ethic promotes loyalty to the nation and respect for those with higher status, especially elders; precedence of the interests of the collective (e.g., family, company, nation) over those of the individual; high esteem within society for bureaucrats, and long hours of work for all able-bodied individuals as a way of life. What enhances this ethic in Japan is the homogeneity of attitudes. Among the similar views Japanese share are "the preference for harmony over conflict"; and a "belief in the beneficent paternalism of governments, bureaucrats, and employers."[8]

The pragmatic policies adopted for foreign trade are a combination of the views held by Adam Smith, David Ricardo, and Frederic List. That is, there has been a recognition of the benefits derived from free trade, but protectionist measures have been imposed and justified in the name of promoting infant industries. Macroeconomic stabilization measures have been neo-Keynesian, with the state providing guidance and some rationalization of investment while vigorously pursuing the goal of full employment. Japan's industrial policy, including domestic trade regulations and support of expanding industries, is a unique blend of stimulative measures. In terms of agricultural supports, Japan's policy is similar to the Common Agricultural Policy of the European Community (see Chapter 14). It should be added that the views of most Japanese economists, as presented in recent economic literature, seem favorably inclined toward competitive market solutions. These same economists, however, are not bashful about rationalizing interventionist or protectionist policies when the purpose is to promote the national interest (as defined by Japanese authorities). This view reflects the economic development of postwar Japan: reliance upon market forces, but introduction of state-sponsored measures when necessary to guide the economy toward achieving the goal of rapid economic growth.

[6]Ibid., p. 22.
[7]Michio Morishima, "Confucianism as a Basis For Capitalism," in Daniel I. Okomoto and Thomas P. Rohlen, *Inside the Japanese System* (Stanford, CA: Stanford University Press, 1988), pp. 36–38.
[8]"A Survey of Japan," *The Economist*, December 5, 1987, p. 5.

SOCIAL UNIQUENESS AND
CONCENTRATED POLITICAL POWER

To develop a realistic view of the Japanese economy, it is essential to understand its social and political structures. Much emphasis has been placed on Japanese social uniqueness, and considerable credit has been given to the contribution of the social and political structures to the economy's performance. Particular features of these structures have complemented economic factors so that relationships within and between the private and public sectors have been conducive to economic growth.

Social Structure

Six general features of Japan's social structure have contributed to the evolution and characteristics of the principal institutions and to the behavior of the economy. First, Japan is a vertical society whose members feel comfortable behaving according to rank order (i.e., status), which is clearly established for relationships such as those within and between families, enterprises, business conglomerates (*keiretsu*—see "Principal Institutions," p. 180), universities, and government institutions. Prestige is accorded to and a dominant position held by those in upper levels of the social structure. Deference and accommodation are demonstrated toward those with higher status, while more aggression and even contempt may be characteristic of relations with persons lower in the social structure or persons from lower (in terms of status) institutions. Some manifestations of this vertical social feature include the seniority-based reward system and the low status of women in private firms. Until recently women were sometimes "forced to wear drab uniforms . . . [be] relegated to subordinate rules and . . . denied certain rights and privileges deemed natural for men."[9] However, emancipation is proceeding as many Japanese women are receiving higher education and aggressively pursuing careers long dominated by males.

Japanese evaluate companies according to when they enter a new market. The first enterprise to do so is considered "original," which confers a status upon the firm that future competitors will have difficulty matching. On a broader level, hierarchical social classification characterizes the nation's industrial organization. Companies, as well as industries, are ranked according to "the business they are in, their size and market share, their affiliations with bigger companies and banks. [The ranking, known as the 'Society of Industry'], is obvious to those involved in industry."[10]

The second feature of the social structure is the importance of collectivity versus individuality. Variously known as groupism, paternalism, or familism,

---

[9]"An Outsider Takes an Inside Look at Japan's Corporate Culture," *The Japanese Economic Journal,* May 3, 1986, p. 40.
[10]Rodney Clark, *The Japanese Company* (New Haven, CT: Yale University Press, 1979), p. 95.

collectivity reinforces vertical ties and social interdependency within a hierarchy. Both children and adults are expected to conform and harmonize with the group rather than assert a separate identity. Japanese classify those with whom they interact as an "insider" (*uchi*), someone within their group with whom they feel comfortable and can trust, or an "outsider" (*soto*). In economic, political, and social relations Japanese have a strong preference for dealing with insiders.

Managers and subordinates alike place the interests of the enterprise above their individual desires. Superiors may take an interest in subordinates to the extent that a subtle personal relationship develops similar to that between a parent and child or between an older and younger sibling. The company (especially a large firm) is paternalistic toward its employees to the extent that it promotes a harmonious family atmosphere in the workplace and provides generous fringe benefits and job security to its regular work force. In return, employees are expected to devote themselves loyally to their enterprise, perhaps even to place the welfare of the company above that of themselves or their families.

The third feature of the social structure is that social relations are long term, broad in scope, and collective. Relations occur within a tight organizational hierarchy, so that the entire social system is built around the individual's place and status within the vertical order. Within many institutions this social ordering is reflected in the lifetime employment social norm and the seniority reward system. Both practices were introduced after World War I in response to shortages of skilled labor and high labor turnover. During the rapid economic growth period (1955–1980s) growing enterprises needed larger labor forces, particularly managerial staff. Therefore, promotion opportunities were readily available and enabled top management to promote more easily on the basis of seniority. Both the lifetime employment social norm and seniority reward system have been (until 1993) efficient means for integrating social mores within the business community.[11] Japanese workers, as members of a company, believe they are part of a type of family, or *ie*. If they believe their corporate family will guarantee social security through lifetime employment, they will demonstrate greater loyalty, more teamwork, and a lesser willingness to switch companies. This behavior is cost-efficient to their employers. A seniority reward system is an easy, efficient way for Japanese companies to establish rank order (i.e., status) among employees, who themselves prefer such a system.

Collective integration within organizations is the fourth feature of the Japanese social structure. The outstanding example of this feature is the consensus nature of decision making, *ringi sei*. The Japanese believe that those ultimately responsible for making decisions are obligated to include the views of their subordinates. In doing so they reconcile competing interests and promote harmony (*wa*) within the organization. An elaborate process of discussion occurs before a consensus is reached. Information will flow down and up within the firm, as consensus is built at every level.

---

[11]The unraveling of these schemes is discussed in "Institutional Change," Chapter 10.

Deep-seated interest in direct and subtle aspects of interpersonal communication and relationships is the fifth feature of the social structure. The network of power, influence, and dependency among and within groups is intricate. Symbiotic relationships exist on many levels, with close ties, or cliques, forming within and between families, schools, and private and public enterprises. The degree of interdependency and group orientation among the Japanese extends to all groups within the social structure, including the *zaikai* (certain prominent business leaders, Parliament, and ministries within the bureaucracy.

Finally, the social structure of Japan is shaped by the nation's homogeneity of language, ethnic origin, and basic values, among other traits. This homogeneity, coupled with the perception among Japanese of being part of a national "family," has created a strong sense of national identity and continuity. In a country with a very high population density, conformity to social mores and working rules is considered a virtue. Japanese are pervasively ethnocentric, with a patriotic sense of common purpose. Many of their "habits of domestic life . . . are still in the main peculiar to themselves."[12]

Relevance of Social Classes

The Japanese work force can be classified by sociologists according to standard definitions of social class, and intertemporal analysis has been performed regarding social mobility among these classes. However, Japanese analysts seem to agree that most Japanese are not willing to think in terms of identifying and distinguishing social classes (e.g., lower, middle, or upper class). According to one Japanese analyst, "stratification is not characteristic of Japanese society: it cannot be sliced horizontally into strata."[13] There is, however, a strong sense of identity with one's company. Status among workers differs within the firm, but all members are integrally linked by a sense of belonging to the *ie* and by reciprocal obligations.

Political Structure

Two authorities have been primarily responsible for establishing rules for economic behavior since World War II: The Occupation Authority and the Parliament (diet)-bureaucracy-business establishment. The Occupation Authority sought to demilitarize and democratize Japan. They introduced new working rules, which imposed institutional change throughout the economy and the social and political structures. The rules provided for the reorganization of *zaibatsu*, and for land reform, labor democratization, and measures for a democratic political system.

Politically, the emperor's position was reduced to that of a ceremonial figurehead. A parliamentary democracy similar to the British system was

---

[12]G. C. Allen, *A Short Economic History of Modern Japan* (London: George Allen & Unwin Ltd., 1960), p. 88.

[13]Haitani, *The Japanese Economic System*, p. 22. While about 90 percent of the Japanese people believe their standard of living is middle class, there are recent signs that growing disparities in wealth are contributing to more Japanese identifying with a lower middle class who believe they possess much fewer material goods and enjoy less leisure time than the nouveau riche Japanese.

introduced. The Occupation Authority's aim was "... to establish a political system in which the political views and interests of the broad mass of the population should be represented through a government whose lines of responsibility were clear."[14] Other specific reforms designed to achieve this goal included lowering the voting age, granting suffrage to women, giving political freedoms to opposition parties including leftists, purging old guard politicians, expanding civil liberties, and increasing the autonomy and authority of municipal governments.

In keeping with Japanese tradition, the foreign-imposed economic rules and political structure were adapted to the social structure. Using the democratic foundations as a base, Japan "erected a superstructure peculiar to herself and fabricated to meet her special needs in her rise to industrial eminence."[15] The political structure that has emerged is conservative and pluralistic, with an effective system of checks and balances. Power within the Japanese political structure is not concentrated within a unified center of command. Rather, there is an intricate web of economic and social as well as political relationships among the ranking members of the Parliament, bureaucracy, and business community who share power within the political structure.

Until recently the Parliament was characterized by single-party dominance. That is, it was dominated by the pro-business views of the Liberal Democratic Party (LDP) from 1955 until the middle of 1993 when apparent corruption within the LDP leadership led to election results that saw the formation of unsteady coalitions with growing power being assumed by the Socialist Party. Spring of 1994 witnessed political turmoil as the shaky government coalition (the Japan Renewal Party) collapsed when the Socialist Party left in protest over a decision by the moderate and conservative coalition members to exclude Socialists from a voting bloc they formed. However, in mid-1994 Tomiichi Murayama became Japan's first socialist prime minister since 1948 to be elected. However, the strong presence of Liberal Democratic Party members was sure to keep the socialist's power in check. Observers believed that with the Socialist Party sharing power political reforms and foreign policy shifts may ensue, but economic reforms would be modest.

Parliament's power comes from its role in approving budgets for the annual operating expenses of the state, special projects, public corporations, and local governments. Since about half of the budget revenue of local governments is allocated in the form of grants and subsidies by the Parliament, the national government has considerable power over municipalities. The other source of power over the economy comes from Parliament's role as the body which passes (although it does not usually propose) the working rules.

Laws are often proposed by senior civil servants within various ministries of the bureaucracy. The ministries directly involved with the economy, especially

[14]J. A. A. Stockwin, *Japan: Divided Politics in a Growth Economy,* 2nd ed. (London: Weidenfeld and Nicolson, 1982), p. 47.

[15]Allen, *The Japanese Economy,* p. 137.

the Ministry of Finance and the Ministry for International Trade and Industry (MITI), have behaved according to a philosophy which includes "a deep sense of conviction of . . . [their] mission to establish world leadership [for Japanese industry] that is hardly found elsewhere."[16] The political power of MITI is extensive vis-à-vis other ministries. MITI's industrial policy of promoting cartels where they would encourage economies of scale have brought it into conflict with the Fair Trade Commission over abuses of the Anti-Monopoly Law. These engagements have been settled, more often than not, in MITI's favor.

PRINCIPAL INSTITUTIONS—
MANY ORIGINATING FROM
JAPAN'S HISTORICAL LEGACY

The principal institutions that affect a majority of the production and distribution decisions within Japan include the Ministry of Finance, MITI, the *keiretsu*, city banks, and small retailers. However, due to Japan's cultural uniqueness, rise to world prominence, and intricate web of relationships, other institutions which affect economic activity are also described in this section.

Two categories of institutions are discussed next: state institutions— Parliament, advisory councils, the cabinet, bureaucracy, public enterprises, and state-owned financial institutions; and private institutions—*keiretsu*, large firms (employing 500 or more workers), medium firms (employing 100–499) and small firms (employing less than 100) that are either independent or associated (as subsidiaries or subcontractors) with a keiretsu, private financial institutions, retail and trade companies, enterprise unions, cooperatives, and the *zaikai*. The organization of Japan's principal institutions is illustrated in Figure 9-1.[17]

State Institutions

State institutions in Japan do not stand alone. The complex interrelationships between and among state and private institutions are intrinsic to their definition. Nevertheless, some of the major state institutions will be described separately to form a basis for understanding their interrelationships with one another and with the private sector.

---

[16]H. Simonis and U. Ernst, eds., *Japan: Economic and Social Studies in Development* (Hamburg: Institute of Asian Affairs, 1974), p. 37. These ministries are discussed further in the following "Principles Institutions" section.

[17]Although these institutions will be discussed individually, it should be kept in mind that the same type of symbiotic relationships that exist among politicians, bureaucrats, and business leaders hold true among members of institutions listed. "In the Japanese establishment, no one group is supreme. . . . [Among the principal institutions] there is an intricate network of power, influence and dependency . . . [which is a] symbiotic relationship. It is further complicated by the elaborate network of interpersonal relations based on school ties, marriage bonds, and ministerial affiliations. . . . These relations contribute to a club-like atmosphere . . . of the Japanese establishment." Haitani, *The Japanese Economic System*, pp. 39–41.

Figure 9-1   Japan's Principal Institutions

State

Prime Minister, Cabinet

Diet (Parliament)   Advisory Councils

Government Bureaucracy
  Ministry of Finance
  Fair Trade Commission
  Ministry of International Trade and Industry
  Economic Planning Agency

                                                State-Owned
                        Public Enterprises   Financial Institutions:
                                                  Bank of Japan
                                                  Japanese Development Bank
                                                  Postal Savings Bank

Private:

Keiretsu
  Large Firms   Subsidiaries   Independent Firms
  Medium Firms   and   Large
  Small Firms   Subcontractors   Medium
                                                      Small

Financial Institutions: Distribution Firms:
  City Banks   General Trading Companies
  Foreign Exchange Bank   **Small Retailers**
  Industrial Bank of Japan

Enterprise Unions   Cooperatives
                        Zaikai (Business World)

Source: Kanji Haitani, *The Japanese Economic System* (Lexington, MA: D. C. Heath & Co.), 1976, p. 40.

PARLIAMENT (DIET).   The legislative branch is comprised of a two-body legislature responsible for policy decisions. Recent charges of corruption against the Liberal Democratic Party (which has represented the right-to-center conservative, private enterprise and economic growth interests) have led to changes in informal rules favoring reform in campaign financing and parliamentary procedures (see "Institutional Change," Chapter 10).

ADVISORY COUNCILS.   These institutions are administratively attached to government ministries and agencies. They serve ministers at the cabinet and bureaucracy level by preparing reports in response to specific questions, rendering opinions in licensing or rate-price change proposals, evaluating appeals of those claiming damages for environmental (e.g., pollution) or trade reasons, supervising qualifying examinations, and granting licenses. Most of their activities are purely advisory, for the major policy decisions are made jointly by politicians, business leaders, and bureaucrats.

CABINET.   The cabinet is the executive branch of the Japanese government. It consists of the prime minister and cabinet ministers, whose number is determined by the diet. Included among the cabinet ministers are heads of the Ministries of Finance, Agriculture and Forestry, International Trade and Industry, Transportation, and Labor. Cabinet responsibilities toward the economy include preparation of the fiscal budget and initiating bills which will be enacted by the Parliament.

BUREAUCRACY.   The bureaucracy consists of institutions involved with Japan's political, economic, judicial, social, and environmental affairs. Each institution's duties include administering rules passed by the diet, drafting new rules for the diet to debate and vote upon, and advising diet members in policy matters. Diet members value such consultation partly because the Japanese bureaucracy is known for the quality of its personnel and for being apolitical. Due to the enormous prestige derived from serving in the bureaucracy, Japan's most gifted university graduates aspire to high positions in the various ministries. Those who are selected adapt to the "internal dynamics within the economic ministries and agencies [which] stress[es] strict adherence to the basic tenants [sic] of Japan's forward progress in economic and technological development."[18]

The Ministry of Finance is one of the most prestigious and powerful bureaucratic agencies, for it holds responsibility for Japan's fiscal and monetary policies. Among its specific duties are supervising tax collection, all aspects of the national budget and the annual fiscal and loan plan, formulating and executing social insurance and pension programs, controlling and managing exchange-rate policies, controlling customs and tariffs, and supervising the carrying out of monetary policy by the Bank of Japan. The enormous power of the Ministry of Finance over the direction of the Japanese economy is a direct result of its very influential involvement in decisions affecting all the major macroeconomic variables.

The Fair Trade Commission was established by the Occupation Authority in 1947 as part of the Anti-Monopoly Act. The commission was designed to prevent unfair business practices in an economy which previously had no formal control over private-sector monopoly. Today it is quasi-autonomous in judicial and legislative matters, with responsibility for investigating unfair trade behavior, initiating judicial proceedings when necessary, and rendering a verdict in each case. If criminal charges are warranted, the Fair Trade Commission files an

---

[18]Charles J. McMillan, *The Japanese Industrial System* (New York: Walter de Gruyter, 1984), p. 5.

indictment with a judicial body. The commission is also responsible for evaluating and either granting or denying proposals for mergers between private firms.

The powerful Ministry of International Trade and Industry (MITI) has the responsibility of giving the Japanese business community order and direction (e.g., promote the growth of heavy industry). MITI regulates the production and distribution activities of firms engaged in such industries as energy production, transportation, mining, cotton textiles, electronics, and machines. There are six specific functions of this ministry: control and promote foreign trade; assure an adequate supply of goods and services for various sectors throughout the economy; promote development while guiding and regulating industries in manufacturing, mining, and distribution; develop and supervise a resource and energy policy to guarantee a stable supply of energy resources and industrial raw materials; administer the government's policy toward small business; and administer matters pertaining to patents and trademarks.[19]

The Economic Planning Agency provides the official (i.e., state) forecast for the nation by drafting plans for the economy. These plans are not documents that oblige private firms to prescribe to certain rules. Rather the plans reflect the state's estimate of the path the economy is likely to follow, identify anticipated problems, and outline future economic policies the state intends to pursue. The plan is intended to serve as a guide for private-sector decision makers by lessening uncertainty about the government's policies and the state of the economy in the future.[20]

STATE-OWNED FINANCIAL INSTITUTIONS.   Japan's financial institutions and the interrelationships among them are similar to those of the manufacturing sector. A vertical hierarchy exists throughout the public (and private) financial sector according to size of institution. The interbank borrowing pattern shows funds flowing from smaller to larger banks, while the allocation of credit from the central bank (Bank of Japan) is exclusively to large commercial banks. Overall, the financial system has distinct Japanese features, despite the fundamental reforms imposed by the Occupation Authority between 1946 and 1952, adapting activities and rules practiced before 1946 to those characteristic of Western models.

The Bank of Japan was established in 1882 for the specific purpose of promoting modernization through channeling funds to industries deemed most important by the state. Its basic functions are similar to those of any central bank: perform financial activities of the government, regulate monetary policy, supervise bond issues, and manage the value of the yen on the international financial market. The bank's policies are shaped by the prestigious Ministry of Finance, which supervises its operations closely.

Two other state-owned and controlled financial institutions with features

---

[19]Haitani, *The Japanese Economic System*, pp. 52, 53.

[20]For further discussion, see Chalmers Johnson, ed., *The Industrial Policy Debate* (San Francisco: ICS Press, 1984), pp. 53 ff.

unique to Japan are the Japan Development Bank and the Postal Savings Bank. The former was instrumental in the postwar recovery effort, first financing reconstruction and economic development of steel, electric power, and shipping industries, and later shifting its emphasis to industries producing for export. It cooperates rather than competes with private banks by making joint loans with private banks to strategic industries. The Postal Savings Bank stimulates savings by offering tax-free interest on virtually any amount of savings in fixed time deposit saving accounts. The importance of these accounts is indicated by the fact that this bank holds over 20 percent of Japan's total savings.[21] The Postal Savings Bank's total deposits (in excess of $1 trillion) make it the world's largest savings institution. The bank's significance is due to Japan's tax rules and the population's high propensity to save disposable income (discussed further in Chapter 10).

Private Institutions

Japan's business institutions must be understood within the context of the organization of the private sector. More than in any other economy, the organization of this sector is an intricate web of competitive and complementary relationships. The unique combination of industrial, distributional, and financial hierarchies, and the gradations of firms within, give the private sector a multifaceted socioeconomic structure.

The industrial organization is characterized by vertical and horizontal forms of integration. Industrial, commercial, and financial firms are interwoven in complex, close-knit associations peculiar to Japan. At the root of the interrelationships among Japanese institutions are the society's orientation toward group behavior and a belief that economic growth will ensue and benefits from competition will derive from an industrial organization pattern where business groups "are cemented by a variety of commercial linkages: between buyer and seller of goods, lender and borrower, shareholder and issuer of equity."[22]

The nature of postwar business institutions was influenced by the Occupation Authority. In the interest of demilitarization and democratization, this authority acted to dissolve the *zaibatsu*. *Zaibatsu* monopoly power was weakened thereafter through a series of rules breaking up their holding companies and purging members of the controlling families from managerial and financial positions. The new rules were effective, ending the ability of these conglomerates to retain control over markets through discriminatory business practices. Easy entry into the manufacturing sector ensued, including the emergence of young and able business leaders who replaced the purged *zaibatsu* managers. Curiously,

[21]McMillan, *The Japanese Industrial System*, p. 290. McMillan points out that "under Japanese law, individuals can deposit up to three million yen without incurring tax on interest; . . . [there is a loophole effectively eliminating any] ceiling on the number of deposit accounts [an individual can have]." Ibid., p. 290. Also refer to "Socking It Away in Japan," *Time*, December 14, 1987, p. 60.

[22]Richard E. Caves and Masu Uekusa, *Industrial Organization in Japan* (Washington, DC: Brookings Institution, 1976), p. 59.

banks and insurance companies escaped the Occupation Authority's dissolution efforts. They emerged from the war intact, except for the losses incurred from loans extended for armaments production.

Recurring themes throughout Japan's economic history are the nation's ability to adapt quickly to changes in authorities and rules for economic behavior; to preserve the unique qualities of its culture, and to subordinate individual interest and work collectively for the national interest. The response to the *zaibatsu* dissolution exemplifies these themes. After regaining independence in 1952, the Japanese government, seeking rapid economic growth and recognizing the benefits from economies of scale, introduced rules facilitating the formation of large business groups. In addition, personal contacts between business leaders from related industries, which had been taking place since 1946, became more formal. The new working rules and discussions among Japan's business leaders led to the formation of its postwar economic institutions. Foremost among these was the new type of affiliated group, or business alignment, known as the *keiretsu*.

KEIRETSU.   A *keiretsu* is a closely affiliated confederation of heterogeneous firms. It is structured both vertically and horizontally, with a large industrial, marketing, or financial concern as the nucleus. Member firms engage in cooperative (i.e., bilaterally negotiated versus free market) buying, selling, and financial activities, some of which are organized and perhaps financed by the central company. The linkages among members of the *keiretsu* are generally loose, or informal, to the extent that interactions depend upon firms in related areas cooperatively pursuing a mutual interest. In the case of an industrial *keiretsu*, the nucleus firm and group firms responsible for producing specific assembly parts engage in transactions characteristic of a bilateral monopolistic market. For the purpose of guaranteeing the huge amounts of capital needed to fund postwar reconstruction and growth (since internal financing could not meet capital needs), affiliation between banks and manufacturing concerns has been necessary. When a bank is the nucleus *keiretsu*, firms will have bank accounts with this group bank, the bank will be their major stockholder and most important lender, as well as overseer and disciplinarian of firms' financial conditions.

In some cases the same companies which formerly comprised the *zaibatsu* have merged the old component industrial or commercial parts into a new grouping. This was the case for Mitsubishi (1954) and Mitsui (1959), as new firms which had been developing since the war ended sought their own affiliates. The result has been an institution distinguishable from the prewar *zaibatsu*. The linkages between firms are looser, the individual *keiretsu* are relatively smaller in scale, and economic power is less concentrated even in the largest *keiretsu* than had been the case with the *zaibatsu*. No central organization, command center, or family is in control of the group. There is no holding company arrangement. Rather, ties are made through interlocking shareholder relationships formed by mutual exchange of relatively small percentages of members' stocks, and by personal agreements to buy and sell. In addition, some interlocking directorships have been established. Coordination has been through informal administrative links such as the periodic meetings of member firms' presidents.

A number of factors influence a firm's willingness to form or join a *keiretsu*. The first is the Japanese propensity toward collectivity. They believe that a diversified industrial grouping comprised of affiliates representing all industries is a source of power, influence, prestige, security, and trust. Building of a trust relationship through mutual cooperation avoids undesirable effects of relying exclusively on one seller (of components to you) or one buyer (of your component). The desire to belong to a group is a cultural rather than an economic phenomenon, as illustrated by the fact that firms belonging to a *keiretsu* generally are not more profitable than large independent firms.[23]

Second, a *keiretsu* enables the central firm to internalize the external economies if it experiences rapid economic growth. The firm can become self-sufficient in regard to its input supplies, and can potentially decrease input costs through avoiding intermediary margins and reducing transportation costs. Opportunity costs due to sudden stoppage of supplier production is avoided. It can establish a subsidiary to serve as a market for its production. For example, Mitsubishi Chemicals, a producer of carbide, sold its output to the newly established Mitsubishi Monsanto Chemical firm. Parent firms can establish a subsidiary to produce a specialty product, as occurred with the establishment of Aichi Steel to produce a special steel for Toyota.[24]

Third, member firms can benefit from the reduction of time and cost by substituting interfirm reciprocal transactions, including subcontracting relationships, for those of a complex, market nature. This would apply for intragroup bank financing, procurement of component parts from smaller group members, and the distribution of group output by its trading company. Fourth, groups can benefit from an exchange of information, the collective talents of its diversified management, and the ability to interchange personnel. Suppliers of parts can participate with final product producer in the design of such components. Finally, the *keiretsu* can potentially close itself off from outsiders, effectively erecting a nontariff trade barrier. Intergroup and interfirm relations, however, are common. Although mergers are unusual, the Japanese have demonstrated a willingness to "engage in cartels with respect to prices, production, or plant and equipment investment, either explicitly on advice from industry associations or administrative guidance from the government (normally MITI), or tacitly on mutual understanding."[25] Cartels and other forms of

---

[23]For further discussion concerning the linkage between cultural foundations, *keiretsu* functions, and the six elements of the Japanese social structure discussed earlier, see M. Y. Yoshino and Thomas B. Lifson, *The Invisible Link: Japan's Sogo Shosha and the Organization of Trade* (Cambridge, MA: MIT Press, 1986).

[24]Kazuo Sato, ed., *Industry and Business in Japan* (New York: M. E. Sharpe, Inc., 1980), pp. 72–73.

[25]Hiroshi Okumura, "Interfirm Relations in an Enterprise Group: The Case of Mitsubishi," *Japanese Economic Studies*, 10 (Summer 1982), p. 72. Members of the Mitsubishi group have formed cartels with members of other groups in their respective industries.

cooperative behavior have shown a tendency to increase during periods of low economic growth, while a high degree of competitive behavior can be observed during the periods of rapid growth.

To summarize, the *keiretsu* is a uniquely Japanese institution. It combines practical management and organizational practices in the pursuit of economic growth and efficiency with an institutional environment heavily imbued with Japanese sociocultural features. The *keiretsu* system

> has succeeded in skillfully combining the collectivist integration principle, such as seen in vertical integration, and the market cooperation principle, such as seen in specialization, and skillfully and judiciously used the two principles in response to different situations within the technique of external procurement control and purchase policy as a catalyst. It achieved this result through full utilization of the intermediate organizational functions.[26]

The remaining principal institutions will be discussed in terms of their size, their relationship with a *keiretsu*, and their primary function (e.g., distribution, finance, labor, lobby). Within the manufacturing sector institutions can be classified according to their legal type of business organization and their relation to a *keiretsu*. Briefly, Japanese firms can be organized as single proprietorships, partnerships distinguishable by the extent to which each partner may be held liable, limited-liability companies with attributes of a partnership and a joint-stock company, and joint-stock companies similar to corporations in the United States. Manufacturing firms within *keiretsu* are themselves subdivided into large, medium, and small enterprises, such as subsidiaries and subcontractors that are affiliated with a *keiretsu*, and independent firms.

LARGE, MEDIUM, AND SMALL FIRMS. The relative importance and status of large, medium, and small manufacturing firms to the Japanese economy can be demonstrated by a number of facts. Small companies account for about 95 percent of all manufacturing establishments, while medium firms comprise an additional 3 percent.[27] In terms of their share of value added, small firms accounted for about 50 percent of manufacturing industries' output between 1959 and 1979.[28] The growth rates and profit rates of small, medium, and large firms were similar to one another between 1967 and 1974. The annual growth rate of sales for all three firm sizes was 16.7 percent, 17.0 percent, and 16.3 percent,

[26]Koichi Shimokawa, "Japan's Keiretsu System: The Case of the Automobile Industry," *Japanese Economic Studies* (Summer 1985), p. 27.

[27]Allen, *The Japanese Economy*, p. 124.

[28]Yataka Kosai and Yoshitaro Ogino, *Contemporary Japanese Economy* (London: Macmillan Press, 1982), pp. 70, 71.

respectively, while the respective profit rate as a percentage of total capital was 6.5 percent (small), 5.1 percent (medium), and 5.0 percent (large firms).[29]

In terms of all Japanese firms, small firms account for 97 percent, mid-sized firms for just less than 3 percent, while large corporations account for only about 0.2 percent of all firms.[30] In terms of earnings, large corporations account for over 53 percent while medium-sized and small firms account for about 20 percent and 27 percent, respectively.[31] It is anticipated that both manufacturing and retailing medium-sized firms will increase in importance, thereby illustrating that the view of Japan as consisting of a dual firm structure (modern large firms and traditional small firms) is outdated.

SUBSIDIARIES AND SUBCONTRACTORS.   Most medium and small Japanese manufacturing firms are linked to a *keiretsu* either as subsidiaries or subcontractors. A subsidiary is defined by the Japanese Fair Trade Commission as a firm whose parent company holds at least 30 percent of its shares, or whose parent holds between 10 percent and 29 percent of the shares while forming an interlocking directorship and/or extending loans to the dependent firm.[32] Subsidiaries are insiders, trusted because they are part of the *keiretsu*. Their relationship to the parent firm is known as *ko-gaisha*, which means "child company." The familial, collectivist relationship involves parent and subsidiary firms exchanging personnel, while the parent can offer technical information, managerial advice, and financial assistance to its subsidiary. In return subsidiaries supply parts, components, or specific factory services to larger firms generally involved with higher stages in the production process.

The Japanese define a subcontractor as a firm which produces a product, part, accessory, or raw material used by the parent firm to produce a final product, or a firm which produces or repairs equipment, machinery, or tools used by the parent firm.[33] In other words, there are exclusive, long-term ties between the parent company and the smaller firm (subcontractor). Conceptually subcontracting and interfirm relationships within a *keiretsu* are similar, and in both cases despite the existence of a bilateral monopoly risks of opportunism are avoided given the cooperative nature of the relationship and reliance upon bilateral negotiations.

While subcontracting is practiced in every industrial nation, it is a dominant feature in Japan. Over half of the roughly 1 million small and medium Japanese manufacturing organizations are subcontractors. They are outsiders and,

---

[29]Sato, *Industry and Business in Japan*, p. 102. A small manufacturing firm has fewer than 300 employees or less than 100 million yen of equity capital, while a small retail trade or service firm has fewer than 50 employees or equity capital that is less than 10 million yen.

[30]Hideichiro Nakamura, "Formation and Development of Mid-Sized Firms," *Japanese Economic Studies*, XXI, 2 (Winter 1992–93), 30.

[31]Ibid.

[32]Haitani, *The Japanese Economic System*, pp. 125, 126.

[33]Hisashi Yaginuma, "The Keiretsu Issue," *Japanese Economic Studies*, XXI, 3 (1993), 4.

consequently, are lower in the hierarchical industrial network. Opinions differ concerning the type of relationship that exists between larger firms, especially those at the center of a *keiretsu*, and their subcontractors. Some believe the larger firms use their greater power to unfair advantage, controlling their relationship with the weaker subcontractors. Others argue that large firms benefit their suppliers, providing support during slow growth periods that might otherwise be devastating to the smaller firm. There is evidence supporting both contentions. What is clear is that subcontracting has the potential to be advantageous to all participants. The subcontractor benefits by receiving orders, eliminating the burden of attracting business. It can receive financial, technical, or marketing assistance from the larger firm to which it is related. In addition, the ability of numerous small subcontracting firms to survive and prosper affords many Japanese the opportunity to organize their own company. Recent surveys indicate that a growing number of males are interested in such entrepreneurial pursuits in lieu of being a member of a large business institution.

Numerous advantages exist for the large firm that chooses to organize its production scheme by relying upon subcontractors. It can benefit from economies of large-scale production without concern for diseconomies of scale. Such decentralization also favors the output of high-quality goods and services where economies of scale are not necessary. The large firm retains control, for it can impose rigid discipline regarding the terms of a contract (e.g., quantity, quality, and delivery schedule). The benefits of market competition are retained, for a large firm can shop around, retaining the option to purchase the necessary parts or services on the open market. The same applies for selecting a new, or replacing an existing, subcontractor. During a recession, subcontractors serve as a buffer, for large firms may discontinue the relationship due to lack of demand for the final product. This enables large firms to retain their own labor, while forcing smaller firms to lay off employees. Large firms have been known to delay payment to subcontractors during periods of slow cash flow. They also have selected subcontractors for projects involving high risk of accident or pollution. Subcontractors also appeal to large firms because they have proven to be inventive, innovative, reliable, and efficient. They pay lower wages, reduce the uncertainties of seeking the subcontracted parts on the open market, and possess the specialized equipment and technology to meet the product specifications. Overall, the subcontracting relationship has been a source of vitality to the Japanese industrial sector, providing benefits of bilaterally negotiated agreements while fostering, rather than inhibiting, competitive forces.

EXAMPLE OF A JAPANESE *KEIRETSU*. A *keiretsu* system from the Japanese automobile industry provides an example of the complex relationship between a central company (e.g., Toyota, Nissan) and the subsidiaries and subcontractors which serve the automobile manufacturer. The *keiretsu* relationship between the parent company and parts manufacturers is one type of subsidiary and subcontracting relationship. A type of semivertical integration network of specialized firms exists. Parent companies concentrate on control, design, model changes, and assembly of the final product. They rely on technologically advanced parts manufacturers for intermediate products.

The network involves specialization at many stages and levels of the production process. Larger firms (most likely subsidiaries) supplying primary parts to the parent company may form their own *keiretsu* for secondary and tertiary parts. The interrelationships and competitive nature of this network extends further.

> Even within the same group there is a vertical within-group competition between the automobile manufacturer and his primary parts producer and between primary parts producers and secondary parts producers; also there is a horizontal competition in the form of placing purchase orders to more than one parts producer within the group. At the same time, there is competition from independent parts producers and from new entrants in the market.[34]

This flexible system offers cooperation and competition on all levels. The *keiretsu*, from the point of view of both the parent and supplier firm, can be monolithic while providing autonomy and adaptability when necessary. As compared to the vertical integration network prevalent in the U.S. automobile industry, the Japanese network provides greater autonomy for management at many levels, adapts better when significant changes in parts specifications are necessary, and fosters a more cooperative, long-term relationship between firms.

INDEPENDENT FIRMS.   Industrial and social development in Japan has enabled both medium and small firms to prosper. Over the past three decades, large and medium-sized enterprises have emerged independent of giant *keiretsu*. These firms have attained a scale which enables them to raise funds through the securities market, to utilize modern management techniques, and to develop and mass produce their own products.

PRIVATE FINANCIAL INSTITUTIONS.   Three of the most important types of private financial institutions are the city banks, the Foreign Exchange Bank (Bank of Tokyo), and the Industrial Bank of Japan. The 13 city banks, ranked according to assets, are among the world's largest financial institutions. The banks are all among the top 15 banks worldwide. Each bank has served to promote rapid growth of Japan's industry by not only providing short-term venture capital, but also playing a role in the management of industrial enterprises. Unlike medium-sized and small banks, the city banks can borrow directly from the Bank of Japan. This has facilitated the allocation of scarce credit (credit was rationed throughout the 1950–1980 period in directions deemed high priority by the Ministry of Finance and MITI).

The Foreign Exchange Bank is a specialized exchange bank. It serves as an agent for the Bank of Japan and the government, although it is privately owned

---

[34]Shimokawa, "Japan's Keiretsu System," p. 26.

and controlled. Its relative importance as a financier of transactions involving foreign exchange has dwindled as the city banks have expanded their international activities. The Industrial Bank of Japan is also specialized, existing to raise capital in foreign markets and to finance medium- and long-range projects for the public corporations and private industry.

RETAIL AND TRADE INSTITUTIONS.   Two important Japanese institutions dominate the sector involved with marketing goods and services: the general trading companies and the small retail firms. The coexistence and prevalence of these radically different institutions can be attributed to Japan's economic history and unique culture. Traditionally, distribution in Japan was carried out by the large merchant houses affiliated with the *zaibatsu* and by small retailers. Postwar dissolution of the *zaibatsu* meant a temporary end to their trading companies. After 1952, however, ties between old constituent firms that had comprised the prewar trading companies were renewed, and large general trading companies reemerged, albeit not as subsidiaries of the *keiretsu* parent company. Other trading companies have also developed as subsidiaries of large financial or manufacturing concerns. They are similar in character to their larger counterparts. An example is the Toyota Sales Company, a subsidiary of Toyota Motor.

The great trading companies (the largest ten) are known as *Sogo Shosha*. They are economically powerful and globally oriented. They handle a wide range of commodities and account for a large portion of Japan's foreign trade (over half of the nation's exports and over three fourths of its imports). The functions they perform include: (1) assisting Japan's growth and development efforts through providing marketing support and purchasing assistance to manufacturers (they have served to coordinate their *keiretsu's* manufacturing and financial strategies with their own trading behavior); (2) specializing in raw materials trade, assuring that necessary inputs are procured for Japanese manufacturers; (3) initiating investment projects (e.g., developing new industries and organizing new business ventures) overseas as well as domestically; (4) collecting foreign and domestic market information for the manufacturers they represent; (5) providing financial assistance to smaller customers; (6) conducting leasing businesses dealing in products ranging from computers to jumbo jets; and (7) aggressively marketing Japanese products abroad.[35] Because of the cultural gap and language barrier separating Japanese manufacturers from foreign markets, the trading firms employ marketing specialists who serve to bridge the cultural gap while promoting their customers' products. This particular function exemplifies the unique importance of the *Sogo Shosha* to the economy. Some analysts argue that these trading firms "have no parallel within the capitalist, communist or socialist

---

[35]Haitani, *The Japanese Economic System*, p. 129. Haitani observes that trading companies send their most competent, promising recruits abroad in search of foreign markets. The recruits are "extremely hard working people, motivated by a strong desire to increase the sales volume of their company, and to contribute to the economic growth of their country." Ibid.

economies. They are concerned with a special structure which seems to be optimally suited to the nature of the Japanese."[36]

An example of a *Sogo Shosha* is Mitsui and Co. Ltd. (Mitsui Bussan), the general trading company for the Mitsui *keiretsu*. Since 1960 it has ranked alongside Mitsubishi as one of the largest trading companies in Japan. Its annual sales revenue exceeds $100 billion, it owns over $30 billion worth of assets, and it employs over 13,000 people in offices around the world.[37] It handles about 10 percent of Japan's imports and exports. Like the other *Sogo Shosha*, about 40 percent of Mitsui Bussan's revenue comes from international trade, with domestic sales and overseas investments accounting for about 50 percent and 10 percent, respectively.[38] Mitsui's comprehensive nature extends to developing new industries and innovatively reorganizing existing production and distribution schemes.

The incidence of small retailers is greater in Japan than in any other large industrial nation. In Japan the ratio of the number of retailers to members of the population is about 1/74 versus a ratio of 1/100 and 1/160 in France and the United States, respectively. There are more than 1.6 million retailers in Japan, and over half of them employ only one or two persons. The predominance of the small retail shop is indicated by the fact that in 1988 shops with fewer than ten employees accounted for over 93 percent of all retail business in Japan.[39]

A number of terms have been used to describe Japan's retail distribution system, including *archaic, traditional,* and *feudal.* The main criticism of retail distribution is that working rules (e.g., the Large-Scale Retail Store Law) existed, which protected small retailers from competition from large retailers who sought to enter a market. This law, amended in 1979, required those seeking to open a retail establishment with sales floor space in excess of 500 square meters (about 5,400 square feet) to request permission from the local government where the store is planned to be located—a government heavily influenced by owners of small retail stores. The retail distribution scheme, therefore, has maintained a traditional way of life, albeit by inflating prices. The 1991 revision of the Large-Scale Retail Store Law may affect the importance of small retailers dramatically as medium-sized stores, which employ 3–19 persons, grow in importance.[40]

There are justifications for the incidence, and importance to the Japanese, of many small retailers that go beyond preservation of tradition. Since Japanese homes are small, storage space is limited. Retailers therefore serve the function of a warehouse. Japanese prefer fresh food daily, so they prefer to visit stores frequently. Given the traffic congestion and shortage of parking spaces in a densely populated nation, having retailers close to one's home so that shopping

---

[36]Simonis and Ernst, eds., *Japan: Economic and Social Studies in Development,* p. 208.

[37]McMillan, *The Japanese Industrial System,* p. 238.

[38]Ibid.

[39]Kaz Miyagiwa, "Reforming the Japanese Distribution System: Will It Boost Exports to Japan?" *Japan and the World Economy,* 5 (1993), 322.

[40]Ibid., pp. 322–323.

on foot can be done is preferable. Close personal relationships can be developed between retailer and customers, and the Japanese preference for quality service can be satisfied. This service includes special packaging, offering credit, and a willingness to serve customers after stated closing time.[41]

ENTERPRISE UNIONS.   Japan's labor unions are typically enterprise unions (i.e., over 90 percent of union members belong to an enterprise union), found primarily in large firms. They are oriented along company interests, rather than being organized at the national level or according to workers' industry, trade, or craft. About one fourth of all employees belong to an enterprise union, and they have their terms and conditions of work established by collective bargaining. Within the union membership, there is an absence of class antagonisms. Class consciousness among the workers is characterized more by a feeling of belonging to the enterprise than by one of alienation from employees of a higher rank. There is little demarcation between white-collar, blue-collar, and clerical workers or between workers in different crafts or occupations.

COOPERATIVES.   The importance of cooperatives in Japan is roughly equivalent to their importance in the United States. Over 30 million Japanese are members of at least one cooperative. Areas in which cooperatives are relatively important include agriculture (particularly rice growers, fisheries, and timber), retail distribution of food, housing, and credit unions. There are signs that in financial services credit unions may grow in importance considering bad debt problems encountered by the financial sector over the past few years.[42]

ZAIKAI.   The special interests of Japan's business community are communicated to elected state officials and bureaucrats by federations of business organizations, of which there are four. Leaders from these organizations comprise a still larger, more powerful institution, the *Zaikai*. The ability of this influential group to influence prominent members of the state higher-order authority stems from the fact that the *Zaikai* serves as the body which allocates campaign funds to political parties and individual office seekers. These business leaders are consulted by the Japanese government before any new rules or policy measures are adopted.

SUMMARY

The working rules for the Japanese economy are best understood in the context of the nation's history and attitudes toward economic activities. Both of these factors

---

[41]Jeroen C. A. Potjes and A. Roy Thurik, "Profit Margins in Japanese Retailing," *Japan and the World Economy,* 5 (1993), 343–344.

[42]Mark Klinedinst and Hitomi Sato, "The Japanese Cooperative Sector," unpublished paper presented at the Allied Social Sciences Meetings, Boston (January 1994).

shaped the principal institutions and the decision making by authorities in the political structure responsible for establishing and interpreting the working rules. The homogeneity and uniqueness of the Japanese culture have created a stable, socially cohesive society willing to accept and unite behind the authorities' macroeconomic policies. Institutions resemble a kinship group characterized by loyalty and dependency among members organized in a strict hierarchy.

The economic, social, and political conditions existing in 1946 provided a firm basis for the introduction of new working rules. The Occupation Authority, without violating the Japanese social structure with its emphasis upon status and collective behavior, introduced democratic reforms in both political and economic institutions which would promote economic growth and development in Japan. Such reforms included conservative monetary policies and the establishment of a parliamentary democracy which led to political stability through the long tenure of the Liberal Democratic Party.

The dual structure of the manufacturing and retail sectors exemplified by the coexistence of modern conglomerate enterprises and small traditional institutions has been maintained, albeit with some modification of institutions (e.g., *keiretsu* replacing *zaibatsu*). As a result, rapid economic growth through expansion of large-scale enterprises has occurred without adversely affecting traditional economic institutions such as small farms and retail units. In addition, MITI emerged as the authority responsible for guiding economic activity, committed to establishing Japan as a world economic power.

The philosophical basis and public acceptance of the state's role in guiding the economy have historical roots, as the state had successfully guided Japan's industrial revolution. Post-World War II attitudes favored the state's complementing private-sector initiatives, a type of Keynesian institutional complementarity. To promote high levels of savings and investment, the Postal Savings Bank and Japan Development Bank were developed to channel communal savings to industries deemed vital (by MITI) to Japan's interests.

Throughout the state's promotion of industrial growth, there has been a noticeable absence of hostility toward large conglomerate business institutions. As a result, institutions such as the *keiretsu* were encouraged to establish complicated forms of integration, thereby maintaining the Japanese preference for belonging to a group and working with insiders. The specific aspects of the economy's behavior, including the performance, are presented in Chapter 10.

KEY TERMS AND CONCEPTS

Confucian Beliefs
Feudal Order
Keiretsu
Ministry of International
    Trade and Industry

Occupation Authority
Sogo Shosha
State Guidance
Zaibatsu

QUESTIONS FOR DISCUSSION

1. Distinguish between a *zaibatsu* and a *keiretsu*.
2. What was the Imperial Rescript on Education?
3. List at least four general features of Japan's social structure that have contributed to the evolution and characteristics of its principal institutions.
4. What is the place of the Ministry of International Trade and Industry (MITI) within Japan's political structure?
5. List three benefits a firm belonging to a *keiretsu* derives from relying upon a subcontractor.
6. How did the Japanese state contribute to the nation's industrial revolution and to the post-1952 rebuilding efforts?
7. Evaluate the role played by the Occupation Authority in the post World-War II (1946–1952) economic recovery of Japan?
8. In what respects does the philosophical basis for the working rules of Japan's economy (post-1952) conform to the teachings of John Maynard Keynes?

REFERENCES

"A Survey of Japan." *The Economist*, December 5, 1987.

Allen, G. C., *The Japanese Economy*. London: Weidenfeld and Nicolson, 1981.

—————, *A Short Economic History of Modern Japan*. London: George Allen & Unwin, 1962.

"An Outsider Takes a Look Inside at Japan's Corporate Culture," *Japanese Economic Journal*, May 3, 1986, pp. 40–41.

Balassa, Bela, and Marcus Noland, *Japan in the World Economy*. Washington, DC: Institute for International Economics, 1988.

Bieda, K., *The Structure and Operation of the Japanese Economy*. Sydney: John Wiley & Sons, 1970.

Caves, Richard E., and Masu Uekusa, *Industrial Organization in Japan*. Washington, DC: Brookings Institution, 1976.

Clark, Rodney, *The Japanese Company*. New Haven, CT: Yale University Press, 1979.

Haitani, Kanji, *The Japanese Economic System*. Lexington, MA: D. C. Heath & Co., 1976.

Hyoe, Murakani, and Johannes Hirschmeier, eds., *Politics and Economics in Contemporary Japan*. Tokyo: Japan Culture Institute, 1979.

Ito, Takatoshi, *The Japanese Economy*. Cambridge, MA: MIT Press, 1992.

Japanese Economic Journal, November 1, 1986, p. 11.

—————, February 14, 1987, p. 6.

—————, December 28, 1985, p. 10.

Johnson, Chalmers, ed., *The Industrial Policy Debate*. San Francisco: Institute for Contemporary Studies, 1984.

Klinedinst, Mark, and Hitomi Sato, "The Japanese Cooperative Sector." Unpublished paper presented at the Allied Social Sciences Meetings, Boston (January 1994).

Kono, Toyohiro, "Competitive Strategy," *Japanese Economic Studies*, 13, 1–2 (1984/85), 45–71.

Kosai, Yataka, and Yoshitaro Ogino, *The Contemporary Japanese Economy*. London: Macmillan Press, 1982.

"Life Expectancy in Japan Continues to Become Longer," *Japanese Economic Journal*, July 19, 1986, p. 24.

Lincoln, Edward J., *Japan: Facing Economic Maturity*. Washington, DC: The Brookings Institution, 1988.

McMillan, Charles J., *The Japanese Industrial System*. New York: Walter de Gruyter, 1984.

Minami, Ryoshin, *The Economic Development of Japan: A Quantitative Study*. London: Macmillan Press, 1986.

Miyagiwa, Kaz, "Reforming the Japanese Distribution System: Will it Boost Exports to Japan?" *Japan and the World Economy*, 5 (1993), 321–336.

Nakamura, Hideichiro, "Formation and Development of Mid-Sized Firms," *Japanese Economic Studies*, XXI, 2 (1992–93), 21–53.

Nakamura, Takafusa, transl. by Jacqueline Kaminski, *The Postwar Japanese Economy: Its Development and Structure*. Tokyo: University of Tokyo Press, 1981.

Okimoto, Daniel I., and Thomas P. Rohlen, eds., *Inside the Japanese System*. Stanford, CA: Stanford University Press, 1988.

Okumura, Hiroshi, "Interfirm Relations in an Enterprise Group: The Case of Mitsubishi," *Japanese Economic Studies*, 10, 4 (Summer 1982), 53–82.

Pascale, Richard Tanner, and Anthony G. Athos, *The Art of Japanese Management*. Middlesex, England: Penguin Books, 1984.

Patrick, Hugh, and Henry Rosovsky, eds., *Asia's New Giant: How the Japanese Economy Works*. Washington, DC: Brookings Institution, 1976.

Potjes, Jeroen C. A., and A. Roy Thurik, "Profit Margins in Japanese Retailing." *Japan and the World Economy*, 5 (1993), 337–362.

Sato, Kazuo, ed., *Industry and Business in Japan*. New York: M. E. Sharpe, 1980.

Shimokawa, Koichi, "Japan's Keiretsu System: The Case of the Automobile Industry," *Japanese Economic Studies*, 13, 4 (Summer 1985), 3–31.

Simonis, Heide, and Udo Ernst, eds., *Japan: Economic and Social Studies in Development*. Hamburg: Institute of Asian Affairs, 1974.

"Socking It Away in Japan," *Time*, December 14, 1987.

Stockwin, J. A. A., *Japan: Divided Politics in a Growth Economy*, 2nd ed. London: Weidenfeld and Nicolson, 1982.

Thurow, Lester P., ed., *The Management Challenge*. Cambridge, MA: The MIT Press, 1986.

Yaginuma, Hisashi., "The *Keiretsu* Issue: A Theoretical Approach," *Japanese Economic Studies*, 21, 3 (Spring 1993), 3–48.

10

BEHAVIOR OF THE JAPANESE ECONOMY

1946–Present

OBJECTIVES

1. Present the cooperative relationship between the state and the private sector in macroeconomic decision making.
2. Explain how the state's role regarding ownership of resources is limited, and has been decreasing since 1952.
3. Evaluate the extent to which the state exerts control over the economy, particularly regarding economic planning, trade policy, and the role of the Ministry of International Trade and Industry.
4. Discuss factors contributing to low import penetration in Japan.
5. Identify where tradition remains a contributing factor regarding social processes for economic coordination.
6. Examine the performance of the economy, discussing the factors that influenced the economy's performance.

The previous chapter outlined those features of Japanese economic history and cultural traits which shaped the principal institutions and the philosophical basis for state-private economic cooperation. In addition, the authorities responsible for establishing and interpreting working rules within Japan's principal institutions were identified. This chapter will focus upon the behavior of the economy, especially as it has been influenced by technological change and adaptation as well as changes in working rules affecting international trade.

LEADERSHIP, COOPERATION, AND PERSUASION IN RESOURCE ALLOCATION DECISIONS

Two significant features of decision making in Japan are that the head of a group (e.g., cabinet, an agency of the bureaucracy, leaders of the *zaikai*) has "enormous symbolic importance,"[1] and that cooperation and persuasion always take precedence over imposition of rules through compulsion. This is reflected by continual consultation among authorities from state, manufacturing, financial, distribution, and academic institutions as they cooperate to achieve harmony (*wa*) by making decisions collectively deemed in Japan's best interest.

Such a decision-making process is possible and effective due to the uniqueness of the Japanese social structure and homogeneity of attitudes. The strong degree of national pride stimulates the Japanese to work within groups and to arrive at decisions cooperatively. The decision-making process is known as *ringi-sei*. All members of a group have an opportunity to contribute. While the process is tedious and lengthy, those involved feel that they had an opportunity to contribute to a decision. Once a consensus is reached, a united effort toward achieving the specified goal is likely to result.

With these decision-making features in mind, the relative power held by politicians, bureaucrats, and business leaders within the political structure is easier to understand. Many Japanese observers have asked the following questions: Can any single group translate its political power to control the path of economic activity? Are the labels such as "Administrative Guidance" or "Japan, Inc." which have been popularized to describe decision making within Japan relevant in the 1990s? One response to this is that since the Japanese culture is complex and its firms have distinctive corporate cultures, no simple categorization of decision making is possible. Another way to answer both questions is to emphasize the importance of persuasion and cooperation to the Japanese.

The state has tried to play a neutral role when coordinating and guiding activities of fiercely competitive private-sector institutions in a direction deemed to be in the nation's best interest. The state's approach has been to encourage (not compel) private institutions voluntarily to comply with rules passed by Parliament and written by the bureaucracy, in consultation with leaders of private and academic institutions, designed to promote the national interest. One analyst argues that decision making between public and private institutions is a process "involving subtle give-and-take, not frontal confrontations which would result in the forcible imposition of one side's will on the other."[2]

This decision-making process has also been described as "patterned pluralism" in which the state and the private sector are both autonomous, but

---

[1]Chalmers Johnson, "Japan the Societal State," in Daniel I. Okimoto and Thomas P. Rohlen, eds., *Inside the Japanese System* (Stanford, CA: Stanford University Press, 1988), p. 214.
[2]Ibid.

their particular interests are coordinated by the bureaucracy in such a manner that a consensus can be reached with voluntary compliance.[3] This process has been effective because there is mutual trust between the public and private sectors and great respect for the judgment of the bureaucracy, especially leaders of the Ministry of International Trade and Industry (MITI) and the Ministry of Finance. The interests of the private sector (e.g., manufacturing, retail, agricultural, labor) are important to the state, but the state is not subservient to the private sector. Rather, through economic planning (see "Social Process," p. 204), the relationship between the state and private sector is a partnership, in which the "*zaikai* represents all business interest, and the spirit is one of cooperation."[4]

The symbiotic relationship among Japanese public authorities (e.g., members of the diet, cabinet, and bureaucracy) and business leaders has prevailed throughout the twentieth century. After regaining political independence in 1952, authorities in the public and private sector were unified in recognizing the supreme importance of economic growth and development for the nation to avoid being dominated by Western economic powers. Given the desire to expand production capacity while facing a shortage of raw materials, scarcity of credit, and threat of foreign competition, the Japanese adopted the most pragmatic policy: cooperation between government and business in the national interest.[5] In the face of the perceived foreign threat, reaching a consensus concerning goals and policies to pursue was an easy, harmonious process.

Regarding the degree of centralized versus decentralized decision making today, one leading Japanese economist argues "the image of a powerful elite of government officials guiding Japan's industries is a far cry from reality . . . the moving force has been the operation of supply and demand."[6] The extent to which public institutions have guided the industrial sector appears to have decreased each decade since independence was achieved. The "Japan, Inc." view of a monolithic state-private sector that plans and executes economic growth policies in a detailed manner is outdated. Such a view overemphasizes the current power of the state and fails to account for the increased contributions of other factors, especially entrepreneurship and market forces. Disagreements between private firms and the state over policy measures have become more common, and

---

[3]Ellis S. Krauss and Muramatsu Michio, "Japanese Political Economy Today: The Patterned Pluralist Model," in Daniel I. Okomoto and Thomas P. Rohlen, eds., *Inside the Japanese System* (Stanford, CA: Stanford University Press, 1988), pp. 209–210.

[4]Stephen Warshaw, *Japan Emerges* (Berkeley, CA: Diablo Press, 1987), p. 132.

[5]Immediately after World War II, most productive resources were especially scarce. Shortages of capital equipment and modern technology, raw materials for industry, energy resources, land, and business leadership, especially marketing expertise, were widespread. On the other hand, resources such as labor, especially the number of educated and skilled persons, and social overhead capital, such as seaports and railroad, irrigation, and communication (e.g., postal, telephone, broadcasting) networks, were relatively abundant.

[6]Yataka Kosai and Yoshitaro Ogino, *The Contemporary Japanese Economy* (London: Macmillan Press, 1982), p. 128.

government economic plans do not necessarily resemble the policies actually implemented. Some state guidance is provided, but decentralized firms have the autonomy to respond to market forces.

An example of the limited power of state bureaucracy decision making (i.e., ability to compel private institutions to behave in a prescribed manner) involved the Ministry of Finance. During the early 1980s, the ministry sought to enforce existing tax laws so as to prevent Japanese citizens from avoiding tax payments through establishing multiple accounts at the postal savings banks. Interest earned on these accounts was not taxable, but there was a legal limit of 3 million yen (roughly $30,000 in the early 1980s) per account. Establishing multiple accounts violated the spirit of the law, according to the Ministry of Finance. Commercial banks, the public (through pressuring authorities in the diet), and postal savings bank officials all protested. In response no change in the rules or enforcement procedures were made. According to one analyst, "[t]he history of the fiasco demonstrates that the Japanese bureaucracy is sometimes far from in control of policy outcomes, contrary to the customary perception by Americans."[7]

In recent years the tight symbiotic Liberal Democratic Party–bureaucrat–business relationship has resulted in charges of overcentralization of decision-making power and corruption as political contributions and bribes have become widespread. This corruption appears to be the result of generations of symbiosis, which has seen second-generation politicians rise within ranks to replace their retiring fathers.[8] Money has become even more important in Japanese politics than in other Organization for Economic Cooperation and Development (OECD) nations, with the power concentrated in Tokyo's Kasumigaseki district where government offices are concentrated.[9] Financial contributions deepen mutual dependence among bureaucrats, political leaders, and business groups whereby authorities are bribed to formulate and implement working rules in favor of business interests. Rent-seeking interests channeled money to party members and bureaucrats, as did newly emerging firms, leading to bureaucratic turf battles and a maze of new and sometimes contradictory working rules. Efforts to reform this organization of decision making are discussed in the "Institutional Change" section.

Overall, without widespread administrative reform of state bureaucracy, cooperative decision making among the ruling elite can be expected to continue. Their close bond will be fostered not only by mutual trust and common pursuit of the national interest, but also by the constant shifting of personnel between high positions in the private and public sectors. Retired ministry officials often are

---

[7]Edward J. Lincoln, *Japan: Facing Economic Maturity* (Washington, DC: The Brookings Institution, 1988), p. 107.

[8]In 1990 47 percent of all Liberal Democratic Party Lower House members were second-generation politicians. See Mizuguchi Hiroshi, "Political Reform: Much Ado About Nothing?" *Japan Quarterly* (July–September 1993), p. 247.

[9]OECD was established to coordinate economic policies among the world's industrial nations. Members include all of Western Europe, Turkey, Japan, New Zealand, Australia, United States, and Canada.

elected to Parliament or are offered a job in the private sector, a process known as *amakudari* ("descending from heaven").[10] The private sector, however, exercises considerable power within the political structure through representatives in the *zaikai*. This organization primarily represents the common interest of large industrial, banking, and commercial enterprises. The *zaikai's* power comes from its unity and financial strength, for it is the funnel through which political donations from Japanese business leaders flow. In the clublike atmosphere that characterizes Japan's establishment, *zaikai* leaders are consulted by government officials before any major economic policy measures are taken.

EXTENSIVE PRIVATE OWNERSHIP
WITH TEMPERED STATE CONTROL
OVER RESOURCES

Private institutions, whether independent or belonging to a *keiretsu*, own and control most resources in Japan. The number of public enterprises has been declining, while government expenditures continually account for a relatively modest percentage of total spending. Formal rules give the state considerable power to intervene in the affairs of private firms, but this power is rarely exercised. While the government's role in international trade is pervasive, its influence over domestic activity in the goods, labor, and money markets is modest. There is also a traditional role for cooperative control in influencing working rules in particular areas of the economy, especially in agriculture and retail trade.

There is no clear, legal definition of public enterprises (state corporations). Essentially, these institutions are partially or wholly owned and controlled by the state (i.e., supervised by a particular ministry), and they are operated as a commercial enterprise. Many were developed by the Occupation Authority as part of the democratization reform program. Prior to the early 1980s public enterprises were prominent on the local and national level in tobacco, salt and energy production, communications, transportation, housing and finance. They accounted for over 60 percent of assets in the Japanese economy in 1955, but this percentage declined to under 40 percent by 1965, and decreased steadily thereafter.[11] In 1985 salt, tobacco, and telephone and telegraph enterprises were privatized, and there are plans to privatize Japan National Railways. Among the currently owned public enterprises are Japan Airlines and major radio and television networks. The economic importance of these public enterprises is in terms of employment. They currently employ about 2 percent of the entire labor force, but account for over 40 percent of public-sector employment. In addition,

---

[10]Hugh Patrick and Henry Rosovsky, eds., *Asia's New Giant: How the Japanese Economy Works* (Washington, DC: The Brookings Institution, 1976), p. 785.

[11]Richard E. Caves and Masu Uekusa, *Industrial Organization in Japan* (Washington, DC: The Brookings Institution, 1976), p. 59.

public enterprises are important to some members of organized labor, since they are the last bastion of militant labor union activity.[12]

When ownership and control are measured by the volume of public finance, it can be concluded that the state has played a "supporting role," limiting the scale of its activities "to a minimum."[13] Relatively little (about 1 percent of gross national product) is spent on national defense, while direct subsidies for research and development as well as social security payments in the form of old-age pension and social insurance are low relative to other members of the Organization for Economic Cooperation and Development (OECD). In addition, total government expenditures as a percentage of gross domestic product are the lowest among OECD members.[14]

Given the history of cooperation between the state and the private sector, informal rules discourage the state from exercising strict control over the private sector except in cases of emergency or perceived threat from foreign powers, as in the early 1950s. The state does have the right to evaluate private enterprises' pricing decisions, inventory levels of raw materials, and production levels, and to use moral suasion to influence private-sector decisions to be in the national interest. Formal working rules also give the state the right to intervene directly in certain areas of the economy. Four of these rules pertain to: (1) trade, giving the state the right to form export and import cartels; (2) smaller firms, giving the state the right to intervene for the purpose of establishing cartels among smaller firms; (3) national emergencies (e.g., an oil crisis), giving the state the right to exercise controls designed to stabilize the national economy; and (4) short-run instability, including rules "that permit government interference in the price of general goods and services in structurally depressed industries, which require concerted action in scrapping surplus equipment."[15] While these formal rules exist, it is private institutions rather than public enterprises and state control through interventionist measures that are responsible primarily for ownership and control of resources in Japan.

A distinguishing feature of Japanese corporate ownership is that the principal stockholders of the large corporations are nearly all corporations with an ownership structure unlike that of other OECD nations. This has advantages. For example, management is free of stockholder influence and can adopt a long-term perspective in decision making rather than feel pressure to continually show short-term profits, since long-term growth is a primary goal of all Japanese large corporations. Low dividends are tolerated as long as the price of the stock does not

---

[12]Public-sector labor unions should not be confused with the private-sector enterprise unions discussed in Chapter 9.

[13]Sakibara Eisuke and Noguchi Yukio, "Organization for Economic Reconstruction," in Okimoto and Rohlen, eds., *Inside the Japanese System*, p. 52.

[14]Organization for Economic Cooperation and Development, *OECD Economic Outlook* (Paris: OECD, 1989), p. 22.

[15]Lester C. Thurow, ed., *The Management Challenge: Japanese Views* (Cambridge, MA: The MIT Press, 1986), pp. 174–175.

decline. However, when stock prices begin to decline and dividends fall, as has occurred since 1990 due to a recessionary trend, there are few individuals and institutional investors interested in investing in Japanese firms. This has resulted in declining stock prices accompanied by low levels of capital investment. Some argue this trend spells an end to the "corporate capitalism" form of ownership in Japan.[16]

Much publicity has been devoted to Japanese working rules pertaining to trade. Conflict between foreign and domestic firms, and subsequently between foreign and Japanese government officials, has grown more intense since the mid-1960s. At the heart of the conflict are Japanese protectionist policies. Such policies, by which the state exercises control over the flow of trade, have in the eyes of foreign firms denied foreign producers of certain goods and services fair access to the Japanese market. Some Western observers cite economic xenophobia as the main reason for current protective trade policies in Japan. They note that since the late nineteenth century when Japan began to industrialize, a national goal has been to establish "an economy owned, operated, and supplied by Japanese firms."[17]

During the postwar reconstruction effort in the early 1950s, Japan faced a severe balance of payments problem and was about to embark on a full-scale industrialization effort to overcome the threat of foreign domination. Nearly all raw materials, fuel supplies, nonprocessed foodstuffs, and some capital equipment had to be imported, so external (i.e., non-Japanese) manufacturers of these goods faced few restrictions. When foreign producers of other manufactured products sought entry into Japan's market, they faced public controls in the form of high tariffs and quotas, especially on those products that had been identified as central to the nation's export promotion and import substitution policies. Japan has been accused of dragging its feet since the early 1960s on measures to facilitate access to its market.

Japanese policymakers, especially leaders of MITI, have been quick to defend their protectionist measures. In the past they used the infant industry argument, and stressed the vital role of export promotion in their reconstruction and growth strategy as a source of needed foreign exchange and as a contributor to the nation's aggregate demand. A casual observer may not appreciate the vital importance the Japanese attach to foreign trade. The fact that the value of exports plus imports as a percentage of GDP are lower in Japan (generally under 20 percent) than every other OECD nation except the United States underestimates international trade's contribution to the economy. Japan is almost completely dependent upon imports for key raw materials, energy supplies, and some basic foodstuffs. Remembering the years of food shortages after World War II, being self-sufficient in rice production is considered vital to the nation's interests.[18]

[16]See Hiroshi Okumura, "Japan's Corporate Capitalism in Peril," *Japanese Economic Studies*, 21, 4 (Summer 1993), 3–24.

[17]Lincoln, *Japan: Facing Economic Maturity*, pp. 74, 75.

[18]It is important to recognize that "Japanese equate national security with food security and food security with rice . . . [and that] many aspects of Japanese life—social, religious, artistic, dietary—are linked somehow with rice." See Ni'ide Makoto, "Rice Imports and Implications," *Japan Quarterly* (January–March 1994), p. 20.

Subsidies to rice farmers led to overproduction and introduction of working rules in the early 1970s to reduce the acreage devoted to rice production. The recent poor harvest (1993) has required that Japan import rice, and this has served to reduce the nation's willingness to open up its agricultural markets to the extent desired by member nations participating in the General Agreement on Tariffs and Trade discussions.

A number of manufacturing industries export a large proportion of their total output. The nation's successful trade policies and the subsequent rapid shift in its balance of trade position vis-à-vis nearly every other nation have prompted foreign firms and their governments to claim they are victims of unfair trade practices. Japan counters by emphasizing that productive efficiency, not public control over the flow of trade, is the source of its trade success and that its own exports face trade restrictions.

In distribution, small retailers have felt threatened by the large department store and supermarket, each of which has begun to appear in Japan over the last two decades. The ability of small retailers to exercise control over their markets and inhibit larger distributors from entering their markets has persisted in the face of rapid economic growth and modernization. This is due to their political influence which led to the introduction of a working rule designed to protect them from competition—The Large-Scale Retail Store Law—passed in 1974. Under this rule large retail stores (either Japanese or foreign owned) must receive government permission to enter a market, and small retailers have considerable influence over the national and local government. Their political power reflects the historical importance of the small retail institution. "Japan's vast distribution system is rooted culturally in the life of its agricultural past and small villages. Even Japan's bigger cities are no more than an assemblage of villages and neighborhoods."[19]

MARKETS, TRADITION, AND STATE GUIDANCE AS SOCIAL PROCESSES FOR COORDINATING ECONOMIC ACTIVITY

Introduction

Overall, unregulated markets are the social process which coordinates a majority of Japan's production and distribution decisions, with a modest role for traditional processes. Neither the state nor the private sector is subservient to the other, but authorities from both sides seek a common ground from which to pursue activities beneficial to the firms and the nation. While guidance of the

[19]Charles J. McMillan, *The Japanese Industrial System* (New York: Walter de Gruyter, 1984), p. 242.

economy from foreign and Japanese public institutions has been prevalent in varying degrees, "direct government involvement" in the Japanese economy has been declining in importance since the late 1950s.[20] Currently state guidance over economic activities is focused primarily on international trade, agriculture, environmental matters, and state-private cooperation in research and development of new technology.

Role of Markets

One Japanese economist describes the private sector as being comprised of both market and organized ("extra-market" institutions—e.g., *keiretsu*) elements.[21] In the case of the *keiretsu* reciprocity among members occurs, which represents a type of transaction used to integrate the social and economic spheres of the economy. The existence of such organizations, however, does not inhibit strong competition for greater market shares, if for no other reason than the Japanese propensity to rank everything and accord the greatest prestige to the largest firm in an industry. The organized elements primarily serve to "provide an orderly structure within which the interplay between private companies takes place."[22] Despite the publicity given to those industries which have prospered under state guidance, there are also many Japanese products (e.g., tape recorders, television sets) that have achieved rapid export growth through market competition without receiving significant state aid.

Role of Tradition

There are two cases in which tradition is important in coordinating production and distribution activities. First, manufacture of cotton and silk textiles and raw silk is still concentrated in the same districts of Japan where output and trade originated before 1868. Second, two principal features of industrial relations in most large Japanese corporations today—a seniority-based system of rewards and lifetime employment expectations—have their roots in the pre-1868 commercial house which was organized as "an artificial or simulated kinship group . . . [where] the employees were quasi-members of the family."[23]

It is widely held that employment relations, like many other interpersonal relationships in Japan, reflect the social relations peculiar to the nation. The Japanese attitude traditionally has been that they are members of a family, associates distinguishable by rank but sharing a common purpose. Their employer is expected to be paternalistic, which today means that high priority is assumed to be placed upon maintenance of employment, fringe benefits such as bonuses, and other benefits agreed upon during collective bargaining. It should be

[20]Lincoln, *Japan: Facing Economic Maturity*, pp. 16, 17.

[21]Okimoto and Rohlen, eds., *Inside the Japanese System*, p. 40.

[22]Ibid.

[23]Kanji Haitani, *The Japanese Economic System* (Lexington, MA: D. C. Heath & Co., 1976), p. 13.

kept in mind that this employment scheme applies to less than half of the labor force—those employed in large firms or by the government. Workers employed in most small- and medium-sized firms face a competitive labor market with no guarantee of job tenure.

Planning

In this section the aspects of state guidance (referred to as *gyosei-shido* by the Japanese) that will be examined are economic planning, industrial and fiscal policies, and agricultural and environmental policies, as these aspects are practiced in Japan. Since 1952, there has been no elite group of authorities engaged in central planning activities. The role of the state has not been to force economic growth or other conditions. The type of guidance provided by the state is "unique," although its impact on the entire economy "should not be overestimated."[24] Japanese "planning" and industrial policy measures consist of establishing guidelines and working cooperatively with the private sector rather than using coercion to direct production and distribution activities. The guidance by the state has taken the form of "intervention without legal endorsement," for there are few formal rules for state guidance activities.[25]

The Japanese state seeks coordination primarily through decentralized decision making by private firms combined with state planning and industrial policies. The market-planning link is assured by the state through the *ringi-sei* decision-making process whereby both sides agree on the goals and policy measures before any actions are taken. Paternalistic guidance of the state has been generally accepted, for the state has a history dating back to 1868 of successfully initiating industrial development through activities such as supplying the initial capital for investment (e.g., for the shipbuilding industry). The lengthy tenure of the Liberal Democratic Party, faith in the efficient, capable bureaucracy, especially MITI, and favorable (as perceived by the Japanese) performance of the economy have served to strengthen acceptance of state guidance of selected industries and economic activities.

Overall, there is not a clear dichotomy in Japan between state guidance and free markets. The Japanese have sought to "link the virtues of planning [and industrial policies] with the virtues of the market, not to use one to thwart the other."[26] Japanese authorities in both the public and private sectors recognize the importance of selected state-directed measures for guiding the economy in a direction deemed desirable by authorities from public and private interest groups.

STATE GUIDANCE—INSTITUTIONS.   The institutions responsible for guidance have been MITI, the Ministry of Finance, the Small and Medium

---

[24]Thurow, *The Management Challenge*, p. 224.
[25]Ibid., p. 173.
[26]Ibid., p. 188.

Enterprise Agency (an affiliate of MITI), and the Economic Planning Agency. MITI has formulated Japan's industrial policy and made some key resource allocation decisions during the early 1950s with the goal of establishing a comparative advantage for selected Japanese firms in international markets. MITI has been instrumental in guiding those sectors and industries deemed most important to national economic goals in the desired direction. Among the reasons for MITI's effectiveness are its immunity from both private- and other public-sector pressure, lengthy tenure with MITI of its top officials, broad authority over most manufacturing sectors, ability to persuade representatives of different groups to reach a consensus, and ability to select the right industries in which to promote economies of scale and protection from foreign competition.[27]

The Ministry of Finance guides particular sectors of the economy. It supervises the activities of the Bank of Japan and, consequently, can influence the economy through monetary policy, credit control, and banking and foreign exchange regulation measures. Its financial power extends further to the supervision of tax collection, drafts and implementation of the national budget, and fiscal investment and loan plan.

Because there are so many small manufacturing and retail firms, the Small and Medium Enterprise Agency was established. Its purpose is to supervise and guide the industrial and commercial behavior of these firms. Among the measures at its disposal are financial assistance at low rates of interest, managerial and technological guidance, and the formation of cooperatives when competition becomes excessive.

STATE GUIDANCE—ECONOMIC PLANNING. Economic planning has been an instrument of Japanese state guidance since the end of World War II. It exemplifies the cooperative interrelationship between the public and private sector. The Economic Planning Agency has customarily drawn up long-range plans. The plans generally consist of macroeconomic guidelines and forecasts, identifying potential problem areas as well as projecting the future value of macroeconomic variables. The economic plans "often do little to influence policy, so that they are far from plans in any real sense"[28] (e.g., French indicative plans— see Chapter 11, or former Soviet Union annual plans—see Chapter 16). The plans have contributed toward furthering Japan's economic development by serving as "the foundation of various public policies like road building, port facilities, and social security";[29] guidelines (i.e., state projections of its future policy measures) which private firms consult when making investment decisions; a device to educate and gain cooperation from those involved (authorities from management, labor, consumer groups, and the academic community) in the planning process.

[27]Ibid., pp. 171–173.
[28]Lincoln, *Japan: Facing Economic Maturity*, p. 22.
[29]Thurow, *The Management Challenge*, pp. 223, 224.

STATE GUIDANCE—INDUSTRIAL POLICY. From 1946–1952 the Occupation Authority was faced with the task of rebuilding and liberalizing an economy suffering from production bottlenecks and rapid inflation. In the classical, free market tradition, Joseph Dodge emphasized and implemented a balanced budget, monetary restraint, low tax rates, and the abolishment of industrial subsidies, while discouraging reliance upon foreign aid. He further emphasized Japanese self-reliance, accumulation of capital, and stable exchange rates. The Japanese subsequently adopted most of these policy measures, effectively preventing cost-push inflation by moderating wage increases for public employees while encouraging heavy capital investment through keeping interest rates low to make labor more productive. Mobility of labor within firms has contributed to stable real wages and rising productivity. Deviations from the free market policy have been most obvious (especially before 1980) in the subsidization of key industries through credit rationing and artificially low rates of interest under the guidance of the Bank of Japan.

After regaining independence, Japanese industrial policy was designed to guide industrial development by allocating key resources, protecting domestic firms from foreign competition, urging voluntary compliance with goals jointly established by the state and affected industries, as well as relying upon competitive markets. After 1952 the Industrial Structure Council drafted a basic strategy proposal, which it submitted to MITI for approval. The role of MITI was to guide selected industries by lending them scarce credit, assist in the acquisition of foreign technology, and recommend production levels and prices. MITI focused upon a few key industries, including steel and coal. In addition to credit, imported raw materials were selectively allocated. MITI also protected certain industries from foreign competition. The intent was to modernize selected industries that could lead an export promotion drive into international markets once they became competitive internationally. In addition, the financial system was "closed and tightly regulated" prior to the 1980s.[30] The purpose was to channel high levels of private savings to satisfy demand for investment funds in the private sector. Thus, the state was able to guide the allocation of credit, and this strengthened the ties between the public and private sectors.

During the 1950s and 1960s there were five factors which enabled MITI to guide the economy effectively.[31] First, Japan's trading partners permitted the nation to impose controls in the name of protecting infant industries. Second, all authorities in the public and private sectors agreed that it was in Japan's (and their own) best interest if the state promoted industrial development. Performance between 1868 and 1946 under state guidance created informal rules in favor of state-private sector cooperation. Third, the price of energy, especially oil, was very low. Fourth, the exchange rate between the dollar and yen remained stable at $1 =

[30]Okimoto and Rohlen, eds., *Inside the Japanese System*, p. 39.
[31]Thurow, *The Management Challenge*, pp. 187, 188.

360 yen. As a result, export (and import) prices remained relatively stable. Finally, Japan was *the* newly industrializing nation, for the "dynamic Asian economies" (e.g., China, Hong Kong, Malaysia, Singapore, South Korea, Taiwan, and Thailand) had not yet experienced rapid economic growth.

After 1960 industrial policy measures focused on the rationalization of industry and maximization of economic growth. MITI argued in favor of an industrial policy emphasizing greater capacity for production, especially for export, of heavy metals and chemical industries over light industries. These industries were chosen as key industries, thereby becoming eligible for state assistance. MITI officials estimated that these industries' products faced a high income elasticity of demand in international markets. Officials also believed these industries had the potential to benefit from economies of scale which, in turn, could be achieved through technological progress. Scarce credit, foreign exchange, imported raw materials and other key inputs, and foreign technology were selectively allocated to guarantee that these high-priority industries could rapidly grow through investing in capital equipment. This was in contrast to recommendations made by the Occupation Authority in the early 1950s that Japan should pursue a development strategy which emphasized the manufacture of labor-intensive goods for export, since the nation had an abundance of labor. In opposition, the combined voices of MITI and big business representatives contended that Japan should develop an industrial structure similar to that of Western industrial nations. Fortunately for Japan the views of MITI and business leaders prevailed. They agreed to cooperate in the implementation of policies whereby the productive capacity of heavy and chemical industries, especially their ability to export goods, would receive highest priority. In addition to establishing working rules for allocating scarce natural resources and credit to selected industries, the government chose to protect domestic infant industries from foreign competition. The state recognized that time was needed for technical and marketing expertise to develop, for the quality of products to be improved, for per unit production costs to decline as economies of scale were realized, and for Japanese firms to establish themselves in foreign markets.

The case of heavy metals and chemical industries illustrates the strong role MITI played in guiding the economy during the 1960s. MITI, relying on the use of moral suasion, helped to shape the structure of these industries, guide their product development, ensure an adequate supply of raw materials and energy, and manage trade relations.[32] The ability of MITI and other state institutions to control Japan's industries should not be overstated, however. While successful in guiding Japanese chemical, steel, and other heavy metals industries to become competitive on international markets, MITI's policies have not succeeded for industries such as commercial aircraft and computer software.

---

[32]Bela Balassa and Marcus Noland, *Japan in the World Economy* (Washington, DC: Institute for International Economics, 1988), pp. 35, 36.

Between 1960–1968 there was a fundamental change in policymaker's attitudes toward fiscal policy. The 1947 Finance Act was amended during this period, bringing an end to strict adherence to the balanced budget principle. "This marked a watershed beyond which fiscal policy underwent great changes, and it became possible to adopt strong policies for dealing with business fluctuations."[33] Significant changes in government spending ensued as a rapidly growing economy and changes in informal rules concerning social welfare led to greater public expenditures. Both in absolute terms and as a percentage of GNP, spending on social security, housing, and environmental and welfare programs increased. Japanese economists, like their Western counterparts, had faith that Keynesian countercyclical policy measures could alleviate serious recession through deficit spending and other means to increase aggregate demand. They were encouraged by the era of high economic growth (1955–1970), during which real GNP had increased over 10 percent annually while prices were relatively stable and unemployment remained low. The public believed their incomes would continue to increase unabated. The attitudes of the public and policymakers were an endorsement of state-private cooperation.

Faith in policymaking was shattered by the oil crises of the 1970s. The oil shocks and international recession hit Japan hard, resulting in persistent inflation, higher unemployment, and lower growth rates (e.g., 4 percent to 5 percent). Personal savings rates fell, capital coefficients rose, and the rate of capital formation declined, as did factor productivity. The public began to blame a lack of antitrust enforcement for rising prices, leading the Japanese courts to rule against MITI's desire to promote collusion among particular firms.[34] Since then MITI's activities for guiding Japanese industry have been curtailed. One other factor contributed to the declining role of the state in coordinating economic activity—concern over a rising government budget deficit. A measure taken to rectify the problem was the reduction of the number of government-owned enterprises while granting permission to privately owned firms to compete with some remaining government-owned enterprises.

Over the past decade, as Japan became a mature economy, state guidance activities have been focused on promoting high-technology industries as well as maintaining certain protective trade practices and providing subsidies, especially to rice producers. The state has promoted development of the computer industry by insisting that public agencies and universities only purchase computers produced by Japanese firms, and by investing heavily in computer research. Changing informal rules within the business community in favor of a diminished role for the state in economic matters led to further changes in formal rules in the early 1980s. The new rules included privatization of a number of public enterprises, which resulted in a decline in the number of government workers as

---

[33]Takafusa Nakamura, *The Postwar Japanese Economy: Its Development and Structure* (Tokyo: University of Tokyo Press, 1981), p. 130.
[34]Lincoln, *Japan: Facing Economic Maturity*, p. 11.

well as a reduction in public funding of health insurance and social security.

STATE GUIDANCE—AGRICULTURAL AND ENVIRONMENTAL POLICIES. Two areas in which state guidance of production and distribution activities either has remained or become more significant are agriculture and environment-growth-leisure issues. The plight of agricultural workers and small farmers has drawn much attention throughout the postwar period. Programs to improve the average income of agricultural families have come at the expense of taxpayers, consumers, and landlords. The conflict has spilled over into the bureaucracy, for the high cost of the agricultural support programs has created difficulties for fiscal policymakers. Conflicts between agricultural (especially rice growers) and nonagricultural interests began immediately after World War II. Occupation Authority forces moved quickly to improve the plight of those workers (nearly half the labor force) engaged in agriculture. Aiming to avoid internal political unrest, the Occupation Authority imposed working rules which effectively changed the status of the agricultural workers from tenants to peasant proprietors with small average land holdings

Two major working rules, the Agricultural Land Act of 1952 and the Basic Agricultural Law of 1961, have served to reinforce the predominance of fragmented, dispersed land holdings and commit the state to public works projects designed to modernize agriculture, such as irrigation, soil improvement, and land conservation. The rules provide security to farmers, albeit at considerable public expense (see "Performance," p. 215) through protective trade barriers and price supports. Farm incomes have been maintained by the agricultural policy which seeks to achieve parity between industrial and agricultural incomes. The conflict concerning government support for Japanese farmers at the expense of taxpayers and consumers can be expected to continue, just as it continues in the United States and the European Community.

Due to the unprecedented rate of economic growth, conflict was bound to arise between proponents of rapid growth and long workweeks and those seeking to protect the environment and provide the average Japanese worker with more hours of leisure. The Japanese decision to maintain rapid economic growth led to the perpetuation of the longest average workweek among the OECD nations, and to inevitable spillover costs in the form of pollution, manifested by rising death rates from lung cancer. The emphasis on growth over environmental interests reached a peak in the late 1960s. Chemical pollutants had fouled Japan's air and water, exacerbating problems such as asthma and lung cancer while creating new health hazards such as Minamata disease, which caused pollution-related birth defects. Urban congestion and automobile pollution also imposed high social costs.

Partial resolution of the growth-environment conflict began in the late 1960s. Societal goals shifted away from an obsession with maximization of output toward greater emphasis on leisure and other qualities of life. People realized that compared to other OECD nations Japan was devoting relatively few funds toward public goods and social services. In response, the Japanese government shifted its industrial policy by facilitating the development of high technology (e.g., computers and other electronic products), fashion, and knowledge industries (e.g., information systems, computer software). State guidance promoted Japanese investment abroad in industries likely to pollute Japan's environment. More public resources were devoted to protecting the environment, longer vacation periods for workers were proposed, and there was greater public spending on housing, hospitals, and schools. These efforts represented a significant reversal of the 1952–1970 approach in which growth of output was given absolute priority and consumer goods and social welfare were treated residually.

Summary of Japanese Economic
Policymaking Since 1952

Overall, there has been a blend of classical supply-side and Keynesian approaches to growth and stabilization, combined with Japanese-style guidance activities (*gyosei-shido*). Since the mid-1960s the extent of guidance has diminished each decade. This has been in direct response to the favorable (in the Japanese view) performance of the economy after state policies (especially those protecting Japanese firms from foreign investment and imports) enabled selected industries to become competitive in the international market. As reflected by the data in the "Performance of the Economy" section, these policies have contributed to keeping inflation, interest rates, and taxes low while offering a conducive, supportive environment for the private sector to achieve growth in all sectors, especially heavy industries.

INSTITUTIONAL CHANGE DRIVEN BY FOREIGN AUTHORITIES AND NEW TECHNOLOGY

Two major factors were instrumental in stimulating changes in Japanese attitudes and, subsequently, the nation's working rules and principal institutions prior to the early 1990s. First, the outsider influence of the Occupation Authority between 1946 and 1952 established a new political structure as well as new legal foundations for business, agriculture, and labor. The major reforms included the breakup of the *zaibatsu*, the antimonopoly laws, land reform, and labor democratization. In order to purge Japan of militaristic, antidemocratic attitudes, wartime national leaders in the bureaucracy, industry, and finance were prohibited from serving in public or corporate office.

The second major factor was the industrial development policies pursued through state-private cooperation in the years following reestablishment of independence, which stimulated introduction of new technology on an unprecedented scale. Policies such as subsidizing key industries to enable them to achieve economies of scale and encouraging the borrowing of Western technology facilitated the rapid expansion of industrial and financial institutions. New financial institutions, such as the Japan Development Bank, were designed to stimulate greater savings and investment levels and to direct investment funds to high-priority industries. While public institutions such as MITI and public enterprises are still prevalent today, their relative influence in the economy has diminished while private-sector institutions have become more important. Among the private institutions that have flourished in postwar Japan are the *keiretsu*, the *sogo shosha*, and independent firms.

Industrial development in Japan has enabled midsized firms independent of the giant *keiretsu* to prosper. These firms have attained a scale which enables them to raise funds through the securities market, to utilize modern management techniques, and to develop and mass produce their own products. The development of independent firms is evidence that rapid economic growth has made the Japanese industrial organization more fluid. Independent firms prospered while adapting to changes in the nation's industrial structure. One Japanese economist observes that these firms "enlarged their scale in answer to it [i.e., growth], and secured a monopolistic character either through a high market share or innovation, and grew into leading enterprises."[35] A working rule introduced in 1983 reformed the over-the-counter securities market and permitted midsized firms to offer their stocks publicly. The ability to raise large sums of capital has enabled some to prosper, for it gave entrepreneurs such as Mesaru Ibuka, founder of Sony Corporation, the opportunity to put into practice his view that technology, research and development, and mass production devoted to producing a specialized product should be the basis for the modern firm to stimulate demand.

Until the early 1990s certain features unique to Japanese institutions had been preserved rather than replaced. Industrial relations, the significance of small firms in distribution, agriculture, and manufacturing, and the *keiretsu* groups all continued to retain elements of traditional Japanese behavior while operating in a dynamic economy. While convenience stores and Western-style shopping centers are becoming established, the pace is very slow.

However, the pattern of institutional stability does not appear to be persisting. The Liberal Democratic Party's 38-year reign ended in the summer of 1993, and since then ruling coalitions have been fragile. The Japan Renewal Party lasted only eight months and suffered from criticism similar to that leveled at the Liberal Democrats—namely, that back-room deals rather than open discussion of issues characterized the political decision-making process. Significant institutional reform will require greatly decreasing the cozy, symbiotic relationship among political party (or parties), bureaucracy, business-sector relationship where mutual assistance based upon money and votes is dominant over open discussion and resolution of Japan's economic problems. It is becoming an informal rule that "[t]riangular power structure may have provided a stable

---

[35]Kazuo Sato, ed., *Industry and Business* (New York: M. E. Sharpe, 1980), p. 280.

foundation for Japan's economic growth, but it is now proving a serious impediment to Japan's continued well-being."[36]

The formation of a trade union confederation known as *Rengo* is leading to tougher negotiations between management and labor. Exacerbating this situation is the impact of the early 1990s' recession, which is leading some firms to deviate from the lifetime employment scheme. Both blue-collar and white-collar workers are being offered incentives to retire early, or have been laid off by firms forced to reduce costs. Such change has been "profoundly disturbing" to the Japanese people who had become accustomed to the informal rule that trusted large firms to provide loyal workers both a livelihood and lifetime security.[37] Slow economic growth, greater competition (particularly from its Asian neighbors) for its exports in the face of a very strong yen, and a large baby-boomer generation reaching maturity meaning a glut of persons qualified for middle- and upper-level management positions have led many Japanese firms to adjust their employment relations. Some firms are moving away from seniority pay schemes in favor of merit pay or individual salary negotiations. Such negotiations are becoming more widely adopted as the globalization of Japanese firms requires different compensation for management depending upon their geographical location. Overall, it appears that lifetime employment and seniority pay will gradually be replaced by new schemes more consistent with the contemporary economy's domestic and external conditions.

There is evidence that changes in attitudes are occurring which favor fewer hours worked and more time spent in leisure; greater emphasis on consumption; less support for agricultural interests in favor of lower food prices; more concern for the environment; better housing; and the provision of greater income security for senior citizens. As a result of growing disparities in wealth, some Japanese are beginning to identify with a lower middle class, believing they possess fewer material goods and enjoy less leisure time than the nouveau riche Japanese. Relaxation of the Large-Scale Retail Store Law has meant expansion of mass retailers and greater availability of lower-priced consumer goods. Small retail establishments likely will persist, for their close relationships with consumers, warehouse function, and quality service plus convenient location are all valued by Japanese shoppers. However, their relative importance may be reduced in future decades should mass retailers be able to offer similar products at reduced prices, as they have throughout Western Europe and the United States.

[36]Hiroshi, "Political Reform: Much Ado About Nothing?" p. 251.
[37]Yamamoto Harumi, "The Lifetime Employment System Unravels," *Japan Quarterly* (October–December 1993), p. 382.

PERFORMANCE OF THE ECONOMY: RISING FROM A POVERTY LEVEL TO BECOME ONE OF THE WORLD'S RICHEST NATIONS[38]

Although suffering from a recession the past few years, in both absolute and relative terms, economic growth in Japan has been more favorable since 1960 than growth in the United States, France, Sweden, or the European Community (EC) (see Table 10-1), although the economy no longer achieves rates in excess of 10 percent that were characteristic of the 1955–1970 period. Although Japan's growth since 1980 generally has exceeded that of its industrial rivals nearly every year, that difference has been narrowing, particularly vis-à-vis the United States.

Unemployment rates have been consistently more favorable in Japan than in the United States, France, and the EC, and slightly better than in Sweden until the last few years when Sweden's rate increased dramatically. As Table 10-2 indicates, Japan's unemployment has been continually below 3 percent, although in recent years the number of overtime hours worked has declined. One practice that contributes to low unemployment is awarding semiannual bonuses that are a sizable portion of a typical worker's annual income. This practice is consistent with the theories of John Maynard Keynes. Keynes, who favored minimizing unemployment, feared that during a recession when prices fell, rising real wages of employees would lead employers to lay off workers if wages were inflexible, since employers would be unable to raise prices so as to maintain constant real wages. In Japan this problem is avoided, for if sales decline semiannual bonuses are reduced or eliminated, effectively cutting wages, while workers are retained.

TABLE 10-1 Real Gross Domestic Product, Average Annual Change, 1960–1994

	1960–68	1967–76	1977–86	1987–94[1]
Japan	10.2%	7.0%	4.0%	3.1%
United States	4.5	2.6	2.7	2.3
France	5.4	4.3	2.2	2.0
Sweden	4.4	3.2	1.7	0.6
EC[2]	4.6	4.0	2.1	2.2

[1]1994 is estimated.

[2]Prior to 1973 member nations included Belgium, France, Italy, Luxembourg, the Netherlands, and West Germany. In 1973 Denmark, Ireland, and the United Kingdom became members. Greece joined the European Community in 1981, with Portugal and Spain following suit in 1986. The EC become the European Union (EU) in 1992.

Source: Organization for Economic Cooperation and Development, *Historical Statistics: 1960–1987* (Paris: OECD, 1989), p. 44; OECD, 54 (December 1993), p. 126.

[38]In the early 1950s Japan and Zambia had a comparable level of economic development.

Inflation in Japan was comparable to that of other nations during the macroeconomic instability problems caused by sharp oil price increases during the 1970s and early 1980s. Since then Japan demonstrated a greater ability than its industrial counterparts to curtail price increases as inflation has consistently fallen below 2 percent (see Table 10-3).

TABLE 10-2   Unemployment,[1] 1973–1994

	1973–82	1983–92	1993	1994
Japan	2.0%	2.5%	2.5%	2.9%
United States	6.9	6.7	6.9	6.5
France	5.2	9.7	11.7	12.2
Sweden	2.2	2.6	8.2	8.3
EC	5.6	9.9	11.3	—

[1]For 1973–1992 figures are averages of standardized unemployment rates. OECD defines the unemployed as persons of working age who are without work, available for work, and actively seeking employment. The unemployment rate is expressed as a percentage of the total labor force, which included all members of the armed forces.

Source: The 1973–1992 and 1993 data are from OECD, 54 (December 1993), p. 144; the 1994 figure is the March figure from *The Economist*, April 16–22, 1994, p. 114.

TABLE 10-3   Inflation,[1] 1974–1994

	1974–82	1983–92	1993	1994[2]
Japan	8.4%	1.8	1.0%	-1.0%
United States	9.0	3.8	2.5	2.6
France	10.4	4.4	1.5	1.6
Sweden	10.4	6.7	1.9	0.3
EC	12.2	5.3	—	—

[1]Average annual percentage change in the consumer prices.

[2]Projection of annual rate based upon first three months.

Source: 1974–92 figures are from OECD, 54 (December 1993), p. 140; the 1993 and 1994 figures are from *The Economist*, April 16–22, 1994, p. 114.

High rates of investment growth (see Table 10-4) have been one factor contributing to prosperity, as Keynes forcefully argued. Japan has maintained growth rates of investment greater than the United States in many years. Investment in capital spending has risen to expand output capacity, the main purpose of which is to increase exports of products such as laser copiers, automobiles, and steel. One factor promoting such rates of capital investment is Japan's historically high gross savings rates, which contribute toward keeping interest rates low. The Japanese anticipate a worst-case scenario when making savings decisions, and due to less government spending on social insurance must finance a larger portion of their retirement income than their counterparts in other industrialized nations. Finally, the semiannual bonuses earned by workers of large enterprises are perceived as transitory income, and as such a high percentage of these earnings is saved.

TABLE 10-4   Growth of Gross Fixed Capital Formation,[1] 1967–1994

	1967–76	1977–86	1987–94
Japan	8.4%	3.3%	5.1%
United States	3.0	4.2	2.5
France	4.4	0.4	2.0
Sweden	1.8	0.8	-1.3
EC	2.9	0.9	2.9

[1]Average annual percentage change.

Source: OECD, 54 (December 1993), p. 130.

Capital stock in Japan has grown rapidly since the mid 1950s, although the prolonged recession of the early 1990s may result in significant declines in industrial capital spending. Continued growth of capital stock, when combined with the nation's technological progress and management skills, has created impressive productivity gains and lower rates of increase in unit labor costs compared to Japan's industrial rivals (see Tables 10-5 and 10-6). Rising productivity, in turn, has contributed to lower inflation over the past decade, since wage increases have lagged behind the growth in labor productivity.

Performance in the international and public sectors provides helpful information about the economy's behavior. Despite appreciation of the yen, Japanese export growth has exceeded that of imports since 1975, outpacing comparable performances in the United States or EC. Average annual contribution of net exports to the growth of Japan's gross national product over the 1980–1987 period was over 3.5 percent, compared to -0.4 percent and about 0.0 percent for the United States and France, respectively.[39] There are signs that the combination of a very strong yen (about 85 yen to $1 in Spring 1995) and competition from the maturing dynamic Asian economies are slowing the growth of Japanese exports. Since 1985 Japan's share of the world merchandise exports has fallen from about 11 percent to 9 percent, while that of the United States has risen from the same 11 percent to almost 14 percent.[40]

[39]Balassa and Noland, *Japan in the World Economy*, p. 11.

[40]For a Japanese perspective on this problem, see Masaki Sato, "The Dulling of Japan's Competitive Edge," *Economic Eye*, 14, 4 (Winter 1993), 25–28.

TABLE 10-5   Productivity in the Business Sector,[1] 1960–1991

	1960–73	1974–79	1980–91
Japan	5.5%	2.1%	1.9%
United States	1.6	0.2	0.5
France	3.9	1.8	1.5
Sweden	2.7	0.3	0.6

[1]Average annual percentage change.

Source: OECD, 54 (December 1992), p. 189.

TABLE 10-6   Unit Labor Costs in the Business Sector[1]

	1970–76	1977–86	1987–94
Japan	12.3%	2.2%	0.9%
United States	6.3	6.2	3.4
France	10.1	8.0	1.8
Sweden	10.2	7.9	4.8

[1]Average annual percentage change.

Source: OECD 54 (December 1992), p. 137.

As a percentage of GNP, central government spending (see Table 10-7), social security transfer payments, and taxes in Japan all have remained comparable or below those of its major industrial competitors, although the gap has been narrowing. Low levels of defense spending also contribute to Japan's ability to hold government expenditures down while still promoting growth. Whereas the United States and France spend about 7 percent and 4 percent, respectively, of their GNP on national defense, the comparable degree of expenditures in Japan has been only about 1 percent since 1946.[41]

TABLE 10-7   General Government Outlays[1]

	1978–86	1987–94	1995 (ESTIMATED)
Japan	32.0%	32.5%	36.4%
United States	32.3	33.7	33.5
France	49.0	51.4	54.5
Sweden	62.0	63.1	69.0

[1]As a percentage of nominal GDP. Current disbursements which consist primarily of final government consumption expenditures, interest on the public debt, subsidies, and social security transfers to households.

Source: OECD, 54 (December 1993), p. 148.

The one sector of the economy that contributed to Japan's immediate postwar development but has since become a drain on government expenditures

[41]*Japanese Economic Journal*, February 14, 1987, p. 6.

is agriculture. Land reform, widespread application of biological and chemical technology, capitalization of agriculture, and price supports for farmers, especially those producing rice, all contributed to dramatic increases in agricultural output. Although the number of person-hours devoted to agriculture has declined by over two thirds since 1946 and the amount of cultivable land has decreased while the number of part-time farmers has increased, growth rates of agricultural production compared favorably to the United States, United Kingdom, and France until the last decade.[42] Production, however, has been achieved at considerable cost to taxpayers and consumers.

As would be expected in any rapidly industrializing nation, agriculture's contribution to gross domestic product has declined steadily—from 18 percent in 1940, to 6 percent in 1970, to less than 3 percent in the late 1980s.[43] Government support policies, which enable farmers to realize parity with those not engaged in agriculture, have recently come under severe criticism. Free trade advocates, while recognizing that the agricultural sector's productivity is the highest in the world, argue for phasing out protectionism due to rising costs of the government support programs. To a degree their cries are being heard, for meager harvests in the early 1990s have meant that emergency rice imports have been required. Rice supports have received the most publicity, for the cost of this program is over 40 percent of the total agricultural support budget. It has been estimated that by subtracting the world price (cost to import) from the domestic producer price, and multiplying this figure by the quantity of each good produced in Japan, the difference (consumer burden) exceeds one-half the value of domestic agricultural production. If one compared the value of gross agricultural output in 1978 (10.4 trillion yen) to the cost of protection as computed previously (6 trillion yen) in higher consumer expenditures plus the local government subsidies (2 trillion yen), the effective protection cost was about 8 trillion yen for a 10 trillion yen industry.[44]

Standard of Living

In terms of four general categories of living standards (health, security, income distribution and consumption, and negative externalities), Japanese living standards have been improving on an absolute basis.

HEALTH.   Average life expectancy in Japan ranks among the highest in the world, while infant mortality rates are among the lowest. There have been, however, rising suicide rates, a greater incidence of heart attacks among chief executives of large Japanese firms, and an increasing number of fatalities and injuries from automobile accidents. This last factor is attributable to the increasing

---

[42]Ryoshin Minami, *The Economic Development of Japan: A Quantitative Study* (London: The Macmillan Press, 1986), Chapter 4.

[43]Ibid., p. 93.

[44]Yoshikazu Kano, "Japanese Agriculture: It Can Be Revitalized," *Japanese Economic Studies*, 13 (Spring 1985), 34–66.

number of automobiles and passenger miles in a densely populated nation.

SECURITY.   Rising incomes and low levels of unemployment have provided economic security to the Japanese. Personal security is high, as indicated by the low incidence of homicides and robberies. Japan has fewer than two murders per 100,000 members of the population versus almost ten in the United States, and only about 1 percent as many robberies compared to the United States.[45] Social security benefits as a percentage of national income are well below those of other industrial nations. It should be noted that personal income taxes are considerably lower in Japan, and that the government is committed to increasing social security spending gradually as part of a program to create a Japanese-style welfare society.

INCOME DISTRIBUTION AND CONSUMPTION.   In terms of income distribution, Japan is slightly below the OECD average. Disposable personal income in Japan has been increasing at over 6 percemt annually in per capita real terms, compared to about 2 percent in the United States.[46] In absolute terms food, housing, and personal assets (e.g., automobiles, electronic goods, home appliances) are all more accessible to the average family today than three decades ago. The percentage of dwellings with telephones and toilets increased over 300 percent and 600 percent, respectively, between 1963 and 1983.[47] Domestic prices in Japan, however, are a growing cause for consternation. Japanese who travel abroad and compare their standard of living with that enjoyed by most Europeans or U.S. residents realize that their material standard of living is lower, especially considering the wealth of their nation and the proportion of their lives they devote to their company rather than to leisure. Two factors which keep prices high have been Japan's trade barriers and traditional retail distribution system.

Evidence indicates that the combined effect of tariff and nontariff barriers has created a relatively higher ratio of Japanese domestic prices to world market prices of agricultural and some nonagricultural products than in the United States or the EC.[48] The Japanese family pays a higher percentage of its income for food, housing, and utilities than do families in other OECD nations. MITI authorities have met with Japanese business leaders to encourage them to reduce the differences in prices between products sold in Japan and similar products sold abroad. There are many consumer products that are more expensive in Tokyo than in U.S. or EC cities. One explanation from Japanese business leaders is that these

---

[45]"The Secret of Japan's Safe Streets," *The Economist*, April 16–22, 1994, pp. 38–40. Factors cited for the low crime rates include cultural homogeneity, no illiteracy or poverty, few immigrants, very low incidence of drug abuse, close relationship between police officers and the public, strict gun control, and the ability to prosecute criminals.

[46]Minami, *The Economic Development of Japan*, pp. 211, 395.

[47]Lincoln, *Japan: Facing Economic Maturity*, p. 51.

[48]For further discussion, see Balassa and Noland, *Japan in the World Economy*, pp. 49–62.

differentials are due to the traditional system of distribution and more demanding product standards in Japan.

Examples of nontariff barriers that inhibit the penetration of foreign products in Japanese markets include arbitrary changes in the size of import quotas; rules which directly limit imports of certain products (e.g., steel); time-consuming procedures, including lot testing of products at the point of entry into Japan; resistance toward foreign construction firms during public procurement bidding procedures; resistance by trading companies to distribute imported goods that would adversely affect Japanese industries; state encouragement of mergers and collusive agreements among Japanese firms to assist depressed domestic industries; and the Japanese buyers' preferences for purchasing Japanese-produced goods from insiders (e.g., computers). These practices have resulted in considerably lower import penetration levels in Japan than in other nations. As a percentage of apparent consumption (i.e., domestic production plus imports, minus exports), imports of manufactured goods are about 5 percent in Japan versus 14 percent and 27 percent in the United States and France, respectively.[49] Finally, the theory of comparative advantage would predict greater intraindustry specialization in Japan than actually exists. Overall, Japan can be considered an outlier relative to trade behavior of other industrialized nations due to her tariff and nontariff barriers, including the ethnocentric tendency to deal with insiders.[50]

Japan's distribution network contributes to high consumer prices due to high labor costs caused by low productivity of retail workers, a large profit margin between the manufacturing and retail level due to the many layers of intermediaries in the traditional distribution channel, the absence of active price competition among small retailers, and the ability (until recently) of small retailers to inhibit entry of larger, more efficient firms (e.g., department stores). In fact, retailers have been able to cooperate with producers so that consumer prices are relatively uniform. One anomaly of this system is that certain Japanese products are cheaper to purchase abroad than domestically.

NEGATIVE EXTERNALITIES.   Some unfortunate by-products of rapid economic growth are evident in Japan. The degree to which they are harmful has been exacerbated by the high population density. The most serious problems have been air and water pollution, traffic congestion, and a lack of parks and other recreation areas. Under state guidance Japan has been devoting more resources toward alleviating each problem, especially pollution. The area devoted to local parks has more than doubled since 1970.

SUMMARY.   Different conclusions have been drawn regarding the extent to which the Japanese people have realized improvements in their well-

---

[49]Ibid., pp. 62, 63.
[50]Mordechai E. Kreinin, "How Closed Is the Japanese Market?" *The World Economy*, 11, 7 (1988), p. 541.

being. Ryoshin Minami argues that post-World War II economic growth has brought about a rapid improvement in "net national welfare." He defends his contention by maintaining that growth has created the necessary resources to "reduce factors detrimental to that welfare."[51]

Mosoko Ozawa believes that greater affluence and equality in Japan are a myth. He recognizes that Japan's Gini coefficient is slowly declining, and that most Japanese believe they are part of a middle class. He analyzes trends in consumption, especially costs of certain goods and services, to determine whether people are becoming better off. Among the negative features he cites are high levels of consumer credit (mostly due to home mortgages), the high cost of lower quality of Japanese housing in terms of area per person and sanitation facilities, long workweeks and few vacation days, and the widening of income differentials between certain groups. The income differential trend has been especially pronounced between males and females, workers in large versus small firms, and older (i.e., those with seniority) versus younger workers. Ozawa further argues that Japan's income distribution is less equally divided than the OECD average, and that government attempts to redistribute income through taxation and income transfer programs have not worked well.[52] Overall, Ozawa believes that the upgrading of consumer demand over the past decades has been limited to the relatively small proportion of wealthy workers. Another critic agrees, arguing "the production-oriented economic policy has neglected people."[53]

The Japanese are beginning to demand more leisure time. Japanese employees work more hours and take fewer vacation days than do workers in any other industrial nation. Although the average workweek in many large firms has been reduced to the five-day workweek typical of most OECD nations, the typical Japanese factory worker and manager continues to spend nearly as much time on the job. This is because free time on week days has become shorter as workers are required to do extra work each day as a trade-off for more free time on weekends. Nonscheduled work required of managers has also increased, requiring some to devote part of their weekend to satisfying their supervisors. Recently these factory workers spent 43.7 hours a week on the job, versus 38.4 and 35.6 spent by their American and West German counterparts, respectively.[54] The average annual holidays (including weekends) are only about 95 days.[55] Employees may work

[51]Minami, *The Economic Development of Japan*, pp. 404–441. Minami defines net national welfare as "personal consumption expenditures (minus expenditure that is not really personal, e.g., commuting expenses) plus an imputed wage for leisure and housework, and the value of services stemming from ownership of consumer durables, minus expenditure on pollution control." Ibid., p. 408.

[52]Mosoko Ozawa, "Myths of Affluence and Equality," *Japanese Economic Studies*, 14 (Winter 85/86), 30–55.

[53]Tomoko Furugori, "Work Hours and the Quality of Life," *Japanese Economic Studies*, 21, 2 (Winter 1992–93), 19.

[54]Urban C. Lehner, "Japanese May Be Rich, But Are They Satisfied With Quality of Life?" *The Wall Street Journal*, January 9, 1990, p. 1.

[55]*Japanese Economic Journal*, November 1, 1986, p. 11.

weekends to satisfy demand for their product while not taking all of the paid vacation days to which they are entitled. There are indications, however, that attitudes may be changing. The degree of loyalty among Japanese workers is waning, especially among those whose career expectations are not being met by their employers.

Factors Contributing to the Economy's Unprecedented Performance

There is no denying that rapid rates of economic growth in Japan have created environmental problems and that prosperity has not been enjoyed evenly. The nation appears to be addressing these issues, although not at a pace consistent with the values of those who emphasize ecological and egalitarian matters. This section will concentrate on the complex interrelationship of economic, political, social, and external (e.g., international) factors which have contributed to the ability of a small country that is poorly endowed with natural resources to rebuild a devastated nation to such a degree that it currently ranks as the second largest economy (in terms of gross national product) in the world.

The elements of Japan's economic growth will be discussed as they affect productive factors. The following equation will serve as a framework for the presentation: $Y = f[K, L: S, R, T]$.[56] While increases in the quantities and quality of two key inputs, capital (K) and labor hours (L) have been the major factors, the social climate (S), resource endowment (R), and technology (T) have also contributed to Japan's rapid growth by enhancing capital and labor productivity.

Japan's high and sustained rates of investment in capital and its achievement of economies of scale were facilitated by firms' willingness to reinvest a high percentage of their profits, high rates of personal savings, and state guidance—including monetary policies. Through activities of the Bank of Japan and the city banks, firms have been able to secure vital credit at low interest rates when seeking to modernize and expand their capacity. Throughout most of the period from 1952 to the late 1970s, credit was selectively allocated to those industries deemed important to the national purpose.

Japan has invested heavily in improving the quality of its workers. Human capital has been developed through an excellent education system, which enrolls a high percentage of children in preschool (63 percent versus 32 percent in the United States), graduates about 90 percent of its students from high schools (versus 77 percent in the United States), and requires its students to attend high school for about 50 days more each year than is required in the United States.[57]

---

[56]For an attempt to quantify the relative contributions of the main elements of growth, see Kosai and Ogino, *Contemporary Japanese Economy*, pp. 8–11; and Lincoln, *Japan: Facing Economic Maturity*, pp. 14–21, regarding causes of high economic growth between 1953 and 1971.

[57]Yasumasa Tomoda, "Japan's School System as a Mirror for America," *Economic Eye*, 14, 1 (Spring 1993), 30. It is estimated that about half of Japanese high school graduates possess a level of knowledge and analytical skills equivalent to the typical American college graduate.

National standards are established, and the depth of requirement for each subject is high by international standards. High literacy rates and an abundant supply of qualified engineers and scientists have contributed to the favorable increases in labor productivity and to the development of innovative, high-quality industrial and consumer products. It is noteworthy that Japan has about six times as many engineers and one fifteenth as many lawyers per capita as the United States. Japan is "a society which values harmony above rivalry and so shuns litigation and the expensive services of legal and financial consultants."[58]

Considering Japan's poor natural resource endowment, credit for progress can be shared throughout the labor force, for Japan's growth record has been achieved through the cumulative efforts of entrepreneurs, technicians, managers, politicians, bureaucrats, and hard-working, loyal laborers. Cooperation between the state, business leaders, and labor leaders is the norm in this homogeneous, unified society. Pragmatic industrial policies provide an example of harmonious cooperation where resources were selectively allocated to certain firms without much complaint from those not designated to receive special consideration.

The period from 1952 to the late 1960s illustrates the effectiveness of Japanese industrial policies. By 1960 Japan had become an industrialized nation. Manufacturers in selected industries were technologically advanced enough to mass produce a relatively limited number of quality products on a scale which made them highly competitive in international markets. These products included steel, petrochemicals, automobiles, and home electrical appliances. Over the 1956–1980 period, the growth rate of real output for heavy (e.g., metals and metal products, machinery) and chemical industries averaged 11.8 percent annually.[59] Agricultural development was successfully promoted through a unimodal strategy that has been offered as a model to underdeveloped nations.[60] Biological and chemical technology has served to make the productivity of Japanese agricultural land the world's highest.

The Japanese also introduced industrial and managerial reforms, some of which were assimilated from Western nations. Institutional reforms imposed by the Occupation Authority liberalized and democratized the economy. One Japanese executive argues that "Japan's success could never have been achieved without the magnanimity of the United States after World War II."[61] Other reforms involved refining their own type of industrial relations and subcontracting system. Western influence has not radically affected Japanese employment relations, for the traditional personal relationships between employees and their firm have not been traded off in the name of greater

---

[58]Warshaw, *Japan Emerges*, p. 134.

[59]Minami, *The Economic Development of Japan*, p. 131.

[60]Bruce F. Johnston, "The Japanese Model of Agricultural Development: Its Relevance to Developing Nations," Kajushi Ozhawa, Bruce Johnston, and Hiromitsu Kaneda, eds., *Agriculture and Economic Growth: Japan's Experience* (Tokyo: University of Tokyo Press, 1969), pp. 58–102.

[61]Shigekuni Kawamura, "Japanese Management Style," *Japan and the World Economy*, 5 (1993), 289.

productive efficiency. However, there is evidence that the presence of foreign employers in Japan has induced some workers to switch jobs for better pay and a more challenging position—one they could not expect to attain with their previous employer for many years. In 1988 over 4 percent of the work force switched employers, an 80 percent increase over 1983.[62] Management has skillfully exploited the special features of the Japanese social structure to obtain employee loyalty. Workers, feeling they have job security and a benign, paternalistic employer, have shown little resistance when asked to adapt to cost-cutting measures, which require their being mobile or learning to perform new tasks. Their willingness to sacrifice their individual needs in the interest of maintaining harmony while promoting long-term development of their firm has contributed to the continued success of Japanese firms. Japanese managers also have managed to dampen the effects of the yen's appreciation (it was less than 100 yen to the dollar in mid-1995) on the nation's trade balance.

Concentration ratios indicate that although some "large oligopolies" exist in Japan today, vigorous competition among firms, not cartels, is the rule.[63] Innovation, risk taking, and a desire among industrial groups to increase market share have made collective efforts to limit competition between domestic producers relatively ineffective. One Japanese economist credits the success of the nation's multinational corporations to their ability to survive and prosper within a highly competitive domestic market.

> In order to survive the competition at home the companies had to improve the quality of their products and had to introduce automated large-scale production to reduce their costs. The size of the market in Japan is sufficiently large that anyone who could survive the competition in the home market found that their products were also competitive in world markets. Japanese consumers are very selective and demand high-quality goods, so the companies continually had to improve quality.[64]

Japan's poor resource endowment has been overcome through growth of exports, which have increased with the nation's ability to acquire necessary foreign exchange for purchasing resources abroad. Japan has used its coastline and small size to its advantage. Concentration of industries and the development of ports and harbors have held down transportation costs.

Within firms workers excel at intimate exchanges of information and sharing of information. Also, despite remaining faithful to their historical legacy and culture, the Japanese have a talent for borrowing and assimilating foreign technology, and such technology transfer and adaptation have increased

---

[62]Masasayoshi Kanabayashi, "In Japan Employees Are Switching Firms For Better Work, Pay," *The Wall Street Journal*, October 11, 1988, p. 1.

[63]G. C. Allen, *The Japanese Economy* (London: Weidenfeld and Nicolson, 1981), pp. 126–130.

[64]Toyohiro Kono, "Competitive Strategy," *Japanese Economic Studies*, 13 (Fall/Winter 1984/85), 45.

productive efficiency. In fact, Japanese are encouraged to borrow technology. This stems from their patent system, which "aim[s] at avoiding conflict and promoting cooperation" by encouraging Japanese firms to borrow from their competitors before trying to invent similar technology themselves.[65]

Exogenous factors are the final element of growth worth considering. International events such as Occupation Authority reforms, the decision to limit defense spending, and the boost to Japanese exports caused by the Korean War as well as global economic growth throughout the 1950s and 1960s all contributed to promoting economic growth. The impact of the Korean War was prodigious because the value of exports more than doubled between 1949 and 1951. The foreign trade multiplier effect in Japan created increased levels of production and employment and greater business profits, triggering a cumulative upswing in the economy. Further stimulus was provided by $4 billion in "special procurement" payments given to United Nations forces stationed in Japan and Korea between 1952 and 1956.[66]

Many of the factors which influenced Japan's economic growth and development are similar to those which shaped other industrial nations during their respective take-off periods. Unique Japanese practices including industrial relations and the unified national efforts toward rapid growth combined with productive government administrative guidance to enhance the nation's ability to save and invest at the unprecedented rates necessary for sustaining high economic growth. Firms have benefited from investment in research and development to pioneer production techniques such as the just-in-time inventory management system (also known as the "lean production" system) and a computer-aided design system which links technicians located across many time zones. The evolution of the lean production system has forged together selected social and economic features to generate enhanced economic performance.[67] Toyota is experimenting with altering assembly-line production so as to be able to tailor each car produced for an individual customer.

Japanese cultural homogeneity, sense of groupism and degree of reciprocal employer-employee loyalty, and the relative absence of class antagonisms combine to promote economic growth and development. The homogeneous culture and strong identification with the enterprise and nation facilitate consensus decision making, especially on the macroeconomic level. The social structure provides "the basis for unity and coordination among government leaders and a variety of business groups along with the public in general, which

[65]George Melloan, "An American Views Japan's Copycat Culture," *The Wall Street Journal*, July 12, 1988, p. 33.

[66]Haitani, *The Japanese Economic System*, p. 7.

[67]For an analysis of the lean production system, especially as it has revolutionized the automobile industry, see James Womack, Daniel T. Jones, and Daniel Roos, *The Machine that Changed the World* (New York: Rawson Associates, 1990); and Sheridan Tatsuno, *Created in Japan* (New York: Harper and Row, 1990).

g[i]ve an additional boost to Japanese technological and economic development."[68] There is a symbiotic relationship among establishment leaders that creates a clublike atmosphere among authorities from Parliament, the bureaucracy, and the *zaikai*. The Japanese people readily accept the decisions of these authorities rather than seeking to defy them. There is mutual respect between management and their employees.

For these and other reasons, labor turnover has been low by international standards. Feeling secure with their firm makes workers more willing to transfer or adapt to new technology as circumstances change. Firms have proven flexible, adapting their economic institutions by systematically transferring employees and changing production methods while maintaining social unity between management and workers. There are few horizontal class antagonisms capable of disrupting production schedules, and there is an absence of me-tooism in wage settlements to create cost-push inflation during expansionary periods. The large number of well-educated, young workers who joined large, growing firms since the early 1950s had strong incentives to remain with firms that were giving them steady salary increases based upon seniority and promotions. Compared to European nations, the low labor turnover in Japan is significantly different among blue-collar workers, while white-collar worker turnover is comparable.[69]

The Japanese social structure is conducive to the achievement of projects with high national priority, such as economic growth in selected industries, partly because there is an absence of hostility toward concentration of economic power (e.g., that within *keiretsu* or city banks). The Japanese excel in

> activities which demand (1) close coordination of all available information, (2) finely coordinated planning and execution involving many parts of a firm or a number of firms, (3) meticulous attention to details, and (4) organizational ability to distribute collective gains to reward the participants in coordinated activities in such a way as not to stifle the inherent competitive spirit of each individual participant.[70]

[68]Asim Sen, "Lessons for Development from the Japanese Experience," *Journal of Economic Issues*, XVII, 2 (June 1983), 421.

[69]Yoshio Higuchi, "Labor Turnover Behavior: Japan versus the West," *Japanese Economic Studies* (Fall 1993), pp. 61–88. Higuchi points out that one factor explaining the lower turnover rate in Japan compared to the United States is the higher education received by Japanese workers, since workers with more education tend to switch jobs less frequently than those with lower levels of education.

[70]Murakani Hyoe and Johannes Hirschmeier, eds., *Politics and Economics in Contemporary Japan* (Tokyo: Japan Culture Institute, 1979), p. 131.

THE JAPANESE ECONOMY AND
THE EVOLUTIONARY-INSTITUTIONAL
PROCESS OF DEVELOPMENT

Japan's isolation from the rest of the world between the seventeenth and midnineteenth century contributed to the evolution of a unified, ethnocentric population that remained culturally homogeneous. This feature, when combined with strict social and political structures and the Confucian philosophy, not only fostered a preference for kinship groups, but also has created a willingness to accept authority, especially the informal and formal rules introduced by the bureaucracy.

The philosophical basis toward the economy was modified in 1946 following a change in the political structure as the Occupation Authority assumed power. This authority introduced working rules, which established new principal institutions and created a more democratic, demilitarized Japan. The emergence of *keiretsu* as well as the growth in importance of MITI and the Ministry of Finance can be attributed to Occupation Authority influence. The philosophical basis of the Occupation Authority was fiscally conservative (i.e., advocated a balanced budget), and economic policies that emphasized supply-side and monetarist measures (e.g., stable, modest growth of the money supply) were introduced.

After Japan regained its independence, pragmatic bureaucrats and business leaders cooperated within the framework of the working rules and institutions introduced by the Occupation Authority to develop industrial policies which introduced new technology and promoted rapid growth while gradually extending the international competitiveness of more and more Japanese firms. High rates of investment combined with state-private sector cooperation were successful in promoting rapid growth. Such performance by the economy fostered acceptance of state guidance over selected economic activities and loyalty rather than hostility toward large business organizations such as the *keiretsu*. Due to the economy's favorable performance (as perceived by the Japanese) and the unified sense that pursuing rapid growth was in the national interest, Japanese attitudes toward the economy, including what the state's role should be, has remained relatively constant. As a result, the political structure remained stable from 1955 until 1993, with the Liberal Democratic Party as the majority authority within Parliament.

The Matsushita Electric Company is a microcosm of the Japanese economy, and its behavior is consistent with the evolutionary-institutional theory. Matsushita illustrates the interrelationship between philosophical basis, social and political structures, economic institutions, and favorable performance. The firm's policy is to treat its employees as *the* critical resource. Its philosophy (the "Matsushita Creed") is in harmony with values inherent in the social structure. Like other Japanese firms, Matsushita seeks to satisfy not only its employees' economic requirements, but their social, psychological, and spiritual needs as well.

Matsushita's training program for management and workers recognizes that Japanese workers seek a familylike ambiance with corresponding spiritual ties at the workplace. Through their ties with Matsushita, employees find a sense of identity and belonging not only in the company but in society as a whole. Matsushita promotes an affiliative consciousness among its workers through the "Matsushita Creed," which stresses the virtues of "combined efforts," "cooperation," and devotion to the company.[71] Among the seven spiritual values, which are inculcated into all Matsushita trainees, are harmony and cooperation, adjustment and assimilation, and gratitude.[72] The success of Matsushita can be attributed in part to its development of a corporate culture that recognizes and builds upon those aspects of the social structure that promote efficient economic behavior.

A FINAL OBSERVATION

Throughout its history, Japan has demonstrated an ability to adapt to changing domestic and international political and economic conditions while preserving a relatively unique culture. The nation will need pragmatic, able leaders in the future to maintain its current position as a world economic power while preserving social cohesion. Optimism for such a scenario is well founded, for the Japanese economy is an excellent illustration of the central importance of human resources. As economic historian G. C. Allen summarizes structural changes and growth in Japan, "Explanations of great achievements in economic affairs as in other kinds of human activity call for a survey of impersonal forces and a statistical and analytical study of the factors that mold the inchoate material of material life. But, in the end, it is men not walls that make a city."[73]

KEY TERMS AND CONCEPTS

Economic Planning	**Ministry of International Trade and Industry**
Import Penetration	**Patterned Pluralism**
Keiretsu	*Ringi-sei* **Decision Making**

QUESTIONS FOR DISCUSSION

1. What are the essential features of the *ringi-sei* decision-making process?
2. Why are the Japanese so concerned with their trade policy?
3. What are some traditional aspects of the Japanese economy's social process for economic coordination?
4. How does decision making in Japan promote cooperation among management and workers?

---

[71]Richard Tanner Pascale and Anthony G. Athos, *The Art of Japanese Management* (Middlesex, England: Penguin Books, 1984), p. 51.
[72]Ibid.
[73]Allen, *The Japanese Economy*, p. 119.

5. Outline the role of the bureaucracy in promoting and regulating economic activity in Japan.
6. Evaluate the performance of the Japanese economy, linking factors contributing to that performance to the performance indicators you select for your evaluation.
7. How has Japan's historical legacy, philosophical basis, and social structure contributed to the economy's performance since 1946?

REFERENCES

Allen, G. C. *The Japanese Economy*. London: Weidenfeld and Nicolson, 1981.

"An Outsider Takes a Look Inside at Japan's Corporate Culture," *Japanese Economic Journal* May 3, 1986, pp. 40–41.

Balassa, Bela, and Marcus Noland, *Japan in the World Economy*. Washington, DC: Institute for International Economics, 1988.

Boltho, Andrea, *Japan: An Economic Survey—1953–1973*. Oxford: Oxford University Press, 1975.

Caves, Richard E., and Masu Uekusa, *Industrial Organization in Japan*. Washington, DC: Brookings Institution, 1976.

Commission of the European Communities, *European Economy Annual Report 1985–86*. Brussels: Directorate-General for Economic & Financial Affairs, 26 (November 1985).

Haitani, Kanji, *The Japanese Economic System*. Lexington, MA: D. C. Heath & Co., 1976.

Harumi, Yamamoto, "The Lifetime Employment System Unravels," *Japan Quarterly* (October–December 1993), pp. 381–386.

Hiroshi, Mizuguchi, "Political Reform: Much Ado About Nothing?" *Japan Quarterly* (July–September 1993), pp. 246–258.

Hyoe, Murakani, and Johannes Hirschmeier, eds., *Politics and Economics in Contemporary Japan*. Tokyo: Japan Culture Institute, 1979.

International Monetary Fund, *World Economic Outlook*. Washington, DC: IMF, 1985.

Japanese Economic Journal. November 1, 1986, p. 11.

————. February 14, 1987, p. 6.

————. December 28, 1985, p. 10.

Johnson, Chalmers, ed., *The Industrial Policy Debate*. San Francisco: Institute for Contemporary Studies, 1984.

Kanabayashi, Masasayoshi, "In Japan Employees Are Switching Firms For Better Work, Pay," *The Wall Street Journal*, October 11, 1988, p. 1.

Kano, Yoshikazu, "Japan Agriculture: It Can Be Revitalized," *Japanese Economic Studies*, 13, 3 (Spring 1985), 34–66.

Kono, Toyohiro, "Competitive Strategy," *Japanese Economic Studies*, 13, 1-2 (1984/85), 45–71.

Kosai, Yataka, and Yoshitaro Ogino, *The Contemporary Japanese Economy*. London: Macmillan Press, 1982.

Kreinin, Mordechai E., "How Closed is the Japanese Market?" *The World Economy*, 11, 7 (1988), 529–542.

Lehner, Urban C., "Japanese May Be Rich, But Are They Satisfied With Quality of Life?" *The Wall Street Journal*, January 9, 1990, p. 1.

"Life Expectancy in Japan Continues to Become Longer," *Japanese Economic Journal*, July 19, 1986, p. 24.

Lincoln, Edward J., *Japan: Facing Economic Maturity.* Washington, DC: The Brookings Institution, 1988.

Makoto, Ni'ide, "Rice Imports and Implications," *Japan Quarterly* (January–March 1994), 16–25.

McMillan, Charles J., *The Japanese Industrial System.* New York: Walter de Gruyter, 1984.

Melloan, George, "An American Views Japan's Copycat Culture," *The Wall Street Journal*, July 12, 1988, p. 33.

Minami, Ryoshin, *The Economic Development of Japan: A Quantitative Study.* London: The Macmillan Press Ltd., 1986.

Nakamura, Takafusa, transl. by Jacqueline Kaminski, *The Postwar Japanese Economy: Its Development and Structure.* Tokyo: University of Tokyo Press, 1981.

Okimoto, Daniel I., and Thomas P. Rohlen, *Inside the Japanese System.* Stanford, CA: Stanford University Press, 1988.

Okumura, Hiroshi, "Japan's Corporate Capitalism in Peril." *Japanese Economic Studies* 21, 4 (Summer 1993), 3–24.

————. "Interfirm Relations in an Enterprise Group: The Case of Mitsubishi," *Japanese Economic Studies*, 10, 4 (Summer 1982), 53–82.

Organization for Economic Cooperation and Development, *OECD Economic Outlook.* Paris: OECD (June 1989).

Ozawa, Mosoko, "Myths of Affluence and Equality," *Japanese Economic Studies*, 14 (Winter 85/86), 30–55.

Ozhawa, Kajushi, Bruce Johnston, and Hiromitsu Kaneda, eds., *Agriculture and Economic Growth: Japan's Experience.* Tokyo: University of Tokyo Press, 1969.

Pascale, Richard Tanner, and Anthony G. Athos, *The Art of Japanese Management.* Middlesex, England: Penguin Books, 1984.

Patrick, Hugh, and Henry Rosovsky, eds., *Asia's New Giant: How the Japanese Economy Works*, Washington, DC: Brookings Institution, 1976.

Sato, Kazuo, ed., *Industry and Business in Japan.* New York: M. E. Sharpe, 1980.

Sen, Asim, "Lessons for Development from the Japanese Experience," *Journal of Economic Issues*, 17, 2 (June 1983), 415–422.

Shimokawa, Koichi, "Japan's Keiretsu System: The Case of the Automobile Industry," *Japanese Economic Studies*, 13, 4 (Summer 1985), 3–31.

"Social Security Payments Post Lowest Growth in 30 Years," *Japanese Economic Journal*, September 20, 1986, p. 24.

Stockwin, J. A. A., *Japan: Divided Politics in a Growth Economy*, 2nd ed. London: Weidenfeld and Nicolson, 1982.

Thurow, Lester P., ed., *The Management Challenge.* Cambridge, MA: The MIT
     Press, 1986.
Warshaw, Steven, *Japan Emerges.* Berkeley, CA: Diablo Press, 1987.

11

THE FRENCH ECONOMY

1946–Present

1. Explain how the contributions of Jean Monnet complemented Keynesian macroeconomic policies.
2. Examine the innovative measures adopted for guiding and controlling economic activity.
3. Examine how French economic policies have been a mixture of free trade measures combined with indicative planning and nationalization of particular industries (recognizing the pervasive influence of policies established by the supranational institutions of the European Union).
4. Demonstrate that despite a very active influence of the state (in terms of percentage of resources it owns and controls) microeconomic efficiency does not appear to have been inhibited.
5. Discuss the contributions of the state to the economy's performance.

INTRODUCTION

The French economy since 1946 illustrates an innovative approach to coordinating and controlling economic activity. The state has introduced guidance and control measures such as indicative planning and nationalization of selected industries. A combination of historical factors contributed to the informal rules which influenced the decision to expand the state's influence over the economy after

1945. This influence has decreased over the past decade as the deepening of integration with the European Union and changing attitudes toward state intervention have seen the emergence of a "decentralized, multinational, free-market, pluralist [French] European state."[1]

A LONG HISTORY OF STATE INTERVENTION

France has a long history of state intervention in economic matters. During the seventeenth century, the chief financial adviser to King Louis XIV, Jean-Baptist Colbert, accepted the philosophical basis of the early mercantilists (i.e., favored accumulation of bullion, see Chapter 5). Colbert was responsible for introducing an ambitious program (what some consider the first consistent industrial strategy) to develop the economy. The program included promoting the manufacturing sector through the protection of domestic industry (e.g., subsidies and interest-free loans to producers, nontariff barriers against foreign shippers), import substitution measures, and an emphasis upon self-reliance and national military and economic strength.[2] In the eighteenth century, Napoleon introduced the civil service, which became a powerful factor in facilitating state intervention as France became unified as a nation-state. The network of civil servants enabled the state to intervene on the regional and local levels to facilitate achievement of national goals, or to correct what were perceived to be imbalances in the private sector.

Although laissez-faire policies were prominent in France as well as in most of Western Europe between 1850 and 1914, informal rules shifted after World War II in favor of reintroducing broad state guidance of the French economy. The performance of the economy from the late nineteenth century to the end of World War II was one reason. During the 1876–1938 period, real national income increased over 400 percent in Germany, over 300 percent in the United Kingdom, but less than 200 percent in France.[3] Even worse was the performance between 1929 and 1938, for while real national income grew about 42 percent and 19 percent in Germany and the United Kingdom, respectively, it declined almost 14 percent in France.[4]

Part of the reason for the low investment rates was France's history of "market sclerosis," that is, low competitive pressure and lack of concern for

---

[1]Elizabeth Haywood, "The European Policy of François Mitterrand," *Journal of Common Market Studies*, 31, 2 (June 1993), 281.

[2]The state program introduced by Colbert was "so ambitious that *colbertisme* is still a popular term for pervasive government initiative at the microeconomic level." See William James Adams, *Restructuring the French Economy* (Washington, DC: The Brookings Institution, 1989), p. 54.

[3]Warren C. Baum, *The French Economy and the State* (Princeton, NJ: Princeton University Press, 1958), p. 16.

[4]Ibid.

productive efficiency.[5] The French government had "aggressively promoted or defended certain industries for centuries,"[6] especially when it believed that France's national independence was threatened. The absence of competitive pressure was also due to protective barriers erected by private firms, which created monopolistic industry structures concentrated in particular regions, and French "hyperconservatism."[7] French merchants and producers have traditionally had a strong propensity for self-employment and for the existing way of life in lieu of structural change, even if it offered greater profitability than the status quo. Such attitudes, when supported by public and private restraints of trade, resulted in the domination of small and medium-sized firms. Under such conditions investment in new technology is less likely, so growth of factor productivity is inhibited.

Although there is a tradition of economic liberalism in France, beginning with the physiocrats and Jean-Baptiste Say, some informal rules survived in the French consciousness from its economic and political history. Laissez-faire policies, although they dominated the 1850–1940 period, were never wholeheartedly embraced; and modernization techniques in the name of efficiency were introduced with only modest enthusiasm. Unregulated market forces were blamed for the poor performance of the economy between 1914 and 1945. In particular, the Great Depression was attributed to "the disorder and malfunctions of the market and its hallowed laws."[8] In addition, laissez-faire policies and private concentration of ownership and control of productive resources were blamed for France's highly skewed distribution of wealth and income. Many French, especially the "left" intellectuals, who historically have influenced the French intelligentsia and the working class, criticized unregulated market forces for producing a mix of output that included the most profitable products rather than producing at affordable prices goods and services a majority of the French society needed.

In 1946 the French economy was suffering from the effects of World War II and decades of low investment and competitiveness. The distribution network was outdated; the industrial, mining, and agricultural sectors were backward; the capital market was weak; there was a dearth of Schumpeterian entrepreneurs; and the state continued to protect weaker firms. There also were serious shortages of raw materials (especially coal); significant imbalances in the economic development of certain regions; low inventory levels; much destruction of industrial capacity, infrastructure, and transportation networks during the war;

---

[5]George Ross, Stanley Hoffman, and Sylvia Malzacher, *The Mitterand Experiment* (Cambridge: Polity Press, 1987), p. 24.

[6]William James Adams and Christian Stoffaes, eds., *French Industrial Policy* (Washington, DC: The Brookings Institution, 1986), p. vii.

[7]Adams, *Restructuring the French Economy*, pp. 2, 3.

[8]Richard F. Kuisel, *Capitalism and the State in Modern France* (Cambridge: Cambridge University Press, 1981), p. 278.

and considerable inflationary pressure.

The experience of World War II convinced the French that the policy of isolationism that they adopted after World War I was a failure. In addition they realized their economy lagged well behind international economic rivals (e.g., West Germany, United Kingdom, and United States) in terms of modernization and structural characteristics. The collective desire to reverse the decline of the national economy and to make France a world power led to a change in informal rules. The French decided to seek an alternative to the state's passive role except for state protection of traditional enterprises. Many French intellectuals and authorities favored the government taking the initiative in promoting economic activity through a state-guided industrial policy committed to modernization and structural change. Planning as a measure to coordinate national efforts was widely advocated as the most efficacious means to allocate resources, control inflation, and improve the unfavorable balance of trade. A foreign policy was needed to establish cooperation with a new Germany. The French solution included measures such as nationalization, planning, integration—both politically and economically—with its European rivals, especially West Germany. The philosophical basis for these measures is discussed next.

A PHILOSOPHY FOR GUIDING MACROECONOMIC ACTIVITY

The philosophical basis upon which working rules were established for the first two decades after World War II was primarily influenced by two factors. The first was the contributions of John Maynard Keynes (see Chapter 8), whom the French had "discovered" by 1946. One Keynesian position that influenced French thinking was his belief that macroeconomic stabilization could be achieved by

> the deliberate control of the currency and of credit by a central institution, and . . . [by] collection and dissemination on a great scale of data relating to the business situation . . . These measures would involve society in exercising directive intelligence through some appropriate organ of action over many of the intricacies of private business, yet it would leave private initiative and enterprise unhindered.[9]

Second, following the experience of the depression and devastation from World War II French authorities were prepared to develop a comprehensive blueprint for restructuring and modernizing the economy. They recognized the need to formulate an alternative philosophical basis and working rules for the economy suitable for the achievement of their goals while consistent with the

---

[9]Saul Estrin and Peter Holmes, *French Planning in Theory and Practice* (London: George Allen and Unwin, 1983), p. 8.

international political and economic realities of the postwar period. They were faced with the task of "find[ing] a way to bypass the sterile debate over the merits of free enterprise or *dirigisme* [central control] and reconcile the market with an interventionist state."[10] Charles de Gaulle sought to enhance his nation's status in the world community through economic growth and modernization within a more just, effective economy with greater economic equality. He turned to Jean Monnet, who ultimately became the father of French economic planning and a prime proponent of integration with other European nations.

Monnet was a modest, charismatic public official dedicated "to bring[ing] men together, to help them solve the problems that divided them."[11] He was directed by de Gaulle to develop a plan for the postwar reconstruction and modernization of the economy. In response to de Gaulle's desire for France to achieve grandeur among nations, Monnet convinced him that a concurrent modernization of the economy was essential. Neither de Gaulle nor Monnet had strong ideological convictions regarding a philosophical basis and working rules for an economy. Monnet was a pragmatist. Assessing the postwar climate, he set out to develop a practical plan designed to attract Marshall Plan funds from the United States for reconstruction purposes. He worked to develop a planning procedure consistent with private enterprise, believing "that effective competition and intelligent planning are natural allies rather than enemies."[12] The primary problem was to devise a process by which the state could guide economic activity, taking advantage of the efficiency of market forces while avoiding domination by bureaucrats and ministerial officials. Monnet's philosophy was similar to that of Japan's *ringi-sei* decision-making process. Rather than a scheme characterized by a few authorities issuing binding commands to subordinate state officials and enterprise managers, Monnet wanted a democratic, collaborative decision-making process for establishing working rules and policies to achieve national goals. All groups ultimately responsible for plan execution (e.g., representatives from government, manufacturing and agricultural enterprises, trade unions, and consumers) were involved.

Persuasion and reason in collective decision making to achieve unanimous consent was Monnet's method for plan formulation. No means for solving a collective problem would be implemented until a consensus was reached among representatives with similar economic interests. Monnet often relied on exhortation to change informal rules, hoping that consensus among all parties would be reached to establish formal rules. In reaching a consensus Monnet believed that those who collaborated to formulate the plan would become more committed to implementing rules and working to achieve goals collectively agreed upon. The plan was intended to be "the agent of economic growth rather

---

[10]Kuisel, *Capitalism and the State in Modern France*, pp. 250, 251.

[11]Ibid., p. 219.

[12]John Sheahan, *Promotion and Control of Industry in Postwar France* (Cambridge, MA: Harvard University Press, 1963), p. 44.

than a step toward socialism . . . [to be the facilitator of] economic development and technological progress but not social or political change . . . [and to be] impartial . . . , aloof from party politics and parliamentary scrutiny."[13]

The French brand of planning was termed indicative. Such planning was intended to complement market forces, the view being that it was possible to control "the [macro and micro level] environment through rational rather than blind economic processes."[14] Proponents of the new process argued that a planning agency could facilitate decision making of investors, consumers, state officials, and laborers, among others, through nonauthoritarian means. The planning method would guide the private sector by forecasting target levels of macroeconomic variables, and after a consensus was reached regarding national goals, stimulating voluntary compliance by all interest groups to achieve the plan's objectives. Planning would help coordinate state activities in a complex, modern economy and also would provide the framework and guidelines for future economic activity by making more information available to decision makers. More information, in turn, would lessen uncertainty of expectations regarding the business environment. Less uncertainty would, it was held, stimulate greater investment within the private sector. The result of this new philosophy was "a Gallic style of economic management that blended state direction, corporatist bodies, and market forces."[15]

While indicative planning is a primary manifestation of the philosophical basis for the French economy, it is not the only one. During the past two decades, nationalization of key industries (e.g., energy, transport) as a means to guide resource allocation in a direction consistent with national interests has been proposed and adopted (see "A Key Role for State Ownership and Control," p. 246). The philosophical basis also justifies economic and political integration with other European Union members, which for the past 30 years has emphasized the importance of less regulated markets for coordinating production and distribution activities. Such markets were to be created by removing trade barriers between member nations while transferring guidance of member nation economies from the national to the supranational level (see Chapter 14—"The European Union").

France's willingness to give up some national sovereignty to a supranational authority was related directly to its decision to abandon isolationism in favor of developing close economic and political links with other European nations, particularly Germany. Among other reasons, France wanted a bigger role in managing a unified European economic and political entity, believing it would give French authorities greater bargaining power in the world community than if they only spoke for France. Beginning in 1951 with the creation of the European Coal and Steel Community, France has been a major voice for a

[13]Kuisel, *Capitalism and the State in Modern France*, p. 246.

[14]John S. Harlow, *French Economic Planning: A Challenge to Reason* (Iowa City: University of Iowa Press, 1966), p. 11.

[15]Kuisel, *Capitalism and the State in Modern France*, p. 248.

united Europe, accepting the benefits that would accrue to the French economy from membership in what is slowly becoming a unity of twelve European economies that, with regard to particular activities and working rules, behave as one economy.

One change in the philosophical basis toward the economy began in 1981 when French voters elected a socialist government—the first time this party had won the national election since the 1930s. There was a conflict between the philosophical basis of Socialist Party authorities, led by President François Mitterrand, and the large private sector which the Socialists "[a]t best . . . saw . . . as an element of the economy to be tolerated rather than cultivated."[16] The Socialists desired to nationalize more industries and virtually all banks, increase social legislation, and reduce the skewed distribution of income and wealth. They believed that more resources should be allocated through state institutions. The Socialists, however, were not in favor of strong guidance from the central government, but wanted close cooperation between the public and private sectors. They favored decentralized decision making by democratically elected regional and local authorities as well as more autonomy for enterprise managers. This brand of decentralization, referred to as *autogestion* by the French, would make those involved responsible for everyday activities.

By the late 1980s Mitterrand, who won reelection in 1988, was successful in gaining acceptance for his long-term philosophy—namely, that France should shift toward "free market integrationism" away from "nationalism and protectionism."[17] This required new working rules, which began to reverse the nationalization trend, place more reliance upon the European Community to govern French economic affairs (particularly through acceptance of the Maastricht proposal to establish a European Union—see Chapter 14), and introduced proposals to reduce state subsidies, particularly in areas of agriculture and employment. Despite Mitterrand's endorsement of reducing the state's role, the 1993 election shifted political power to conservatives. This has meant a further shift away from the deeply ingrained preference for statism (*dirigisme*) in economic affairs, the most significant example being the decision to expand privatization efforts by the state selling off more than 20 large state-owned companies (see "A Key Role for State Ownership and Control," p. 246).

[16]Ross, Hoffman, and Malzacher, *The Mitterrand Experiment*, p. 70.
[17]Haywood, "The European Policy of François Mitterrand," p. 282.

SOCIAL AND POLITICAL STRUCTURES: MERITOCRACY AND A PRESIDENTIAL REPUBLIC

In France there is a close link between rank (or degree of influence within the circle of high-ranking authorities) and status. Both informal and formal rules exist which perpetuate this link as well as the composition of the social and political structures.

Social Structure

France's social structure is divided into three classes according to a person's (or family's) activity in the production process and his or her "social practices:" the bourgeoisie, middle class, and working class.[18] The bourgeoisie include political authorities, owners of industrial and commercial means of production and distribution and their senior managers, and university professors. Between the property owners and the working class is the middle class, whose members include petty bourgeoisie (e.g., artisans, shopkeepers), middle- and lower-level supervisors, technical staff members, engineers, primary school teachers, and any other white-collar workers. The working class includes manual workers, farmers, and agricultural workers. Factors defining gradations within this class include nationality and skill level. For example, migrant, unskilled workers from non-European Union nations (e.g., Turkey, Algeria) have lowest status, while highly skilled manual workers who are natural French citizens and born in a more developed region (e.g., Paris) have the highest status within the working class.

Membership within these classes is perpetuated by informal and formal rules favoring meritocracy. In 1980 only about 4 percent of the school-age population in France received a bachelor's or advanced university degree, as compared to 14 percent and 17 percent in Japan and the United States, respectively.[19] The close positive correlation between level of education, ability to receive a favorable distribution of the income created by the economy, and social class is justified by informal rules held by the French "that each person, and hence group, appears in its 'natural' place."[20] In a study of French society between 1947 and 1975, it was found that those with higher incomes not only could purchase more material goods and services, but received a more favorable share of redistributed benefits (e.g., "social transfer payments") than lower income individuals.[21] The Gini coefficient in France is considerably above that of Japan

---

[18]For a detailed discussion of French social classes, see Jane Marceau, *Class and Status in France* (Oxford: Clarendon Press, 1977), pp. 7 ff.

[19]*Living Conditions in OECD Countries* (Paris: OECD, 1986).

[20]Marceau, *Class and Status in France*, p. 39.

[21]Ibid.

and Sweden, as well as that of most of the other OECD nations.[22] There is a lack of mobility between social classes perpetuated by an "overwhelming predominance of professional heredity over the generations, particularly of occupational position but also of occupation itself."[23] Due to this occupational rigidity, immobility between social classes is common, and since nearly all French authorities are from the bourgeoisie class the lack of social mobility perpetuates rule by those with high status.

Political Structure

France is a republic whose central government maintained a strong presence, especially between 1958 (following the election of Charles de Gaulle as president and approval of a new constitution establishing a Fifth Republic) and 1981 (after which socialist François Mitterrand assumed the presidency). The president is elected for a seven-year term by popular vote. Since more than 50 percent of the vote is required to win, and there have been four main political parties (Gaullist Party, an independent center-right coalition, Socialist Party, and Communist Party) with other smaller parties as well, a second round of voting between the top two vote recipients has often been necessary. Until 1981 this rule inhibited the left (i.e., Socialist and Communist Parties), which received the most votes in some elections but were unable to receive more than 50 percent in the runoff election. Once elected the president appoints a prime minister.

A new constitution passed in 1958 gave greater authority to the president, including the power to dissolve the Parliament (the body which must approve all legislative and financial measures), whose members are elected for four-year terms, and to call a new election within 20 to 40 days. This act of dissolution occurred in 1958, 1968, and 1981. In each case the president (de Gaulle, Pompidou, and Mitterrand) sought to improve their support within the legislature by increasing the percentage of the Parliament (National Assembly and Senate) loyal and beholden to them.

The interrelationship between authorities who make the working rules, public officials who administer and enforce the rules and manage public enterprises, private-sector leaders (e.g., manufacturing, commercial, agricultural, trade union leaders), and those who are usually responsible for the informal working rules (political party leaders, bourgeoisie intellectuals, representatives of the media, and the National Assembly) is depicted in Figure 11-1. This hexagon is one analyst's depiction of pluralist power in France. The "partisan national executives" are the president, prime minister, and ministry leaders, who deal with major changes in working rules and state policies for macroeconomic stabilization (e.g., decisions to nationalize or privatize an industry, accept or reject certain

---

[22]In the late 1970s France's Gini coefficient was about 0.43 compared to about 0.30 for Sweden and less than 0.20 for Japan. *Living Conditions in OECD Countries* (Paris: OECD, 1986), p. 119.

[23]Marceau, *Class and Status in France,* p. 81.

European Union working rules).

The French political structure is more complex than depicted in Figure 11-1 because France belongs to the European Union, a supranational economy whose political structure consists of supranational institutions with authorities appointed or elected from the 12 member nations (see Chapter 14). At the national administrative and management levels, there is a symbiotic relationship between public-sector authorities and private-sector executives to the extent that top public-sector authorities often are recruited from among top managers in

Figure 11-1   The Political Structure as National Economic Policy Is Formulated

Political Decisions (Heads of the partisan national executive)	**Administrative, Adjudication, and Enforcement** (Heads of the "permanent" senior civil service, judiciary, police, and military)
Democratic mobilization, communication, and legitimation (Leaders of political parties, elite and mass media, parliament)	**Public economic management** (Heads of the public financial and industrial corporations)
Labor market organization (Leaders of the trade unions and professional organizations)	**Private economic management** (Leaders of the financial, industrial and agricultural corporations, trade associations, and peak organizations)

Source: Jack Hayward, *The State and the Market Economy* (New York: New York University Press, 1986), p. 49.

private enterprises. This relationship can be traced to the "meritocratic, bureaucratic and technocratic traditions [which] are . . . firmly and operationally institutionalized and accepted in France."[24] The result is a strong "interface between the most conspicuously capitalist pressure group in French society and the major techno-bureaucratic agencies of the French state, who focused on group-government links."[25] This pertains most often to public economic management, partly because of the extent of nationalization in the financial and industrial sectors, and partly because management of French public enterprises is encouraged to be active in policy decisions.

Influence of private-sector interest groups, especially from large business enterprises, comes from financial contributions to political parties and from the exchange of positions between top-level business managers and government bureaucrats. The influence of trade unions has not been significant. For much of the postwar period the relationship between trade union leaders and authorities has been quite antagonistic, for the union leaders generally have been committed

[24]Hayward, *The State and the Market Economy*, p. 50.
[25]Ibid., p. 2.

to replacing those public-sector "elites" who serve bourgeoisie interests while perpetuating the capitalist system in France.[26] Under the Mitterrand regime government-trade union antagonism has lessened considerably, although the state's willingness to open the economy to international competitive forces may conflict with union leaders' desire to preserve job security, as manifested by occasional strikes or violent protests. Time lost due to labor disputes during the early 1990s reflects growing job insecurity partially stimulated by state attempts to introduce new working rules designed to counteract the recession and mounting unemployment.

Members of the last group (e.g., media) are considered part of the political structure because of their close contact with and influence among the French people. The extent of the media's influence over informal rules is due to its ability to provide open information about the decision-making process. The public, consequently, has time to react in advance of legislation being voted upon.

PUBLIC INSTITUTIONS ON THE NATIONAL AND SUPRANATIONAL LEVEL

The relative importance of France's principal institutions has varied since 1946 according to the economic and political problems, relative strength of the executive branch (president, prime minister, and cabinet), political party to which authorities belong, and the level of economic integration of the European Union. Five institutions (or group of interrelated institutions) have been instrumental in establishing and coordinating France's major production and distribution patterns. These are the executive branch, public enterprises, Ministry of Finance, supranational institutions of the European Union, and planning institutions.

The political party to which the executive branch authorities belong is significant due to the gulf in ideology (at least until recently) between the leftist and rightist parties. Changes in the political structure have been followed by institutional change as new authorities introduce working rules consistent with their own philosophical basis. Gaullists have sought to strengthen executive power so that decision making was highly centralized. During the 1981–1993 period, the Socialist Party executive authorities emphasized decentralization and changed a number of working rules, especially those pertaining to social insurance and welfare coverage and the extent to which industries and financial institutions are nationalized (see "A Key Role for State Ownership and Control," p. 246). Public enterprises or state-owned enterprises (SOEs) increased considerably over the decade of the 1980s when the socialist authorities nationalized enterprises in many sectors—especially financial. The rise to power

[26]Ibid., p. 53.

of the Conservative Party is reversing the privatization trend as well as expanding efforts to implement significant reductions in the generous social welfare benefits enjoyed by the French.[27]

The Ministry of Finance is the state's second most powerful institution. It has been especially powerful since de Gaulle increased the finance minister's powers in 1958, after which this ministry became a "superministry and the center for economic management."[28] The Ministry of Finance's power is enhanced by its virtual monopoly over macroeconomic information and the extensive funds it receives to support its forecasting and research and development divisions. It uses the information and research findings to fulfill its responsibility for the national budget, monetary and fiscal policy, monitoring the effectiveness of public and private investment projects, forecasting key macroeconomic variables, and (when necessary) price control. As the working rules of the European Union level of integration are all implemented, coordination of France's macroeconomic policies will shift to the supranational level, and the relative importance of the French Ministry of Finance should decline. This change will be consistent with the evolution of the French economy for the past five decades. The influence of European Union institutions (see "Principal Institutions," Chapter 14) on the French economy has increased each decade since 1951. Although the EU allocates funds equivalent to 3 percent of its members' combined gross national product, working rules which support farmers (the Common Agricultural Policy), liberalize trade, and permit member nation workers and firms easier access to French markets (e.g., Germans and Belgians can invest or work in France subject to the same rules that apply to French firms and citizens) all have a profound affect on the French economy.

The type of planning institutions introduced during the late 1940s distinguished France's social process for coordinating production and distribution activities from that of other guided market economies. While planning at the national level is becoming less important in France, understanding the nature of their planning institutions is essential for understanding the evolutionary path the economy has followed since the late 1940s. Prior to the late 1960s authorities were committed to planning, primarily because of their lack of faith in unregulated market forces and also because planning enhanced the state's power. While Monnet was commissioner of planning, this institution was the primary locus of the nation's economic policy making. The Planning Commission, while having no executive power, orchestrated the process of research, consultation, and identification of national objectives and priorities as the plan was being constructed. The commission assembles information, drafts outline proposals to be considered by other planning institutions, mediates disputes between

---

[27]These benefits are among the most generous of any economy and are discussed further on pp. 251–254.
[28]Kuisel, *Capitalism and the State in Modern France*, p. 253.

ministries over priorities and resources allocation, and facilitates an exchange of information between state (e.g., civil servants, managers of public enterprises), business, agriculture, and labor representatives. The commission has no executive power. It has been, however, influential in getting different parties to agree to act in a manner consistent with the realization of agreed-upon goals.

Under the Planning Commission are about 30 modernization commissions. The name *modernization* was chosen to remind all concerned that a postwar national goal was modernization of the economy. Modernization commissions link planners with enterprises responsible for plan implementation. After broad economic objectives are established by leading authorities, they are disaggregated by sector and industry by vertical modernization commissions, under the supervision of the Planning Commission. There are also horizontal modernization commissions, which aggregate detailed plans at the industry and sector levels. The horizontal commissions study the broad needs of the economy in terms of financial, labor, energy, and other needs. Many interest groups have some influence, so that the entire planning process is a concerted effort of all these commissions.

The other important planning institution is the Economic and Social Council. The council is comprised of over 100 experts in economic and social policy, many from the private sector, and performs a consulting function. After the plan is formulated by the Planning Commission and modernization commissions, the council renders its opinion on the plan (or on any policy measures suggested by authorities pertaining to economic and social matters). In doing so it links the other planning institutions with the National Assembly.

BEHAVIOR OF THE ECONOMY: TRANSFORMATION AT THE NATIONAL AND EUROPEAN UNION LEVEL

The French economy has been transformed from a "protected, colonial economy"[29] by factors such as indicative planning, a nationalization (and recently a privatization) program, membership in the European Union, and a more open economy that gives foreigners greater access to French markets and requires French producers to be competitive on world markets. To make this transformation France reorganized decision making, made major changes in working rules governing ownership and control of resources, and introduced institutions which implemented a new social process for coordinating economic activities.

[29]Ross, Hoffman, and Malzacher, *The Mitterrand Experiment*, p. 18.

Plurality in Resource Allocation Decision Making

There is a plurality of participants in economic policy decision making, as indicated by Figure 11-1. The influence of each participant over major resource allocation decisions depends on their ability to influence authorities in the executive branch, the Ministry of Finance, or members of Parliament. Acceptance of greater centralization of economic policy decision making, with considerable powers concentrated in the executive branch, was widespread for about two decades after the war. There remains a degree of centralization, primarily because of France's membership within the European Union, the power of the executive branch (relative to Parliament) and the Ministry of Finance, and the growth of public enterprises. Since the major policies of the European Union are initiated by the European Council (of which the French president is a member), the primary stimulus for economic and political integration is concentrated within the executive branch.

Beginning in the late 1960s, and accelerating in the 1990s, decision making has become more decentralized. Reasons for greater decentralization are that the economy has become more modernized, many of the necessary structural transformations have been achieved (especially more market competition), the nation has become more economically integrated within the European Union, the importance of indicative planning has declined, and Mitterrand and the new conservative parliament have introduced political reforms granting more autonomy to regional and local government. A more competitive, open French economy has meant that market forces and thereby decentralized decisions, as opposed to guidelines contained in the economic plan are becoming the supreme factor in most resource allocation decisions.

A Key Role for State Ownership and Control

In terms of both ownership and control the state as well as the European Union play an important role as owner and/or controller of enterprises involved with all sectors of the French economy. While privately owned and controlled enterprises account for over three quarters of France's gross domestic output, state ownership and control through state-owned enterprises (SOEs), the Ministry of Treasury, and the Planning Commission affect more economic activities in France than does the state in most OECD nations. In 1994 France ranked seventh among 24 OECD members in terms of general government outlays as a percentage of gross domestic product, with 54.8 percent.[30] The importance of the state has grown in absolute terms over the past two decades but has actually declined relative to other OECD members.[31] Much of the growth of government spending has come

---

[30]*OECD in Figures,* 54 (Paris: OECD, 1993), p. 148.

[31]In 1959 France ranked first in terms of taxation as a percentage of gross national product (at about 34 percent), and third in 1967 (about 37 percent). See Graeme M. Holmes and Peter O. Fawcett, *The Contemporary French Economy* (London: The Macmillan Press, 1983), p. 159.

from increases in social expenditures, which have risen faster than the rate of growth of real GNP. While state purchases of goods and services has remained fairly constant over the past three decades, social expenditures rose from an average of 13.4 percent of GDP over the 1960–1975 period to almost 30 percent of GDP by 1980 (compared to the 1980 OECD average of about 26 percent), and to over 35 percent in the late 1980s.[32] Efforts to reduce this percentage have met stiff public resistance.

There are a number of means used by the state to control the economy. The most pervasive influence prior to the 1990s was through nationalization of enterprises, which resulted in a significant revision of the structure of many French industries. In addition, planning, state purchases of private-sector goods and services, subsidies, working rules introduced by the European Union, as well as monetary and fiscal policy have been other important means. The European Union control has increased in importance. It has been significant in controlling the agricultural sector, for while nearly all French farmers are freeholders of their land, most are affected profoundly by the Common Agricultural Policy (see Chapter 14).

Nationalization of business enterprises is not exclusively a postwar phenomenon, for there are examples of state ownership from as early as the seventeenth century. Most nationalization of enterprises occurred during two periods: immediately after World War II and after 1981, when the socialist authorities assumed power. In the interim years the extent of nationalization increased slowly. There were a number of motives underlying the 1946 nationalization wave, including dissatisfaction with the performance of an economy that had many features of a laissez-faire market economy, determination of authorities to guide a modernization and structural change effort, desire to punish those private enterprises believed to have collaborated with the Germans during the war, and desire to control sectors of the economy providing essential public services (e.g., energy, transport). From the point of view of authorities who introduced the working rules, "[n]ationaliztion . . . , besides liberating democracy from the trusts ['capitalist oligarchy'], was mainly a step toward economic recovery, growth, and independence."[33]

At first only a few sectors were nationalized. In order to have control over allocation of credit and insurance, financial and insurance enterprises were nationalized. Control was exercised through the state-owned Bank of France, the Treasury, a National Credit Council, and the Banking Control Commission, which collectively "chartered and applied credit policy and retrained private banks from acting contrary to public economic policy."[34] Electricity and gas enterprises were nationalized to give the state control over energy supplies, while the coal industry

[32]*OECD in Figures* (Paris: OECD, 1989), pp. 16, 17.
[33]Kuisel, *Capitalism and the State in Modern France*, p. 203.
[34]Ibid., p. 214.

became state owned in order to spearhead the restructuring drive. A few manufacturing enterprises also were nationalized, including Renault and Air France.

By 1958 the state owned most of France's financial system, while SOEs accounted for about 20 percent of the country's industrial capacity. Although there was not a broad nationalization drive comparable to that of 1946, by the late 1970s the state gradually had extended its ownership in areas ranging from stud farms for horses, to public ground and rail transport, to steel and computer enterprises. Meanwhile existing SOEs were permitted to diversify. The extent of state influence varied by industry. Industries in which the state had a "monopoly" position (over 80 percent of total production) included tobacco, coal, natural gas, electricity, and telecommunication services. The state was "very important" (produced between 40 percent and 80 percent) in the aeronautic, electrical and mechanical auto equipment, armaments, and land, air, and sea transport; "important" (produced between 20 percent and 40 percent) in crude oil, automobiles, and health services; and of "secondary" importance in other areas, which included household appliances and services rendered to enterprises.[35]

Despite the broad range of industries in which there were SOEs (38 by 1980), public enterprises accounted for more than 5 percent of the value added in only nine of these industries when the Socialist authorities were elected.[36] This changed dramatically in 1982. The Socialist authorities' philosophical basis included the belief that private ownership was the cause of two major problems plaguing France—high unemployment and a very unequal distribution of income. This belief, as well as the relatively poor performance of the economy during the 1970s, prompted the socialists to propose closer state-private sector coordination (especially manufacturers and banks), seeking to emulate the Japanese success with "a new economic dynamism that would spread throughout the French economy."[37] Consequently, a large-scale nationalization program was launched during the 1980s.

The dramatic expansion of state ownership occurred directly, through formal rules giving the state the right to acquire enterprises (usually by compensating the previous private shareholders after negotiations), and indirectly, as the state became the owner of subsidiaries of the private enterprises that were nationalized. Nationalized enterprises included 38 banks and finance companies and 7 of the largest 20 firms in France—companies that were involved in producing goods such as ships, telecommunications equipment, computers, aluminum, iron and steel, and pharmaceuticals.[38] A number of facts illustrate the

[35]For additional information see J. R. Hough, *The French Economy* (New York: Holmes and Meier, 1982), p. 44.

[36]Adams, *Restructuring the French Economy*, pp. 62, 287.

[37]Volkmar Lauber, *The Political Economy of France* (New York: Praeger, 1983), p. 164.

[38]Howard Machin and Vincent Wright, eds., *Economic Policy and Policy-Making under the Mitterrand Presidency 1981–1984* (New York: St. Martin's Press, 1985), p. 144.

extent of nationalization by the late 1980s. SOEs account for almost 20 percent of GDP and about 40 percent of all investment.[39] Almost 25 percent of all workers are employed by SOEs, while these enterprises are responsible for about one third of domestic sales and a like proportion of all exports.[40] Among large firms employing over 2,000 employees, nearly half are SOEs.[41] However, in the face of a prolonged recession since 1991, efforts have been underway to privatize firms, including those in automobile and air transport industries.

The impact of the post-1981 nationalizations was felt most acutely in heavy industries such as iron and steel, iron ore, and basic chemicals. In the case of these three industries the percentage of total output accounted for by SOEs rose from about 16 percent in chemicals and about 1 percent in each of the other two industries prior to 1981 to over 50 percent in chemicals and more than 70 percent in both the iron and steel and the iron ore industries.[42] Finally, by owning enterprises that are multinational, the state owns and controls firms doing business in countries that are its economic rivals. The overall impact of the SOEs is difficult to assess without analyzing each enterprise's control of the market supply, the price elasticity of demand for their goods or services, their pricing strategy, and the amount of state subsidies they receive.[43] However, some observations are in order.

Evidence indicates that prior to 1990 in France, unlike the Central and East European experience, SOEs were as productive, and perhaps more productive, than many private enterprises. One indicator is that the percentage of value added by all SOEs is greater than the percentage of the work force they employ. In addition, the effect of state ownership on the seven largest nonfinancial firms nationalized has been effective to the extent that all but one of them showed a profit in 1985, while only one was making a profit in 1982.[44] Part of the success is due to the management of SOEs, for the national authorities have been reluctant to intervene actively in the management of these enterprises. In fact, many SOEs, particularly the ones dealing with private enterprises in and outside of France, "have behaved as independently of government as d[o] . . . their private counterparts."[45]

Consistent with the evolutionary nature of economies, there have been waves of French privatization. In 1986–1988 15 large industrial and financial trusts were privatized. These trusts control over 1,300 affiliated enterprises with

---

[39]See Hayward, *The State and the Market Economy*, p. 51, and Bela Balassa, *The First Year of Socialist Government in France*. (Washington, DC: American Enterprise Institute, 1982), p. 164.

[40]Ross, Hoffmann, and Malzacher, *The Mitterrand Experiment*, p. 59.

[41]Machin and Wright, *Economic Policy and Policy-Making*, p. 146.

[42]Balassa, *The First Year of Socialist Government in France*, pp. 2–5.

[43]For further discussion, see Adams, *Restructuring the French Economy*, pp. 54–79.

[44]Ross, Hoffmann, and Malzacher, *The Mitterrand Experiment*, p. 64.

[45]Ibid., p. 74.

over 300,000 employees. Their combined assets were about $24 billion.[46] In 1993 there began a second wave of privatization as the newly elected conservative government began to formulate plans to sell off 21 large state-owned companies. These included Renault; Air France; Rhone-Poulene, the world's largest chemical company; Banque Nationale de Paris, which ranks among the top 20 banks in the world in terms of assets; Credit Lyonnais; Group Bull (computers); Elf Aquitaine, sixth largest petroleum refiner in the world; and Thomson (electronics) so as to reduce the state's role in France's industrial and financial sectors. Privatization would also help reduce the large government budget deficit (about 6 percent of gross domestic product in early 1994), and if the conservatives are successful in privatizing all state-owned companies the receipts could total over $50 billion.[47]

The economic strength of these companies is mixed. Some such as Renault are profitable and able to compete on the world market. Others such as petroleum, pharmaceutical, and insurance companies have been managed as private firms and may be suffering the effects of prolonged recession in Europe. Some, however, are overstaffed and suffer from bureaucratization, and are currently in need of government subsidization to remain viable. Included among these companies are Air France, Group Bull (which lost about $3 billion during 1988–1993), and Thomson.[48] Therefore, the government must continue to fund these weak, unprofitable companies to keep them viable until buyers can be enticed to purchase them.

Sales began in late 1993, with Banque Nationale de Paris and Elf Aquitaine being among the first to be privatized. In the case of industries deemed in the national interest such as Elf Aquitaine, the state is seeking to reduce its ownership (in this case from just over 50 percent to about 13 percent) so as to retain some national control. The fear is that foreign owners will assume ownership and control over producers of vital products. The pace of privatization will be slower than first expected due to considerable labor unrest stimulated by the inevitable job insecurity which privatization entails.[49] Overall, privatization in France has been successful, especially in comparison with similar efforts throughout Central and Eastern Europe (see Chapter 16). The ingredients for the French success have been "utilizing the tender price offer technique at a fixed price . . . ; a diversified offer to various 'blocks' of shareholders (individuals, wage earners, domestic and foreign institutional investors, and a hard core of stable shareholders); . . . [and] privation public enterprises when they are profitable."[50]

State control over French enterprises, in addition to ownership, is in the

[46]Wladimir Andreff, "East European Privatization in the Light of Western Experience," *Journal of Transforming Economies and Societies* 1, 1 (Summer 1994), 23.

[47]"France for Sale," *Fortune*, September 6, 1993, p. 11.

[48]Steward Toy, "The CEO Guillotine Is Busy Again," *Business Week*, November 1, 1993, p. 54.

[49]When Air France laid off about 8 percent of its work force in late 1993 strikes erupted, costing the firm about $12 million a day.

[50]Andreff, "East European Privatization in the Light of Western Experience," p. 24.

form of equity financing, credit policies, subsidies and tax incentives (e.g., lower value-added taxes imposed on particular products), state purchases of goods and services, and public support of research and development. There are only a few SOEs which are heavily dependent upon equity finance, and most are financial institutions. Subsidies which are intended to guide a SOE's behavior or supplement deficit earnings nearly all go to nonfinancial enterprises. Farmers, food processors, food distributors, rail transport, nuclear weapons, and nuclear power received about 80 percent of all state subsidies. While the amount of these subsidies was "considerable," no enterprises relied upon state subsidies to pay a majority of their costs. As a buyer of goods and services the state is not important in terms of the percentage of nondefense manufacturing enterprises' output. Over 75 percent of state procurement funds are concentrated in four industries: electrical equipment, electronic equipment, ships, and airplanes.[51] The sponsorship of research and development by the state has been concentrated in a few industries, especially aerospace and electronics. Overall, the extent of state control over French industry is most prominent in heavy industry and high-technology electrical and electronic areas; of moderate importance in the automobile, shipbuilding, construction (e.g., railways), wood and paper, and pharmaceutical industries; and of modest importance in the consumer goods (e.g., clothing, shoes, furniture), food processing, and production of light machine tools industries.[52] State control is marginal in retail services, commerce, and distribution of goods and services.

French Alternatives for Economic Coordination

Since 1945 the French have sought alternatives to heavy reliance upon either unregulated markets or centrally directed state controls to coordinate economic activities. The state has taken the initiative to guide the economy by adopting an industrial policy designed to complement market forces while providing extensive social insurance and welfare services.[53] To guide private-sector decisions, the state has adopted measures with which it would "nudge . . . private parties toward elastic responses to market signals, and . . . compensate for remaining private conservatism by escalating direct government participation in the allocation of resources."[54]

Themes of French industrial policy have included an "active role for government in the economy, . . . that government should intervene selectively as well as generally . . . [and] bring about 'a strategic consensus among government, industry, and labor as to the basic directions in which the economy ought to

---

[51]Toy, "The CEO Guillotine Is Busy Again," p. 54.

[52]Machin and Vincent, *Economic Policy and Policy-Making*, p. 150.

[53]Any state policy which seeks to alter the composition of a nation's output and distribution of that output (from what unregulated market forces would generate) can be considered an industrial policy.

[54]Adams, *Restructuring the French Economy*, p. 43.

move."[55] In recent years the theme has been to reduce state influence in favor of greater reliance upon free market rules and European Union working rules. The goals of France's industrial policy have varied over the period from 1945 to the present. Initially they were to promote structural change and modernization so as to achieve economies of scale, thereby making French products competitive with products sold by the major industrial powers on the world market. Less emphasis was placed upon macroeconomic stabilization. Between 1958 and 1981 the relative emphasis placed upon particular industries changed, with the nuclear, electronics, and aerospace industries receiving considerable attention and state resources. After 1981 French industrial policy focused upon making mature industries more competitive internationally. In addition, the Mitterrand government increased the state-directed redistribution of income and wealth as well as the realignment of economic power. Since the late 1980s the policy has been one of competitive disinflation under which inflation is reduced so as to make French products more competitive, thereby stimulating exports while lowering unemployment.

Indirect means of control and voluntary compliance with state proposals rather than commanding private-sector managers and workers are main features of the industrial policy measures. The broad interrelated industrial policy and redistributional measures introduced in France include nationalization; price discrimination by SOEs;[56] contracts with SOEs specifying desired output targets and extent of state support the SOE would receive; moral suasion (e.g., provide SOEs with a public study of the impact of their activities on the economy);[57] promotion of one or two large firms in each key industry;[58] price controls to prevent inflation; extensive social insurance and welfare services; greater international cooperation through European Union membership; export subsidies; tariffs and quotas to promote import substitution and export promotion policies; public procurement; funding of research and development; cash subsidies; regulation of financial markets (a 1947 working rule permits the treasury to veto any new bond or equity issue it believed was not in the national interest); foreign exchange controls; selective monetary and fiscal policy; various incentives (e.g., accelerated depreciation write-offs, investment tax credits); selective allocation of credit; construction permits; marketing selected products

---

[55]Adams and Stoffaes, *French Industrial Policy*, p. 167.

[56]Some SOEs, especially public utilities, discriminate according to the amount of their good or service used by client. Low prices can be set to promote public consumption, with a corresponding subsidy granted to the SOE producing the low-priced good or service.

[57]While these studies were not binding on the SOEs, evidence indicates that management decisions were influenced. "Very often the studies show the companies how much they could contribute to the public interest without jeopardizing their ability to compete." Ibid., p. 124. The state's role in the contract process is to monitor if SOE objectives are consistent with national economic objectives.

[58]This is popularly referred to as "the strategy of national champions." Adams, *Restructuring the French Economy*, p. 54. Subsidies and other government favors would be concentrated on only one or two enterprises in each industry until the 1970s when a more egalitarian treatment of enterprises was adopted.

and services; regulation of labor markets (the state could set minimum wages and had the right to disprove an enterprise's decision to lay off workers); and indicative planning.

The relative importance of these measures has varied since 1945. Membership in the European Union has meant the end of some protective practices (e.g., foreign exchange controls), creating a more open, competitive French economy coordinated to a large extent by market forces and working rules established by the supranational institutions of the European Union. Financial controls, especially selective allocation of credit, have played a crucial role for most of the period. The significance of indicative planning has declined from being *the* primary means of control for the first two decades after World War II to being a minor factor in recent years.

Between 1946 and the late 1960s France practiced the most elaborate and detailed planning process among the industrialized guided market economies. For a few years in the late 1940s strong central control (heavy *dirigiste*) was the management style, becoming an indicative style after the immediate reconstruction objectives were achieved. Since then French planning has been a process for coordinating economic activities, not a means for extensive state intervention in the matters of private enterprises. Planning has been "decentralized, horizontal, and hortatory—decentralized in that regional governments participate actively, horizontal in that policies are designed to be applied in a neutral manner to all industries, and hortatory in that planners enjoy no powers other than persuasion."[59]

A trend established in the early 1970s has been for market forces to become more important than planning for coordinating production activities, although expanded social insurance and welfare programs have made the state more active in the distribution of France's national income. President Valery Giscard d'Estaing was a primary leader in the shift toward unregulated markets, for he believed that "complex social systems have to rely also on automatic mechanisms."[60] Planning no longer is a "third way between dirigisme and liberalism,"[61] but is being used to facilitate the transformation to a more open economy.

Since the late 1980s French macroeconomic policy of "competitiveness through disinflation" has emphasized maintaining the value of the franc and reducing inflation so as to make French products more competitive, thereby reducing unemployment while maintaining a favorable balance of trade. Coordination has become more difficult in the 1990s due to a prolonged recession with unemployment hovering around 12 percent. The budget deficit is spiraling out of control, partly due to France having the most generous social insurance and

[59]Adams and Stoffaes, *French Industrial Policy*, p. 119.
[60]Lauber, *The Political Economy of France*, p. 21.
[61]Ross, Hoffmann, and Malzacher, *The Mitterrand Experiment*, p. 27.

welfare schemes in the world. For example, public day care may cost as little as $2 daily, annual university tuition is under $300, some workers receive an extra month's pay for Christmas and for summer vacation, workers who lose their job can receive 60 percent of their pay for up to five years, and the family of a deceased individual may receive over $6,000 for burial costs.[62] Seeking to reduce the tax burden while stimulating employment and reducing the budget deficit, the government is left with very unpopular policy options. French policymakers chose to raise taxes (increased income tax surcharges, increased duties on petrol and alcohol) while cutting government spending and freezing public-sector wages, and raising user fees for health care.

Such conservative policies are required for macroeconomic stabilization to be achieved and for France to satisfy the requirements for European Union membership established by the 1992 Maastricht, Netherlands Treaty. The treaty, which each European Union member has to ratify, establishes fiscal and monetary rules for eligibility. These rules pertain to domestic monetary policy and interest rates, stating that they be targeted so as to maintain external value of currency. Another working rule was that gross public debt as a percentage of nominal gross domestic product must not exceed 50 percent. Finally, the ratio of government deficit on current public expenditure to gross domestic product must not exceed 3 percent. During the early 1990s France was the only member of the European Union to satisfy all of these requirements until the deficit problem worsened. The performance of the nation's economy in other areas is discussed next.

PRIVATIZATION, THE EUROPEAN UNION, AND REDUCED PLANNING: FACTORS PROMOTING INSTITUTIONAL CHANGE

Changes in the executive branch, especially the rise of de Gaulle, Giscard d'Estaing, and Mitterrand led to the adoption of new institutions or the extension of existing institutions, both of which influenced the behavior of the economy. In addition to the change in executive branch authorities, the most important institutional changes in France were the extension of the SOEs (see "A Key Role for State Ownership and Control," p. 246), the growing importance of European Union supranational institutions (see Chapter 14), and the decline in importance of planning institutions. Factors which have combined to lessen the importance of planning include: the difficulty of coordinating a more complex, open economy through consensus agreements with representatives of interest groups, more discrepancies between plan forecasts and the economy's actual performance; concern about bureaucratization of economic decision making and the threat of

---

[62]"Are the French Spoiled?" *Newsweek*, March 22, 1993, p. 45.

collusion between enterprises; the pro-market philosophical basis of Giscard d'Estaing as well as Mitterrand in the early 1990s; and the lack of "'proof' that economic planning was responsible for the exceptional success of the French economy in the post-war period,"[63] rather than credit the government with fostering an improved competitive environment in which French firms were prodded to become competitive.[64]

The institutional change which has the most significance for the direction the French economy as it evolves into the twenty-first century has been the election of the conservative (center-right coalition) government in 1993 and 1995. The 1993 government won 460 out of 577 seats in Parliament, with 24 additional seats going to conservative independent candidates while a significant decline was experienced by the Socialists, Communists, and other leftist parties (who combined won only 93 seats).[65] The Conservatives are pro-Maastricht and advocate policies designed to make France qualify for membership in the European Monetary Union. Such policies must be consistent with provisions contained in the Single European Act of 1986 (see Chapter 14), which harmonize working rules throughout the European Union primarily in a direction consistent with a greater role for the private sector. Consistent with the conservative government's goal of deepening French involvement with the European Union is the Bank of France, the nation's central bank, gaining its independence in early 1994. As an independent bank it will set the nation's monetary and interest-rate policy.

PERFORMANCE: A LONG PERIOD OF FAVORABLE GROWTH BUT UNEMPLOYMENT PERSISTS

Analysts agree that throughout the 1945–1990 period the performance of the French economy was quite favorable in terms of the objectives France has established for itself under different authorities and in terms of comparison to other major European nations (e.g., West Germany, United Kingdom, Italy). Between 1960 and 1976 the French economy grew faster than any other major industrial nation with the exception of Japan (see Table 10-1). From 1976–1986 France's economic growth exceeded that of the European Union (EU) average, while its unemployment rates have remained slightly below the EU level (see Table 10-2). Inflation was lower in France during 1974–1992 than the EU average, but higher than its main industrial competitors (see Table 10-3).

---

[63]For a detailed discussion of the combination of factors contributing to the decline of French planning importance, see Hough, *The French Economy*, pp. 120, 121.

[64]An analysis of the impact of the French government on the economy performance is provided by Adams, *Restructuring the French Economy*, 1989.

[65]The government is described as "cohabitation" since there is a socialist president and conservative prime minister and parliament, at least until the 1995 presidential elections.

What reasons can be cited for the French "success" in terms of the nation satisfying its economic goals from 1945 to 1990? While recognizing that France has benefited from belonging to the European Union, much credit has been given to the state-guided modernization and structural improvement drive initiated in the 1940s. France was able to introduce an effective planning scheme while simultaneously increasing the degree of competition in many industries. It is difficult to isolate the effects of planning on the economy's performance, for there are no easy indicators with which to make such an assessment. This has been more so as the economy has grown more open and complex, while its scope has enlarged to encompass social as well as economic objectives.[66] What can be said is that planning appears to have mobilized investment and savings, and to have successfully implanted the informal rule that French citizens had a civic responsibility to contribute toward making their nation a world economic power. Since targets of early plans were achieved, the public's confidence in the planning process increased. Workers accepted state guidance and modernization efforts in return for promises of an improved standard of living. This they received, for real income per capita grew at an annual average rate of just below 3 percent between 1960 and 1985,[67] while the percentage of households that owned an automobile, refrigerator, washing machine, and a television set increased from less than 3 percent in 1960 to over 50 percent by 1977.[68] The state was successful in prodding French firms to become more competitive in international markets.

Since 1991 France has been mired in a serious recession. Economic growth has been below 2 percent each year, and was negative in 1993. Although inflation has been very low, unemployment has increased from less than 9 percent in 1990 to almost 12 percent. In addition, youth unemployment (i.e., those under 25 years of age who are seeking work) remains a serious problem. It has exceeded 20 percent since the late 1980s, reaching about 24 percent in 1994. Gross fixed capital formation has been negative each year prior to 1995, while factor productivity continues to decline. Exports and industrial production also have been unfavorable during the early 1990s.

Evaluating the overall performance since 1991 reveals that one primary aim of competitive disinflation has been achieved, namely, reduction of inflation, albeit with only modest improvement in France's competitiveness. Business profits have increased, and the balance of trade reestablished, but little has been done to reduce unemployment.[69] Persistence of unemployment is due, among

---

[66]J. Carre, P. Dubois, and E. Malinvaud, *French Economic Growth* (Stanford, CA: Stanford University Press, 1975), p. 474. Some analysts credit planning with stimulating higher levels of investment in capital (that was able to increase labor productivity), improving utilization of production facilities, and guiding enterprises toward becoming more competitive on international markets.

[67]Adams, *Restructuring the French Economy*, p. 4.

[68]Holmes and Fawcett, *The Contemporary French Economy*, p. 23.

[69]For a detailed evaluation of this policy, see Olivier Jean Blanchard and Pierre Alain Muet, "Competitiveness Through Disinflation: An Assessment of the French Macroeconomic Strategy," *Economic Policy*, 16 (April 1993), 11–56.

other reasons, to only modest improvements in competitiveness where large differentials are required to reduce unemployment levels substantially. Also, since some of France's trading partners have devalued their currency while the franc has remained relatively strong, the improved competitiveness due to lower inflation is partially offset. Government attempts at structural reform include new working rules pertaining to reduced social expenditures (such as paying 80 percent of previous earnings for up to two years for those who become unemployed) and income taxes, or reducing payroll taxes (by up to 40 percent) for firms that reduce the workweek from 39 to 32 hours (so that more workers will be hired). However, both changes have met with stiff resistance from those who fear a "dismantling of the [French] welfare state" to employers who argue that reducing the workweek will put them at a disadvantage vis-à-vis their competitors.[70] Having succeeded in reducing inflation through tough measures, it remains to be seen if French authorities have the will and ability to do likewise for the employment problem.

A SUMMARY OF THE EVOLUTIONARY-INSTITUTIONAL PROCESS OF DEVELOPMENT IN FRANCE

The post-World War II French philosophical basis and principal institutions were heavily influenced by the poor performance of the economy prior to that time. The prewar economy had featured little state guidance (in the Keynesian sense) and formal and informal protective barriers which perpetuated traditional production and distribution practices, leaving many French firms unable to compete in world markets. The state of the economy in 1945, combined with vivid memories of defeat at the hands of Germany, drove French authorities to adopt a philosophical basis which favored planning, nationalization, and other industrial policy measures to promote modernization and structural change. In addition, the failure of isolation convinced French authorities to establish close ties by integrating politically and economically with its European neighbors.

The philosophical basis held by authorities from the late 1940s to the early 1970s was a combination of a desire for state guidance with respect for decentralized, voluntary decision making, and belief in the efficiency of markets. This basis led to the establishment of planning institutions and SOEs, and to working rules providing for a strong Ministry of the Treasury. The informal and formal rules for these institutions focused on measures to guide enterprises to behave in a manner consistent with national goals by providing incentives rather than by issuing directives. Successful performance of the economy for more than two decades after the new policies were implemented promoted widespread faith

---

[70]William Echikson, "Unemployment: Working It Out," *France Today,* 9, 3 (April 1994), p. e.

in planning and compliance by most interest groups with the recommended behavior (e.g., level of investment for modernization purposes) suggested by the planners. Some analysts observed that "[a]s economic success became more certain, public opinion and politicians changed their views. Social progress and economic efficiency were no longer perceived as competitors."[71]

A change in the political structure occurred in 1974 following a brief period of poor economic performance (primarily due to the first of two oil crises). The new government of Giscard d'Estaing, which was elected by a small margin, introduced a philosophical basis emphasizing markets as the primary process for economic coordination. An interrelated factor strengthening the shift to working rules promoting competition through unregulated markets while not pursuing further nationalizations was France's deeper integration within the European Union. Community working rules required a more open, competitive economy with the exception of the agricultural sector. However, planning institutions were not abandoned, for sentiments against laissez-faire policies remained strong in some political and intellectual circles.

In 1981, after seven years of modest economic performance and disputes over economic policy, which split the center-right coalition while leading to less investment as rising costs of social services put a squeeze on enterprise profits, Socialist authorities were elected. One performance indicator that the Socialists found unacceptable was the highly skewed (compared to the OECD average) distribution of income. The Socialist and Communist authorities attributed most economic imbalances to unequal or insufficient democratic rights in the workplace. As a result they wanted better integration of state regulatory measures and competitive market mechanisms. This resulted in widespread institutional change as more private enterprises became SOEs. Meanwhile, spending on social insurance and welfare programs increased. The authorities were able to introduce these measures without meeting public resistance because of the improved economic performance throughout the 1980s. Rapid economic growth provided the state with sufficient resources to fund its enterprises and provide social insurance and welfare payments to those in need (e.g., miners, peasants, small shopkeepers who lost their jobs due to more international competition) without having to tax workers and employers more heavily. Class antagonism and meritocracy were not a serious problem despite the continuing unequal distribution of income because the state assisted those in need to achieve an acceptable standard of living. The problematic performance of the economy since 1991 has stimulated election of a conservative government with new working rules which provide for greater reliance upon market forces and instilling more discipline in monetary and fiscal policies as France seeks to comply with European Union provisions.

---

[71]Ross, Hoffmann, and Malzacher, *The Mitterrand Experiment*, pp. 34, 35.

LOOKING AHEAD

The French economy demonstrates that state guidance in the form of indicative planning and nationalization, combined with measures such as selective allocation of credit, is not inconsistent with the relatively favorable performance of an economy (in terms of standard indicators). Another type of economy that extends state influence over production and distribution activities is the democratically controlled social economy. The philosophical basis for this type of economy is presented in Chapter 12.

KEY TERMS AND CONCEPTS

European Union   Public Enterprises
Indicative Planning   State Intervention
Nationalization

QUESTIONS FOR DISCUSSION

1. What is indicative planning? How does it differ as a social process for economic coordination from other processes presented in earlier chapters?
2. Why are the French disinclined toward laissez-faire policies?
3. What role does the Ministry of Finance play in guiding the French economy?
4. Why were some French industries nationalized?
5. In what respects does the role of the state in economic activities differ between France and Japan?
6. Evaluate the extent to which French economic policymaking since 1946 has been consistent with the policy prescriptions of John Maynard Keynes.

REFERENCES

Adams, William James, *Restructuring the French Economy.* Washington, DC: The Brookings Institution, 1989.

Adams, William J., and Christian Stoffaes, eds., *French Industrial Policy.* Washington, DC: The Brookings Institution, 1986.

Andreff, Wladimir, "East European Privatization in the Light of Western Experience," *Journal of Transforming Economies and Societies* 1, 1 (Summer 1994), 21–33.

"Are the French Spoiled?" *Newsweek*, March 22, 1993, p. 45.

Balassa, Bela, *The First Year of Socialist Government in France.* Washington, DC: American Enterprise Institute, 1982.

Baum, Warren C., *The French Economy and the State.* Princeton, NJ: Princeton University Press, 1958.

Blanchard, Olivier Jean, and Pierre Alain Muet, "Competitiveness Through

Disinflation: An Assessment of the French Macroeconomic Strategy," *Economic Policy*, 16 (April 1993), 11–56.

Carre, J., P. Dubois, and E. Malinvaud, *French Economic Growth.* Stanford, CA: Stanford University Press, 1975.

Cohen, Stephen S., *Modern Capitalist Planning: The French Model.* Berkeley, CA: University of California Press, 1977.

Estrin, Saul, and Peter Holmes, *French Planning in Theory and Practice.* London: George Allen and Unwin, 1983.

"France for Sale," *Fortune*, September 6, 1993, p. 11.

"France's Economy Gets Strong Grade in Report by OECD," *The Wall Street Journal*, April 12, 1990, p. A11.

Harlow, John S., *French Economic Planning: A Challenge to Reason.* Iowa City: University of Iowa Press, 1966.

Hayward, Jack, *The State and the Market Economy.* New York: New York University Press, 1986.

Holmes, Graeme M., and Peter O. Fawcett, *The Contemporary French Economy.* London: The Macmillan Press, 1983.

Hough, J. R., *The French Economy.* New York: Holmes and Meier, 1982.

Kuisel, Richard F., *Capitalism and the State in Modern France.* Cambridge: Cambridge University Press, 1981.

Lauber, Volkmar, *The Political Economy of France.* New York: Praeger, 1983.

Living Conditions in OECD Countries. Paris: OECD, 1986.

Machin, Howard, and Vincent Wright, eds., *Economic Policy and Policy-Making under the Mitterrand Presidency 1981–1984.* New York: St. Martin's Press, 1985.

Marceau, Jane, *Class and Status in France.* Oxford: Clarendon Press, 1977.

McCarthy, Patrick, ed., *The French Socialists in Power, 1981–1986.* New York: Greenwood Press, 1987.

OECD in Figures. Paris: OECD, 1989.

Ross, George, Stanley Hoffman, and Sylvia Malzacher, *The Mitterrand Experiment.* Cambridge: Polity Press, 1987.

Salin, Pascal, "Some Lessons for France's Conservatives," *The Wall Street Journal*, June 15, 1988, p. 25.

Sheahan, John, *Promotion and Control of Industry in Postwar France.* Cambridge, MA: Harvard University Press, 1963.

Social Expenditure: 1960–1990. Paris: OECD, 1985.

Toy, Stewart, "The CEO Guillotine Is Busy Again," *Business Week*, November 1, 1993, p. 54.

12

THE PHILOSOPHICAL BASIS FOR A DEMOCRATICALLY CONTROLLED SOCIAL ECONOMY

OBJECTIVES

1. Explain how the views of Robert Owen, John Stuart Mill, the Fabians, and William Beveridge developed as a reaction to what they perceived as negative consequences of laissez-faire policies in an economy whose primary social process for economic coordination was unregulated markets.
2. Explain the justification offered by philosophers for state intervention as a necessary means to complement market activity.
3. Discuss the specific reform measures proposed that would extend state influence throughout the economy, measures which offered protection to citizens from the adverse effects of unregulated market forces.

INTRODUCTION

The philosophical basis for a democratically controlled social economy (DCSE) developed simultaneously with Marxian philosophy (see Chapter 15). However, while the Marxian philosophy foresaw inevitable confrontation between the bourgeoisie and proletariat, the DCSE philosophy was designed to reform the new industrial economies gradually and peacefully. The DCSE philosophy is a synthesis of moral, political, and economic beliefs. The earliest proponents of this synthesis of beliefs included the Early Reformers (Robert Owen and John Stuart Mill) and members of the Fabian Society (among whom were George Bernard

Shaw and Sidney Webb). Later philosophers and intellectuals who articulated the DCSE philosophy in the twentieth century included leaders of the Social Democratic Party in Sweden and the primary author of England's "Beveridge Report," William Beveridge.

The Early Reformers, Fabians, and Beveridge perceived negative economic and social effects of industrialization within England's laissez-faire market economy (LFME). These social critics observed that a majority of the growing urban population lived in unhealthy, crime-ridden factory towns with no source of support (except for charity) should they experience misfortune such as unemployment or injury from industrial accidents. It appeared that economic growth throughout the first half of the nineteenth century, while improving the standard of living of the middle and upper classes, was not accompanied by an improved standard of living for most factory workers. Mill stated that "hitherto it is questionable if all the mechanical inventions yet made have lightened the day's toil of any human beings. They have enabled a greater population to live the same life of drudgery and imprisonment, and an increased number of manufacturers and others to make fortunes."[1]

The primary goal of these reformers was the establishment of an egalitarian society with greater freedom, less inequality of income and wealth, and universal protection from unemployment and poverty. The state should complement the private economy where necessary. "Collective intervention by the democratic state"[2] through interventionist monetary and fiscal policy was advocated to mitigate the effects of macroeconomic instability and for the purpose of lessening income inequalities. DCSE proponents believed it was the state's responsibility to establish working rules for the purpose of decreasing unemployment, especially among the poor, and to provide general support (e.g., social and economic services) for those less fortunate.

Markets and private ownership were condoned, but these were to be subordinate to conscious social control of private ownership and investment, redistribution of income through progressive taxation, transfer payments, and provision of public education and public goods. Nationalization was not generally the suggested means for social control over the economy. Instead, the economic power of entrepreneurs and stockholders would be dispersed among democratic organizations whose interests were more representative of the entire society. Such organizations included producers' and consumers' cooperatives, labor unions, and voluntary associations.

Unlike the typical classical economists, some DCSE advocates, including Mill, believed that the distribution of output should not be regulated by the natural laws of economics (i.e., physical laws of nature and competitive markets). They also argued that economic growth in an LFME would not guarantee the

---

[1]Jacob Oser and Stanley L. Brue, *The Evolution of Economic Thought*, 4th ed. (San Diego: Harcourt Brace Jovanovich, 1988), p. 148.

[2]Jay Douglas, *Socialism in the New Society* (New York: St. Martin's Press, 1963), p. 31.

alleviation of poverty. According to DCSE proponents, an LFME was unjust, irrational, and dehumanizing: People were treated as commodities—productive inputs subject to the laws of demand and supply for the purpose of generating profits that relatively few property owners would enjoy.

The essential intent of DCSE proponents can be summarized as follows.

> Socialism [i.e., a DCSE] is, essentially, the tendency inherent in an industrial civilization to transcend the self-regulating market by consciously subordinating it to a democratic society. It is the solution natural to the industrial workers who see no reason why production should not be regulated directly and why markets should be more than a useful but subordinate trait in a free society. From the point of view of the community as a whole, . . . [a DCSE] is merely the continuation of that endeavor to make society a distinctively human relationship of persons.[3]

This chapter will focus on three principal contributors to the DCSE philosophy: the Early Reformers, the Fabian Society, and William Beveridge. These contributors provided informal rules which eventually became the basis for the formal working rules of twentieth-century DCSEs, including Sweden and some other members of the European Union (e.g., Denmark, the United Kingdom), and in Australia, Canada, and New Zealand, among other nations. The specific contributions of the Swedish intellectuals and labor leaders toward reforming the Swedish economy are discussed in Chapter 13.

THE EARLY REFORMERS

Robert Owen

Robert Owen (1771–1858) was an entrepreneur, philosopher, and early advocate of the DCSE's underlying principles. Owen's contributions to DCSE philosophy are contained in his philosophy of social reform, the reforms he introduced or advocated, and the impact of his views and reforms on the nineteenth- and twentieth-century institutions and working rules adopted by the industrial economies.

PHILOSOPHY.   There were three features of Owen's philosophy: his conception of happiness within a community, criticisms of the philosophy and working rules of an LFME, and evaluation of society's behavior. Owen believed that happiness depends upon a person's living arrangements and the living conditions enjoyed by others within the same environment. Consequently, a person could become happier "only by endeavoring to increase the happiness of all around

---

[3]Karl Polanyi, *The Great Transformation* (Boston: Beacon Press, 1957), p. 234. Polanyi's use of the term *socialism* has been replaced by *a DCSE* for reasons outlined in this chapter.

him."[4] The pursuit of pleasure by individuals or families without concern for their surrounding social environment would, according to Owen, foster a competitive society with disharmony and lower levels of happiness. He believed families were an "autonomous and alien element in society . . . [which] served to isolate men from each other, and to breed loneliness and self-centredness."[5] Owen's alternative for social reform, which would raise happiness and enhance social harmony, was "communitarianism." He advocated the establishment of experimental communities, "scientific associations of men, women and children . . . from about four or five hundred to about two thousand, arranged to be as one family."[6]

Owen's most notable experimental community venture was in New Lanark, Scotland. This industrial textile community was created by Owen's father-in-law in the late eighteenth century in response to a labor shortage. He built textile mills and houses with which to entice workers to settle in New Lanark. When Owen took over the community he saw an opportunity to extend his concept of community to industrial relations as well as living arrangements.

Believing that behavior could be improved through changing living and working conditions, Owen introduced social and economic reforms into the community that would become widespread throughout DCSEs in the twentieth century. These reforms included free education, child labor rules prohibiting children under the age of 10 from working, sickness and old-age insurance, community recreational facilities, higher wages combined with a shorter workweek, and a company store that offered goods at prices below those prevailing in the area. Although the degree to which inhabitants of New Lanark became "happier" cannot be determined, more desirable behavior (e.g., greater sobriety) ensued. The community's inhabitants enjoyed above-average living standards compared to other industrial workers in that era, and the community prospered as long as Owen was able to provide his personality and management skills toward its everyday operations.

Owen was critical of the philosophical basis of an LFME. He disagreed with the inherent belief that natural laws governed society. He also lamented the negative effects of the early industrial market economy, especially the dehumanization of laborers and the extent of poverty endured by a majority of the society's members. Owen expressed moral indignation toward the basic assumptions of LFME philosophy, believing that "[i]f individuals pursue their aims opposed to and in competition with their fellow men, angry and malevolent passions are nurtured, the divisive forces in society are strengthened, and all superior and valuable qualities of human nature are repressed."[7]

The classical economists' emphasis on the maximization of wealth rather

---

[4]Henry William Spiegel, *The Growth of Economic Thought* (Durham, NC: Duke University Press, 1983), p. 441.

[5]J. F. C. Harrison, *Quest for the New Moral World* (New York: Charles Scribner, 1969), p. 60.

[6]Ibid.

[7]Spiegel, *The Growth of Economic Thought*, p. 441.

than happiness was rejected by Owen. He criticized the substitution of machinery for labor, which had the effect of displacing some laborers while driving down the wages of others and increasing the profits of the manufacturer. In addition, Owen criticized the "business civilization" which "compelled small children to work long hours and allowed them to grow up warped in mind and body without an adequate education, . . . [while forcing employers] to persevere in the maintenance of a system imposed on them by the competitive struggle, a system making for disharmony and dooming the worker to a life that had lost its dignity."[8]

The third feature of Owen's philosophy was his "science of society." Owen assumed it possible to reconstruct society on a "scientific basis" if the reformer knew the laws of social dynamics.[9] In formulating his laws concerning behavior in society, Owen identified a conception of behavior and of the forces which could improve behavior. He believed man's behavior was a product of the environment; therefore, undesirable institutions (e.g., competitive markets, the family) would have a corrupting influence. Owen argued that by changing the environment, especially through educational reform and cooperative living and working arrangements, people could become happier and more productive.

Owen's agent of change would be an association of the most rational members of all socioeconomic groups and principal institutions. He rejected revolutionary measures of change; consequently, he did not seek to promote class struggle. Instead, Owen hoped that "universal togetherness"[10] would ensue from "cordial cooperation and unity of action between the government, Parliament, the church, and the people."[11] He advocated peaceful, gradual, marginal social and economic reforms that would progressively repeal existing undesirable institutions, rules, and conditions. If impediments to reform were removed one at a time, Owen believed, there would be fewer objections toward the subsequent removal of other problems.

REFORMS.   The reforms advocated by Owen were designed to protect and assist the working class. These measures included public provision of social security, public training programs with a commitment to reduce unemployment, and producer cooperatives. Owen presumed that happiness would be raised if the results of each worker's efforts were shared with the community. Public provision of social security, with the community's wealth distributed on a need basis, was such a measure. The selfish pursuit of individual wealth maximization would erode, Owen assumed, if people recognized that their own happiness was dependent on the happiness of the entire community.

Owen believed the attainment of full employment would reduce "the

---

[8]Ibid., p. 440.

[9]Harrison, *Quest for the New Moral World*, p. 78.

[10]Oser and Brue, *The Evolution of Economic Thought*, p. 148.

[11]William Ebenstein and Edwin Fogelman, *Today's Isms: Communism, Fascism, Capitalism, Socialism*, 8th ed. (Englewood Cliffs, NJ: Prentice-Hall, 1980), p. 211.

temptation to commit crimes"[12] and lower the incidence of unhealthy and unsavory habits (e.g., drunkenness, violent acts) common among paupers. An innovative reformer, he proposed free public education and training for all children. Education and training, Owen believed, would bring about full employment, which, in turn, would alleviate the drunkenness and crime that were widespread within the English lower classes. Other than the national education system, Owen did not advocate active state intervention in terms of providing public employment, relief payments to the poor, or nationalization of industry. Producers would be encouraged to establish cooperatives voluntarily, thereby avoiding direct competition in favor of cooperation.

IMPACT.   What impact did Robert Owen have on the evolution of the DCSE in the twentieth century? His critique of the LFME, efforts to pass factory legislation,[13] and support of trade unions influenced the growth of the labor movement in the United Kingdom. While Owen's attempt to establish producer cooperatives was not a lasting success, a consumer cooperative movement in which he had a mild interest became established. This movement would contribute to the growth of the Labor Party in Britain.

Owen was the first to use the term *socialism*. He did not, however, contribute any formal working rules for a new economy based upon an economic theory he had developed. The informal rules embodied in his theory of society and conception of happiness and community provided inspiration to those who sought to reform an LFME.

John Stuart Mill

John Stuart Mill (1806–1873), a brilliant scholar who made contributions both as a philosopher and as an economist, generally has been associated with the classical school of economics (see Chapter 5). He believed there were benefits to society from the LFME, especially from private property and competition. He adopted and articulated the conventional economic principles of his classical predecessors in seeking scientific solutions to social problems.

As a moral philosopher, however, he was considered a philosophical radical. He had "strong and deep feelings about the injustices of the capitalist economy."[14] Mill believed there were potential social benefits from state intervention, which would guide self-interest,[15] and from institutional reform,

---

[12]Robert Owen, *A New View of Society and Other Writings* (London: J. M. Dent and Sons, 1927), p. 35.

[13]Owen helped promote Factory Acts, which imposed standards on all employers, such as the minimum age for workers in textile mills and a limit on the number of hours per day an individual could work in a factory.

[14]Harry Landreth, *History of Economic Theory* (Boston: Houghton Mifflin, 1976), p. 150.

[15]In this regard the intent is to encourage people "to identify their own long-run interest with that of the state and thus recognize that by promoting the public interest they promote their own." Spiegel, *The Growth of Economic Thought*, p. 85.

which would result in greater emphasis upon the development of people than on profits earned by business.

Mill's vision of the ideal society included greater happiness and well-being for all individuals. He did not, however, measure these features in material terms. He stressed the importance of high moral development for all individuals, with the poor and the working class being elevated in noneconomic as well as economic terms. All individuals would possess greater wisdom, virtue (e.g., altruism), and the ability to manage their own lives. These conditions would not be accomplished by the use of force, but through peaceful, democratic procedures.

Continued economic and population growth were limited by nature, as Thomas Malthus and David Ricardo had argued (see Chapter 5), and were neither necessary nor desirable in an ideal state. Mill envisioned a "stationary state" as superior to an LFME in which relatively few enjoyed the benefits from economic growth. Mill's state would be characterized by a "less materialistic culture"[16] and a more equitable distribution of income. In this society "no one is poor, no one desires to be richer, [and no one] . . . has any reason to fear being thrust back by the efforts of others to push themselves forward."[17]

Among the problems Mill identified as being exacerbated by England's LFME were class conflict and poverty. Although he held both employers and employees responsible for the hostility and disharmony between the property-owning and working classes, Mill placed greater responsibility upon the former for their unfair, unjust treatment of their workers. While Mill accepted the LFME tenet that production was governed by nature, he argued that the distribution of personal income was subject to modification. Income distribution, while partially influenced by competitive forces, was also determined by society's customs, laws, and institutional arrangements. Consequently, authorities could change the distribution of income through introducing working rules related to subsidies, maximum work hours per day, expropriation of land and other productive assets, state ownership of natural monopolies, and wealth and inheritance taxes—the revenue from which could be reallocated to selected groups in any proportion desired. The distinction Mill drew between production and distribution was significant. It gave "resonance to the clarion call for economic reorganization and reform which resounds through his work. . . . Unlike Smith, Mill view[ed] laissez-faire [LFME] not as a natural system of liberty, but as a man-made institution and as such subject to the test of social usefulness."[18]

Mill was an eclectic, blending the views of the economic liberals who favored the LFME with his desire for social reforms through government policies. He faced the same dilemmas that all DCSE proponents have faced: how to retain the positive features of competitive markets while avoiding the adverse effects of

---

[16]Landreth, *History of Economic Theory,* p. 139.
[17]Ibid., p. 140.
[18]Spiegel, *The Growth of Economic Thought,* p. 385.

competition upon society; and how to reap the benefits of the LFME, especially economic freedoms and greater output and productive efficiency, while expanding the state's agenda to protect the working class and the indigent. This expansion was necessary, he argued, because the LFME created a nonharmonious social order (due to a skewed distribution of income) and accentuated the virtues of wealth and selfishness.

A slow pace of reform was necessary, for genuine reform would not stem from changes in only one factor. Rather, Mill believed that social problems required many-sided reform measures. Like Owen, Mill recognized that folkways follow stateways. He recommended that reforms be introduced slowly to give those fearing change time to observe and accept the new working rules.

Mill was not dogmatic regarding the role of the state in reforming an LFME. He did not advocate state nationalization of industry (except for natural monopolies) or any form of economic planning. He continually extolled the contributions to productive efficiency of competition and private property. Mill did argue in favor of state provision of public goods (e.g., lighthouses) and for state support of public education. He stated that if he had to choose between "communism" and the LFME which created suffering and injustices endured by the working class and the indigent (in the 1840s), and if private property would perpetuate the poverty endured by these groups, then he would prefer "communism." For Mill, however, the choice of an economy was not between capitalism, socialism, or communism, but between the existing LFME and the type of economy which could be established through social reform. His preference was for an economy whose social process for economic coordination was primarily competitive markets, but whose working rules concerning the benefits derived through ownership of private property were modified by public authorities to create a more equitable distribution of income.

Other changes in the working rules of an LFME advocated by Mill included his advocacy of trade unions, producer cooperatives, voluntary associations of citizens, and universal education. Mill believed trade unions would enhance the bargaining power of workers. Otherwise, competitive forces, especially as they were influenced by the growth of the labor force, would overwhelmingly favor the employers during wage disputes. Mill advocated the formation of producer cooperatives, an "association of the labourers themselves on terms of equality, collectively owning the capital with which they carry on their operations, and working under managers elected and removable by themselves."[19] He believed that the growth of such institutions would promote greater harmony and cooperation as well as greater profits through the attainment of economies of scale. As a result, workers' wages would be higher than under an LFME.

To encourage a more democratic, cooperative, socially involved society, Mill supported voluntary participation in the form of local and municipal

---

[19]Graeme Duncan, *Marx and Mill* (Cambridge: Cambridge University Press, 1973), p. 247.

associations. While Mill was vague regarding the specific activities and rules that would characterize such associations, he assumed participation in them would enhance citizenship and social cohesion, decrease class conflict, raise the ability of people to manage their own lives, and increase the sense of community. This form of public education would serve to "lift men beyond their narrow private interests and their exclusive private circles."[20] Voluntary associations, schools, and universities were part of the network of social institutions Mill believed necessary to "transform people . . . into rational beings."[21] Both state and private educational institutions were necessary. This would prevent a state monopoly from shaping individuals without the benefits provided by an alternative, competing viewpoint.

Education was a primary measure for social reform, Mill argued, because he believed that behavior could be conditioned. More rational attitudes would provide a basis for the development of firmer moral convictions and beliefs. Mill claimed that people with convictions and beliefs would be likelier to initiate social reforms than those motivated by material interests. To the extent that rapid population growth was attributable to ignorance, education would help mitigate the harmful effects of excess population. Better-educated workers would become happier and realize greater fulfillment from their work and leisure activities. Finally, education would increase the appeal of noneconomic aspects of human behavior. In Mill's reformed society educated people would use their wealth to stimulate appreciation of the objects and desires (e.g., the arts) which wealth could not purchase.

Summary

What effect did the Early Reformers have on the evolution of the DCSE? Since England experienced a favorable economic performance for more than two decades after 1850, with the working class realizing an increased standard of living as well, few reforms advocated by either Owen or Mill were adopted before the late nineteenth century. That substantive reforms similar to those contained in the Early Reformers' preachings were not introduced in many societies until after the Great Depression of the 1930s illustrates the role played by authorities in changing the working rules of an economy. There were no sympathetic, influential authorities in nineteenth-century England who would champion Owen's proposed reforms. The introduction of such reforms coincided with the rise to authority status of Labor-Party leaders in Scandinavia and Britain after the Great Depression of 1929–1932 and World War II. Some state regulation and reforms of factories and education consistent with Mill's proposals were introduced in England during the nineteenth century. Overall, however, Mill's main contribution was the informal rules and process of change he advocated, and which influenced later philosophers and political activists—most significantly in England and Sweden.

The DCSEs have peacefully evolved through gradual reforms after

[20]Ibid., p. 250.
[21]Ibid., p. 253.

considerable compromise between competing groups. Twentieth-century DCSE proponents have been nondogmatic, eclectic, open-minded, pragmatic, willing to compromise, and sentimental—all qualities consistent with John Stuart Mill. The first formal group sympathetic to a DCSE were the Fabians, who hailed Mill "as a forerunner and kindred thinker."[22]

THE FABIAN SOCIETY

The performance of England's economy during the depression of 1873 to 1896 stimulated considerable unrest among workers, unemployed and indigent, and intellectuals. The labor movement became more cohesive as workers were no longer willing to accept some basic tenets of the LFME philosophy. In this climate arose a "new generation of intellectuals" who would provide a philosophical basis and propose working rules for a DCSE.[23]

The leading intellectuals of this "new generation" were Henry George, Sidney and Beatrice Webb, and George Bernard Shaw. Influenced by George, Shaw and some fellow reformers formed the Fabian Society in 1884. The name *Fabian* was taken from Fabius Cunctator, a successful Roman general noted for his exercise of caution during military campaigns.[24] Sidney Webb joined the society in 1885.

Henry George was an American writer and social reformer who analyzed reasons for the increasing gap between the affluent upper class and the lower class in LFMEs. George concluded that private ownership of land exacerbated the wealth differential between the two classes. Basing his appeal for reform on his views concerning "social justice, natural rights, and the teachings of Christianity,"[25] George used the Ricardian theory of rent to argue for high taxes on landowners. Since income created by land was "a gift of God," George believed the community, rather than private owners, should receive most of that income.[26] Despite his willingness to redistribute income from the property-owning class to the working class, George was not an advocate of Marxian principles (see Chapter 15). He rejected class struggle and believed competition among private enterprises and free trade was beneficial to society. He did, however, advocate public ownership of natural monopolies (e.g., public utilities, common carriers).

Among the intellectuals influenced by George was Sidney Webb, considered the father of British socialism. Webb was one of the first members of the Fabian Society and was instrumental in formulating its platform. Much of Webb's lifelong involvement with social reform was shared with his wife, author Beatrice Potter Webb. She was active in developing the platform of the Fabian

---

[22]Spiegel, *The Growth of Economic Thought*, p. 393.

[23]Peter Mathias, *The First Industrial Nation*, 2nd ed. (London: Methuen, 1983), p. 341.

[24]Lisanne Radice, *Beatrice and Sidney Webb* (London and Basingstoke: Macmillan Press, 1984), p. 55.

[25]Spiegel, *The Growth of Economic Thought*, p. 498.

[26]Ibid., p. 497.

Society and worked with her husband to build the British Labor Party. George Bernard Shaw was a journalist and playwright whose skill as an orator and originator of ideas complemented Sidney Webb's "encyclopedic knowledge and debating and organization skills."[27]

The Fabians strove to create an economy in which affiliation and cooperation would replace competition, and where poverty would be replaced by greater economic equality, and everyone would enjoy a "national minimum standard of civilized life."[28] Five features of the Fabian philosophy are noteworthy. First, Fabians preferred morally stimulated beliefs as opposed to those arrived at following economic analysis. Fabians did not accept the basic assumptions and values of the LFME philosophy, lamenting that in an LFME economy considerable poverty could exist despite high, sustained rates of economic growth. Second, the Fabians adopted an eclectic, pragmatic approach to social reform. They reflected many of the views of Karl Marx, believing his interpretation of behavior was too narrow, and that he failed to recognize the contribution to greater industrial efficiency and output made by entrepreneurs. Third, Fabians held a preference for reform through democratic and parliamentary political institutions. They preferred peaceful elections to the assumption of control through revolution. Fourth, Fabians believed that in the interests of maintaining harmony, reforms should be on a small scale and gradual. They recognized the lengthy process involved before social reforms would become politically and morally acceptable to a majority of the population. Fabians saw themselves, in conjunction with the nation's education system, as teachers who would convince the property-owning classes that there were virtues in reforming an LFME according to the Fabian program. Finally, they believed that progress toward a more collectivized, socially conscious society was inevitable.

Following are specific reforms advocated by the Fabians. First, a national social insurance program would be financed out of general revenues, with benefits distributed to all members of society without any means test. Second, public education, technical training, museums, parks, and art galleries would all be designed to serve the entire population rather than a small elite class. Third, Fabians advocated collective control over the primary means of production. The most radical reform Fabians proposed was the socialization of rents earned on land. Taxes on rents would serve to reallocate income away from private owners to be shared among the entire population. This reform would promote a collectivist spirit while fulfilling the ethical right Fabians believed workers possessed to the full value of what they produced. Fourth, public enterprises would be established, financed with taxes on rents and interest income, at the national, county, and municipal levels. Such enterprises could afford to pay workers higher wages since they would not be subject to taxes on rent or interest.

---

[27]Radice, *Beatrice and Sidney Webb*, p. 56.
[28]Spiegel, *The Growth of Economic Thought*, p. 250.

Among the enterprises recommended were those concerned with transportation, banking, laundry, baking, and entertainment (e.g., public houses). Fifth, nationalization of industries and resources where local administration was impractical was proposed. These included railways and other common carriers, public utilities, insurance enterprises, land, and mines. One benefit which could ensue from nationalization was that those who otherwise would have remained unemployed under an LFME could be given the opportunity to work— something Fabians believed was every individual's right.

The means by which Fabians sought to reform society was for their group of intellectual elite to provide the informal rules that would influence British authorities (e.g., Parliament, political party leaders) to propose formal rules to reform the economy consistent with the Fabian proposals. "Fabian permeation," led by a "small educated elite, [could supply] ideas and principles of social reconstruction to each of the great political parties in turn, as the changing results of English politics [brought] them alternatively into power."[29] The Fabians provided their informal rules by publishing articles and pamphlets and by delivering lectures, each of which provided a philosophical and factual basis for Fabian reforms.

Summary

What impact did the Fabian Society have on the evolution of the DCSE in the twentieth century? The Fabians influenced informal rules throughout northern Europe, while some of the specific reforms they proposed were eventually adopted in Britain.[30] They were able to change the informal rules concerning social and economic reforms by providing steady discussion, propagating their ideals in a consistent, nondogmatic manner, and providing facts concerning the extent of poverty under an LFME. Perhaps the most important attitudinal change they promulgated was the view that poverty was the fault of society and, therefore, preventable. This stood in contrast to the LFME view that poverty was attributable to a person's character and willingness to malinger—a view the Fabians steadily rejected. In addition, the Fabians offered a convincing argument concerning democracy as the proper means to introduce gradual social reforms. In doing so they provided an alternative to the Marxian view that the state was a tool of the bourgeoisie and had to be eliminated before reforms were possible.

The development of the modern British Labor Party can be traced to the efforts of the Fabians. Sidney Webb coauthored the constitution and platform of the party in 1918. Included in the platform was a call for a minimum standard of living for all British citizens and for "social control of resources, including . . . the

---

[29]Radice, *Beatrice and Sidney Webb*, p. 61.

[30]One reason that the Fabians had limited influence beyond Britain was the absence of a formal (in the sense of the classical economic and Keynesian paradigms, which contained a body of economic theory as well as a philosophical basis—see Chapters 5 and 8) Fabian paradigm, which could serve as a specific platform for social reform in other nations. Fabian writings, especially the facts used to support their proposals, were particularly relevant to Britain.

method of progressive taxation."[31] The Fabians were instrumental in changing the informal rules leading to subsequent reforms in Britain, such as the system of modern education, the adoption of a universal social insurance and a national health service, the abolishment of a means test for social welfare benefits, and the nationalization of selected industries.

It should be added that these reforms were introduced following the ascent to power of authorities representing the British Labor Party. This party became the majority party after the 1945 general election, when it won over 60 percent of the seats in Parliament. At this time the Labor Party authorities had another formal reform proposal whose authors were influenced by ideals held by the Early Reformers and members of the Fabian Society—the Beveridge Report.

THE BEVERIDGE REPORT

The "Beveridge Report" is so named because it was written primarily by Sir William Beveridge, Director of the London School of Economics and Political Science. The background, preparation, main features, and impact of the report are presented here.

There were two principal factors responsible for the establishment of the Beveridge Committee on Social Insurance and Allied Services which prepared the report. First, there was concern throughout Britain about the efficacy of the existing (1940) administration of social welfare and insurance programs. These programs were administered by seven different institutions operating under different rules. For example, the Ministry of Labor administered unemployment insurance, the Ministry of Health administered national health insurance, and three different agencies were responsible for administering various pension schemes. The result was that services overlapped, were duplicated, or did not provide for certain people in need—especially the elderly and children.

Unemployment insurance and sickness allowances illustrate the variation in the size and scope of coverage. The unemployment insurance benefit was determined by "subsistence needs," and a person receiving this benefit was eligible to receive an allowance for dependents.[32] However, if the same person were unable to work due to sickness, he or she would receive a benefit below subsistence and would receive no "statutory allowance" for dependents.[33] The Beveridge Committee was established in response to such problems and anomalies.

The second factor was the rising tide of public opinion, heightened by living conditions during World War II, in favor of extending social insurance and welfare services. The extra burden of wartime taxes had exacerbated the extent to which poverty prevailed, especially among urban children. As would be expected,

---

[31]Roy C. Macridis, *Contemporary Political Ideologies,* 2nd ed. (Boston: Little, Brown, and Co., 1983), p. 231.
[32]Jose Harris, *William Beveridge* (Oxford: Clarendon Press, 1977), p. 378.
[33]Ibid.

solidarity extended beyond the working class during the wartime crisis. The general public joined the trade unions as advocates of extended social insurance and welfare, and the government recognized these new informal rules. Social research findings changed attitudes concerning the cause of poverty. Prior to 1900 poverty was attributable to lower earnings, but by 1940 unemployment, combined with "inadequate provision for childhood and old age," were considered the prime causes.[34]

It was against this background that the government approved the formation of the Beveridge Committee. The Beveridge Committee was established to analyze "technical details" concerning the overlapping, incomplete coverage of existing social welfare schemes.[35] There was fear among government officials that too much publicity for such a study would dramatically increase the public's expectations of expanded social reforms beyond what the state could afford, or beyond what many members of Parliament preferred. In contrast, Beveridge saw the committee as an opportunity for him to establish goals of social policy and the means to achieve them, thereby provoking the state to broaden social welfare measures. He dominated the proceedings of the committee, discussing technical issues in meetings while developing his own analysis, which amounted to a fundamental reassessment of the entire social insurance and welfare system.

Like Owen, Mill, and the Fabians, Beveridge was a pragmatic social reformer who favored democratic means to create a more egalitarian society where poverty is abolished. His vision of the ideal economy, conception of the behavior of the existing economy, and means to reform Britain did not have a theoretical economic basis. Beveridge did not draw from any specific doctrine when he identified pragmatic means to achieve his ideal society.

The cornerstone of his reform program was a comprehensive social insurance system. This system featured a "national health service for prevention and comprehensive treatment available to all members of the community."[36] Other features included the lack of a means test (based upon the informal rule that social insurance should be available to the entire population regardless of family income); national versus municipal financing and administration of social programs; child allowances, paid out of general funds, payable to all families with children regardless of their family income; and public measures to achieve low levels of unemployment. The goal of full employment (i.e., 3 percent unemployment) should become a top priority of the state. Like the Fabians, Beveridge was impressed by the reduction of unemployment in the Soviet Union through increased public expenditures during a depression. Beveridge favored planning to coordinate certain economic activities, but he advocated democratic rather than coercive means to implement corresponding working rules.

[34]Ibid., p. 439.
[35]Ibid., p. 383.
[36]Ibid., p. 390.

The committee published the report in late 1942. Its hallmark, according to Beveridge, was its "economy in administration, adequacy in benefits, [and] universality in scope."[37] Economy would follow from the unification of various agencies responsible for administering social insurance and welfare programs under a single ministry. The methods for financing the proposed programs were, in part, contributed by John Maynard Keynes, who enthusiastically endorsed the thrust of the Beveridge proposals. Keynes recommended that pensions be financed on a pay-as-you-earn basis (i.e., out of current government revenue), and that employers, not workers, should bear a greater share (than Beveridge had originally proposed) of the pension scheme's cost. In particular, Keynes advocated a substantial tax on employers who dismissed workers. Finally, Keynes recommended that expanded social insurance and welfare programs gradually be phased in to avoid the need for deficit financing or significant tax increases.

Adequacy of benefits would be assured, since the state would establish and fund national minimum levels for family income, health care, unemployment, pensions, and social insurance. Many benefits would be paid on a flat-rate basis according to family size. These benefits would guarantee a subsistence income to all citizens without a means test while complying with the public's informal rules that government programs should foster "privacy, independence, and thrift."[38] Individuals, therefore, would remain free to purchase supplemental insurance (e.g., health, disability) from private suppliers.

The scope of coverage was designed to be universal. The entire British population was divided into six classifications, with corresponding contribution rates and benefit rights defined for each group: (1) wage and salary earners; (2) others gainfully occupied; (3) housewives; (4) others of working age; (5) those below working age; and (6) retired persons above working age.[39] Every British citizen would be eligible for the national health service and the children's allowance program. Benefits or grants would be provided to those who needed assistance due to unemployment, sickness, workmen's disability, old age, funeral of a family member, and maternity. Additional funds were to be available for widows and orphans.

Impact

Unlike the work of Owen and Mill, the "Beveridge Report" was published when the public mood and state of the economy were conducive to the introduction of new working rules for the economy.[40] Over 100,000 copies of the report were sold soon after its completion in late 1942, and the press gave the report considerable

---

[37]Ibid., p. 413.

[38]Ibid.

[39]Sydney Pollard, *The Development of the British Economy: 1914–1980,* 3rd ed. (London: Edward Arnold, 1985), p. 230.

[40]One contributing factor was Beveridge's "mingled tone of optimism, patriotism, high principle and pragmatism [which] exactly fitted the prevailing popular mood." Harris, *William Beveridge,* p. 421.

publicity. Discussions and debates concerning the efficacy of the proposals were sparked throughout Britain.

Authorities within Parliament and the bureaucracy, as well as representatives of the Labor Party, were cautious about endorsing the ideological implications and economic viability of the report's reform proposals. Beatrice Webb criticized the report as offering "reform within a context of capitalism."[41] After debating the reforms in early 1943, Parliament implemented none of the proposals as formal working rules.

The public responded critically toward the absence of new reform measures and voted the Labor Party into power in 1945. This victory over the Liberal Party (with which Beveridge was aligned) has been attributed to the strong desire of the Labor Party's followers for reform and to an effectively organized and funded political campaign. It might appear that Beveridge's reform proposals, greeted with such enthusiasm two and one-half years prior to the election, had little impact throughout Britain.

It is true that Beveridge was neither involved with social reform policy discussions after the 1945 election nor directly responsible for the new formal rules introduced between 1945 and 1948.[42] However, the main principles (albeit with modifications) in these new working rules were similar to those contained in the "Beveridge Report." Beveridge, in his role as a "synthesizer and publicist" can be credited with having "interpreted the mainstream of public opinion and . . . [with having] transformed an incoherent mass of popular feeling into a blueprint for social reform."[43] Beveridge's work, combined with the efforts of Owen, Mill, and the Fabians (through the Labor Party) provided the informal and formal rules which comprise the "core" of Britain's DCSE.[44]

LOOKING AHEAD

The actual cases of economies with a philosophical basis, principal institutions, and working rules consistent to varying degrees with those discussed in this chapter (e.g., Australia, Canada, Denmark, New Zealand, Norway, Sweden, and the United Kingdom) have been based upon "an alliance between . . . intellectuals and the labor union movement."[45] Although many of the specific working rules adopted in DCSE have been in response to labor movement demands for relatively narrow reforms, broad reform proposals from intellectuals, influenced

[41]Ibid., p. 424.

[42]The Family Allowance Act of 1945, National Insurance and National Health Service Acts of 1946, and National Assistance Act of 1948.

[43]Harris, *William Beveridge*, p. 449.

[44]Walter C. Neale, *The British Economy: Towards a Decent Society* (Columbus, OH: Grid Publishing, 1980), p. 170.

[45]John E. Elliott, *Comparative Economic Systems*, 2nd ed. (Belmont, CA: Wadsworth, 1985), p. 255.

by the work of Owen, Mill, the Fabian Society, and (for the United Kingdom) the Beveridge Report have been indispensable. The following chapter (the case of Sweden after 1932) illustrates the intellectual-labor alliance and the process by which another economy having many features similar to an LFME was gradually and peacefully transformed into an economy based upon the principles of Owen, Mill, Webb, and others discussed in this chapter. Chapter 14, "The European Union," provides a creative experiment of nations, some of whose economies are consistent with democratic social principles, establishing a supranational economy that contains elements of the DCSE partly as an attempt to counter perceived (and actual) problems created by free trade working rules.

KEY TERMS AND CONCEPTS

**Democratically Controlled
Social Economy
Means Test**

**Social Economy
Socialism**

QUESTIONS FOR DISCUSSION

1. According to the views of Robert Owen, what was socialism?
2. How did Owen's community in New Lanark differ from the typical factory town of its era?
3. How does John Stuart Mill's argument that natural laws do not govern the distribution of income provide the basis for abandoning laissez-faire economic policies?
4. According to Henry George, what was the cause of the skewed distribution of wealth in England? What did he propose as a means to reduce the disparity?
5. What were the principal tenets of the Fabian Society?
6. How does the philosophical basis for a DCSE differ from that of an LFME?
7. What was the role of education in the DCSE philosophers' programs for economic reform?

REFERENCES

Cole, Margaret, *The Story of Fabian Socialism.* London: Heinemann, 1961.

Douglas, Jay, *Socialism in the New Society.* New York: St. Martin's Press, 1963.

Duncan, Graeme, *Marx and Mill.* Cambridge: Cambridge University Press, 1973.

Ebenstein, William, and Edwin Fogelman, *Today's Isms,* 8th ed. Englewood Cliffs, NJ: Prentice-Hall, 1980.

Elliott, John E., *Comparative Economic Systems,* 2nd ed. Belmont, CA: Wadsworth, 1985.

Harris, Jose, *William Beveridge.* Oxford: Clarendon Press, 1977.

Harrison, J. F. C. *Quest for the New Moral World.* New York: Charles Scribner, 1969.

Landreth, Harry, *History of Economic Theory*. Boston: Houghton Mifflin, 1976.

Macridis, Roy C., *Contemporary Political Ideologies*, 2nd ed. Boston: Little, Brown, and Co., 1983.

Mathias, Peter, *The First Industrial Nation*, 2nd ed. London: Methuen, 1983.

Neale, Walter C., *The British Economy: Towards a Decent Society*. Columbus, OH: Grid Publishing, 1980.

Oser, Jacob, and Stanley L. Brue, *The Evolution of Economic Thought*, 4th ed., San Diego: Harcourt Brace Jovanovich, 1988.

Owen, Robert, *A New View of Society and Other Writings*. London: J. M. Dent & Sons, 1927.

Polanyi, Karl, *The Great Transformation*. Boston: Beacon Press, 1957.

Pollard, Sydney, *The Development of the British Economy: 1914–1980*, 3rd ed. London: Edward Arnold, 1985.

Radice, Lisanne, *Beatrice and Sidney Webb*. London and Basingstoke: Macmillan Press, 1984.

Spiegel, Henry William, *The Growth of Economic Thought*. Durham, NC: Duke University Press, 1984.

13

THE SWEDISH ECONOMY*

1932–Present

OBJECTIVES

1. Demonstrate how an economy can, for a number of decades, perform favorably in the opinion of a majority of the population, while simultaneously relying heavily upon private ownership and competitive markets for production and also providing extensive social insurance and welfare programs.
2. Describe the evolution of the Swedish economy as a gradual, democratic, peaceful process.
3. Analyze the wage bargaining agreements between employers and organized labor characteristic of the 1938–1990 period.
4. Describe the cooperative institutions that are important to the Swedish economy.
5. Examine the changing relationship between the Swedish philosophical basis and the working rules for the economy, and how these rules evolved in response to changing ideals and performance of the economy.
6. Identify the causes of the sharp reversal in performance indicators after 1990 and the impact upon the philosophical basis, political structure, and working rules for principal institutions.

*Portions of this chapter are based on James Angresano, "Sweden: An Example of a Viable Social Economy?" *International Journal of Social Economics*, XVII, 4 (1990), 12–31.

INTRODUCTION

The Swedish economy, or model, has often been described as a welfare state or as an example of democratic socialism. Such descriptions obscure the underlying and complex interrelationships among economic, social, and political factors in Sweden. The nation's historical legacy, combined with a philosophical basis that, prior to the early 1990s, emphasized egalitarian values achieved through state-private sector cooperation, have been instrumental in the process by which the economy's working rules have been established, interpreted, and enforced. Of particular interest are Sweden's exhaustive and imaginative social insurance and welfare policies, through which the state has redistributed income effectively so that the widespread poverty existing in the early 1930s was abolished, while the forces of free enterprise within the private sector have created a material standard of living that is the envy of many nations.

THE ROOTS OF WELFARE REFORM

Certain factors that shaped the nation's consciousness during the rebuilding of the economy after 1932 were already in place before the landmark elections of that year: the role of the state in economic matters, the lateness of Sweden's industrial revolution, and the poor performance of the economy between the end of World War I and 1932.

Role of the State

Prior to the twentieth century the Swedish state began to assume a paternalistic role toward its citizens' well-being. State intervention in social and economic matters and the existence of a rudimentary scheme of welfare policies were introduced well before 1932. Included among these policies were Poor Laws (introduced in 1847), public health policies (1874), a publicly financed pension system (1913), and a working rule limiting the work day to 8 hours (1919). Many social insurance and welfare policies were administered effectively on the local government level, fostering a cohesive spirit within communities and faith that an effective, honest bureaucracy was capable of alleviating social and economic problems equitably and efficiently. Views toward local authorities gave them impetus to extend and administer social insurance and welfare programs throughout the twentieth century.

     Despite Sweden's historically paternalistic attitude in terms of responsibility for the welfare of its citizens, there was little state ownership of the means of production, and a pervasive, strong work ethic prevailed among the citizenry. Swedes believed that work was good in and of itself. Other influential attitudes that remained in the nation's consciousness after 1932 were the tradition of self-help and the antagonisms between social classes exacerbated by increasing income inequality throughout the late nineteenth and early twentieth centuries. Although Sweden was homogeneous in terms of its culture, language, and the absence of significant national minorities, members of the aristocracy were able to translate their social status into economic and political power, and this was a factor that stimulated the popular political movements that began in the late nineteenth century.

Industrial Revolution

Such movements were one by-product of Sweden's industrial revolution. This revolution occurred relatively late (post 1870), but was rapid and effective. The groundwork in terms of the existence of state-sponsored infrastructure (canals, railways), banks, a literate and skilled labor force, and aristocrats able to participate or contribute to the entrepreneurial efforts of Swedish or foreign investors was in place by 1870. Stimulus came from Swedish inventions, or from innovations using foreign products. The pace and extent of industrialization in Sweden were impressive. Between 1870 and 1914 the size of the industrial labor force quadrupled, while the rate of economic growth in Sweden was exceeded only by those of Japan and the United States.[1] The impact of the industrial revolution, especially the increasing income differentials between classes and the growing antagonism between management and labor, stimulated popular movements on the local level and the subsequent emergence of institutions such as the Social Democratic Party, national trade union and employer organizations, and producer and consumer cooperatives. While state authorities sided with the wealthy property owners, most Swedes became active in popular movements. When the industrial revolution occurred, many small centers of industry emerged, and such towns "offered a social structure that was a fertile ground for the growth of popular movements."[2] Such movements were stimulated by the strong intellectual life in Sweden, which emphasized rationality and practicality in commercial and public affairs.

Industrialization and the growth of industrial towns led to "organizations broadly supported by ordinary citizens, with a democratic structure and an ideology which often combine[d] cultural aims with protection of material interests of the members."[3] Among the institutions that emerged was the Social Democratic Party, founded in 1889. This party was instrumental in establishing the LO (central trade union confederation) in 1898.

By 1902 employers, responding to growing worker militancy, founded the SAF (Swedish Employers' Confederation). When employers formed a central organization, trade unions were stimulated to work together within the LO. This led to struggles between workers and employers, with general strikes, lockouts, and antagonism prevailing between 1900 and the early 1930s. The trade union

[1]Henry Milner, *Sweden: Social Democracy in Practice* (Oxford: Oxford University Press, 1989), p. 54. Also see Ryoshin Minami, *The Economic Development of Japan* (London: The Macmillan Press Ltd., 1986), pp. 36–43.
[2]Lennart Forseback, *Industrial Relations and Employment in Sweden* (Uppsala: Swedish Institute, 1980), p. 6.
[3]Ibid.

movement began to have a significant effect upon the political structure in 1917, when Social Democratic authorities were represented in the Swedish cabinet for the first time. About this time there was a shift in attitudes away from antagonism in favor of pragmatic working rules designed to reform the industrial society.

Another by-product of the Swedish industrial revolution was the popular reaction against private monopoly power. As safety and security were important features in Swedish households, workers expected their employers to provide these same features in the workplace. However, these features were absent in many firms. In addition, many Swedes sought lower-priced and higher-quality products than privately owned, profit-seeking firms were providing. In response, consumer and producer cooperatives began to develop to address these needs. Individual cooperative societies formed retail stores. In 1899, many small, struggling cooperatives banded together to form The Cooperative Union, known familiarly throughout Sweden as "K.F." The history of cooperatives illustrates "the remarkable ability of the Swedes to concentrate upon an immediate, practical problem, bringing to the issue of the price of potatoes not only intelligence and acumen but even a kind of ardor."[4]

A Poor Economy

Poverty was prevalent throughout Sweden prior to the 1930s, and many Swedes emigrated to the United States between 1850 and the early 1930s because they were starving. There was a continual decline in the birth rate between 1870 and 1930, and family poverty became associated with having too many children. Between 1919–1923 Sweden experienced inflation, then deflation and a foreign exchange crisis. Due to the Great Depression, there was high unemployment and another foreign exchange crisis, as well as a 25 percent decline in industrial output. Overall, the economy's performance between 1917 and 1932 heightened public concern over the efficacy of laissez-faire market economy policies. Vivid experiences with poverty stimulated a number of Social Democratic Party leaders to offer both a new philosophical basis and a reformist program aimed toward the gradual socialization of the economy.

THE EVOLUTION OF SOCIAL DEMOCRATIC PHILOSOPHY

Swedish attitudes toward the appropriate role of the state in economic activity, especially concerning the issue of providing health care, social insurance, and welfare services, developed over centuries and are "deeply woven into the fabric of Swedish tradition and custom."[5] These attitudes are embodied in ideals

---

[4]Marquis Childs, *Sweden: The Middle Way* (New Haven, CT: Yale University Press, 1936), p. 2.

[5]Albert H. Rosenthal, *The Social Programs of Sweden* (Minneapolis: The University of Minnesota Press, 1967), p. 92.

(informal rules), which have served to legitimize economic policies, social insurance programs, and welfare policy measures (formal rules). The ideals evolved in response to growing empathy toward the poor and disadvantaged. Each ideal, in turn, fostered a further desire to reallocate resources from a higher level (i.e., local or central government) to the level of the household, and reinforced the willingness to place the cause and responsibility for social and economic problems on the Swedish society, not on the individual.

The first ideal, embodied in the poor laws of the eighteenth century, was to relieve the poor from distress. Swedish authorities accepted the view that state intervention was necessary to assist families suffering from the effects of adverse economic and social forces beyond their control.[6] The extent of assistance provided was meager, partly because it was held that those suffering from poverty were primarily responsible for their condition. However, the Swedish poor laws were an important first step toward more comprehensive state-provided assistance, since financial responsibility shifted to the local government and away from charity provided by individuals or the Church.[7]

A new philosophy toward social assistance to the poor developed in the late nineteenth and early twentieth centuries. The main proponents were the Social Democrats, who challenged the conventional wisdom that low wages were necessary to ensure full employment.[8] The party leaders felt that a move toward self-help would become necessary because as long as poverty remained a function of economic and social conditions, it could not be alleviated by the provisions contained in the poor laws. Consequently, they sought to create a system that would increase opportunities for the poor by stimulating employment while promoting family welfare. Social Democrats believed that such a humanitarian system should be founded upon three basic principles:

> 1) legislation to guarantee to every Swedish citizen a simple and decent standard of living . . . [Social Democrats hold that] it is the duty of society to provide for the needs of the aged, invalids, widows, and those who have lost their income through no fault of their own; 2) housing and child benefits for needy families so that they should not be forced to lower their standard of living because they have children to raise. [The] idea is to distribute the expense over the entire population as a collective responsibility; 3) social welfare to be . . . the inherent right of every citizen irrespective of his financial status.[9]

---

[6]Steven Koblik, ed., *Sweden's Development from Poverty to Affluence: 1750–1970* (Minneapolis: University of Minnesota Press, 1975), p. 336.

[7]Rosenthal, *The Social Programs of Sweden*, pp. 8–9.

[8]See Wilfred Fleisher, *Sweden: The Welfare State* (Westport, CT: Greenwood Press, 1973), p. 158. This belief was based upon research which indicated there was no "empirical relationship between low wages and high employment." Social Democrats argued that publicly funded distress relief and job opportunities would alleviate poverty.

[9]Ibid., pp. 159–160.

In 1913 the National Pension Act was passed, providing all Swedes with social insurance. This became the basis for subsequent retirement, disability and old-age schemes. In 1918, a new poor law was adopted, forming the basis for social insurance and welfare measures in Sweden until the early 1960s. Its significance was the underlying concept of placing responsibility with the local government for providing "adequate care and relief"[10] to anyone in need, while the central government would contribute by providing counselors to assist with administration.

The ideals of integration and equality became the foundation of the Social Democratic Party platform in 1932. To Social Democrats, integration meant an end to class conflict by "end[ing] the exploitation of labor, . . . subject[ing] the economy to democratic control . . . [and] resolv[ing] the psychological problems associated with industrial labor."[11] Integration also meant that all segments of the Swedish population would become the common responsibility of the state. Social Democratic leaders such as Ernst Wigforss, Gunnar and Alva Myrdal, and Gustav Moeller stressed the need for state-supported social and economic reform for the purpose of promoting the well-being of lower middle-income and low-income families. Moeller exemplified the conviction that the party must strive to create a regime which would provide for its less fortunate members. In reference to his childhood, most of which was spent as an orphan in a slum inhabited by uneducated, impoverished, often drunk individuals, he stated that "society offered my mother no help against overwork, illness, and poor housing conditions . . . She was overpowered by the circumstances and died prematurely [age 27]. I felt then that something had to be done about it."[12]

In reference to the problems of poverty and low population growth (especially among low-income families) plaguing Sweden after World War I, the Social Democrats believed society needed redistributional reforms to strengthen family and marriage bonds. According to Alva Myrdal, a "population" (i.e., family) policy can be nothing less than a social program at large.[13] The Social Democrats emphasized the importance of equality, believing it was the state's role to create a more egalitarian society through an expansion of social services and welfare policies.

The equality ideal, implicit in the ideal of integration, had various connotations. These ranged from the view "that people should be regarded as equals in the sense of 'equal value' . . . to the idea that all citizens should live under completely equal circumstances" (e.g., equal distribution of freedom, power, security, and wealth).[14] This ideal is contained in the Swedish term *folkhem*, which means the "people's home." Social Democratic advocates of the equality ideal believed all

[10]Ibid., p. 158.

[11]Timothy Tilton, "A Swedish Road to Socialism: Ernst Wigforss and the Ideological Foundations of Swedish Social Democracy," *The American Political Science Review*, 73 (June 1979), 514.

[12]Fleisher, *Sweden: The Welfare State*, p. 16.

[13]Alva Myrdal, *Nation and Family: The Swedish Experiment in Democratic Family and Population Policy* (Cambridge, MA: The MIT Press, 1968), p. viii.

[14]Koblik, *Sweden's Development from Poverty to Affluence*, p. 346.

citizens should receive equal treatment (e.g., universal coverage under a national pension scheme) and live in harmony without "antipathy among social classes."[15]

The ideals of social security and social justice became popular in the 1950s and 1960s, respectively. Like equality, both ideals are implicit in the concept of integration. Social security reflects the humanitarian philosophy that a "welfare state" should provide all Swedes with the "means of meeting the financial hazards of loss of regular income because of age, [serious illness], disability, or death of the breadwinner."[16] It was believed that individuals were helpless and therefore not responsible in the event that competitive economic forces or unforeseen social catastrophes adversely affected them. The state would ensure that all citizens had security and opportunity through publicly funded health and welfare programs, including the provision of adequate housing, employment, pensions, and cultural amenities. Rules such as the Social Assistance Act of 1957 were designed to guarantee security while respecting the dignity of all individuals.

The social justice ideal, for which the slogan *Jamlikhet* appeared in the late 1960's, contains the belief that

> all individuals have an equal right to a rich and evolving life . . . [meaning] security, freedom, happiness, the right to cultural opportunities, employment, and influence in the community. This [means] an approach to equalization of income. [It calls for reforms] directed against the privileged for the advantage of the underprivileged and the bettering of their conditions of life."[17]

Based upon a 1969 report by Alva Myrdal, this ideal stresses that Social Democrats should proceed beyond the promotion of full employment and social security. Minimization of class differentials should be a "permanent ambition" of policy.[18] It was held that all citizens, especially those who lacked the talent or temperament to acquire a normal amount of resources in a competitive economy, had "the right to compensation" either through redistribution of income or expanded social services to "neutralize any loss of normal income."[19]

Overall, the social insurance and welfare policies prevalent throughout Sweden until the early 1990s were designed to satisfy the popular ideals by meeting specific problems as they arose, with protective and redistributive measures designed to appeal to all social classes. There was no specific dogma to fulfill. Instead, authorities relied upon Swedes to be pragmatic, sensible, and responsible when faced with choosing specific redistribution measures.

[15]Franklin D. Scott, *Sweden: The Nation's History* (Minneapolis: The University of Minnesota Press, 1977), p. 584.

[16]Rosenthal, *The Social Programs of Sweden*, p. 12.

[17]Scott, *Sweden: The Nation's History*, p. 547.

[18]Gunnar Heckscher, *The Welfare State and Beyond* (Minneapolis: The University of Minnesota Press, 1984), p. 227.

[19]Ibid., pp. 228–229.

Socialization measures were the means toward the pursuit of a classless society, achieved through measures designed to create greater equality of living standards. The intent was to banish poverty and to provide all Swedes with a decent standard of living. Therefore, policies created a comprehensive (to cover all Swedes) economic security system. Programs were available on a general basis to the whole population, with the general population contributing toward paying for these programs—many of which everyone is entitled to benefit from regardless of their household income (e.g., child allowances).

During the late 1960s some elements of the Social Democratic Party began to advocate an even greater emphasis on equality, industrial democracy, and social control of investment. These advocates believed Sweden enjoyed general welfare due to achievement of full employment and a social insurance and welfare safety net which protected all Swedes from poverty. They sought introduction of measures (see "Social Process for Economic Coordination," p. 304) to erode further the inequalities of a "bourgeois capitalist society." However, working rules which would change radically the ownership of the means of production have not been introduced, partly due to Swedish informal attitudes which reject extensive state ownership and control of the means of production, and to the performance of the economy since 1990.

This performance, which included a dramatic reduction in growth and sharp increase in unemployment (see Tables 10-1 and 10-2 in Chapter 10 and "Performance," pp. 316–323 in this chapter) sparked concern among many Swedes that the ideals of integration, equality, social security, and social justice may not provide a realistic basis for maintaining and establishing working rules that will continue to promote the favorable performance of the Swedish economy that has evolved since 1932. The contemporary Social Democratic view regarding the concentration of economic and political power over the economy's working rules may be the same as that held in 1932, but large firms are more dominant over the Swedish economy today, and the extent to which people suffer from poverty and lack of job opportunities is very different from 1930's conditions. Sweden's economy today is service oriented, must compete in the international economy, and has a very large public sector. Newly developing attitudes in Sweden place greater faith in market solutions to coordinate production and distribution, and reproach the state for going too far in raising taxes and imposing rules to regulate economic and social activities. The belief that state interference is better than markets for coordinating production and distribution decisions rapidly is being accepted by fewer Swedes.

The Social Democrats retain their belief that state-directed distribution should remain an essential part of the Swedish economy, reflecting their preference for a society characterized by a more egalitarian distribution of income, property, and political influence. They recognize the need to change some working rules to alleviate macroeconomic problems plaguing Sweden in the early 1990s, but resist abandoning the goal of guaranteeing all Swedes a decent income and state-funded social insurance and welfare measures. Many retain the belief that it is possible to steer distribution while avoiding the negative impact of such state activity on economic growth and efficiency.

However, opponents have argued (and convinced a majority of voters) that a broad redistribution policy is not compatible with the poor performance of the economy, particularly declining growth rates and loss of competitiveness in world markets, experienced by Sweden since 1990. They point out that the increasingly ambitious distribution policy created an organization of decision making that was more politicized and collectivized, with adverse effects on the economy and Swedes' well-being. Most Swedes recognize that the lack of public funds and their desire for greater freedom of choice means that changes in the pre-1990 philosophical basis and working rules of institutions are inevitable and necessary. While the universal social welfare policy will be retained, it is widely regarded that its disadvantages (such as overregulation by a monolithic public sector) must be eliminated.

A new philosophical basis has been offered stemming from a belief that Sweden has suffered from a growing bureaucratization of economic life. This basis advocates a "clear division of responsibilities among agents, pluralism, and active leadership."[20] The basic position is to increase production efficiency and lower costs by subjecting all economic institutions to as much competition as possible while making individuals assume greater responsibility for their own well-being and increasing incentives to stimulate greater work effort. Proponents of this philosophy call for the transformation of Sweden's publicly managed social welfare systems by increasing the range and freedom of choices Swedes have concerning social insurance and welfare services (especially education, health care, child care, and care of the elderly) while also encouraging competition in these areas as well. Also proposed is privatization of state-owned companies and abolition of wage-earner investment funds (see "Extensive Private and Cooperative Ownership and Control of Resources," pp. 299–304) to reduce the power of trade unions.

AN EGALITARIAN SOCIETY WITH A PARLIAMENTARY DEMOCRACY

Social Structure

Prior to the twentieth century Swedes assumed that social class distinctions were "inherent in the natural order" of society."[21] Children from lower class families (e.g. farmers, blue-collar workers) were supposed to aspire to similar occupations following only an elementary education. Throughout the twentieth century, attitudes favoring an egalitarian social structure have become widespread. Men

---

[20]For a detailed presentation of many proposals based upon this position, see Assar Lindbeck, Per Molander, Torsten Persson, Olof Peterson, Agnar Sandmo, Birgitta Swedenborg and Niels Thygesen, "Options for Economic and Political Reform in Sweden," *Economic Policy,* 17 (October 1993), 219–264.

[21]Milner, *Sweden: Social Democracy in Practice,* p. 51.

and women are considered as equals, all occupations are considered to be of equal worth, and children are encouraged to realize their potential regardless of their family's social status.

To achieve equality Sweden has relied heavily upon democratic institutions and state-sponsored reform measures. Public education, in particular, has been looked upon as the "medium for the dissemination of egalitarian ideas."[22] There are very few private schools in Sweden. The nation spends a higher percentage of its GDP on education than any other OECD member, and has created the most educated society in Europe. School systems have been reformed to eliminate vestiges of elitism. The same quality of education is offered to all of Sweden's inhabitants regardless of their economic and social status. There are uniform schools at the municipal level with standardized teaching methods and expectations. The intent is to enable everyone to benefit equally from education regardless of socioeconomic background.

Besides using education to change attitudes and provide necessary qualifications for occupations, Sweden has promoted egalitarianism through narrowing income differentials and leveling material standards of living (e.g., housing, access to cars and household appliances). A solidaristic wage policy and a large public sector, which redistributed benefits through extensive public control of income distribution (see pp. 299–304), including a very progressive income tax scheme, facilitated a more equitable distribution of income and living conditions. In addition, the relatively high degree of social equality is enhanced through the Swedish emphasis upon organizations. There are many associations throughout Sweden, including those representing the interests of laborers, employers, teachers, nurses, engineers, and women. Nearly all workers belong to some worker organization. "Few countries can show such solidarity in organization, and in few countries are the organizations and the folk movements so directly influential in government."[23] While complete social equality has not yet been attained, Swedish society is among the most egalitarian in Europe in terms of income distribution and opportunities afforded to all inhabitants of Sweden to qualify for different occupations and to receive comparable social insurance and welfare benefits.

SOCIAL STRUCTURE TODAY.   In terms of social classes, Sweden's social structure resembles an ace of spades.[24] The upper class contains about 90 percent of the population, and consists of entrepreneurs who employ at least 20 people;

---

[22]Heckscher, *The Welfare State and Beyond*, p. 185.

[23]Scott, *Sweden: The Nation's History*, p. 586.

[24]See P. C. Jersild, "The Good Old Social Pyramid, 1988 Style," *Inside Sweden*, 2 May-June 1988), 16; and Robert. Erikson and Rune Aberg, eds., *Welfare in Transition: A Survey of Living Conditions in Sweden 1969–1981* (Oxford: Clarendon Press, 1987), pp. 18–26. Classification of Swedish society into three classes according to occupation (upper—I, middle—II, lower—III) was done first in 1911. Rather subjective criteria were used to classify people. However, when this was done in 1968, stratification of classes resulted in nearly the same groups being placed in either Class I, II, or III.

executives and upper-level managers in the private and public sector; professions (e.g., doctors, lawyers) whose occupations require higher education; university students whose education is expected to lead them to an "upper-class" occupation; pensioners whose previous occupation was an "upper-class" one; and housewives whose spouses are considered as part of this class. Some argue that there is a high concentration of wealth and power within this group so that their working and living conditions, consumption patterns, and political participation are significantly different from the rest of the Swedish population.

The middle class consists of farmers, small proprietors, lower-salaried management in the private and public sectors, as well as students, pensioners, and housewives whose expected, past, or husband's occupation corresponds to "middle-class" occupations. This class comprises about 37 percent of the Swedish population. The working class consists of about 53 percent of the population. Its members have occupations such as factory workers; agricultural workers; small landholders; service workers in the private-sector; nearly all public-sector employees; low-level white-collar employees; pensioners whose occupation was "working class"; housewives whose husbands hold a "working-class" position; and most pupils with only a primary or a few years of secondary education. Finally, there is a small fourth class of Swedes (about 1 percent). This underclass which includes jobless youth and those unable to support themselves (e.g., senior citizens or disabled Swedes who do not receive adequate health care or social benefits to enable them to enjoy a standard of living equivalent to those in the middle or working classes).

Over the past few decades, the social structure has changed. There are now more white-collar workers and fewer blue-collar workers and farmers. There is greater social mobility, as "the correlation between parents' and children's class identity has declined,"[25] as well as the correlation between social class and occupation, and between parent's social class and the class of one's friends or spouse. However, there is some evidence that since the mid-1980s the trend is reversing as more people become high-income earners while more receive social assistance. In addition, the lower classes are underrepresented in universities despite school reforms designed to provide equal education and greater financial aid to needy students.

GENDER ISSUES.   While Sweden is a relatively classless society, and women, by law, have the right to employment in all occupations, shortcomings remain in the relative status of women versus men. In terms of membership in Parliament, only 38 percent of the representatives are women. Women continue to bear a much greater responsibility for care of the children and household. In the private sector, men hold about 95 percent of the highest-paying positions. In addition, there is low status attached to the public-sector jobs many women hold.

---

[25]Joachim Vogel, "Are Class Differences Increasing or Decreasing?" *Inside Sweden*, 2 (1990), 10.

Earnings differentials between men and women persist. This is attributable to different occupations and length of workday differentials. About one half of Sweden's work force are women, but about half of them have part-time positions (versus only about 6 percent of men who work part-time). Informal rules exist concerning goals to increase the percentage of women in management positions, especially senior positions in private and public institutions. Some believe that if these goals are not reached formal rules will be introduced requiring that they be reached.

IMMIGRANTS.   Currently foreign nationals (immigrants) comprise about 10 percent of the Swedish population and about 5 percent of the work force. While immigrants enjoy a reasonably good standard of living and have functioned well within their own cultural context (e.g., Swedish Greek), they are not fully integrated into Swedish society. Although immigrants have a higher labor force participation rate than Swedes, the unemployment rate for immigrants is higher. In addition, while income differentials between Swedes and immigrants are relatively small (partly because immigrants receive the same quality education as all Swedes), it is far more common for immigrants to work in occupations requiring irregular working hours (especially health care work). In addition, immigrants are overrepresented in industries with below-average working environments. While immigrant housing is similar to that of most Swedes, due to larger families they often live under more crowded conditions.

SUMMARY.   Prior to the 1990s Sweden worked enthusiastically to implement the Social Democratic philosophical basis in working toward creating a more egalitarian society. As a result, Swedish society is more egalitarian than any other industrialized nation. However, some Swedes wonder why class differences survive in terms of status between sexes, education, language, social segregation in cities, and the status of immigrants. Some attribute lingering social class differentials to the characteristics of Swedish social relationships. Due to historical factors such as the absence of community social institutions (e.g., English pub) or prevalence of many small farmers working independently, Swedes tend to be reserved and uncommunicative, and to have a preference for social autonomy. As a result, "the Swedish system does little to contribute to the development of a socially active and energetic way of approaching people outside the social sphere."[26] This point, however, should not be interpreted as a criticism of a Swedish society whose emphasis upon minimizing social-class differentials is reflected in the views of leading authorities.

Political Structure

Sweden's government is a parliamentary democracy, so the authorities responsible

---

[26]Vogel, "Are Class Difference Increasing or Decreasing?" p. 10.

for establishing, modifying, and replacing the economy's working rules are determined by popular vote.[27] The Parliament is unicameral, with 349 members elected for three-year terms. Members of Parliament generally are elected from one of the six main political parties: Social Democratic, Communist, Moderate (formerly Conservative), Liberal, Center (formerly Agrarian), and Green (environmental). Each party has its own well-defined philosophy, and the main features of each philosophy have been retained since the early 1930s (with the exception of the Green Party, which was formed in 1981, and the Christian Democratic Party and New Democracy Party, which first gained seats in Parliament in 1991). While no party binds itself to the philosophy of Adam Smith, Karl Marx, or John Stuart Mill, there is a clear distinction between the socialist (i.e., Social Democrats and Communist) parties and the nonsocialist parties, especially regarding the issue of how Sweden's wealth should be distributed. The Social Democratic and Communist Parties emphasize the need for democratic control over production and distribution, while nonsocialist parties emphasize unregulated markets as the desirable means to promote economic efficiency and preserve democracy. The Green Party emphasizes the ecological impact of the production process, and advocates some state-directed measures to control undesirable externalities.

Cabinet members are the main authorities. There is a prime minister (selected from the majority party), and 20 ministers, 13 of whom are heads of particular ministries. All ministers are appointed by Parliament, and are usually representatives of the political party or parties (in the case of a coalition government) in power. Nearly all ministers are members of Parliament who retained their seats while serving as ministers.

Allocation of seats among the parties is by proportional representation based upon the percentage of the national vote cast for each political party. Rules, both informal and formal, serve to perpetuate the domination of the leading political parties. A party must receive at least 4 percent of the national vote before it can have any representatives in Parliament. Parties are allotted state subsidies in proportion to the percentage of the votes received in the previous election. If Swedes choose to vote by postal ballot, which enables them to vote up to one month in advance of the election, only the six parties currently having representatives in Parliament will be listed on the ballot. Another factor inhibiting the emergence of other political parties is that relatively few Swedish votes are "swing votes." About 80 percent (down from 90 percent a few decades ago) of Swedes are closely linked to a party. While the Social Democrats and Communists together received between about 47 percent and 51 percent of the votes in each election between 1970 and 1990, in the 1991 election they combined to receive only 38 percent. In 1994, however, they received over 45 percent of the vote as voters rejected the nonsocialist coalition's attempt to include social insurance and welfare programs in its budget cuts.

---

[27]There is a monarch, but since 1971, when the new constitution came into effect, the rank of the monarch was reduced to ceremonial head of state, possessing no power over the economy's working rules.

There has been a trend toward decentralizing Parliament's authority. The main issue concerns where to concentrate decision-making powers and resources. The emphasis recently has been upon transferring authority to the county and municipal (*Kommun*) level. The justification for decentralization is to "systematically abolish . . . unnecessary and burdensome detailed State controls which continue to restrict the scope for maneuvre at local and regional levels."[28] On the county level, governors are appointed by the national cabinet, while county residents elect their remaining authorities who assume responsibility for providing a large part of Sweden's health care, education, and vocational training, among other services. On the municipal level, 286 municipalities provide public services, social insurance, and welfare benefits pertaining to housing, infrastructure, education, child welfare, and family assistance. Parliament establishes minimum standards for all services, and the municipality has the discretion of providing more comprehensive, generous services. In 1992 the relative importance of the counties within the three-layered scheme was reduced. The municipalities took over provision of home health care and geriatric services from the county councils, and may receive more autonomy once the ability of the central government to impose a ceiling on municipal tax rates is removed. Further changes can be expected since a fourth layer of government representation is inevitable—Swedish membership in the Union (see "Institutional Stability until the 1990s," pp. 314–315).

For all but six years between 1932 and 1991, the Social Democrats served as the party in power, albeit sometimes as part of a coalition government. Consequently, most of the working rules that were implemented between 1932 and 1991 evolved through the political process from the ideals, aspirations, and goal-oriented actions of the founders and leaders of the Social Democratic Party. The rules developed are not consistent with any particular model of an economy. Unlike advocates of laissez-faire market economies or command over social economies (see Chapters 15–18), Swedish policymakers have not been obliged to be dogmatic, since most Swedes do not believe they are bound to adhere to any particular dogma. Instead the economy's working rules have been developed in a pragmatic manner, with the intent to redress existing social and economic problems, eliminate poverty, and provide all Swedes with a decent standard of living.

The attitude of the Social Democrats has been that state intervention is warranted if unregulated market forces do not satisfy the ideals of the Social Democrats and the needs of organized labor. Their strategy has included socialization, that is, expanding the state's power by increasing its responsibility for macroeconomic stability and providing universal social and welfare services by redistributing income. This strategy has been acceptable to a society which prefers social reforms and social welfare without the working rules associated with command over social economies. As a result, over 90 percent of Swedish firms today remain privately owned and controlled. Electoral realities have

---

[28] Agne Gustafsson, "Decentralisation in Sweden," *Current Sweden*, 316 (April 1984), 5.

prevented the Social Democrats from introducing highly partisan measures. Instead, they continually have had to reach political compromises with representatives of competing special-interest groups.

Beginning in the 1930s the Social Democrats concluded that in lieu of radical policies leading to extensive public ownership and control of the means of production, their party should propose a series of compromise measures that would quietly but steadily erode the "capitalist" domination of the economy.[29] Each one of these measures was not to be considered a panacea in itself, but only one of the means that the Social Democrats might employ to construct their version of a decent society gradually, while curbing what they deemed to be excessive power held by private firms and individuals.

The Social Democrats recognized that the achievement of their ideals through reformist measures required not only political compromise, but also a growing national economy. Since their political control has been tenuous over the past half-century and tempered by special-interest politics, their ability to replace the institutional autonomy of large private enterprises with state control has been limited. Recognizing both this limitation and their dependence upon industrial development to promote social and economic ends, the Social Democrats and representatives of labor reached a compromise with owners of private enterprises. The economic policy deliberations of the 1930s led each group to assume the following roles: The state would focus on macroeconomic policies such as stabilization and modification of the distribution of income. Meanwhile, firms would remain independent and freely competing enterprises.

In 1991 a four-party coalition led by the Conservative Party (along with the Liberal, Center, and Christian Democratic Parties) assumed power. There is, however, no clear majority on the right or left of the political spectrum since this coalition won only 170 of the 349 seats in Parliament (versus 138 seats for the Social Democrats). Consequently, they have had to court the right-wing New Democracy Party, which won 25 seats. Since the Conservative prime minister and the rest of his party disapprove of most positions held by the New Democrats, compromise has been difficult. However, as in the rest of the Nordic countries, compromise among competing interest groups is the nature of the political process. For example, the New Democrats supported a budget that called for reductions in public spending more modest than they preferred in return for a reduction in the value-added tax.

The 1991 shift in sentiment against the Social Democrats plus the ability of two new parties, the antisocialist Christian Democrats and populist New Democrats, to win seats in Parliament are largely a reflection of economic problems—particularly a growing government budget deficit—and social concerns (the New Democrats advocated curbs on immigration and foreign aid). The Conservatives want to balance the budget by 1998, while the Social

---

[29]Tilton, "A Swedish Road to Socialism," p. 515.

Democrats believe more taxes are necessary to reduce the deficit. This and other issues have triggered a power struggle between different interest groups. Not only are political parties at odds, but politicians, bureaucrats, and interest-group representatives are also debating over the type of working rules necessary to alleviate the nation's economic woes. It appears that the lack of consensus is working in the Social Democrats' favor, for opinion polls indicate that they are likely to regain power in the next election. This may reflect the public's unwillingness to give up the benefits they derive from state-funded social insurance and welfare schemes. Recognizing the difficulty of alleviating the nation's economic problems, Social Democrats have become less ideological and have courted groups formerly outside of their power base—including wealthy property owners and unorganized workers.

PRINCIPAL INSTITUTIONS: IMPORTANT ROLE FOR ORGANIZED LABOR, MANAGEMENT, AND COOPERATIVES

Four institutions have been particularly noteworthy since the early 1930s: the Social Democratic Party; the trade union organizations, namely, the Swedish Trade Union Confederations (LO), the Central Organization of Salaried Employees (TCO), and the Swedish Confederation of Professional Associations (SACO); the Swedish Employers' Confederation (SAF); and cooperatives. Sweden's principal institutions have their roots in the nation's history. Factors such as Sweden's relatively small size as a nation, an independent peasant class, the tendency for people to belong to organizations, and the widespread acceptance of many basic tenets contained in the philosophical basis underlying a democratically controlled social economy (see Chapter 12) combined to shape these institutions. Factors such as Swedish membership into the European Union and changes in working rules affecting these and other institutions could lead to the emergence of other principal institutions, most likely multinational or supranational in nature, before the end of this century.

The Swedish Trade Union Confederations (LO, TCO, and SACO)

About 85 percent of Sweden's 4.3 million person labor force belong to a trade union. The labor union movement began about 1850 as Swedish workers began organizing themselves into unions to offset the power of (private) owners of capital. By 1898 there were 27 unions, and most of them joined to form a central organization—the LO. Membership in the LO has grown from about 400,000 in 1920 to over 2.25 million members today, including 500,000 pensioners. About 90 percent of blue collar workers, roughly two thirds of whom work in the private sector, belong to the LO.

The LO is closely tied to the Social Democratic Party. It is the dominant institution of the Swedish trade union movement. Through its link with the Social Democratic Party, the LO has been instrumental in shaping the working rules of the economy. Overall, its acceptance of the Social Democrats' philosophical basis, size, and tight organizational structure gives the LO a dominant position in terms of its ability to influence the economy's working rules.

Any strike that will involve more than 3 percent of membership requires LO leaders' approval. The LO leaders collectively bargain for pay and work conditions for the membership, holding the position that the state should not intervene in the collective bargaining process. Since they represent workers from many areas, LO leaders (as well as TCO leaders) cannot make agreements that benefit a few at the expense of other interest groups.

The TCO, founded in 1944, currently has over 1 million active members. About 75 to 80 percent of all white-collar workers, half of whom work in the private sector, belong to TCO. The TCO is not linked to any political party, although TCO members tend to support the Social Democratic Party to the extent that the Social Democrats emphasize state measures designed to maintain full employment. The SACO, which has about 250,000 members, also does not have close ties to any political party. Many professional associations are in SACO, including university-trained professionals (teachers, physicians, pharmacists), and many of its members are employed in the public sector.

The Swedish Employer's Confederation

The Swedish Employer's Confederation (SAF) is the dominant employer organization in the private sector, and has about 42,000 members that employ about 1.5 million persons. Like the LO, TCO, and SACO, SAF not only engages in collective bargaining but spends considerable time trying to influence informal rules (i.e., public opinion). SAF is divided into 35 branch associations, each of which is consistent with its sphere of activity in the private sector.

Cooperatives

A cooperative is an economic association operated on the basis of joint action and self-help. It is organized by and for groups of people who wish to satisfy their self-interest as consumers, suppliers, employees, or residents through their own efforts. The rules of conduct for Swedish cooperatives typically have included: open membership, independence from any political party, one member/one vote, expectation of a modest return on the investment of one's time and capital, and teamwork. The purposes of Swedish cooperatives are to foster economic development while achieving independence from private owners of capital, and to provide high-quality goods and services while bringing down prices of private producers and distributors. Cooperatives are an alternative countervailing force to both private-sector and public-sector activities in the economy. They are intended to offset private economic power in certain sectors where economic concentration inhibits competitive behavior in the marketplace. They do not seek to eliminate the private sector, but to check the spread of monopoly power. Swedish cooperatives provide an alternative institution where cooperation and emphasis upon satisfying consumers and producers in a nonprofit atmosphere are provided.

The Swedish cooperative movement emerged in the mid-nineteenth century, but did not prosper due to a lack of widespread support. Beginning with those movements of the late ninteenth century that reacted against the concentration of capital and fear of rising prices due to Sweden's industrial revolution, the cooperative movement quickly gained broad public support with individual members seeking a sense of involvement and influence over their economic well-being. Members of a growing urban-based working class began to form cooperatives at the grass-roots level to satisfy their housing, consumer goods, agricultural production and distribution, and insurance needs. As the success of the reform measures introduced by the Social Democratic-Agrarian alliance (1932) fostered solidarity among antimarket economy laborers and antisocial economy agricultural workers, cooperatives gained popularity.

Housing cooperatives were founded in the 1870s, and grew rapidly after 1920. Their objective has been to build better housing while ensuring employment to construction workers and to workers involved with supplying building materials. Members pool their own savings and borrow funds to construct and manage one-family or apartment dwellings. Typically, members pay a 5 percent down payment (financing the rest through a mortgage loan) and an annual fee to cover their share of the cooperative's loan payments and operating expenses. The residents receive a "dwelling right" in return, entitling them to reside in their housing unit for as long as they wish, while having the right to rent or sell the unit. In addition, the resident becomes eligible to participate in managing the cooperative. The importance of Sweden's housing cooperative (HSB) is indicated by its current membership (over 500,000 persons), and the fact that annual sales of consumer housing cooperatives are equivalent to about 20 percent of the value of all consumer goods purchased annually.

Consumer cooperatives are responsible for purchasing, producing, banking, publishing, travel services, and food processing, among other areas. Such cooperatives were founded in 1899. The purpose of consumer cooperatives is to provide high-quality, low-cost goods and services to people who might otherwise not have been able to afford such goods and services, and to provide consumer education to Swedish consumers to enable them to get the most value for their income. Cooperatives developed extensively for food and everyday necessities (e.g., light bulbs) first, and gradually expanded to include insurance and retail services, among others. During the same period producer cooperatives emerged, especially throughout the agricultural sector. Farmers involved with dairy, livestock, and timber production formed these economic associations for mutual benefit.

Cooperatives for agricultural products became widespread at the beginning of the twentieth century. Farmers seeking to avoid the detrimental effect of active price competition looked to cooperatives to protect their economic status. Associations specializing in dairy, meat, eggs, timber, and crops were formed. Such institutions guaranteed fee-paying members stable prices for their output (75 percent of which currently passes through agricultural cooperatives). Product development, marketing, and distribution were also handled by the cooperative, thereby enabling farmers to concentrate on production and to avoid dealing with wholesalers and retailers. These cooperatives, guided by the nation's agricultural policy, regulate the market, assuring the availability of adequate food supplies while smoothing out the effects of surpluses and shortages in production. State-funded support for farmers, which began in the early 1930s, is apportioned by the agricultural cooperatives.

Among other types of Swedish cooperatives are those that provide insurance and burial services. The insurance cooperative was formed in 1925. It provides practically all types of insurance (e.g., personal, life, motorist, travel, and homeowners) to about half of Swedish households. The purpose of burial cooperatives, like other cooperatives, is to offer Swedes an alternative to private, profit-oriented enterprises in this field. Currently this cooperative is responsible for about one third of Sweden's burials.

AN ECONOMY INFLUENCED BY COLLECTIVE BARGAINING

Centralized and Decentralized Resource Allocation Decision Making

Resource allocation decision making in Sweden is a curious blend of popular decisions arrived at democratically on a decentralized basis and highly centralized decision making by the national government and national associations of special-interest groups. Swedish decision making has been described as an example of "corporatist democracy."[30] Such a process gives economic interest groups considerable influence over establishment of the economy's working rules because the leaders of their national confederations serve as formal or informal advisors to state authorities. These authorities, in turn, are bound by formal or informal working rules to take into account the views of the centrally organized interest groups.

Swedes prefer to arrive at decisions following open discussion in which representatives of many interest groups participate. By adopting such a cooperative (versus competitive) approach, it is believed that organized interest groups have the opportunity to further their members' interests while minimizing

[30]Milner, *Sweden: Social Democracy in Practice*, pp. 73, 74.

the adverse effects their interests may have on competing parties. The Swedish preference for participation in interest groups, whether economic, educational, or recreational, is illustrated by the fact that each Swedish adult is affiliated, on the average, with 1.6 organized associations. (e.g., trade unions, consumer and housing cooperatives, sports clubs, study groups).

While decentralized decision making was preferable to many Swedes during the first half of the twentieth century, there has been a tendency in the private sector toward the centralization of decision-making authority through leadership of more recently developed larger institutions, especially since the late 1960s. Two purposes of the centralization movement have been to coordinate policy decisions in a more complex economy (or what one analyst calls the "progressive implementation of representative democracy"), and to achieve greater economic efficiency.[31] The latter purpose has become important to associations such as cooperatives, which must compete with growing, more centralized profit-oriented private institutions. As an extension of nineteenth-century popular movements designed to provide members with independence and protection from private monopoly forces, cooperatives have been organized to foster participatory democracy. However, in the face of competition with expanding private firms the cooperatives have been forced to abandon local, decentralized decision making and "emulate the emphasis on efficiency among their private competitors."[32]

In general, decision making within government has been divided into the state, county, and municipal levels. Each provides the services for which it is most efficient. For example, prior to the early 1990s health care and certain types of educational services were provided on the 24 county levels, while municipalities provide basic personal services such as primary education and day care. There has been a consolidation of municipalities, with the number being reduced from about 1,000 in 1962 to about 286 in 1994 so as to give greater responsibility to municipal authorities regarding provision of social and welfare services and ability to impose taxes. This shift reflects the changing philosophical basis in favor of greater reliance upon individual autonomy and discipline imposed by market forces. The move away from state decision making also reflects the view that the state had assumed too many different obligations and was unable to fulfill most of them.

From the late 1930s to early 1990s decision making concerning wages was centralized, with leaders of the LO, TCO, and SACO bargaining with SAF representatives. In 1938 at Saltsjobaden an historic compromise was reached between authorities representing labor (LO) and owners of Swedish capital (SAF), leading to highly centralized cooperation in decision making pertaining to wages. Over the past decade this bargaining model has come under criticism, resulting in a trend toward more decentralized wage settlements (see "Performance," pp.

---

[31]Nils Elvander, "The Future of Swedish Wage Negotiating System," *Inside Sweden*, 2 (October 1985), 304.
[32]Ibid., p. 312. Elvander observes "the continuing transfer of economic power to the central organization has made efforts to preserve and strengthen democracy within the cooperative movement extremely difficult."

316–323), as more workers and employers express a preference for decentralization (i.e., at the individual workplace level) of the wage bargaining process.

Most decisions affecting production are made on a decentralized basis by managers of privately owned firms. There is virtually no role for central planning by state authorities with regard to production decisions. The role of the public sector has been primarily in decisions pertaining to the distribution, or redistribution, of income so as to raise consumption levels or protect all Swedish citizens from misfortunes beyond their control. Representatives of the state, private-sector management, labor, and consumer groups have engaged actively in a cooperative manner to make decisions pertaining to the distribution of national income. In recent years interest groups have gained more control over decision-making bodies and pursued their respective group's agenda at the expense of the general public. Their ability to do this is due to their realizing that the combination of short terms in office (three years between elections) and a succession of weak coalition governments has shifted power in their favor as politicians have sought to appease more groups of marginal voters. Some refer to the decision-making organization that has evolved as a "corporatist demand mechanism" and argue that it has become increasingly difficult to control—with adverse effects upon the Swedish economy.

Extensive Private and Cooperative Ownership and Control of Resources

There is not a strict dichotomy between private-sector and state activities. Just as cooperation between private owners and labor interests was institutionalized with the Saltsjobaden agreement, there is a voluntary cooperation between business and the state in the production and distribution of resources. One analyst has noted "that industry and labor (SAF and LO) sidestepped state regulation by making the state a silent partner in the concerns that affected them and all of society."[33] The extent of cooperation, however, appears to be declining throughout the 1990s.

In terms of the relative importance of private versus cooperative versus state ownership and control of resources, the private sector is dominant in the production of goods and services, with cooperatives playing a relatively important role (compared to other OECD nations). Over 90 percent of Swedish enterprises are privately owned (with cooperative ownership accounting for about 5 percent of all these enterprises), while state-owned enterprises account for less than 10 percent—with the trend toward privatization growing. Sales of goods and services produced by private firms comprise about 65 percent of all sales, with government-owned enterprises and cooperatives accounting for about 20 percent and 15 percent, respectively. Of the 4 million Swedes in the labor force, about 60 percent work in the private sector (including cooperatives), while the rest are employed by the state. The public sector exerts considerable influence over the distribution of income throughout Sweden. Private consumption in Sweden is just

---

[33]Scott, *Sweden: The Nation's History*, p. 521.

over 50 percent of gross national product, as compared to the OECD average of 60 percent. Meanwhile public consumption accounts for nearly 30 percent of Sweden's GNP versus an average of 20 percent for all OECD nations.

PRIVATE SECTOR (EXCLUDING COOPERATIVES).   The percentage of enterprises privately owned in Sweden is similar to that in the United States. In Sweden's economy the wealthy, influential entrepreneur has not been eliminated. The most noteworthy was Marcus Wallenberg who, at the time of his death in 1983, controlled companies whose 1982 sales were almost $25 billion. The extent of his family's economic power is illustrated by the fact that about one out of every four Swedes in the labor force work for a company owned and controlled by the Wallenbergs.

Concentration of stock ownership is a feature of Sweden. There are indications that the structure of ownership of Swedish firms is becoming even more concentrated as these firms seek greater economic efficiency in an attempt to remain competitive on the international market. Of the total market value of companies that are listed on the Stockholm Stock Exchange, about 75 percent is held by institutional owners while only 25 percent is owned by individuals.[34] Individual ownership is very concentrated, for 90 percent of Swedish households own no stock while 1 percent own about 75 percent. Meanwhile, the richest 2 percent of Swedish households own 62 percent of all shares of stock traded on the stock exchange.[35] As of the mid-1990s the Wallenberg empire's concentration of economic power had increased, for the family owns about 40 percent of stock shares sold on the Swedish stock market—a concentration of ownership unequaled anywhere in Europe.[36]

Stock ownership has become a national issue since the mid-1970s, for workers have been pressing for a national profit-sharing scheme. Here ownership of private enterprises with corresponding rights to establish rules pertaining to the possession, use, and disposal of an enterprise's assets and goods and services produced would become collective ownership. The political impetus toward such a scheme came from the radical element of the Social Democratic Party, which began to reappraise "the degree to which party goals could be achieved within the parameters of a capitalist society."[37] This group believed that, having introduced extensive social insurance and welfare measures, the Social Democratic Party needed to further the labor movement through passage of working rules providing for some form of state-worker private ownership and control over the means of production.

[34]Mats Isaksson and Rolf Skog, "Ownership, Influence and Efficiency," *Skandinaviska Enskilda Banken Quarterly Review,* 1 (1989), 4–9.

[35]Kenneth Hermele, "The End of the Middle Road: What Happened to the Swedish Model?" *Monthly Review,* 44, 10 (March 1993), 18. He also points out the growing concentration trend, noting that the five biggest owners in each of the 50 most important Swedish companies listed on the stock market increased their voting control from 47 percent to 61 percent between 1978 and 1988.

[36]"Whither the Wallenbergs?" *The Economist,* December 25, 1993–January 7, 1994, p. 89.

[37]Richard Scase, *Social Democracy in Capitalist Society* (London: Croom Helm, 1977), p. 166.

A number of working rules have been proposed. One would utilize the large government pension fund, which had grown to about 50 percent of GNP by the mid-1970s, to purchase shares of stock from companies, thereby permitting workers to assume control of firms. The schemes were not consistent with the democratic, decentralized, pragmatic approach preferred by Swedish policymakers since 1932. In particular, there has been an aversion to centrally planned and enforced measures. In 1976, after years of study, the Labor Organization endorsed an innovative scheme for transferring ownership and control of privately held firms to their workers. This scheme became known as the Meidner Plan, with collective wage-earner funds as the key component.

Essentially the plan would gradually transfer ownership and control of the means of production to trade union workers, thereby giving workers a greater voice in the management of industry. The transfer would occur through the purchase of companies' stock through a fund controlled by the trade unions. Sources of funds would come from a tax at about 20 percent on companies' profits as well as from a modest payroll tax. Transfer of power would satisfy the workers' desire to assume greater control. In addition, it would further socialize investment by enabling workers to make decisions which would guarantee (from their viewpoint) investment levels consistent with economic growth rates necessary for maintaining full employment and state-controlled redistributional measures intended to minimize standard of living differentials among households.

A modified, less powerful version of the original Meidner Plan was established as a working rule in 1982 and went into effect in late 1983. Six wage-earner funds instead of one large fund were established. One provision of the use of these funds to purchase voting stock of Swedish corporations was that the workers' combined ownership of stock in any one Swedish corporation had to be less than 50 percent. Another provision was that the use of tax revenues to support the fund will end after 1990. Thereafter, the fund would be permitted to grow only if an enterprise's profits exceed "a required, annual 3 percent real return transferred into the supplementary pension system."[38] Overall, the extent to which this alternative form of ownership and control, referred to by some as "economic democracy," will affect management of private enterprises may be modest. This is because labor will have a greater, but not majority, voice in controlling the decision making of any particular private enterprise. Given the adverse performance of the economy since 1990, the sentiment against trade union ownership and power has shifted so that the pace of employee ownership decreased considerably and may cease to grow altogether.

COOPERATIVES.   Cooperatives are an important alternative type of private ownership and control of Swedish enterprises. They have "served in

---

[38]Charles P. Rock, "Recent Reforms Democratizing Swedish Economic Institutions," *Journal of Economic Issues*, XXI, no. 2 (June, 1987), 840. Also refer to Hans-Goran Myrdal, "The Swedish Model— Will it Survive?" *British Journal of Industrial Relations*, 18, 1 (March 1980), for additional information about wage-earner funds.

practice as brake and corrective"[39] on private monopoly power. They provide consumers with a variety of high-quality, modestly priced goods and services. Through popular movements that have become institutionalized on a large scale, cooperatives have promoted the egalitarian, integration ideals so prominent in the philosophical basis for the Swedish economy. Finally, cooperatives have remained apolitical and are not perceived as a threat to the autonomy of the private sector. The extent of acceptance within Sweden is illustrated by the fact that about two thirds of Sweden's households have at least one person who belongs to a producer or consumer cooperative.

Cooperatives employ over 5 percent of the labor force, including over 15 percent of retail workers. More than 7 percent of Sweden's industrial production is accounted for by cooperatives, including about one third of the nation's annual housing production. Cooperatives are especially important in the agricultural sector, where more than three quarters of agricultural output passes through producer cooperatives. In addition, more than half of the food consumed in Sweden is produced by farmers belonging to a cooperative.

About 1 million Swedes (out of the entire population of about 8.4 million) live in cooperative housing units, while more than half of Sweden's citizens are covered by insurance purchased through cooperative insurance enterprises. Sales of consumer cooperatives comprise about 20 percent of the sales of everyday goods and services. One prominent cooperative is the Swedish Co-operative Union and Wholesale Society. This institution is Sweden's third largest enterprise, with about 2 million members and 90,000 employees.[40] Almost one fourth of Sweden's retail trade is accounted for by *Konsum*, the retail outlet of the Society.

PUBLIC OWNERSHIP.   State ownership of the means of production is quite modest (less than 10 percent of all enterprises). There are two forms of public ownership: majority-owned (or "limited" companies), and nationalized but semiautonomous enterprises in terms of their financial and staffing decisions. The state owns seven public utilities, nine credit institutions, and over 100 other firms, most of which are engaged in the mining, forestry, engineering, pharmaceutical, shipbuilding, and steel industries. All public enterprises are expected to cover their operating costs as well as show a return on invested capital. The source of public enterprise funds is user fees.

In terms of the proportion of the labor force that works for the public sector, plus tax receipts and government spending as a percentage of gross domestic product, the Swedish state exerts considerable control over the economy. Prior to the early 1990s, whenever Sweden experienced recessions, state control had been extended. In the early 1960s the state involvement in the economy was equivalent to that in most OECD nations. However, following the economic

---

[39]Scott, *Sweden: The Nation's History*, p. 494.
[40]Milner, *Sweden: Social Democracy in Practice*, p. 77.

slowdowns of the past two decades (see "Performance," pp. 316–323), public employment as a percentage of the labor force increased to over 38 percent in 1985, by far the highest in the OECD. The relative proportion of government expenditures and tax receipts to GDP are likewise higher in Sweden than France, Japan, and the United States, as well as all other OECD nations.

A primary factor for the growth of state control over Sweden's resources has been the extension of income redistributed in the form of pensions (about 60 percent of public-sector transfers), sick pay benefits (15 percent), child allowances, study grants, and housing allowances, among other transfer programs. In addition, Swedish public expenditures on labor market measures to retrain or support those who have lost their jobs account for a relatively higher proportion of GDP than in any other nation.

As of 1960 Sweden's public expenditures accounted for about 30 percent of GDP, which was similar to the average for OECD countries. Beginning in the mid-1960s the state extended its control over Swedish resources and public employment, as a percentage of the labor force, nearly doubled from about 20 percent in 1965 to just under 40 percent by the mid-1980s. During the 1970s central government and local government employment rolls grew 40 percent and 80 percent, respectively, versus less than 10 percent growth of employment in the private sector.[41] Meanwhile, state subsidies to industry rose dramatically. The impetus for the post-1960 increase was the philosophical principle of *Jamlikhet*, which justified the extension of social insurance and welfare programs, combined with a decline in overall economic performance. Between 1970 and 1982 social security transfers grew over 20 percent on an annual basis, while central government transfers to business (about half of which were price subsidies) and households increased over 20 percent and 13 percent, respectively.[42]

During the recession in the early 1970s the Swedish government extended its control over manufacturing in an effort to mitigate the effects of a decline in the economy's performance on unemployment. To finance these activities taxes increased from 24 percent of GDP in 1950 to 48 percent in 1970, and to 61 percent of GDP by 1982. Despite the tax increases, the state government's budget deficit reached as high as 13.0 percent of GDP in 1982.[43] The severity of this percentage can be appreciated if one observes that as late as 1977 the budget deficit had never exceeded 5 percent of GDP. As a percentage of GNP public-sector spending (much in the form of income redistribution and provision of social insurance and welfare benefits) reached 70 percent in 1994, the highest proportion of any industrial country. This growth has coincided with a growing government budget deficit which reached about 15 percent of GNP in 1994—more than double the 1992 level.[44]

---

[41]*Growth or Stagnation? The Swedish Economy 1981–1985* (Stockholm: Ministry of Economic Affairs, 1982), p. 77.

[42]Bosworth and Rivlin, *The Swedish Economy*, p. 263.

[43]Ibid., pp. 263, 312, 313.

[44]Meanwhile, taxes as a share of gross domestic product are about 50 percent in 1994 compared to about 30 percent in the United States.

Reformers who accept the philosophical basis of the Swedish Conservative Party call for decentralization of political authorities' control over the economy, especially regarding social insurance and welfare services, in favor of municipal control. They also advocate private-sector alternatives to public services, such as retirement homes and preschools, in the interest of reducing costs and boosting quality. Another reform proposed is reducing government control over housing and construction by dismantling price regulation in the housing market. Finally, voucher schemes are recommended to reallocate central government subsidies. In general, the proposal is for subsidies to be paid directly to the user in the form of a voucher for use (at the individual's discretion) in either the public or private sector. The choice is to be determined in a competitive environment by alternative providers of the service in question.

Swedish corporations pay a 52 percent tax on profits and are required to finance nearly all social insurance benefits by a payroll tax which exceeds 35 percent of their total wage bill, about twice what an employer in the United States would pay.[45] Taxes on income earners are progressive, ranging from 5 percent to 42 percent of income. Top marginal tax rates have been the subject of much debate. They have ranged from about 50 percent in 1959, to 80 percent in 1981, to about 60 percent in 1989, and were be reduced to about 50 percent in 1991. There is strong sentiment not to increase them, and to eventually reduce them further as the budget deficit is brought under control. In addition, local tax rates vary according to decisions made by municipal authorities, although no Swede can be required to pay more than 72 percent of his or her income for local and national income taxes. Swedish consumers faced a stiff 19 percent value-added tax (23.46 percent of the pretax price of a taxable item) before the 1991 tax reform. Although the rate has been reduced, relative to other OECD nations it remains high. Such high tax rates permit the state, through an extensive scheme of publicly controlled measures, to continue coordinating many of Sweden's distribution (but not generally production) decisions.

Social Process for Economic
Coordination: Extensive State
Measures to Influence Distribution

Sweden's economy is characterized by a unique blend of unregulated and regulated markets, combined with state intervention for stabilization and redistribution purposes. To varying degrees the state has guaranteed all Swedes a certain degree of welfare (i.e., housing, employment, health care, and cultural advantages), while taking steps to equalize opportunity so as to alleviate tension between social groups. The private sector is relatively autonomous in terms of production decisions, while there is considerable cooperation between labor and management over wage policy. The predominantly market-coordinated production and state-regulated distribution must interact so that the economy

---

[45]Ibid., p. 187.

performs favorably to the extent that greater equality and a high standard of living for all Swedes can be achieved while sufficient incentives for greater efficiency and flexibility in the private sector are encouraged. This was something not achieved during the early 1990s. As a small open economy Sweden's economic performance is significantly affected by the international economy. Consequently, state measures to redistribute income cannot adversely affect the private sector's profitability (thereby reducing employment levels) without necessitating countermeasures (e.g., a government deficit) to maintain full employment.

Since 1932 three broad types of policy measures have been introduced. The first concerns macroeconomic stabilization, with the attainment of full employment as the principal objective. The second includes redistributional measures designed to created a more equitable distribution of income and higher levels of consumption of both private and public goods for all Swedish families. Swedish policies to coordinate production and distribution decisions have been introduced mainly in response to the philosophical basis promoted by the Social Democrats. However, electoral realities have prevented the Social Democrats from introducing highly partisan measures, and democratically determined reform measures have gradually been introduced. Poor performance of the economy during the early 1990s has stimulated a third type of policy measures which reflect a more conservative philosophical basis. The measures are designed to increase work incentives, reduce the level of state guarantees for all individuals, and promote growth through private-sector initiatives.

Influenced by the Social Democrats' philosophical basis and the cooperative wage bargaining process, Sweden became during the 1930s what one scholar describes as a "solidaristic market economy" with a "'social partnership' between . . . encompassing representative organizations."[46] Because a high percentage of Sweden's work force belongs to centrally organized unions, the flow of information necessary to make this partnership work is greatly facilitated. The decision making at higher levels includes consultation among representatives of labor, management, and the state who are authorities of "'corporatist' societal institutions."[47]

Overall, Sweden's social process for economic coordination consists of five main ingredients. The first is an active Keynesian-type fiscal policy, which emphasizes maintenance of a high level of aggregate demand to minimize the severity of business cycles and unemployment. The focus is on consumption, not investment, to maintain adequate demand levels. Second, the process relies on extensive private ownership and control over production. Despite centralized decision making, a large bureaucracy, and a state committed to monitoring and intervening in economic matters, there is not any trace of centralized economic

---

[46]Milner, *Sweden: Social Democracy in Practice,* p. 23.

[47]Ibid., p. 40. The type of long-range policies discussed include those pertaining to education, transit, energy, health care, and consumer information, among other areas.

planning and virtually no production planning. Sweden, as a small open economy, is highly dependent on international trade. Therefore, it places considerable emphasis upon unregulated markets to impose microeconomic efficiency so that its producers can be competitive in an international economy whose prices Sweden must take as given.

The third ingredient is a solidaristic wage policy, the purpose of which is to reduce wage differentials and change the structure of the economy to improve the international competitiveness of the nation's small open economy. As a measure to coordinate management and labor decisions, this policy "reduces uncertainty by channeling market competition to those spheres of activity where they are seen to contribute to aggregate productivity, while fostering relations of social solidarity in other spheres to complement that productivity."[48] Wage restraint is exercised by unions who seek full employment without inflation. The unions are willing to settle for wages that are set in the more competitive sector of the Swedish economy that must compete in the international market. Fourth, Sweden employs active labor market measures to promote full employment and increase the mobility of labor. There is an informal rule favoring a work ethic so that state-funded measures designed to minimize unemployment are preferable to high unemployment rates requiring large public expenditures. Among the market-support measures to maintain full employment, given that wages cannot be reduced, are vocational retraining for "redundant" workers, and subsidies for workers who are transferring jobs.

During the 1990s a fifth ingredient has been introduced designed to offset some of the other four ingredients. Essentially there is reduced emphasis being placed on labor market measures, new working rules to stimulate work initiative, and reductions in social insurance and welfare payments. Therefore, as the evolutionary-institutional theory predicts, the nature and expansion of the types of policy measures coincidental to these five ingredients changed over the period from 1932 to the present. Five phases can be identified. Each will be discussed in turn.

STABILIZATION PHASE (1932 TO MID-1950S).   During the first phase stabilization policies were emphasized, although some "welfare-reformist" measures were introduced.[49] The Social Democrats were distrustful of the self-regulating market economy, blaming it for causing the periodic recessions experienced in Sweden during the 1920–1932 period. In particular, the "free-market system" was criticized for "its negative effects on the distribution of income and wealth,"[50] and its Swedish proponents were chastised for advocating the classical economic view that a skewed distribution of income was necessary to generate profits to entrepreneurs so as to stimulate economic growth. Social Democratic

---

[48]Ibid., p. 37.

[49]Scott, *Sweden: The Nation's History*, p. 523.

[50]Erik Lundberg, "The Rise and Fall of the Swedish Model," *Journal of Economic Literature*, 23 (March 1985), 14.

leaders, including Gunnar Myrdal, believed that the LFME was incapable of rectifying problems plaguing Sweden in the areas of low population growth among low-income families, housing, agriculture, international trade, and poverty.

The Social Democrats proposed an economic program that was designed not only to resolve the impending economic crisis, but to establish their party unequivocally as a party of full employment. They intended to substitute public investment financed through various forms of collective savings for deficient private initiative, significantly increasing the state's expenditures (especially on social insurance, collectivized housing, and preschool education) and raising income and wealth taxes. Social Democrats were supported by the research of the Stockholm School of economists, which included Knut Wicksell and Myrdal. These economists anticipated Keynes by advocating a stabilization policy based upon deficit public spending, lower taxes, and public works projects to alleviate chronic unemployment caused by a prolonged recession. The Social Democrats used this theory to encourage state intervention if the private sector could not generate full employment. While public works were encouraged, nationalization of industry was rejected by authorities.

Social Democrats believed that deficit spending was necessary to expand aggregate demand, which would stimulate economic activity to the extent that social reforms could be financed. Increased household spending as a result of these reforms, which included unemployment benefits, would support the anticipated economic expansion. It was believed that programs such as a privately financed (by employer contributions), publicly distributed unemployment insurance scheme were sufficient to guarantee that the wealth created by the economy would be redistributed according to the ideals of integration and equality.

The ability of the Social Democrats to implement their program in 1932 was tempered by the political reality that they had to form a compromise coalition with the Agrarian Party, resulting in the following "cow trade." The Agrarians agreed to accept the Social Democrats' proposals for alleviating unemployment, while the Social Democrats agreed to endorse agricultural price supports, including a "detestable excise tax on margarine."[51] The subsequent performance of the economy, which included higher rates of economic growth, declining unemployment, and rising incomes among industrial and agricultural workers after 1932, promoted solidarity among industrial and agricultural workers. Both sides realized that generally rising incomes could be mutually beneficial to all Swedes, since each group's well-being was influenced by the other sector's purchasing power.

The Social Democrats' ability to implement radical redistributional reforms was also tempered by other nonsocialist parties. The necessity for compromise among all political parties has meant that practical politics would prevail. The ability of competing interest groups to work together led to reforms aimed at transforming society in favor of social equalization. The Social

[51]Koblik, *Sweden's Development from Poverty to Affluence*, p. 270.

Democrats pragmatically proposed a series of compromise measures that would quietly but steadily erode what they referred to as the "capitalist" domination of the economy.[52] Each one of these measures was not to be considered a panacea in itself, but only one of the means that the Social Democrats might employ to construct gradually their version of a decent society.

Therefore, the coalition government focused on macroeconomic policies such as demand stabilization and measures to modify the distribution of income. The Social Democrats also focused on alleviating poverty, especially as this condition was exacerbated by unemployment. Meanwhile, labor unions and employers agreed in 1938 to establish the rules for cooperative industrial labor relations. The solidaristic wage policy was based upon the philosophy of "equal pay for equal work: workers performing the same job should receive the same wage, irrespective of the inter-firm or inter-industry differences in productivity and profitability."[53] Both sides respected the power of the other. The LO agreed to hold the strike weapon in reserve, while employers agreed to the equal-pay objective. This centralization of collective bargaining, combined with LO and SAF influence in state decision making, facilitated working rules designed to secure employment and high rates of economic growth at wage and profit levels acceptable to workers and employers. Workers, recognizing Sweden's need to be competitive internationally, would exercise wage restraint rather than stimulate inflation or force layoffs. Management would continue to make decisions regarding what, how, and how much to produce, while providing their share of funding for social programs—the extent of which would be determined by state authorities.

Under the solidaristic wage agreement firms characterized by low productivity and profits would no longer be able to reduce wages, nor could they increase wages to attract better workers. Rather, less productive firms would face cost pressures that would force them out of the market. Workers would shift employment to more productive firms, and would receive assistance through state-funded active labor market measures. Meanwhile, more efficient firms would reap high profits since the solidaristic wage agreement would hold down wage increases that workers in such a firm might otherwise have been able to receive through collective bargaining on the local level. The success of this type of industrial democracy requires that the threat of unemployment be minimized while workers and owners agree not to haggle endlessly over wages, for "[t]hreats of redundancy are not conducive to the development of a sense of community and belongingness at work."[54]

As a result of the solidaristic collective wage agreement, the Social Democrats and labor unions paradoxically endorsed big business. Meanwhile the private sector quietly acquiesced to provide its share of funding for social programs. The subsequent ability of the Social Democrats to introduce gradual

---

[52]Tilton, "A Swedish Road to Socialism," p. 515.

[53]Bosworth and Rivlin, *The Swedish Economy*, p. 131.

[54]Geoffrey M. Hodgson, *Economics and Institutions* (Cambridge: Polity Press, 1988).

"socialization" measures into the economy without a revolution or large-scale nationalization shaped attitudes within and outside of Sweden. Citizens began to accept that their own fate was tied to the fate of all Swedes, while the rest of the world began to pay attention to Sweden's "middle way."

By the mid-1950s, the combined effect of the stabilization policies, social insurance schemes, Swedish neutrality during World War II, and the devaluation of the Swedish krona in the late 1940s (which stimulated exports) contributed to a healthy economy and realization of the goal to abolish poverty. This performance contributed to the Swedish people becoming accustomed to full employment as well as high rates of economic growth. They looked to the future with even greater expectations and demanded improvements in health care, pensions, education, and housing subsidies. Consequently, the Social Democrats would meet less political resistance to future social insurance and welfare proposals.

SECOND PHASE (MID-1950s TO MID-1960s).   During this phase stabilization measures which had been introduced in the 1930s were supplemented by active labor market policies, a collective savings scheme, and expanded social insurance and welfare programs. Macroeconomic policymakers, labor union leaders, and Social Democrats had different but reconcilable interests at the beginning of the 1950s. Policymakers were concerned about maintaining full employment without fueling inflation. Years of wage restraint by labor in response to Social Democrat appeals combined with labor's fear that adjustments to structural imbalances in industry would stimulate unemployment inspired an innovative policy proposal by the LO in 1951—the Rehn Model.

Named after Gosta Rehn, an LO economist, the policy was an alternative to the Keynesian and Stockholm School aggregate demand management scheme. The LO agreed that general fiscal policy was necessary to achieve full employment. However, the LO believed that supplementary measures would become necessary before the solidaristic wage policy could be effective. To achieve the equal pay for similar work objective while maintaining full employment would require state-funded active labor market policies aimed at specific areas. These policies (e.g., temporary subsidies to improve the geographical mobility of laborers in declining industries, and funds for retraining of "redundant" workers) would help alleviate problems incurred while structural imbalances between industries were corrected.

It was accepted that there would always be some industries experiencing excess capacity, high unemployment, and noncompetitive production costs, while other industries would be operating beyond efficient capacity utilization. Labor market policies would be necessary to support workers in less profitable firms that had to shut down (while more profitable firms expanded), for under the solidaristic wage policy less profitable firms could not reduce wages. The state-funded labor market policies would shift the cost for structural change from workers to society. In return for state measures to promote full employment, the unions agreed to temper wage demands to a level consistent with price stability.

The Rehn model also called for savings and investment to be, as Keynes suggested, "socialized." This would be achieved through higher taxes imposed on employers to enable the state to channel these savings effectively into investment. In 1959 the political alliance between the Social Democrats and the Communist Party was sufficient to pass a formal working rule which expanded the national pension scheme. Increased employer contributions into the pension fund came from an increase in indirect taxes, especially payroll taxes. These taxes provided the source for significantly greater public savings, thereby enabling the state to socialize investment, and to expand active labor market measures and social insurance and welfare coverage.

Examples of social programs financed by higher indirect taxes and fees imposed on employers included the adoption of general health insurance (1955) and the general supplementary pension scheme (1959). The pension scheme was a "universal, compulsory, inflation-indexed, earnings related supplementary pension."[55] The scheme was superimposed on the universal pension scheme introduced in 1947, which provided flat-rate pensions financed out of general taxation. The 1959 pension scheme was quite ambitious, for all citizens were guaranteed a pension regardless of their employment history.

THIRD PHASE (MID-1960S TO EARLY 1970S).   At the beginning of this phase there was a change in "policy ambitions."[56] A broader concept of full employment emerged along with a stronger commitment toward a more egalitarian distribution of income. Measures to achieve full employment and to support lower-income families required an expansion of public expenditures, with employers and wealthier Swedish families bearing the greatest burden. Measures introduced to assist lower-income families included a decrease in the cost of visiting a physician, subsidies for the purchase of medicine, and general dental insurance. Employers faced new restrictions designed to create greater job security for workers. In particular, employers' discretion to discharge their workers became more restricted.

An increase in the female labor force participation rate coincided with a greater commitment to maintaining full employment, which included measures to maintain workers in their current place of residence, and the slowdown in economic growth during the early 1970s.[57] The result was rapid growth of public-sector employment and other publicly financed measures, including training programs and early retirement. These measures were costly, but were justified for being a "positive and humane method of taking care of those who otherwise would be counted as 'unemployed.'"[58]

---

[55]P. Gourevitch, A. Martin, G. Ross, C. Allen, S. Bornstein, and A. Markovits, *Unions and Economic Crisis: Britain, West Germany, and Sweden* (London: George Allen and Unwin, 1984), p. 213.

[56]Lundberg, "The Rise and Fall of the Swedish Model," p. 21.

[57]Ibid. The female labor force participation rate increased from about 50 percent in 1960 to roughly 75 percent in 1980 (versus a 1980 OECD average of 50 percent).

[58]Ibid.

In 1970 the LO and SAF jointly developed a new model according to which wages would be determined. The model divides the economy into two sectors: the "competitive sector" (about one third of the economy) in which prices are established in international markets; and the "sheltered sector" which is influenced both by competitive-sector prices and Sweden's domestic conditions. Prices in the latter sector are established on a markup-over-cost basis. Wages in the competitive sector are established according to world prices and productivity of competitive-sector workers. Wages in the competitive sector would serve as the basis for wages in the sheltered sector. These wages would be set through centralized collective bargaining according to the solidaristic principle.[59]

FOURTH PHASE (EARLY 1970S TO 1990).   During the fourth phase Sweden had to face two serious recessions due to supply-side shocks. Commitment to full employment has remained strong, although the trade-off has been rising taxes. Stabilization measures such as price controls and an industrial policy were introduced, for many Swedish firms found it difficult to remain competitive internationally in the face of an upward wage drift combined with slow productivity growth. Meanwhile workers sought greater control over investment through the wage-earner fund proposal.

Marginal tax rates rose to over 80 percent in the early 1980s, while government expenditures and transfer payments exceeded two thirds of GNP, coinciding with the rapid growth of public-sector employment. Beginning in the late 1970s a rising portion of government spending was for active labor market programs. This period is significant. For the first time in 44 years a nonsocialist government was elected to power, ruling from 1976 to 1982. During this period labor market expenditures grew from about 2.5 percent to about 3 percent of Sweden's GDP. The growth of these expenditures under nonsocialist authorities reflects the deep Swedish commitment to the ideal of integration through allocating funds for the retraining and relocation of workers whose jobs were redundant. The percentage of the Swedish labor force receiving assistance through any labor market program (e.g., relief work, retraining) grew from 1.8 percent in 1970, to 3.6 percent in 1979, to 4.1 percent in 1984.[60]

Beginning in 1970 Sweden extended the bargaining feature of its economy to include price monitoring. The National Swedish Price and Cartel Office (SPK) was established, charged with responsibility for price controls. This institution had the authority to monitor all domestic prices except for housing. This was not a scheme of strict price control. Rather, firms wishing to market new consumer products or to make price adjustments due to changes in the quality, packaging,

[59]Philip Arestis, "Post-Keynesian Economic Policies: The Case of Sweden," *Journal of Economic Issues,* 20, no. 3 (September 1986), 711.

[60]For further discussion, see Stephen McBride, "The Comparative Politics of Unemployment," *Comparative Politics* (April 1988), 303–323.

or terms of payment for existing products had to file a report with the SPK.[61] In about 25 percent of the cases the firm is required to provide additional information, while in about 10 percent of all requested price increases SPK has "consulted" with the firm, seeking to reduce the price increases in the name of protecting consumers, holding down inflation, and maintaining full employment. The negotiation process favors the larger firms, for those able to enlist trade union members and other employees on its side during negotiations are likelier to win approval than smaller firms who have less bargaining power.

In the late 1970s, during a deep recession, Sweden adopted an industrial policy designed to combat rising unemployment while keeping Sweden competitive on the international market and maintaining free-trade policies. The state chose to subsidize declining industries on a selective basis, and over $10 billion was allocated to such industries between 1975 and 1985, while between 1975 and 1983 government funds allocated to declining industries grew from 0.3 percent of GNP to 28 percent of GNP in 1982.[62] Funds were shifted from emphasis on "growth-renewal" to "restructuring-reduction" payments. These payments provided operating funds for selected industries and funds to retrain and compensate workers who had to relocate. The extent of selectivity is illustrated by the fact that between fiscal 1976–1977 and 1982–1983 "[i]ndustries that accounted for 22.5 percent of manufacturing employment received 92.7 percent of the subsidies, and just two industries, steel and shipbuilding, representing only 8.8 percent of manufacturing employment, received 69 percent of the subsidies."[63]

It is interesting that even with the election of a nonsocialist government in 1976, the mainstays of the Social Democrats means for achieving their goals were continued rather than a new set of coordinating mechanisms being introduced. Therefore, industrial subsidies grew while public employment levels increased. After the Social Democratic reelection in 1979 a drastic devaluation of the krona was permitted so as to promote domestic employment. This led to a rapid expansion of industry as Swedish exports became more competitive in international markets. Meanwhile, public-sector programs were reduced modestly. Overall, the means of keeping unemployment low and funding social programs—expansionary fiscal policy, growth of the large Swedish firms (particularly those producing for foreign markets), and labor market programs— were still affordable.

However, there was a breakdown in centralized wage bargaining. Unions were not able to agree on national averages, so many wages were determined on the local level, and then tended to drift upwards. Part of the change reflected the growth of public-sector employment where workers are immune to international

---

[61]Lars Jonung, "The System of Price Controls as a Bargaining Process," *Skandinaviska Enskilda Banken Quarterly Review*, 3 (1984), 69.

[62]Bosworth and Rivlin, *The Swedish Economy*, p. 72.

[63]Ibid., p. 71.

competition. Consequently, they do not have to exercise wage restraint. Faced with rising taxes and inflation, nongovernment union workers broke from the centralized scheme to seek higher wages. The breakdown in the support of a labor-capital alliance, with the old rules of wage bargaining, also was due to rising unemployment. Policies designed to stimulate growth of Sweden's multinational corporations (MNCs) were tolerated as long as their expansions coincided with job security for workers. However, despite the fact that the top 20 Swedish MNCs grew to account for about half the nation's exports, these firms began to invest most of their profits abroad to the detriment of Swedish employment levels.

FIFTH PHASE. (1991 TO PRESENT).   Events of the preceding period initiated a round of policymaking, which began in 1991 with the election of the four-party conservative coalition. Faced with a serious recession, members of the coalition and Swedish voters recognized that the nation no longer could afford to accept rapid growth of the public sector and other means for minimizing unemployment without further hampering economic growth. Previous policy involving a large currency devaluation had stimulated inflation, and repetition of such a policy in 1989 was not as effective in curtailing rising unemployment as it had been in previous decades.

The time had come whereby low rates of private-sector growth no longer provided a source for funding public-sector growth and existing social insurance and welfare measures. The coalition was forced to first introduce measures designed to reestablish macroeconomic stability and restore confidence in the economy. Marginal tax rates were reduced, while the growth of public spending was curtailed. Measures to reduce the budget deficit include making dramatic reductions in social insurance and welfare programs, reducing public spending in other areas, and requiring Swedes to pay more for all publicly provided benefits. Other reforms include reducing the level of income guaranteed an individual or family and replacing it with something resembling a flat fee (a type of negative income tax), and providing fewer benefits for those unemployed, in labor market programs, or sick. Long-term goals are to reduce overall taxes as well as public spending (both these rates are the highest among OECD nations) and to facilitate noninflationary wage settlements. The latter goal can be achieved, it is argued, by establishing only one level for wage bargaining, the sectoral level, except for large corporations, whereby it is proposed to make the firm the level for wage agreements.

The second objective of the new policymakers is to introduce comprehensive changes in working rules consistent with their philosophical basis. A number of comprehensive reforms have been recommended which, if introduced, would effect dramatically the nature of the Swedish economy.[64] More autonomy has been shifted to the municipalities regarding taxation rights and

[64]For a detailed presentation of the recommendations for reform, see Lindbeck et al., "Options for Economic and Political Reform in Sweden."

provision of social and welfare services. Competition in the provision of public services is being encouraged so as to achieve more efficient resource use in both the public and private sectors. Providing fewer regulations promoting job security are under consideration as part of an effort to stimulate work initiative. Implementation of such reforms would demonstrate an evolution of the economy toward the guided market economies with relatively more reliance placed upon market forces to regulate distribution of benefits to society members.

Policymakers have constraints placed upon them by the need to maintain international competitiveness. They continually are faced with external economic pressures while having a small, open economy with a public which desires continuation of large social welfare insurance expenditures. These pressures have contributed to the nation's labor market policies, trade policies, and macroeconomic policy programs to be crafted in particular ways best suited to Sweden's economic philosophy and institutions.

INSTITUTIONAL STABILITY
UNTIL THE 1990s

Relative to other industrialized economies, there was little institutional change in Sweden between 1932 and 1991. This can be attributed, in part, to the impact of a generally favorable economic performance (in the opinion of most Swedes), for the economy was able to satisfy many of the ideals contained in the Social Democrats' philosophical basis (see "Performance of the Economy," pp. 316–323). The performance reinforced support for the Social Democrats among their primary supporters—trade union members. While Social Democratic influence in Parliament is no longer dominant, they were the ruling party for all but six of 60 years (1932–1991). Given their unwavering philosophical basis in terms of emphasis upon gradual, redistribution reforms to equalize living conditions and opportunities, Sweden experienced relatively few institutional changes. Another reason for institutional stability (i.e., the "continuity of Swedish values" as contained in the philosophical basis for the economy) is inherent in the values themselves. One scholar argues that "Swedish values are, comparatively speaking, more integrative and harmonious . . . [and] contain few internal conflicts . . . ."[65]

Some institutional changes can be identified, although nearly every case represents a modification rather than replacement of a principal institution. There were changes in the relative importance of the LO and SAF. Their importance increased following the 1938 historical compromise and the adoption of the Rehn model in the early 1950s. However, the 1980s trend toward decentralization of collective bargaining has meant a reduced role for the LO and SAF (and their authorities).

[65]Milner, *Sweden: Social Democracy in Practice*, p. 72.

Cooperatives increased in importance in terms of the proportion of Sweden's domestically produced goods and services they provided. However, they have had to adjust their decision-making process in an expanding world economy. In response to their need to compete with large centralized national and international producers of goods and services, cooperatives have become more highly centralized, thereby diminishing the popular, democratic decision-making feature upon which many cooperatives were established.

Meanwhile, the role of the Social Democrats in terms of their control over Sweden's working rules and resources increased almost steadily throughout the 1932–1991 period, with the exception of the election of the nonsocialist coalition in 1976. This change brought no sweeping reforms in the working rules, and some social insurance and welfare measures (e.g., active labor market measures) actually grew proportionately during this period. Since 1991, however, institutional changes of a political and economic nature have been introduced to cope with the serious economic problems.

While Sweden seeks to retain universal social insurance and welfare policies, there is recognition of the need to eliminate the disadvantages in the delivery of these services due to monolithic public institutions and their working rules. In response, efforts are underway to stimulate introduction of private and cooperative alternatives to public institutions providing these services. The objective is to provide more competition, better-quality services, and more freedom of choice for recipients. Some large public institutions, such as those providing care for the elderly, are being phased out. Also, proposals have been introduced designed to reduce the role of interest groups (especially trade unions) in government decision making.

Significant institutional changes will ensue from the November 1994 decision by Swedish voters to join the European Union (EU). Being part of the EU means that Sweden will become subject to the working rules of EU supranational institutions (see Chapter 14). Thus, in addition to benefiting from being part of a major trade bloc to which nearly all of its major trading partners will belong, Sweden will face the discipline that membership in the EU requires. It will no longer be able to rely on unilateral devaluation of the krona as a means to restore economic competitiveness and reduce unemployment. It will also be required to further reduce its value-added tax and other taxes and subsidies so as to achieve harmony with EU working rules. Thus, EU membership will impose discipline on Swedish economic policymakers and more competition within the economy (partly through easing entry barriers for firms from other EU member nations). This discipline, some Swedes believe, is necessary for the nation to implement the needed institutional reform so as to reestablish favorable performance of the economy.

PERFORMANCE OF THE ECONOMY:
ALLEVIATION OF POVERTY, BUT
NEW PROBLEMS HAVE ARISEN

The economy's performance will be evaluated first according to its ability to attain the goals it established for itself (goals which have been consistent with those of social economics). Second, performance will be judged according to whether sufficient revenue has been generated to finance economic and social programs, especially those designed to maintain full employment and enhance family and worker welfare without adversely affecting economic growth, price stability, and the government budget deficit. Evaluating whether Sweden has attained its goals of banishing poverty, integrating all socioeconomic groups while minimizing class conflict and decreasing the exploitation of labor, and establishing social and economic security requires that performance indicators corresponding to each goal be identified. In addition, data describing the behavior of these indicators are also necessary. This will be done for each of the three broad goals Sweden has chosen to pursue. Due to the dramatic change in economic performance since 1990, an evaluation will be made for two periods (before and after 1990), followed by a summary of performance from a long-run perspective.

1932–1989

The degree to which poverty has been banished and a decent standard of living provided for all Swedes is reflected by rates of unemployment, the standard of living of the poorest (i.e., 20 percent) segment of the population, and international standard of living comparisons. Unemployment rates in Sweden declined rapidly after the Social Democrats rose to power, falling from 22.8 percent in 1932 to less than 2 percent by the mid 1950s.[66] A low rate of unemployment (i.e., less than 3.3 percent, and often below 2 percent) was experienced for most of the 1960–1989 period, although labor market measures including rapid expansion of public-sector employment were necessary to maintain the low rates since the early 1970s. Between 1970 and 1989 Sweden's unemployment exceeded 3 percent only in 1984, and averaged 2.2 percent for the 1978–1987 decade.[67] For the same period the unemployment rate in Sweden was well below the OECD average. It should be noted, however, that Sweden spent considerably more as a percentage of its GDP on active labor market measures than any other OECD nation. When workers covered by active labor market measures are added to those who have received early retirement pensions, then Swedish employment conditions were similar to the OECD average.

     To the degree that per capita gross domestic product (and the Gini coefficient) is an indicator of well-being, poverty was banished in Sweden. From

[66]B. R. Mitchell, *European Historical Statistics: 1750–1970* (New York: Columbia University Press, 1975), p. 171.
[67]*OECD Economic Surveys: Sweden 1988/89* (Paris: OECD, 1989), p. 104.

the midnineteenth century, when impoverished Swedes were emigrating in search of economic opportunity, to 1981, Sweden developed into a nation whose per capita gross domestic product was greater than that of any European nation, the United States, and Japan (taking into account that exchange rate fluctuations can alter international rankings). However, by 1987 Sweden's ranking fell below Japan's (and that of Switzerland, Denmark, and Norway), but still exceeded that of the United States.[68]

A set of related goals Sweden chose to pursue was to integrate all socioeconomic groups, minimize class conflict and the exploitation of labor, and equalize income and wages. One indication of the degree of class conflict is the relative share of factor income which is received by employees as compared to the percentage received by "owners" (proprietors, landlords, and stockholders). Between 1955 and the mid-1970s employee compensation as a percentage of factor income rose (from about 60 percent to 67 percent), as did social insurance receipts.[69]

On an absolute basis, the average number of hours worked declined from 48 hours in 1932 to about 36 in the late 1980s, while the number of weeks of paid vacation to which employees are legally entitled has risen from two in the 1930s to five in the 1980s. Income distribution became more equal after 1932. The percentage of income received by the poorest 20 percent of Swedish households increased from 4.6 percent in 1965 to 7.4 percent in 1986.[70] An international comparison of income distribution for the late 1970s indicated that Sweden's distribution was more equal than that of either the United Kingdom or West Germany.[71] The health and physical development of children across the spectrum of incomes is equal, indicating that Sweden has become a classless society.[72]

The final goal was the establishment of social and economic security. Quantifiable performance indicators are more difficult to identify, since the primary goal is to protect citizens from misfortune beyond their control. As indicated by the growth of public consumption and services, especially the national pension scheme and health care system, one could argue that this aim was achieved. The social insurance fund grew from less than 1 percent to nearly 40 percent of net national savings between 1960 and the mid-1970s.[73] Meanwhile, the rate of growth of public consumption has been roughly double that of private consumption since 1970.

[68]See "International Comparisons," *OECD Economic Surveys: Sweden 1988/1989* (Paris: OECD, 1989).

[69]Joint Economic Committee, *Monetary Policy, Selective Credit Policy, and Industrial Policy in France, Britain, West Germany, and Sweden* (Washington, DC: U.S. Government Printing Office, 1981), p. 168.

[70]The World Bank, *World Development Report 1987* (Oxford: Oxford University Press), p. 128.

[71]Dorothy Wilson, *The Welfare State in Sweden* (London: Heinemann, 1979), p. 148. For Sweden its Gini coefficient was 30.2 in 1977, compared with 33.3 and 36.8 for the United Kingdom and West Germany, respectively.

[72]Christopher Hitchens, in "Minority Report," *The Nation*, January 30, 1989, p. 116, discussed this achievement. He argues that "[i]n Sweden a few years ago, it was claimed by social scientists and physicians that for the first time in history you could not tell the social class of a child by examining its health record and rate of growth."

[73]Joint Economic Committee, *Monetary Policy*, p. 169.

The performance of Sweden's economy from 1932 to 1989 was influenced not only by the nature of the working rules but by policymakers' decisions and the national and political environment within which the economy must operate. For example, after the 1973 oil crisis (an international economic factor), Swedish policymakers adopted a demand expansion strategy, including higher wages, to combat the economic slowdown. Such a policy contributed to the subsequent adverse performance of the economy. Economic growth rates declined to about 1.3 percent for the next decade, the rate of inflation doubled (partly due to protectionist trade policies and high taxes), Sweden's foreign debt increased, budget deficits grew, and marginal tax rates rose to about 80 percent on personal income. This performance has been attributed to poor policy decisions as well as the problem of seeking to maintain full employment under a solidaristic wage policy, which keeps wages at a level that inhibits the nation's exporters from being competitive on the world market. In fairness, it should be noted that the policymakers' decision in 1982 to devalue the krona and to cut budget deficits stimulated exports and maintained low unemployment while promoting economic recovery during the mid- to late 1980s.

An evaluation of the Swedish economy's performance from three viewpoints illustrates the subjective, value-laden aspect of such an exercise. According to many Social Democrats, the reformist strategies were successful. They point to positive effects of social insurance and welfare reforms, such as the abolishment of poverty and unemployment, which prior to 1932 had been a fact of Swedish life. Other noted positive results have been the combined effect of active labor market policies, a tax scheme that falls most heavily on employers and upper-income households, the solidaristic collective bargaining agreement, and expanded education for equalizing household incomes and opportunities.

One study (by a Social Democrat) that ranked the provision of welfare by OECD nations according to four criteria (government revenue/GDP; public spending/GDP; infant mortality rates; and GDP per capita) concluded that Sweden ranked first in the OECD.[74] Proponents of Social Democratic policies credit these measures with reducing the risk of losing income through injury or economic forces, with promoting equality of status, and with providing for economically weak and socially handicapped Swedish citizens. Overall, Social Democratic proponents argue that the comprehensive social welfare policies created a society in which there is employment security, education, and health care available to everyone.

From two other perspectives, however, the performance of the economy has either failed to eliminate or has created problems that alternative policies would have avoided. Those of a Marxist persuasion, while recognizing Sweden's social and economic achievements, argue that class conflicts still prevail and that

---

[74]Francis G. Castles, *The Social Democratic Image of Society* (London: Routledge and Kegan Paul, 1978), pp. 61–66.

a disproportionate share of the social and economic rewards fall into the hands of the capitalist class. They call for more rapid and extensive transfer of control to the labor class through worker funds.

Advocates of a market-oriented economy, who rank economic efficiency higher than economic security and equality, are critical of the economic and social trends in Sweden over the 1970–1979 period. They attribute the stagflation of the 1970s and the declining savings and investment rates to the effects of Social Democratic economic policies. In response to the stagflation, government expenditures rose (as a percentage of GDP) from 31 percent in 1960 to 67 percent in 1982, the highest rate among industrialized nations. This growth coincided with rising taxes, as tax revenues increased from about 30 percent of GNP in 1960 to over 60 percent by the mid-1980s.

The impact of rising marginal tax rates included a rise in nonmarket transactions (e.g., barter, where people perform services for one another without reporting any income earned), and reduced incentives to be efficient and productive. (Most Swedes believe that the earnings of efficient workers are not appreciably higher than earnings of less efficient workers.) There was a decline in the official number of hours worked in Sweden after the mid-1970s, partly due to people engaging in tax-free transactions and partly due to an unwillingness to work extra hours because of the high marginal tax rates. Swedish authorities addressed these problems by agreeing to reduce taxes, including the top marginal tax rate, from about 75 percent in 1988 to 60 percent in 1989 to 50 percent by 1990.

Critics point to the increase in the size of the public sector where there was a "transfer [of] about 75 percent of gross income earned on the margin to the public sector—mainly for retransfer back to the private sector."[75] Rising tax rates failed to balance the central government budget, however. The central government's budget deficit increased dramatically in the late 1970s and early 1980s, reaching 13 percent of GDP in 1983 before declining to roughly 5 percent in 1987.[76] Part of the deficit was due to expenditures for the government's labor market policies, which increased from roughly 1 percent to 4 percent of GNP between 1960 and the mid-1980s. Among other adverse effects, the growing deficit has reduced savings and investment in capital.

Growing public expenditures were accompanied by extended intervention in the economy. Market distortions ensued, with an adverse effect on work incentives, entrepreneurship, savings, and investment. State subsidization of weaker industries inhibited mobility of labor and increased the difficulty for employers to lay off employees. Government policies were also blamed for an erosion of workers' attitudes away from strong adherence to a work ethic, egalitarianism, and conformity with the rule for reporting income (so characteristic of the 1950–1970 period) toward a more complacent attitude

[75]Lundberg, "The Rise and Fall of the Swedish Model," p. 28.
[76]Bosworth and Rivlin, *The Swedish Economy,* p. 312.

concerning work combined with a shift toward individualism and a willingness to take jobs in Sweden's informal economy.

The solidaristic wage policy came under criticism in the 1980s for exacerbating youth unemployment, promoting disincentives to work, and having only a modest impact on reducing wage differentials between men and women.[77] When minimum wages are relatively higher, young workers without experience are less attractive to employers. Critics of the wage policy argue that the narrowing of the wage differential between more skilled and less skilled workers has eroded work incentives, especially when combined with Sweden's income redistribution policies. Evidence indicates that the decrease in the male-female wage differential is more attributable to women's gains in productivity (due to their receiving more education).

Additional information about this period was presented in Chapter 10 (Table 10-1 through Table 10-7).

The 1990s

For nearly every economic and social indicator, the Swedish economy's performance has been poor during this period. While this is unfortunate for the Swedes, such a reversal in fortune is consistent with the evolutionary nature of economies, which exhibits ebb and flow regarding performance. Most Swedes did not foresee such a possibility, however, believing that once the trend of favorable performance was established it would continue. Therefore, they did not question the deepening involvement of the state in terms of rising tax rates and incidence of public spending, assuming that favorable economic growth would enable the private sector to be able to pay for increasing social insurance and welfare programs.

Beginning in 1990 economic indicators reflected that a serious recession was being experienced. The average annual rate of GDP growth during 1990 to 1994 was -0.6. percent. Unemployment rose from about 2 percent to over 8 percent (with another 4 percent of the labor force in government-subsidized work programs). Labor productivity, which grew about 4 percent annually from 1950 to 1970, and about 1 percent for the next 20 years, began declining—particularly in the domestic manufacturing sector. Growing Swedish MNCs invested heavily abroad, continuing a trend that started in the 1970s.[78] This had disastrous effects on the domestic economy in terms of output and demand.

Meanwhile, the banking industry was in a crisis and many banks required government subsidies to remain solvent. Public-sector jobs were being cut, user fees for medicine increased, while real disposable income and private consumption declined. The burden wan not felt equally. Since 1961 blue-collar workers have

---

[77]For further discussion, refer to Bosworth and Rivlin, *The Swedish Economy*, pp. 126, 141, 153, 173.

[78]While manufacturing output grew about 180 percent for Swedish-owned MNCs, domestic output during the 1974–1990 period grew only 16 percent for domestic firms. See "Sweden: Worse and Worse," *The Economist*, October 9, 1993, pp. 58–59. Capital flight was so extensive that it reached about 7 percent of GNP in 1989 and 1990.

experienced a slight rise in premature death rates, while those of white collar workers declined 25 percent.[79] Sweden saw its per capita GNP ranking fall from third to fourteenth among OECD nations during this five-year period.

What factors contributed to such a dramatic and rapid reversal of the economy's performance? A combination of many unfavorable factors—some systemic, some due to poor policymaking, and some due to the European recession—contributed to the decline. In 1990 Sweden faced numerous problems that stimulated a debate concerning the future of existing working rules—a portend of what was to come. Inflation and unit labor costs were well above the OECD average, while growth of GDP had fallen much below the rest of Europe. Youth unemployment persisted, while real income of most families had not risen over the past two decades. Absenteeism was estimated at one fourth of the work force on a given day, with sickness and need to look after children cited as the main reasons. Workers protested economic conditions by staging a two-week walkout, and LO members (but not LO leaders) asked for large wage increases. As the evolutionary-institutional model predicts, there was a growing number of advocates for changes in the working rules. In particular, some authorities suggested that marginal tax rates be cut even further to as low as 30 percent in an effort to stimulate greater number of hours worked and higher savings.

Recent evaluations of the economic crisis cite numerous causes. Orthodox economists point to systemic reasons, including the Social Democrats' equality goals, which these economists argued placed too much emphasis on distribution and too little on incentives for production or the contributions individuals should be expected to make. Other factors include the increased politicization and collectivization of decision making, the highest tax and government spending rates in the OECD, and the loss of productive efficiency in both the public and private sectors. This loss was partly due to a declining work ethic fueled by generous benefits offered to "sick" workers, which many claimed distorted their incentive to perform their job. For example, these workers could receive about 60 percent of their pay the first three days out of work, and this percentage rose to about 90 percent thereafter depending upon the number of days out of work. Absenteeism was particularly high among younger workers, exceeding that of older workers by 50 percent.

Policy errors included the abrupt deregulation of financial markets coinciding with tax reform, both of which exacerbated the decline in domestic income. Fiscal policies were not restrictive enough during the high-growth periods of the late 1980s to prevent inflation from rising. Hourly wages were permitted to grow at the same rate they had during the 1960–1980 period despite large decreases in labor productivity. When these policy mistakes are combined with the systemic problems and European recession, understanding the dramatic reversal of Sweden's economic performance is not difficult to comprehend.

[79]Hermele, "The End of the Middle Road," p. 16.

Summary of Performance:
A Long-Run Evaluation

Conservative economists conclude that Swedish economic policies have generated changing values which are not conducive to sustaining the nation's standard of living. These attitudinal changes include worker complacency, loss of family responsibility, and loss of entrepreneurial spirit. Blame is placed on the state for doing so many things *for* the individual, consequently diminishing individual initiative.[80]

To some observers, the Swedish economy is an anomaly, for compared to other industrialized nations Sweden's prosperous economy has the largest public sector (with the ratio of government expenditures to GNP exceeding 66 percent); the most progressive income tax system (the effective marginal tax rate on income above $46,000 exceeds 80 percent); very generous social welfare programs; narrow wage differentials, especially among blue-collar workers; and powerful labor unions to which over 80 percent of all workers belong.

If the Swedish economy's performance is defined in terms of economic growth, inflation, unemployment, and savings and investment rates, then it has performed well on an absolute and relative basis (to the rest of Europe's OECD members and the United States) over the 1932–1989 period. The evidence indicates that these indicators were favorable between 1932 and 1975, somewhat unfavorable for the next decade, and satisfactory for the late 1980s. The rates of both economic growth and inflation have followed this trend.

Swedish economic growth has been exceptional for more than a century. Over its modern economic growth phase, Sweden's per capita growth was higher (2.6 percent) than that of any other industrialized nation during a comparable period.[81] Sweden's economic growth has been slightly below the average European growth rate after 1960. Swedish inflation has generally matched that of Europe since 1960, while unemployment in Sweden had been lower, especially 1983–1989. It should be noted that when the number of Swedes retained and employed by public labor market measures (e.g., vocational training, public relief work, including jobs created in archives, and youth teams) are accounted for, the unemployment differential is 2 to 3 percent narrower.

Credit for the performance can be attributed to Sweden's largest firms, whose research and development and foreign investment efforts have stimulated exports and employment levels. Other factors include the homogeneous nature of the society during the 1930–1980 period, which enhanced the willingness to finance redistributional social welfare measures, political stability with complementarity and cooperation between state, employer, and labor institutions, and the nation's economic policies. Sweden's successful recovery from the oil price shocks of the 1970s, which led to inflation and a widening government

---

[80]Scott, *Sweden: The Nation's History,* pp. 545–546.
[81]Minami, *The Economic Development of Japan: A Quantitative Study,* p. 37.

budget deficit, illustrates the efficacy of the type of policies introduced by the Social Democrats. After the 1982 elections, when the Social Democrats returned to power after six years of nonsocialist rule, policymakers eschewed orthodox, anti-inflationary measures whereby unemployment levels would be permitted to rise for the purpose of reducing inflation. Instead, a more pragmatic, humane approach characteristic of Swedish economic policies since the 1930s was adopted. The krona was devalued, government expenditures reduced (thereby reducing the budget deficit to about 5 percent of GNP), and subsidies to noncompetitive firms were phased out, while labor market policies prevented a sharp rise in unemployment. The results would be deemed favorable by those who accept the Social Democratic philosophical basis.

The current problems invariably will lead to institutional changes and a reversal of the growing trend of state-provided benefits. Most analysts would agree with the conservative coalition that, in the name of egalitarian goals, counterproductive policies were introduced. Therefore, while having succeeded in alleviating poverty and creating a wealthy society, redistribution policies reached their limit and contributed to a dramatic reversal in fortune.

DEVELOPMENT OF SWEDEN'S ECONOMY AS AN ILLUSTRATION OF THE EVOLUTIONARY-INSTITUTIONAL THEORY

The development of the Swedish economy conforms to the evolutionary-institutional theory, for the economy's performance has continually shaped informal rules, some of which were translated into new working rules and institutions. As one Swedish analyst observes, "The Swedish Model was never conceived as a political program for all time. . . . I see it as a product of an ongoing historical process, as continuous social reform in order to produce a more and more all-encompassing welfare society."[82]

Part of the nation's historical legacy included a paternalistic attitude held by the state toward its citizens, and the desire of citizens to influence local institutions through participatory democracy. While maintaining this aspect of historical legacy, the Social Democrats rejected the pre-1932 institutions and performance of the economy, especially the degree of social class division, unemployment, and poverty. The philosophical basis of the party was shaped by old attitudes it retained and old attitudes it opposed. After 1932 this new philosophical basis could be applied to economic reforms due to the change in the political structure resulting from the election of the Social Democrats.

---

[82]Per-Martin Meyerson, "Where Is Sweden Heading?" *Viewpoint Sweden*, 10 (New York: Swedish Information Service, January 1992), p. 4.

Working rules were gradually modified between 1932 and 1970 in favor of extended social insurance and welfare programs as well as the equalization of incomes and opportunities. The favorable performance of the economy (from the viewpoint of most Swedes) led to stability within the political structure and the extension of measures designed to satisfy the Social Democrats' desire to provide security and equalize incomes and opportunities. Centralized wage bargaining worked well when strong national organizations (i.e., LO and SAF) engaged in centralized decision making. Wage increases were consistent with macroeconomic stabilization, and Swedish exporters were competitive on the world market to the extent that exports contributed to high rates of economic growth.

After 1970, however, unfavorable performance indicators led to changes in first the informal, then formal working rules. Partly due to the worldwide recession, Swedish exports suffered and the public sector grew rapidly, while workers experienced declining real wages in the face of inflation and moderate wage demands. These conditions put pressure on the cooperative working agreement between labor and employers. In addition, tension and division has grown between private and public labor unions as public-sector workers seek to receive wages comparable to their private-sector counterparts. Since the early 1980s there has been a trend toward decentralized wage bargaining as more highly skilled workers and employers prefer local wage negotiations.

Early 1990 witnessed the resignation of Social Democratic Premier Ingvar Carlsson after he lost a vote in Parliament over economic policy, although he later returned to the office as a result of the 1994 elections. Poor performance of the economy was the main reason, and many Swedes were changing their attitudes regarding the efficacy of continuing the working rules introduced under Social Democratic leadership between 1932 and 1990. In particular, it was believed that the tax burden was excessive and that further increases in taxes to deal with "resource and quality-related problems of public-sector institutions and transfer payment systems" was not the answer.[83]

As a result of these changes in the informal rules and the very poor performance of the economy in the 1990s, the new coalition government is proposing new working rules that permit decentralized decision making and free-market forces to coordinate more production and distribution decisions for the Swedish economy. These same authorities may be required by Swedes to continue adhering to the principal values contained in the philosophical basis introduced by the Social Democrats, but with some redefinition and clarification of ideals (e.g., equality, integration). There does not appear to be widespread preference for radically new working rules that would eliminate the essence of the Social Democratic vision, for most Swedes recognize that Social Democratic policies throughout the 1932–1990 period "created a society that has achieved more in terms of social equality, economic security and freedom than many other . . .

---

[83]Kjell-Olof Feldt, "What Shall We Do With Capitalism?" *Inside Sweden*, no. 3 (July 1989), p. 4.

[economies]."[84] There is, however, need for institutional reform and fiscal discipline to restore competitiveness to the domestic economy.

LOOKING AHEAD

Sweden is not the only European nation in which social insurance and welfare measures have been introduced. In fact, a strong role for the state is the rule rather than the exception in terms of both the production and distribution of resources in European nations. This point will be illustrated in Chapter 14, which focuses on a supranational economy that has grown to include 15 European nations—The European Union.

KEY TERMS AND CONCEPTS

Collective Wage Bargaining   **Meidner Plan**
Cooperatives   **Solidaristic Wage Policy**
Folkhem   **State Paternalism**
Jamlikhet

QUESTIONS FOR DISCUSSION

1. What were the objectives of the Saltsjobaden agreement?
2. Why is Sweden so concerned with inflation?
3. How important are cooperatives to the Swedish economy?
4. Are Swedish rates of unemployment comparable to those in the United States? (Hint: How is unemployment measured in each country?)
5. What were the ideals of Sweden as contained in the philosophical basis for the economy held by the Social Democrats?
6. What are the new ideals held by the conservative political parties?
7. How did the solidaristic wage policy contribute to making Sweden more competitive in international markets?
8. How can the Swedish state be considered paternalistic when it owns or directly controls a very small proportion of private-sector production facilities?
9. Do the economic problems of the early 1990s and subsequent change in working rules imply that elements of the Swedish democratically controlled social economy are not efficacious for any other economy? Reconcile your answer with the evolutionary-institutional theory.

---

[84]Ibid., p. 5.

REFERENCES

"A Change of Course: A Survey of Sweden's Economy," *The Economist*, March 3–9, 1990.

Arestis, Philip, "Post-Keynesian Economic Policies: The Case of Sweden," *Journal of Economic Issues*, 20, 3 (September 1986).

Bosworth, Barry P., and Alice Rivlin, eds., *The Swedish Economy*. Washington, DC: The Brookings Institution, 1987.

Castles, Francis G., *The Social Democratic Image of Society*. London: Routledge and Kegan Paul, 1978.

Childs, Marquis, *Sweden: The Middle Way*. New Haven, CT: Yale University Press, 1936.

Conradson, Bridgett, Lis Granlund, and Hans Medelius, *And So They Became Welfare Swedes*. Stockholm: Nordiska Museum, 1970.

Elvander, Nils, "The Future of Swedish Wage Negotiating System," *Inside Sweden*, 2 (October 1985) 12–13.

———, "Interest Groups in Sweden," *Annals of the American Academy of Political Science*, 413 (1974), 27–43.

Erikson, Robert, and Rune Aberg, eds., *Welfare in Transition*. Oxford: Clarendon Press, 1987.

Feldt, Kjell-Olof, "What Shall We Do With Capitalism?" *Inside Sweden*, 3 (July 1989), 3–5.

Fleisher, Wilfred, *Sweden: The Welfare State*. Westport, CT: Greenwood Press, 1973.

Forseback, Lennart, *Industrial Relations and Employment in Sweden*. Uppsala: Swedish Institute, 1980.

Govrevitch, P., A. Martin, G. Ross, C. Allen, S. Bornstein, and A. Markovits, *Unions and Economic Crisis: Britain, West Germany, and Sweden*. London: George Allen and Unwin, 1984.

Growth or Stagnation? The Swedish Economy 1981–1985. Stockholm: Ministry of Economic Affairs, 1982.

Gustafsson, Agne, "Decentralisation in Sweden," *Current Sweden*. Stockholm: Swedish Institute, 316 (April 1984), 5.

Heckscher, Gunnar, *The Welfare State and Beyond*. Minneapolis: University of Minnesota Press, 1984.

Hermele, Kenneth, "The End of the Middle Road: What Happened to the Swedish Model?" *Monthly Review*, 44, 10 (March 1993), 14–24.

Hitchens, Christopher, "Minority Report," *The Nation*, January 30, 1989, p. 116.

Hodgson, Geoffrey M., *Economics and Institutions*. Cambridge: Polity Press, 1988.

Isaksson, Mats och Rolf Skog, "Ownership, Influence and Efficiency," *Skandinaviska Enskilda Banken Quarterly Review*, 1, (1989), 4–9.

Jersild, P.C., "The Good Old Social Pyramid, 1988 Style," *Inside Sweden*, 2 (May–June 1988), 16.

Joint Economic Committee, *Monetary Policy, Selective Credit Policy, and Industrial Policy in France, Britain, West Germany, and Sweden*. Washington, DC: US. Government Printing Office, 1981.

Jonung, Lars, "The System of Price Controls as a Bargaining Process," *Skandinaviska*

Enskilda Banken Quarterly Review, 3 (1984), 68–73.

Koblik, Steven, ed., *Sweden's Development from Poverty to Affluence: 1750–1970*. Minneapolis: University of Minnesota Press, 1975.

Lindbeck, Assar, "Income Distributions in Sweden," *Skandinaviska Enskilda Banken Quarterly Review*, 1 (January 1983).

————, *Swedish Economic Policy*. Berkeley: University of California Press, 1974.

————, Per Molander, Torsten Persson, Olof Peterson, Agnar Sandmo, Birgitta Swedenborg and Niels Thygesen, "Options for Economic and Political Reform in Sweden," *Economic Policy*, 17 (October 1993), 219–264.

Lundberg, Erik, "The Rise and Fall of the Swedish Model," *Journal of Economic Literature*, 23 (March 1985).

McBride, Stephen, "The Comparative Politics of Unemployment," *Comparative Politics* (April, 1988), pp. 303–323.

Meyerson, Per-Martin, "Where Is Sweden Heading?" *Viewpoint Sweden*, 10. New York: Swedish Information Service, (January 1992).

Milner, Henry, *Sweden: Social Democracy in Practice*. Oxford: Oxford University Press, 1989.

Minami, Ryoshin, *The Economic Development of Japan*. London: Macmillan Press, 1986.

Mitchell, B. R., *European Historical Statistics: 1750–1970*. New York: Columbia University Press, 1975.

Myerson, P. M., *The Swedish Economy at the Crossroads*. Stockholm: Federation of Swedish Industries, 1980.

————, *The Welfare State in Crisis—the Case of Sweden*. Stockholm: Federation of Swedish Industries, 1982.

Myrdal, Alva, *Nation and Family: The Swedish Experiment in Democratic Family and Population Policy*. Cambridge: The MIT Press, 1968.

Myrdal, Hans-Goran, "The Swedish Model—Will it Survive?" *British Journal of Industrial Relations*, 18, 1 (March 1980).

Myrdal, Gunnar, *Value in Social Theory*. London: Routledge and Kegan Paul, 1978.

OECD Economic Surveys: Sweden 1988/89. Paris: OECD, 1989.

OECD in Figures, Supplement to the OECD Observer No. 158. Paris: OECD, June/July 1989.

OECD. Main Economic Indicators. Paris: OECD, February 1994.

Ramaswamy, Rama, "Wage Bargaining Institutions, Adaptability, and Structural Change: The Swedish Experience," *Journal of Economic Issues*, 26, 4 (December 1992), 1041–1062.

Rosenthal, Albert H., *The Social Programs of Sweden*. Minneapolis: The University of Minnesota Press, 1967.

Scase, Richard, *Social Democracy in Capitalist Society*. London: Croom Helm, 1977.

Scott, Franklin D. *Sweden: The Nation's History*. Minneapolis: University of Minnesota Press, 1977.

Statistical Abstract of Sweden: 1990. Stockholm, Statistiska Centralbyran, 1990.

Statistical Abstract of Sweden: 1989. Stockholm, Statistiska Centralbyran, 1989.

Stuart, Charles E., "Swedish Tax Rates, Labor Supply, and Tax Revenues,"

Journal of Political Economy, 89 (October 1981).

"Sweden's Economy: The Nonconformist State," *Economist,* March 7, 1987.

"Sweden: Worse and Worse," *The Economist.,* October 9, 1993, pp. 58–59.

"Swedish Industry," *Fact Sheets on Sweden.* Stockholm: The Swedish Institute, June 1989.

"Taxes in Sweden," *Fact Sheets on Sweden.* Stockholm: The Swedish Institute, June 1989.

"The Cooperative Movement in Sweden," *Fact Sheets on Sweden.* Stockholm: The Swedish Institute, May 1988.

The Swedish Economy. Stockholm: National Institute of Economic Research, 1986.

The Swedish Economy, 1983. Stockholm: Swedish Institute, June 1983.

"The Swedish Political Parties," *Fact Sheets on Sweden.* Stockholm: The Swedish Institute, February 1989.

Tilton, Timothy, "A Swedish Road to Socialism: Ernst Wigforss and the Ideological Foundations of Swedish Social Democracy," *The American Political Science Review,* 73 (June 1979).

Vogel, Joachim, "Are Class Differences Increasing or Decreasing?" *Inside Sweden.* (1990), p. 10.

Walters, Peter, "Distributing Decline: Sweden's Social Democrats and the Crisis of the Welfare State," *Government and Opposition,* 20 (Summer 1985).

"Whither the Wallenbergs?" *The Economist,* December 25, 1993–January 7, 1994, pp. 89–90.

Wilson, Dorothy, *The Welfare State in Sweden.* London: Heinemann, 1979.

The World Bank. *World Development Report 1987.* Oxford: Oxford University Press, 1988.

14

THE EUROPEAN UNION

Fifteen Economies or One,
or Will It Be Both?

OBJECTIVES

1. Use the evolutionary-institutional framework to explain how the European Union (EU) can be considered as one economy.
2. Explain the enlargement process, evaluating the positive and negative features of enlargement from the point of view of member nations.
3. Identify the factors that stimulated certain European nations to integrate economically and politically.
4. Explain how resource allocation decision making is carried out through supranational institutions.
5. Discuss particular EU policies for controlling resources, including the Common Agricultural Policy, Competition Policy, Transport Policy, and Social Policy.

To attempt a description of the European Community [now European Union] is rather like trying to explain a psychic experience. It exists on so many different planes: the one on which it presents itself; the way in which politicians try to mold it; the actual; and the potential. The overlap between them is often small, and the first two vie with each other in unreality.

CHRISTOPHER TUGENDHAT,
former member of the European Commission

INTRODUCTION

A better understanding of the European Union (EU)[1] can be gained if the EU as an economy is adequately described.[2] Such an understanding will provide a more comprehensive perspective than is provided by orthodox economists regarding both the present nature of the EU and what the EU is likely to evolve toward in the future. Will the EU be 15 separate economies, one fully integrated economy, or a new interrelationship, as yet to be defined among member nations?

Two descriptions of the EU often appear in orthodox economic literature. The first describes the EU as one economy, comprised of the combination of member nations' economic performances. Performance typically includes growth of gross national product, rates of unemployment and inflation, investment levels, trade flows, and other standard indicators of macroeconomic activity, as periodically reported by the Organization for Economic Cooperation and Development (OECD) or the EU, among others. The second description of the EU pertains to the level of economic integration.[3] From this point of view the EU is considered to be 15 economies seeking to achieve the economic and monetary union level of integration. This chapter will use the evolutionary-institutional framework to demonstrate that the EU is both individual member-nation economies and an evolving supranational economy guided by multinational political institutions that develop working rules for economic behavior.[4]

The EU is comprised of three separate organizations: the European Coal and Steel Community (ECSC), the European Atomic Energy Community (Euratom), and the European Economic Community (EEC). In reality the three organizations are one entity. A unique innovative aspect of the EU relative to other international bodies is that its members have relinquished to supranational authorities some of their national sovereignty in the interests of forming an

---

[1]As members have integrated further economically and politically (while enlarging their number), the group has changed its description of itself from European Coal and Steel Community to European Economic Community, to European Community, to European Union. Throughout most of this chapter European Union (EU) will be used to describe the member nations. It should be kept in mind that this level of integration has evolved in the 1990s, and that in prior decades the other descriptions were operative.

[2]During 1994 the European Union was comprised of 12 member nations, including Belgium, Denmark, France, Greece, Ireland, Italy, Luxembourg, the Netherlands, Portugal, Spain, United Kingdom, and West Germany. In addition, Austria, Finland, Norway, and Sweden had been accepted for membership beginning January 1, 1995 (subject to voters in each of those countries accepting the terms of membership). Meanwhile, Cyprus, the Czech Republic, Hungary, Malta, Poland, Slovakia, Switzerland, and Turkey have formally applied for membership and are waiting for the EU to accept their applications.

[3]For further discussion of economic integration, see Appendix A at the end of this chapter.

[4]The political concept of supranationalism has been defined as " . . . a situation in which international administrative institutions exercise power over, for example, the economies of the nation states." Power of the authority can be exercised in response to a majority vote rather than to a unanimous agreement. Dennis Swann, *The Economics of the Common Market*, 4th ed. (Middlesex, England: Penguin Books, 1978), p. 17.

economic and political entity that is both cohesive and indissoluble.[5] The EU is governed by supranational democratic institutions which handle administrative, legislative, budget, and judicial matters. During the process of economic and political integration, the EU has adopted rules for economic behavior, including common policies regarding trade with nonmember nations and other regional concerns such as transportation and agriculture.

The cornerstone of the EU is the Treaty of Rome, signed by the original six member nations (Belgium, France, Italy, Luxembourg, the Netherlands, and West Germany) on March 25, 1957.[6] This treaty established the goals and formal working rules which provided the basic tenets for European economic integration. The broad philosophical agreement was to seek economic and political integration in Europe through mutual consent of the member nations. Informal rules of member nations, such as a willingness to lessen social-class differentials through redistributional programs, and a commitment to democratic ideals and free trade within the union, guided the EU's founders in writing the Treaty of Rome.

HISTORICAL LEGACY: INTEGRATION AS A MEANS FOR MAINTAINING PEACE

The concept of a united Europe was first formally proposed in 1834 by an organization known as Young Europe. After World War I, another unification movement began, calling for the establishment of a Pan-European Union. Although neither movement led directly to the establishment of the EU, they provided "important precedents" (e.g., Europe-wide organizations that dealt with issues such as communications and trade), which facilitated the spread of informal rules concerning the efficacy of European unity.[7]

After World War II, Europe was declining as a center of political and economic power, particularly in relation to the United States and the Soviet Union. Prominent European leaders sought to change the attitudes and formal rules in order to create international instruments of cooperation among all European nations—particularly between France and what had become West Germany. In 1946 Winston Churchill called for the establishment of a United States of Europe. Within the next decade, formal means for unification, including the OECD, the

---

[5]In one expert's opinion, the EU is "a *sui generis* association of sovereign states. . . . The relationship between the nation-state and the Community has been by and large a relationship of symbiosis rather than a zero-sum game. But the kind of cooperation which has been established between member countries on a voluntary basis has no parallel elsewhere in the world." See Loukas Tsoukalis, "Looking into the Crystal," *Journal of Common Market Studies*, 21, 1 & 2 (September/December 1982), 229.

[6]The Treaty of Rome refers to the European Economic Community (EEC) Treaty and the European Atomic Energy Community (Euratom) Treaty. In 1951 the European Coal and Steel Community (ECSC) Treaty had been signed. In this chapter the term *Treaties* will be used to refer to all three treaties.

[7]W. Hartley, *The Politics of the Common Market* (Englewood Cliffs, NJ: Prentice-Hall, 1967), p. 4.

Western European Union, the North Atlantic Treaty Organization (NATO), the Council of Europe, and the European Community emerged.

The European Coal and Steel Community

Formal rules upon which a European community would be based were first proposed in 1950 by Robert Schumann, the French Minister of Foreign Affairs. The Schumann Plan was intended to initiate political and economic unification between France and West Germany, thereby enhancing the prospects for European (and world) peace.[8] The plan called for the establishment of a European Coal and Steel Community (ECSC). Nations choosing to join had to be willing to relinquish some national sovereignty to a new supranational institution, the High Authority, which would supervise their entire coal and steel production.

The establishment of the High Authority was a significant step toward European unification. Member nations had taken the unique step of delegating authority to a supranational institution whose representatives were selected by the members, but who had the authority to make independent and collective decisions that were in the member states' common interest. It was believed that the ECSC would establish both a common base for economic development and a first step toward a federation of European nations, thereby lessening tension through peaceful cooperation. Three other institutions were founded for establishing and interpreting the rules of the ECSC: the Council of Ministers, Court of Justice, and Parliamentary Assembly.

The limited objective of the ECSC was to ensure maximum efficient output and a rational distribution of coal and steel within member countries. The High Authority was given the power to regulate prices, secure needed raw materials, improve living and working conditions for coal and steel workers, and promote trade and investment. The formal rules of the ECSC were designed to promote free trade through the elimination of those trade restrictions (e.g., tariffs, quotas, national subsidies, and discriminatory policies pertaining to transportation or prices) that worked against the achievement of economies of scale or lower consumer prices. Specific measures were proposed to achieve lower transportation costs, sufficient supplies of raw materials, modernization and expansion of production facilities, higher living standards for coal and steel workers, as well as to promote mergers.

The Treaty of Rome

The favorable economic performance of the ECSC stimulated further negotiations concerning cooperative trade and production schemes among European nations.

---

[8]This plan was formulated by a staff headed by Jean Monnet. Monnet believed that European relations could be improved (e.g., less antagonism and the hastening of reconciliation between France and Germany) through organizations such as the ECSC. Monnet argued that "it is institutions which control the relations between men, it is they which are the true support of civilization." Michael Curtis, *Western European Integration* (New York: Harper & Row, 1965), p. 16.

Most Western European nations participated. The negotiations culminated in 1957 with the emergence of two mutually exclusive groups. One was the European Free Trade Association. The other group consisted of the original six members of the ECSC—Belgium, France, Italy, Luxembourg, the Netherlands, and West Germany. These six nations integrated further by signing the Treaty of Rome.

The aim of the founders of the EEC was to promote economic integration "by means of four progressive harmonization processes."[9] These processes were: first, the elimination of internal barriers to trade through removing customs barriers; second, the achievement of a customs union through applying a common external tariff toward nonmember nations; third, the establishment of a common market by permitting the free flow of factors of production plus goods and services; fourth, the attainment of further integration by adopting common policies (e.g., agriculture, competition, social, transport), which would contribute to the establishment of a single market.

The basis for trade among members was established by the ECSC Treaty (1951) and the Treaty of Rome (1957). In each case working rules pertaining to a customs union were formulated, with policies designed to facilitate the achievement of a common market level of integration. The Treaty of Rome aimed to achieve the common market level of integration by 1970, specifying that common working rules and policies should be implemented which would apply to all aspects of economic and social life in member nations.

Two series of events which have affected the present nature of the EU economy occurred after 1957. First, the incremental enlargement to include 15 nations has increased the potential for trade creation considerably. The second series of events started in the late 1960s when global monetary stability had ended, Japan had emerged as an economic power, and EU leaders recognized they were experiencing a "loss of sovereignty in macroeconomic and monetary policies."[10] At the Hague Summit in 1969 formal steps were taken towards becoming an economic and monetary union. Although the original target date of 1980 was overly ambitious, the fact that attitudes among the members were receptive to such a union indicates the degree to which economic integration had progressed throughout member nations.

There were no provisions in the Treaty of Rome concerning integration of monetary and fiscal policies throughout the Community. During the 1960s the formation of the European Economic Community prompted members to pursue the prospect of cooperating in monetary and fiscal matters, leading to the consideration of an integrated monetary system. When the heads of state committed themselves to working toward an economic and monetary union, it became necessary to consider innovations such as a common currency and means to stabilize exchange rates between members. During the 1970s the oil crises and

---

[9]G. N. Munshell, *The New Europe* (London: Hodder and Stoughton, 1985), p. 11.
[10]Peter Ludlow, "Beyond 1992," *European Affairs*, 2, no. 3 (Autumn 1988), 14–30.

the collapse of the Bretton Woods international monetary mechanism contributed to high rates of inflation and volatile exchange rates throughout Europe. In response, member nations decided to work collectively toward more stable monetary conditions, resulting in the 1979 establishment of a scheme—the European Monetary System (EMS) designed to reduce currency fluctuations through its exchange-rate mechanism.[11]

In 1981 the Commission sought to initiate a new movement towards achieving the economic and monetary union, while in 1984 the European Parliament drafted a constitution calling for the establishment of this higher level of integration. These actions culminated in 1986 with the signing of the Single European Act. The purpose of this act was to amend the Treaties so as to extend the scope of member cooperation while improving the decision-making mechanisms which foster integrated efforts. The central economic feature of the act was the commitment to establish working rules creating a single European market by 1992.

At the Hague Summit in June 1988 the heads of state (with the exception of British Prime Minister Margaret Thatcher) enthusiastically agreed to set up a committee to analyze and propose measures for establishing an economic and monetary union, which would necessitate the establishment of a central bank and a common currency. In August 1990, the commission made its final proposal for Economic and Monetary Union (EMU) with the primary purpose of creating a basis for tighter coordination of economic and monetary policies throughout the EU. It drafted treaties establishing the provisions for both an EMU and Political Union. The EMU treaty designated that there should be a common currency, a central bank (EuroFed), single monetary policy, close coordination of fiscal and monetary policies, prohibition of monetizing public deficits, and avoidance of large fiscal deficits for all members. This proposal was approved by member-nation representatives at Maastricht, the Netherlands, in December 1991, with January 1, 1999 set as the desired completion of the EMU and Political Union. However, difficulties with the exchange-rate mechanism (the EMS all but collapsed in 1993) and enlargement issues (pp. 364–368) have delayed progress toward this goal.

[11]The formation of the EMS must be distinguished from the goal of establishing an economic and monetary union or a common currency. The EMS has more limited specific objectives, namely to foster monetary stability in Europe by close monetary cooperation, serving as a means for mitigating excessive fluctuations in exchange rates. In doing so the EMS can reduce uncertainty in intra-EC investments, trade, and payments.

A PHILOSOPHY FOR
INTEGRATING ECONOMIES

The formal and informal attitudes which provide the basis for the working rules of the EU are a combination of broad ideals and practical considerations concerning the benefits of economic and political integration. In general, there has been a philosophical struggle between social democratic adherents and single-market proponents. EU economic policy has reflected the desire to integrate according to "market principles," tempered by most members' preference for democratic control over an economy which features state-sponsored redistributional programs, including extensive social welfare and insurance schemes.[12] There are relatively few authorities within the member nations who favor adopting economic policies for their individual countries which place strict adherence upon laissez-faire economic policies, especially as these policies would influence the distribution of income. Nor are there many authorities in EU member states who believe in the need for more government control over an economy through central planning and nationalization of industry and services.[13] There are, however, differences of opinion concerning the path of future integration. The debate centers about the relative efficacy of a unified internal market and single currency guided by EU institutions with an emphasis upon economic management through harmonization policies versus a single market and individual currencies where market forces are the primary social process for economic coordination.

During the 1950s and 1960s, the spirit of John Stuart Mill, the Fabian Society, the Scandinavian Social Democratic parties, and the French planners, especially Jean Monnet, influenced most economic policymakers in member nations. There was a common desire to end Europe's political and economic rivalries by establishing attitudes promoting mutual interest, and from there it followed that some economic and political objectives could best be attained by member nations working together—establishing supranational institutions to which national governments would transfer some of their power.

Debate within the EU reflected the economic philosophy of national economies—a bias towards economic management, state intervention, and increased government expenditures. The Common Agricultural Policy (see pp. 351–354) was a logical outcome of such a view. The approach to European unification originally proposed by Schuman and Monnet was "functionalist."[14]

[12]Jeffrey Harrop, *The Political Economy of Integration in the European Community* (Hants, England: Edward Elgar, 1989), p. 4.

[13]For a description of the difference between *laissez-faire, social market,* and *neosocialism* economic philosophies in EC nations, see John Pinder, "The Political Economy of Integration in Europe," *Journal of Common Market Studies*, 25, 1 (September 1986), 1–14.

[14]Victoria Curzon Price, "Three Models of European Integration," *Whose Europe?* (London: The Institute of Economic Affairs, 1989), pp. 26–29.

The basic principle was that economic management from the center (i.e., EU supranational institutions) was efficacious, and that sovereignty of nation states would slowly wither away as successful cooperative efforts, taken in "small functional steps," would convince members of the benefits of integration.[15] The problem with this formula was its emphasis upon harmonization of economic, social, and political institutions, for it was argued that further harmonization was a prerequisite for free and fair trade. The decision-making process (see "Political Structure," pp. 339–342), especially the unanimity principle, which required that all members must agree on any proposal before it became a working rule, mitigated against changes in working rules that would create substantive harmonization measures. The result was little integration, while numerous barriers remained which inhibited the free flow of trade throughout member nations.

The macroeconomic problems of the 1970s, coupled with rising dissatisfaction with the performance of those member economies with extensive social insurance and welfare schemes (e.g., United Kingdom), led to a "fundamental shift" in attitudes toward guidance of economies throughout Europe.[16] Emphasis began to be placed upon market forces and deregulation in lieu of expensive government interventionist policies. Thus, the view that the state's economic power had to be checked through more liberal trade policies won out over the view that national governments should protect their sovereignty and narrow economic interests.

The market-oriented view, championed by Thatcher, proposed a "principle of competing jurisdictions" as a basis for determining the nature of the single European market and the degree of power and accountability of EU institutions.[17] Greater resource mobility and competition between member states, lower tariffs, and a "customs union between sovereign states"[18] were proposed as the best means for the EU economy to achieve both efficiency and fairness. Thatcher in particular was outspoken against economic planning and controls, favoring working rules that foster free enterprise competitive conditions and that reward personal endeavor and initiative. This view offered a model of integration which replaced the concept of harmonization by emphasizing "mutual recognition and equivalence."[19] Under this model the systems of government as well as the distinctive social and economic institutions in each member state would be maintained. EU members would pursue common ends through different means chosen by themselves. They would also be willing to relinquish some authority to EU institutions as long as member differences are mutually

[15]"The essence of the strategy, according to Monnet, was to stick to technical, functional matters as much as possible, for technicians from different countries [but not politicians] would generally be able to agree on a technical solution to a problem." Ibid., p. 27.

[16]Ludlow, "Beyond 1992," *European Affairs*, p. 20.

[17]Cento Veljanovski, "Foreword," *Whose Europe*, pp. ix, x.

[18]Ben Roberts, "The Social Dimension of European Labour Markets," *Whose Europe*, p. 40.

[19]Price, "Three Models of European Integration," *Whose Europe*, p. 29.

recognized and respected and as long as it is agreed that EU institutions can better perform a particular function than some lower-level (e.g., national) entity.

The opposing philosophy is a modification of the prevalent view from the 1950s and 1960s. There is no emphasis upon socialism and other social engineering methods of the 1960s. There is, however, the belief that uniform institutional arrangements (e.g., one currency, one central bank, and common policies) controlled at the EU level are necessary for the successful completion of the single market. Integration should be pursued by focusing on industrial relations, better working conditions, and centralization (i.e., EU economic policies). Included among the policies recommended is increased EU spending on technological development to assist selected "national champion" industries. Jacques Delors, former president of the commission, not only supported the achievement of the single market, but called for the establishment of an EMU before the end of this century. He saw the EU political structure evolving in the federal direction with EU institutions assuming control over about 80 percent of member states' economic, fiscal, and social matters. Delors's philosophy was that the EU is "an instrument not merely to promote economic ends, but like Jean Monnet [Delors believes greater integration is] . . . a stepping stone to the creation of a democratic socialist European super state that will be able to maintain the cultural identity of European civilization against the capitalist threat of the USA and Japan and the Communist threat of the USSR."[20]

Political events, particularly throughout Europe since 1989, have rendered much of this view obsolete—and may reduce the likelihood of significant further integration. The philosophical basis underlying the Maastrict Treaty was toward federalism/central control—that member nations, in sharing sovereignty, were more likely to achieve certain goals through the EMU and Political Union than by members relying upon their own macroeconomic and political programs. Views in favor of "subsidiarity" as a guiding EU principle became the informal rules. Broadly, subsidiarity contained the belief that the EU should undertake only activities it could perform better than member states acting individually.[21] More specifically, subsidiarity embodies views (depending upon the political ideology in question) concerning the constitutional relationship between state and society.[22] There is evidence of a growing fear throughout member nations of bureaucrats within supranational institutions seeking to arrogate to the center functions which individual member states may better (many citizens believe) undertake themselves. Polls taken in 1994 indicate that less than one third of EU citizens favor a more federal Europe, and that subsidiarity as an informal rule needs to be replaced. The Maastrict philosophy in favor of more federalism is meeting

---

[20]Roberts, "The Social Dimension," *Whose Europe*, p. 40.

[21]Critics argue that if subsidiarity were to become an operative principle, costly and ineffective programs such as the Common Agricultural Policy would have to be eliminated.

[22]For a detailed discussion, see Kees Van Kersbergen and Bertjan Verbeek, "The Politics of Subsidiarity in the European Union," *Journal of Common Market Studies*, 32, no. 2 (June 1994), 215–236.

resistance from those who note the EU member nations' relatively poor economic performance compared to the United States and many Asian nations (see "EU Economic Performance," pp. 368–376). These citizens believe EU bureaucrats are seeking to transfer power to themselves and that more central control by EU institutions cannot promote more favorable economic performance than individual economies. Thus, the EU is faced with the problem of questioning its purpose in the twenty-first century in the face of emerging economic power in Asia, its own economic problems, and the realignment of Europe and the former Soviet Union.

Lingering attitudes favoring economic management and welfare schemes help to explain the dilemma many member governments encounter when deciding whether or not to accept an EU proposal for establishing rules providing for freer trade in the interest of further integration, for such policies expose all firms (especially those currently protected) to greater competition. Member nations must resolve the conflict between offering protection from self-regulating market forces and agreeing to accept the rules required for further economic integration, a conflict not unlike the double movement described by Karl Polanyi.[23] In terms of being guaranteed the same type of protection from competitive forces beyond their control, some EU citizens fear the effects from further integration, which would include a competitive internal market, one central bank, and one currency for all members. In this respect many authorities in member nations would prefer that the EU be 15 economies, each responsible for its own fiscal and monetary policy.

The practical considerations in favor of further integration can be traced to the recognized political and economic benefits. Politically, integration offers greater protection from larger world powers which may not be of Western European origin. In addition, tension between member states is lessened through greater economic cooperation, something Polanyi argued concerning the 1815–1914 hundred years of peace when the gold standard unified the international economy. Economically, the benefits of integration include greater bargaining power in world trade negotiations, trade creation following the removal of trade barriers, gains from specialization given wider markets, economies of scale, and an expansion of interindustry linkages.

Another economic consideration influencing the evolution toward one economy is the recognition that while an expansion of world trade requires more open economies, such economies face limits when domestic macroeconomic policies are introduced (see appendix to this chapter). The impact of international forces may swamp domestic policies, creating a bifurcation of economic policymaking and implementation. This results in the impetus to shift some policies to the international level where supranational institutions are authorities. The completion of the internal market, which embodies movement away from protectionism and national isolation, represents such a shift of policy, as does the

---

[23]See Karl Polanyi, *The Great Transformation* (Boston: Beacon Press, 1957).

agreement between the United States and Canada to form a free trade area. In this regard there is impetus in favor of one economy, not 15, as members accept that macroeconomic policymaking needs to be shifted to the supranational (EU) level.

PROMOTING SOCIAL AND POLITICAL HARMONY

Social Structure

Social and regional considerations play an important role in the EU. There are more than 15 separate social structures due to social, economic, and cultural heterogeneity between regions within member nations. Among EU nations, especially northern and southern members, there exist differentials such as language, culture, degree of social class hierarchy, the extent of poverty, the role of women, the status and rights of workers, as well as different senses of nationality and identity. These differences are widening as more immigrants from Central and Eastern Europe settle in EU nations. However, there is some uniformity throughout the EU, partly due to the presence of a large middle class, the extent of trade union and professional organization influence, the importance attached to social and regional considerations, and the virtual absence of poverty in most member nations. Overall, EU countries feature "highly pluralistic societies in which well-organized trade unions and other professional organizations play a major role."[24]

Political Structure

As a political entity the EU is "a union of states"[25] with a political structure that extends from regional authorities to the supranational level. EU law that falls within the sphere of the Court of Justice supersedes any national law which conflicts with an EU law. Therefore, EU principal institutions (discussed shortly) not only are vested with the power to pursue objectives considered to be in the interest of the entire community but can pass legislation that will become binding upon all members. These institutions are adopting and implementing working rules that have shifted major economic policy decision making from 15 individual nations to one decision-making structure representative of all member nations.

The EU political structure is based upon a tripartite division of powers whereby no individual or group is *the* authority in more than one division of government. The EU has three distinct branches of government: an executive branch which drafts proposals (the commission); a judicial branch over which the

---

[24]Loukas Tsoukalis, "Looking into the Crystal Ball," *Journal of Common Market Studies*, 21, 1 & 2 (September/December 1982), 231.

[25]Christopher Brewin, "The European Community: A Union of States Without Unity of Government," *Journal of Common Market Studies*, 26, 1 (September 1987), 12.

Court of Justice is the authority; and a legislative branch which consists of an institution for enacting proposals (the council), and institutions which provide consultation on legislative matters (the Parliament, the Permanent Representative Committee, and the Economic and Social Committee). The basic interrelationships among these institutions are shown in Figure 14-1.

The nature of decision making is of paramount importance in the EU, for member states still prefer a degree of national sovereignty and are averse to the imposition of rules not in their particular interest by a supranational authority. At the EU level member states continually debate and bargain for concessions when common policy rules are being established. EU decision making has been most effective when the objectives have been "limited, explicit, and mutually compatible, involving only those countries whose interests are 'directly at stake.' "[26] When all members' interests are affected, and agreement among all 15 is required, the pace of decision making inevitably slows down while the thrust of original proposals may be diluted until everyone has been appeased. Attempts to reform the Common Agricultural Policy illustrate this process.

Figure 14-1   The European Community's Decision-Making Process

Decisions		
	COUNCIL	
	Permanent Representatives Committee	ENACTMENT
	Working Parties	
ECONOMIC AND SOCIAL COMMITTEE	PARLIAMENT	
		CONSULTATION
Specialized Sections	Committees	
	COMMISSION	DRAFTING OF PROPOSAL

Source: Emile Noel, *Working Together: The Institutions of the European Community* (Luxembourg: Office for Publications of the European Communities, 1985), p. 6.

[26]Christopher Tugendhat, *Making Sense of Europe* (New York: Columbia University Press, 1988), pp. 53, 54.

One informal rule (in the spirit of Monnet) that influences the policymaking process in Brussels is that authorities should go slowly, not pushing or offending anyone. Such a process is consistent with the overall objective of the EU to achieve unity through mutual consent. The decision-making process will most likely proceed slowly, and numerous compromises are inevitable. Economic policymaking is a positive-sum game requiring multiple trade-offs between members.[27] This becomes more prevalent as EU membership grows, creating a more politically and socially diverse community. One anomaly of EU integration is that while enlargement provides distinct economic advantages, political problems are multiplied. Federalist proponents of greater integration believe patience and compromise are necessary in order to realize their goal of a highly unified and integrated community in which a body of European law is recognized and freely accepted by all EU citizens.

In recent years cracks in the system have appeared. The original political structure was based upon having "consensus about political representation, political process and the definition of public goods, some of which might be better provided . . . by EC [EU]-level policies."[28] But the political structure has been one in which there is no independence or direct political authority at the EU level. There is, however, considerably easier access to the EU decision makers by

---

[27]Unanimity is required for new initiatives or objectives (e.g., completion of the internal market), for any council act constituting an amendment to a commission proposal, to override a vote by the European Parliament rejecting a council decision taken by majority vote, and for a proposal from the commission for approximation of laws not concerned with the establishment of the internal market. The unanimity rule is based upon the principle that majority voting should not be the means to require member nations to pursue goals against their will. However, Article 100A of the Single European Act specifies that qualified majority votes by the council should be taken when considering the adoption of measures, regulations or administrative actions in member states which have as their objective the establishment and functioning of the internal market. Only after a unanimous agreement committing every member in principle to pursue a specific objective does qualified majority voting (for means to achieve the objective) become efficacious. Majority voting then serves as "an administrative and management tool within an agreed political framework to which the member states have explicitly committed themselves." Tugendhut, *Making Sense of Europe*, p. 165. If majority voting replaced unanimity as the means for establishing broad objectives, then council ministers and heads of state might be placed in the position of supporting an EU-wide objective after having voted (with the minority) against the objective. When there were 12 members this meant that such a qualified majority was 54 votes out of a possible 76, with at least six member nations voting in favor of a measure. The weighting of votes by the council is according to a nation's relative size (e.g., population, economy) as follows: West Germany, France, Italy, and the United Kingdom—10 votes each; Spain—8 votes; Belgium, Greece, Portugal, and the Netherlands—5 votes each; Denmark and Ireland—3 votes each; and Luxembourg—2 votes. After 1996 Austria and Sweden will each have 4 votes, while Finland and Norway each receive 3. The number of votes needed for a qualified majority rises to 64 (and the number of votes needed to defeat a proposal—the "blocking minority"—becomes 27). The intent of this procedure is to protect smaller members from being dominated by a bloc vote of the larger nations. With enlargement to 16 members, the total number of votes in the council increases to 90. The largest five nations, with about two thirds of the EU population, have only 48 votes. A qualified majority now, as before, will require votes from nations with roughly 70 percent of the EU population. Therefore, the political power of the smaller members has increased after enlargement.

[28]Helen Wallace, "European Governance in Turbulent Times," *Journal of Common Market Studies*, 31, no. 3 (September 1993), 299.

special-interest groups who have made their presence felt. The general public has slowly realized that the technocrat-elite symbiosis has contributed to an erosion of national rights and may not result in working rules in the general public's best interest. The mood among EU citizens is waning enthusiasm for greater concentration of political power within EU institutions, and for the EU in general (as indicated by the lowest voter turnout ever in the 1994 European Parliament elections, as just over 56 percent of eligible EU voters chose to participate in the election).

SUPRANATIONAL INSTITUTIONS

The degree of integration which evolved from the early 1950s to the present has required a structure of institutions that transcends those national institutions serving international cooperative and consultative purposes. The establishment and enforcement of the EU's working rules are carried out through four principal institutions: the European Commission; the Council of Ministers; the European Parliament; and the Court of Justice.

The European Commission

The European Commission is the EU's "intellectual leader, . . . problem solver and trouble shooter."[29] It ensures that the provisions of the Treaties are upheld, initiates and formulates policy proposals, and serves as the executive branch in charge of administering the legislation (i.e., ensuring that member states enforce EU laws) adopted by the Council of Ministers or contained in the Treaties. After the 1996 enlargement it will be comprised of 21 commissioners, two from each of the large members (France, Italy, Spain, United Kingdom, and West Germany), and one from each of the other 11 members. Commission members are appointed for a four-year term by unanimous agreement of all member nations. Once appointed they are expected to act in the EU's common interest, upholding EU objectives in the welter of member nation interests.

The Council

The Council of Ministers is the principal decision-making body and ultimate authority in the EU, responsible for acting on the proposals it receives from the commission. It has the power to reject such proposals. Membership in this institution consists of national ministers from relevant areas (e.g., agriculture, finance, and foreign affairs), one from each member nation. They attend meetings periodically in response to proposals submitted by the commission.

In addition, the heads of state of member nations comprise the European Council. This group holds summit meetings, which provide political guidance

---

[29]Tugendhat, *Making Sense of Europe*, p. 137.

and major impetus for further integration of the EU. As the ultimate political authority in the EU, the European Council establishes informal rules in the form of goals and objectives, which provide the basis for discussion and debate within the commission and Parliament. The impetus for the completion of the internal market by 1992 and the commitment to explore the efficacy of an economic and monetary union came from the European Council. The significance of institutionalizing meetings between heads of state is that only they have the ability "to strike a final balance between different and conflicting interests, [and to] establish goals and set guidelines within which the member states and Community must work."[30]

The European Parliament

Perhaps the most innovative institution in the EU is the European Parliament. As a democratically elected assembly of individuals belonging to European (versus national) political parties, the Parliament "represents the ultimate embodiment of the European ideal" to transcend national frontiers.[31] Prior to enlargement it was comprised of 567 members elected to five-year terms from EU member states. This number will increase to over 600 after Austria, Finland, and Sweden become active members of the EU in 1995. National representation is according to population.[32] Parliament members represent EU political groups (e.g., Socialists, European People's Party, European Democrats, Communists) rather than national parties.

The primary function of the Parliament is to consult. It renders its opinion to the council on proposals made by the commission; it can amend legislation; it may veto appointments of EU authorities; it determines the EU's budget (in conjunction with the council); it supervises the work of the council and commission; and it may dismiss the commission, if it so chooses, by a two-thirds majority vote. The role of this body in the adoption of new policy measures was expanded by the Single European Act (1986), which included new procedures pertaining to decision making (e.g., the cooperation procedure, see "Institutional Change," pp. 362–368). Although these new rules do not give equal authority for policy adoption to this institution representative of the European electorate, they do make the council more accountable for its policy decisions.

The Court of Justice

The Court of Justice, comprised of one judge from each member nation, is the highest court in the EU.[33] Like the Parliament, the court's role is to act in the interest

---

[30]Ibid., p. 166.

[31]Ibid., p. 146.

[32]Prior to 1996 the number of seats will be allocated as follows: Germany (99); France, Britain, and Italy (87 each); Spain (64); the Netherlands (31); Belgium, Greece, and Portugal (25 each); Denmark (16); Ireland (15); and Luxembourg (6). Beginning in 1996 these numbers will remain the same while Sweden will have 21, Austria 20, Finland 16, and Norway 15 seats.

[33]If there is an even number of members, then an additional judge will be selected from either Germany, France, Italy, Spain, or the United Kingdom on a rotating basis.

of the entire community, not in the interest of any particular country. The primary function of the court is to pass judgment on legal disputes pertaining to the application and interpretation of EU law (including the economy's working rules as specified in the Treaties and subsequent regulations and directives). In particular, the court interprets the Treaties to ensure compatibility between their provisions and any measures proposed by the commission, the council, or any national government. Overall, the court's rulings, in conjunction with the provisions of the Treaties, constitute a set of working rules (i.e., European law) binding on all EU institutions, member states and their national courts, and EU citizens.

WORKING RULES AND
THE BEHAVIOR OF THE EU

The basic working rules for integration and economic behavior, including common policies, are outlined in the *Treaties Establishing the European Communities*.[34] Four types of rules comprise EU legislation: (1) *regulations* are EU laws to which all member states must adhere, although application of regulations remain within each member state; (2) *directives* bind members to the stated objective, but permit national authorities to determine means for introducing these rules; (3) *decisions* pertain to a specific issue (e.g., refusal of one member to purchase goods produced by another member) which bind the specific group in question to comply; (4) *recommendations* and *opinions* are informal rules which are not legally binding. As the rules are modified and amended, the EU evolves. The European Court can overcome national resistance to regulations, directives, and decisions by enforcing EU working rules. For example, the court can require a member whose actions (e.g., subsidizing a state industry) distort competition in violation of EU Competition Policy (see "Behavior of Economy," pp. 354–356) to eliminate the subsidy. One such case involved French and Italian state monopolies over the sale of cigarettes and tobacco. Only state-produced products were sold by certain retailers who were privileged merchants, not civil servants, with an exclusive license. The court ruled that such an arrangement violated the Competition Policy, especially by restricting sales of cigarettes and tobacco products produced in other member nations. As a result, the French and Italian licensed merchants had to stock these other products as well.[35]

The dynamic effects of integration include the influence of changes in EU working rules on the nature of policymaking (e.g., relinquishing some authority to the EU) in member nations. As integration within the EU increases, the degree of interdependence between member nations' economies will also increase,

---

[34]*Treaties Establishing the European Communities* (Luxembourg: Office for Official Publications of the European Communities, 1987). The 1991 Maastricht Treaty sought to amend the earlier treaties.

[35]Anthony J. C. Kerr, *The Common Market and How It Works* (Oxford: Pergamon Press, 1987), p. 96.

thereby affecting the ability of one nation to have effective control over its fiscal and monetary policies. The evolutionary process of institutional change also is influenced by the impact of the EU performance upon the informal attitudes of EU citizens, especially business leaders, and the subsequent changes in formal attitudes held by authorities within principal institutions and the heads of national governments. Such changes have stimulated proposals for establishing new working rules and institutions to govern the means by which conflicting interests of member nations can be resolved, including the organization of resource allocation decisions, ownership and control of resources, and the processes by which economic decisions will be coordinated.

Organization of Resource Allocation
Decision Making

In most respects organization of resource allocation decisions throughout the EU is decentralized among 15 economies, although there has been a gradual centralization trend within EU supranational institutions, albeit at a reduced pace since the early 1990s recession and monetary problems. There has been centralization of industrial and trade policies, particularly since the decision to complete the internal market by 1992 was made by the European Council. Council members had been encouraged to do so by members of the European Commission and the European Parliament. These EU authorities, in turn, were responding to lobbying efforts by representatives of the private sector who perceived a common challenge to their domestic markets. Business leaders, especially from the automobile and electronics industries, recognized the relatively poor performance of the EU, leading to Europe's eroding competitive position vis-à-vis Japan and the United States since the early 1980s. These leaders wanted centralized decision making by EU authorities for the purpose of coordinating research and development efforts, while leaving each nation's industries free to pursue microeconomic aspects of high technology, and the establishment of EU working rules consistent with a free market (e.g., reduction of border checks, and harmonization of national technical standards and procurement policies). In effect, business leaders wanted the EU to assume a decision-making role vis-à-vis member nations similar to that of Japan's Ministry of International Trade and Industry. This change in informal rules ultimately led to a significant formal rule—the Single European Act (1986). More centralized decision making, particularly in trade matters, ensued, since the act provided for an extension of qualified majority voting in four fields that previously required unanimity: "the creation of a real internal market by 1992, technological research and development, economic and social cohesion and the improvement of working conditions."[36] However, harmonization of fiscal matters, including value-added

[36]*Steps to European Unity*, 6th ed. (Luxembourg: Office for Official Publications of the European Communities, 1987).

tax rates and excise tax rates, is proceeding more slowly since unanimity is required before working rules in such matters can be changed.

In terms of the centralization of resource allocation, EU finance consists of the budget for the European Coal and Steel Community, whose funds are derived from a levy paid to the commission by producers on the value of coal and steel manufactured, and the budget for Euratom and the EEC, both of which are funded out of the EU's "own resources." EU financing is unique, as resources are transferred from the national to the supranational level to fund integration policies and the means to administer them.[37] The revenue for the EU budget comes from four main sources. First, a part of member nations' value-added tax (VAT) is paid by EU citizens. Each member nation contributes the first 1.4 percent regardless of the VAT rates charged on purchases within its borders (these rates range from 12 percent to 25 percent). This source contributes about 55 percent of EU revenue. Second, customs duties from the EU's common external tariff provide about 22 percent of EU revenue. The revenue from customs duties is reduced by the fact that since the duties are paid at the EU border, member states are reimbursed for 10 percent of the customs duties they collect. It should be noted that the relative contribution of customs duties to the EU budget has been declining as world trade negotiations lead to the gradual reduction of such duties.

The last two sources of revenue are GNP-based resources from each member nation (20 percent), and agricultural and sugar levies, which together contribute just under 4 percent of EU revenue. The agricultural levies are paid by exporters to equate world prices with EU target prices (see pp. 351–354). The amount collected will be influenced by a number of factors beyond the EU's control, including world weather conditions. The sugar levy is contributed by EU sugar producers as part of the coresponsibility measure introduced in the late 1970s for the purpose of limiting the EU's cost when financing products perpetually in surplus. The distribution of funds is roughly as follows: CAP (50 percent); structural operations (32 percent); internal policies (6 percent); external policies (6 percent); administration (4 percent); and monetary reserves (2 percent). In terms of total expenditures, the EU budget is over 35 billion ECU, or approximately $40 billion (in winter, 1994 exchange rates).

As measured by the ratio of the EU budget to the combined GDP of all member nations (about 1.2 percent), centralization of EU economic power is currently quite modest.[38] Rather than the size of the budget or which institutions

---

[37]EU finance has been described as "haphazard and chaotic" by one analyst, who observes that ". . . the EC has a budget which derives revenue and distributes benefits in a manner entirely unrelated to levels of national wealth. Moreover, to make matters worse, the Community also lacks any accurate means of assessing the national incidence of such costs and benefits." See Brian Ardy, "The National Incidence of the European Community Budget," *Journal of Common Market Studies*, 26, no. 4 (June 1988), 425, 426.

[38]Although this 1.2 percentage is modest compared to the average spending of each member relative to its GDP, 48 percent, EU decisions have a significant impact on many economic, social, and political aspects of each member.

allocate funds, the degree of centralization must be evaluated according to the impact of the rules established by the EU, including the common policies, especially the extent to which these rules influence flows of resources. EU goals and policies effectively control a sizable percentage of all public expenditure, given the importance of support schemes in national budgets. In addition, the EU has control in macroeconomic policy matters via moral suasion and working rules which carry penalties for noncompliance.

An example of increased centralization of decision making, which created favorable results for over three decades until the 1993 crisis, has been in the area of financial cooperation. Beginning with the European Investment Bank and Monetary Committee in 1958, the EU has slowly been attempting to assume control of exchange-rate stability among most members. The first mechanism was the "snake in the tunnel" monetary arrangement, created in 1972, which linked currencies within a narrow range (± 2.25 percent) against other currencies. This mechanism was superseded in 1979 by the European Monetary System (EMS) exchange-rate mechanism whose basic features were held in place until 1993.

The main objectives of the EMS have been to minimize exchange-rate instability; to fight inflation through a convergence of macroeconomic policies; to serve as another link between EU economics and politics; and to provide closer monetary cooperation among EU members while fostering deeper political and economic integration. The EMS was designed as a cooperative measure to foster interdependence of EU economies in need of more monetary policy coordination and exchange rate stabilization. Both France and Italy benefited. Following currency realignments in 1983, the EMS helped mitigate the effects of currency speculation which might otherwise have contributed to the depreciation of the franc and lira. This would have stimulated inflation and budget deficits in both nations.

Three key features of the EMS designed to promote monetary stability within the EU are the exchange-rate mechanism, a set of credit mechanisms, and the European Fund for Monetary Cooperation. The central feature of the EMS which unites these three features is the European Currency Unit (ECU). The ECU is the accounting unit of the EMS. It consists of a basket of member nations' currencies, with each currency being weighted according to a formula which calculates each nation's share of EU gross domestic product, intracommunity trade, and monetary support to the EU. Based on the formula the relative share of the West German mark is about 30 percent, while that of the French franc and the Greek drachma are roughly 20 percent and 1 percent, respectively. The ECU's value is calculated daily by the commission on the basis of market exchange rates at the close of trading.[39]

The ECU serves many functions. It is the *numeraire* for EU financial statements, since the EU budget, members' exchange rates, the divergence between these exchange rates, credit operations, and the settlement of accounts

---

[39]In early 1994 1 ECU equaled about $1.15.

are each denominated in ECUs. As the numeraire for the EMS exchange-rate mechanism, the ECU is used to establish fixed central rates for each member's currency. These rates serve as the basis for computing a grid of bilateral exchange rates between members. The EMS goal of promoting monetary stability requires some means for monitoring exchange-rate variability. The degree of fluctuation permitted around bilateral exchange rates was (prior to 1993) ±2.25 percent (6 percent for the Italian lira). Denominating exchange rates in ECUs is necessary to establish a basis for comparison.

The next function of the ECU is to serve as a reference unit for measurement of the divergence between exchange rates. The divergence indicator is "the ratio of a member currency's ECU price, which is based on actual exchange rates and is therefore variable, to the fixed ECU price, based on the central rates."[40] If a currency crosses a "threshold of divergence," the member nation's central bank is obligated to intervene (e.g., buy or sell the currency, taking immediate steps to curb inflation, impose taxes) so as to maintain its currency's relative value within the accepted range. Such a commitment toward exchange-rate stability requires that member nations' central banks be able to intervene and receive credit when necessary. The ECU serves as the denominator for credit operations involving creditor and debtor balances during currency intervention activities. Some EU firms use ECUs for accounting purposes, while it is possible for EU citizens to open bank accounts denominated in ECUs.

A credit mechanism exists by which central banks can extend members' credit on a very short-term basis (e.g., less than three months) to finance obligatory currency intervention activities. ECUs are the unit of account for these bilateral credit transactions. The final major function of the ECU in the EMS concerns settling accounts between monetary authorities. Interest paid to creditor banks is partially (i.e., at least 50 percent) payable in ECUs. The applicable interest rate is equal to a weighted average of official discount rates for member currencies.

Another feature of the EU financial system worth noting is the European Monetary Cooperation Fund (EMC Fund). Established to facilitate progress toward the economic and monetary union level of integration, the EMC Fund provides the basis for a common currency and financial reserve. Each member state deposits 20 percent of its gold and dollar reserves with the EMC Fund. In return they receive an equivalent value of ECUs. These ECUs thus serve as a reserve instrument, used for settling debts between member banks that were incurred through adhering to requirements of the EMS (e.g., short-term loans during central bank intervention are conducted through the EMC Fund).

Prior to 1993 the EMS system was successful in terms of reducing inflation and exchange-rate variability. It was estimated that it saved member nations about $15 to $25 billion in currency losses by stabilizing rates and boosted

---

[40]George Zis, "The European Monetary System 1979–84: An Assessment," *Journal of Common Market Studies*, 23, 1 (September 1984), 45–71.

inflation (through reduced risk of currency loss). As a result, informal rules favoring the establishment of an economic and monetary union (EMU) were accepted by EU heads of state in the late 1980s, then formalized with the approval of the Maastrict Treaty on European Union 1991, which formally commits EU members to work toward the establishment of an economic and monetary union by January 1, 1999.[41] Among the treaty's provisions were increasing the power of the European Parliament, extending the decision-making rule of qualified majority to certain areas of social policy, and the key feature—establishing for the EU a monetary system comparable to that of Germany.[42] This system would include a central bank independent of political authorities capable of introducing measures to establish price stability.[43]

Those drafting the Maastrict Treaty did not fully comprehend the problems with the EMS in the "new Europe" following German reunification and the Cold War's end. What maintained the EMS, particularly the "permanently fixed exchange rates," was modest differences in inflation and interest rates among members (especially between Germany and the rest of the EU). When German unification induced a recession and fiscal problems, interest rates rose there in the face of deficit problems and the desire to fight inflation. Currency speculators realized how fragile the system was and that many currencies were overvalued. Calls for lower interest rates in Germany were ignored by the independent Bundesbank, partly because its authorities refused to place EU interests before domestic concerns, and also (some speculate) because they feared a loss of power if the proposed EMU featuring an EU central bank became reality.

During 1992 and 1993 there were recommendations to alter the EMS working rules by permitting wider fluctuation margins in member currencies, but the proposal was rejected since it represented a step away from the achievement of an EMU. Meanwhile recession outside of Germany increased, culminating in the September 1992 currency crisis. During a frantic weekend of meetings, EU monetary authorities agreed to establish new working rules whereby most EU member currencies could fluctuate within a 15 percent range about a central rate. While preserving some sense of monetary coordination and stability, the new rules made clear that the goal of a relatively quick transition from a common market to an EMU was unrealistic and unlikely to be achieved during this century. Critics argue that the 15 percent fluctuation bands mock the basic intent of the EMS. They also believe that the idea of a federal Europe achieved through provisions of the Maastrict Treaty is unrealistic and that the EU needs to redefine its goals and rethink the means to achieve those goals and its organization of decision making, particularly in regards to monetary matters. EU members do not

[41]EMU is discussed further in the following sections.

[42]For a detailed discussion, see Geoffrey Garrett, "The Politics of Maastricht," *Economics and Politics*, 5, no. 2 (July 1993), 105–123.

[43]Other features are discussed in "Institutional Change," p. 362.

seem ready to place European interest ahead of domestic concerns, which is vital for an EMU to be achieved. Authorities realize that while harmonizing trade and certain policies (see pp. 351–357) in an incremental manner has been successful, such an approach does not work for greater monetary integration.[44]

There are additional obstacles to the achievement of an EMU and the type of decision making required. One concerns harmonization of tax policies, including excise and value-added taxes, and removal of material and technical barriers between members. Each nation has its own rationale for particular policies and trade barriers and continues to resist mandatory changes that would affect their power of taxation. Consequently, harmonization will require considerable political will to elevate EU interests over national and sectoral interests. The United Kingdom refuses to tax purchases of children's clothing or food. Italy has a 38 percent tax on luxuries, while the United Kingdom and the Netherlands have no luxury taxes. Ireland and Denmark insist on maintaining their value-added taxes at rates of about 20 percent, while Spain sets its rate at 12 percent. However, once border controls are removed, countries with higher taxes will lose sales if their citizens choose to shop in neighboring member nations with lower taxes.

Members have different perceptions of macroeconomic problems. In Italy, for instance, high inflation is not considered as serious as it would be in West Germany. In nations such as Denmark curtailing unemployment, perhaps through increased public spending, is accorded top priority in macroeconomic policymaking. Some EU members fear that supranational macroeconomic policymaking within an economic and monetary union would impose stringent monetary and fiscal policies upon them, perhaps creating a recession in those member states experiencing high inflation. Overall, the path toward more centralized decision making is likely to be longer than anticipated.[45]

---

[44]Ratification of this treaty will mean that greater centralization of decisions would ensue since responsibility for all members' fiscal and monetary policies would shift to EU institutions. And prior to its implementation it also means more power to member nations' parliaments, since each must ratify the treaty's provisions. The money supply, management of exchange rates, fiscal policy, and some redistribution programs would be controlled at the supranational level. As a result, policy decisions would be made according to what EU officials deem to be in the entire EU's interest. It has been estimated that the EMU level of integration would require members to redistribute funds equal to between 5 percent and 7 percent of member nations' combined gross national products. This larger EU budget would be necessary for administering monetary and fiscal policies as well as for financing transfer payments that would stimulate economic growth and development in lower-income regions.

[45]This should not be surprising. During the 1950s it was proposed that the common market level of integration be realized by 1968—but it took until 1992. The informal rules broadly favoring an EMU generally are acceptable given the recognition of the economic benefits that would result. What is necessary is the combination of the right economic environment (period of stable growth and modest, common rates of inflation in most EU members) and a political environment in member nations conducive to relinquishing some sovereignty over fiscal and monetary policy to further centralize decision making.

National Ownership (Public, Private,
and Cooperative) with Supranational
Control of Resources

While there is public ownership of the means of production in many EU nations, especially within northern members, there is no ownership at the supranational (EU) level. The degree of EU control over flows of resources is directly related to the impact of rules such as those permitting transnational mergers—especially in chemical, pharmaceutical, heavy truck, luxury automobiles, and electronics industries, those prohibiting national subsidies that were designed to protect certain sectors and particular firms from the effects of integration and from external competition, and those requiring the removal of technical conditions which inhibited trade (e.g., restriction on the sale of beer in Germany not brewed according to strict German standards).

Through the Common External Policy, the EU has acted as a bloc bargaining agent providing external protectionist measures for selected industries in decline, including steel and textiles. For steel the EU has set production quotas, prices, subsidies, as well as establishing trade agreements with non-EU trading partners—particularly with Central and Eastern European nations since 1989. The intent has been to allow EU producers time to adjust to foreign competitive pressure. The assistance to the textile industry includes adopting rules designed to decrease national aid in member nations, using social and regional funds to pay textile workers who suffered from EU textile policies. Included also is a multifibre agreement in the common external trade policy. Part of the multifibre pact includes bilateral trade agreements limiting textile imports into the EU from about 30 non-EU supplier nations whose low wage rates for textile workers give them a comparative cost advantage.

EU control has been growing due to the breadth of the common policies' influence and the impact of rules creating a single EU-wide market. The Common Agricultural Policy is the most prominent example. However, the extent to which the EU can exercise control in social, competition, and transport (among other) areas has also been increasing.

COMMON AGRICULTURAL POLICY.   The Common Agricultural Policy (CAP) represents the most integrated, expensive (over 20 billion ECU a year), and fully developed EU policy in terms of supranational control. EU decisions apply throughout the agricultural sectors of member nations. The EU makes major price and production decisions for most outputs produced, including nearly all fruits and vegetables, dairy products, meat, cereals, sugar, olive oil, and wine.

The EU founders decided to include agriculture among the economic activities the proposed Common Market would cover because of a desire to ensure that the EU satisfy a high percentage of its agricultural needs from its own resources rather than being dependent upon external sources. It is also desired to lessen the risk of food shortages, such as those which plagued Europe during the post-World War II period; prevent costly social upheavals should the rate of rural-urban migration suddenly increase if farming as a way of life became unfeasible to many citizens; stabilize food prices and agricultural incomes in the face of wide fluctuations in supplies (often due to erratic natural conditions); increase the size of the internal market for farmers, thereby encouraging specialization of goods produced (leading to productivity gains and lower food prices);[46] increase the variety of foods available for consumers; and promote harmony within the EU by reconciling differences (e.g., costs of producing) between competing member nations. Such differences are bound to arise due to differences in existing agricultural policies as well as geographical factors. In addition, the founders recognized that achieving the common market level of integration would not be possible without a policy that integrated the agricultural sectors of member nations, especially since farmers were politically powerful.

One major purpose of the CAP deserving further mention is the protection of farmers' incomes. Such an objective was put forth during the period of the early 1950s when farmers' political clout was especially pronounced, for a relatively high percentage of the labor force was employed in agriculture.[47] It was recognized that government intervention was necessary to guarantee some degree of parity between farm and nonfarm incomes in rapidly industrializing nations.

The CAP basically is an interventionist scheme whereby the market price of nearly all agricultural products within the EU is manipulated so that desired price levels (those consistent with higher farmer incomes) are attained. Specific means for accomplishing this is through protective devices imposed at the EU border and through the EU measures to purchase excess supplies at a specific support-price level. In response to higher prices, output of cereals has exceeded EU requirements for the past decade, with annual surpluses of 20 percent not unusual. Other products typically in excess supply include butter, milk powder, and wine. Furthermore, different market organizations have been created. In each case producers of different products are supported through various support-price and direct-aid schemes.

There are other forms of support, including export refunds paid by the EU to its farmers if the world price they receive for exports falls below the market price within the EU (including transport costs to the point of export). Minimum prices set above free-market equilibrium prices encourage surpluses. In 1984 excess output included 27 percent for dairy products, 19 percent for sugar, and 15 percent for cereals. Rather than store all, the EU provides export subsidies to enable farmers to sell their products on world markets, thereby decreasing the world market price—perhaps at the expense of farmers of Third World nations.

---

[46]Member nations would concentrate on producing those products well suited to their prevailing climatic and physical conditions. For example, Spain and Greece would produce wine, olive oil, and citrus fruits while the United Kingdom would specialize in livestock and cereals production.

[47]As of 1958 the percentage of the labor force employed in agriculture was about 23 percent in France, 15 percent in West Germany, 12 percent in the Netherlands, and over 40 percent in Italy. See Munshull, *The New Europe*, p. 115.

Such subsidies may account for one third of the CAP budget.[48] The provision of such support measures has required a system for financing the CAP. The EU created the European Agricultural and Guidance Fund (EAGF), whose costs are shared jointly by the members, to be responsible for all financing of measures to organize and support those agricultural markets designated as eligible by the council. There are two sections of the EAGF. The Guarantee Section finances support purchase and export refund measures, while the Guidance Section finances measures designed to create structural improvements for promoting agricultural production.

The Guarantee Section finances interventionist measures designed to control markets and prices (e.g., purchasing surpluses at the intervention price, financing refunds paid to exporters of member nations). Its revenue comes from import levies, from levies paid by producers of particular products (e.g., sugar, dairy products, cereals) to help finance their own support measures, from customs duties receipts, and from general EU funds. About two thirds of all EU expenditures are for financing the Guarantee Section of the CAP. A much smaller percentage (less than 3 percent) of total EU funds is allocated to the Guidance Section. Structural policy projects are generally cofinanced with member nations, since the individual projects funded are for specific areas generally located in poorer regions of EU nations, especially in Greece, Ireland, southern Italy, and Portugal.

Since 1992 the CAP has been influenced by endogenous and exogenous forces, most of which have exacerbated existing problems. In the face of expanding capital-intensive farming (in response to CAP working rules which encouraged doing so), new rules were introduced to alleviate the pressure of farming on the EU environment. Such measures included incentives for farmers to adopt more environmentally friendly production techniques, and reduced prices for products such as cereals with the aim of reducing the number of acres devoted to such crops, thereby reducing the intensity of soil cultivation.

The General Agreement on Tariffs and Trade (GATT) negotiations have focused on CAP subsidies. Seeking to reduce protectionism in agriculture worldwide, GATT's members (which include the EU) voted to permit a GATT authority review of all agricultural policies around the world to ensure they conform to GATT working rules. EU farmers, particularly the French, have resisted implementation of GATT's rules vehemently. The EU also is resisting opening their markets to exports from Central and East European nations, many of which can offer quality agricultural goods at low prices. The extent of the CAP's protectionist nature is such that it has turned Poland's surplus in farm trade (realized in 1990) into a deficit by 1994.

The EMS breakdown has meant that CAP costs will rise. This is due to the rule that gives farmers in member countries whose currency is depreciating vis-à-vis the ECU a "monetary compensatory amount" in the face of falling agricultural

---

[48]Tugendhat, *Making Sense of Europe*, p. 45.

prices. The cost of this program, which was about 6 billion ECUs per year from 1984 to 1992, has gone up to over 7.5 billion ECUs since the EMS crisis. In addition, German farmers protested a reduction in CAP payments in response to the German mark appreciating. Consequently, a new rule was passed to give all EU farmers compensatory payments in the face of currency fluctuations. This rule adds over 300 million ECUs to the CAP budget for each 1 percent appreciation of the German mark.

While the CAP has been the EU's most significant and widespread effort to further integration over the past three decades, it is fraught with problems today. In the face of rising farm payments and administrative costs, two other products (bananas and potatoes) were added to the list of produce eligible for subsidies. The combination of subsidies and many thousands of producers invites fraud, which some estimate to cost over 3 billion ECUs per year. Therefore, while the CAP has offered protection to the rural sector and boosted farm incomes while sustaining the price of farm land, it has done so at the expense of EU consumers and nonmember nations anxious to export lower-priced agricultural goods to the EU.[49] Consequently, further changes in CAP working rules can be expected. The same can be said for other interrelated policies provided for by the Treaty of Rome. The objectives and some key features of three such policies—competition, transport, and social—are discussed next.

COMPETITION POLICY.   The EU's attempt to create a single market within which goods, services, and productive resources flow freely among the member nations requires that artificial barriers to trade be eliminated. The Competition Policy was introduced for this purpose. Specifically, the policy seeks to establish working rules designed to give all EU traders access to any internal market. There are rules which prohibit firms from establishing restraints of trade (e.g., collusive agreements to set prices, limit quality, or prohibit exports). Other rules prohibit member nations from providing their firms any favored treatment which would give these firms, sometimes referred to as "national champions," a competitive advantage vis-à-vis other EU producers.

Some of the key features of the Competition Policy involve the Commission's role as enforcement authority, the Commission's observation and regulation of state-owned enterprises, its policing of state-aid programs, and the limitations of the Commission's power to promote competitive structures that would be in the community's (versus individual member's) best interests. The Commission has been granted the power to prohibit price-fixing and cartel

---

[49] An example of a subsidy program that benefited farmers (at taxpayer expense) concerned canola (rapeseed) oil. EU farmers were given a subsidy if they planted the crop on land designated as idle "set aside" fields. Justifying the program in the name of fuel (which canola oil can be converted into), farmers receive an EU subsidy plus revenue from selling the seed to a crusher (who produces the oil). Farmers can earn about $350 per acre on what was intended to be idle land (the setting aside itself a justification for maintaining high CAP support payments), while the amount of fossil fuel required in the production process is almost equal to the amount of oil produced.

agreements, ban subsidies deemed to be a distortion of trade, veto mergers and takeovers that restrict trade, and prohibit any other form of anticompetitive behavior that involves firms operating across member nations' borders.

As enforcement authority, the Commission can take the initiative in response to complaints lodged by EU citizens, enterprises, or member nations. The Commission has the right to impose fines against enterprises that violate EU fair trade or antitrust laws. For example, the British government was required by the Commission to reduce the amount of debt the Rover Group was permitted to write off prior to its being privatized. Another decision involving Rover was the Commission requiring British Aerospace to return to the British government more than $75 million which it had received as an incentive to purchase the state-owned car maker.

State-owned enterprises (e.g., alcohol in West Germany and France; petroleum in France; salt and bananas in Italy) are prohibited by the Treaty of Rome from discriminating against enterprises from other member nations when purchasing or marketing their goods and services. Practices such as refusing to import from other members, restricting the quantities of members' imports, or imposing burdensome marketing conditions or bans on advertising against member nations' enterprises are strictly prohibited by the Competition Policy rules. Any state aids that distort trade between member nation firms are prohibited. For example, direct subsidization of a producer (e.g., through low-interest loans, government grants, or tax concessions) that gives the producer's product a competitive advantage is prohibited. Those aid programs that are permitted, including those for regional development or environmental purposes, must be designed to be phased out within a reasonable period of time.

With its weak political clout and modest budget, the commission is limited in its ability to encourage the formation of competitive structures like cartels in industries such as shipbuilding or petrochemicals. Such conglomerates have the potential to compete against nonmember enterprises. However, national governments have preferred to promote expansion of their own industries rather than encourage collusive agreements that would be in the EU's best interests, such as enhancing the EU's collective competitive position vis-à-vis the rest of the world.

Reducing subsidies is a stated goal of the Competition Policy, since the extent of subsidization varies widely throughout the EU. In Germany and Belgium subsidy payments to firms amount to over 20 percent of GNP, while in Denmark, Ireland, Portugal, and Luxembourg the comparable payments account to is less than 1 percent. A recent case, which arose as a result of a British and German protest, involved two French firms. The state-owned bank Credit Lyonnais invested over $400 million in the state-owned steel manufacturer Usinor Sacilor—an investment the commission permitted despite claims that it amounted to a subsidy.

This decision and other controversies have left the commission open to criticism that it is too easily influenced by political pressure. Some have advocated establishment of a EU antitrust authority that would be independent of EU and national authorities. Such an agency could arrive at and publish its decisions, then send these to the commission for its approval. If the commission reversed the decision, it would be required to explain publicly the reasons for doing so. Such a process, some believe, would reduce the actual (and appearance of) political meddling in major competition policy matters.

TRANSPORT POLICY.   The transport policy is an essential component of integrating the EU economies into a single market, for it is integrally linked with the trade, agriculture, and competitive policies. In addition, transportation is an important sector whose contribution to the gross domestic product of the EU outweighs that of agriculture. The overall objective of the EU's Transport Policy is to provide an inexpensive, efficient, and rapid-transport system that will facilitate intra-EU trade. The policy seeks (1) to promote the unification of transportation networks throughout the EU; (2) to prevent member nations from intervening with discriminatory measures (e.g., artificially raising transport cost, and import prices by delaying shipments at their borders) designed to give their country a competitive advantage over others; and (3) to improve infrastructure (e.g., bridges, waterways, tunnels) throughout the EU. In recent years it has been recognized that alternative modes of transport must be promoted for environmental reasons, and that a truly integrated and intermodal transport system (for example, to offer a high-speed railroad link throughout the EU) should become a long-term policy goal.

Specific measures have been suggested or introduced to simplify procedures for commercial traffic crossing borders within the EU. These measures include a more efficient organization of existing border checkpoints (e.g., through increased staffing and longer hours of station operation) and a uniform passport for all EU citizens and commercial vehicles. Overall, progress has been slow. Some EU members continue to resist more liberalized commercial road transport schemes in an effort to protect their national railway transport interests. In addition, nations prefer to have control over the number of licenses they grant to foreign carriers giving these carriers access to their market. The numerous bilateral license agreements serve to exclude cheaper carriers of peripheral EU nations, which is discriminatory and promotes inefficiency. For example, the number of licenses granted by West Germany permitting Dutch trucks to transport goods into Germany exceeds 700,000 annually, while carriers in lower-cost, peripheral EU members such as Greece and Portugal are in a weak bargaining position to receive licenses on a reciprocal basis. The single internal market will improve this situation, for in 1993 greater freedoms to transport goods were extended to carriers throughout the EU. Truck drivers will be able to transport goods from the Netherlands to Portugal with a single piece of paper as a permit, versus about two pounds of assorted documents required for the same route today.

SOCIAL POLICY.   The Treaty of Rome contains provisions that necessitate the adoption of a social policy. The objectives of this policy are to improve the standard of living and working conditions of EU citizens, attempting to mitigate large differentials in such conditions among different countries and between men and women; to enhance occupational and geographic labor mobility through guaranteeing that workers have equal rights to apply for vacant jobs anywhere in the EU, by ensuring that migrant workers receive the same social security rights enjoyed by nationals, and through equalizing employers' contributions to their nation's social security revenue; and to protect cultural minorities and regional diversity. This last objective is significant, for since 1992 there are some fears that the encouragement of greater economic competition may become an excuse for intolerance toward minorities.

Two principal features of the Social Policy are the promotion of full employment and the financing of social programs through the European Social Fund. The employment program consists of a range of employment, unemployment, and income maintenance policies, including finance for training and retraining schemes. Promoting full employment, especially among young EU citizens, has attracted considerable attention because during the mid-1980s over 10 percent of the EU's labor force has been unemployed, while the rate for youth (i.e., people under 25 years of age) has been about twice that figure.

To combat this problem, the EU Social (and Regional) Policy has focused on increasing employment opportunities for young people through funding vocational education or self-employment training programs in member nations, especially in regions hard hit by unemployment. These include southern Italy and much of Spain and Portugal. The European Social Fund extends grants totaling about 1.5 billion ECU (i.e, about $2 billion) annually toward measures designed to achieve the policy's objectives, with over 90 percent of the funds allocated for vocational training schemes.

The Social Policy also focuses on encouraging all EU nations to adopt formal rules regarding employment policy that are consistent with goals of improving living and working conditions and providing equal pay and social security benefits for comparable work regardless of nationality or gender. The importance of harmonizing benefits is to prevent migrant workers from the aforementioned poorer regions flocking to nations, especially West Germany, which offer better working conditions and social security benefits. Reaching a consensus on social policy harmonization often proves more difficult than doing so for trade and currency matters, as some habits are deeply ingrained in each nation. For example, years of debate failed to resolve the proposal to establish a 48-hour workweek with a ban on Sunday labor so ultimately no final decision was reached.

Coordination of the Production and Distribution Activities of 15 Economies

Evaluated in terms of 15 economies, extensive social insurance and welfare schemes as well as cases of (indicative) economic planning complement market coordination of economic activity in member nations. When the EU is considered as one economy, the emphasis has been upon the establishment of an integrated, large-scale, competitive economy operating according to market principles, with a modest role for redistributing income through common policies. Until the provisions of the Single European Act are implemented effectively, most economic decisions will be coordinated by the 15 separate economies except for matters included in the EU Trade Policy (discussed later), for particular products having considerable market coordination and protective measures provided through EU institutions [e.g., agricultural (CAP), steel (European Coal and Steel Community), and textiles (common external tariff), and for EU-sponsored research. Implementation of the working rules contained in the Single European Act will establish a common internal market for the 15 economies, with the EU assuming greater responsibility for coordinating economic activity. The complexity of this coordination will increase geometrically as fiscal and monetary objectives, policy schemes, programs, management of projects, and consultation shift to the EU level.

The trade policy is the foundation of the EU economy. Broadly speaking this policy, as stated in the EEC Treaty, specifies the rules and objectives for economic integration within the community, for trade relations between the EU and the rest of the world. Common external tariffs against nonmember nations, no customs duties between EU members, and free movement of productive factors, especially labor, capital, and goods and services, are the goals of the trade policy. Free movement of labor means that job seekers can move between member nations and face no discrimination regarding access to employment, remuneration, or working conditions. The EU seeks to facilitate this flow through an administrative office, which channels labor market information to all member nations. This office also assists members to develop training programs consistent with estimated future needs of the EU labor market.

Achieving the objective of free, undistorted flows of capital between members has been more difficult. One major problem has been the tendency for excessive capital to flow primarily from members with weaker currencies to those with a strong currency (e.g., West Germany) when exchange-rate fluctuations indicate an impending depreciation of currency in the former members. The EU permits member governments to impose exchange controls if the member believes its capital market will be disturbed by the free flow of capital. For example, any nation experiencing excessive inflows of capital could impose exchange controls to avoid a dramatic appreciation of its currency (thereby leading to a loss of exports or domestic inflation). Meanwhile nations with a weaker currency would seek to impose curbs on the outflow of their domestic savings.

Since the Treaty of Rome the goal of establishing a single EU market has been difficult to realize. Larger volumes of free trade and further degrees of integration have been hampered by the persistence of customs formalities and procedures as well as member nations' interventionist measures imposed during times of domestic recession. Members wishing to slow the inflow of goods from any other EU member (or from any nonmember nation) could increase the number of technical conditions required for a shipment to enter its country, assign relatively few personnel to its border for customs inspection purposes, restrict competition for state contracts by only considering bids from its national suppliers, or restrict entry of service enterprises, especially in the area of transport and finance. In each case the time and cost of shipping goods from trading partners would increase, as would the purchase price of some goods and services from other members. A willingness among all member nations to integrate to the level of an economic and monetary union would significantly alleviate current problems pertaining to the free flow of the factors of production. Such a willingness is formally embodied in the Single European Act (SEA) of 1986.

The SEA evolved from a "White Paper" prepared in 1985 for the EU Commission. This paper included a list of nearly 300 working rules designed to create an internal market through the removal of fiscal, technical, and physical trade barriers between EU members. Rules were designed to lessen border controls to permit greater freedom of movement of persons, goods, services, and capital; harmonize technical requirements for products to decrease nontariff barriers; streamline the EU decision-making process; and harmonize national standards for product quality and tax rates. Examples include the removal of controls on capital movements, thereby permitting EU residents to select any banking or investment service offered within the EU; and uniform standards and regulations for products such as electrical appliances and foodstuffs, thus decreasing shipping time spent at borders.

The goal of completing the internal market by having all of its provisions implemented and enforced by each member nation was not achieved in 1992 as desired, but should be reality by the late 1990s. Despite almost 100 percent of the provisions having been approved by the Council and over 90 percent of them transposed into national law in all member nations, as late as 1994 less than half were actually established as a formal working rule in every member nation (12 in 1994) and even fewer have been implemented effectively.[50] More rapid implementation has been inhibited by bureaucratic resistance at the national level by civil servants and members of the business community who either do not understand the EU directive or resist supervision by supranational authorities (and their loss of power at the national level). Specific areas in which compliance with the SEA has been slow include reducing border checks,[51] harmonizing indirect taxation, standardizing a set of rules that would apply to the establishment of a European limited company, and ensuring that bidders from all EU nations interested in obtaining a public procurement contract are treated with equal fairness as a bidder from the member nation soliciting bids. Ultimately, effective completion of an EU single market depends upon the willingness and ability of member states to be responsible for compliance with and enforcement of SEA working rules.

[50]Garrick Holmes, ed., "European Trends: Regional Monitor, 1993 1st Quarter," London: *The Economist Intelligence Unit* (1993), p. 82. The passage of SEA working rules has occurred at a faster pace than implementation, for once the council passes a legislative measure it takes as long as two years for the measure to be incorporated into national law.

[51]Great Britain, Ireland, and Denmark have resisted more liberal treatment of individuals at their borders—the first two undoubtedly in response to the threat of terrorism.

Concerning EU trade relations with various groups of nonmember nations is the other component of EU trade policy. To achieve a level of integration in which member nations behave uniformly within a single trading bloc, the EU has established rules which seek to avoid significant distortions of competition and obstacles to trade when EU members engage in trade with nonmember nations. The EU adjusts its common external trade barriers through internal bargaining and behaves as a bloc in world trade negotiations. The EU claims that its average level of import duties for nonagricultural products is lower than those of its chief trading partners, namely the United States and Japan. In addition, the EU bargains as a bloc to establish special trade agreements with the EFTA, Central and East European countries, and blocs of Third World Nations.[52]

Among the improved decision-making features introduced at the EU level in recent years, which are noteworthy in terms of their affecting economic coordination, are the Cooperation Procedure and Codecision Procedure (see Institutional Change," pp. 362–368), and the principle of competing jurisdictions. This principle affects the means adopted in member nations to comply with EU directives for achieving the objectives specified in the SEA by January 1, 1993. At issue is the extent to which members will be coerced into harmonization by adopting EU specified means versus "managing" their own economies through a "mutual recognition and equivalence" scheme.[53] Under this scheme member nations are not required to harmonize prices, taxes, and quality of goods by edict. Rather, once members agree on broad "essential requirements" of a particular directive, such as minimum safety standards for automobiles, each member can adopt safety standards at or above EU requirements. The basis for each member's decision will be influenced by its being a "competing jurisdiction" with other EU nations. Proponents of this scheme argue that competitive forces of a single EU market will establish norms and deviations based upon consumers' preferences. If automobiles with low safety standards are in demand, then members which choose to legislate standards well above EU minimum levels will put their own automobile industry at a competitive disadvantage.

Regarding value-added tax (VAT) rates, some harmonization has been necessary. Until 1996 a 15 percent minimum VAT rate was established as a "political agreement" (it being difficult to approve an EU directive since tax matters require unanimity of council members). Differences in standard VAT rates and tax rates on necessities and luxuries among nations are permitted, as have different excise tax rates on products such as cigarettes, beer, wine, and petrol. EU

---

[52]For example, in 1975 the EU established a special trade agreement with 46 African, Caribbean, and Pacific (ACP) nations (all former colonies of EU member nations). This agreement offered these ACP nations preferential treatment for many of their agricultural (e.g., cocoa, tea, peanuts) and nonagricultural products originating in ACP nations, but not for ACP agricultural exports which compete with EU-grown agricultural products. However, the impact of these measures on ACP exports to the EU has been modest. The ACP share of EU imports has declined gradually. In addition, the ACP share of manufactured products imported by the EU has fallen from about 5 percent in 1970 to about 1 percent currently.

[53]Price, *Whose Europe*, p. 30.

legislation has reduced the differential. However, as the internal market is effectively completed, the principle of competing jurisdictions should lead to an even greater convergence of rates. Otherwise if neighboring EU members had widely different rates, shoppers in both nations would flock to the EU member with lower value-added taxes to the detriment of the economy of its higher-taxed neighbor.[54] Finally, completion of the internal market requires that VAT be paid in country of purchase rather than country of consumption (if these differ), which will speed up border crossings for EU citizens within the union since nations will not have the justification of detaining someone while seeking to ensure that value-added taxes on any goods purchased have been paid.

The principle of competing jurisdictions holds for matters which have no negative externalities across borders. For those cases where negative spillover effects occur, such as automobile emission control standards, EU harmonization is more acceptable to proponents of the competing jurisdiction principle, including Mrs. Thatcher. An EU directive requires members to inform the commission of national rules that affect environmental matters, with the commission having the right to prohibit the national legislation if it believes the measure represents a nontariff barrier. For most other matters, many argue competitive forces rather than EU coercion should be the process which establishes the means for further economic integration.

In the face of a long recession, much discussion has occurred in the mid-1990s regarding coordinating economic policies. It is recognized that Keynesian measures will be ineffective for a number of reasons. The EU nations already have had fiscal budget deficits, savings rates are low, and interest rates are relatively high. To follow the Keynesian advice and borrow to finance public works projects (to reduce the chronic unemployment) is likely to further increase budget deficits, drive up interest rates, take money from potentially more productive education and training schemes, and wind up funding unproductive projects. In an effort to maintain the integration momentum, EU authorities continually offer members broad guidelines of economic policy designed to coordinate members' economic policies. The EU goals are to stimulate employment; lower unemployment; maintain stable prices and exchange rates, achieve fiscal stability, and complete the internal market. Some argue that the achievement of the EMU level of integration will facilitate realization of these goals.

---

[54]The same principle holds for worker safety standards. Rather than EU directives requiring members to harmonize such standards, which might result in the coercion of Portuguese producers to match the high (and costly) West German standards, each nation is free to allocate its national income between competing objectives.

INSTITUTIONAL CHANGE:
A TRIAL-AND-ERROR PROCESS

According to one observer, EU integration is a "good example of the Hayekian thesis that it is not only the economy that proceeds by trial and error, but that the same principle applies to the unconscious formation of other institutions."[55] Institutional changes that are unique to the EU economy have occurred with relative frequency. In addition to reforms for the purpose of establishing a single market, four particular institutional changes affecting the entire EU have occurred since 1990. These are German unification, the proposed economic and monetary union, enlargement from the original six members to 15 members (with most remaining European nations interested in joining), and reform of EU decision making. These changes are dynamic, influencing one another, existing EU institutions, and the economy's performance.

German Unification

Integration of the West and East German economies began almost immediately after the November 1989 political revolution, symbolized by the tearing down of the Berlin Wall. In July 1990 a monetary union was formed with the deutsche mark becoming the common currency. With the virtual collapse of the East German economy following the end of intra-East European trade (see Chapter 16), the West Germans inherited a poor economy with many overstaffed, heavily subsidized firms producing products of low quality while causing considerable ecological damage in the process. Consequently, the commitment to unification has required far greater investment to restructure the East German economy (particularly infrastructure such as streets and railways) than the West Germans anticipated, including considerable subsidies to alleviate the impact of poverty.[56] The annual amount spent by the West Germans in East Germany amounted to about 6 percent of its national income, and a corresponding tax increase or expenditure reduction was not forthcoming. This required monetization of the debt, with higher inflation and interest ensuing. As discussed earlier, this was a prime reason for the EMS breakdown in 1992–1993.

Attempts to unify a rich democratic nation with a poor nation subject to an authoritarian political structure are unprecedented, and even the wealth and organization skills of the West Germans combined with the absence of a language barrier has not prevented extensive poverty throughout the East (and some resentment of West German "imperialism" in the unification process). The EU's future is tied to the success of German unification, given that Germany is the largest in population and wealthiest EU member. One pillar of the EMS was

---

[55]Price, "Three Models of European Integration," p. 23.

[56]Initial cost estimates were about $25 billion per year for four years, but these were quickly revised to over $100 billion per year for at least ten years in order to bring the East German economy to the level of the poorest regions of West Germany.

German hegemony in monetary matters. However, with the cost of unification contributing to a German fiscal deficit and inflationary pressures that push up interest rates to the detriment of other EU currencies, the Germans were unable to give EU matters top priority. This contributed to the 1992–1993 monetary crisis, which required new working rules for the EMS, and pessimism regarding the efficacy of an EMU.

Maastrict Treaty: The Economic and Monetary Union

Prior to the early 1990s creation of a functioning single market was at the center of EU concerns. With that market all but complete, emphasis has shifted to the establishment of an economic and political union—the EMU level of integration. This would strengthen and modify existing EU institutions and redefine the EU's purpose. Among its features would be the ECU becoming the single EU currency, a common foreign and defense policy, and virtual European citizenship for EU member citizens with more power transferred to the European Parliament. EMU proponents argue that members would benefit from greater efficiency and growth through the elimination of exchange-rate variability and uncertainty as well as reduced transactions costs because of multiple currencies. Other benefits would be more price stability, more responsible public finance, and more potential for employment creation. It is believed that the creation of the EMU also will establish the basis for more coherent fiscal and monetary policy to enable the EU to better withstand external macroeconomic shocks.

Principal institutions would be modified or created by an EMU. The Council of Ministers would be known as the Council of Ministers of the European Union, the commission to be called the European Commission, and the judicial power called the Court of Justice of the Communities. Two new institutions would be the European Monetary Institute (established in 1994) to strengthen arrangements for coordinating members' monetary policies and the EMS. A European System of Central Banks, known popularly as EuroFed, comprised of 15 governors of the members' central banks would be under council supervision. Together with some EU finance authorities they would comprise the monetary board of directors responsible for determining EU monetary policy.

There are many opponents of EMU who oppose this higher level of integration on both economic and political grounds. First, they are skeptical regarding how many members will be able to satisfy the following standards required for entry into the EMU according to the Maastrict Treaty: inflation rate for one year prior to membership must be less than 1.5 percentage points higher than that of the three lowest national inflation rates in the EU; long-term interest rates for the previous year are less than 2 percentage points higher than those of the three member states with the lowest inflation rates; the ratio of public debt to GDP must not exceed 60 percent; the ratio of planned or actual government deficit to GDP at market prices should not exceed 3 percent; and for the previous two years no devaluations in the member's currency beyond the plus or minus 2.25

percentage bands. (The currency crisis of 1992–1993 has stimulated much rethinking on this last requirement.)

Second, some analysts argue there is "neither economic theory nor economic evidence [which] provides a clear case for or against monetary unification,"[57] and that additional economic and political analysis is necessary. Others believe the 15 percent currency fluctuation bands currently established as an EMS working rule will stimulate currency instability and divergence, thereby postponing the realization of the EMU standards. Still another refutes the EU estimate that an EMU will boost EU GNP by 10 percent, claiming that the most likely impact will be a low (perhaps as little as 0.1 percent of GDP) savings in transactions costs.[58]

On political grounds critics believe the former European Community has not been effective in foreign policy matters, since its members have divergent national interests, and that the EU as a whole would lack political credibility. They believe that the EMU proposal is the outcome of a political process stimulated by narrow interest groups interested in facilitating trade (especially large firms exporting throughout the EU), and does not have broad public support. The Maastrict proposal to strengthen the European Parliament so as to make citizens feel more involved with EU affairs was not greeted with enthusiasm in the 1994 European Parliament election (in which voter turnout for this election was the lowest ever—56.4 percent). Overall, critics of EMU see, at best for EMU proponents, a long evolutionary process in which modest EMU requirements are met by most members (likely after individual nations' currencies stabilize within a 2.25 percent band around central rates) and a political redefinition of the EU is offered by authorities in recognition of the new Europe and monetary realities.

Enlargement

As an evolving entity the EU economy has increased its population and geographical area significantly since 1973. Denmark, Ireland, and the United Kingdom joined in 1973, followed by Greece (1981), then Portugal and Spain (1986). In 1994 the European Parliament voted overwhelmingly (almost 95 percent of the votes cast) to approve membership applications from Austria, Finland, Norway, and Sweden. However, only voters in Austria, Finland, and Sweden approved a referendum for EU membership permitting their respective nations to become full members in 1995. Meanwhile, Malta, Cyprus, Switzerland, and Turkey are waiting to have their applications approved. The procedure for becoming an EU member is as follows: First, the prospective member nation's government submits a formal request to the council. Second, the commission studies and evaluates the request before it renders a detailed opinion regarding

[57]Barry Eichengreen and Jeffry Frieden, "The Political Economy of European Monetary Unification: An Analytical Introduction," *Economics & Politics*, 5, no. 2 (July 1993), 89.

[58]Patrick Minford, "The Path to Monetary Union in Europe," *The World Economy*, 16, no. 1 (January 1993), 17.

the rules and necessary internal structural reforms in the prospective nation under which the Commission believes the applicant should be granted membership. Third, this opinion is sent to the council, which decides whether further negotiations between the EU and the applicant would be feasible.

Three broad criteria serve as the basis for evaluation of an applicant country's eligibility for membership. First, its economy must have an institutional structure and level of development to be able to adapt to greater competition after accession, and its firms must conform to EU working rules. Second, the applicant nation must have a political structure that is both democratic and able to implement and enforce EU rules. Any new members of the EU must share the ideals of the original six members as stated in the Treaties. These ideals include a commitment to democratic institutions, which has precluded some nations (e.g., Greece) from applying for membership while under the authority of a dictatorship. Finally, the aspiring member must demonstrate it is compatible with the EU by being able to accept the EU's treaty obligations and principal institution decisions, and adopting the *acquis politique*—a vague concept which has meant that the nation's broad economic and political goals conform to those of the EU's aim of political, economic, and monetary union. In practice this last criterion enables the EU to admit new members more on political grounds (toward nations they are favorably inclined to politically) than technical, economic grounds.

Once council decides to pursue negotiations, the fourth step begins. Negotiations concerning conditions for entry occur between delegations from the applicant nation and EU members. After these negotiations are completed, accession treaties are prepared and signed by the negotiators. National parliaments of each member must approve the terms of the accession treaties.

The relative advantages and disadvantages of an enlarged European Union are the basis for approval. Advantages include economic benefits (i.e., dynamic effects realized by participants in a larger market, including trade creation and gains from specialization of labor) and a greater political bond between members, which can serve to lessen internal tensions or enhance EU bargaining power during international trade negotiations. In the case of Austria (where about two thirds of the more than 80 percent of the votes cast were in favor of joining the EU), it was recognized that membership would reduce transport costs, enable its farmers to receive CAP subsidies, and tie the nation's economy to the EU which accounts for over 60 percent of its exports and almost 70 percent of its imports. On the other hand, Austria has to end its trade agreement with the United States concerning importing hormone-fed beef because this violates EU regulations.

From the point of view of EU members, there are numerous disadvantages, real or perceived, that can exist when new members join the union. During negotiations each of these problems must be resolved to the satisfaction of each member before new applicants can expect approval. Five particular disadvantages can be identified.

First, enlargement requires adjusting political institutions. For example, the size and relative voting power of each nation changes (e.g., Parliament increased from 476 to 518 members after Spain and Portugal became members). In addition, enlargement results in a change in the sharing of costs and benefits, and it requires the EU to become more flexible with the possibility that new nations may be granted an exception to a particular EU working rule.[59] Second, enlargement can result in a greater political, social, and economic divergence between members. The per capita incomes of Greece and Portugal are far below the EU average. There are different rules pertaining to working conditions and pay for women in the Mediterranean members (Greece, Portugal, and Spain) as compared to other EU members.

Third, increased membership means a larger agricultural sector. In the case of the Mediterranean enlargement, the potential for higher CAP expenditures was significant given the large increase in farmland and the ability of the Mediterranean countries to produce large volumes of products heavily subsidized under the CAP (e.g., Spain—olive oil). EU farmers fear a loss of income following enlargement due to competition from new members whose products cost less (e.g., citrus fruits grown in Greece, Portugal, and Spain).

The fourth disadvantage perceived by wealthier members with lower unemployment rates is the threat of a large migration of labor from members experiencing high unemployment and whose wages, working conditions, and benefits from social welfare programs are well below the EU average. Finally, members fear that allowing poorer nations to join the EU will result in financial burdens. The EU commitment to fund redistributional policies (e.g., regional, social, and common agricultural) out of its "own resources" obligates all members to contribute to the EU budget. Existing EU members with domestic economic problems may be unwilling to finance redistributional programs which will primarily benefit new member nations. In addition, EU financial assistance is available to new members who are expected to begin adopting EU policies (e.g., adhere to rules for competition, agriculture) before they officially become members. Portugal received funds prior to entering the EU in 1986 for structural reforms to assist its industries toward becoming competitive with other EU industries. The case of the Central and East European nations is important, especially in light of this last perceived disadvantage.

Interest in joining the EU has been expressed throughout Central and Eastern Europe (CEE), with the EU informing the Czech Republic, Hungary, Poland, Slovakia, Albania, Bulgaria, Romania, Slovenia and the three Baltic nations (Estonia, Latvia, and Lithuania) that they are eligible for future membership. At present the EU has established associate membership agreements with each of these nations—which essentially are ad hoc bilateral trade agreements without other stipulations concerning CEE nations' trade relations with non-EU nations. The EU fears competition from lower-priced steel, textiles,

[59]Austria has a strong neutrality stance concerning foreign policy, so it had to be assured this could not be violated by a qualified majority decision in an EU foreign policy matter.

and food products produced throughout CEE—products all these nations are anxious to export. Consequently, these agreements offer only slow reduction in EU-imposed tariffs and quotas against CEE exports, including antidumping rules that have been detrimental to some CEE firms' efforts to increase exports to EU. This has been especially true in the case of steel, where competitive CEE producers have faced barriers to the EU market on the basis of their being accused of dumping—something they have denied.

The Czech Republic, Hungary, and Poland are likely to be the first successful applicants, albeit well beyond the year 2000 which they have set as their target goal for full EU membership. However, it is highly unlikely that such a goal will be achieved. First, the EU needs time to absorb its most recent members. Then the establishment of the EMU must be dealt with as well as the applications of Cyprus, Malta, Switzerland, and Turkey. Second, the cost to the EU of admitting even these three (wealthiest) CEE nations would be prohibitive. The main increases in EU budgetary outlays would be in extending the CAP and structural funds to CEE nations which are relatively poor (even the wealthiest is at a standard of living only half of the EU average) and heavily dependent upon agriculture—with countless environmental, infrastructure, and poverty problems (see Chapters 15–17). One estimate claims it would raise the EU budget in these areas 60 percent just to admit the Czech Republic, Hungary, Poland, and Slovakia. Another estimate cites over $12 billion as the cost just in extra structural funds of admitting the first three of these four nations. There is a new commitment to increase structural funds in poorer EU regions (particularly in Portugal and Spain). Applying the same rules to all eligible CEE nations would require increasing the EU budget by 0.85 percent of GDP (note that the present percentage for all member nation spending on EU matters is 1.2 percent of GDP). Third, CEE firms are not yet able to compete with EU firms, nor are the governments able to comply with EU welfare and labor regulations. Other EU requirements CEE nations will not be able to satisfy in the near future are demonstrating they have stable institutions that can guarantee democracy, a rule of law, and human rights (as defined by the EU), and an economy primarily characterized by private ownership and competitive markets.

Given these constraints some suggest that the EU and CEE recognize that CEE membership is unlikely in the near future. The EU might agree to liberalize gradually trade agreements with CEE nations and permit them the decades they will need to meet the entry requirements—and perhaps exempt the incoming CEE nation from agricultural or social and regional support as a condition of entry. A more radical suggestion is for the EU to significantly reduce CAP and structural fund spending—a proposal sure to enrage many EU special interests. In any case, unless the Czech Republic, Hungary, or Poland experiences an economic performance similar to that of Japan in the late 1950s or China (see Chapter 18) more recently, the EU likely will have no CEE members for another decade.

The EU has committed over $6 billion in economic aid for the rest of the 1990s to CEE and has approved the start of 14 multimillion-dollar construction infrastructure projects designed to link CEE with the EU through modern highway, railway, and electricity grids. Meanwhile, no timetable for expansion has been offered these aspiring members. Trade concessions will be provided, as will a checklist for reforms CEE members must introduce in order to prepare them for the rigorous competition they will face once they join the EU's single market.

Decision-Making Reform

The most significant institutional changes as they can affect decision making in the EU are the cooperation procedure contained in the Single European Act (see Figure 14-2), and the codecision procedure contained in the Maastrict Treaty (see Figure 14-3). The first procedure enhances the influence of the European Parliament (EP) in the decision-making process. Such a change, while falling short of making the EP the EU's legislative body, should improve decision-making efficiency, especially in removing barriers to the internal market. In addition, greater EP influence can mobilize members' citizens to focus more allegiance and expectations on their EP representatives rather than on their national parliaments, thereby increasing informal attitudes favoring supranational (versus national) interests. The codecision procedure further enhances the European Parliament's influence over EU decisions. It cannot be overridden if it rejects a council proposal. Amendments to proposals made by the Parliament no longer have to pass through the commission, but go directly to the council. Finally, when Parliament's amendments are rejected by council, the new conciliation committees act to seek to resolve differences by searching for a compromise piece of legislation acceptable to a majority of Parliament and a qualified majority of the council.[60]

While the Council of Ministers and the European Council remain the ultimate authorities concerning important EU decisions, the European Commission makes most decisions. The decision-making process can be slow and inefficient as long as members, pursuing national interests, are able to insist on decisions being taken by a unanimous vote of the council. (This gives the most reluctant member considerable power in negotiating sessions.) Completion of the internal market and the ability of the EU to become one economy requires considerable dialogue and compromise among the principal institutions. The cooperation and codecision procedures, by fostering closer cooperation between the decision-making institutions while increasing the power of the EP should enhance efficiency of EU decision making, thereby hastening the integration process.

[60]Lisa L. Martin, "International and Domestic Institutions in the EMU Process," *Economics and Politics*, 5, no. 2 (July 1993), 138–140.

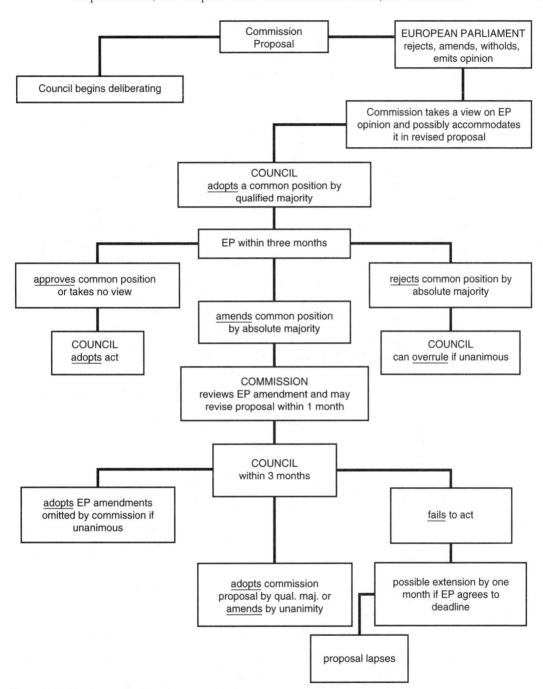

Figure 14-2   The Cooperation Procedure

Source: Juliet Lodge, "The Single European Act and the New Legislative Cooperation Procedure: A Critical Analysis," *Journal of European Integration*, XI, 1 (Fall 1987), 12.

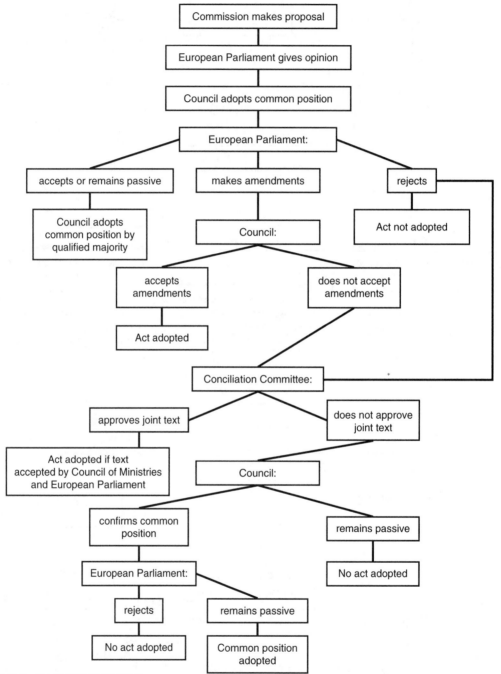

Figure 14-3   The Codecision Procedure

Source: Lisa L. Martin, "International and Domestic Institutions in the EMU Process," *Economics and Politics*, 5, no. 2 (July 1993), 139.

EU ECONOMIC PERFORMANCE: BENEFITS FROM INTEGRATION

Some indicators of performance which have affected attitudes of EU and national authorities include a comparison of EU economic performance, especially economic growth and unemployment rates as well as world market share of certain products, with comparable rates and shares of the United States and Japan; estimates of the extent of trade creation and the effect of integration upon the economic growth of EU nations; estimated costs incurred due to existing barriers to free trade throughout the EU; the performance of the EMS; and estimates of benefits to be derived from completion of the internal market.

Compared to the United States and Japan, EU economic growth and unemployment rates have been unfavorable, especially unemployment since the early 1980s (Table 14-1). Other indicators of performance have become less favorable for EU nations since 1970 (Table 14-2). In addition, profitability as measured by the net rate of return on invested capital has also declined for the EU as a whole. A number of factors have contributed to these adverse trends, including rising energy costs (the EU is heavily dependent upon imported energy sources); structural and social rigidities in the labor market; the absence of a dynamic, modern approach to research and development; and lack of economic policy coordination within the EU as it attempts to compete in the world economy with the United States, Japan, and newly industrializing Asian nations, among others.

The unemployment problem is chronic, as over 20 million people in the 15 EU nations were unemployed as of 1995. Low growth rates with a lingering recession have been one cause of high unemployment. Other causes include: creation of mainly part-time jobs over the last 25 years; higher minimum wages, more worker benefits, longer vacations, shorter workweeks, and higher costs to lay off a worker than in the EU's major competitors (the United States or Asian nations). The comparison with the United States is interesting, for while unemployment rates and length of time the typical worker is unemployed are both lower in the United States, so are the incidence of poverty and job insecurity—as is the gap between the earnings of workers relative to median earnings as compared to the EU.

TABLE 14-1   Economic Growth and Unemployment: EU, United States, Japan, 1973–1994

	ECONOMIC GROWTH[1]		UNEMPLOYMENT RATE[2]	
	1977–86	1987–94	1973–82	1983–94
EU	2.1 %	2.2 %	5.6 %	10.2 %
United States	2.7	2.3	6.9	6.7
Japan	4.0	3.1	2.0	2.5

[1]Average annual percentage of real gross domestic product.
[2]Average annual rate.

Sources: OECD, *Historical Statistics, 1960–1987*; European Union data.

TABLE 14-2   EU Inflation, Investment, and Productivity, 1961–1994
(average annual % growth rates)

		LABOR	
PERIOD	INFLATION[1]	INVESTMENT[2]	PRODUCTIVITY[3]
1961–70	4.4%	6.0%	4.6%
1971–80	10.9	1.5	2.8
1981–86	8.0		1.9
1987–91			1.9
1977–86		0.9	
1987–94		2.9	1.8
1983–94	5.3		

[1]Gross domestic product deflator.
[2]Gross fixed capital formation.
[3]Real gross domestic product per person.

Source: The EU Commission, *European Economy: Annual Economic Report* (Belgium: Directorate-General for Economic and Financial Affairs, July 1987), p. 16; European Union data.

This performance reflects and has contributed to, EU losses of world market share in high-valued goods (Table 14-3). In particular, EU business firms have been facing increased market domination from Japanese "screwdriver factories" (Japanese-owned firms located in the EU which assemble finished products using component parts imported from Japan).[61]

TABLE 14-3   EU Loss in Market Share:[1] 1979–85

Electrical Goods	-4.39%
Motor Vehicles	-4.25
Rubber and Plastic Products	-2.53
Industrial and Agricultural Machinery	-2.49

[1]Market share is the exports of the EU (ten members, not including Spain and Portugal) to the rest of the world compared with exports of OECD countries to the rest of the world.

Source: *European Economy: The Economies of 1992* (Brussels: Commission of the European Communities, no. 35, March 1988), p. 29.

One indicator of performance that has been instrumental in influencing authorities to pursue further integration is the rate of return on investment in research. There are those who believe that the fragmentation of EU economies has resulted in less efficient research results than in the United States and Japan. In 1984 one report stated that a comparison of the cost to develop digital switching systems was as follows: in Japan two firms jointly spent $1.5 billion; in the United States three firms spent $3 billion; while in Europe numerous firms spent $10

[61]For a discussion of the EU's efforts to foster technological progress at the supranational level, see Anthony Scaperlanda, "The European Community and Multinational Enterprises: Lessons in the Social Control of Industry," *Journal of Economic Issues*, 26, 2 (June 1992), 421–432.

billion.[62] This report stimulated EU heads of state to pursue means to jointly promote selected industries, especially those requiring high technology. Their solution was further integration through the working rules defined in the SEA.

Estimates of the effect of integration on overall trade and growth of EU members have been favorable. Not only has considerable trade creation ensued from further integration, but the contribution to the rate of economic growth attributable to integration has been estimated to be about 40 percent of total EU growth over the 1961–1972 period, and 30 percent between 1974–1981.[63] It should be noted that enlargement and worldwide protectionism also were contributing factors to the 1974–1981 period of growth, for each stimulated member nations' exports (especially within the EU). The growth of EU exports over the 1978–1986 period exceeded import growth (215.5 percent versus 205.6 percent), while the EU trade balance improved from a deficit of 32.4 million ECU in 1979 to a 10.9 million ECU surplus in 1986.[64] However, from 1988–1992 the EU trade balance was negative each year, growing from almost 24 billion ECU in 1988 to over 80 billion ECU in 1991.

Overall, it is believed the effect of integration on the economic performance of most EU nations has been "quite substantial and mostly positive,"[65] with it being estimated that 1972 GDP of the EU was 2.2 percent higher than it would have been without integration, while the 1981 figure was estimated at 5.9 percent. In addition to evidence of poorer performance of the EU vis-à-vis its major competitors and of the favorable impact of economic and monetary integration, national and EU authorities can consider estimates of the additional costs borne by EU business firms from the absence of an internal market. These additional costs, which are due to complex customs barriers, protectionist procurement policies, divergent product standards, and the inability of small firms to achieve economies of scale, have been estimated to add about 15 percent to total costs.[66] Meanwhile, both the real and potential benefits to be derived from further monetary and economic integration have been illustrated by the favorable performance of the EMS and studies such as the Cecchini Report.[67]

[62]Tugendhat, *Making Sense of Europe*, pp. 206, 207.

[63]Studies indicate that trade creation outweighed trade diversion by more than 5 to 1 (about $10 billion trade creation compared to under $2 billion trade diversion) for the original six EU members over the 1969–1970 period. Following enlargement to nine members, it has been estimated that trade creation increased by $28 billion versus $5 billion for trade diversion over the 1977–1978 period. Note that all figures are in current dollars. See Mordechai E. Kreinin, *International Economics*, 5th ed. (New York: Harcourt Brace Jovanovich, 1987), pp. 320–321. Concerning integration's contribution to growth, see A. J. Marques Mendes, "The Contribution of the European Community to Economic Growth," *Journal of Common Market Studies*, 24, no. 4 (June 1986), 266–270.

[64]Eurostat, *Basic Statistics of the Community*, 25th ed. (Luxembourg: Office for Official Publications of the European Communities, 1988), pp. 257–277.

[65]Mendes, *Contribution of the European Community*, p. 268.

[66]Jeffrey Harrop, *The Political Economy of Integration in the European Community* (Southampton, Great Britain: Edward Elgar), pp. 55, 56. Small firms face administrative costs and regulations when seeking to meet cross-national technical standards or to merge with firms whose owners reside within another EU member nation.

[67]Paulo Cecchini, *The European Challenge: 1992—The Benefits of a Single Market* (Hants, England: Wildwood House, 1988), p. 97.

In terms of its objectives, namely, exchange-rate stabilization and promotion of monetary cooperation among the central banks of participating EU members, the EMS was a success prior to 1992. Evidence indicates that following the introduction of the EMS in 1979 the volatility of exchange rates declined for the next 13 years. The EMS also provided a framework within which member states could more effectively pursue anti-inflationary policies. The result was that inflation rates in those member states belonging to the EMS "declined significantly, became increasingly convergent," and were less variable.[68] According to one analyst, prior to 1992 the success of the EMS had "done more than any other single European initiative to induce actual convergence and habits of cooperation in macroeconomic policy management which ten years ago seemed to be beyond our grasp."[69]

The Cecchini study estimates that the completion of the internal market will raise EU national income by about 4.5 percent, lower inflation by 6 percent, and reduce unemployment by about 1.5 percent as 1.8 million new jobs are projected to be created after 1992.[70] These indicators of performance have been influencing informal and formal attitudes regarding further integration. Slow growth and high unemployment have mobilized opinion throughout the 1980s for pan-European solutions to meet increased foreign competition, including new working rules fostering mergers and joint ventures among firms owned by EU members. The evidence that improved EU performance can ensue from integration and enlargement has stimulated the desire to integrate closer to one economy rather than to remain 15 small or medium-sized (relative to the U.S. or Japanese) open economies. An EU research unit predicts that the potential from an EMU is considerable, and that 1994–2000 performance in terms of real GDP growth and unemployment would be enhanced by member nations converging in terms of satisfying Maastrict Treaty fiscal and monetary policy criteria.[71] Analysts

[68]Frank McDonald and George Zis, "The European Monetary System: Towards 1992 and Beyond," *Journal of Common Market Studies*, 27, no. 3 (March 1989), 183. A recent empirical study, however, concludes that EMS countries experienced reduced inflation at the expense of a worsening trade-off between inflation and unemployment. See Paul De Grauwe, "The Cost of Disinflation and the European Monetary System," paper presented at the Meeting of the Money Study Group, Eighteenth Annual Oxford Conference, Oxford, September 19–21, 1989.

[69]Ludlow, "Beyond 1992," p. 19.

[70]Cecchini, *The European Challenge: 1992*, p. 97. This study was an exercise in comparative static analysis. Studies of the dynamic effects of a single market suggested greater gains in economic growth coming from increased technological change, investment, competition, and economies of scale. See Richard Baldwin, "The Growth Effects of 1992," *Economic Policy*, 9, (October 1989), 248–281. In this study Baldwin estimates the single market might permanently add 0.25 to 0.9 percent to the annual EU growth rate.

[71]It has been estimated that with convergence 1994–2000 real growth will be almost 3 percent annually, but less than 2 percent without convergence. For unemployment, convergence is predicted to bring the rate below 10 percent, but that it will continue climbing to over 11.5 percent without convergence.

argue that the Maastrict criteria, while politically motivated, serve as a useful guideline in terms of providing EU members with targets (albeit difficult to realize) for responsible monetary and fiscal policies. Stringent criteria all but assure that the EU will not achieve the EMU level of integration before its members' budgets and currencies are sound.

SUMMARY—BEHAVIOR OF THE ECONOMY.   Since 1960 the performance of the EU economy has lagged behind that of its major competitors, namely the United States, Japan, and members of the EFTA. The major problems are the high rate of unemployment; the absence of labor mobility; declining rates of investment and labor productivity; falling profitability of investment; and rising public debt, as a percentage of gross domestic product. These conditions combined with the degree of welfare programs and state intervention in economic matters throughout the EU inhibit the introduction of rapid technological changes capable of increasing labor productivity. There has been a conflict between the laissez-faire market economy rules the EU founders established as goals, with the social programs and history of state involvement which pervade nearly every EU member nation. The slowdown in economic growth since the early 1970s has exacerbated this conflict.

Two final features of the EU economy that will affect future economic and political developments are the economic effects of German unification throughout the EU and the recent surge of economic growth and development within southern European nations (e.g., Italy, Greece, Portugal, and Spain). Analysts predict that reunification of Germany will increase EU economic growth by about 0.5 percent, and that all members but West Germany will reap the benefit of higher growth without facing the burden (e.g., higher taxes and inflation) of reconstructing the East German economy.

The rates of economic growth and foreign investment experienced by "sun belt" EU members have recently exceeded those of their northern counterparts. Southern EU nations offer advantages to industrialists seeking to establish manufacturing facilities, including a large supply of labor that is generally not very militant or politically powerful, and that is willing to work for lower wages. Spain's economic growth in 1987 was the second highest in the EU, partly due to rising foreign investment by French, German, and American automobile producers as well as by AT&T, which invested $200 million in a microchip-producing facility. Some predict that after 1995, when all internal barriers to the free flow of goods and productive resources within the EU are scheduled to have been removed, the southern EU members will experience more rapid economic growth than northern EU members.

CONCLUDING REMARKS

Is the EU 15 economies, one economy, or both? The EU has yet to become a United States of Europe, and it should not yet be considered as one economy, despite the considerable rhetoric describing it as one entity with coordinated business strategies vis-à-vis the United States and Japan, a modest role for national economic goals, and a unified political structure. However, the member nations are united in their willingness to relinquish some authority to the EU level for agreed-upon common purposes believed to be better pursued at the supranational level.

In terms of principal institutions the EU is moving toward one economy, but until an EMU is established with a central bank and supranational authorities responsible for fiscal policy to organize and coordinate resource allocation, decisions will be shared between supranational institutions and national institutions. The pace of further monetary and fiscal integration after 1995 is likely to proceed slowly, for unanimous council approval (as well as national parliament ratification) will be required. In addition, national, regional, and sectoral interests will have to agree to subordinate their interests for the common interest of the EU.[72] Partly due to the number of diverse EU members and the centuries of strong nationalism, combined with the recent poor performances of EU member economies, there is not a strong political will (especially among citizens of the United Kingdom) to become more European, that is, to become one economy.

As enlargement continues, the social structure of the EU is likely to become more heterogeneous, divided along national and regional lines. Evidence indicates that factor mobility's contribution to economic growth has been negligible, so encouragement of labor migration will likely not be promoted at the EU level on those grounds. Broader migration could result in the same type of "melting pot" society created by labor migration throughout the United States, which would have implications for attitudes toward a more integrated EU under a federal government.

Perhaps the principle of subsidiarity will provide the basis for member nations and EU authorities to find a way to determine what economic activities each can perform more effectively. Many national authorities still believe that common EU policies can be implemented without transferring control over resources from 15 national governments to a central, federal government. Given the current degree of authority, the political structure of the EU is both one

---

[72]Adam Smith recognized the difficulty of removing protective measures against foreign competition, which had existed for a considerable period of time and which involved industries employing "a great multitude of hands." He argued in favor of "humanity," stating that "the freedom of trade should be restored only by slow gradations, and with a good deal of reserve and circumspection" so as to prevent sudden significant increases in unemployment. He did, however, favor their removal, arguing that competitive market adjustments would restore equilibrium in the labor market. It is such competitive adjustments, however, that most people do not wish to subject themselves to, preferring national protective measures to maintain their economic and social security.

integrated economy and 15 separate nations, with an association of states achieving unity through consenting to transfer some sovereignty and control over resources to a supranational authority. The philosophical basis for the EU working rules is also divided between the democratic social ideals held by nearly all 15 members and the EU commitment to integrate according to market principles.

Overall, the EU is unique, for it is simultaneously 15 separate and one constantly evolving supranational economy. It is a peculiar interaction of economic and political integration—each at a different stage and evolving at a different rate. The EU, while currently a federation of 15 distinguishable economies, has achieved a degree of economic (and political) integration well beyond that of any other international agency. The likelihood of accurately predicting the nature of this evolving supranational economy beyond 1995 is similar to the success rate of traditional economic forecasters. Like those who predict the weather, economic forecasters have roughly a 60 percent chance of being correct concerning the state of an economy one month into the future. Beyond that period future scenarios are anybody's guess. Those who are disappointed by the absence of a more definitive prediction might take comfort from the EU official who, recognizing that economic integration is an ambivalent, ambiguous, and partial process, stated that "[a]s the Community itself is without precedent, so the forms it will adopt are likely to be so as well."[73]

APPENDIX:
LEVELS OF
ECONOMIC INTEGRATION[74]

Economic integration is a process whereby participating economies merge economic and political rules and decision-making institutions to varying degrees. There are many forms, or levels, which economic integration can take, varying according to the type of common rules for economic behavior adopted by participating nations. The history of the EU reflects several examples of the economic integration process.

[73]Ibid., p. 230. It has also been argued that each enlargement brings a new member, new traditions, political and social preferences, interests, and economic strengths and weaknesses into the EU— thereby influencing the behavior and evolution of the EU.

[74]This appendix focuses on trading blocs established by political fiat and defined by national geographic borders. For an interesting perspective regarding the rise of the *region state* (a natural economic zone that extends across borders such as between Hong Kong and China and parts of small Asian nations) and the advantages it offers (particularly for those favoring free-enterprise zones with an absence of government intervention), see Kenichi Ohmae, "The Rise of the Region State," *Foreign Affairs*, 72, no. 2 (Spring 1993), 78–87.

There are five levels of economic integration. In increasing order of significance they include:

1. *A Free-Trade Area*   Nations abolish trade barriers among members, but each nation retains its own particular barriers vis-à-vis nonmember nations. Examples: (1) the European Free Trade Area, formed in 1960, which was initially comprised of Austria, Denmark, Norway, Portugal, Sweden, Switzerland, and the United Kingdom—all of which (with the exception of Switzerland) have joined the EU; (2) the North American Free Trade Area (NAFTA).

The United States, Canada, and Mexico formed NAFTA, which went into effect in 1994. Canada has been the chief trading partner of the United States, with Mexico third in importance (after Japan). Under the NAFTA provisions, all quotas and import restrictions were abolished as well as most tariffs. The remaining tariffs (primarily on automobile and agricultural products) will be phased out by the year 2009 at the latest. This free trade area stimulated much populist debate in the United States, with considerable fear expressed over the loss of jobs to Mexican industry. Analysis by economic experts indicates there is little to fear in this regard.[75]

First, NAFTA is primarily a tool of foreign policy with the United States seeking to assist its poorer southern neighbor. The economic impact on the United States is likely to be modest. The U.S. GNP is 9 and 25 times greater than that of Canada and Mexico, respectively. Tariffs against Canadian products have been all but eliminated since 1990, while the average against Mexican products was 4 percent before NAFTA. There will be little net change in the number of jobs gained or lost for U.S. manufacturing workers, as the losses in unskilled, low-paying and wage-intensive areas (shoes, textile, and some labor-intensive agricultural products) should be offset by U.S. gains in high technology (especially telecommunications), automobile, and financial services firms.[76] The gain in real income for the United States should be quite modest, while there is evidence that the U. S. environment (along the Mexican border) may actually improve as a result of NAFTA.

During the first quarter of 1994 (immediately as NAFTA became operative), Mexican exports to the United States rose over 22 percent while U.S. exports to Mexico increased about 15 percent. Some of this reflects previous orders that had been made in anticipation of NAFTA going into effect, and some represents the United States shifting purchases of goods such as petroleum and coffee to Mexico as a lower-cost supplier. The growth of trade reflects an acceleration of a recent trend in which U.S. imports from Mexico and exports to that nation have been rising much faster than U.S. trade with the rest of the world.

[75]For an excellent political economy analysis, see Paul Krugman, "The Uncomfortable Truth about NAFTA," *Foreign Affairs*, 72, no. 5 (November/December 1993), 13–19.

[76]For the past 25 years the number of U.S. manufacturing jobs has declined from about 19.5 million in 1970 to just over 17.5 million in 1995—although the value of manufactured goods produced has increased due to rising labor and capital productivity.

It is anticipated that the more rapidly rising import volume from Mexico will be offset in the long run by the income gains in Mexico's middle class who will, it is anticipated, purchase more U.S. products and begin to reverse the trade deficit.

2. *A Customs Union* This level of integration extends the free-trade area by incorporating common external trade barriers between member nations and the rest of the world.

3. *A Common Market* Further integration is achieved through the removal of barriers against the free flow of the factors of production (e.g., labor and capital) among member nations. Example: The European Economic Community began evolving toward becoming a common market after the Treaty of Rome in 1957. All barriers to the free internal flow of factors are expected to be removed by 1995, creating a single market.

4. *An Economic and Monetary Union* Members of a common market adopt a common currency and agree to give a supranational authority the power to establish harmonious, coordinated monetary and fiscal policies. At the Hague Summit in 1969 heads of state of EU members established as an EU goal the formation of such a union. More recently (1988) a majority of the heads of state agreed that the establishment of an EU central bank and a common currency should be seriously considered for adoption, and the 1991 Maastrict Treaty set 1999 as the completion date. As discussed earlier in this chapter, this date is optimistic.

5. *Full Economic Integration* Member nations of a monetary union relinquish some individual autonomy and form one government, which establishes and integrates the primary political and economic working rules for all members. Example: The United States since the late eighteenth century.

As an economy the EU is a unique institution. It is one intermediate stage between several national economies and one supranational economy. For the past 45 years it has been in the process of integrating both politically and economically. Currently, it is a peculiar interaction of market integration and political integration. Each type of integration is at a different stage (i.e., the degree of economic integration has proceeded further than the degree of political integration). It is noteworthy that although the extent of cooperation varies among economic and social policies, the degree of integration among EU members is beyond that of any other international agency.

There are two basic political advantages of greater, more formal interdependence where unity is achieved through acting on behalf of members' general interest while achieving maximum consensus. First, there is a lessening of tension between nations with a history of rivalry so as to decrease the possibility of war and to protect themselves from foreign invasion. Second, the individual nation's political influence is strengthened (i.e., reestablishing Europe as a political power) when such influence is expressed through a collective institution.

Economic advantages accrue through the benefits derived from free trade within an enlarged entity. These advantages include greater specialization of labor; economies of large-scale production; greater efficiency and availability of goods and services due to an increase in areawide competition; the stimulation of investment in response to the wider market, as firms move production and distribution facilities closer to the new markets; and trade creation, as the tariff-free trade within the integrated community results in more trade with new, lower-cost suppliers.

The economic benefits for a customs union are not the same as those benefits from universal free trade (see Chapter 5 for Adam Smith's and David Ricardo's arguments in favor of free trade). Formation of a customs union creates free trade among members, but a common barrier is imposed against imports from nonmember nations. The positive effect from a customs union, known as *trade creation*, stems from an increased volume of imports from member nations when the market price of a good or service within the union is less than the domestic price initially prevailing in the member nation in question. However, if trade is diverted away from lower-cost, nonmember producers (whose imports face the custom union's tariff) toward higher-cost member nation producers, *trade diversion* occurs. Whether gains from trade creation outweigh the welfare losses of trade diversion depends upon factors such as elasticities of demand and supply in the member nations and the differential in prices among trading partners. Studies have indicated that trade creation has outweighed trade diversion since the formation of the customs union in 1957.

KEY TERMS AND CONCEPTS

Common Agricultural Policy
Economic Integration
European Coal and Steel Community
European Community
European Currency Unit
European Monetary System
European Union

Maastricht Treaty
Single European Act
Supranational Institutions
Trade Creation
Trade Diversion
Treaty of Rome

QUESTIONS FOR DISCUSSION

1. What is the ECU?
2. How is the ECU related to the European Monetary System?
3. What is the procedure by which the EU undergoes enlargement?
4. Name the countries currently applying for EU membership.
5. Distinguish between an economic and monetary union and a common market.
6. Is the EU 15 economies, one economy, or both?
7. Discuss the evolution of the EU from the European Coal and Steel Community

to the common market using the evolutionary-institutional framework.

8. Explain how decisions regarding resource allocation are made by the EU's supranational institutions.

9. What does the philosophical basis of the EU have in common with the views of the reformers discussed in Chapter 12?

REFERENCES

Angresano, James, "An Evolutionary-Institutional Approach to the Study of Comparative Economies," *Journal of Economic Issues*, 23, 2 (June, 1989), 511–518.

Borchardt, Klaus-Dieter, *European Unification*, 2nd ed. Luxembourg: Office for Official Publications of the European Communities, 1987.

Bos, Marko, and Hans Nelson, "Indirect Taxation and the Completion of the Internal Market of the EC," *Journal of Common Market Studies*, 27, 1 (September 1988), 27–44.

Brewin, Christopher, "The European Community: A Union of States Without Unity of Government," *Journal of Common Market Studies*, 26, 1 (September 1987), 1–23.

Brewin, Christopher, and Richard McAllister, "Annual Review of the Activities of the European Communities in 1988," *Journal of Common Market Studies*, 27, 4 (June, 1989), 323–357.

Cecchini, Paolo, with Michael Catinat, and Alexis Jacquemin, *The European Challenge: 1992—The Benefits of a Single Market*. Hants, England: Wildwood House, 1988.

Commons, John R., *Institutional Economics*, Madison, WS: University of Wisconsin Press, 1959.

Corbett, Richard, "Testing the New Procedures: The European Parliament's First Experience with Its New 'Single Act' Powers," *Journal of Common Market Studies*, 27, 4 (June 1989), 359–384.

Curtis, Michael, *Western European Integration*. New York: Harper & Row, 1965.

De Grauwe, Paul, "The Cost of Disinflation and the European Monetary System," paper presented at the Meeting of the Money Study Group, Eighteenth Annual Oxford Conference, Oxford, September 19–21, 1989.

"The EC's Competition Policy," *The Economist*, March 14, 1993, pp. 55–56.

Eichengreen, Barry, and Jeffry Frieden, "The Political Economy of European Monetary Unification: An Analytical Introduction," *Economics & Politics*, 5, 2 (July 1993), 85–104.

Emerson, Michael, "The Economics of 1992," *European Economy*, 35. Brussels: Commission of the European Communities, Directorate-General for Economic and Financial Affairs (March 1988).

European Economic and Monetary Union, Luxembourg: Office for Publications of the European Communities, 1981.

European Economy: The Economics of 1992, Brussels: Commission of the European Communities, no. 35 (March 1989).

Eurostat, *Basic Statistics of the Community*, 25th ed. Luxembourg: Office for Official Publications of the European Communities, 1988.

Garrett, Geoffrey, "The Politics of Maastricht," *Economics and Politics*, 5, 2 (July 1993), 105–123.

Hartley, W., *The Politics of the Common Market*. Englewood Cliffs, NJ: Prentice-Hall, 1967.

Harrop, Jeffrey, *The Political Economy of Integration in the European Community*. Hants, England: Edward Elgar, 1989.

Holmes, Garrick, ed., "European Trends: Regional Monitor, 1993 1st Quarter," London: *The Economist Intelligence Unit*, 1993.

Kreinin, Mordechai E., *International Economics*, 5th ed. New York: Harcourt Brace Jovanovich, 1987.

Krugman, Paul, "The Uncomfortable Truth About NAFTA," *Foreign Affairs*, 72, 5 (November/December 1993), 13–19.

Lodge, Juliet. "The Single European Act and the New Legislative Cooperation Procedure: A Critical Analysis," *Journal of European Integration*, 11, 1 (Fall 1987), 5–28.

Martin, Lisa L., "International and Domestic Institutions in the EMU Process," *Economics and Politics*, 5, 2 (July 1993), 125–144.

McDonald, Frank, and George Zis, "The European Monetary System: Towards 1992 and Beyond," *Journal of Common Market Studies*, 27, 3 (March 1989), 183–202.

Mendes, A. J. Marques, "The Contribution of the European Community to Economic Growth," *Journal of Common Market Studies*, 24, 4 (June 1986), 261–277.

Minford, Patrick, "The Path to Monetary Union in Europe," *The World Economy*, 16, 1 (January 1993), 17–28.

Munshull, G. N., *The New Europe*. London: Hodder and Stoughton, 1985.

Nicoll, William, "Paths for European Unity," *Journal of Common Market Studies*, 23, 3 (March 1985), 199–206.

Noel, Emile, *Working Together: The Institutions of the European Community*. Luxembourg: Office for Official Publications for the European Communities, 1985.

Ohmae, Kenichi, "The Rise of the Region State," *Foreign Affairs*, 72, 2 (Spring 1993), 78–87.

Pinder, John, "The Political Economy of Integration in Europe," *Journal of Common Market Studies*, 25, 1 (September 1986), 1–14.

Polanyi, Karl, *The Great Transformation*. Boston: Beacon Press, 1957.

Portes, Richard, "EMS and EMU After the Fall," *The World Economy*, 16, 1 (January 1993), 1–16.

Swann, Dennis, *The Economics of the Common Market*, 4th ed. Middlesex, England: Penguin Books, 1981.

Taylor, Paul, *The Limits of European Integration*. New York: Columbia University Press, 1983.

Tsoukalis, Loukas, *The European Community and Its Mediterranean Enlargement*. London: George Allen & Unwin, 1981.

_____, "Looking into the Crystal Ball," *Journal of Common Market Studies*, 21, 1 & 2 (September/December 1982), 229–244.

Tugendhat, Christopher, *Making Sense of Europe*. New York: Columbia University Press, 1988.

Van Kersbergen, Kees, and Bertjan Verbeek, "The Politics of Subsidiarity in the European Union," *Journal of Common Market Studies*, 32, 2 (June,1994), 215–236.

Wallace, Hellen, "European Governance in Turbulent Times," *Journal of Common Market Studies*, 31, 3 (September 1993), 293–304.

Zis, George, "The European Monetary System 1979–84: An Assessment," *Journal of Common Market Studies*, 23, 1 (September 1984), 45–71.

15

THE PHILOSOPHICAL BASIS FOR COMMAND OVER A SOCIAL ECONOMY, AND THE CASE OF THE SOVIET UNION

1928–1989

OBJECTIVES

1. Explain the factors which influenced Karl Marx's vision of the ideal economy and conception of the society in which he lived.
2. Outline and discuss Marx's theory of history and model of *capitalism's* demise.
3. Discuss the features of the economies (*crude communism* and *true communism*) that Marx predicted would supersede *capitalism*.
4. Explain the historical legacy and attitudes of the Soviet Union which contributed to the establishment of principal institutions and working rules consistent with the philosophies of Karl Marx, Vladimir Lenin, and Joseph Stalin.
5. Explain how central planning influenced the organization of decision making, ownership and control of resources, and the social process for coordinating production and distribution activities.
6. Discuss the main features of the 1985–1989 reforms.
7. Outline the evolution of the Russian economy since 1989.
8. In what respects does the legacy of the pre-1989 economy influence efforts to reform the Russian economy?

INTRODUCTION TO CHAPTERS 15–18

The pace and extent of reforms characteristic of all Central and Eastern European (CEE) economies, as well as China, since 1989 require a slightly different presentation than for other economies discussed earlier. This section begins with a discussion of the philosophical basis upon which the former state-controlled social economies were based (Chapter 15). While this philosophy remains the basis for only two small economies (Cuba and North Korea—both of which may follow the CEE path in the near future), its imprint upon the historical legacy of the transforming CEE nations and China is significant. This has been particularly true regarding the political structures of these nations, for in many cases former members of the Communist Party recently have been freely elected to serve as political and economic authorities—with some public sentiment to reintroduce certain pre-1989 institutions and working rules.

The case of the former Soviet Union follows later in this chapter, illustrating the nature of a command over social economy and introducing the complex issue of transformation as it has applied to Russia in the 1990s. Transformation issues as they have affected the CEE economies, including Russia, are presented in Chapter 16, followed by a detailed analysis of the Hungarian economy (Chapter 17). Chapter 18 focuses on characteristics of China's transformation and reasons for its being the world's fastest growing economy since 1979.

As indicated by the subsequent performance of these economies, results have been mixed. It is apparent the initial (i.e., 1989) belief that the transformation from a "planned" to a "market" economy would be relatively quick and not too painful (a belief inherent in recommended transformation policy such as the "shock therapy" program) was unrealistic—reflecting the simplistic dichotomy perspective discussed in Chapter 1.

The following four chapters provide a vivid illustration of the usefulness of the evolutionary-institutional theory. In response to poor performance and the introduction of more flexible political structures, these economies radically have altered their principal institutions and corresponding working rules. The evolving economies contain institutions and rules that reflect the respective nations' historical legacy. While these economies can be expected to evolve in a more democratic direction with greater reliance upon private enterprise, the nature of CEE and China's economies will follow an unknown path in response to the new institutions and rules adopted, priorities and policies of their authorities, and the external economic environment (such as trade relations with the European Union, technical and financial assistance from wealthier nations, and activities of foreign investors in these nations). They currently are not, nor can they be expected to be in the near future, market economies simply because the philosophical basis of Karl Marx is no longer their beacon.

KARL MARX

During the 1820s, the economic and social impact of industrialization on the working class, especially in England and France, aroused criticism of the existing political, economic, and social order in some intellectual circles. Over the next 60 years this criticism would be articulated into a long, intricate, and powerful argument that would become the philosophical basis for the economies of nations inhabited by about one third of the world's population during much of the twentieth century. Due to the strength, logic, and integrated features of his theories, Karl Marx was the leading proponent of this argument.

While Marx was not "infallible" as an historian, philosopher, or economist, his views are invaluable, and "unavoidable,"[1] to anyone seeking to understand the dynamic field of comparative economies. The following presentation focuses on Marx as the intellectual who provided the basis for the command over a social economy (CSE). His desire for radical transformation of the mid-nineteenth century laissez-faire market economy (LFME) into his vision of an ideal society ("true communism") was intense, and his philosophy encompasses his interpretation of history, conception of society, and economic theories.

In addition to the social and economic conditions prevalent throughout northern Europe during his formative years (i.e., the first half of the nineteenth century), Marx was influenced by George Wilhelm Friedrich Hegel's philosophy, the classical economists, and French utopian socialists (e.g., Charles Fourier, Henri Comte De Saint-Simon). The social and economic conditions prevalent during the early years of England's LFME (circa 1840–1860) shaped Marx's conceptualization of the behavior and performance of such an economy. He witnessed poor living and factory conditions—especially the long hours and low wages endured by nearly all workers, including children. He also witnessed the owners of the means of production enjoying, from his viewpoint, a disproportionate share of the value of the goods produced by the industrial working class.

From Hegel, Marx developed a theory of history that was based upon conflict between the property-owning class and the working class. This evolutionary theory held that economic forces shaped the consciousness of society's classes as well as the principal institutions through which production and distribution decisions are made. The classical economists, especially David Ricardo, provided Marx with a basis for departure and analysis. Specifically and central to Marx's analysis of the dynamic behavior of economies were the labor theory of value and the classical school's abstract method for analyzing the interrelationship among economic factors (e.g., land, labor, output) and quantifying these relationships in economic laws.

Marx believed that his mission was to inform the proletariat (propertyless working class) that history was on their side. He sought to further their cause by assisting them to form workers' organizations and by teaching them his evolutionary theory of societal change. In doing so Marx believed he was planting the seeds for the "inevitable" working-class revolution. Central to his teaching was an explanation of what he called the "laws of motion of capitalism." Assisted by Friedrich Engels, Marx applied economic analysis to his theory of history,

---

[1]Robert L. Heilbroner, *The Worldly Philosophers*, 6th ed. (New York: W. W. Norton, 1986), p. 170.

which included his belief that societies continually evolve by the process of dialectical materialism (discussed later), to the working class that *capitalism*, thus, was only a stage in the evolution to higher economic orders, namely *crude communism* (which some refer to as *socialism*), and ultimately *true communism*. (Marx's use of the term *capitalism* is based on his description of England's industrial laissez-faire market economy in the early nineteenth century, which was characterized by a highly concentrated ownership and control of productive resources by a small bourgeoisie class.) Marx's philosophy regarding the evolution of these higher stages is presented as the interaction of many social, political, and economic factors. This complex but logical argument follows from his conception of society and human behavior, and of the relationship of economic factors to noneconomic factors (e.g., social and political structures, culture). Marx's theory of history focuses on his model of capitalism's demise, and he projects a model of crude communism and a vision of true communism.

MARX'S CONCEPTION OF SOCIETY

Marx argued that society consists of an economic base that functions within a superstructure of legal, cultural, social (e.g., the family), and philosophical activities and thought. The superstructure provides the informal and formal working rules that bind society together. Included within the superstructure are a system of education, laws of inheritance, literature, music, and works of art—all of which were supervised by the state for the purpose of perpetuating the social and political structure by maintaining existing working rules, which at that time were "the sanctity and justice of capitalist property ownership."[2] Contemporary authorities were, in Marx's view, instruments of the capitalist class—those members of society who owned and controlled the primary means of acquiring and accumulating wealth, i.e., capital. Under the LFME, these authorities introduced working rules (such as those governing the educational system) that reinforced acceptance and respect for the working rules that perpetuated a skewed distribution of wealth—especially rules protecting private property. In reference to the relationship between the property-owning class and the authorities, Marx argued that "[t]he bourgeoisie has agglomerated population, centralized means of production, and has concentrated property in a few hands. The necessary consequence of this was political centralization . . . one nation, with one government, one code of laws, one national class interest, one frontier, and one customs tariff."[3] In effect it was the bourgeoisie who established, modified, and interpreted all working rules. Consequently, in Marx's view of society not

[2]William Ebenstein and Edwin Fogelman, *Today's Isms*, 8th ed. (Englewood Cliffs, NJ: Prentice-Hall, 1980), p. 3.
[3]Karl Marx and Friedrich Engels, *Manifesto of the Communist Party* (New York: International Publishers, 1971), p. 13.

only economic concepts but political, social, and cultural concepts as well were a reflection of the bourgeoisie's dominant position over the working class.

The economic base was comprised of the forces of production and relations of production. The forces included the main instruments of production such as labor skills, tools, and capital. These forces, however, were not considered simply as economic concepts. The technical abilities and views of the property-owning and working classes, including their view toward the philosophical basis and working rules of the economy, were a reflection of the culture of their society. The relations of production included social and working relations between people who interacted through society's principal institutions. These relations "necessarily embrace[d] the legal and political, [religious,] and social bonds that legitimate and enforce the roles of different classes."[4]

From Marx's perspective society was divided into two classes (the bourgeoisie and the proletariat), which were engaged continually in class struggle. Their struggle was a function of the conflict between the dynamic forces of production and the relatively static relations of production (e.g., principal institutions of the economy). This belief follows from Marx's view that a person is a product of his or her material conditions and social relations, whereas under the philosophical basis of an LFME, a person was conceived as an isolated individual in pursuit of his or her own self-interest. Marx believed in the perfectibility of behavior, and that since behavior was a result of society's material conditions and principal institutions, reforming these conditions and institutions (i.e., replacing the existing economy with a new economy under a different philosophical basis, authorities, and working rules) would lead to different behavior.

MARX'S THEORY OF HISTORY

Marx offered a materialist interpretation of history in which social, political, and philosophical aspects of society are conditioned by the forces and relations of production. He argued that the forces and relations of production, taken together, constitute the economic base of society. This base, in turn, generates a corresponding legal and political superstructure. The consciousness of society will correspond to the existing economic base and superstructure. Marx argued that the stimulus for change throughout history could be found in the interaction between the forces and relations of production, with the forces of production being the dynamic element. This theory is referred to as dialectical materialism, which Marx developed, in part, from the philosophy of Hegel. In particular, Marx accepted the Hegelian notion that every ideal and force bred its opposite, so that history "was nothing but the expression of this flux of conflicting and resolving ideas and forces. Change—dialectical change—was imminent in human affairs."[5]

[4]Robert L. Heilbroner, *Marxism: For and Against* (New York: W. W. Norton, 1980) p. 65.
[5]Heilbroner, *The Worldly Philosophers*, pp. 142, 143.

From Marx's point of view there is historical causation; that is societies are continually evolving toward some higher stage of development, the ultimate stage being true communism. The process of change is both evolutionary and revolutionary, initiated by a change in an economic factor which thereby alters the mode of production. The process intensifies class struggle, and there are changes in the relations of production as a new social structure emerges. Those classes threatened by change are pitted against those who stand to improve their social, political, and economic position following change. Class struggle ensues, and the relations of production change as a result, leading to changes in the superstructure. Marx described this process (what he referred to as the "laws of motion" of society) for evolution from "feudalism" to "capitalism" and from "capitalism" to "crude communism."

The industrial revolution began in the early eighteenth century, introducing new technology that was incompatible with the existing feudal society. In particular, a radically different mode of production was made possible through the development of a new principal institution—the factory. Higher output, more trade, and lower prices conflicted with the handicraft scheme of production and the relative importance of the feudal manor. The conflict between the rising capitalist class and the artisans and landowners resulted in changes in the relations of production. After a long struggle, the power held by artisans and landlords diminished, with greater economic and therefore political power being concentrated within the capitalist class. Meanwhile many agricultural tenants and handicraft workers became members of the industrial working class, partly due to the effect of enclosures. The end result was the industrial revolution and changes in the working rules, resulting in a new superstructure with a capitalist economic base—the LFME. The enclosures, poor laws, gold standard, and trade legislation were informal and formal working rules that emphasized and maintained free trade, private property, and the capitalist class.

Thus, feudalism evolved into what Marx called capitalism. He accepted the existence of the latter as an inevitable, necessary stage in the evolution toward the highest stage of society—true communism. He praised the dynamic capitalist society, with its emphasis upon accumulation of wealth by individuals who were consumed with the profit motive, for providing the means for the proletariat to enjoy a higher standard of living once they became authorities and could assume control over the means of production. In (considering the source) what has been one of the most glowing praises of capitalism, Marx evaluated the performance of England between about 1750 and the late 1840s in the following manner.

> The bourgeoisie, during its rule of scarce one hundred years, has created more massive and more colossal productive forces than have all preceding generations together. Subjection of nature's forces to man, machinery, application of chemistry to industry and agriculture, steam-navigation, railways, electric telegraphs, clearing of whole continents for cultivation, canalization of rivers, whole populations conjured out of the

ground—what earlier century had even a presentiment that such productive forces slumbered in the lap of social labor?[6]

However, Marx argued that the conflict between the bourgeoisie and proletariat classes would increase during the more advanced stages of capitalism. This was inevitable, for the desire for accumulation on the part of the property-owning class would result in greater disparities in wealth between them and an oppressed proletariat. The workers, in turn, would be brought together into urban industrial areas, hastening the inevitable overthrow of the existing mode of production, relations of production, and superstructure that maintained them: This is the process of capitalism's demise.

MARX'S MODEL OF CAPITALISM'S DEMISE

The process by which capitalism would develop and then be overthrown is depicted in Figure 15-1. The schematic outlines Marx's interpretation and analysis of capitalism's laws of motion. Due to the dialectic nature of the process, at each stage the degree of class conflict is increased. The process begins with the exploitation of labor.

EXPLOITATION OF LABOR.   The transformation from capitalism to crude communism occurs over decades of economic development during which the means of production expand while the proletariat eventually unites and initiates a political revolution to overthrow the existing superstructure. To illustrate exploitation, Marx took David Ricardo's labor theory of value and articulated it further. He argued that since the only social cost of producing products is labor, it is the amount of labor time embodied in producing a commodity that measured the value of a commodity. In response to the question of how differences in skills could be measured, Marx argued that those differences would be reflected in the quantity of output workers produced.

Exploitation arises because of the difference between wages received by a worker and the value of the commodities that worker produced. This difference, or profit, Marx referred to as surplus value, which he claimed the capitalists expropriate from the proletariat for the purpose of enjoying a higher standard of living and accumulating more capital. Marx observed that the capitalist has the advantage during the wage bargaining process, and seeks to prosper through paying workers less than the value of their output. Workers can only sell their labor power, while the capitalist controls the product of that labor power. Thus, the proletariat toils while the bourgeoisie hold claims (i.e., private property) to

---

[6]Marx and Engels, *Manifesto of the Communist Party*, pp. 13, 14.

ownership of the primary means of production—claims that are sanctioned and maintained by the superstructure. Such a scheme of social relations exacerbates the conflict between the two classes, while each commodity produced represents the "congelation of forces locked in combat, not in cooperation."[7] This exploitation of labor produces two immediate effects: capital accumulation and an unequal distribution of income.

ACCUMULATION OF CAPITAL AND A HIGHLY SKEWED DISTRIBUTION OF INCOME. In order to continue to prosper and to meet competition, capitalists compete by introducing labor-saving technology in the form of capital. They are able to invest in capital because, through exploitation of labor, they receive a surplus value (i.e., profits). In other words, the capitalists extract surplus value and use that income to accumulate more capital. In Marx's dialectical theory, the accumulation of capital by a private owner means that capital, rather than a physical entity, is a "social relation of domination, an expression of the hierarchy of ['capitalist'] class structure."[8] Meanwhile, the distribution of income is highly unequal, and the degree of inequality increases over the decades of capitalist development as some owners of capital (of less efficient enterprises) and all workers suffer from the effects of capital accumulation and an unequal distribution of income under working rules by which the means of production are privately owned.

Figure 15-1 Marx's Model of Capitalism's Development and Demise

---

Exploitation of Labor
(labor theory of value; surplus value)

Capital Accumulation   **Skewed Distribution of Income**

Falling Rate of Profit   **Unemployment**   **Business Cycles**
            (substitute capital for labor)   (lack of purchasing power)

Centralization of Capital and   **Reserve Army of the Unemployed and Immiseration**
Concentration of Wealth   **of the Proletariat**
                                              (alienation; organize and unite)

Increased Class Conflict

Social Revolution

FALLING RATE OF PROFIT, UNEMPLOYMENT, AND BUSINESS CYCLES.   According to Marx, capitalists compete by introducing labor-saving capital, seeking to avoid an upward wage drift. Lower interest rates and profit rates would ensue because labor is the only source of profit; thus, displacing workers (thereby creating

[7]Heilbroner, *Marxism: For and Against*, p. 105.
[8]Ibid., p. 117.

unemployment) drives profits down by replacing the profitable factor of production with capital that is, according to the labor theory of value, nonprofitable. In addition, substituting capital for labor exacerbates the severity of business cycles (capitalist crises) due to a growing inadequacy of purchasing power and the uncertain rate at which investment will occur. Marx disagreed with Jean-Baptiste Say's law of markets, arguing that this law was "tautological" and relevant only under special, basic circumstances.[9] Marx did not believe that those who sold a good or service would necessarily purchase other goods and services within a short period of time, or that as the interval between receipt of income from a sale and another purchase increased, the likelihood of a business crisis grew.

The dialectic nature of the process by which capitalism develops and then suffers demise is further illustrated by the effect of the falling rate of profit on the extent of exploitation. Using the following equation

$$R' = \frac{\text{labor (\# of people employed) x (output per worker – wage)}}{\text{total cost of capital + total wage bill}}$$

where R' is the rate of return on inventory turnover, Marx said that as capitalists, competing with one another, purchase more capital, the total cost of capital increases. In order to maintain R' either the difference between output per worker and the wage must increase, or wages must decline, while the same output per worker is maintained. In either case the degree of exploitation increases. Over time, unemployment keeps rising (as capital is substituted for labor), while business cycles become more severe—partly due to the growing lack of purchasing power among the proletariat.

CENTRALIZATION OF CAPITAL, CONCENTRATION OF WEALTH, AND RESERVE ARMY OF UNEMPLOYED.   One outcome of the business cycles is that larger firms take over smaller, less successful enterprises. The larger firms prosper further from taking advantage of greater economies of scale. In the process of capital accumulation, the number of unemployed becomes a large, reserve army waiting to be recalled to work or to replace those already employed (who were unable or unwilling to work at the prevailing wage and working conditions). The existence of this army, among other effects, would keep wages at a subsistence level. Marx believed that as the severity of the cycles increased, ownership and control over capital and wealth are further concentrated within a shrinking class of powerful capitalists, while the degree of alienation within the proletariat increases.

The concept of alienation is central to Marx's model of capitalism's demise. Alienation is the result of conflict between the proletariat and bourgeoisie in the work process. Workers sell their labor power but have no control over the

[9]Jacob User and Stanley L. Brue, *The Evolution of Economic Thought* (San Diego: Harcourt, Brace, and Jovanovich, 1988), p. 183.

product that their efforts produce. Since the capitalists retain ownership and control over commodities produced, workers become alienated from their output, as well as from the capital they work to create, from each other (as they compete with one another for favors from their employer in the form of wages and other benefits), and ultimately become alienated from themselves as they lose personal identity. Overall, workers increasingly become indifferent and hostile toward their work, fellow workers, and their employer. According to Marx, in a "capitalist society" the proletariat "have lost their understanding and control of the world around them and have, in the process, been stunted and perverted into something less than full human beings."[10]

The main sources of alienation are private property and exploitation. Since ownership and control of private property become more concentrated and the extent of alienation increases during capitalism's development, immiseration of the proletariat is inevitable. That is, exploitation and alienation drives workers to organize and unite—exacerbating the growing tension between them and the bourgeoisie.

CLASS CONFLICT AND SOCIAL REVOLUTION.   Ultimately, there is a revolutionary proletariat movement against the existing social and political structures that maintain working rules perpetuating capitalism. Marx believed his mission was to inform the proletariat about the laws of motion of the industrial society in which they lived, hoping to free them from capitalist domination. This freedom will be achieved, he argued, at a very advanced stage of technological development when class conflicts reach such a height that a social revolution, either peaceful or violent, will be led by the proletariat. The working classes' numbers would have been increased by the industrialization of their society. Such a process is inevitable due to the scientific socialism of Marx, who argued that his theory of history supported the inevitable class conflicts that would end in revolution. In his words,

> Hand in hand with this . . . expropriation of many capitalists by a few, other developments take place on an ever-expanding scale, such as the growth of the co-operative form of the labor process, the conscious technical application of science, the planned exploitation of the soil, the transformation of the means of labor into forms in which they can be used in common, the economizing of all means of production by their use as the means of production of combined, socialized labor, the entanglement of all peoples in the net of the world market, and, with this, the growth of the international character of the capitalist regime. Along with the constant decrease in the number of capitalist magnates, who usurp and monopolize all the advantages of this process of transformation, the mass

[10]John G. Gurley, *Challengers to Capitalism: Marx, Lenin, Stalin, and Mao* (New York: W. W. Norton, 1979), p. 42.

of misery, oppression, slavery, degradation and exploitation grows; but with this there also grows the revolt of the working class, a class constantly increasing in numbers, and trained, united and organized by the very mechanism of the capitalist process of production. The monopoly of capital becomes a fetter upon the mode of production which has flourished alongside and under it. The centralization of the means of production and the socialization of labor reach a point at which they become incompatible with their capitalist integument [outer cover]. The integument is burst asunder. The knell of capitalist private property sounds. The expropriators are expropriated.[11]

MARX'S MODEL OF SOCIALISM

The historical context from which socialism (what Marx referred to as "crude communism") will emerge consists of the final stage of capitalism's demise. This is a period when people's consciousness (or informal rules) has not been raised to a level consistent with acceptance of the philosophical basis of true communism. In particular, under crude communism the set of relations of production would include working rules based upon the belief that income differentials were deemed necessary to motivate workers during this stage—in other words, "from each according to his ability, to each according to his labor."[12] Marx believed that the highest form of society (i.e., true communism) would only be possible when there was widespread acceptance of working rules that would eliminate differences in workers' incomes. At this point the prevailing informal rule would be "from each according to his ability, to each according to his needs."

The central feature of the philosophical basis of crude communism was the belief that private property should be abolished. Cooperation would replace competition, with emphasis placed upon the development of all individuals instead of upon the maximization of the market value of goods and services produced. Under the new relations of production, individuals associate within institutions whose purpose is to produce goods and services that provide social utility as determined by those selected to plan economic activities.

The social structure would evolve toward a classless society. Marx believed this could be accomplished through socially provided education, abolition of the distinction between rural and urban areas, and changes in the working rules for the economy, which would eliminate exploitation and

---

[11]Karl Marx, *Capital*, Volume I, p. 929, in Heilbroner, *Marxism: For and Against*, p. 126.

[12]See John E. Elliott, *Comparative Economic Systems* (Belmont, CA: Wadsworth Publishing, 1985), p. 246. Workers would not receive money, but would be given a "certificate" at the workplace specifying the quantity of labor provided. This certificate has value in the sense that a worker "draws from the social stocks of means of consumption as much as costs the same amount of labour." Taken from Karl Marx, *Selected Works*, Volume II (New York: International Publishers, 1932).

alienation through the abolition of private property and development of new principal institutions not under the control of a small, property-owning class. Since surplus value would no longer exist, the standard of living of the proletariat would rise well above the subsistence level characteristic of the capitalist society.

A new political structure would be established once political and economic power had been wrested from the bourgeoisie. By forbidding private ownership and control of the means of production, no individuals or small property-owning class could significantly affect the superstructure by translating their economic power into political power. There would be a dictatorship of the proletariat in which worker representatives would be the authorities, charged with pursuing collective interests. Controlled by the workers, the state would be responsible to the proletariat who comprise a large majority of the population. While Marx did not articulate either a clear process of transformation or specific features of the new political structure, Engels's description of the political structure of this stage of society is similar to the structure of contemporary (i.e., late twentieth century) parliamentary democracies.

In addition to political institutions, the institutions directly responsible for the production and distribution of goods and services would be similar in nature to contemporary Swedish cooperatives (see Chapter 13). Organization of decision making would be both centralized and decentralized. Plans for establishing social goals and broad means to satisfy them would be drawn up in a centralized manner, while decision making on the enterprise level would be decentralized in the form of collective worker control.

The means of production (especially capital and land) would be owned and controlled socially (i.e., by the workers through state supervision). In addition, rights of inheritance would be abolished, income earners would face steep progressive tax rates, property of emigrants would be confiscated, and the state would control ownership and allocation of credit institutions. Everyone would be expected to work. Control of communication and transportation would be from the state level. Overall, Marx believed these working rules would eliminate exploitation of the proletariat. In addition, a social surplus would be generated to provide funds for investment and for goods that would be consumed collectively.

The social process for coordinating production and distribution decisions would be a combination of central planning (to focus on investment) and democratic control by workers of individual enterprises. Meanwhile, the profit motive and free markets would be eliminated as means to coordinate economic activities. That Marx's writings lack specific treatment of the coordinating mechanism is partly due to his conviction that crude communism would only emerge in an advanced capitalist nation. Consequently, he did not foresee the need for a society at the stage of crude communism to make significant sacrifices for the purpose of rapidly expanding the means of production (as was the case for every command over a social economy following the consolidation of political power by a communist government).

Under crude communism Marx predicted that the performance of the economy would be superior to that under capitalism. Due to social ownership, the elimination of wasteful competition, and a more equal distribution of income, capitalist crises in the form of severe fluctuations in the rates of growth, inflation, and unemployment would be diminished, if not eliminated. Workers would be less alienated, for they would be the central figures in cooperative planning and the execution of production and distribution decisions, as well as the social owners of all they produced. Healthier, more stimulated workers in an economy characterized by full employment would contribute to higher rates of economic growth than occurred under capitalism. One product of higher growth rates would be that more goods that could be collectively consumed would be available, with a declining need for goods exchanged through traditional markets. In the process, the satisfaction of social rather than individual needs would be emphasized.

According to the dialectical theory of history, institutional change would gradually occur, primarily as class distinctions disappeared, which Marx believed was inevitable following the abolition of private property, and the state as an institution of central control "withered away." The two factors that would enable true communism to emerge would be the superior performance of the crude communism economy and the change in consciousness that would follow from changes in the workers' material conditions and cooperative social institutions (e.g., full employment, higher standard of living, education) as well as their ability to enjoy more leisure time.

MARX'S VISION OF TRUE COMMUNISM

In Marx's writings specific features of this ultimate stage of society are not described in detail. He offers a vision of a future society, not a blueprint for a real economy. He predicted that true communism would evolve as part of the process of dialectical materialism during the highest stages of crude communism when technology was advanced, workers were motivated for affiliative rather than achievement purposes, and feelings of alienation had been eliminated. The new society consequently would reap the benefits of industrialization without bearing the social costs endured under capitalism (e.g., exploitation, alienation).

The social structure would be a classless society, for status differentials will have disappeared. Human beings will fully develop in terms of achieving self-realization. They will be free, and collectively in control of the political, economic, and social institutions. The political structure does not feature authorities separated in rank and status from their constituents. Rather, representatives of the proletariat would perform purely administrative functions. In Marx's ideal society "[t]he Communists do not form a separate party opposed to other working-class parties. They have no interests separate and apart from those of the proletariat as a whole."[13]

---

[13]Marx and Engels, *Manifesto of the Communist Party*, p. 22.

Ownership and control of what Marx referred to as "bourgeois property" would be abolished, for no property would be acquired through private ownership of capital. Community ownership and control would ensure that exploitation was eliminated, and that production was for collective purposes. Concerning specific working rules and institutions for coordinating production and distribution decisions, Marx and Engels do not address resource allocation methods for true communism in their writings.

Marx did provide, however, views regarding activities of labor. The division of labor will be replaced with a system whereby individuals become adept at a variety of occupations through education and improved technology. This would enable workers to contribute to the production process by engaging in tasks at different branches of different industries (e.g., hunting, fishing, education, farming, production) according to their natural and acquired abilities, rather than having to specialize in a particular task.[14] Under true communism, labor (i.e., a person's contribution to the total output) would not determine the distribution of necessities. Rather, affiliative consciousness would result from changes in the forces and relations of production, making need-based distribution acceptable to everyone.

Such a stage of true communism would be characterized by a favorable (from Marx's viewpoint) performance of the economy. Due to technological advances labor will become more productive, while work will be more enjoyable in a cooperative environment where workers are not alienated from the product they produce. Greater productivity and affluence would enable people to take advantage of publicly provided education as well as more leisure time. Class conflict will cease to exist due to the abolition of private property and competition (which, in turn, eliminates exploitation, alienation, and severe business cycles). Due to society having become united and classless, the collective will can shape its own institutions and working rules.

Overall, under true communism Marx optimistically held that

> [c]rime would disappear, the span of life would increase, brotherhood and cooperation would inculcate a new morality, scientific progress would grow by leaps and bounds. Above all, with . . . ["true communism" existing world wide], war, the greatest blight of humankind, and its twin, nationalism, would have no place.[15]

CONCLUDING REMARKS

No economy has evolved from an advanced capitalist state to a crude communist state as Marx predicted. However, his philosophy either was or remains the core of

---

[14]For further reading, see Elliott, *Comparative Economic Systems*, p. 248.

[15]Roy L. Macridis, *Contemporary Political Ideologies* (Boston: Little, Brown, and Company, 1983), p. 209.

the philosophical basis of many nations (e.g., former Soviet Union, China, Cuba, Hungary) which were relatively undeveloped at the time authorities sympathetic to Marx's views rose to power. These authorities used Marx's philosophy as a justification for new working rules—especially rules pertaining to the organization of decision making, ownership and control of resources, and social process for economic coordination. In each of these nations the Marxian philosophical basis was supplemented by contributions from ruling authorities such as Vladimir Lenin, Joseph Stalin, and Mikhail Gorbachev in the Soviet Union, and Mao Tse Tung and Deng Xiaoping in China. These hybrid philosophical bases, as well as the other components of the CSEs of selected Central and Eastern European nations, Hungary, and China are presented later and in Chapters 16–18.

THE SOVIET ECONOMY: 1928–1989

INTRODUCTION

The Soviet Union has been one focal point of the most rapid, widespread, and significant transformation of economies in history.[16] The economic reforms currently occurring in CEE surpass the events of the 1917–1945 period, which witnessed the abandonment of the laissez-faire market economy and development of the alternative economies (discussed in Chapters 7–14) as well as the command over a social economy (CSE). Every CEE nation has been undergoing major political and economic reform since 1989, and in most cases the break from the Marxian philosophical basis and the working rules of a CSE are on the verge of being complete, even if the establishment of new economies is not. This section will evaluate the Soviet economy from 1928 to 1989 as *the* primary example of a CSE, then focus upon the dramatic reform movement through the middle of 1990. Undoubtedly as you read this chapter, additional reforms and perhaps a completely new economy (i.e., new philosophical basis, social and political structure, principal institutions, and working rules for the behavior of the economy) will have become established in Russia (and perhaps in the former Soviet republics). On the other hand, if poor performance of the economy continues, the reforms may be blamed and a backlash of conservatism may result in the reestablishment of previous working rules and institutions.

---

[16]The official name Union of Soviet Socialist Republics (USSR, or Soviet) was not adopted until 1924. For events occurring prior to that time, the nation will be referred to as Russia.

HISTORICAL LEGACY AND
CONTEXT: 1917–1928

Prior to 1860, the Russian economy had many characteristics common to England's feudal economy, followed by a period of industrialization after 1860. By 1917, although the Russian economy had developed beyond the stage of a contemporary underdeveloped country, the nation's per capita income was low, and the economy was very backward compared to the Western capitalist powers. The nation had nevertheless become the fifth most industrialized nation in the world in terms of total industrial production; there were well-trained factory managers, scientists, engineers, and technicians. And the agricultural sector had developed to the extent that peasants were capable of exporting their produce outside of their villages and Russia as well. However, a large majority of the population (about 80 percent) remained illiterate peasants.

In 1917, there was political unity within the revolutionary Bolshevik government with control centered in Moscow, although czarist forces maintained control of the countryside. The Bolshevik leaders needed to introduce policies which would further their ability to win the revolution. Several factors induced the Bolsheviks to believe that they could introduce working rules consistent with the Marxian philosophical basis and propel the predominantly peasant society into the stage of crude communism: (1) They possessed the ability to exert control over regions their military forces held. (2) The Russians feared the outside world due to their history of being invaded by foreign powers. (3) The Russian people were traditionally hardy, patient, able to endure difficult living conditions, and generally willing to be led rather than to take the initiative. (4) The state historically had intervened in economic matters. The search for the correct development began simultaneously with the revolution with the introduction of a new economy known as war communism.[17]

The authorities, led by Vladimir Lenin, sought to achieve crude communism in a society which lacked a large proletariat due to Russia's modest industrial base relative to the size of the agricultural sector. Therefore, they identified their first task as the development of the industrial sector. Lenin believed in the primacy of politics over economics—that the will of the authorities would prevail over economic forces. By 1919, he and the small group of revolutionaries who had initiated the revolution were in control of the political structure, and thereby the economy. Their skills were mainly political, and they lacked a coherent philosophical basis and blueprint for developing an economy characterized by the material conditions present in Russia in 1918. They could not draw heavily from Marxian philosophy, for it did not offer guidance regarding how Russian society could be transformed into a modern industrial power.

---

[17]This name was appropriate since the Bolshevik forces needed to introduce economic policies that would enable them to win the revolution.

While there has been some conformity of the economy with Marx's philosophical basis (e.g., state ownership and control of enterprises and prices; discouragement of private economic activity; antagonism toward the philosophical basis and working rules of capitalism), the economy has been developed according to a philosophical basis that is (especially since the mid-1920s) "Soviet first of all."[18] Russian history, including the events of the 1920s, influenced the development of the philosophical basis and working rules for the economy that were firmly established by Joseph Stalin after he solidified his power in 1928 (see "Philosophical Basis," pp. 403–404). The significant events of the 1920s were the period of war communism (1918–1921), the New Economic Policy (1921–1924), and the Great Industrialization Debate (1924–1928).

War Communism

Seeking to bypass the stage of capitalism, the authorities introduced a system of administrative control. This social process to coordinate production and distribution efforts was chosen not only because it was consistent with the Marxian philosophical basis, but because authorities believed it was the most efficacious means to guide the economy while pursuing a Bolshevik victory in the revolution. Some of the features of war communism included a bureaucratic social process with highly centralized decision making; extensive state ownership and control (all industries employing 20 or more persons were nationalized, land and banks were nationalized, private trade was abolished and replaced with allocation by central authorities and requisitioning of materials through state monopolies and monopsonies), and a state-established monopoly over foreign trade; little use of money; and free public services. Under the working rules of war communism, the performance of the economy was favorable to the extent that the Bolsheviks were able to win the revolution. However, by 1920 the peasants and trade union members were revolting against the state's monopoly over production and distribution decision making. In response to this discontent, informal rules changed toward the efficacy of war communism policies as the correct development path. In 1921, the authorities introduced a new program based upon a different philosophical basis and set of working rules—the New Economic Policy (NEP).

New Economic Policy

In a pragmatic move, Lenin repudiated the working rules of war communism, as he recognized the absence of Marxian preconditions for the achievement of crude communism. In order to solidify their political power and stimulate the economy through promoting industrialization (in a world where they faced hostile foreign capitalist powers), he and other Bolshevik authorities introduced the working rules of the NEP.

---

[18]Raymond Hutchings, *Soviet Economic Development*, 2nd ed. (New York: New York University Press, 1982), pp. 26, 27.

> The logic of the situation clearly demanded that they [authorities] create the prerequisites for their existence and survival. They had to effect a rapid industrialization, both in order to generate political support and to become strong enough to defend themselves against a hostile and economically advanced capitalist world.[19]

Ironically, the NEP has been described as a type of "state capitalism." Although the state retained ownership and control of the major industries, many reforms were introduced. Communal services and free distribution of foodstuffs were discontinued. Relatively heavy emphasis upon markets as the social process for economic coordination was restored along with privatization and decentralization of decision making, especially in agriculture and trade. Small industries (i.e., employing fewer than 20 workers) were denationalized. A significant working rule was the proportional agricultural tax under which a fixed proportion of a peasant's net produce (above the family's subsistence needs) was payable to the state in taxes. The peasants then were free to sell whatever surplus remained to private dealers, cooperatives, or the state. Peasants were also permitted to lease land and to hire laborers.

Two historic events in 1924 would shape the nature of the post-1928 Soviet economy. The first was the "scissors crisis." Due to increased agricultural output and state pricing policies that raised the prices of industrial goods, the terms of trade faced by farmers (prices of goods they produced relative to the prices of industrial products they sought to purchase) declined. The Bolsheviks feared that the peasants would withhold their agricultural output in response to the decline in prices, thus reducing the payments of agricultural taxes so desperately needed to finance the industrialization drive. Unfortunately, the data are inconclusive regarding whether they did so or not. Industrial output grew favorably between 1921 and 1928, although unemployment increased after 1925. However, in terms of guaranteeing a steady supply of revenue to the state, the behavior of the peasants under the NEP was perceived as a threat by many authorities. In their minds, "[t]he attempt to pit the State monopoly of industry against the decentralized responses of the peasants had failed. The government held the 'commanding heights' but it could not at present use them to achieve the breakthrough towards industrialization which the Bolsheviks wanted."[20]

Great Industrialization Debate

The second major event was the death of Lenin, which triggered a long debate among authorities and economists over the type of economy to create in order to introduce a correct development strategy. Central issues in the debate concerned the type of philosophical basis, political structure, and principal institutions to

---

[19]Robert W. Campbell, *The Soviet-Type Economies*, 3rd ed. (Boston: Houghton Mifflin, 1974), p. 6.

[20]Hutchings, *Soviet Economic Development*, p. 38. "Commanding heights" refers to state control over energy, transport, communications, financial, and key manufacturing industries.

adopt, as well as the relative importance of the state in economic decision making, ownership and control, and coordination of production and distribution decisions. Interrelated with these issues were the issues of which sectors (i.e., industrial, agricultural) to focus upon and what should be the pace at which each sector would be developed. Also, there were many factions within the Communist Party, and some members of these factions shifted positions in response to the evidence provided by economists and to the shifting of the political wind. The latter point is important, for the death of Lenin created a power gap that rival authorities were seeking to fill. The debate gave rise to two broad factions.

Proponents of the radical position (which Stalin eventually advocated) argued that the NEP, while a necessary stage to prepare the economy for a large-scale industrialization drive, demonstrated the precarious nature of control over the economy held by authorities primarily because peasants were granted many freedoms. Favoring rapid industrial growth through state-controlled rather than market measures, radicals identified the need for the state to be guaranteed the ability to obtain a reliable grain supply from millions of scattered peasant farms. Radicals were concerned that no guarantee was possible unless authorities could control peasant production and distribution activities. It was argued that a massive industrialization drive should begin with a three- to five-year period for capital and labor to build plants, equipment, and infrastructure. There would be no surplus of industrial goods sold to peasants for a few years, but peasants would be required to sell grain through the state and provide labor for the expanding industrial sector. Peasants were not trusted, as they had been under the NEP policy of supporting peasant agriculture, to save large sums voluntarily. Radicals feared that those peasants and individuals who prospered from market activity would rise in social status and lead a revolution to take control of the political structure.

The conservative view was that since the performance of the economy under the NEP was successful and a workable relationship between authorities and those engaged in agriculture and industry had occurred, the NEP policies should be continued. Proponents of this view held that to abandon the NEP and radically reorganize the agricultural sector would risk alienating the peasants who had supported the Bolsheviks during the revolution. They favored gradual expansion of industry, believing that modest growth of the agricultural sector would provide the raw materials and food for industrial workers and a surplus for export purposes. Funds obtained from the exports could be used to invest domestically or through purchases of imports in needed capital equipment for the industrialization drive.

The result of the Great Industrialization Debate favored the radicals. Under Stalin's leadership, a massive industrialization drive was embarked upon after 1928, and agricultural units were collectivized. This enabled the authorities to maintain control over the peasants' economic and political activities. State farms (see "State-Controlled Principal Institutions," pp. 406–408) were established to mass-produce large quantities of grain and other agricultural products for domestic supply and to export for needed foreign exchange. It was decided that a large supply of savings was necessary to finance the massive industrialization effort, and that the agricultural sector would be the source of the surplus.

The experience of war communism and the NEP influenced the authorities to choose the radical position. A number of "precedents of the 1920s" remained in the consciousness of Stalin and other authorities who were the chief architects of the Soviet CSE, as well as authorities who succeeded them.[21] One was that centralization of decision making, state ownership and control, and planning as a social process were possible and efficacious under the right conditions. Based upon the experience of war communism planning efforts, authorities recognized that for planning to be successful central planners needed "detailed and coordinate[d] information from the enterprise level and up and the political and economic muscle to ensure compliance, [otherwise] planning will be ineffective."[22] Authorities also learned that planned objectives were likelier to be achieved if resources were allocated by central authorities in the desired direction. Second, authorities learned that if agriculture was necessary to provide funds for industrialization, then collectivization was preferable to privatization, as peasants could not be trusted to comply voluntarily with state wishes. Third, while it was believed that industrial laborers should be left free to choose their occupations, the state should maintain control over trade unions. Finally, markets were not trusted as a means to allocate goods and services, for it was recognized that market forces (e.g., prices and output levels) as a social process were not likely to stimulate production and distribution patterns consistent with the preference of authorities.[23]

A MARXIST-LENINIST-STALINIST PHILOSOPHY

Prior to the late 1980s, the justification for the institutions and working rules that characterize the Soviet economy was the Marxian philosophy primarily complemented by the views of Stalin. Beginning in 1928, Stalin established a rigid doctrine which only he was permitted to change, imprisoning or killing those who dissented from his political and economic views. Stalin was obsessed with the need for the Soviet Union to industrialize rapidly to catch up with Western capitalist powers. According to Stalin "[w]e have lagged fifty to a hundred years behind the leading countries. We must cover this distance in ten years. Either we do that, or they crush us."[24]

---

[21]For a detailed discussion of the "precedents," see Paul R. Gregory and Robert C. Stuart, *Soviet Economic Structure and Performance*, 4th ed. (New York: Harper & Row, 1990), pp. 68–71.

[22]Ibid., p. 69.

[23]For a theoretical discussion of the incompatibility between a political structure where authorities seek tight control over economic activity through planning and reliance upon unregulated market forces, see Charles E. Lindblom, *Politics and Markets* (New York: Basic Books, 1977).

[24]Hutchings, *Soviet Economic Development*, p. 48.

Stalin's means to close the gap was a centrally planned economy that included state ownership and control over all the means of production. This would require a rapid and violent (if necessary) reorganization of the agricultural sector in which collectivized farming would replace individually managed units. Stalin believed collective farming was imperative for the state to be able to control the peasants (whom Stalin distrusted). In particular, the peasants were required to make material sacrifices (receive modest payment for their output) so as to provide a surplus which the state could use for investment purposes. In addition, collectivization would fulfill Stalin's desire to eliminate the rich peasant class (*kulaks*) whose interests he believed were counter to those of the Communist Party.

From Stalin's death in 1953 until the late 1980s, the philosophical basis has softened to the extent that some reforms were introduced by Soviet authorities (see "Modest Institutional Change," pp. 413–418). However, since the principal institutions and most working rules remained intact (as has Communist Party control over political and economic matters), most of these reforms were too modest to have a significant impact on the economy's performance. Seeking to retain their power and for want of any alternative, authorities reiterated stale Marxian principles—thereby rationalizing the continuation of the basic working rules of a CSE. The "guiding principle" underlying these rules as well as the overall "design" of the Soviet economy was "that the Communist Party should have institutionalized control over all major aspects of economic activity in the USSR. This goal clearly dominates other possible considerations, most notably economic efficiency. . . ."[25]

CONGRUENT SOCIAL AND POLITICAL STRUCTURES

The social and political structures mirrored themselves more closely in the Soviet Union than in any economy since ancient Rome. This was primarily due to the fact that status follows from access to goods and services rather than income earned. Access, in turn, was according to working rules established by authorities with a virtual monopoly over both political power and economic activities. The result was that when distribution occurs, the rules heavily favor the "status elite" members of the Communist Party.[26]

---

[25]Ed A. Hewett, *Reforming the Soviet Economy*. Washington, DC: The Brookings Institution, 1988, p. 101.

[26]Such a scheme gave rise to the Soviet joke comparing capitalism and communism. Some Soviet citizens claim that the difference between these two systems is that under capitalism man exploits man, while under communism it is just the opposite.

Social Structure

The structure of Soviet society in the late 1980s is best described as "a radical social pyramid."[27] At the apex were the wealthy families who comprise under 2.5 percent of the population. This group included elite political authorities, retired political elites, leading diplomats, scientists, artists, and athletes; and enterprising managers of cooperatives as well as very successful black marketeers. This last group consisted of persons able to acquire supplies of higher-quality consumer goods (especially those embodying the latest electronic technology). These goods were in considerable demand, but their price was fixed by the state (at below equilibrium levels). Therefore, those who had control over the supply of such goods (authorities and black marketeers) could resell them for large profits.

Consumption of all types of goods and services was disproportionately enjoyed (relative to their income) by the elite Soviet class. There is considerable anecdotal evidence that members of this class received the most advanced health care, the best educational institutions for themselves and their children, and easy access to state-subsidized recreational facilities. One particular example illustrates the skewed nature of consumption. In one region of central Russia the elite (i.e., local and regional Communist Party officials) accounted for just 0.04 percent of the population, but supposedly "consumed between 56 percent and 100 percent of all the high-quality food in their region."[28]

If the middle class is considered to be the percentage of households owning their own house or apartment, plus a car, furniture and appliances, then the Soviet middle class was very small by standards of industrialized nations. Whereas in 1989 most Japanese and about half the people in Hungary and Czechoslovakia would have been considered middle class, in the Soviet Union the comparable proportion was about 11 percent.[29] Since everyone else in the Soviet Union was considered to be in the lower class, then over 86 percent of the Soviet Union's members were relatively poor. The aged were highly represented in the lower class, for their income remained fixed. The behavior of this group during the open debates and demonstrations of the late 1980s indicated the extent to which they, ironically, have become immiserised by the upper-class authorities. This was especially true in the republics (e.g., Lithuania, Armenia, and central Asian republics) which claimed they were subjected to economic exploitation and cultural imperialism by the central authorities. The perpetuation of poverty in these republics was reinforced by the very high incidence (above 90 percent) of intermarriage within Soviet ethnic groups.

---

[27]Andrei Kuteinikov, "Soviet Society—Much More Unequal Than US," *The Wall Street Journal*, January 26, 1990, p. A14.

[28]Ibid.

[29]Ibid.

Political Structure

Prior to the mid-1990s, the Communist Party maintained a monopoly over political power, but during 1990, political reform became imminent. The political structure that characterized the Soviet Union prior to 1990 is discussed next and is outlined in Figure 15-2. At all levels Communist Party authorities and government authorities overlapped and interlocked with one another, with party members monitoring government activities. Control by the party was assured, for many members of leading political institutions simultaneously held high-authority positions within the government (e.g., until 1990, Mikhail Gorbachev was General Secretary of the Communist Party as well as President of the Supreme Soviet). Leading party authorities established the philosophical basis and goals for the economy, the means by which they would be achieved, and appointed officials to head principal institutions and to oversee the economy to ensure that party policies were implemented and carried through. Implementation was guided by the Soviet government, which served as the "administration organ" for the Communist Party, and in many respects its structure "replicated the party hierarchy."[30]

Some features of the political structure should be noted. The Party Congress was the ultimate source of authority. It elected the Central Committee, which consisted of national leaders with expertise in the fields of politics, economics, science, and literature, and trade union, worker, and farmer representatives. The Central Committee monitored and supervised national-level ministries which, in turn, oversaw specific industries and sectors of the economy. The Central Committee also was responsible for electing the Politburo (see p. 407), which was the main body for establishing the goals and priorities for the economy.

Figure 15-2   The Pre-1990 Political Structure

COMMUNIST PARTY STRUCTURE	GOVERNMENT STRUCTURE
Politburo of the Central Committee	Ministers and Presidium of the Supreme Soviet
Central Committee, General Secretary	
Party Congress—national level	
Party Congress—republic level	Republic Ministers and Supreme Soviet Central Committee
Party Congress—region level	Regional Executive Committee
Party Congress—city level	City Executive Committee
Party Committees—local (village) level	Village Executive Committee
All other party members	General public

[30]Hewett, *Reforming the Soviet Economy*, p. 107.

STATE-CONTROLLED PRINCIPAL INSTITUTIONS

The institutions with primary responsibility for establishing and coordinating the major production and distribution patterns were the Politburo, the planning bureaucracy, state-owned industrial enterprises, and agricultural units.

Politburo

The Politburo was the center of Communist authority power. Membership in the Politburo consisted of about 20 leading authorities from the Central Committee. The Politburo selected from among its members the General Secretary, who presided over this institution. The main goals for the economy (e.g., target rates of overall growth and for particular sectors and goods; target levels of investment and consumption) were set by the Politburo. Its influence over the economy was twofold. First, "all the strategic decisions that drive the entire planning process" were made by this institution.[31] Second, control over the implementation of its decisions and achievement of high-priority goals was ensured because of the control Politburo members had over government officials responsible for implementing and carrying through the Politburo's directives. Since these government officials, in turn, had considerable control over enterprise managers, the Politburo exerted control over all aspects of production and distribution.

The Planning Bureaucracy

In a CSE, involvement with the central plans extended from the highest authorities to all workers. The principal institutions responsible for the formulation and implementation of the plan included the Politburo and state committees and ministries. Once the goals and priorities had been established by party authorities, a plan had to be formulated capable of achieving authorities' wishes while being feasible and internally consistent. (That is, the resources necessary to produce targeted levels of outputs for all sectors of the economy were available.) The primary responsibility for formulating such a plan was given to the State Planning Committee (*Gosplan*), established in 1921 to coordinate central planning machinery. Its main purpose was to translate guidelines established from above into a detailed plan identifying what, how, and how much to produce and for whom to produce it.

Other state committees were responsible for allocating resources to enterprises or establishing value indicators to guide the behavior of enterprises while establishing a common standard which enabled authorities to measure (and control) economic activity. There was a committee responsible for allocating raw materials and intermediate products (*Gossnab*), setting prices (*Goskomtsen*), for establishing wage scales for enterprises (*Goskomtrud*), and for all central and

---

[31]Ibid., p. 106.

commercial bank functions (*Gosbank*). Finally, there were ministries (e.g., industry, agriculture, foreign trade) responsible for managing specific sectors and activities in compliance with the directives established in the plan.

State-Owned Industrial Enterprises

Nearly all production and distribution activities were performed by enterprises owned by the state. The party controlled the appointment of managers of such enterprises, and these managers were required to adhere to the guidelines established by authorities, as specified in the plan (e.g., target level of output). This system created a management style "characterized by centralism, verticalism, and one-[person] management."[32]

Agricultural Units

Agricultural institutions were important to the Soviet economy for a number of reasons. First, about one fourth of the Soviet labor force was involved with agriculture. Second, since private enterprise was permitted on a limited scale, the agricultural sector offered the opportunity to compare factor productivity of different institutions that coexist within one sector. These institutions were the state farm, the collective farm, and private plots.

The state farm was an agricultural factory owned, directly controlled, and operated as a government enterprise with hired labor, and it sold its output to state procurement agencies. During the collectivization drive initiated by Stalin, virgin land was opened up as "grain factories" were established. Due to their poor performance, state farms declined in importance from the mid-1930s until the late 1950s when their size and relative importance was increased. As of 1989 state farms accounted for over 50 percent of all sown area in the Soviet Union.[33]

Collective farms (*kolkhoz*) comprised over 40 percent of all sown area. While theoretically more autonomous than the state farm, the collective was still under the supervision of party members. Peasant participation in such a farm was voluntary, but in reality peasants had few other alternatives unless they chose to move to an urban area. Collectives produced according to state guidelines, using collectively owned buildings and equipment supplied by state-managed machine tractor stations. While wages paid to peasants were relatively low, each family was allocated an area of land to use as they wished. This land became a private plot. While some factory workers and state farm workers were also allocated some land for their own use, the size of such plots was about four to five times larger for collective farm workers. Overall, these plots accounted for less than 3 percent of all sown land, but they were an important source of the Soviet Union's supply of meat, milk, and eggs.

---

[32]Gregory and Stuart, *Soviet Economic Structure and Performance*, p. 208.
[33]Ibid., p. 295.

COMMUNIST PARTY CONTROL
OF THE ECONOMY

Prior to the late 1980s, the Soviet economy exhibited a clear relationship between the philosophical basis, political structure, and working rules for principal institutions. The Communist Party was in complete control of the economy and of the information and education people received. In addition, government authorities provided leading party authorities with the information they needed to manage the economy. Compliance with the goals and priorities established was required of all enterprise managers and workers—with little opportunity for individually determined, owned, and controlled economic activity.

Concentrated Resource Allocation
Decision Making

Decision making was highly centralized, concentrated within a complex administrative hierarchy, the extreme expression occurring during Stalin's regime, when he personally assumed responsibility for all major economic (and political) decisions. There was a strict hierarchy of decision making throughout the bureaucracy as directives flowed from the top authorities (Politburo) through government planning committees, to controlling and supervising agencies, and finally to individual enterprises. Together the party and government authorities were linked through a system of interlocking directorates with the Politburo making all important decisions. Authorities at upper levels administered, supervised, and inspected the activities of the next lower-level authorities, and this scheme repeated itself throughout the economy.

> The philosophy behind the design [was] clear: the center controls economic activity on the supply side, on a branch-by-branch basis. This, it seems, [was] a logical extension of the philosophy within the party, which advocate[d] direct control of a broad range of performance indicators.[34]

Overall, prior to *perestroika* (see "Modest Institutional Change," pp. 413–418) Communist Party members, especially high authorities, were the dominant decision makers. They established economic goals and priorities, and planned the means to achieve these goals down to the level of each enterprise. A system of *nomenklatura* (party control over authority appointments—including ministry officials and enterprise managers) assured that managers loyal to authorities were in charge of enterprises. The only decision-making power which enterprises had involved residual matters pertaining to minor administrative details which the state permits them to decide.

---

[34]Hewett, *Reforming the Soviet Economy*, pp. 109, 111.

Dominance of State Ownership and Control of Resources

With the exception of private plots, handicrafts, a few minor rural activities (e.g., food processing), and some services (e.g., repair of automobiles or household items), there was state ownership and control over the means of production. All private activities were individually or family operated, for no one was permitted to hire labor (so as not to "exploit" them for personal gain). Prior to the late 1980s, the attitudes of authorities toward private property were not favorable, for such property was "regarded as transitory . . . and tolerated only out of necessity" (e.g., the need for the food produced on private plots).[35]

In practice, ownership and control were not simply an omnipotent state dominating a very small private sector. As the Soviet economy became more complex over the past few decades, the ability of the Communist Party to control economic activity was likened to a "spotlight."[36] When there was a particular objective to achieve, the party was capable of focusing on relevant projects by quickly organizing party and government authorities to reallocate resources in that direction. One case in point occurred during the early 1980s when the Soviet authorities mobilized industries to produce equipment necessary for the completion of a natural gas pipeline from the Soviet Union to Western Europe.

Processes Planned and Underground Processes for Economic Coordination

There were three distinctive social processes for economic coordination: (1) the primary process of central planning where the influence (if not complete control) of party authorities was ubiquitous throughout the economy; (2) the shadow economy; and (3) the "second economy." Although only the first was official, the other two enabled enterprises to meet their output targets and consumers to satisfy their demand.

CENTRAL PLANNING.   The most noteworthy distinction between CSEs and other types of economies was that authorities' (or planners') preferences guided production and distribution activities, not market forces. A command form of planning administered through a strict hierarchy (in which compliance with the plan became law) was introduced by Stalin in 1928. With some modest reforms this scheme was the primary means to coordinate economic activities throughout the Soviet Union until the reform drive which began in 1990.

In terms of what is to be produced, the Politburo established goals and priorities. This group made decisions concerning the relative emphasis to be placed upon capital (versus consumer) goods; on defense versus nondefense

---

[35]Jan S. Prybyla, *Market and Plan Under Socialism: The Bird in the Cage* (Stanford, CA: Hoover Institution Press, 1987), p. 33.
[36]Hewett, *Reforming the Soviet Economy*, p. 168.

goods; on the extent of investment in infrastructure versus health and human services; on the relative importance of industrial versus agricultural growth and modernization; and many other decisions requiring trade-offs involving key aspects of the economy. The planning organs received directives from the Politburo and had to formulate a plan that would give directions to every state enterprise in the industrial and agricultural sectors.

There were annual, five-year, and long-range plans which had to be formulated. The most noteworthy was the five-year plan, a period selected because of the time an average project took to be completed and the time within which the effects of a shift in policy could be realized. In formulating the plan the planners (i.e., authorities at *Gosplan*) were attempting to translate political goals provided by the Politburo into precise, detailed, and consistent production targets and directives for enterprises.

Assume the Politburo favored growth of capital goods, weaponry, and consumer goods by a given percentage for each. Planners then set goals for the next five years concerning the desired level of gross national output, output targets for key sectors, the distribution of gross national output among consumption, investment, and other uses for the output, the distribution of investment to key industries, and the level of consumer goods that will be produced. Next, the planners translated the goals into targets and directives by drawing up output targets and supply plans with which to allocate material and equipment. Coordination of the plan was through a material-balances method by which the planners sought to equate supplies with demand without relying upon prices (which reflect relative scarcity) to bring supply and demand into equilibrium. The problem was to make the plan internally consistent (i.e., the sum of the required inputs for each enterprise must be equal to the supply of inputs available from current inventory, imports, and current period production).

The tool relied upon was an input-output table. This table depicted the interrelationship between producers and users of all goods and services. The planners first translated aggregate guidelines into a detailed plan, which identified necessary inputs for all sectors. It then had to make the plan feasible by balancing materials, generally by allocating necessary resources to help achieve higher-priority goals (as defined by the Politburo), while lower-priority items (usually housing and consumer goods) were treated residually in terms of resource allocation.

Throughout the formulation of the plan, there was a bargaining process between planners and ministry authorities and between ministry authorities and industry authorities and so on down the hierarchy to the enterprise level. At each level both sides arrived at a request for resources and target output level. However, the *Gosplan* ultimately adjusted, coordinated, and reconciled differences in requests by enterprises and formulated the final plan. Then directives were issued, which were legally binding on all enterprises. Enterprises were expected to meet their target quota as specified in the National Economic Plan.

The plan was disaggregated at the ministry level for distribution to enterprises. Once the plan was distributed, how did authorities coordinate resource allocation so as to achieve all specified goals? One perpetual problem was that due to some or all of the following—exogenous factors which affected supply, mistakes in the planning process, inadequate or misguided incentives, or poor performance—the production of inputs may not have been sufficient to meet the need for them. Uncertainty and bottlenecks of supplies throughout industries would ensue. Planners could respond by shifting resources to higher-priority industries (e.g., reduce supply of cement for housing construction—a lower-priority item—and reallocate it for a higher-priority item such as construction of a steel foundry).

In the Soviet scheme prices generally served a measurement and control function. They were established by planning authorities in the *Goskomtsen*. Since there were over 20 million different products, the authorities established prices for those goods deemed to be important to the entire economy (finished goods and inputs such as fuel, energy, and raw materials).[37] Once prices were established, they tended to remain rigid despite shifts in demand or supply. The only legal activities for which demand and supply had an influence occurred in the market for food produced on private plots and in the retail sector. Given that the supply of retail goods is fixed, the Soviet authorities established a lump-sum (turnover) tax which was added to the cost of production. In theory, the amount of the tax would be sufficient to reduce quantity demanded so that it just equaled the fixed quantity supplied. However, this was not usually accomplished, leading to shortages or surpluses of various goods.

In terms of how income was distributed, there were wage differentials established by authorities in the State Commission for Labor and Social Questions (*Goskomtrud*). The factors used to determine the differentials included the skill required for the occupation, the number of years a worker had been employed, the particular industry, the geographical region, and the working conditions. Bonuses for exceeding output levels were more widely used as incentives after 1970. The state supplemented worker incomes by providing a broad range of subsidized necessities (food, rent) and free services (health, education, transportation).

Central planning as a coordinating mechanism was effective in enabling the Soviet Union to force rapid industrialization and development in selected high-priority areas (e.g., defense). However, the mounting criticism of central planning, which culminated with the dramatic reform movements in 1989–1990, focused on a number of problems. First, bureaucratization of economic life impinged upon individual initiative and failed to allow for consumer preference. The result was often overproduction of low-quality goods and shortages of desired goods. Second, the number of administrators relative to workers was very high, as in the case of Soviet agriculture where about 3 million bureaucrats administrated a sector with about 14 million farmers. Third, planning permitted authorities to make

---

[37]Hewett, *Restructuring the Soviet Economy*, p. 113.

decisions arbitrarily, compelling subordinates to follow directives which may lack economic rationale. Fourth, planning created inflexibility in that adjustments to disequilibrium situations were slow. Fifth, enterprise managers and workers (who did not fear losing their jobs) engaged in dysfunctional behavior by responding to incentives that did not take profit maximization into account. Finally, mistakes by the planners were magnified throughout the economy. The frequent occurrence of these problems led to the emergence of two alternative processes for coordinating Soviet production and distribution activities.

SHADOW ECONOMY. Due to shortages of raw materials, intermediate goods, and consumer goods that plagued the Soviet economy for many decades, other means of resource control emerged. To provide materials and services which the formal planned sector did not or could not provide, enterprise managers and workers developed a "shadow economy" through which they sought to comply with the directives given to them by the planners.[38] For example, to obtain equipment necessary for an enterprise to meet its output target, managers bartered with one another, bribed government officials responsible for allocating needed materials, or purchased the equipment without planners' knowledge from another enterprise.

SECOND ECONOMY. The black market was an alternative social process through which "second-economy" activities were coordinated. Soviet citizens who were unable to satisfy their demand for high-quality consumer goods could obtain such goods on the black market. Analysts claimed there was considerable pent-up demand, since Soviet citizens were unable to obtain high quality goods from state suppliers. For example, a black marketeer able to obtain a Sony Walkman, which retails in Western nations for under $60 but is not available in Soviet retail stores, could receive over $600 for the product.[39] It was believed that the size of the second economy increased each year (as the formal economy failed to satisfy consumer demand), and it has been estimated that as much as 15 percent of the labor force were engaged full time or part time in second-economy activities.[40] In the case of repairs of apartment, appliances, automobiles, and clothing, about a third or more expenditures were through the second economy.[41]

---

[38]Ibid., p. 177.
[39]"Special Report—The Soviet Union," *Business Week*, November 11, 1985, p. 94.
[40]Hewett, *Reforming the Soviet Economy*, p. 180.
[41]Ibid.

MODEST INSTITUTIONAL CHANGE
UNTIL THE 1989 POLITICAL AND
ECONOMIC REVOLUTION

1928–1984

Between 1928 and the mid-1950s there was little institutional change. The absence of institutional change did not mean that the Soviet economy's performance received widespread acceptance from the population. While there is evidence that the standard of living for most Soviet citizens improved only modestly between 1928 and the mid-1950s (see "Performance of the Economy," pp. 418–420), the authorities were able to screen and "edit" information concerning the Soviet economy's performance in absolute and relative terms (to the non-CSEs), while retaining a monopoly over political power and using force against those who criticized the Communist Party and its economic policies. Thus, there was little pressure for institutional change.

After Stalin's death in 1953 and the consolidation of power by Nikita Khrushchev, more openness was permitted regarding discussion of the economy's performance and possible means for reform. While the record concerning economic growth and technological achievement, especially of capital goods, weaponry, and space exploration was impressive, the growing complexity of the economy made it increasingly more difficult for the central authorities to plan and coordinate most economic activities effectively. Khrushchev, therefore, sought to promote greater productive efficiency by decentralizing administrative decision making, replacing central ministries in Moscow with *sovnarkhozy*, "new regional economic councils."[42] The provisions of this reform were greeted with a negative reaction by bureaucrats and SOE managers, initiating a "treadmill of reforms" pattern which persisted since the late 1940s.[43] This pattern was characterized by the lack of a coherent philosophical basis and corresponding economic theory upon which the reform was based; by resistance from authorities who lost some power over decision making (and did not fully comply with the provisions of the reform); and by a subsequent decline in the rate of economic growth and productivity (without a noticeable improvement in the quality of output). This was partly because coordination between producers of final products and those supplying raw materials and intermediate goods was poor.

After Leonid Brezhnev became the leading authority in 1964, the main economic authority was Premier Alexei Kosygin. Although he introduced incentives for SOEs to stimulate production, he also introduced reforms in 1965 which began to reverse Khrushchev's decentralization measures. Kosygin was

---

[42]"Survey *Perestroika*: And now for the hard part," *Special Report—The Economist*, April 28, 1990.

[43]Gertrude E. Schroeder, "Economic Reform of Socialism: The Soviet Record," in Jan S. Prybyla, ed., "Privatizing and Marketizing Socialism," *The Annals of the American Academy of Political and Social Science*, 507 (January 1990), 37.

reacting to a decline in key economic performance indicators in the early 1960s (e.g., economic growth, labor productivity), and recognized that the standard of living of most Soviet families lagged well behind that of typical Western families. Autonomy that managers previously had been granted regarding the awarding of worker bonuses was reduced. Administrative decision making was further recentralized when the regional councils were amalgamated into "one coordinating agency."[44] A similar pattern occurred in the agricultural sector, although working rules permitting the use of private plots were liberalized by Kosygin.

One effect of the Kosygin reforms was that a high percentage of the SOE incentive fund was being distributed as bonuses to managers and workers and investment funds were allocated for projects not consistent with the preferences of central planners. Kosygin's desired result to improve labor productivity and product quality was not achieved, however. Some experts argued this was not surprising, for the Kosygin reforms did not change the essential features of the Soviet CSE. Thus, the behavior of central planners, enterprise managers, and workers was not altered significantly. In 1971, the "treadmill of reforms" process continued with attempts to modify previously introduced reforms. The authorities' objectives were similar to those of Khrushchev and Kosygin: to make the economy perform more efficiently through modest institutional reform, which would change the behavior of SOE managers and workers. However, their reforms failed to eliminate the inherent problems of the CSE, especially overcentralization of decision making and the absence of meaningful performance indicators.

Additional working rules reversed the effect of the Kosygin reforms.[45] Central planners were given control over the size and use of SOE incentive funds, more plan targets were reintroduced (e.g., improvements in labor productivity), the size of the incentive fund was more closely tied to the enterprise's ability to satisfy the plan's quotas, and the ability of SOEs to receive bank credit without planners' approval was reduced. In addition, due to bureaucratic resistance some of the reforms proposed by Kosygin never were implemented.

In 1979 the Program to Improve the Economic Mechanism introduced another round of reforms. As with earlier reforms there were few, if any, substantive provisions. The intent was to improve the economy's performance, especially labor productivity and the quality of goods produced, by "changes in the arrangements for the choice of output [permitting SOEs to contract with one another for supplies], the allocation of resources to produce it, and the distribution of the associated personal income."[46] These reforms were not sufficient to prevent the declining performance of the economy throughout the 1980s. Overcentralization of decision making and rigid planner control were not

[44]Ibid,. p. 36.

[45]For a detailed discussion, see Gregory and Stuart, *Soviet Economic Structure and Performance*, pp. 447–450.

[46]Morris Bornstein, "Improving the Soviet Economic Mechanism," *Soviet Studies*, 37, 1 (January 1985), 2, in Gregory and Stuart, *Soviet Economic Structure and Performance*, p. 451.

changed, and prices continued to be administered by the state according to average cost of production plus an average markup over cost (rather than reflecting relative scarcity). Rationing of producer goods was the primary means to allocate inputs among SOEs, and meeting the target level of output remained the main indicator of enterprise performance.

Another "large-scale experiment" introduced in 1984 to increase enterprise autonomy met the same fate.[47] The planners, ministry officials, and SOE managers were able to thwart the introduction of these reforms because, as with earlier reforms, the essential features of the CSE remained intact. Enterprise managers still faced shortages of needed inputs; consumer demand had no influence regarding what was produced. There was little concern for the quality of what was produced, and incentives were too weak to stimulate managers and workers to fulfill the plan's targets. One lesson of institutional reform prior to 1985 was that tinkering with the economy through piecemeal, hybrid reforms was not effective as reflected by subsequent changes in the economy's performance. More Soviet authorities and Western analysts recognized that a "comprehensive 'restructuring' of the Soviet economy"[48] was necessary before significant performance improvements could be expected.

Post-1985 Reforms: The Gorbachev Era

Each of the principal institutions—Politburo, planning bureaucracy, SOEs, and agricultural units—experienced considerable change after Mikhail Gorbachev became the supreme political and economic authority in 1985. His informal rules, particularly *Perestroika* (restructuring of the economy), *Glasnost* (more openness in society), and *Demokratizatsia* (greater democracy), stimulated a wave of political and economic reform that began to transform the Soviet economy. One significant difference between the wave of reforms in the Gorbachev era and those reform movements since the mid-1950s was that significant political reform accompanied the economic reforms.

POLITICAL REFORM.   By 1989 Gorbachev demonstrated his skill as a bureaucratic tactician. He consolidated his power within the Communist Party and the Soviet government, and reduced the power of the Politburo by removing seven of its nine members. They were replaced by loyalists who used their power not only to select Gorbachev as chairman of the Presidium of the Supreme Soviet, but also as chairman of the Supreme Soviet. This was significant, for it meant that Gorbachev could only be removed from office by vote of the entire party congress (rather than through political infighting and pressure from the small group of Politburo members).

[47]Leonore Shever Taga, "The Soviet Firm in the 'Large-Scale Experiment,'" *Comparative Economic Studies*, 31, 2 (Summer 1989), 92–94.
[48]Ibid., p. 134.

Consistent with the spread of democracy throughout CEE, there were many new challenges to the monopoly of power over the political structure held by the Soviet Communist Party. The most significant challenge came from Boris Yeltsin who, after being elected president of the Russian republic left the Communist Party, becoming the first noncommunist authority in Soviet history in 72 years. Mayors from Moscow and Leningrad followed suit. Yeltsin issued direct challenges to the Communist Party, seeking to end its "policy of imperial centralism."[49] He called for dismantling the Communist bureaucracy in order to break the link between the party organs and government institutions. Yeltsin objected to the power over resource allocation held by the Politburo and planning bureaucracy members (these authorities control about 95 percent of the Soviet economy's output), preferring republic autonomy instead.

Unlike other Soviet authorities, Yeltsin's economic reforms were supported by a broad philosophical basis and accepted economic principles. Some of his aides proposed the views and types of reforms introduced into British economy by Margaret Thatcher (e.g., privatization of SOEs, tight fiscal and monetary discipline, a central bank for each republic) as a philosophy and model for reforming their republic, if not the entire country. Yeltsin favored a convertible ruble, permitting SOEs to sell surplus produced in excess of a target output level on the open market, and greater SOE autonomy regarding using any profits for higher salaries, investment, or educating and training workers. His challenge to Gorbachev and other leading Soviet authorities was significant, for not only is Russia the largest republic in the Soviet Union, but all 15 republics had their own political structure and then were expressing the nationalistic spirit which Yeltsin appealed to in his own republic.

Gorbachev's response to the growing anti-Soviet, nationalistic movements throughout the Soviet Union was to propose a loose federation of republics with sovereign rights for each republic, but such a proposal lacked a clear blueprint. Gorbachev sought to preserve the union of republics, but at the time appeared to be heading toward the same position as that of the Queen of England over the British Empire—holding very loose control over a confederation of increasingly autonomous political entities ruled by their own authorities. Recognizing the need for further radical political reform, he preached to Communist Party conservatives that their dogmatic interpretation of the Marxian-Leninist-Stalinist philosophical basis would stimulate the drive within republics for greater autonomy and would doom the economic reform movement as well.

REFORM OF STATE-OWNED ENTERPRISES.   While foreign analysts give Gorbachev high marks for his political reforms, his economic reforms were ineffective. There was considerable rhetoric regarding moving toward a "regulated market

---

[49]Adrian Karatnycky, "Yeltsin's Win Foreshadows End of Empire," *The Wall Street Journal*, May 30, 1990, p. A12.

economy," but Soviet authorities lacked understanding of the behavior of markets and the willingness to give up any power. Since an economy in which markets are *the* primary social process for coordinating production and distribution activities is inconsistent with the desire of authorities in a CSE to maintain control through planning, the implementation of substantive reforms was inhibited.

Beginning in 1985 Gorbachev called for permitting bankruptcy of SOEs unable to finance their own operations, reducing the percentage of SOE output regulated by the plan (to about 30 percent), giving SOE managers the right to contract for supplies among themselves without first receiving the planners' permission, and raising the material incentives in the workplace (e.g., permit the awarding of bonuses up to 50 percent of a worker's base income). Overall, Gorbachev sought to introduce a new business culture (set of informal rules) where greater economic efficiency and pursuit of profit for individual gain was important. Other suggested reforms included privatizing over 75 percent of the SOEs "mainly by leasing factories or converting them into joint stock companies with shares being sold to the work force,"[50] establishing new banks independent of the *Gosbank*, reforming the tax system, developing a securities market, and introducing free-enterprise zones for foreign trade. Gorbachev encouraged more joint ventures with Western firms in an attempt to eliminate the monopoly of Soviet SOEs over production and to attract new technology and management expertise to an economy with obsolete production facilities.

AGRICULTURAL REFORM.   Consistent with his predecessors, Gorbachev introduced few major reforms in agriculture, although he focused on improving the effectiveness of the existing agricultural sector. Farm procurement prices were increased, but losing farms were still subsidized rather than being permitted to go bankrupt. The Gorbachev response to losing agricultural enterprises was to advocate merging losing farms with another farm. He proposed improving horizontal communication between farms and their suppliers by decentralizing decision making, but this met considerable resistance from local party authorities unwilling to refrain from interfering with day-to-day farm operations.

One potentially substantive reform was lease contracting, under which the state leased land to one or a few families. However, farmer autonomy was inhibited by the state's right to manage administration of these leases, farmers' use of equipment, storage of produce, and transportation of supplies and produce. Like other economic reforms proposed by Soviet authorities, leasing could not be effective until significant price reform, combined with steadier availability of inputs and reduced centralized decision making, became a reality.

[50]Peter Gumbel, "Soviets Change Economic Plan, Bar Price Rises," *The Wall Street Journal*, July 20, 1990, p. A8.

PERFORMANCE OF THE ECONOMY: ASSESSMENT DIFFICULTIES DUE TO POLITICIZATION OF DATA

It is difficult to evaluate the performance of the Soviet economy. This is due in part to the absence of prices which reflect relative scarcity or which remain fixed (e.g., the prices of meat and milk, which remained unchanged from 1962 to the late 1980s) and the difficulty of obtaining accurate information. The consensus of those who evaluated the economy's performance is that in terms of average annual growth of gross national product, unemployment, job security, and technological developments in selected areas (e.g., defense), the Soviet economy performed well between 1928 and the mid-1950s, fair between the 1950s and the mid-1980s, but poorly thereafter.

1928–1984 Performance

The average annual rate of GNP growth in the Soviet Union during this time period exceeded the annual average growth of GNP in all the leading industrial nations during their respective industrialization drives (e.g., 1834–1843 in the United States) with the exception of Japan which had a comparable growth rate.[51] In terms of changes in the consumer price index, inflation was considerably lower in the Soviet Union between 1960 and the late 1980s than in OECD nations.[52] In addition, during the period of the late 1920s to mid-1960s, factor productivity in the Soviet Union was comparable to the average of the leading Western industrialized nations during their industrialization periods.[53] By the late 1950s the Soviet Union had risen to second in the world in combined industrial and agricultural output, and was virtually equal to the United States in military and ideological power.

To most Western observers, unfavorable indicators of performance between 1928 and the mid-1980s included the absence of economic freedoms, a limited supply of consumer goods, long waiting lines for the purchase of such goods, and the existence of illegal markets in which the prevailing prices were considerably higher than official prices (but which offered goods consumers could not purchase officially). These higher prices were not recorded in official inflation estimates, and consequently the reported low rates of inflation understate the true changes in the cost of living for the typical Soviet family.

Beginning in the late 1960s, most indicators of performance started to become less favorable, leading to the very poor performance (in the opinion of both Soviet authorities and citizens) of the economy in the late 1980s. The average annual rate of growth of real GNP fell from a 1961–1970 average of about 5 percent

[51]See Simon Kuznets, *Economic Growth of Nations* (Cambridge, MA: Harvard University Press, 1971, pp. 11–14), from Gregory and Stuart, *Soviet Economic Structure and Performance*, p. 359 .

[52]Alan P. Pollard, ed., *USSR Facts and Figures Annual*, 12 (New York: Academic International Press, 1988), p. 144.

[53]Ibid., pp. 364–367.

to about 2.6 percent for the period from 1970 to the mid-1980s.[54] The divergence between planned and actual growth rates increased between 1966 and 1990, being about 25 percent lower in 1966–1970 (5.1 percent actual versus 6.5 percent to 7.0 percent planned), but over 50 percent lower for the 1981–1985 period (1.9 percent actual versus 4.0 percent planned).[55] One other factor to note is that since unofficial inflation has increased during the past few decades, the real rates of growth as officially reported are overstated. In fairness to the Soviet Union, there was a slowdown of economic growth experienced by most economies. The average annual rate of real GDP growth for 16 OECD nations fell from 4.9 percent from 1950–1973 to 3.4 percent from 1973–1987.[56] During the same periods the comparable figures for the Soviet Union were 5.0 percent and 2.1 percent.[57]

Other unfavorable indicators of the economy's performance included a severe housing shortage (to the extent that many divorced couples were forced to continue sharing the same apartment for lack of alternative housing), and a declining average life expectancy for adult males (the Soviet Union was the only industrialized nation to experience this unfavorable trend over the period from 1960 to the mid-1980s). The quality of housing was poor, and many families (about 20 percent) lived in apartments that did not have a supply of hot water or a bathroom.[58] Alcohol abuse, poor medical care, and environmental problems contributed to the declining average life expectancy.

Death from alcohol poisoning was the main factor cited for the declining adult male life expectancy. The poisoning was attributed to high alcohol consumption rates and the low quality of ethanol used to produce alcoholic beverages in the Soviet Union. When the state attempted to reduce consumption, people purchased alcohol on the black market where the quality may be even poorer than that in state stores.[59] Those suffering from alcohol problems received slow and improper medical treatment from a substandard health care system (relative to Western facilities).[60] Although care was "free" to users, the health care system was characterized by doctors who were poorly paid and whose training typically was comparable to that of a nurse in the United States, a lack of modern equipment and medicine, and shortages of medicine.

The growing health problem was also due to environmental decay

---

[54]Ibid., p. 134.

[55]Ibid., p. 136.

[56]Robert L. Bartley, "The Great International Growth Slowdown," *The Wall Street Journal*, July 10, 1990, p. A16.

[57]Ibid.

[58]Pollard, *USSR Facts and Figures*, p. 484.

[59]During one period in the 1980s when consumption of vodka was prohibited, consumption actually increased.

[60]For a discussion of alcohol illness and Soviet health care, see Vladimir G. Treml, "Death From Alcohol Poisoning in the USSR," *The Wall Street Journal*, November 10, 1981, p. 26; and Walter Clemens, Jr., "A Soviet Melting Pot? Nyet," *The Wall Street Journal*, June 8, 1990, p. A10.

throughout the Soviet Union. According to one Soviet expert, 20 percent of the Soviet citizens resided in "ecological disaster zones," while another 40 percent lived under "ecologically unfavorable conditions."[61] The heavy incidence of steel and chemical production in urban areas contributed to this problem, as did the obsession of central planners and Politburo authorities with rapid economic growth and self-sufficiency (ignoring the theory of comparative advantage in the process). Because they had a monopoly over economic decision making and lacked access to environmental decay information (or received inaccurate information from those seeking to cover up the problem), these authorities were not accountable to anyone for the decaying environment. A classic example was the Soviet decision to grow cotton in Uzbekistan, which has contributed to the rapid recession of the Aral Sea and numerous ecological problems.[62]

The Economy's Performance During the
Gorbachev Era

Whether because of or in spite of the economic and political reforms introduced after Gorbachev assumed power, the performance of the Soviet economy declined steadily. The economy suffered not only from problems common to CSEs (e.g., shortages of goods), but also from two of the worst problems (i.e., inflation and unemployment) experienced by many economies characterized by a high degree of decentralized decision making, private ownership and control of resources, and markets as the major social process for economic coordination. In addition, the economy experienced a balance of trade deficit and a rapidly growing state budget deficit, creating a mounting debt problem. All of these problems triggered considerable labor and ethnic unrest throughout the Soviet Union.

In terms of economic growth, the percentage change of GNP was -1.0 percent and -2.5 percent in 1989 and the first half of 1990, respectively.[63] Industrial output fell 1.0 percent in the first half of 1990 (especially for coal and housing) after growing only 1.7 percent in 1989.[64] Meanwhile, rates of growth of factor productivity continued to decline as the growth of the labor force was very slow and Soviet industry failed to modernize its technology. One indicator of Soviet industrial inefficiency was the use of raw materials. The case of copper production, where Soviet producers used triple the energy used by their West German counterparts to manufacture one ton, was not unusual.[65]

Concerning output, distribution, and offering citizens a balanced diet, the agricultural sector's performance was poor. Output rose only 1.9 percent in 1989

---

[61]"Russia's Greens: The Poisoned Giant Wakes Up," *The Economist*, November 4, 1989, p. 24.
[62]Ibid.
[63]Laurie Hays, "Gorbachev Plan May Curb State, Double Prices," *The Wall Street Journal*, April 13, 1990, p. A1.
[64]Ibid.
[65]"Russia's Greens: The Poisoned Giant Wakes Up," *The Economist*, p. 24.

and 1.0 percent in the first half of 1990.[66] The amount of state subsidies paid to losing agricultural institutions grew, and nearly one third of the farms extended credit were unable to repay their loans. In terms of distribution, it was estimated that about 30 percent of all agricultural output in the Soviet Union spoiled before it could be consumed.[67] Given the low rate of growth and distribution problems, it was not surprising that the diet of a typical Soviet family was deficient in terms of dairy products, eggs, meat, fruits, and vegetables.[68] Policies attempting to alleviate problems in this sector exacerbated other problems. For example, seeking to boost output, authorities ordered high applications of chemical pesticides, resulting in a high incidence of infant mortality and childhood ailments (e.g., anemia) in affected agricultural regions.[69]

Shortages of consumer goods became more chronic. One report (from late 1989) stated that over 1,000 consumer goods used every day by typical families were consistently "in short supply."[70] The quality of what is available remained poor. One leading Soviet economist estimated that the value of unusable products (primarily consumer goods) stored in warehouses throughout the nation is about $700 billion.[71] A vivid indication of the plight of the Soviet consumer is that the wait to purchase a hamburger at the Moscow McDonald's restaurant which opened in 1989 was typically 4 hours, and the cost of the hamburger for the average worker was equivalent to a half-day's pay.

Numerous problems ensued from these shortages. The state was forced to use scarce foreign exchange to increase imports, especially of items such as soap, detergent, vegetable oil, and grain so as to satisfy consumer demand. These heavy expenditures (about $16 billion in 1989) contributed to the rising trade deficit (discussed later). Corruption in distribution has also increased. Faced with continual shortages, some state retail stores began issuing special invitations without which consumers were unable to purchase goods. These invitations often were received by factory managers who, in theory, were supposed to allocate them to workers with above-average productivity. In reality a black market emerged in which SOE managers and Communist Party officials acquired and sold these invitations on the black market. An options market also emerged as speculators began purchasing the invitations, obtaining the particular consumer good, then reselling the good for a profit.[72]

[66]Hays, "Gorbachev Plan May Curb State, Double Prices," p. A1.

[67]William Moskoff, "Introduction" to "Perestroika In The Countryside: Agricultural Reform In The Gorbachev Era," *Comparative Economic Studies*, 32, 2 (Summer 1990), 3.

[68]Ibid.

[69]"Russia's Greens: The Poisoned Giant Wakes Up," *The Economist*, p. 24.

[70]Peter Gumbel, "How Gorbachev's Plan Has Left Soviet Union Without Much Soap," *The Wall Street Journal*, November 20, 1989, pp. A1, A14.

[71]Peter Gumbel, "Soviets Testing Limited Private Initiative at State-Run Plants That Didn't Hack It," *The Wall Street Journal*, October 7, 1990, p. A12.

[72]Peter Gumbel, "Soviet Retail System Gets Strikingly Worse in Era of Perestroika," *The Wall Street Journal*, July 23, 1990, p. A1.

Inflation surged as consumer prices rose an estimated 20 percent in 1989 and about 25 percent in the first half of 1990.[73] Factors contributing to price increases included reforms increasing enterprise managers' control over prices, considerable cash balances held by the public (which people tended to use when consumer goods were available), shortages of lower-priced goods (thereby requiring that consumers purchase higher-priced but not necessarily higher-quality goods), and a wage drift partly fueled by inflationary expectations. The last problem was caused by wage increases well in excess of productivity gains since 1987. Managers, given more autonomy to grant wage increases to increasingly disgruntled workers (who were dissatisfied with declining real wages), opted to retain stability within the enterprise by seeking to placate workers without having regard for worker productivity or the impact of wage drift on inflation.

In the face of declining output and some enterprise failure (part of the reform process to eliminate inefficient SOEs), unemployment became a serious problem. The estimated unemployment for the entire labor force was 17 percent, with over 25 percent unemployment in some of the non-Russian republics.[74] Part of the rapid rise of unemployment was due to the decline in output of major products such as oil, coal, and steel. Exports of these products have fallen during the past two years, and combined with rising imports of consumer goods contributed to the Soviet Union's first trade deficit since the mid-1970s—and a strain on foreign reserves.

Due to the combination of lower growth, more enterprise autonomy (with a corresponding lower percentage of enterprise funds passing through state authority hands), greater demands on the state to import needed consumer goods and support the unemployed, and the authorities' decision to expand defense expenditures, the government budget deficit and total government debt both rose dramatically during the 1980s. In 1980, as a percentage of GNP, the Soviet government budget deficit and total debt were 2.9 percent and 14.4 percent, respectively.[75] In 1986 these percentages had grown to 6.5 percent and 21.0 percent, respectively, and by 1989 the state budget deficit as a percentage of GNP was 13.1 percent, while debt had mushroomed to 45.9 percent.[76] Lacking a market in which to sell government bonds, the state monetized its debt, thereby exacerbating the inflation problem.

Summary of Performance During the Gorbachev Era

While it is difficult to isolate the impact of the economic reforms introduced by Gorbachev from the inherent characteristics of CSE economic policies and the

---

[73]Hays, "Gorbachev Plan May Curb State, Double Prices," p. A1.

[74]"Soviet Unemployment," *The Wall Street Journal*, November 1, 1989, p. A10.

[75]Ronald I. McKinnon, "Stabilizing the Ruble," paper presented at the Association for Comparative Economic Studies Meetings, Atlanta, December 28–30, 1989, p. 2.

[76]Ibid.

economic environment external to the Soviet Union, there is no doubt that most Soviet authorities and citizens believed that the impact of the reforms has been a lower standard of living due to more severe shortages (especially food), more labor unrest, higher inflation and unemployment, and a rapidly increasing budget deficit. However, in the face of this poor performance the authorities continued to devote a high percentage of annual GNP (some estimate well over 20 percent) to defense and foreign policy matters. It is no wonder that among Soviet citizens "[t]he Communist myth . . . lost all credibility. Everyone [knew] the system [didn't] work and everyone [knew] that Mr. Gorbachev . . . [had not found] a way to make it work."[77] In response, people did little work but were not penalized for such behavior. This led to lower output levels, so people saw less reason to work hard if there was nothing to buy—and the vicious circle continued.

Many analysts believe that the combination of inherent defects of the CSE, especially its inability to allocate resources efficiently, and Gorbachev's evolving hybrid economy with its ineffective reforms shared the blame. Among the many problems with the reforms was their inability to make enterprise managers conserve resources. Rather, the demand for inputs increased after 1985. More autonomy also stimulated managers to meet their targets by raising prices, since they were being evaluated according to the "value" of what they produced. Combined with the wage drift, management autonomy fueled inflation.

Under Gorbachev the main features of the CSE remained in place. One lesson of the 1960–1989 period is that Soviet authorities, faced with a recession, sought to increase central control, which exacerbated efficiency and incentive problems. Due to the incentive structure, which rewarded party authorities whose sector, industry, or enterprise complied with the plan, these authorities continued to intervene in the management of enterprises. Fear of penalty for failure throughout the Soviet Union stimulated SOE managers to do what they believed necessary to protect themselves. For example, managers tended to stockpile inputs to increase their chances of satisfying central planners' targets, while those unable to obtain inputs were at a loss as to how to obtain them.

While there may have been considerable cooperation between ministry authorities and their enterprise managers, the same may not have been true between ministry officials who competed with one another for scarce resources (e.g., raw materials, credit), the allocation of which was under central planner control. The lack of cooperation between ministries was attributed to the Soviet people's inherent

> desire to keep contacts with the outside to a minimum [which pervaded] the entire system, from the ministries to the enterprises themselves. Individual enterprises, and their ministries, strove for vertical integration by producing most of the inputs and services required to produce the output for which they were held responsible in the plan. This was a

[77]George Melloan, "Big Macs Yes, But Don't Wait Up for Russian Capitalism," *The Wall Street Journal*, February 5, 1990, p. A15.

natural consequence of an uncertain material-technical supply system in which even enterprises with the authorization and rubles necessary to purchase an important input may have found they could not acquire it.[78]

Central authorities also manifested a preference against dealing with foreign suppliers of key products, and such behavior resulted in significant opportunity costs to the rest of the economy. A case in point was the previously discussed objective of raising cotton in Uzbekistan rather than to trade for cotton by producing a good for which the Soviet Union has more of a comparative advantage.

THE RISE AND FALL OF A STATE-COMMANDED ECONOMY AS AN ILLUSTRATION OF THE EVOLUTIONARY-INSTITUTIONAL THEORY

The absence of reform during the period from 1928 to the late 1950s is attributable to the favorable performance of the economy in terms of satisfying the objectives of the leading authorities—especially Stalin. Other reasons include the screening of information to the general public who was not aware of its low standard of living relative to industrialized Western nations, the monopoly over political power held by the Communist Party, and the strong ideological convictions of Stalin, which inhibited any alternative philosophical basis from being discussed. These conditions began to change in the late 1950s.

Recognizing some inefficient aspects of centralized planning as a social process as well as the poor variety and quality of Soviet consumer and producer goods, Soviet authorities introduced economic reforms throughout the post-Stalin era. Unfortunately for Soviet citizens, these reforms followed a "treadmill" pattern, for while authorities recognized the gradually declining performance of the economy, their unwillingness to relinquish tight control—for political and ideological reasons—contributed to continuation of the poor performance. The resistance by party officials and bureaucrats to reform is understandable, for they were the primary beneficiaries of their ability to exert control over the CSE, no matter how poorly the economy performed. Being in a position to distort or refuse to implement reforms (given their ability to appoint and influence ministers and SOE managers) while controlling the distribution of wealth, Soviet authorities were able to perpetuate their position within the social and political structure. Soviet authorities realized that their own standard of living did "not depend primarily upon the creation of wealth but upon interference in the wealth-creation process."[79] To his credit Gorbachev

---

[78]Hewett, *Reforming the Soviet Economy*, p. 170.

[79]Jan Winiecki, "Obstacles to Economic Reform of Socialism: A Property-Rights Approach," in Jan S. Prybyla, ed., "Privatizing and Marketing Socialism," *The Annals of the American Academy of Political and Social Science*, 507 (January 1990), 67.

recognized that the combination of a political monopoly, a virtually bankrupt philosophical basis, and an increasingly wasteful planning process that failed to perform adequately necessitated substantive economic and political reforms.

One result of the openness encouraged by Gorbachev throughout CEE was the widespread recognition of how poor citizens of these nations were relative to their Western counterparts. Throughout these nations informal attitudes began to favor radical political and economic reform, and by the late 1980s such reforms had been introduced either peacefully (East Germany, Hungary, Poland), or following violent civil strife (Romania). This revolutionary movement swept through the Soviet republics, many of which (including Russia) sought to secede from the Soviet Union.

LOOKING AHEAD

In the face of this movement, and recognizing that the Soviet economy was, figuratively, imploding, Gorbachev and other Communist authorities grudgingly ended the Communist Party's monopoly over political power while committing themselves to a new, although as yet only vaguely defined, philosophical basis— a "regulated market economy," which included promises of new property rights and more autonomy on the republic and local level. The reforms that were introduced have altered the social and political structures, and working rules for the economy are being changed weekly. Many new principal institutions were considered, most of which were part of a privatization movement. Many uncertainties lay ahead for Soviet authorities, for reforming a CSE is fraught with problems. These will be analyzed in Chapter 16.

KEY TERMS AND CONCEPTS

Alienation	New Economic Policy
Capitalism	*Perestroika*
Central Planning	Privatization
Crude Communism	Second Economy
Economic Base	Superstructure
Exploitation	Treadmill of Reforms
Gosplan	True Communism
Great Industrialization Debate	

QUESTIONS FOR DISCUSSION

1. What did Marx mean by exploitation?
2. What factors influenced Marx's conception of England's industrializing economy?

3. How are the economic base, superstructure, mode of production, and relations of production interrelated?
4. Why did Marx believe that crude communism was a superior economy to capitalism?
5. How did Marx's theory of history influence his critique of capitalism?
6. What were the main issues involved in the Great Industrialization Debate?
7. Why was the Soviet Union's agricultural sector collectivized in the late 1920s?
8. What is the second ("shadow") economy, and how did it contribute to the Soviet economy?
9. Was the Soviet economy before 1989 consistent with the philosophy of Karl Marx?
10. How was central planning used as a social process for economic coordination?
11. How did the political structure contribute to the ability of the Communist Party to control the Soviet economy?
12. Why was it so difficult to introduce meaningful economic reforms in the Soviet Union?
13. Evaluate the performance of the Soviet economy between 1928 and 1989.

REFERENCES

Bartley, Robert L., "The Great International Growth Slowdown," *The Wall Street Journal,* July 10, 1990, p. A16.

Bergson, Abraham, *Productivity and the Social System—The USSR and the West.* Cambridge, MA: Harvard University Press, 1978.

"Beyond Perestroika," *The Economist,* June 9, 1990, pp. 49–50.

Campbell, Robert W., *The Soviet-Type Economies: Performance and Evolution,* 3rd ed. Boston: Houghton Mifflin, 1974.

Clemens, Jr., Walter, "A Soviet Melting Pot? Nyet," *The Wall Street Journal,* June 8, 1990, p. A10.

————,"Perestroika Needs a Work Ethic to Work," *The Wall Street Journal,* December 5, 1989, p. A22.

Ebenstein, William, and Edwin Fogelman, *Today's ISMS,* 8th ed. Englewood Cliffs, NJ: Prentice-Hall, 1980.

Elliott, John E., *Comparative Economic Systems,* 2nd ed. Belmont, CA: Wadsworth, 1985.

Engels, Frederick, *Socialism: Utopian and Scientific.* New York: International Publishers, 1972.

Fusfeld, Daniel R., *The Age of the Economist,* 4th ed. Glenview, IL: Scott, Foresman and Company, 1982.

Freedman, Robert, ed., *Marx on Economics.* New York: Harcourt, Brace, and World, 1961.

Gregory, Paul R., and Robert C. Stuart, *Soviet Economic Structure and Performance,* 4th ed. New York: Harper & Row, 1990.

Gumbel, Peter, "Soviet Retail System Gets Strikingly Worse in Era of Perestroika," *The Wall Street Journal,* July 23, 1990, pp. A1, A8.

_____, "Soviets Change Economic Plan, Bar Price Rises," *The Wall Street Journal*, July 20, 1990, p. A8.

_____, "How Gorbachev's Plan Has Left Soviet Union Without Much Soap," *The Wall Street Journal*, November 20, 1989, pp. A1, A14.

_____, "Soviet Economists Charting New Reform Face Grim Opinion About Change So Far," *The Wall Street Journal*, November 14, 1989, p. A153.

_____, "Soviets Testing Limited Private Initiative at State-Run Plants That Didn't Hack It," *The Wall Street Journal*, October 7, 1989, p. 12.

Gumbel, Peter, and Laurie Hays, "Soviet Sideshow: Perestroika Bombs at Its Big Tryout in the Trade Arena," *The Wall Street Journal*, June 21, 1990, pp. A1, A10.

Gurley, John G., *Challengers to Capitalism: Marx, Lenin, Stalin, and Mao*, 2nd ed. New York: W. W. Norton, 1979.

Hays, Laurie, "Gorbachev Plan May Curb State, Double Prices," *The Wall Street Journal*, April 13, 1990, p. 1.

Heilbroner, Robert L., *The Worldly Philosophers*, 6th ed. New York: W. W. Norton, 1986.

_____, *Marxism: For and Against*. W. W. Norton, 1980.

Hewett, Ed A., *Reforming the Soviet Economy*. Washington, DC: The Brookings Institution, 1988.

Hough, Jerry F., "The Politics of Successful Economic Reform," *Soviet Economy*, 5, 1 (January-March 1989), 3–46.

Hutchings, Raymond, *Soviet Economic Development*, 2nd ed. New York: New York University Press, 1982.

Ickes, Barry W., "Obstacles to Economic Reform of Socialism: An Institutional Choice Approach," Jan S. Prybyla, ed., "Privatizing and Marketizing Socialism," *The Annals of the American Academy of Political and Social Science*, 507 (January 1990), 53–64.

Jensen, Hans E., "Marxism and Keynes: Alternative Views on Capitalism?" *Atlantic Economic Journal*, 17, 4 (December1989), 29–37.

Karatnycky, Adrian, "Yeltsin's Win Foreshadows End of Empire," *The Wall Street Journal*, May 30, 1990, p. A12.

Kuteinikov, Andrei, "Soviet Society—Much More Unequal Than US," *The Wall Street Journal*, January 26, 1990, p. A14.

Landreth, Harry, and David C. Colander, *History of Economic Theory*, 2nd ed. Boston: Houghton Mifflin, 1989.

Lindblom, Charles, *Politics and Markets*. New York: Basic Books, 1977.

Macridis, Roy L., *Contemporary Political Ideologies*, 2nd ed. Boston: Little, Brown, and Company, 1983.

Marx, Karl, and Frederick Engels, *Manifesto of the Communist Party*. New York: International Publishers, 1971.

McKinnon, Ronald I., "Stabilizing the Ruble," Paper presented at the Association for Comparative Economic Studies Meetings, Atlanta, December 28–30, 1989.

George Melloan, "Private Property: Will Russia Permit It?" *The Wall Street Journal*, February 12, 1990, p. A15.

_____, "Big Macs Yes, But Don't Wait Up for Russian Capitalism," *The Wall*

Street Journal, February 5, 1990, p. A15.

_____, "Gorbachev's Race Against Economic Chaos Isn't Going Well," *The Wall Street Journal,* September 12, 1989, p. A27.

Moskoff, William, "Introduction" to "Special Issue: *Perestroika* in the Countryside: Agricultural Reform in the Gorbachev Era," *Comparative Economic Studies,* 32, 2 (Summer 1990), 1–6.

Pollard, Alan P., ed., *USSR Facts & Figures Annual,* New York: Academic International Press, 1988.

Prybyla, Jan S., *Market and Plan Under Socialism: The Bird in the Cage.* Stanford, CA: Hoover Institution Press, 1987.

_____, "Preface" to Jan S. Prybyla, ed., "Privatizing and Marketizing Socialism," *The Annals of the American Academy of Political and Social Science,* 507 (January 1990), 9–17.

Prybyla, Jan S., ed., *Comparative Economic Systems.* New York: Appleton-Century-Crofts, 1969.

"Russia's Greens: The Poisoned Giant Wakes Up," *The Economist,* November 4, 1989, pp. 23–25.

Schroeder, Gertrude E., "Economic Reform of Socialism: The Soviet Record," Jan S. Prybyla, ed., "Privatizing and Marketizing Socialism," *The Annals of the American Academy of Political and Social Science,* 507 (January 1990), 35–43.

Sherman, Howard, *Radical Political Economy.* New York: Basic Books, 1972.

"Soviet Economy—Too Little, Too Late," *The Economist,* May 9, 1990, pp. 57–58.

"Soviet Unemployment," *The Wall Street Journal,* November 1, 1989, p. A 10.

"Special Report—The Soviet Union." *Business Week,* November 11, 1985, p. 94.

Staley, Charles E., *A History of Economic Thought: From Aristotle to Arrow.* Oxford: Basil Blackwell, 1989.

"Survey Perestroika: And Now for the Hard Part," Special Report in *The Economist,* April 28, 1990.

Taga, Leonore Shever, "The Soviet Firm in the 'Large-Scale Experiment,'" *Comparative Economic Studies,* 31, 2 (Summer 1989), 92–134.

Toumanoff, Peter, "Economic Reform and Industrial Performance in the Soviet Union: 1950–1984, *Comparative Economic Studies,* 29, 4 (Winter 1987), 128–172.

Tremel, Vladimir G., "Death From Alcohol Poisoning in the USSR," *The Wall Street Journal,* November 10, 1981, p. 26.

Wilczynski, J., *The Economics of Socialism,* 2nd ed. London: George Allen & Unwin, 1972.

Winiecki, Jan, "Obstacles to Economic Reform of Socialism: A Property-Rights Approach," in Jan S. Prybyla, ed., "Privatizing and Marketizing Socialism," *The Annals of the American Academy of Political and Social Science,* 507 (January 1990), 65–71.

16

TRANSFORMATION ISSUES

OBJECTIVES

1. Compare the perspective toward transforming CEE economies immediately after the political revolutions of 1989 and five years later.
2. Identify the lessons to be learned from the transformation experience.
3. Identify changes in CEE economies' social and political structures, philosophical bases, principal institutions, and behavior of the economy—particularly ownership and control and social processes for economic coordination.
4. Evaluate the performance of the transforming economies.

INTRODUCTION[1]

Having committed to abandon the philosophical basis and working rules of a CSE, the Soviet Union and the rest of CEE were faced with introducing reforms that would facilitate a dramatically improved performance of their economies. The reforms contemplated included changes in the working rules pertaining to the organization of decision making, production and distribution institutions, the degree of decentralization (versus centralization) of decision making, the nature of property rights (extent of private ownership and control permitted) for

---

[1]Much of the material in this chapter is taken from Angresano 1994a, 1994b, 1994c, 1994d, 1993, 1992a, 1992b.

430

productive resources, and the extent to which markets (versus cooperatives or some form of planning) were to be relied upon as a social process to coordinate production and distribution activities. Such a reform movement was without parallel. The obstacles reformers faced are discussed here.

IN THE AFTERMATH OF THE 1989 REVOLUTIONS

The rapidity and comprehensive nature of the 1989 political revolutions left analysts and policymakers in both CEE and the rest of the world unprepared to propose radical reforms. Policymakers did not have the benefit of learning how other European CSEs were reformed in the past, and nearly all chose to ignore the case of China. They did, however, recognize comprehensive reform would be difficult and would dramatically alter the distribution of income and power throughout their respective societies.

Conventional Wisdom in 1990

Policymakers recognized that many obstacles had to be overcome before a successful transformation of the former CSE economy could occur. First, it was believed that attempts by authorities to reduce state influence over particular sectors in the name of greater economic efficiency and distributional equity (e.g., removing trade barriers or subsidies to the agricultural sector, reducing defense spending) would encounter considerable political resistance.[2] Second, there was resistance to abandoning all aspects of the Marxian philosophical basis, especially state ownership of property, for fear that a "capitalist" class would emerge to exploit the working class and assume control over authorities through dominating the superstructure, just as Marx had argued. Third, there was fear and lack of knowledge concerning how to behave in a competitive economy where unregulated markets became predominant concerning the flow of production and distribution. Many authorities and other citizens believed competitive markets cause higher prices and unemployment, so whenever price reforms were announced it was feared panic buying would ensue. It was (accurately) believed that widespread fear of competitive markets would result in strikes throughout CEE, since many thought radical economic reform would result in considerable hardships—including unemployment and poverty.

Fourth, it was realized that it would be difficult for CEE authorities to establish a social and psychological environment in which faith in government was sufficient to give it the possibility of leading the country out of its economic

---

[2]It is noteworthy that obstacles discussed in this section are applicable not only to CSEs in the process of being reformed, but to other types of economies which sought to reform inefficient or partially redundant sectors (e.g., agricultural sectors in the United States, Western Europe, and Japan; the defense industry or savings and loan institutions in the United States).

difficulties. As a result, some authorities initially believed it best to introduce reforms in a piecemeal manner following suggestions from some Western economists, with a "tendency to pick and choose bits of 'capitalism' [e.g., make the nation's currency freely convertible on the international market] to be grafted on to the brain-dead socialist economy."[3] Fifth, political realities were believed to pose another obstacle for resisting reforms, for ruling bureaucrats would fight a shift of their authority to those lower in the social structure, or to the workings of an institution (a market) they feared and did not understand. Serious reformers feared these same authorities would seek to reintroduce central controls if the economy failed to perform well immediately after reforms were introduced, thereby aborting the reforms "that threaten[ed] the current property-rights structure" from which they had directly benefited.[4] Many of these same authorities were unwilling to introduce comprehensive price reform by changing the system by which most prices were administered either by planners or enterprise managers without regard for relative scarcities—fearing that such reform would stimulate inflation.

Concerning privatization, the sixth recognized obstacle was that an inevitable increase in unemployment would ensue if obsolete, revenue-losing enterprises were permitted to go bankrupt. Fear of inflation was the seventh obstacle, for it was believed that if producers were free to sell their products on the open market and state-subsidized prices were eliminated, rapid price increases would follow without the elimination of shortages or improvements in quality. This was expected particularly for agricultural products. In one pre-1989 instance in the Soviet Union, after collective farms were given greater autonomy the result was a 300 percent to 500 percent increase in the price of certain agricultural goods.

The second economy was believed to be another obstacle to reform, for many citizens, managers, and authorities had come to accept and depend upon it. Those involved with the second economy had reason to resist reform of the traditional CSE. Their competitive position vis-à-vis legal suppliers and their profit margin on goods sold would be adversely affected if free entry of other suppliers were permitted. For example, those who profited from exchanging hard currency they could obtain for local currency at exchange rates well above the official rate would suffer after the local currency becomes freely convertible to hard currency at international market exchange rates. Consequently, many of the literally millions of people engaged in the second economy would, in a manner consistent with the theory of rent-seeking behavior, seek to retain "their little illegal or gray niches and rackets," which had been carefully "cultivated" over the years, rather than become subject to unknown competitive forces.[5] The second-

[3]"Survey Perestroika: And Now for the Hard Part," *The Economist*, April 28, 1990, p. 19.
[4]Ibid.
[5]Gregory Grossman, "Sub-Rosa Privatization and Marketization in the USSR," in Jan S. Prybyla, ed., *The Annals of the American Academy of Political and Social Science*, 507 (January 1990), 51.

economy network also extended beyond petty black marketeers. Many of those involved in such activity on a large scale had links with Communist Party authorities (just as drug dealers in Western nations have ties to political authorities), so that both stood to suffer opportunity losses should privatization reforms become widespread to the extent that their area of (illegal) business was affected.[6]

The eighth obstacle concerned COMECON (Council for Mutual Economic Assistance), the trading system that linked CEE economies after World War II. Abandoning the working rules of COMECON, which had bound CEE nations in their foreign trade activities, meant a sudden decrease in trade volume due to the loss of guaranteed buyers for goods produced and guaranteed sources of low-cost supplies (particularly for those receiving natural resources from the Soviet Union). Another perceived obstacle was that workers and managers were inexperienced and unskilled for functioning effectively in a more competitive economy. The prevailing work ethic was inferior to that present in England's nineteenth-century LFME or in Germany or Japan during their respective twentieth-century industrialization drives.[7] CEE workers and managers trusted very few people, and the social structure encouraged this. The practice of nomenklatura created strict divisions between party members and workers. Workers and state-owned enterprise managers recognized few incentives to work hard or innovate in the face of low, rigid wages and the absence of quality goods and services to purchase. Widespread corruption replaced honest work in many enterprises, as many state-owned enterprise managers became "trickster-magicians juggling statistics to fulfill quotas—quality be damned."[8] As a result of the extensive network linking corrupt managers and authorities, it was feared that the new reform programs would not only be resisted, but defied.

The tenth anticipated obstacle concerned the monopoly structures and obsolete technology pervasive among state-owned enterprises. These conditions, when combined with indifferent management and worker attitudes, resulted in the production of low-quality goods at high cost per unit produced. Such conditions would discourage these firms from adapting to the foreign technology as well as inhibit foreign investment in them. It was expected that foreign investment would also be inhibited by bureaucratic delays and the absence of local finance for those foreign firms seeking working capital. The anticipated bureaucratic delays were attributable to the retention of ministries and large staffs, which were expected to continue interfering in the production and distribution process.

---

[6]In 1990 a waiter at a prominent Budapest hotel informed me that reforms would bring an end to his comparative advantage of having access to "hard" currency and ability to purchase "Western" goods, and reduce his relative standard of living. Two years later we met, and his prediction was correct.

[7]The standard joke told by CEE workers was that "we pretend to work and they pretend to pay us."

[8]Walter C. Clemens, Jr., "Perestroika Needs a Work Ethic to Work," *The Wall Street Journal*, December 5, 1989, p. A22. Clemens argues that "[e]conomic growth cannot be imparted by terror, sticking to rules, or bribes. It requires a climate of freedom and of mutual trust—both curbed by the traditions and structures of Soviet life."

Summary to Conventional Wisdom

Recognition of these obstacles had two effects on CEE during the early 1990s. In some nations reforms were resisted as fear of change and ability of authorities to retain control resulted in superficial, hybrid reforms designed to maintain many existing institutions and working rules as well as the pre-1990 position of authorities.[9] In other CEE nations reformers, stimulated by Western advisors who were influenced by recognition of these obstacles, introduced sudden comprehensive changes in working rules and principal institutions. Nearly all reformers suffered from having a dichotomy viewpoint of economies (i.e., capitalism versus socialism), and from perceiving economic transformation as a linear process ensuing from the satisfaction of specific prerequisites rather than as an evolutionary process influenced by endogenous and exogenous factors. With this conventional wisdom in mind, it is interesting to evaluate the lessons from the first five years of transformation policies.

Lessons from the 1990–1994 Experiences

The transformation experiences of CEE nations have differed from one another, partly due to each country's having a peculiar institutional structure and historical legacy. However, many similarities indicate that lessons from economic policies, which have and have not worked in both CEE and other nations, are relevant for the region. In addition, the historical experiences of some non-CEE nations shed light on the effectiveness of policies based upon a neoclassical philosophical basis and the desirability of establishing a "free market economy" (FME) in CEE.

1. TRANSFORMATION OF CEE ECONOMIES WILL REQUIRE FAR MORE TIME THAN ORIGINALLY ANTICIPATED.   Based upon the performance of the CEE economies since 1989 and the development experiences of Organization for Economic Cooperation and Development (OECD) nations and the newly industrialized Asian countries, the initial forecasts were wildly optimistic concerning the time required before CEE nations would experience both significant economic development and dramatic structural transformation. As

---

[9]Recognizing these obstacles, many CEE authorities sought to retain elements of the past philosophy and made half-hearted efforts to introduce reforms designed to guide their economy toward a regulated market economy. This resulted in a cacophony of different and often conflicting reforms in different parts of the country, while the major issues required for a comprehensive restructuring of the economy were not addressed. In this regard not only were the authorities to blame for the poor results that ensued, but also the trade union members, who (correctly) fear job insecurity if substantive reforms of SOEs are implemented. They have been successful in watering down the price reforms that have been introduced, winning compensation in the form of a partial indexing (about 70 percent) of their wages in the face of price increases— thus fueling the inflationary spiral. As of mid-1990 the Soviet authorities retained control over 80 percent of the Soviet Union's prices, and were afraid to decontrol retail prices further because of the anticipated 50 percent or greater price increases that would ensue.

illustrated in previous chapters, decades rather than a few years are usually required for any substantial transformation of an economy—particularly if a democratic form of government characterizes the political structure.[10] Many factors inhibit rapid reform. The first is the enormity of the problem. The following, highly interrelated factors must be introduced—new types of entrants into the production process (such as private and international firms), new property rights, a new philosophical basis and business ethics, and new distributional schemes featuring different incentives. Other factors inhibiting rapid reform are large populations unfamiliar with the working rules and culture of a commercial society in which markets play a dominant role in economic activity, and bureaucratic resistance to change.

Concerning this resistance, the case of CEE transformation illustrates that people tend to resist institutional change if: (1) such change is forced before they are fully informed and trust that there will be rewards for adopting the new institutions; (2) their attitudes include learned helplessness due to decades of being discouraged from taking any initiative; and (3) there exist entrenched bureaucracies (both within and outside of the political structure) whose members fear that they will lose jobs, income, and privileges as a result of change. The widespread existence of these conditions has inhibited rapid institutional change. It is clear that institutional change does not quickly or even necessarily follow legislation. Since the desired societal transformation requires that members radically change their way of thinking, habits and work patterns, sense of duty, and values regarding self-reliance, such change will occur slowly. Public cynicism towards authorities (particularly when charges of corruption are made) has delayed the process. Without credibility and legitimacy of authorities, legal changes will be ignored or violated.

2. PUBLIC SUPPORT IS NECESSARY FOR SUCCESSFUL IMPLEMENTATION OF INSTITUTIONAL CHANGE.   The introduction of democracy has, in many respects, complicated and reduced the pace of transformation. This is because it has created political fragmentation (see "Political Structure," pp. 444–445). As a result, elected authorities have difficulty arriving at consensus when faced with complex decisions. Given the comprehensive nature of required institutional changes, some form of political pluralism with interest-group representation or the emergence of a dominating political party is necessary. The public also must believe it has a partnership with its authorities through some formal or informal social contract, thereby agreeing to cooperate by making the sacrifices required for successful transformation policies, as vividly illustrated by the Japanese (see Chapters 9 and 10).

---

[10]Transformation was relatively swift when former LFMEs became CSEs due to state-directed and enforced mobilization of resources, changes in working rules and principal institutions, and state supervision and enforcement of all economic activity without having to face political opposition.

3. MUCH WESTERN ADVICE HAS BEEN INAPPROPRIATE, MISGUIDED, AND COSTLY.   The dominant stream of advice provided by the International Monetary Fund (IMF) and Harvard University advisors, some World Bank officials, and leading authorities in CEE has been from a dogmatic, neoclassical perspective. The basis for the advice was faith in policies that were never tested and not supported by any substantive evidence. There was considerable pressure on CEE authorities to accept the advice without any discourse regarding alternative perspectives. As was the case for development economists who introduced their growth models in underdeveloped nations during the 1950s and 1960s, Western advisors to CEE governments overemphasized technical solutions and paid too little attention to problems associated with institutional change. Their social engineering programs emphasized radical stabilization as they naively assumed economic growth would ensue once unregulated market forces were decreed and investment in capital increased.

The FME perceived in these advisors' proposals was an abstraction and became a "mantra . . . [they] composed . . . for recitation by elites in countries targeted for reform. Promising a new utopia to replace an earlier one, the free market plans stumble[d] on their own magisterial pretensions."[11] The grand reform schemes proposed were generally as unsuccessful as similar schemes have been in underdeveloped nations. A prime example was the $100 billion plan for reforming the former Soviet Union devised by Harvard experts. Known as the "window of opportunity," it perceived the CEE transition to an FME occurring in a linear fashion in stages, with the completion of one stage being a prerequisite for the next phase. The plan called for three phases, with 34 separate activities in the first phase alone. This first phase included institution building with reductions in social spending and subsidies to firms. Then the focus was on the achievement of macroeconomic stabilization and market reforms. Finally, the emphasis shifted to consolidating stabilization efforts, large-scale privatization, and the beginning of broad structural reforms. It was assumed that this would be completed by 1994, at which time Russian authorities would take over. A technically elegant plan that lacked a realistic perspective of economies and the process by which they evolve, it was a dismal failure.

4. ACTIVE STATE POLICIES CAN BE PRODUCTIVE.   The performance of CEE economies for the previous four decades prior to 1990 and the ideological content of Western advice led CEE authorities to believe that state intervention and poor performance of the economy are reciprocal causes. However, the experiences of industrialized economies indicate that some state intervention throughout the transformation process can be more effective than relying upon unregulated market activities. Evidence from the development experiences of other nations indicates that

---

[11]Howard Wachtel, "Common Sense About Post-Soviet Economic Reforms," *Challenge* (January-February 1992), p. 46.

organized markets (rather than unregulated, pure competition) and cooperation among corporations can be effective and efficient forms of industrial organization.

State intervention can be productive in a number of areas. The Asian experience illustrates the potential for effective state-guided industrial and trade policies. The state is also necessary, particularly now in CEE, to prevent competition of the quality of goods and services offered from becoming "savage." The extensive network of organized crime prevalent today in CEE illustrates the pressing need for greater state regulation of economic activity. The state is also necessary for providing a social safety net to its citizens who have come to expect social insurance and welfare schemes, much as they are provided by Western nations. State activity in this regard will become more necessary as privatization of previously state-owned enterprises continues and new owners have neither the desire nor willingness to provide similar schemes for their workers.

5. STUDYING THE DEVELOPMENT EXPERIENCE OF OTHER NATIONS IS USEFUL. Such a study would indicate that there has been a multitude of solutions to nations' economic problems in terms of philosophical basis, working rules for principal institutions as well as for organization of decision making, ownership and control of resources, and social processes for coordinating economic activity. CEE authorities could draw from those experiences in devising imaginative, innovative goals and policies with their own blend of state, private, and cooperative activity appropriate for their nation's conditions. For example, many economies—particularly those of Japan and South Korea—have benefited from a favorable coexistence and cooperation between the public and private sectors. State initiative has been effective in developing an industrialization strategy to expand infrastructure and establish industries deemed to be of strategic importance by authorities. Selective promotion of exports and imports has also contributed to high growth rates. Overall, Asian nations illustrate a nondogmatic view that markets need to be governed to support entrepreneurial initiatives identified as important by the state.

The French, Austrian, German, and Italian experiences indicate that some type of economic planning and state ownership of enterprises can provide productive efficiency as well. In fact, nearly all of Western Europe's economies were reconstructed after World War II through reliance upon widespread controls and regulations and a significant amount of public ownership of enterprises. The states managed exchange rates, capital flows, some prices, promotion of exports and some restrictions on imports, and did not emphasize achievement of abstract monetary targets. Sweden's post-1932 development (see Chapter 13) illustrates how a small, open economy required to be competitive on world markets and whose population would come to expect social insurance and welfare measures could develop a unique blend of institutions and rules to become a wealthy nation that alleviated poverty.[12]

[12]It is interesting that the level of economic development in Poland in 1990 was similar to that of Sweden in 1932. For further discussion of the relevance of Sweden for CEE, see James Angresano, "A Mixed Economy in Hungary? Lessons from the Swedish Experience," *Comparative Economic Studies*, 34, 1 (Spring 1992), 41–57.

The case of China (see Chapter 18), where the economy has grown at a rate of over 10 percent annually since 1990 is interesting (while many economies of CEE nations have declined by roughly that percentage during the same period). It illustrates that rapid establishment of FME conditions in lieu of state support for enterprises is not necessary to transform an economy that previously relied heavily upon economic planning and state ownership of assets. Some unique, effective principal institutions have evolved, such as the township and village enterprises. China also demonstrates that neither massive privatization nor significant disruption of state-owned enterprise activity is necessary for rapid economic growth. It should be noted that China's pragmatic policies have been introduced by a strong, authoritarian leadership at the expense of certain democratic freedoms.

6. PRIVATIZATION IS A SLOW, UNCERTAIN PROCESS FOR PROVIDING STABILIZATION AND ECONOMIC RECOVERY.   With the exception of small-scale trading firms and small parcels of land, the growth of private-sector institutions will be slow, particularly for large-scale manufacturing. Unfortunately, throughout CEE many foreign advisors and CEE authorities believe privatization is the panacea for all transformation ills. As a result they have neglected suggesting alternatives to state ownership such as worker-owned and managed firms. Evidence indicates such alternatives can be productive and some workers in CEE would prefer these alternative forms of ownership and control.

Privatization is more complicated, and its pace has been slower and more uncertain than anticipated. Due to low levels of domestic savings and investment, a much greater interest in trade than production, capital markets remaining underdeveloped, and wariness on the part of foreign investors, levels of investment have been insufficient to contribute significantly to expanding the size of the CEE private sector. Privatization also creates new problems. The managers of some state-owned firms (about to be privatized) deliberately reduced production in order to drive down what bidders would offer to buy those enterprises for—then purchased the firms themselves at a bargain price. An increasingly cynical public is beginning to associate privatization with enriching the already privileged class as well as with greater unemployment and declining social and welfare benefits. They fear that if their state authorities direct the privatization process, then only those connected to political authorities will reap any benefits.

Researchers have identified some positive lessons from small-scale privatization efforts in the Czech Republic, Hungary, and Poland.[13] One is that real estate interests are essential in the privatization process. Since the value of the state-owned retail enterprise assets was low and of poor quality, when the new

[13]See John S. Earle, Roman Frydman, Andrzej Rapaczynski, and Joel Turkewitz, *Small Privatization: The Transformation of Retail Trade and Consumer Services in the Czech Republic, Hungary and Poland* (Budapest: Central European University Press, 1994), especially pp. xv–xxx.

owner was transferred rights to the real estate in question, he or she was much likelier to invest in upgrading the new enterprise. This was particularly true when those to whom the retail establishment was privatized were permitted to purchase the real estate upon which that enterprise was located. Another lesson is that privatization programs were more successful when new entrepreneurs (not connected to any previously existing retail enterprises) emerged to offer competition to owners of the privatized enterprises.

7. SIGNIFICANT FOREIGN AID AND INVESTMENT SHOULD NEITHER BE RELIED UPON NOR EXPECTED. While considerable aid was "committed" by Western leaders, less than one quarter was used in CEE during the first few years after the political revolutions. This was due to the inability of CEE nations to comply with the terms of the grants and loans. Meanwhile, despite CEE efforts in liberalizing trade, reducing tariffs, making their currencies convertible for trade purposes, stabilizing exchange rates, and encouraging foreign investment in nearly every CEE nation, foreign investment has been much lower than anticipated. Most investors continue to wait for more economic, social, and political stability throughout the region. A large proportion of the investments which have been made concern trade of consumer goods, with relatively little devoted to manufacturing. The competition to attract foreign investment has increased throughout CEE and nations are offering large tax breaks for firms to invest, which have reduced the potential benefits from foreign direct investment for the CEE nations.

8. TRADE LIBERALIZATION DOES NOT MEAN MORE TRADE WITH THE WEST. It has become clear that while Western nations pressed CEE nations to open their markets to Western goods, services, and investment, the reverse has not been the case. CEE producers of certain products (particularly agricultural goods, steel, and textiles) have been denied access to large Western markets. Therefore, although an export-oriented policy has been implemented throughout CEE, positive effects from trade have been modest. When coupled with the loss of trade due to the breakup of COMECON, most CEE nations have been experiencing more trade diversion than trade creation since 1990.

THE PHILOSOPHY OF THE NEW RULING CLASS AND THEIR WESTERN ADVISORS

Stale "Marxisim-Leninism" served as the philosophical basis for the pre-1989 economies, elevated to the level of state religion so as to indoctrinate citizens with a strictly conformist way of thinking. The result of conformity was a lack of real stringency, learning, and logic, particularly when comparisons with alternative, Western economies were made. After 1989 the new political regimes in CEE, assuming that the only alternative to their previous economy was a "market economy," welcomed advice (and aid) from international agencies and Western university professors.

A Western Philosophical Basis

A large majority of these economic advisors were from the United States. Most lacked experience or familiarity either with CEE or the process by which economies undergo transition (i.e., evolve). Whether advising authorities or teaching CEE students in the classroom, the overwhelming philosophical basis embodied the textbook, neoclassical perspective. Inherent in this perspective are four basic views. First, a strict dichotomy characterizes alternative economies, namely that economies are either centrally planned or "free market."[14] Second, transformation from a centrally planned economy to an FME would be relatively easy, and not too costly, once the right prerequisites were met (such as liberalized prices, free markets, and privatized enterprises). A cookbook approach to developing transformation policies was adopted, whereby it was assumed that transformation could be accomplished much as a master chef prepares a recipe, that is, obtain the proper ingredients and, using appropriate policies, the desired result would follow. What such advocates failed to realize is that transformation of economies needs to be carried out much as one plays a game of chess, with moves being made in response to the economy's reaction to previous moves (policies).[15] The myth was that free-market institutions could be established quickly, and then within a few years economic growth and a well-functioning FME would ensue.[16] The reality has been a slow institutional buildup, slow embracing of democratic and market principles, and chaotic activity throughout some parts of each CEE economy. A third basic view is that human behavior is characterized by rational, profit maximizing economic agents who respond to changes in economic variables in a universal, predictable manner. Finally, policies embodied the focus of theory on movements toward or attainment of equilibrium rather than on an evolutionary process of societal change within an historical context.

The result was the introduction of a narrow, neoclassical perspective, particularly the tendency to arrive at theoretical conclusions and postulate them

[14]I have had the opportunity to challenge many American and Western European economists regarding their dichotomous views. In nearly every case they have been unable to conceive of any alternative for CEE transformation other than their abstract notion of a "free-market economy"—the particular institutions and working rules for which few are able or willing to articulate.

[15]Typical of the Western philosophy was the proposal put forth by Harvard's Graham Allison and Grigory Yavlinsky—the "Joint Program for Western Cooperation in the Soviet Transformation to Democracy and the Market Economy." The architects established a six-year timetable for transformation (1991–1997), which they outlined would occur in a linear manner if the proper ingredients were introduced. For further information concerning this proposal, see Graham Allison and Grigory Yavlinsky, "Should the West Keep the Soviet Economy From Toppling?" *The Washington Post*, July 7, 1991, p. B3.

[16]Those putting forth such an argument gained support, while those advocating a more reasoned, gradual approach to transformation were labeled conservative and discredited.

as valid for every time, place, and culture. In justifying transformation programs or teaching CEE students, nearly all emphasis was placed upon orthodox economic theory and acquisition of technical skills with which to analyze "economic problems," that is, reducing societal problems to only economic components. The emphasis upon technical skills and the strong belief in natural law resulted in a fund of knowledge and an orientation which inhibited a more innovative pragmatic approach to analysis of societal issues and more creative policies.

Among the numerous problems that ensued from introducing only the neoclassical philosophical basis throughout CEE was that CEE authorities and students were not taught the lessons of economic history, including the fact that many countries have experienced problems when inappropriate economic models based upon unrealistic (neoclassical) assumptions of behavior are introduced. It was not made explicit that economies are constantly changing their working rules and institutions. Perhaps most significant, it was not taught that China has been able to implement significant, alternative transformation policies while experiencing positive changes in the same economic and welfare indicators which have been negative for CEE since 1989.

Toward a Different Philosophical Basis[17]

An appropriate philosophical basis for any CEE nation must go well beyond specifying methods for achieving macroeconomic stabilization and establishing an FME. It must incorporate acceptance of certain lessons from the development experiences of other nations, recognize the essential features of a realistic theory of societal change, and initiate social interaction through a dialogue among interest-group representatives. This process can provide much-needed legitimacy to the government. It can articulate ultimate and instrumental goals, which are buttressed by historical experience, and also stimulate trust and loyalty throughout the cross section of the population represented by the interest groups.

It would be in the interest of CEE nations for their authorities to recognize that some Western advice has been inappropriate and costly—particularly that neoclassical theory is of little relevance to transformation issues, and that the competitive market model is an abstract ideal which Western nations have not chosen to maintain. CEE authorities then could begin a period of studying the development experiences of other nations, from which a new philosophical basis could be developed. Such a basis might incorporate the following: (1) Change government institutions early in the process for reasons of legitimacy and efficiency. A quasi-autonomous agency similar to Japan's Ministry of International Trade and Industry could be established. (2) Restructure state-owned enterprises by replacing top management to overcome institutional rigidities and putting managers familiar with modern production techniques into

---

[17]Note that in 1994 Poland initiated a process similar to that recommended here.

positions of authority—much as was done by the Occupation Authority in Japan. (3) Focus on export promotion as an industrial policy, while negotiating a labor agreement that would trade off wage restraint for job security. (4) Form a regional trade agreement with other CEE nations since entry into the European Union with widespread access to EU members' markets is unlikely for more than a decade. (5) Emphasize a code of ethics combined with a concerted effort to fight economic crime. (6) Suggest alternative institutions (to private or state-owned firms) such as worker-managed firms and producer and consumer cooperatives.

There appears to be a need for, and potential of, negotiations in which widespread participation of interest-group representatives in both the formation and implementation of transformation programs would occur. Key issues are how authoritative and centralized state decision making needs to be, who should be involved in a negotiation process, and how to achieve macroeconomic stabilization. There is evidence that interest-group leaders can obstruct necessary reforms, so that in the absence of widespread support for public leaders there may be justification for more authoritarian state leadership during the early stages of the transformation. It may be necessary for state authorities to replace recalcitrant enterprise and labor leaders (while reducing the power of local government authorities) with interest-group leaders who have been educated concerning the need for and process of negotiation. A similar process occurred in Japan after World War II when the Occupation Authority replaced government authorities and *zaibatsu* management with a younger generation of leaders. An increase in state authority over economic policy (preferably only until macroeconomic stability can be established) strengthens the case for dialogue and negotiations if a return to permanent state-dominated economic decision making is to be avoided. While implementing a negotiated process under strong state supervision is not claimed to be a panacea for CEE problems, this alternative merits serious consideration (as Poland is doing in the mid-1990s) given the performance of the region's economies under the philosophical basis and policies established in the early 1990s.

EMERGING SOCIAL CLASSES AND SHIFTING POLITICAL STRUCTURES

Although the depth of recession, social unrest, and political stability has differed among CEE nations since 1989, nearly all nations in the region currently are experiencing a number of similar problems, albeit to varying degrees. Some of these problems pertain to the changing social structure, particularly an increase in poverty, and political decision making and state legitimacy.

Social Structure

Changes in the social structures throughout CEE have occurred since 1989 with more ethnic strife, poverty, and a more skewed distribution of income. Rising unemployment and poverty rates, especially among children and the elderly, have increased the demand for income maintenance and financial support. Privatization has contributed to the problem. As state-owned enterprises which had funded social insurance and welfare programs and provided some public services are replaced by private firms, the latter firms are less likely to continue providing such financial support. Partly as a result, there has been a growing lower class throughout CEE as poverty has increased, particularly in rural areas. Homelessness is becoming a growing problem. Children and the elderly have been affected the most, especially from falling health and education standards, which are partly due to large decreases in government expenditures for social services and welfare programs. A survey taken in Bulgaria during the early 1990s indicated that almost half of the nation's children lived below the officially defined poverty line and were undernourished.

Although some state-funded redistribution measures seek to reduce income inequalities, there appear to be sharp divisions in the standards of living throughout CEE. There are former authorities and shrewd individuals who are profiting from expanded market opportunities, but many are not. Opportunities for quick profit have been seized by the old nomenklatura, a rising business class, and members of organized crime. Some with access to materials such as coal, nickel, magnesium, petroleum and other commodities for export are becoming the nouveau riche, albeit by stripping their country of valuable resources. Only about one fourth of CEE citizens believe they are economically better off since 1990, while over half believe they are worse off.

Overall, people's attitudes are reversing from their overly optimistic expectations of late 1989 during the postrevolutionary euphoria, reverting to the "helpless envy" attitude toward individuals whose material standard of living has improved considerably. Declining living standards and the end of autocratic rule have coincided with rising crime. Organized crime is rapidly expanding. In Russia the emerging organized crime network is estimated to control over 40,000 businesses. Criminal activities throughout CEE include stolen automobile and art rings, smuggling of immigrants, the sale of drugs and nuclear weapons, police corruption, extortion, and abuses that occur in the absence of formal or informal consensus regarding business ethics.

Political Structure

In the first enthusiastic response to democracy, CEE found itself deeply fragmented politically. Authorities, who had little experience in open, honest communication, have had difficulty uniting these factions to arrive at a consensus when faced with difficult decisions—a problem exacerbated by the existence of many political parties. This has been compounded by a vacuum in political and economic (as well as legal and social) structures so that social forces and institutions have not emerged capable of shaping, selecting, and implementing necessary strategic projects. What have emerged throughout CEE are political structures which may lack legitimate political authority, thereby creating decentralization of political power. This, in turn, has given more power to local-level authorities as well as organized crime syndicates. In the case of Russia industrial lobbies have gained considerable power.

Many CEE citizens blamed their political authorities and Western advisors for the declining standards of living experienced throughout the region after the initial transformation policies were introduced beginning in 1990 (see "Performance of the New Economies," pp. 464–476). This occurred despite the fact that the adverse economic trends prevalent during the early 1990s did so partly in response to the legacy of the previous regime and economy. The feelings of opposition and alienation from transformation policymakers were manifested in the election of former Communist Party authorities in some CEE nations, including the Ukraine, Hungary, and Poland.[18] In Russia some authorities were outspoken in criticizing the IMF's "free market policies," placing some blame for the adverse economic conditions in Russia on the fund's advisors. Instability remains prevalent in Russia, where civil order has broken down—particularly in regions with ethnic divisions. In Bulgaria political instability has prevailed with a continual turnover of top government officials and the formation of a Turkish minority/Socialist coalition, which had difficulty passing reform measures. Eventually, political gridlock contributed to the Bulgarian Socialist Party winning an absolute majority in the parliament. Even in the Czech Republic where a relatively stable political structure exists under Vaclav Havel, there are legitimacy problems, as indicated by one poll which found that a majority of Czech citizens believe the new authorities do not behave in a more moral manner than the previous Communist authorities, and that it is widely believed the new authorities enjoy more benefits than their predecessors.[19]

Political instability is increasing in some CEE nations. There are two pillars of democracy missing—stable political parties and a legitimate constitution. Throughout CEE there is an absence of stability and predictability, although these can be expected to occur when there are established informal and formal working rules which give structure to the political process. Some CEE citizens perceive their government to be in a crisis. Many "apparatchiks" retain their pre-1989 authority positions and disproportionately high living standards. They are suspected not only of putting personal interests before the public

---

[18]In the 1994 Ukrainian parliamentary elections, 118 of the 175 seats won by candidates with clear party affiliations were won by members of the Ukrainian Communist Party or its members of the allied Socialist Party or Peasant Party—all of which favor a return to central planning. The Polish party which received the most votes in the 1994 election was the Democratic Left Alliance, the successor to the Communist Party. It formed a coalition government with the Polish Peasant Party. This coalition has given the nation a greater degree of political stability than exists in most of CEE, although there is tension between the moderate reformers in the coalition and Populists.

[19]Czech Parliament members granted themselves diplomatic status. Since a working rule had been passed exempting those with such status from having to pay the value-added tax on imports (which was 23 percent on luxury goods), a significant competitive advantage could be gained by such authorities vis-à-vis other Czech merchants should they choose to set up a trade-import firm.

interest, but also of subverting democratic and market reform measures. Such a perception has eroded the legitimacy of CEE political structures and contributed to rising anarchistic behavior and emergence of Populist authorities. These hard-line, ethnocentric, antireform authorities, some of whom argue there is nothing their nation can learn from the economic development experiences of other nations, seek to reestablish some economic and political institutions and working rules which prevailed before 1989. In certain CEE nations, some such authorities are gaining public support.

Some argue that the political structures now existing throughout CEE are closer to a mutation than a transformation. Others believe that this state of affairs may not be short-lived. According to two analysts,

> [w]ith so much in transition and thus so much uncertain, the new political formations in Eastern Europe can hardly be understood as regimes in transition to capitalism and liberal democracy. Rather, these are post-communist in nature, and their future is unknown. Indeed, there are good reasons to presume that this transitional state will last a long time. This is because so much is in formation and such structures take a long time to evolve.[20]

COEXISTENCE OF OLD INSTITUTIONS WITH EVOLVING INSTITUTIONS

With the dramatic transformation of CEE occurring, a number of new institutions have emerged, while others have endured, albeit in modified form. The latter include cooperatives and state-owned enterprises. The four most prominent institutions since 1989 have been foreign institutions (governments, international agencies, consultants, nonprofit educational organizations), state-owned enterprises, private-sector firms, and institutions in the "social and uncivil economy."

In retrospect, many analysts and authorities within and outside of CEE nations have criticized the advice they received from **foreign institutions** for being misguided, dogmatic, and based upon a simplistic view that laissez-faire policies are generally and self-evidently true. In their own defense, those seeking to transform CEE economies would point out that they inherited overstaffed **state-owned enterprises** that typically were energy intensive and dependent upon cheap raw materials and energy supplies from the former Soviet Union. The outlets for what these enterprises produced were no longer guaranteed with the breakdown of the bilateral trade agreements throughout the former Eastern Bloc

---

[20]Valerie Bunce and Maria Csanadi, "Uncertainty in the Transition: Post-Communism in Hungary," *East European Politics and Societies*, 7, 2 (Spring 1993), 274.

nations. In addition, there was no business culture among management, and institutional rigidities were pervasive. The extent of these institutional rigidities was grossly underestimated, for such rigidities have played a crucial role in inhibiting the effectiveness of well-intentioned reforms. When combined with the low rate of domestic and foreign investment in manufacturing, a weak credit market, and the poor potential that many state-owned enterprises offer to an investor, rapid change of these enterprises has been slow. In addition, permitting these heavily subsidized institutions to go bankrupt would create massive unemployment in particular regions given the heavy degree of concentration of industry throughout CEE prior to 1989. Since a dramatic transformation of CEE economies requires that members radically change their way of thinking, habits and work patterns, sense of duty, and values regarding self-reliance, such change will occur slowly. Public cynicism toward authorities (some of whom are believed to be corrupt) delays the process, for "legal changes that are not attended by credible commitments will be variously ignored, suppressed, violated, and otherwise distorted."[21]

Another institutional legacy is the pursuit of self-interest and clientism between political authorities and enterprise managers. This remains rampant, as do manifestations of the power of omnipotent and omnipresent former CSE bureaucracy. Many enterprises are still managed by poorly trained former nomenklatura, and profiteering due to corrupt management in such firms has contributed to growing cynicism among the public and a growing distaste for their public officials.

Legal private-sector firms have been developing since 1989, most heavily in the trade and agricultural sectors.[22] The percentage of GDP accounted for by the private sector is gradually increasing due to growth of existing firms, entry of new firms, and transformation of state-owned enterprises. As of the mid-1990s, private-sector activity accounted for over half of Poland's GDP and a lesser percentage for other CEE nations.

There is widespread involvement in what are referred to as **"social" and "uncivil" economies**.[23] Income received from sources other than the "official economy" (monetized, legal) is classified into income from these two other "economies." The social economy is characterized by activities which are nonmonetized and unrecorded, but not illegal, such as households growing their own food or bartering for goods and services with friends and relatives. A 1992 survey taken in Bulgaria, then Czechoslovakia, and Russia indicates that

[21]Oliver Williamson, "Institutional Aspects of Economic Reform: The Transaction Cost Economics Perspective," Seminar paper for *Transformation Processes in Eastern Europe—Challenges for Socio-Economic Theory* (Krakow: Cracow Academy of Economics, June 1992), p. 32.

[22]Some economic activity confined to the black market has been directed into the legal private sector. Other activity is part of the civil and uncivil economy, as discussed here.

[23]For a detailed analysis of these "economies," see Richard Rose, *Divisions and Contradictions in Economies in Transition: Household Portfolios in Russia, Bulgaria and Czechoslovakia*, Studies in Public Policy Number 206 (Glasgow: University of Strathclyde, 1992).

participation in this economy is over 90 percent in each country. The other economy is "uncivil," characterized by smuggling, taking bribes, exchanging currency, and any other activity that is monetized and illegal. The same survey reveals that participation in Bulgaria, the Czech Republic and Slovakia, and Russia in this economy is 50 percent, 73 percent, and 48 percent, respectively.[24] It was also discovered that the typical household is involved in all three economies.

There are strong indications that throughout CEE the breakdown in civil authority combined with growing poverty, job insecurity, and expanded opportunities for quick profits have contributed to an expansion of criminal activity (although some argue corruption may have always been high, but is now more openly acknowledged). Some Russians believe they have traded the former Communist Party authorities for another unsavory set of masters—organized crime lords. In all countries the sharp, steady growth of crime rates has been of "precipitous proportions."[25] Smuggling, sale of narcotics, and organized crime networks are pervasive. Opinion polls indicate this is particularly true in Russia where murders in retaliation for legitimate merchants refusing to pay protection money are not uncommon.[26] The murder rate in Estonia, which was insignificant before 1989, now is comparable to that of New York City.

Public officials taking bribes, tax and bank officers stealing money, as well as authorities being blackmailed are also widespread. Throughout CEE the extent of organized crime and bureaucratic corruption, along with the inability of authorities to take effective measures against organized crime, is such that bribery pays and has become a necessary part of doing business, particularly in Bulgaria, the Czech Republic, and Russia.[27] Unfortunately, the "gangsterization" of CEE economy inhibits foreign investment and drains public treasuries of funds needed for infrastructure as well as social insurance and welfare measures, among other pressing needs.

THE NEW ECONOMIES

Few regions in history have experienced the dramatic changes in organization of decision making, working rules governing ownership and control of resources, and the social processes for coordinating production and distribution decisions as CEE economies have since 1989. Following the euphoria of the political

---

[24]Rose, *Divisions and Contradictions*, pp. 12, 18, 19.

[25]UNICEF, *Central and Eastern Europe in Transition: Public Policy and Social Conditions*, p. 30.

[26]See Rose Brady, "Four Years That Shook My World," *Business Week* July 26, 1993, p. 48; "Rotten to the Core," *The Economist*, August 7, 1993, pp. 47–48; and "Trouble on the Farm," *The Economist*, August 7, 1993, pp. 68–69. There has been "open physical violence" against commercial bank officials perpetrated by organized crime networks seeking to control these institutions. In 1993 alone ten senior Russian bankers were shot in Moscow.

[27]Even members of Russia's Parliament are threatened with bodily harm if they refuse to meet mobsters' demand for tribute.

revolutions it soon became apparent, as one Czech authority astutely perceived, that a successful economic revolution to bring the economies of CEE up to the level of the poorest European Union member would be 1,000 times more difficult than the achievement of dramatic political reform. In each country dozens of political parties emerged, nearly all with a different agenda for economic reform. Meanwhile foreign governments, international agencies, Western academics, and private consultants (many of which were paid by their own governments) offered their services and "expertise" to CEE nations desperate for financial and technical assistance. The ongoing transformation process continues to be analyzed by the international academic and business community. Some aspects of the first half-decade of this process follow.

Shifting Organization of Resource Allocation Decision Making

Throughout the region the nature of decision making has shifted from Communist Party authorities and central planners to political authorities operating within a new democratic political structure, representatives of international institutions (both intergovernmental and private), individuals acting within the private sector, and members of organized crime syndicates. Macroeconomic policymaking and working rules concerning areas such as ownership, trade policy, and financial institutions remain highly centralized, albeit with considerable foreign influence. CEE authorities, lacking expertise in alternative methods of economic policymaking, turned to the IMF, World Bank, and academics and consultants from Western nations for advice. All have offered CEE authorities a plethora of suggestions with one common theme—move quickly to establish an FME.[28] As a condition of foreign aid, particularly desperately needed credit, CEE authorities had to comply with certain IMF and World Bank conditions (see "Experimenting with Social Processes for Economic Coordination," pp. 458–463).

Inhibiting the evolution of certain types of institutions was common throughout CEE prior to 1989. Authorities prevented the development of a civil society with support institutions necessary for markets to function. Democratic cooperatives and business alliances such as a *keiretsu* also were not permitted. These and other types of institutions consistent with the values and culture of each CEE nation need to emerge with new decision-making mechanisms before a new type of economy can be effective.

On the microeconomic level, the expanding private sector means more decisions are being made by individuals. The opening of economies to

---

[28]Discourse regarding any "third way" alternatives for CEE has been discouraged, particularly in Poland. There has been a noticeable absence of IMF support for cooperatives, despite the historical importance of these institutions to CEE economies. The long tradition of cooperatives in Bulgaria, for example, partly reflects the people's desire for equity and recognition that cooperatives are advantageous given few sources of capital and the lack of foreign investment in areas where cooperatives have been prominent.

international trade and investment has meant that more decisions affecting the economy are being made by foreigners representing private firms. However, these decisions are being made within an environment that includes a combination of remaining working rules from the past, and a systemic vacuum (particularly in terms of business ethics) with weak central governments in terms of their ability to enforce a code of business behavior. The lack of legitimacy of state authorities has meant more power for local authorities, with the result being a virtual laissez-faire decision-making environment for those engaged in business throughout CEE.[29]

The new democratic political structure complicates the transformation of CEE economies. Authoritarian governments (note Russia after 1928, Asian Tigers) or governments with very broad popular support (Japan after 1952, France after 1946) effectively can introduce comprehensive reform measures that require the public to make sacrifices in the short term. However, democracy throughout CEE has led to people using their new freedom to oppose reform when the cost of reforms is deemed too great. For example, CEE states are trying to decentralize the degree of control they exert on the economy, but faced with regions of high unemployment and large SOEs, find that continued subsidies are necessary or the result will be massive increases in poverty.

Transformation of Ownership and Control:
Coexistence of Private, State, and Cooperative

Following the 1989 political revolutions, strong ideological arguments were offered concerning privatization. It was agreed among CEE policymakers that for a successful transformation to an FME new working rules and institutions had to be established that would give clear property rights to autonomous individuals— most of whom should be private. The assets in question, for which ownership and control rights would change, included state-owned enterprises in industry, other business assets, construction, trade, other services, financial institutions, land, real estate, and agricultural institutions. Privatization of enterprises and cooperatives was believed to be necessary, and ideological and efficiency arguments were offered in support of this belief. The focus was on form of ownership and control, as reformers failed to recognize the important role played by culture, technology, education, and the material resources and institutions to complement entrepreneurial efforts. Reformers assumed that privatization would be completed within five years. However, they failed to recognize obstacles. One obstacle is that privatization is a lengthy and highly political process which the relatively weak CEE authorities could not easily control. Second, there was considerable public support for worker ownership and control and maintenance of cooperatives. Third, absence of the proper business culture along with poor credit conditions and subsequent weak performance of CEE economies would

---

[29]In Prague it has not been uncommon for landlords to rent someone a flat, then evict the tenant when someone willing to pay a higher rent was found. Those evicted had no recourse.

inhibit emergence of a large entrepreneurial class—particularly in the manufacturing sector.

Once the decision was made to privatize, the pace and scope became the topic of debate. Some argued for a rapid, wholesale approach. This would involve quickly selling state-owned assets or creating a "mixed" ownership enterprise in which the state continued to hold control of assets and manage the firm until ownership and control could be transferred into private hands. Others believed the approach should be gradual, pragmatic, with new forms of ownership evolving slowly at a rate consistent with the availability of private capital and willingness of investors. Still another view was not to be concerned with trying to privatize existing enterprises, since they were obsolete and close to worthless if one compared most enterprises' expected rate of return to the value of their resources. Those holding this view argued for liquidating these enterprises and building new firms.[30] Proponents of this last view underestimated the enormous cost of this alternative, which would have to include retraining and public support for those who lost their jobs, and the absence of investors or shortage of investment funds to rebuild the firms. In particular, they grossly overestimated the extent of foreign capital that would be invested in CEE. Given political instability, poor infrastructure, and unattractive assets, the slow rate of foreign investment throughout CEE since 1989 should not be surprising.

Debates arose as to whether or not state-owned firms should be privatized first, with the new owners becoming responsible for the inevitable restructuring and modernization efforts required, or if restructuring should precede attempts to privatize. Arguments for privatizing first included that poor management decisions might reduce the value and attractiveness of a firm after it was restructured without being under private ownership; layoffs were inevitable during restructuring, and a private owner can implement the decision to do so more easily than the state; and the resources were not available to restructure all state-owned enterprises before they could be privatized. On the other hand, restructuring first offered the advantages of boosting the sales price of the firm, and avoiding further deterioration of its ability to produce.

In retrospect, a diversified, pragmatic approach would have been the best choice. Rather than commit to one form of privatization, policymakers could have devised a program which included privatization and restructuring where funds permitted combined with measures to support the remaining state-owned enterprises so that huge social costs of sudden, massive unemployment (usually concentrated in regions) could be avoided. By ignoring the Chinese experience, CEE policymakers did not believe that a gradual, evolutionary approach where efforts would be focused on gradually building a private sector and very slowly reducing support of state-owned enterprises could be effective. This requires recognizing that it would be necessary to maintain such enterprises for at least a

---

[30]Management expert Peter Drucker made this argument.

decade (and likely longer) and focus on managing these enterprises while devoting other resources, especially seed capital, for budding entrepreneurs to build up the private sector. Such a strategy relies on gradual growth of the private sector to overtake the state sector in importance, and seeks to minimize social costs during the transformation.

THE PROCESS OF PRIVATIZATION.   Privatization can occur in one step when ownership and control rights are transferred to a private party who then can establish management objectives and policies such as replacing assets, restructuring the firm, changing the composition of output, selecting potential buyers, and reselling the enterprise. It can also occur in stages with the state retaining ownership and a state agency or private management firm (see p. 452) becoming the agent responsible for managing the enterprise assets until ownership rights and control can be transferred to a private individual or group of individuals. The interim enterprise becomes a state-owned joint-stock or limited-liability company. Some methods of transferring ownership include open auction, sealed bids, management or employee buyouts, vouchers, restitution, restructuring by breaking up conglomerates and modernizing the production, marketing, and financial methods of individual enterprises—then privatizing—and management contracts. Each has been adopted to varying degrees throughout CEE.

The voucher method can quickly transfer ownership rights to individuals. However, since ownership is dispersed, management of the firm may remain under control of previous managers (as is the case with the Czech voucher scheme which transfers ownership of state-owned joint-stock companies to private hands). In addition, given lack of information, many voucher holders in CEE countries where they have been introduced entrust their holdings to an investment intermediary, some of which promise huge returns.[31]

Management contracts are a method of bringing in private management firms whose reward will be linked to the firm's subsequent performance until it can be sold to private owners. Management firms engage in competitive bidding against one another for the contract. Their bid includes establishing a value for the firm at the time they assume control. The successful bidder is then given management autonomy but is required to observe a hard budget constraint. Their ultimate profit will depend upon a percentage of the difference between the value they place on the state-owned firm in their bid and the value of the transformed joint-stock or limited-liability firm when it is privatized about four to five years later.

New definitions and working rules for enterprises have been written by every CEE nation, embodied in a commercial code that defines rules such as those governing foreign ownership of CEE assets, transfer of assets, restitution, and

---

[31]Some argue these funds are creating pyramid schemes and that it is a matter of time before they go bankrupt. Such was the case of a Russian fund which attracted people's life savings with promises of large profits—only to collapse.

bankruptcy. While these differ, they are similar enough to enable generalizations to be offered. The new forms of business organization are presented next, while the following section highlights the privatization process in Bulgaria, the Czech Republic, and Poland with some reference to the Romanian and Russian experiences.[32]

Concerning private firms, individuals have the right to register to become private merchants, and many have chosen to do so while retaining a primary (and in some cases secondary) job. In terms of incidence of new private firms, the overwhelming majority of them established throughout CEE have been merchants engaged in trade—many at a kiosk or small table selling retail items. General and limited partnerships are a second form of organization. In the general case, partners face unlimited liability (which may be shared equally), while limited partnerships have a general partner with unlimited liability and other partners liable only to the full extent of their contributions to the firm. A limited-liability company founded by private investors requires them to raise all capital themselves and be liable up to what they contribute. The joint-stock company founded by private individuals is permitted to raise capital through public subscription, with all shareholders' liability limited by the value of their shares. These should not be confused with the state-owned joint-stock and limited-liability companies formed from state-owned enterprises in the "*corporatization*" process as interim institutions before they can be privatized. In addition, some state-owned and municipal-owned enterprises remain, as do some cooperatives, although nearly all of the latter are in the process of being broken up or restructured under new working rules.

New working rules pertaining to foreign ownership have been established. In the typical case foreigners enjoy almost the same rights as citizens of the CEE nation in question concerning establishment of a recognized form of business organization. Any exceptions generally pertain to ownership of land. There is freedom to invest, foreigners can purchase foreign currency from banks under the same rules as citizens, and foreign-owned assets are protected from expropriation. Remission of after-tax profits generally is permitted.

Each CEE nation's privatization program is coordinated and regulated by a new principal institution—the privatization agency. Bulgaria's agency is supervised by the Council of Ministers, with land restitution handled by the Ministry of Agriculture. The Czech Federal Finance Ministry approves only large privatization projects and makes decisions concerning restitution awards, while the Ministries of National Property Administration and Privatization oversees all other projects. In addition, there are about 75 local privatization commissions involved with small-scale privatization. Poland has established a Ministry of Ownership

---

[32]Much of the information contained in the remainder of this section is drawn from Roman Frydman, Andrzej Rapaczynski, John S. Earle, et al., *The Privatization Process in Central Europe* (London: Central European University Press, 1993); and Roman Frydman, Andrzej Rapaczynski, John S. Earle et al., *The Privatization Process in Russia, Ukraine and the Baltic States* (London: Central European University Press, 1993).

Transformations office to supervise their privatization process in consultation with the Ministry of Industry when large state enterprises are involved.

THE PRIVATIZATION EXPERIENCE IN BULGARIA. Privatization has proceeded slowly in Bulgaria, despite incentives in the form of aid packages from the World Bank and IMF which are linked to the pace of privatization. The slow pace is primarily due to "sharp political controversies,"[33] as well as a lack of foreign investment, modest amount of domestic capital combined with high interest rates, and lingering recession. Since Bulgaria was highly industrialized, with a 1989 share of labor in manufacturing that was equal to the highest in Europe (38 percent of the labor force), the extent of large state-owned enterprises is considerable.

To privatize such enterprises, Bulgaria chose to rely on sales programs after a "value" which served as the selling price had been established. The program has had little impact. The initial sales program to privatize small-scale enterprises also was a failure due to poor organization and promotion of the sale, unrealistic selling prices, and the absence of foreign investors. There was some success privatizing tourist services, retail establishments, and restaurants. Some success has been realized in the privatization of housing, although this was not a pressing problem since well over 80 percent of Bulgaria's housing was privately owned as of 1989. Land restitution has occurred, albeit not in coordination with changing the rules pertaining to agricultural cooperatives. The result has been many small land holdings (and greater output on such small farms), but with some retention of the cooperative method of farming.[34] The same result has occurred in Romania where most rural farmers, rather than farm individually after restitution of land, continue to pool their land and have formed a new type of cooperative while producing collectively.[35]

One restitution problem encountered, which may have occurred throughout CEE, has been the difficulty of verification of land titles on land that has been collectivized for farming. Verification of previous ownership has not been a problem concerning restitution of other property (e.g., factories, retail shops). However, difficulties arise since most of this property is no longer in the same condition it was at the time ownership was transferred into state hands. This has resulted in considerable debate regarding either the financial amount to award as restitution, or if former owners should be given their property including the improvements without having to pay anything in addition.

---

[33]Frydman, Rapaczynski, Earle et al., *The Privatization Process in Central Europe*, p. 24.

[34]Bulgarian farmers cannot afford to purchase their own machinery, and given the absence of economies of scale, many have decided to share equipment collectively.

[35]Karen Brooks and Mieke Meurs, "Romanian Land Reform: 1991–1993," *Comparative Economic Studies*, 36, 2 (Summer 1994), 17. The authors found that the behavior of farmers was even slower in response to "competitive markets" than was behavior of private farmers.

A legacy of the previous political structure throughout CEE has manifested itself with "spontaneous" (quiet and illegal) privatization. In Bulgaria former authorities sought to transfer ownership of state-owned property to themselves or friends at a low price without a public auction. The transfer of ownership is considered "quiet" if information concerning the sale is not made public, or "illegal" if working rules are violated. Partly in response to such practices *corporatization* was introduced throughout CEE. This is a process which converts state-owned enterprises into joint-stock companies owned by the state, but with a management structure and working rules not unlike private corporations. This conversion is intended as an interim stage before the enterprise ownership and control can be transferred into private hands. There has been a very slow pace of such conversions in Bulgaria, and those that have been corporatized exhibit only modest changes in management style and methods of operation.

An example of a Bulgarian firm that sought to restructure before attempting to be privatized illustrates the enormity of transferring ownership and control of an entire economy's enterprises. AgroPolychim was part of a huge chemical conglomerate that was broken up in 1991. The firm produces agricultural chemicals and relies heavily on imported fuel (obtained from the former Soviet Union as part of the COMECON pact prior to 1989) and urea which it had purchased from another Bulgarian firm. The new conditions in CEE meant that the firm had to purchase its fuel at world market prices with hard currency from Russia or other suppliers, and had to produce its own urea (its former supplier having chosen to export the urea it produced for hard currency). Having been a highly energy-intensive production process and producing agricultural chemicals which are in a very competitive world market, AgroPolychim had to restructure and modernize if it were to survive and continue employing 20,000 Bulgarians.[36] It sought, and eventually obtained, over $80 million from the European Bank for Reconstruction and Development, an institution established by the World Bank for financing such projects in CEE. It was able to receive funding because it could produce a homogeneous product that had buyers on the world market. Unfortunately, limited credit from the European Bank for Reconstruction and Development and the inability to produce a product attractive on the international market precludes many other Bulgarian firms from being transformed in a similar manner.

THE PRIVATIZATION EXPERIENCE IN THE CZECH REPUBLIC.   The Czech government decided to emphasize rapid privatization, transferring ownership to

---

[36]The firm had to purchase modern equipment to produce its own urea, and had to become more fuel efficient to reduce production costs so that it could retain a modest profit after selling its agricultural chemicals at prevailing prices on the international market.

private individuals and letting them assume the task of restructuring. This decision, a significant part of the nation's "radical" transformation program, reflected considerable faith in private entrepreneurs and markets to quickly stimulate favorable economic performance from the rubble of the previous economy. To accomplish their objectives two methods were adopted. The first involved selling the state-owned enterprises in their early 1990s' condition to foreigners (either outright or through a joint venture with a Czech partner). The voucher method was selected as the second method, with free distribution of state-owned enterprise shares to Czech citizens. Sales of enterprises through various methods (e.g., auctions) would be a secondary means to privatize. The voucher privatization for large state-owned enterprises was done in waves, and became a learning process for all involved. Individuals could choose to bid directly or entrust their vouchers to a financial intermediary. A corporatization drive was initiated early in the transformation program through giving firms more financial independence and control over profits generated with the intention of preparing them for subsequent privatization. This was done through the creation of joint-stock companies privatized under the voucher program (although the Czech government retained some shares on a temporary basis).

The Czechs were successful in selling small-scale firms such as restaurants and shops, often through auction. Owners of the land retained property rights, so purchasers of the small enterprises had to pay rent. There was considerable growth of private retail and trade establishments, particularly in Prague. Housing was almost 50 percent privately owned, with another 30 percent being either cooperative housing or owned by enterprises. The state has gradually increased rents and utilities, and is seeking to give occupants the first option to purchase their flats. Concerning land privatization, restitution was established as a high priority which, when the preference for retaining agricultural cooperatives is considered, has meant a slow transfer of ownership. Other property such as apartment houses and about 80,000 retail and service firms have been returned to original owners, and the Catholic Church has received a considerable amount of property that had been nationalized.

THE PRIVATIZATION EXPERIENCE IN POLAND.   A somewhat unique situation existed here compared to the rest of CEE, for Polish workers wanted to assume ownership and control over enterprises as they had been led to believe would occur according to the pre-1989 philosophical basis. The relative power of labor enabled them to gain veto power over corporatization decisions. The subsequent slow pace of privatization since 1990, with the exception of small-scale firms and private entry into the retail trade and service sectors, is attributable to the unstable political structure and the struggle between labor and the state.

The type of privatization programs and relative emphasis in Poland have shifted with the changes in political authorities. There was a strong desire to limit "spontaneous" privatization after some early abuses were publicized. Methods selected included selling state-owned enterprises, a slow process given the usual problems such as inadequate valuation techniques and lack of attractive firms, and distributing shares to workers as part of a mass-privatization program. Restitution was not emphasized because of anticipated political and social problems—not the least of which are extensive claims for return of property by the powerful Catholic Church. More than in other CEE nations Poland has relied upon preprivatization management contracts to prepare firms for ownership transfer. In Poland the management firm that is awarded the contract can retain 70 percent of the firm's increased value while under its direction, with 20 percent going to workers and another 10 percent to a state supervisory agency—but only if at least 51 percent of the enterprise's shares of stock are sold by the end of the management contract (typically four years).[37] While leveraged buyouts by management or employees were expected to be popular, only a few occurred in fact. In Russia, however, employee buyouts have been the primary means of large-scale privatization. Analysts have concluded that the resulting form of "corporate governance" has been able "to create a versatile institution capable of evolving into an effective industrial institution."[38]

Small-scale firms that were the property of municipalities were either sold or rented, according to local authorities' decisions. A key issue became what rent to charge (market or a below-market, administered rate), with some concerns that insiders would obtain property rights and be given low rents. Reports of spontaneous privatization soon after the 1989 political revolution enhanced these concerns. Some Polish nomenklatura were able to obtain private ownership of enterprises by settling very low values on the former state-owned enterprise or its assets, then either purchasing the entire firm or obtaining its best machinery and equipment at little cost. Such activity stimulated a corporatization drive so that the traditional management control was restructured into a scheme similar to that of Western corporations. Some firms remained state-owned enterprises but with a different management structure, while others were converted into either joint-stock or limited-liability companies in preparation for privatization. In reality it appears that substantive changes in management did not occur and budgets remained soft, although hard budget constraints would have exacerbated a serious unemployment problem (see pp. 466–469).

EFFECTIVENESS OF PRIVATIZATION EFFORTS.   In general, transfer of ownership of large state-owned enterprises has moved slowly, although many have become joint-stock companies and some have been restructured. There has

---

[37]Frydman, Rapaczynski, Earle et al., *The Privatization Process in Central Europe*, pp. 199–201.

[38]Trevor Buck, Igor Filatochev, and Mike Wright, "Employee Buyouts and the Transformation of Russian Industry," *Comparative Economic Studies*, 36, 2 (Summer 1994), 13. In Russia policymakers tried to push privatization before restructuring and prior to development of capital markets. The result, with the exception of some enterprises where employee buyouts occurred, has been little substantive change in managerial practices and maintenance of the "old coalition of enterprise managers and ministerial officials."

been rapid growth of private activity in small private retail trade and services, with many people becoming part-time merchants while holding another job. Where voucher privatization has been employed, the state sector has been reduced, although substantive changes in management and nature and quality of products have lagged behind. Cooperatives have been increasing in number, particularly in agriculture. Meanwhile, foreign ownership, with the exception of joint ventures between either Austrian or German firms with Czech firms, has been modest.[39]

Poland may attract the most foreign investment to produce mass-market consumer goods, since its market is the largest in CEE and (like the rest of CEE) its labor force is well educated and trained and willing to work for wages that are less than 20 percent of Western European wages. Concerning the percentage of GDP accounted for by the private sector, Poland appears to have the largest percentage—estimated to be over 50 percent in 1994. While this is encouraging concerning the objective of increasing private-sector influence throughout CEE, there are three caveats. First, a higher percentage of GDP was produced in Poland by private hands before 1989 due to property rights in land remaining with individuals. In addition, nearly all of the private-sector growth has been in retail trade, agriculture, and construction with privately owned large-scale manufacturing contributing little. By late 1994 the state still owned about 60 percent of Polish industry. Finally, the GDP of all CEE nations fell precipitously from 1989 through 1992 so that the amount contributed by the private sector is being compared to a much smaller base.

Experimenting with Social Processes for
Economic Coordination[40]

The processes which have coordinated economic activity throughout Central Europe since 1989 have been a combination of unregulated markets (both legal and illegal), state regulations (legacies of the past and new working rules), organized crime activity, negotiated agreements between interest groups, plus Western policies. The means selected to stimulate transformation, primarily stabilization policies, have become short-run goals in themselves. It was assumed that achievement of stabilization established the basis for the realization of the long-run goal—establishment of an FME, although the meaning of this term has not been clearly articulated either by CEE policymakers or their Western advisors. Authorities throughout CEE have confused some actual Western economies with the textbook model of pure competition, while to most CEE citizens FME means "getting rich," rather than an economy based upon "individual liberty, self-

---

[39]Adam Smith would have predicted this, for he argued that people preferred to invest close to where they could observe the activity of the business.
[40]This section includes some material from James Angresano, "A Myrdalian View of Evolving Socio-Economic Conditions in Central and East Europe," *Development Policy Review*, 12, 3 (September 1994), 251–275.

responsibility, and self-determination in a world where the role of government is to enforce and maintain a stable set of rules."[41]

Realizing that the philosophical basis and performance of their pre-1989 economies were both bankrupt and inadequate, CEE authorities sought a new ideology. No pragmatic alternatives (such as state-guided industrial policies adopted by Japan in the 1950s) were given serious consideration. Instead, the choice was seen as "either socialism or a market economy." It was unfortunate that it became a "reductionist debate, implying a simplistic choice between shock and gradualism, [which] hid the necessary sequencing and speed of the components of an overall policy package."[42] Intellectual dogmatism led to the dichotomy view and simple, "catch slogans like 'shock therapy' versus 'gradualism' as they derive from simple intellectual schemes or models incapable of handling country-specific complexities."[43] Comprehensive privatization has been stressed even in the agricultural sector where evidence exists that cooperative and collective institutions have been productive and preferred by farmers.

The key issues faced at the beginning of the transformation were which new institutions and corresponding working rules would be chosen, how this choice would be made, and what would be the rate by which the selected institutions and rules would replace existing ones. Since the "shock approach" and its inherent economic political ideology consistent with laissez-faire provided a simple resolution to these issues consistent with the prevailing political philosophy, it became the most pervasive set of policies introduced.[44] It was proposed initially by Polish authorities, Western academics serving as their advisors, and international agency "experts." They argued that "the introduction of a set of simple initial macroeconomic conditions" such as rapidly privatizing state property, eliminating subsidies to enterprises and households, restricting growth of the money supply, reducing the budget deficit, reforming the tax system and rules for accounting, liberalizing prices, making the currency internally convertible while stabilizing the exchange rate, holding down wage increases, and opening up the domestic market by eliminating tariffs and subsidies "would provide the framework in which the operation of individual initiative rewarded by economic success in competitive market conditions would be sufficient to initiate the transformation process."[45] Liberalization of domestic and international markets and macroeconomic stabilization through restrictive

---

[41]Svetozar Pejovich, "Institutions, Nationalism, and the Transition Process in Eastern Europe," *Social Philosophy and Policy*, 10 (1993), 76.

[42]Shafiqul Islam, "Russia's Rough Road to Capitalism," *Foreign Affairs* (Spring 1993), p. 60.

[43]Kazimierz Laski, "Transition from the Command to the Market System: What Went Wrong and What to Do Now?" (Vienna: The Vienna Institute for Comparative Economic Studies, March 1993), p. 2.

[44]Simple solutions such as "shock therapy" for CEE or cutting taxes to reduce the U.S. federal budget deficit offered by "experts" and purported to be scientific often gain broad appeal, for as Thorstein Veblen once noted "the bearer of the universal solvent is irresistible."

[45]J. Kregel and Egon Matzner, "Agenda for the Reconstruction of Central and Eastern Europe," *Challenge* (September-October 1992), p. 33.

monetary and fiscal policies were viewed as the most urgent problems. The two nominal "anchors" for these programs were stabilization of the exchange rate, the goal being to reduce inflationary expectations by linking the CEE nation's currency with foreign currencies, and restraint of nominal wages with the intention being to discipline state-owned enterprises and reduce inflationary pressure.

A variety of these policies have been formulated and implemented in sequence throughout CEE, with some variation among nations regarding the extent of privatization and reduction of subsidies to state-owned enterprises. It was decided throughout CEE (with the exception of Hungary which adopted a five-year transformation program) that management of the transformation would be "top-down . . . rigorously structured and regulated by a central plan."[46] Meanwhile, policy implementation would be rapid to break the "treadmill of reforms" characteristic of the pre-1989 period and to take advantage of public acquiescence to "radical, pro-capitalist reform" while refusing to permit time for interest groups opposed to the reform to "coalesce into effective blocs."[47] The plan was bold and created an aura that transformation was a technical, "economic" problem. What was not taken into consideration, however, was the ability of interest groups to take advantage of quick schemes by obtaining assets cheaply and reselling them for substantial profit. Rather, it was widely assumed that economic efficiency gains would be realized once privatization, price liberalization, elimination of subsidies, and opening the domestic economy to international competition were in effect.

The underlying assumption regarding how the adopted policies for CEE transformation would lead to the realization of the chosen goal(s) was that supply-side responses would emerge automatically once the "social energy" inhibited before 1989 was released and "natural" market mechanisms such as freely fluctuating prices were introduced.[48] Foreigners advising CEE believed that transformation of the economies would occur in a mechanical, simplified way. They adopted an inductive method to reform, believing that certain stimuli, consisting of such available tools as stringent monetary and fiscal policy and liberalized prices, would induce desired changes throughout CEE economies. It was assumed that using the proposed stabilization measures as stimuli, the desired induction to changes in economic behavior was virtually guaranteed, as a chemist's combining of particular elements is certain to produce a specific reaction. The main advisors to Poland and Russia (prior to their being replaced in 1994) continued to predict that "the service sector will ultimately expand to

[46]Bruno Dallago, "Debate on the Transition of Post-Communist Economies to a Market Economy," *Acta Oeconomica*, 44 (1992), 273.

[47]Leif Rosenberger, "Economic Transition in Eastern Europe: Paying the Price for Freedom," *East European Quarterly*, 26 (Fall 1992), 273.

[48]Edmund Mokrzycki, "The Social Limits of East European Economic Reform," *The Journal of Socio-Economics*, 22 (Spring 1993), 29–30.

provide jobs for [unemployed] workers who, inevitably, will be released from the industrial sector."[49] It was assumed that the principles of free trade would operate so that encouraging import competition would be a stimulus for very low levels of internal competition, and that state-owned enterprises would become more efficient as a result. Widespread structural problems were recognized, and it was assumed that privatization, macroeconomic stabilization, and price and trade liberalization were prerequisites for industrial and institutional restructuring.[50] Unfortunately, reformers failed to recognize the enormous magnitude of structural adjustment required, particularly in the industrial sector. Despite evidence that China has experienced the world's highest rate of sustained economic growth since introducing different transformation policies in 1979, Western advisors argued that Chinese gradualism has "little relevance" for CEE.[51]

The "shock" transformation packages did have some successes. There was considerable reduction of sellers' influence (versus buyers) in CEE economies while queues for consumer goods have been eliminated. Inflation fell after initial rapid increases, and trade balances began to improve. However, responding to the overall performance of their economies, particularly the disparity from 1989 expectations and early 1990s' reality (see pp. 464–473), stagflation, and reduced levels of consumption, CEE citizens elected new authorities. These new leaders have introduced different policies, considered additional processes (such as a state-directed industrial policy for the many large enterprises unlikely to be privatized in the near future), while changing the relative emphasis of initial transformation programs. One Polish analyst argues that the double distress of macroeconomic and political instability that is plaguing his country has been aggravated by the fact that the shock therapy approach was not "negotiated with the representatives of the most important social groups . . . [and therefore it was] difficult to regain society's support for necessary reforms."[52]

[49]David Lipton and Jeffrey D. Sachs, "Prospects for Russia's Economic Reforms," in William C. Brainard and George L. Perry, eds., *Brookings Papers on Economic Activity*, 2 (1992), 245.

[50]The "consensus view of the transition problem" now includes recognition that the CEE nations face a multitude of unique, interrelated problems and need a social safety net plus considerable Western assistance. See Stanley Fischer, "Stabilization and Economic Reform in Russia," in William C. Brainard and George L. Perry, eds., *Brookings Papers on Economic Activity*, 2 (1992), 112.

[51]Lipton and Sachs, "Prospects for Russia's Economic Reforms," p. 246. These authors offered no further justification for this assertion. On the contrary, the case of China is significant. China has implemented a gradual transformation program characterized by slow pace of privatization and development of the private sector. Very few state-owned enterprises have been privatized, thereby reducing the social costs of transformation caused by sudden increases in unemployment. The policy has been to stimulate the private and communal/cooperative sector while continuing to plan for, and support, state-owned enterprises. Progress in price reform since 1992 has been "quiet and steady" with greater emphasis placed upon "development of markets." Peter Harrold, "The Future of China's Economic Reforms," *The Chinese Business Review* (July-August 1993), pp. 8–9.

[52]Tadeusz Kowalik, "The Great Transformation & Privatization: Two Years of Poland's Experience," working paper prepared for a seminar at the Stockholm Institute of Soviet and East European Economics, April 1992.

In Poland an "integrative method" of social change has been implemented under the guidance of Jerzy Hausner, the newly appointed Chief Advisor to the Deputy Prime Minister for Economic Affairs. This approach "consists in eliciting the desired changes by generating a process of social innovation resulting from social interaction."[53] Emphasis is placed upon developing social cooperation through gaining a consensus among the interest-group representatives of the main economic actors, building consensus for economic policies, and recognizing that state involvement in the transformation—especially in regard to industrial policy—can be productive. Polish policymakers deem it essential for an active role to be played by the state and interest groups to engage in public dialogue to develop goals and policy measures appropriate for their own conditions. These groups would negotiate, viewing it as an active learning process, for the purpose of forming social and political institutions and their respective working rules.

Negotiated decisions based upon social consensus can be efficacious. New working rules for institutions trigger processes of adaptation as well as processes of resistance. Since results from early transformation based upon orthodox theory were much worse than expectations, behavioral rigidity against change can be expected to increase. However, other analysts contributing to the growing body of institutional theory have argued that a negotiation process can counter this problem. "If some basic institutions . . . facilitate class and interest-group communication and compromising, then employee resistance to organizational change may be turned into active cooperation."[54]

Another factor which inhibits transformation of CEE economies is the cognitive restraints which put limits on the speed of behavioral change. Economic behavior evolves as a result of a learning process. Human beings require time to absorb new information, technology, and forms of organization. An open dialogue with negotiations among interest groups, by stimulating a learning process, can increase the speed by which behavioral change occurs. The state also needs to educate interest groups, particularly labor, regarding how to participate in a creative negotiation process.

Support and evidence, partly based upon comparative performances of economies, is growing in favor of active state involvement in the transformation process. One analyst argues that "during the transition there might be a case for direct controls on state enterprises to promote macroeconomic stability, rather than relying upon solely market-based measures. . . . for the state sector, price and

---

[53]Jerzy Hausner, "Imperative versus Interactive Strategy of Systemic Change in Central and Eastern Europe," paper presented at the European Association for Evolutionary Political Economy conference, Barcelona, October 28–30, 1993.

[54]Bjorn Johnson and Bengt-Ake Lundvall, "Catching Up and Institutional Learning under Post Socialism," paper presented at Aalborg University, May 1992.

wage controls, direct credit restrictions, and exchange controls must be considered as potential candidates for use by macroeconomic policy makers."[55] There are studies which indicate that for competitive economies the state will be the gatekeeper between the domestic and international economy in seeking to increase the market share of its nation's multinational corporations. Finally, there is evidence that countries with many negotiated and other forms of "market-plus" coordinating mechanisms are performing better than countries with much reliance on market mechanisms.[56]

Some critics of a "negotiated economy" argue that interest-group leaders will obstruct necessary reforms, so that in the absence of widespread support for public leaders there may be justification for more authoritarian state leadership during the early stages of the transformation. It may be necessary for state authorities to replace recalcitrant enterprise and labor leaders (while reducing the power of local government authorities) with interest-group leaders who have been educated concerning the need for and process of negotiation. A similar process occurred in Japan after World War II when the Occupation Authority replaced government authorities and *zaibatsu* management with a younger generation of leaders. An increase in state authority over economic policy (preferably only until macroeconomic stability can be established) strengthens the case for dialogue and negotiations if a return to permanent state-dominated economic decision making is to be avoided.

In Bulgaria and Russia the rapid reform schemes recommended in the early 1990s have been abandoned. The Bulgarians have been critical of the stabilization phase of the transformation policies introduced by their authorities, under the auspices of the IMF. The policies were intended to quickly reduce macroeconomic imbalances while establishing prices which reflected market forces. Opening up Bulgaria's markets to imports (with the intention of stimulating competition to enhance domestic competition) was combined with measures to reduce aggregate demand, decrease support for state-owned enterprises, and stabilize the Bulgarian lev. Following implementation of these policies, Bulgarian output dropped precipitously and investment was discouraged, since domestic firms were unable to compete on international markets.

The Russian decision to halt the reforms which had been introduced under the advice of Western advisors invited a critical analysis of the reform program. The advisors blamed the IMF and other Western donors from imposing

---

[55]Peter Murrell, "Evolution in Economies and in the Economic Reform of the Centrally Planned Economies," in Christopher Clague and G. C. Raussen eds., *The Emergence of Market Economies in Eastern Europe* (Cambridge, MA: Blackwell, 1992), p. 47.

[56]John Campbell, "Reflections on the Fiscal Crisis of the Post-Communist States," Seminar Paper Number 11, *Transformation Processes in Eastern Europe—Challenges for Socio-Economic Theory* (Krakow: Cracow Academy of Economics, April 24, 1992), pp. 29, 30. He points out that when Western nations faced stagflation during the 1970s and early 1980s, as CEE economies have since 1990, the nations that alleviated problems while inducing relatively less pain on their citizens were those that had developed "negotiated" economies (e.g., Sweden and Denmark).

conditions on aid granted. Others point to the historical legacy which made comprehensive, rapid reforms in Russia after 1990 a daunting task. The subsequent drastic decline in economic indicators and breakdown in political stability (see "Performance of the New Economies," pp. 464–473) led to the "demise of the government who wanted genuinely free markets."[57] The Russians looked to former allies for assistance, and in 1994 signed a peace accord with China that included economic agreements. The significance of this event is that Russia's authorities publicly acknowledged the apparent success of the slower-paced Chinese economic reforms, and began to look to China for lessons regarding how to develop and implement gradual economic reforms in phases.[58]

RAPID, WIDESPREAD
INSTITUTIONAL CHANGE

Nearly every pre-1989 principal institution—especially those pertaining to economic decision making, the legal system, legal forms of business organization, labor regulations, banking, and ownership—has been changed radically throughout CEE, as the efficacy of all political, social, and economic institutions was called into question. The Politburo and avowed Communist authorities have been removed from office, although in countries such as Ukraine and to a lesser extent in Hungary and Poland some have resurfaced in "socialist" or "democratic left" parties and gained reelection. Planning bureaucracies have been dismantled. State-owned enterprises are in the process of becoming state-owned joint-liability companies or have been privatized, while nearly all of the agricultural, retail, and service sectors are dominated by private enterprises. New principal institutions can be expected to emerge, particularly as CEE relationships with the European Union and international agencies evolve, while currently existing ones are almost certain to undergo substantive modifications as the new CEE economies evolve. One example of such evolution is occurring in Poland where the newly privatized large enterprises are forming interrelated networks not unlike Japanese *keiretsu*.

---

[57]"The Road to Ruin," *The Economist*, January 29, 1994, pp. 23–25.

[58]Boris Yeltsin told Chinese President Jiang Zemin, "We pay much attention to studying the experience of economic reforms in China." The Chinese response was that "the international community should acknowledge that there is no single pattern for the development of all countries." See "Russia Signs Peace Agreement with China," *Austin American-Statesman*, September 4, 1994, pp. A1, A12.

PERFORMANCE OF THE NEW ECONOMIES[59]

Since the dramatic political revolutions throughout Central and Eastern Europe (CEE) stimulated the development and implementation of transformation programs for each economy, the expected consequences of these programs have been at the center of controversy and intense examination. Much of the data and information for both quantifiable and nonquantifiable performance indicators are only partially complete and not totally reliable. Nevertheless, conclusions have been and will continue to be made from similar information for the purpose of evaluating transformation policies and determining their efficacy for being continued or implemented in another CEE nation.

Those concluding that CEE transformation policies have had a favorable effect point to the positive trends in Poland where transformation policies were first introduced on a wide scale. They argue Poland now has positive growth of industrial production, increased exports, a falling rate of inflation, a growing private sector in which over half the labor force is involved, liberalized prices, and wide availability of goods and services with few, if any, queues. In addition, they point to newly achieved guarantees of civil rights, freedom of expression, political pluralism, and more self-government by mutual agreement of competing interest groups. Critics of the shock therapy are chided for having "exaggerated the severity of current economic problems and . . . blame[ing] them on the reforms" rather than on institutional resistance to reforms and other negative economic legacies of the past.[60] The architects of Poland's initial transformation program, David Lipton and Jeffrey Sachs, believe that estimates of Polish households' decline in standard of living, which allege a fall of about 33 percent since 1989, are "based on a superficial interpretation of the change in the statistical real wage."[61] By considering changes in consumer purchases since 1989, they conclude that the decline is closer to 5 percent.

The critics, on the other hand, claim that four years since shock therapy (or similar policies) was introduced throughout CEE most of the region is mired in a deep recession. Inflation continues to persist, unemployment is rising, average life expectancy at birth is declining, poverty and income disparities are increasing, while capital flight, crime and an overall pattern of lawlessness are

---

[59]This section draws heavily from Angresano, "A Myrdalian View of Evolving Socio-Economic Conditions in Central and East Europe."

[60]William C. Brainard and George L. Perry, eds., "Editor's Summary," *Brookings Papers on Economic Activity*, 2 (Washington, DC: Brookings Institution, 1992), pp. xii–xxiii.

[61]Lipton and Sachs, "Prospects for Russia's Economic Reforms," p. 247.

pervasive, and faith in political authorities is waning.[62] They claim that Western policymakers have casually accepted the social and economic hardships experienced throughout CEE by proposing and implementing harsher measures within a shorter period of time than any OECD nation would dare to impose.[63]

In the interest of scrutinizing these programs as well as contributing to the understanding of societal change, an evaluation of the evolving CEE economies will be useful. The CEE countries selected for analysis are Bulgaria, the Czech Republic, Hungary, Poland, and Russia. The evaluation process begins by specifying the performance indicators selected, followed by an evaluation of the selected economies' actual performance. Finally, a critique of selected CEE economies' goals and policies and of suggested alternative policies to improve the CEE transformation process is provided.

Consequences of Transformation Policies

The criteria selected, and their corresponding indicators of performance, are presented in Table 16-1.[64] Including social and economic equalization reflects egalitarian values which are held by many CEE citizens. The existence of political democracy rather than an authoritarian regime, while preferred, is not considered essential for positive trends of other performance indicators.

When using these criteria to evaluate and compare the selected CEE economies a few problems arise. Only the first four correspond to performance indicators for which data are available. Furthermore, some of the data available,

---

[62]For an in-depth, comprehensive analysis of changes in social and economic conditions throughout Central and Eastern Europe, see UNICEF, *Central and Eastern Europe in Transition: Public Policy and Social Conditions*. Overall, the study concluded that coinciding with transformation policies have been a "considerable and lasting decline in output, employment and incomes and by the worsening of many social indicators . . . [as well as] the spread of poverty, birth contraction, escalation of death rates, decline in school enrollments and an unstoppable crime wave [which] have reached truly alarming proportions" (UNICEF, 1993, p. iii). This is particularly true in Russia where the impact of the economic crisis includes a reduction in average life expectancy for men from 62 to 59 years since 1989.

[63]In fairness to the policymakers, both institutional legacies and domestic and international environmental factors have been unfavorable for CEE economies. The old political elites remain and have effectively delayed or blunted substantive reforms in many nations. Outmoded state-owned enterprises combined with management and worker attitudes not suited to competitive market conditions have inhibited performance. International economic factors have also contributed to the poor performance of CEE economies. The most damaging have been the collapse of CMEA trade and the Russian economy, German reunification, which has diverted German investment and trade away from CEE, recession in nearly all OECD nations, Western trade barriers, and the difficulty faced by CEE firms adapting to the rules of business designed and practiced by firms outside of its borders. This last problem has affected adversely the former East Germany where "the destruction of its national economy, and the transformation of this economy into an adjunct of another economy with competing interests has been devastating." Roy Vogt, "Transforming the Former GDR into a Market Economy," *Comparative Economic Studies*, 34 (Fall-Winter 1992), 79.

[64]These criteria and performance indicators are similar to those used by the Swedish social scientist, Gunnar Myrdal, who had extensive experience with transformation issues throughout the world. Having selected similar criteria of performance, or what he called "value premises," as "relevant and significant" for countries as diverse as Sweden, the United States, and Asian underdeveloped countries, he undoubtedly would have applied these same criteria to CEE.

particularly those pertaining to wealth and income distribution, poverty rates, involvement in the "social" and "uncivil" economies (see p. 471) and tax avoidance are not very reliable. Table 16-2 has been constructed with these caveats in mind. Where possible, data provided by organizations not directly involved with CEE policymaking, such as the OECD and *The Economist* Intelligence Unit, and UNICEF have been selected in the interest of greater objectivity. Rather than compiling an index for each CEE economy, they will be evaluated together. Emphasis will be placed upon identification of common features and tendencies.

Further elaboration of Table 16-2 performance indicators is warranted. Some argue that the extent of participation in the "social" economy and "uncivil" economy means that GDP, poverty, real income, and unemployment data overstate the degree of misery. While this may be the case, one must be careful not to overestimate the ability of a typical household to supplement its income through such participation (beyond what it did before 1989), since many households' members have been engaged in these unofficial economies for the past four decades (and even longer in Russia). Some households actively involved in these economies before 1989 have actually suffered from the transformation. Their previous ability to supplement their official income was due to their having access to hard currency and the means to obtain consumer goods not available in their country, both of which were inaccessible to the typical CEE household at the time, but neither of which is inaccessible today.

TABLE 16-1 Criteria of Performance and Corresponding Performance Indicators

CRITERIA	PERFORMANCE INDICATOR
Social and Economic Equalization: Regarding status, opportunities,wealth, income, and levels of living.	Distribution of wealth and income.
Rise of Productivity: Increased output per capita.	Percent change in GDP/capita.
Rise of Levels of Living: Prerequisites for rising efficiency and improved productivity of labor.	Percent of poverty. Real wages. Unemployment. Inflation.
Improved Institutions and Attitudes: Want people who are efficient, diligent, orderly, punctual, honest, rational, self-reliant, energetic and enterprising, and have a long run outlook.	Number of new firms developed. Crime rates. Involvement in social and uncivil economies. Tax avoidance.
Social Discipline, Rational Planning: Establish coordinated economic policies by democratic procedures based upon sound critical reasoning. Compliance does not require compulsion.	Procedure and basis for development (transformation) policies.
National Independence: Effective formation and execution of national policies.	Political stability and ability to pass laws.
National Consolidation: United, cohesive, and effective national system of government, courts, administration with unchallenged authority within boundaries of the state.	Ability to enforce laws.
Political Democracy: National regime viewed as legitimate and is willingly accepted by a majority of the public.	Extent of democracy in political system and public attitude toward governing authorities.

TABLE 16-2　Performance of Selected CEE Nations

GDP[1]	BULGARIA	CZECHOSLOVAKIA	HUNGARY	POLAND	RUSSIA
1985–1988	3.7 %	2.5 %	1.0 %	3.8 %	2.5 %
1989	-0.3	2.4	0.4	0.2	1.6
1990	-9.1	0.8	-3.3	-11.6	-4.0
1991	-12.0	-14.9	-10.0	-9.0	-17.0
1992	-8.0	-7.0	-5.0	1.0	-20.0
1993	-4.0	-1.0	-1.0	4.6	-12.0
1994*	-4.0	-1.0	1.0	4.5	-9.0

POVERTY[2]					
1989	—	5.7 %	10.1 %	20.5 %	27.1 %
1991	—	19.4	21.3	38.8	28.7
1992	62.7 %	18.2	—	42.5	77.1

REAL INCOME[3]					
1989	100.0	100.0	100.0	100.0	100.0
1991	58.5	88.5	96.5	71.8	105.3
1992	60.8	94.0	91.8	70.3	61.7

UNEMPLOYMENT[4]					
1990	1.6%	—	1.6%	6.1%	0.0%
1991	11.7	—	7.5	11.5	0.0
1992	15.0	3.0%	12.0	15.0	1.0
1993	17.0	3.5	12.0	17.0	1.0
1994*	17.0	8.0	13.0	16.0	6.0

INFLATION					
1990	26.0%	—	28.0%	585.0%	5.0%
1991	334.0	—	35.0	70.0	103.0
1992	90.0	11.0%	23.0	43.0	2,000.0
1993	64.0	18.0	23.0	37.0	1,000.0
1994*	75.0	14.0	21.0	28.0	400.0

*Estimated—Some figures are the average of the OECD and *The Economist* Intelligence Unit forecasts.

[1]Annual percentage change in per capita real GDP. In Bulgaria, Hungary, and Russia the population has declined slightly since 1989. Pre-1989 data are for Czechoslovakia.

[2]Percentage of households earning less than 45 percent of 1989 average wage (35 percent for Czechoslovakia).

[3]Index of per capital real income; 1989 is the base year.

[4]If those working on partial shifts and those on paid or unpaid leave are included, 10.4 percent of the labor force is either unemployed or partially employed.

Sources: OECD, *The Economist* Intelligence Unit, 1993, 1994; UNICEF, 1993; World Bank, 1993; Lipton and Sachs, 1992; Mokrzycki, 1993; Surdej, 1992; Klusak and Mertlik, 1992; and Brady, 1993.

POVERTY.   Indicators such as declining real incomes,[65] rising percentages of consumption devoted to food, changing composition of food purchased (which indicates an aggravated dietary imbalance), reduced average calories consumed, and growing inability to pay rent demonstrate that poverty has "increased massively" throughout CEE, particularly in rural areas.[66] Homelessness is becoming a growing problem. In Poland an estimated 200,000 to 300,000 persons have lost their homes,[67] some because they could not afford the rent, which rose dramatically after privatization and restitution. Only the Czech Republic is experiencing improved welfare conditions. Although deterioration in welfare conditions has "stabilized" in Poland the past two years, the levels are below those which prevailed in 1989 for many Poles.[68] When the ratio of Poland's unemployed plus pensioners divided by those engaged in economic activity (the nation's "dependency ratio") for 1994 is compared with the ratio prevailing five years earlier, a rapid increase in dependency has occurred.[69] Some argue, however, that when ownership of material goods and estimated income from the social and uncivil economies are considered, people actually are better off. A 1992 survey indicated that 85 percent to 90 percent of adult Poles are worried about their survival, partly due to the new working rules which create job insecurity and place greater importance on education in securing a high-paying position—a condition that did not exist prior to 1989. Poverty among children is growing throughout the region, while health and educational standards are falling as well—with pervasive per capita cuts in health and education—among other social services, and extensive structural unemployment exacerbating the problem.

DISTRIBUTION OF WEALTH AND INCOME.   There appears to be growing "sharp divisions in standards of living" in all CEE nations.[70] However, state-funded income redistribution measures reduce the inequality. While some stronger and shrewder individuals are profiting from expanded market opportunities, many are not. Opportunities for quick profit have been seized by the old nomenklatura, new *buzinesmen*, members of organized crime, and emerging entrepreneurs. The few Russians with access to coal, nickel, magnesium, and other commodities for export are becoming the nouveau riche, albeit by

---

[65]Throughout CEE, without exception, "real wages have fallen massively . . . . Wage survey data show that, in general, the sharpest falls coincided with the introduction of 'big bang' reforms on price and trade liberalization." UNICEF, *Central and Eastern Europe in Transition: Public Policy and Social Conditions*, p. 37. As of early 1995, there was a lower per capita income in every CEE nation compared to 1989 levels.

[66]UNICEF, *Central and Eastern Europe in Transition: Public Policy and Social Conditions*, pp. 7–20, 81.

[67]Stein Ringen and Claire Wallace, *Societies in Transition: East-Central Europe Today: Prague Papers on Social Responses to Transformation*, 1 (Prague: Central European University, 1993), p. 54.

[68]UNICEF, *Central and Eastern Europe in Transition: Public Policy and Social Conditions*, p. 50.

[69]In 1989 this ratio was about 1 pensioner (and no unemployed) to 2.3 workers. Five years later, the ratio of workers to pensioners and unemployed is about 1:4.

[70]Ringen and Wallace, *Societies in Transition: East-Central Europe Today*, p. 7.

stripping the country of valuable resources. In Hungary, it is estimated that 50 percent of households have experienced a decline in their real income since 1991, while fewer than 20 percent claim they are slightly better or much better off.[71] Throughout CEE state governments are passing along responsibility for providing social services to local governments and private firms, as well as asking the public to pay a greater share of the costs. Since many firms cannot afford to provide such services and a growing number of households are unable to pay, the effects of growing disparity in wealth and income are exacerbated.

DEVELOPMENT OF NEW FIRMS.   In each CEE country with the exception of Russia, the number of newly privatized firms or newly created firms is considerable. In Bulgaria an estimated 200,000 new private firms had been created by early 1992, although many employ only one or two persons and the owner may also work in the official economy. Nearly 1 million new firms are present in the Czech Republic, and it is estimated that the private sector accounts for over 30 percent of the value of total output. The rate of development of such firms is similar in Hungary, while in Poland it is estimated that over 35 percent of the value of output is already accounted for by new private firms. When illegal activity is included, the percentage increases considerably.

Evidence throughout CEE indicates that while private firms are "burgeoning" in retail, service, and light industry, development of private ownership of medium- and large-scale manufacturing enterprises will be prolonged, even where the government is committed to "rapid" privatization. In part this is due to high capital requirements and inability of family members to provide the labor and financial needs for larger firms. Another factor is recognition of state authorities that there are significant economic and social costs to privatization and that delaying privatization is viable and efficacious, as long as other transformation policies contribute to stable or rising levels of living.

CRIME.   There are strong indications that throughout CEE the breakdown in civil authority combined with growing poverty, job insecurity, and expanded opportunities for quick profits have contributed to an expansion of criminal activity (although some argue corruption may have always been high but is now more openly acknowledged). In all countries the sharp, steady growth of crime rates has been of "precipitous proportions." Using 1989 as the base year to compute an index (100.0) for the number of crimes reported, the index in 1992 was 394.6 in Bulgaria, 285.8 in the Czech Republic, 198.4 in Hungary, 178.1 in Poland, and 169.4 in Russia.[72] Smuggling, sale of narcotics, and organized crime networks are pervasive. Opinion polls indicate this is particularly true in Russia where murders in retaliation for legitimate merchants refusing to pay protection money

[71]Ibid., p. 7.
[72]UNICEF, *Central and Eastern Europe in Transition: Public Policy and Social Conditions*, p. 87.

are not uncommon.[73] Public officials taking bribes and tax and bank officers stealing money are also widespread. Throughout CEE the extent of organized crime and bureaucratic corruption is such that bribery has become a necessary part of doing business, particularly in Bulgaria, the Czech Republic, and Russia.

INVOLVEMENT IN SOCIAL AND UNCIVIL ECONOMIES.   As discussed in "Principal Institutions," the typical household is involved in the official, social, and uncivil economies. Therefore, income from one household member working in the official sector is the only source of income in a minority of households. Participation in the multiplicity of economies offers protection, a safety net for many households to defend themselves against growing economic insecurity and falling real incomes earned in the official economy. It also offers enterprising individuals the opportunity to supplement their incomes. However, the combination of rising crime and participation in the social and uncivil economies has led not only to higher incomes, but to tax avoidance, thereby exacerbating the state's fiscal problems. It is relatively easy for those engaged in the alternative economies to avoid paying income, social security, and value-added taxes, which are the primary sources of tax revenue.

PROCEDURE AND BASIS FOR TRANSFORMATION POLICIES.   The transformation policies introduced in Poland, and to a lesser degree in Bulgaria and the Czech Republic, have their basis in the previously discussed assumptions. The approach was essentially "cookbook," with considerable faith that private-sector supply-side adjustments led by an emerging entrepreneurial class will compensate for the destruction of the state sector. In Russia this approach had been advocated by advisors (who since have resigned), but the reality has been reforms that are patchwork, piecemeal, and primarily destructive.

POLITICAL STABILITY.   In Bulgaria this has been particularly low, with continual turnover of top government officials. The Turkish-Socialist coalition was fragile and unable to pass substantive reform measures; in the 1994 parliamentary elections, the Socialist party emerged as the dominant political authority. Instability remains prevalent in Russia, where civil order has broken down, particularly in regions with ethnic divisions. Relative stability is predicted for the Czech Republic, but indicators for potential unrest exist in Hungary, where the Socialist Party is growing in popularity, and Poland, where tension over the budget and unfilled radical promises by the early 1990s' government led to the rise to power of the Democratic Left Alliance, the successor to the Communist Party, which formed a coalition government with the Polish Peasant Party in 1994.

---

[73]See Brady, "Four Years That Shook My World," p. 48, and "Rotten to the Core," and "No Foreigners Need Apply," *The Economist*, August 7, 1993, pp. 47–48, 68–69. There has been "open physical violence" against commercial bank officials perpetrated by organized crime networks seeking to control these institutions. In 1993 alone ten senior Russian bankers were shot in Moscow.

ABILITY TO ENFORCE LAWS.   Given the financial crises experienced by all CEE governments, partly a manifestation of weak regimes, tax avoidance, and rising crime, law enforcement is weak—particularly when crime or corruption is involved. As a result, it is not unusual for one party engaged in a contract to renege, or to demand new terms, with little recourse for the aggrieved party.

DEMOCRACY AND PUBLIC SUPPORT FOR AUTHORITIES.   Democratically elected regimes characterize CEE, but with growing negative public attitudes in the face of the economic crisis. Workers are growing more opposed to privatization, viewing it as a threat to their security and standard of living as real wages decline and jobs become less secure. Ethnocentrism is rising within CEE nations due to people's lack of faith in their ruling authorities. In an environment of "institutional instability," manifested by the government's inability to enforce laws and growing corruption on all levels, people linked by a common culture and language band together since they can understand and predict one another's behavior. Seeking to retain their power, the ruling elite fuels ethnic or nationalistic feelings by "creating the perception of an external threat to their respective ethnic groups."[74] Feelings of hopelessness and the persistent stagflation make conditions ripe, in the opinion of some, for a dictatorial government to assume power while blaming free market reforms for the declining standards of living. This has occurred already in Russia, and is threatening to occur in Bulgaria, where the political authorities suffer from lack of legitimacy. In the other three CEE nations the popularity of the ruling party may be declining but appears secure for the immediate future.

Summary

The debate about the effect of transformation policies will continue given the impossibility of isolating their impact while holding other factors responsible for performance constant, such as the economic environment throughout Europe and lingering institutions from the past. However, using comparable performance indicators, one conclusion that can be drawn is that trends in China, except for inflation and political democracy, are either more positive or similar than corresponding results in CEE.[75] (See Chapter 18, "Performance.") In nearly every year since 1978 China's actual performance has exceeded planned performance, while in CEE the decline in economic activity following implementation of

---

[74]Svetozar Pejovich, "Institutions, Nationalism, and the Transition Process in Eastern Europe," *Social Philosophy and Policy*, 10 (Summer 1993), 72–73.

[75]Comparable performance indicators for China indicate high rates of GDP and real income growth, low incidence of poverty and unemployment, and lower rates of inflation than in CEE. New firms are developing rapidly in importance. The transformation policy adopted has been pragmatic, less ideological than in CEE, and there has been political stability. On the negative side, the distribution of wealth and income is becoming more unequal, and there is no democracy. For a comparative analysis of East Asian economies and the lessons to be learned from their development path, see The World Bank, *The East Asian Miracle* (Washington, DC: World Bank, 1993).

transformation measures consistently has exceeded the most pessimistic forecasts of policymakers and their foreign advisors. Consequently, the social and economic costs borne by the Chinese during their transformation have been much less than in CEE.

Based upon the criteria for performance and performance indicators, the performance of CEE economies can be considered as relatively poor.[76] Negative assessments would be given to social and economic equalization, rise of productivity, rise of levels of living, and social discipline and rational planning. Positive and negative aspects can be identified for each of the other four criteria. Overall, the performance indicator's "tendencies" appear to be unfavorable due to the absence of any clear, positive trends throughout CEE. This evaluation, combined with the comparison with China, calls into question the efficacy of CEE policies based upon the assumption that transformation requires rapid privatization, elimination of subsidies to state-owned enterprises, and stabilization measures prior to institutional reforms, or that the state should assume a passive role concerning supply-side responses during the transformation process.

What Went Wrong? A Critique of CEE Transformation Goals and Policies

GOALS.   Some critics argue that transformation goals for CEE in the early 1990s were biased toward Western interests, ridden with ideological assumptions inherent in neoclassical theory such as a desire to secure markets for Western exports and access to CEE's raw materials, and to strengthen political influence throughout the region.[77] The treatment of stabilization measures as ends in themselves for the short run and the claim that these are means which can be separated from the ultimate goal (namely, the specific type of economy to be established) run counter to the belief that development should be defined by societies' needs, not abstract targets, and that means and ends cannot be separated.[78] Finally, some CEE analysts oppose establishment of an FME in which the state plays a passive role coordinating economic activity. They believe CEE citizens prefer a society in which the social welfare of all citizens would be the

[76]Note that the conclusion drawn by UNICEF is that the gravity and relative extent of the decline in CEE nations' social and economic indicators is both "unprecedented and more pronounced, in relative terms, than those observed in Latin America and Africa" during the 1980s (UNICEF, *Central and Eastern Europe in Transition: Public Policy and Social Conditions*, p. 2). The study also concludes that the "largely unexpected deterioration in human welfare" (especially rising poverty, mortality, and crime rates) has been "certainly aggravated" by "policy design problems" (Ibid., p. 45).

[77]In a spring 1993 meeting in Prague, a member of the European Community Commission, while admitting that CEE exporters faced high barriers when seeking to trade with the European Union (EU), told CEE officials that they should not retaliate or the EU would raise barriers even higher.

[78]Some social scientists see a continuum (i.e., what is a means in one situation becomes an end in another, and vice versa) between ultimate and instrumental goals, the method chosen to satisfy a chosen goal is not neutral since it reflects the policymaker's (and perhaps the analyst's) viewpoint. Consequently, they argue that ends and means cannot be separated.

common responsibility of the state. That is, while private ownership and control would be the rule, everyone would be guaranteed a simple and decent standard of living—particularly housing, social insurance, and welfare programs such as family services (child care, home allowances, home care for the ill and elderly), health care, and pensions. There would be state-funded relief from distress for the poor, particularly that due to economic conditions beyond their control. Advocates of such goals conclude that CEE populations, having been influenced by the demonstration effect of living standards and the extent of state support provided to all interest groups throughout OECD nations, will not tolerate the wide income disparities and reduced state responsibility for employment, education, and other social and welfare services which are inevitable under current policies.

POLICIES.   There are five areas in which CEE policies have come under criticism. The first concerns the uniformity of the policy measures introduced throughout the region. Critics agree that no single set of "economic" policies can serve as a "universal panacea" for CEE.[79] Lipton and Sachs's transformation policies are a prime target, since they "make no allowances for cultural and historical differences between the countries and ethnic groups . . . [they have] been advising."[80] Unfortunately, the "arrogant messianism of shock therapy" was accepted throughout CEE as a "sweeping prescription."[81] Yale Professor William Nordhaus admittedly finds the underlying premises of these policies "disturbing," describing them as a "canonical five-plan for stabilization" which Western advisors seek to "apply everywhere from Azerbaijan to Zaire."[82] He cites the case of Russia which is burdened with a depressed economy despite faithfully adhering to the IMF "cookbook recipe" for transformation.

The second criticism would be that the strong technical bent of Western advisors, combined with behavioral assumptions and policy prescriptions which have their roots in traditional neoclassical theory, are at best questionable and at worst completely inappropriate for CEE. This neoclassical approach leads to policies which seek to introduce institutions common to the textbook FME model, reduce all economic problems as a matter of optimum allocation of resources, and assume that efficiency will be established once perfectly competitive markets and free individuals seeking to maximize utility are created or emerge. The approach is both "simplistic" in its formulation of policies and representative of a "revival of a monolithic and deterministic vision of the economic system and the way it works."[83]

[79]Norman Barry, "The Social Market Economy," *Social Philosophy and Policy*, 10 (Summer 1993), 2.

[80]Pejovich, "Institutions, Nationalism, and the Transition Process in Eastern Europe," p. 76.

[81]A. Koves, "Shock Therapy Versus Gradual Change," *Acta Oeconomica*, 44 (1992), 17, 29.

[82]Stanley Fischer, "Stabilization and Economic Reform in Russia," in William C. Brainard and George L. Perry, eds., *Brookings Papers on Economic Activity*, 1 (Washington, DC: Brookings Institution, 1992), p. 117.

[83]Bruno Dallago, "Debate on the Transition of Post-Communist Economies to a Market Economy," p. 268.

One egregious assumption concerns the belief that Schumpeterian-type entrepreneurs will emerge and provide the necessary supply-side creation of new processes to stimulate economic recovery. One regional expert argues it is incorrect to assume a latent "capitalist" class exists which will respond spontaneously and "rationally to investment opportunities."[84] Instead, the richest segments of CEE societies—political authorities, nomenklatura, and organized crime leaders—are attracted by profit opportunities through short-term deals, being afforded such opportunities due to the retention of monopoly position by many state-owned enterprises even if they are privatized. A study of each pre-1989 CEE society would have made that outcome easy to predict, for as two Czech economists point out, "the whole economic system of the central planning . . . [was] based on power relations and on distribution of power. And all this complex system of inequalities of agents was not at all broken in the transition process—it was rather enforced."[85]

Third, CEE policymakers were naive to expect economic rationality to be the only guiding force of the transition, an assumption which followed from their "underestimat[ing what de Tocqueville called] the 'soft' factors of habits, mentalities, cultural routines."[86] From CEE nations' historical legacy many values, norms, and standards for behavior persist which are the primary impediment to development. These include the absence of individualistic competitiveness that is achievement oriented, lack of a civic culture by which people willingly adhere to a rule of law, and absence of a business culture whereby people would be clean, orderly, neat, and eager to satisfy consumers. Where legislation was passed and implemented with the intention of creating the desired "free market" institutions, policymakers failed to account for the institutional legacy of the previous economy whose participants continue to defend themselves from the threat of market forces through lobbying efforts to receive state support. The CEE legacy of "behavioral shortcomings" and "economic incompetence" (including inept managerial and marketing skills) means a long learning process is necessary to permit skills to be developed that will enable CEE firms to become competitive in the international economy.

The decision to reduce rapidly the role of the state in the transformation process is the fourth criticism. It was a simplistic conception of policymakers to believe that since the political structure of CEE caused the economic conditions prevailing in 1989, its removal would open the road to prosperity. There was an ideological commitment to laissez-faire policies which has stood in the way of

[84]Alec Nove, "Economics of the Transition Period," *Forum*, 5, 11-12 (July 1992), 6–7.

[85]Miroslav Klusak and Pavel Mertlik, "Transformation and Macroeconomic Stabilization of the Czechoslovak Economy," paper presented at the "Negotiated Economy and Neo-Liberalism as Institutional Frameworks for a Market Economy" conference, Ambleside, Cumbria, UK, July 4–5, 1992, pp. 11–12.

[86]Piotr Sztompka, "Civilizational Competence: The Prerequisite of Post-Communist Transition," unpublished paper presented at Jagiellonian University, Krakow, November 1992, p. 2.

devising and implementing an investment and overall industrial development. The belief that state involvement in economic development is always counterproductive contradicts the experiences of almost every OECD nation. Where states have been actively engaged in industrial policy, "market conditions" were created and did not emerge naturally following the release of social energy and removal of political and legal barriers, and "ideological sanctification was almost an afterthought."[87] It has become apparent that completion of the privatization process in CEE will take many years, and that attempts to privatize rapidly induce problems which are harmful to economic performance.

According to a renowned expert the Western-designed policies aimed at rapid transformation of the Russian economy were a "recipe for speedy disaster."[88] Unfortunately, he was correct. The level of investment, medical services, supplies of food, and quality of transportation all fell dramatically. The liberalization of trade combined with currency convertibility encouraged those with accumulated rubles to either transfer them to foreign financial institutions where they would be protected from inflation (which ensued), or purchase consumer goods at fixed state prices for resale after such activity was permitted. The extent of foreign assistance and investment was far too little to have any appreciable impact on the economy.

CEE TRANSFORMATION AND THE EVOLUTIONARY-INSTITUTIONAL THEORY

The political revolutions of 1989 and subsequent radical changes and attempts to transform CEE economies illustrate the five themes embodied in the evolutionary-institutional theory (see Chapter 1). Knowledge of CEE history, particularly how the dominant political and economic institutions were established and perceived, provides a sound basis for understanding transformation decisions which sought to quickly escape from the ideological, bureaucratic hold former authorities exerted over the economy. Since 1989 CEE economies have been significantly affected by their political structure, either by permitting substantive reforms in nations such as the Czech Republic where the government is stable, or inhibiting reforms in less stable political environments such as Bulgaria. The rapid changes in CEE social structures, particularly the emergence of widespread poverty, has led to changes in authorities in recent elections—some of which will introduce changes in the economy's working rules that will shift the early direction and nature of transformation efforts.

[87]Barry, "The Social Market Economy," p. 1.
[88]See Nove, "Economics of the Transition Period," pp. 1–15.

That economies are fluid with new working rules creating new institutions emphatically is illustrated, particularly how these institutions are responding to shifts in the different philosophical bases that have been held at different points since 1989 by ruling CEE authorities and their advisors. Finally, it cannot be concluded that an advanced level of economic development in the Western nations' "market economies" means that similar working rules and institutions in CEE will generate a comparable level of performance. This has been apparent in the performance of CEE economies since 1989.

LOOKING AHEAD

The specific example of Hungary as a CEE economy undergoing transformation is presented in Chapter 17, while the subsequent chapter focuses on China as the world's fastest growing economy. China offers an interesting contrast to CEE transformation, for it has been gradually transforming itself by replacing many aspects of the command over a social economy with working rules and institutions that blend private, cooperative, and state-directed features while remaining consistent with the nation's culture.

KEY TERMS AND CONCEPTS

Corporatization
Free Market Economy
Macroeconomic Stabilization Policies
Negotiated Economy

Privatization
Restitution
Social Economy
Uncivil Economy

QUESTIONS FOR DISCUSSION

1. How has the historical legacy of the pre-1989 CEE economies inhibited transformation efforts?
2. Provide an evaluation of the philosophical basis contained in the early transformation programs.
3. What were the main elements of the transformation programs proposed to CEE nations by Western advisors?
4. Why is the privatization process likely to take a few decades to complete?
5. Using your own criteria, evaluate the performance of the CEE economies since 1989.
6. Compare the transformation programs proposed by Western advisors with the gradual program now being introduced in Poland. Using what you have learned earlier in the book, explain which approach you believe would be likelier to transform a particular CEE economy in a desired direction.

REFERENCES

Allison, Graham, and Grigory Yavlinsky, "Should the West Keep the Soviet Economy From Toppling?" *The Washington Post*, July 7, 1991, p. B3.

Amoroso, Bruno, "Is the 'Scandinavian Model' an Alternative to Communism in Eastern Europe?" in Amoroso and Jesper Jespersen, *Macroeconomic Theory and Policy for the 90s*. London: Macmillan, 1992, pp. 117–140.

Angresano, James, "Institutional Change in Bulgaria—A Socio-Economic Approach," *The Journal of Socio-Economics*, 23 (Spring/Summer 1994a), 79–100.

_____, "A Myrdalian View of Evolving Socio-Economic Conditions in Central and East Europe," *Development Policy Review*, 12, 3 (September 1994b), 251–275.

_____, "Pedagogy of the Transformation: Economic Education in Central and East Europe," *Higher Education in Europe*, 19, 2 (1994c), 112–118.

_____, "An Alternative Scenario for Central and East European Transformation," *Journal of Economic Studies*, 21, 3 (1994d), 22–38.

_____, "Bulgarian Transformation: The Need for an Evolutionary-Institutional Approach," in *Transformation Processes in Eastern Europe: Challenges for Socio-Economic Theory*. Seminar Paper Number 20. Krakow: Cracow Academy of Economics, 1993.

_____, "A Mixed Economy for Hungary? Lessons from the Swedish Experience," *Comparative Economic Studies*, 34, 2 (Summer 1992a), 41–57.

_____, "Political and Economic Obstacles Inhibiting Comprehensive Reform in Hungary," *East European Quarterly*, 26, 1 (March 1992b), 55–76.

"A Survey of Poland," *The Economist*, April 16, 1994.

Austin American-Statesman, "Russia Signs Peace Agreement with China," September 4, 1994, pp. A1, A12.

Brady, Rose, "Four Years That Shook My World," *Business Week*, July 26, 1993, p. 48.

Brainard, William C., and George L. Perry, "Editor's Summary," *Brookings Papers on Economic Activity*, 2 (1992), ix–xxv.

Barry, Norman, "The Social Market Economy," *Social Philosophy and Policy*, 10 (Summer 1993), 1–25.

Brooks, Karen, and Mieke Meurs, "Romanian Land Reform: 1991–1993," *Comparative Economic Studies*, 36, 2 (Summer 1994), 17–32.

Buchanan, James, "Asymmetrical Reciprocity in Market Exchange: Implications for Economies in Transition," *Social Philosophy and Policy*, 10 (Summer 1993), 51–64.

Buck, Trevor, Igor Filatochev, and Mike Wright, "Employee Buyouts and the Transformation of Russian Industry," *Comparative Economic Studies*, 36, 2 (Summer 1994), 1–17.

Bunce, Valerie, and Maria Csanadi, "Uncertainty in the Transition: Post-Communism in Hungary," *East European Politics and Societies*, 7, 2 (Spring 1993), 240–275.

Campbell, John L., "Institutional Theory and the Influence of Foreign Actors on

Reform in Capitalist and Post-Socialist Societies," paper presented at conference on "Post-Socialism: Problems and Prospects," Ambleside, Cumbria, UK, July 1992.

Campbell, John L., "Reflections on the Fiscal Crisis of the Post-Communist States," *Seminar Papers No. 11 Transformation Processes in Eastern Europe— Challenges for Socio-Economic Theory.* Krakow, Cracow Academy of Economics, April 24, 1992, pp. 5–40.

Clague, Christopher, and Gordon C. Rausser, eds., *The Emergence of Market Economies in Eastern Europe.* Cambridge, MA: Blackwell, 1992.

Clemens, Jr., Walter C., "Perestroika Needs a Work Ethic to Work," *The Wall Street Journal,* December 5, 1989, p. A22.

Dallago, Bruno, "Debate on the Transition of Post-Communist Economies to a Market Economy," *Acta Oeconomica,* 44 (1992), 273.

Earle, John S., Roman Frydman, Andrzej Rapaczynski, and Joel Turkewitz, *Small Privatization: The Transformation of Retail Trade and Consumer Services in the Czech Republic, Hungary and Poland.* Budapest: Central European University Press, 1994.

The Economist Intelligence Unit, *Business Eastern Europe* (Selected Issues, 1993, 1994).

_____, Country Reports for Czech Republic, Hungary, Poland, and Russia, 1993, 1994.

Erdos, Tomas, "The Chances of Economic Revival," *Acta Oeconomica,* 44 (1992), 1–12.

Fischer, Stanley, "Stabilization and Economic Reform in Russia," in William C. Brainard and George L. Perry, eds., *Brookings Papers on Economic Activity,* 1. Washington DC: Brookings Institution, 1992, pp. 77–126.

Frydman, Roman, Andrez Rapaczynski, John S. Earle, et al., *The Privatization Process in Central Europe.* Budapest: Central European University Press, 1993.

Frydman, Roman, Andrzej Rapaczynski, John S. Earle, et al., *The Privatization Process in Russia, Ukraine and the Baltic States.* London: Central European University Press, 1993.

Grossman, Gregory "Sub-Rosa Privatization and Marketization in the USSR," in Jan S. Prybyla, ed., *The Annals of the American Academy of Political and Social Science,* 507 (January 1990), 44–52.

Harrold, Peter, "The Future of China's Economic Reforms," *The Chinese Business Review* (July-August 1993), pp. 8–9.

Hausner, Jerzy, "Imperative versus Interactive Strategy of Systemic Change in Central and Eastern Europe," paper presented at the European Association for Evolutionary Political Economy conference, Barcelona, October 28–30, 1993.

_____, "Doctrinal Aspects of the Transformation Process and Factors Affecting the Financial Crisis of the State," paper presented at conference on "Post-Socialism: Problems and Prospects," Ambleside, Cumbria, July 1992.

Hausner, Jerzy, and Andrzej Wojtyna, "Privatization as a Restructuring Device:

Can It Substitute for Industrial Policy in the Transforming Economies? Some Lessons from Poland," paper presented at the European Association for Evolutionary Political Economy Conference, Paris, November 1992.

Hausner, Jerzy, Bob Jessop, and Klaus Nielsen, eds., *Markets, Politics and the Negotiated Economy—Scandinavian and Post-Socialist Perspectives.* Krakow, Cracow Academy of Economics, 1991.

Hodgson, Geoffrey M., *Economics and Institutions.* Cambridge: Polity Press, 1988.

Islam, Shafiqul, "Russia's Rough Road to Capitalism," *Foreign Affairs* (Spring 1993), 57–65.

Jones, Derek C., and Mieke Meurs, "Worker Participation and Worker Self-Management in Bulgaria," *Comparative Economic Studies*, 33, 4 (Winter 1991), 47–81.

Johnson, Bjorn, and Bengt-Ake Lundvall, "Catching Up and Institutional Learning under Post Socialism," paper presented at Aalborg University, May 1992.

Klusak, Miroslav, and Pavel Mertlik, "Transformation and Macroeconomic Stabilization of the Czechoslovak Economy," paper presented at the "Negotiated Economy and Neo-Liberalism as Institutional Frameworks for a Market Economy" conference, Ambleside, Cumbria, UK, July 4–5, 1992.

Komarek, Valtr, "Shock Therapy and Its Victims," *The New York Times*, January 5, 1992, p. 14.

Koves, A., "Shock Therapy Versus Gradual Change," *Acta Oeconomica*, 44 (1992), 13–34.

Kowalik, Tadeusz, "Can Poland Afford the Swedish Model? Social Contract as the Basis for Systemic Transformation," paper presented at conference on "Post-Socialism: Problems and Prospects," Ambleside, Cumbria, UK, July 1992.

————, "The Great Transformation & Privatization: Two Years of Poland's Experience," working paper prepared for a seminar at the Stockholm Institute of Soviet and East European Economics, April 1992.

Kregel, J. A., and Egon Matzner, "Agenda for the Reconstruction of Central and Eastern Europe," *Challenge* (September-October 1992), 33–40.

Kregel, J. A., Egon Matzner, and Gernot Grabher, eds., *Market Shock: An Agenda for the Socio-Economic Reconstruction of Central and Eastern Europe.* Vienna: Austrian Academy of Sciences, 1992.

Laski, Kazimierz, "Transition from the Command to the Market System: What Went Wrong and What to Do Now?" Vienna: The Vienna Institute for Comparative Economic Studies, March 1993, p. 2.

Lipton, David, and Jeffrey D. Sachs, "Prospects for Russia's Economic Reforms," in William C. Brainard and George L. Perry, eds., *Brookings Papers on Economic Activity* 2, (1992), 213–284.

McIntyre, Robert, "The Phantom of Transition: Privatization of Agriculture in the Former Soviet Union and Eastern Europe," *Comparative Economic Studies*, 34 (Fall-Winter 1992), 54–67.

Mokrzycki, Edmund, "The Social Limits of East European Economic Reforms," *The Journal of Socio-Economics*, 22 (Spring 1993), 23–30.

Murrell, Peter, "Evolution in Economies and in the Economic Reform of the Centrally Planned Economies," in Christopher Clague and G. C. Raussen, eds., *The Emergence of Market Economies in Eastern Europe.* Cambridge, MA: Blackwell, 1992.

Murrell, Peter, and Yijiang Wang, "When Privatization Should Be Delayed: The Effect of Communist Legacies on Organizational and Institutional Reforms," *Journal of Comparative Economics*, 17 (June 1993), 385–406.

Mujzel, Jan, "Polish Economic Reforms and the Dilemma of Privatization," *Comparative Economic Studies*, 33, 2 (Summer 1991), 29–51.

Nielsen, Klaus, "The Mixed Economy, the Neoliberal Challenge, and the Negotiated Economy," *The Journal of Socio-Economics*, 21, 3 (Fall 1992), 283–309.

"No Foreigners Need Apply," *The Economist*, August 7, 1993, pp. 57–58, 68–69.

Nove, Alec, "Economics of the Transition Period," *Forum*, 5, 11-12 (July 1992), 1–15.

Pejovich, Svetozar, "Institutions, Nationalism, and the Transition Process in Eastern Europe," *Social Philosophy and Policy*, 10 (Summer 1993), 65–78.

Pestoff, Victor A., "Third Sector and Co-Operative Services—An Alternative to Privatization," *Journal of Consumer Policy*, 15 (1992), 21–45.

Porter, Michael E., *The Competitive Advantage of Nations.* London: Macmillan, 1990.

Ringen, Stein, and Claire Wallace, *Societies in Transition: East-Central Europe Today: Prague Papers on Social Responses to Transformation*, 1. Prague: Central European University, 1993.

"The Road to Ruin," *The Economist*, January 29, 1994, pp. 23–25.

Rosati, Dariusz K., "The Politics of Economic Reform in Central and Eastern Europe." London: Centre for Economic Policy Research, 1993.

Rose, Richard, *Divisions and Contradictions in Economies in Transition: Household Portfolios in Russia, Bulgaria and Czechoslovakia*, Studies in Public Policy Number 206. Glasgow: University of Strathclyde, 1992.

Rosenberger, Leif, "Economic Transition in Eastern Europe: Paying the Price for Freedom," *East European Quarterly*, 26 (Fall 1992), 261–278.

"Rotten to the Core," *The Economist*, August 7, 1993, pp. 47–48.

Rusmich, Ladislav, "A Consequence of the Communist Economy: The Disintegration," paper presented at the European Association for Evolutionary Political Economy Conference, Paris, November 1992.

Rychetnik, Ludek, "Can Czechoslovakia Grow a Negotiated Economy?" paper presented at conference on "Post-Socialism: Problems and Prospects," Ambleside, Cumbria, UK, July 1992.

Schaffer, Mark E., "The Polish State-Owned Enterprise Sector and the Recession in 1990," *Comparative Economic Studies*, 34, 1 (Spring 1992), 58–85.

Special Report: "Survey Perestroika: And Now for the Hard Part," *The Economist*, April 28, 1990.

Surdej, Aleksander, "Politics of the Stabilization in Poland," *Seminar Paper for*

Transformation Processes in Eastern Europe—Challenges for Socio-Economic Theory. Krakow: Cracow Academy of Economics, 1992.

Swaan, Wim, and Maria Lissowska, "Enterprise Behavior in Hungary and Poland in the Transition to a Market Economy: Individual and Organizational Routines as a Barrier to Change," in Wolfgang Blass and John Foster, eds., *Mixed Economies in Europe.* Aldershot, UK: Edward Elgar, 1992.

Sztompka, Piotr, "Civilizational Competence: The Prerequisite of Post-Communist Transition," unpublished paper presented at Jagiellonian University, Krakow, November 1992.

UNICEF, *Central and Eastern Europe in Transition: Public Policy and Social Conditions.* Florence: UNICEF International Child Development Centre, 1993.

Vogt, Roy, "Transforming the Former GDR into a Market Economy," *Comparative Economic Studies,* 34 (Fall-Winter 1992), 79.

Wachtel, Howard, "Common Sense About Post-Soviet Economic Reforms," *Challenge* (January-February 1992), 46–48.

Williamson, Oliver, "Institutional Aspects of Economic Reform: The Transaction Cost Economics Perspective," Seminar Paper for *Transformation Processes in Eastern Europe—Challenges for Socio-Economic Theory.* Krakow: Cracow Academy of Economics, June 1992.

17

THE HUNGARIAN ECONOMY SINCE 1946

OBJECTIVES

1. Present the evolution of an economy whose 1946–1989 working rules and principal institutions were imposed upon the nation by Soviet authorities.
2. Explain the factors which contributed to Hungary's becoming the first command over a social economy to introduce economic reforms.
3. Evaluate the effectiveness of Hungary's pre-1989 reforms and post-1989 transformation efforts, identifying obstacles faced and lessons learned.

INTRODUCTION

Political and economic events throughout Central and Eastern Europe (CEE) since late 1989 lend considerable support to the evolutionary-institutional theory, and Hungary is a striking example. This chapter will analyze the 1946–1989 and post-1989 Hungarian economy. Drawing from the discussion of the theoretical obstacles faced by those seeking to reform a command over a social economy (CSE), the focus will be upon what Hungary has had to overcome (i.e., its historical legacy before 1990), alternative philosophical bases which have been adopted, the shifting political structure, and alternative proposals for the organization of resource allocation decision making, ownership and control of the means of production, and social process for coordinating production and distribution decisions.

HISTORICAL LEGACY:
FROM SOVIET DOMINATION
TO TRANSFORMATION

Three features of Hungary's history that influenced the post-World War II economy are land tenure, state intervention, and foreign occupation. Prior to the late 1940s the distribution of land was highly skewed. A majority of Hungary's labor force toiled on rural estates as wage laborers, with only about one third owning enough land to produce a level of output necessary to maintain a subsistence standard of living. The remaining two thirds of the rural labor force were either landless or owned so little land that they, along with the landless, were forced to work for low wages which prevailed throughout the rural sector. A "stagnant" social structure maintained high rates of underemployment and hidden unemployment that plagued rural Hungarian society.[1] This condition differs from the Russian experience, where peasants had a deep attachment to their land prior to the collectivization movement of the late 1920s. Most Hungarians never developed such an attachment. Consequently, in the 1950s when the communist government introduced the collectivization movement, which broke up the large land holdings that were similar in practice to the Roman latifundia, the reform was met with gratitude, not stiff resistance, from most Hungarian peasants.

The history of state intervention in the Hungarian economy throughout the twentieth century is not unlike the experience of most European nations prior to the end of World War II. There was a relatively small role for the state before World War I, followed by the introduction of temporary measures designed to combat typical postwar problems (e.g., rationing of scarce goods, credit controls). After the Great Depression the state's agenda was expanded for economic reasons. The prevailing philosophical basis advocated more state intervention than had the Keynesian philosophy. Since Hungary was a small nation that was deficient in natural resources and dependent upon trade to complement its domestic economy, the state sought to expand its ownership and control of the key areas of finance and foreign trade. In addition, "some type of planning"[2] was advocated as a means to supplement market coordination of production—including armaments—and to provide measures that would prevent the destabilization problems created by the depression. The extent of intervention expanded during World War II as measures like price controls, state allocation of raw materials, rationing of agricultural products, and screening of loan applications by state authorities were introduced.

The nation had become partially industrialized by the late 1930s, but by the end of World War II Hungary had lost nearly a quarter of its industrial capacity, while much damage had been inflicted upon the remaining factories and

---

[1] Paul Ignotus, *Hungary* (New York: Praeger, 1972), pp. 172, 173.
[2] Peter Van Ness, ed., *Market Reforms in Socialist Societies* (Boulder, CO: Lynne Rienner, 1989), p. 32.

infrastructure (especially transportation networks). Defeat also left Hungary without a strong political structure or a corresponding philosophical basis with which to rebuild its economy. Having been an ally, albeit unwillingly, of Nazi Germany, Hungary was invaded by Russian troops, who remained after the war. Foreign occupation and domination such as this have occurred frequently throughout Hungary's history, and "may help to explain both periodic uprisings expressing fierce nationalism (as in 1956) as well as extended times of resignation and relative political tranquility."[3]

In 1945 Hungary was forced to develop close economic and political ties with the Soviet Union. While noncommunist parties received most of the popular support in both the 1945 and 1947 elections (the Smallholders Party won the 1947 election with about 50 percent of the popular vote), 1948 featured a change in Hungary's political structure when the Communist Party established itself as the monopoly party. In 1949 a new constitution changed the nation's name to the Hungarian People's Republic. The philosophy of the Communist Party was that the Hungarian state was "a dictatorship of the proletariat, and its main aim was . . . to build socialism in Hungary."[4] As with all nations whose communist parties assumed control during Joseph Stalin's reign as the political authority in the Soviet Union (1928–1953), Hungary was forced to emulate (and remain loyal and subservient to) the Soviet political structure, foreign policy, and working rules for the economy.

The state introduced working rules similar to those which characterized the CSE of the Soviet Union, replacing the rules which prevailed immediately after the war, when maintenance of free enterprise had been deemed the best remedy for the depressed state of the economy. After 1948 decision making became highly centralized within the state planning commission. State ownership and control over the private sector were extended, in the face of a strong tradition of private small-scale industries, and a centrally directed planning scheme to coordinate production and distribution was adopted. Specific working rules gave the state control over the ten largest banks and the power to nationalize all private firms employing more than 100 persons, which was extended to firms employing as few as ten workers in late 1948. By early 1949 the state owned and controlled nearly all Hungarian mining and metallurgy firms, about 90 percent of engineering and construction enterprises, over 80 percent of heavy industry, and about half of the textile, paper, and food industries.[5] The imposition of the Marxian philosophical basis meant informal and formal rules precluded both the pursuit of profit by entrepreneurs and individual ownership of the means of production. Meanwhile principles of central planning, as opposed to neoclassical principles of efficient resource allocation, were taught to Hungarian managers and students.

---

[3]Andrew Zimbalist, Howard J. Sherman, and Stuart Brown, *Comparing Economic Systems: A Political-Economic Approach,* 2nd ed. (San Diego: Harcourt Brace Jovanovich, 1989), p. 398.

[4]Van Ness, *Market Reforms in Socialist Societies,* p. 35.

[5]Ibid.

Following the death of Stalin in 1953 there was a reaction against the Stalinist heritage (i.e., excessive centralization of state decision making and control of the economy). Leading the reaction which brought about changes in the informal rules toward the economy were some Hungarian intellectuals. In 1956 the Writers' Union held unprecedented (since 1947) elections, and their revolutionary zeal and willingness to assert Hungarian nationalism stimulated other groups to join them— professionals, followed by industrial and service workers, then peasants.[6] Blame for the poor performance of the Hungarian economy was attributed to "blunders, waste, and inefficiency of the . . . [Soviet-type planning process]; . . . and a politically repressive regime subservient to the Soviet Union."[7] Fewer planning and compulsory measures were advocated, with market reforms to coordinate economic activity proposed in their place. Widespread demonstrations in favor of greater freedom and a higher standard of living ensued, stimulating a Soviet military invasion in October 1956 to restore political order.

A new political structure led by Janos Kadar was put in place by the Soviets. Kadar, who would become sympathetic to economic reforms, remained in power until 1988. He was partially successful in easing resentment against Communist Party rule by special interest groups (e.g., the Church, artisans, farmers), and in unifying the nation so that there was widespread acceptance (or at least a minimum of resistance) of Communist Party control. However, due to centralized decision making and control over the economy's working rules, the workers felt increasingly alienated from the party that was supposed to represent their interests, and the rift never healed.

A decade later there was widespread recognition that the working rules for a CSE were wasteful and ineffective, so piecemeal reforms of the planning process were gradually introduced between 1957 and 1967 (see "Social Processes for Coordinating Production and Distribution Activities," pp. 505–507). These reforms included more emphasis on producing consumer goods than was typical for CSEs, and measures to stimulate agricultural output (e.g., abolish compulsory agricultural quotas). The collectivization movement was phased in slowly, and peasants who were well off were not coerced into joining. In addition, members of collectives were permitted to elect their own management, and farmers were given the right to purchase and sell up to seven acres of land.[8] That these reforms were retained can be credited to the subsequent favorable performance of the economy prior to 1980 (compared to the rest of East Europe), Kadar's ability to maintain a semblance of unity among Hungarians, and his ability to avoid repression by the Soviet Union while introducing piecemeal economic reforms in Hungary. The informal rules favoring significant reform would not become formal rules, however, until a "blanket revision"[9] in the form of the New Economic Mechanism (NEM) was introduced in 1968.

---

[6]Ignotus, *Hungary*, pp. 234, 235.

[7]Jan S. Prybla, *Market and Plan Under Socialism: The Bird in the Cage* (Stanford, CA: Hoover Institution Press, 1987), p. 215.

[8]Zimbalist, Sherman, and Brown, *Comparing Economic Systems*, p. 400.

[9]Prybla, *Market and Plan Under Socialism*, p. 215.

Continued unfavorable performance of the economy and the political mood throughout Central and Eastern Europe (CEE) led to political revolution, which culminated in parliamentary elections in spring 1990. The newly elected Hungarian authorities inherited an economy plagued by macroeconomic instability. There was low growth, accelerating inflation, rising unemployment, and the highest debt per capita in Europe—each of which was exacerbated by other adverse conditions. These conditions included structural weaknesses— particularly large, overstaffed, energy-intensive state-owned enterprises, environmental degradation, an inefficient tax system plagued by widespread avoidance of paying taxes,[10] the lack of effective capital markets, and the absence of a business culture oriented toward production efficiency or appealing to consumers. There also was lack of consensus regarding a coherent philosophical basis upon which a transformation program could be established.

DEVELOPMENT OF AN ECLECTIC PHILOSOPHICAL BASIS

Between 1945 and 1948 the attitudes toward the economy's working rules were similar to those which prevailed during the previous decade. State involvement in economic matters was widespread, partly in response to the need to guide the postwar reconstruction effort and partly because authorities "accepted the view that politics comes before economics."[11] The inability of the Communist Party to receive a majority of the votes in either the 1945 or 1947 election meant that the Marxian-Stalinist philosophical basis was not introduced until 1948.

From 1948 to 1968 the attitudes of Hungarian authorities were similar to those of Soviet authorities. That is, production and distribution decision making should be highly centralized, the state should own and control most means of production, and central planning should be the means to coordinate most production and distribution decisions. In addition, the authorities held egalitarian values, which were taught to all Hungarians, in terms of the distribution of income and the nature of the social structure (see "Nonegalitarian Social and Political Structures," pp. 490–494). Following the death of Stalin in 1953, informal rules favoring economic reforms began to be discussed by authorities and economists more openly.

In 1968 Hungarian authorities sought to combine party control through central planning with market coordination of domestic and international production and trade. There began a continual struggle among three reformist views: the conservative view, which favored modifications in the planning scheme while retaining "planner preference" through strong control by the state; the radical position, which sought to replace the CSE philosophical basis and

---

[10]Some estimate that in 1990 state revenues would have been 30 percent greater if all taxes that were due to be paid had been collected.

[11]Van Ness, *Market Reforms in Socialist Societies,* p. 42.

working rules with an alternative economy based upon a democratic political structure and widespread reliance upon the market mechanism, including the pursuit of profit by individuals; and the reformer view, which proposed that major variables (e.g., prices, wages, interest rates) regulate economic activity, and that these variables be meaningful (i.e., determined by free market forces). Another tenet of reformers was that enterprises which were perpetual losers should be permitted to go bankrupt by eliminating state subsidies to such firms.

For most of the 1968–1989 period the conservative philosophy prevailed, partly due to the adequate performance of the economy relative to other Eastern European economies (see "Performance of the Hungarian Economy," pp. 515–520), and partly due to the vested interest of Communist Party members in retaining central control over the economy. The party exhibited "adaptive capacities" so that recessions were not followed by political upheaval.[12] This political structure in which there was a monopoly party and centralized decision making created barriers to political and economic reform. Nevertheless, by the mid-1980s the chronic poor performance of the economy led to growing pressure on authorities to legitimize their position, since they held sole control of the planning process. Failure of the political authorities to justify their position eventually resulted in the acceptance among the people of new informal rules. The political structure which had been monopolized by the Communist Party fell as a result of its economic failures.

Since the 1989 political revolution there has been a broad consensus that two goals need to be achieved. These are greater economic freedoms for individuals and higher living standards. Greater freedom has been described in terms of more decision-making rights held by individuals (e.g., to seek employment anywhere in or outside of Hungary) without having to receive permission from the state, and in terms of fewer bureaucratic constraints facing individuals. Nearly all authorities and economists have favored a reduced (albeit in some cases not radically reduced) role for the state. Some have endorsed the view that the state must participate in the economy as the leading institution organically and structurally. They believe the state's functions should be to promote growth while avoiding structural imbalance, guide macroeconomic stabilization policies, ensure macroeconomic efficiency so that markets function in a socially acceptable manner, and regulate the primary distribution of income and the proportion of private versus public goods produced.

However, there have been political cleavages concerning what philosophical basis to adopt, especially as it pertains to the role of the state, the role of the Church, property rights, liberalization of trade and prices, the tax system, the system of establishing wages, and membership in international

---

[12]Charles E. Lindblom, *Politics and Markets* (New York: Basic Books, 1977), p. 282.

organizations such as the European Union.[13] Substantive differences have existed among three groups, to each of which a number of political parties identify: the conservatives, liberals, and socialists. The conservatives have populist views in favor of a return to the pre-1940 aristocratic culture. The liberals are primarily urban intellectuals who oppose feudal elements in Hungary and want to emulate Western political and economic models. The socialists, who hold some views in common with each of the other two groups, are mostly trade union workers.

The more conservative view believes Hungary has to restore its national identity, while liberals favor establishing close economic and political ties with Western nations. Conservative political party members tend to be more ethnocentric, advocating collectivism and a strong role for the Church. Liberal party members favor individualism and a secular society. Regarding the economy, conservatives prefer some form of social democracy while liberals favor a market economy with a limited role for the state. Centralization of political power and maintenance of client mentality is advocated by conservatives, while liberals argue for decentralization of power. The socialists argue for very gradual transformation, particularly in regard to the rate at which state-owned enterprises are permitted to go bankrupt, and maintenance of social insurance and welfare programs.

In 1990 there were pleas from some members of the Hungarian and American academic communities for rapid transformation to quickly establish a "free market economy."[14] The integrated transformation program they recommended to the newly elected government when it assumed office that year included implementing a bankruptcy law to permit widespread bankruptcies so as to eliminate inefficient state-owned enterprises; establishing a private agricultural sector; quickly increasing competition throughout the banking, health, education, and public services; introducing a program to attract significant foreign investment; providing rules guaranteeing freedom for entrepreneurs; reducing taxes considerably; establishing the forint as a freely convertible currency; and drastically reducing public subsidies to enterprises, consumers, and homeowners or renters. It was believed that adoption of such a plan would stimulate rapid transformation and make Hungary attractive to foreign investment as well as the recipient of considerable aid from international organizations such as the International Monetary Fund and World Bank.

Another alternative, which was adopted by authorities elected in 1990, was the introduction of a gradual transformation program. The intention was to minimize the hardships Hungarians would inevitably have to endure. Consequently, widespread bankruptcies were not permitted, and the privatization

[13]The remainder of this section draws from James Angresano, "A Mixed Economy for Hungary? Lessons from the Swedish Experience," *Comparative Economic Studies*, 34, 2 (Summer 1992), 41–57.

[14]Two widely circulated proposals were Janos Kornai, *The Road to a Free Economy: Shifting from a Socialist System—the Example of Hungary* (New York: W. W. Norton, 1991); and Blue Ribbon Commission—Project Hungary, Action Program for "Hungary in Transformation to Freedom and Prosperity" (Indianapolis: Hudson Institute, 1990).

program was implemented gradually. The lingering recession from 1990 through 1994 and unstable political parties resulted in the rise to power of conservative parties in 1994 (see p. 493).[15] They pledged to proceed with economic reforms and to integrate Hungary with the European Union, as well as to join NATO, but advocated a philosophical basis which contained elements from the pre-1989 economy—as well as social democratic ideals to an increasingly insecure population. Such ideals, which embody egalitarian and community concern, may hold an almost magical aura to Hungarians who share these ideals. Having been imbued with Marxian ideals, Hungarians may wish to create a society in which social policy is assumed as a government responsibility, people receive social insurance and welfare benefits while enjoying economic and political freedoms, income and wealth differentials are minimized while social inequalities are reduced, equal pay for equal work is the rule, the state commits to maintaining full employment, and individuals are compensated for loss of income resulting from economic risks to which they are exposed. However, Hungarians, who possess a high degree of individualism, likely would not care for state involvement comparable to the extensive Swedish state paternalism.[16]

NONEGALITARIAN SOCIAL AND POLITICAL STRUCTURES

The pre-1989 philosophical basis contained the promise that an egalitarian social structure would not prevail in Hungary. This had not been achieved by 1990, partly because status, rank in the political structure, and distribution of income were closely interrelated, and entrance into the political structure was not open to many Hungarians prior to 1990. As expected, the social structure mirrored the distribution of power within the political structure. In terms of the distribution of income, however, the degree of inequality in Hungary was considerably less than in most Western nations—a reflection of the political commitment to an egalitarian social structure through control over distribution of income, pricing policies (e.g., heavily subsidized housing), and extensive publicly funded social services. One interesting feature of the post-1990 economy is the growth in income inequality— a condition which has contributed directly to the shifting political structure.

Social Structure

The nationality with which Hungarians identify is Magyar, although they are descended from Asian nomads, Rumanians, Austro-Germans, and various Slavic

---

[15]At the time of the May 1994 elections unemployment was 12 percent (the rate mainly caused by bankruptcies and enterprise closures), inflation 22 percent, and GDP had declined 23 percent since 1990.

[16]It is interesting that, despite a lingering recession, the Swedish Social Democrats received more votes than any other party in the summer 1994 election.

groups, each of which is a mixture of other ethnic groups as well. Their unifying feature is the Magyar language primarily spoken by Hungarians residing in Hungary and "Magyars" residing in neighboring countries (e.g., Czechoslovakia, Rumania, Yugoslavia). The only non-European language spoken in most of Europe, Magyar contributes to the Hungarian sense of isolation and may stimulate their aggressive sense of independence.[17]

The official policy prior to 1989 stated that social equality should exist between men and women. However, Hungarian women tended to enjoy much less leisure time than men. About 90 percent of working-age women held jobs. If married, these women were expected to be responsible for the household as well. Women were underrepresented within higher levels of the political structure, and generally tended to hold jobs for which they were overqualified and which traditionally pay below-average wages. In an attempt to reduce this inequality in the workplace and to stimulate population growth in a nation with a negative population growth rate, the state-funded maternity leaves for both parents are very generous. Both parents are given up to three years' release time from work to care for the child without losing their jobs.

While the working class was expected to be the foundation of the new social structure following the Communist Party assumption of power in 1948, the reality was that a majority of the Hungarian people were still peasants. However, the state's emphasis upon rapid industrialization saw a dramatic shift in the distribution of population between industry and agriculture. Whereas in 1960 about half the work force was employed in the agricultural sector, by 1980 it was less than one fourth. The peasant population has declined steadily from about half the population in 1945 to less than 15 percent today. The manual workers and their families currently account for about half of the population, having grown rapidly as Hungary rebuilt and expanded its industrial base after the war. The distinctions within this class are attributable to the social class of workers' forefathers, the industry in which workers are employed, and degree of skill. The new entrepreneurial class, nonmanual employees (e.g., service workers, lower-ranking members of the bureaucracy), the intelligentsia, and their families comprise about one fourth of the population. Prior to 1990 senior Communist Party authorities were at the apex of the social structure, comprising only about 8 percent of the population. Many remain active authorities.

Evidence indicates that since 1990 the distribution of income has become more skewed. One executive of a private enterprise estimated that about 50 percent of Hungary's purchasing is controlled by only 10 percent of the population.[18] This primarily has been due to the divergence in incomes between a small, successful entrepreneurial class and the expanding lower class suffering

---

[17]Ignotus, *Hungary*, p. 21.

[18]"Bring Back the Goulash: Hungary's Elections," *The Economist*, May 7, 1994, pp. 57–58. The conspicuous consumption of the new elite has served to make many Hungarians feel poorer and resentful of the new working rules.

from unemployment (particularly structural unemployment) and reduction in real wages, pensions, and other social services and welfare programs. Farmers have suffered from the decline in agricultural output and lack of access to European Union markets.

Political Structure

Between 1948 and 1985 the Hungarian Socialist Workers' Party had a monopoly over political power. The meaning and significance of the party's monopoly over the political structure is "that the party's views were dominant and solely legitimate."[19] As in other CSEs, the institutions and working rules of the economy are "fundamentally the result of politics."[20] The party exercised control over the economy through the central planning process, constant intervention in production and distribution matters—on both the macro and microlevels, and through monopolizing ideological education, which inculcated the entire population with the Marxian philosophical basis. The authorities (party leaders, state bureaucrats, and economic planners) were in a position to secure considerable political and material benefits for themselves through "extending control, ensuring that information circulates . . . and co-opting each other."[21] Communist Party membership comprised between 5 percent and 8 percent of the population, and these members were responsible for electing all important authorities. There were only three First Secretaries during the 1946–1989 period (one of whom was in power for less than a year), with Janos Kadar serving as chief authority from 1956 until 1988.

This highly centralized control over the positions of authority, and thereby the economy's working rules, remained unchallenged under the Kadar regime until the early 1980s. At that time a series of events began which would culminate in the decline of the Communist Party's power in Hungary, followed by presidential and parliamentary elections in the spring of 1990. Perhaps the most significant were the economy's worsening performance and Soviet Premier Mikhail Gorbachev convincing authorities throughout CEE not to interfere with political reform movements. In response the Hungarian Communist Party "decided to share out responsibility and to seek a much-needed respectability through democratic elections."[22] The pace of political events quickened in late 1989. The ruling Communist authorities sought to schedule a presidential election in December of that year, and the first parliamentary elections since 1948 were scheduled for March and April 1990. As 51 new parties had emerged in 1989, this meant Hungary would experience multiparty elections and a revision of the

---

[19]Ibid., p. 180.

[20]Xavier Richet, translated by J. C. Whitehouse, *The Hungarian Model: Markets and Planning in a Socialist Economy* (Cambridge: Cambridge University Press, 1989), p. 181.

[21]Ibid., p. 182.

[22]Tibour Fischer, "Hungary: The Self-Destruction of the Party," *The Wall Street Journal*, November 6, 1989, p. A 17.

constitution. Fearing a victory by the Socialists (i.e., renamed Communists from the Hungarian Socialist Workers Party), a referendum on the presidential election was forced by two of the major new political parties—the Democratic Forum and the Free Democrats. The referendum required that the next president would be chosen in the spring of 1990 by the newly elected parliament. The referendum passed, postponing the presidential election until spring of 1990.

In March and April of that year the gradual shift in the political structure to democratic pluralism was nearly complete. In the parliamentary elections on March 25 and April 8, the Democratic Forum won about 42 percent of the vote, with the Free Democrats receiving about 24 percent. The Smallholders, winners of the last election in 1947, were third with 11 percent, while the Socialist Party (Communist reformers) received only 8 percent of all votes cast, giving them 24 of the 386 seats in the new parliament. A coalition between the two leading parties was formed, which required compromises between the gradual economic reform approach favored by the Forum and the Free Democrats' preference for more rapid change. Jozsef Antall (leader of the Democratic Forum) became the new prime minister.

The new authorities lacked experience, were not enlightened regarding economic matters, and had few qualified experts advising them. There was much discussion of establishing a "market economy" without substantive explanations of what the nature of the principal institutions and rules regarding ownership of private property should be. Lengthy debate inhibited adoption of comprehensive reform measures and contributed to public cynicism toward authorities they believed were inexperienced and opportunistic. The corresponding decline in the government's legitimacy impaired the state's capacity to design and successfully implement reforms that will reduce and restructure its own role.

In the early 1990s the authorities appeared to want the unattainable—the introduction of genuine economic reform measures in a painless manner. They opted for gradualism, and nurtured the illusion that reforms could be implemented quickly, with a favorable impact at little social cost. It was (accurately) predicted then that Hungarians would blame the reform measures for the very problems that gave rise to the need for reforms intended to increase economic freedom while providing a higher standard of living. The ruling coalition led by the Democratic Forum, in failing to deliver on its economic promises, saw its popularity fall. Some analysts believed that "the neo-liberal instincts of the party's intellectuals . . . inhibited a move to the more promising electoral grounds of social democracy and abandoned the left of the political spectrum to the Socialists."[23] In the May 1994 elections the Democratic Forum received only about 10 percent of the votes, while the Socialist Party received over 30 percent. Similar electoral triumphs occurred throughout CEE, with parties led by ex-Communist authorities being elected in Lithuania, Poland, and Romania as well. In Hungary and these nations as well, the "free market" reformers were

[23]"Bring Back the Goulash," *The Economist,* pp. 57–58.

voted out of office in favor of authorities whose philosophical basis included social democratic ideals and elements from the collectivist era prior to 1989.

TRANSFORMATION OF STATE-DOMINATED INSTITUTIONS

1946–1989

Throughout the 1946–1989 period the principal institutions were the leaders of Hungary's Communist Party; state organs responsible for proposing, implementing and enforcing the economy's working rules; state-owned manufacturing enterprises; and agricultural collectives. These institutions were organized in a hierarchical, centralized, and bureaucratized manner. Such an organization was made necessary by the extensive state ownership and control of productive resources, the highly centralized decision-making process, and the use of central planning to coordinate most production and distribution decisions. The management of Hungary's economy was by Communist Party authorities, with implementation and enforcement of their objectives through authorities in governing institutions. These authorities responded to instructions from the "single-centered hierarchical [communist] party,"[24] enabling the state to manage the economy as a board of directors of an American or Japanese enterprise would manage a large, diversified corporation.

COMMUNIST PARTY LEADERSHIP.   This group was responsible for defining the long- and medium-range political and economic goals for Hungary, as well as proposing broad policy measures for achieving the goals, often (but not always in the case of economic matters) with guidance and approval from the Soviet Union. The inner circle was the Central Committee, consisting of the First Secretary of the Communist Party, a president, and other committee members. The government's cabinet (Council of Ministers) was a rule-implementing body that could approve the annual plan. It consisted of a premier, four deputy premiers, heads of 14 ministries (e.g., industry, agriculture), and the chief authority in the National Planning Office. Most of these authorities were chosen for their party loyalty, although many had served as managers of state enterprises.[25]

STATE ORGANS FOR COORDINATING ECONOMIC ACTIVITY.   Following the assumption of power by the Communist Party in 1948, institutions (main organs of the state) were established that would facilitate rapid industrialization and

---

[24]Richet, *The Hungarian Model*, p. 53.

[25]Joni Lovenduski and Jean Woodall, *Politics and Society in Eastern Europe* (Bloomington, IN: Indiana University Press, 1987), p. 253.

collectivization while enabling the state to manage and control the economy. The National Planning Office was established as "the supreme directive organ of all economic activity."[26] It was responsible for organizing and supervising the national plans, making sure the plan was internally consistent (i.e., sufficient inputs were available to produce the desired outputs). The office set targets for the economy, coordinated high-priority industrial and agricultural activities, and supervised investment projects designed to promote rapid economic growth. This institution drew up the national plans (annual, five-year, and long-range plans) for the economy, and disaggregated the plan for the industry level by specifying quantitative output targets. In implementing the plan the National Planning Office was assisted by the Ministry of Industry. This ministry and the "direct-control organs" it supervised also assisted with formulating the plans and was responsible for prices and resource allocation on the enterprise level.

INDUSTRIAL AND AGRICULTURAL ENTERPRISES. State-owned manufacturing enterprises formulated their own plans within the parameters defined by the national plan. In terms of the average number of workers employed by each industrial enterprise (roughly 1,250 between 1970 and 1989) and the value of output of the largest enterprises relative to the smaller state-owned enterprises and cooperative industrial enterprises (in most industries the largest three firms supply over two thirds of all output), the state-owned manufacturing sector in Hungary was the most highly concentrated in Eastern Europe. Even by Western standards the size distribution of Hungarian industrial firms was highly skewed, for the average Hungarian firm has over 180 employees, while the typical manufacturing enterprise in a capitalist nation has about 80 employees.[27]

Agriculture is a key sector in Hungary, where over half the land is arable (compared to the world average of 10 percent arable land) and where trading partners are nations who rely on food imports. Between 1948 and 1956 collective farms were established and managed in a similar fashion to state-controlled industrial enterprises. After some modest decentralization reforms between 1956 and 1958, mass recollectivization occurred. However, most of the collective institutions were reformed into agricultural cooperatives so that in the late 1980s these cooperatives accounted for about half the total agricultural output (versus about 15 percent for state-owned farms). Peasants could join a cooperative voluntarily, compulsory deliveries of output to the state did not exist, and peasants could produce as they wished on small private plots and sell the output in unregulated markets. Peasants had autonomy to select the cooperative's manager, determine the production techniques to adopt, and set their own target levels of output. Many agricultural cooperatives diversified by developing other

[26]Van Ness, *Market Reforms in Socialist Societies,* p. 38.
[27]Janos Kornai, "The Hungarian Reform Process: Visions, Hopes, and Reality," *Journal of Economic Literature,* 24 (December 1986), 1698.

enterprises within the cooperative, which engaged in activities such as food processing, food retail trade, and production of farm equipment and parts. Overall, this principal institution was one of the few Hungarian examples of a "genuine market mechanism" prior to the late 1980s.[28]

Post-1989[29]

Following the 1990 elections the institutions most important in shaping the transforming Hungarian economy have been the two political coalitions which have controlled the government, private-sector firms along with individuals and enterprises in the social and uncivil economies, foreign institutions (particularly governments, international agencies, consultants, nonprofit educational organizations, and investors), state-owned enterprises, and cooperatives. The relative importance of each has been shifting. While the private sector has assumed a dominant position in retail trade and some services, state-owned enterprises continue to remain significant in manufacturing, while cooperatives in a different legal form continue to be important in agriculture. The continued importance of state-owned enterprises is attributable to their size, which makes them more difficult to privatize, the political strength of labor which has strongly resisted bankruptcy measures, and that these enterprises were much more autonomous prior to 1989 than anywhere else in CEE. This autonomy further reduces the perception that there is a pressing need to rapidly transform them.

BEHAVIOR OF THE ECONOMY

From a Hierarchical,
Centralized to a Decentralized
Organization of Resource
Allocation Decision Making

From 1948 until the late 1960s hierarchical decision making was the rule, as all production and distribution decisions of significance were made at the Central Committee level and carried out by lower-level bureaucrats.[30] In 1968 as part of the New Economic Mechanism, the authorities introduced reform measures to decentralize decision making. The purpose of decentralization was to give enterprises "a real degree of autonomy, particularly as regards investment, [and] to

---

[28]Van Ness, *Market Reforms in Socialist Societies*, p. 109. There was "genuine market activity" in the informal economy (especially the black market), but this was not officially acknowledged by the authorities.

[29]Additional information about most of these institutions is presented in the "Ownership and Control of Resources" section, pp. 499–505.

[30]Hungary's organization of decision making was quite similar to that of the Soviet Union between 1928 and the mid-1980s. (See Chapter 16 for further discussion.)

help them become the real centres of maximization."[31] Enterprise autonomy was increased by eliminating quantitative planning directives and detailed procedures from top authorities. Enterprise managers were permitted to make decisions pertaining to their enterprise's production level, scale of production facility, inputs needed including imported raw materials, and where to sell their output.

Unfortunately, the decentralization measures only preceded the first oil crisis by a few years. By the mid-1970s, in the face of a deteriorating economic performance, especially in terms of rising government debt and balance of payments difficulties, the authorities introduced rules designed to recentralize decision making.[32] In 1979 another reform period began during which decentralized decision making was given another boost. Managers of enterprises were to be elected by the workers, while industrial enterprises could emulate agricultural cooperatives by setting up "subsidiaries and joint undertakings in Hungary or abroad with Hungarian or Western firms," or with enterprises in other Eastern European nations.[33] In addition, new rules ended the state monopoly over the banking system so that enterprises could choose among alternative sources of finance.

Overall, the decentralization measures introduced between 1968 and 1989 are best described as partial decentralization of decision making, for they did not eliminate the problem of central authority influence, nor did they provide rational criteria (e.g., meaningful regulators such as prices and interest rates) to assist planners and enterprise managers to make more efficient resource allocation decisions. While rules granting enterprises more autonomy were introduced, the central authorities retained the power to control production and distribution activities, especially investment. On the macro level the planners still remained active, making investment decisions pertaining to infrastructure (e.g., energy or cement-producing facilities), and the coordination of activities (e.g., a transportation link between two or more enterprises). The central authorities had substituted control over the granting of investment funds and scarce inputs for quantitative targets and compulsory compliance with state directives by enterprises.

On the micro level, enterprise managers had objectives that differed from the macroeconomic objectives (e.g., target rates of growth) of central authorities. The allocation of investment funds to state-owned enterprises (SOEs) took place within a "multi-decisional framework," the outcome of which was determined by

[31]Richet, *The Hungarian Model,* p. 126.

[32]This pattern has been repeated in other CSEs (e.g., China in 1989) where, following some democratic economic reforms, the central authorities introduce rules to recentralize decision making, thereby regaining control over an economy whose poor performance was stimulating pressure for political reform. The authorities justified recentralization measures by blaming the decentralization reforms for contributing to the economy's poor performance.

[33]Ibid., pp. 6, 7.

the relative bargaining power of each enterprise.[34] As one analyst observed, "[t]rying to determine whether enterprises were now in a position to impose their will on the centre or [whether] intermediate bodies shaped the decision of central planners is a question with no straightforward answer."[35]

Since 1989 organization of decision making in Hungary generally has followed a similar pattern to that of other CEE nations. New political authorities operating within a new democratic political structure have considerable influence, as do representatives of international institutions (both intergovernmental and private). There is a growing role for individuals (both Hungarians and foreigners) acting within the private sector as well as members or organized crime syndicates. Foreign influence is present as well. In February 1991 Hungary signed a three-year agreement with the International Monetary Fund under which Hungary would qualify for $1.6 billion in credit depending upon its ability to meet specified targets pertaining to reduced budget deficit, balances on current and capital accounts, and reduced state subsidies while laying the foundation for privatization of state-owned enterprises.

Hungarian policymaking concerning macroeconomic issues and working rules for principal institutions remains highly centralized. Following the 1990 elections the new political authorities believed that to break the influence of those who would resist economic reforms, namely nomenklatura as well as enterprise managers and labor, it was "essential for the state to regain control over the redistributive processes and the major macroeconomic decisions."[36] The new authorities wanted to strengthen their own position, and they feared that an alliance against reform would be formed between enterprise managers and workers seeking continued state paternalism. As a result, the ruling coalition (Democratic Forum and Free Democrats) took measures to recentralize economic decision making while insulating themselves from parliamentary opposition.

After recentralization of decision making the central authorities did not focus on implementing a coherent economic reform program. Instead they used their new control for short-term political purposes and, therefore, were responsible for the "repolitization of the economy."[37] Public assets were redistributed so as to create patron-client relations within the economy, and selected large state-owned enterprises continued to be heavily subsidized (although subsidies were reduced overall). A new institution was created, the State Property Agency, which would control privatization and have the right to assume control over any public enterprise.

---

[34]Ibid., pp. 120–123. According to Richet, while the official percentage of investments made by the central government declined from 42 percent to 32 percent between 1970 and 1985, only about 12 percent to 15 percent of all enterprise investment was made *autonomously* by enterprise managers.

[35]Ibid., pp. 126–128.

[36]Laszlo Bruszt, "Workers, Managers and State Bureaucrats and the Economic Transformation in Hungary," Working paper prepared at Central European University, Prague, 1993.

[37]Ibid.

Enterprise management decision-making power was weakened by making enterprises more dependent upon the central government, then by transforming property relations through corporatization. Labor strength was reduced by the abolition of enterprise councils and by granting them little influence in privatization decision making. Central authorities, having insulated their decision-making power from other economic actors, "created the political conditions of its exclusionary reform strategy."[38] Rather than negotiate with interest-group representatives, a climate of political and economic alienation was created and stimulated resistance to government reform efforts. As the economic recession which began in 1989 continued, the government lost popularity. There were further attempts to centralize decision making, some of which was used for short-term political gains. Ultimately, the 1994 elections placed the Socialist Party in charge of decision making. A more open process with greater involvement from management and labor was promised.

It has become apparent in Hungary, as in the rest of CEE, that the new democratic political structure complicates the transformation of CEE economies, particularly as decision making is organized. Democracy throughout CEE has led to people using their new freedom to oppose reform when the cost of reforms is deemed too great. For example, CEE states are trying to decentralize the degree of control they exert on the economy, but faced with growing poverty, unemployment, and insecurity among the population, they have found it necessary for the state to continue redistributing income to enterprises and individuals.

Ownership and Control of
Resources: Privatization and
a Place for Cooperatives

Prior to the late 1980s, Hungary's economy has been described as "multisectoral."[39] In addition to large and small state-owned industrial and agricultural enterprises, there was a formal private sector, an informal private sector which included black market activities, agricultural and industrial cooperatives, and combinations of these, such as a private enterprise renting space from an SOE, or a joint venture between a state-owned and foreign firm. In terms of relative importance of the "first economy" (state-owned enterprises and cooperatives) versus the "second economy" (formal and informal private sector), Hungarians spent about 67 percent of their "active" work time in the first economy versus 33 percent in the second economy, with many people working in both sectors.[40] Measured according to total net material product, however, the percentage contributed by the first economy was about 90 percent, while that of the private sector including the second economy was about 10 percent.[41] If income

[38]Ibid.

[39]Kornai, "The Hungarian Reform Process," p. 1714.

[40]Ibid., p. 1707.

[41]*East European Economic Handbook* (London: Euromonitor Publications, Ltd., 1985), p. 137.

from private agricultural plots is included, the private-sector/second-economy contribution was over 10 percent.

For industrial state-owned enterprises ownership, control, and concentration of industries were consistent with the state's desire to manage the economy and with the informal rule favoring "gigantomania" (i.e., large economies of scale) common to CSEs. Thus, in the interests of "socializing the forces of production" and satisfying the authorities' desire to control economic activity, a high degree of industrial concentration was the natural consequence.[42] There was virtually no impact on state ownership of enterprises after the New Economic Mechanism was introduced, nor was state control of these institutions significantly reduced after 1968. Tight state management of the economy was manifested by the control it maintained over "regulators" such as prices, allocation of credit, taxes, and subsidies to enterprises.[43]

The formal private sector consisted of small firms, since the number of workers a firm could hire was limited to no more than seven. However, given the low level of wages in state-owned enterprises and the absence of controls on private-sector wages, many Hungarians (an estimated 75 percent of the work force) worked part time or full time in the formal or informal private sector. Areas of importance include construction (about 90 percent of housing construction), production of parts for other industrial enterprises, personal services (e.g., hairdressers), professional services (attorneys), repair services (automobile, clothing), transport (especially taxis), all types of retail trade (about 20 percent of all retail sales), restaurants, and hotels.[44] Prior to 1989 this sector was tolerated, but not enthusiastically encouraged by the state because private firms violated the Marxian philosophical basis as well as the authorities' desire to maintain control over economic activities. Consequently, the state would inhibit the spread of private enterprises by denying or delaying licenses through bureaucratic means or by imposing high taxes on profits. Other constraints inhibiting the spread of the formal private sector included the difficulty in obtaining credit or foreign exchange to purchase imported goods, the absence of available office space, telephone service, and data processing equipment, a general lack of confidence in the economy's performance, and the ease with which people could enter the informal private sector.

Concerning the informal private sector, many workers took jobs in the private sector on a part-time basis, working in a state-owned or cooperative enterprise and joining the private sector after work. In addition to the private-sector activities listed earlier, another important area in which uncontrolled production and distribution activities were the rule was private agricultural plots.

[42]Richet, *The Hungarian Model*, p. 171.

[43]While Hungary's average income tax rates are relatively low (12 precent), marginal rates were as high as 60 percent in the late 1980s.

[44]See Van Ness, *Market Reforms in Socialist Societies*, pp. 88–96; and U.S. Department of State, *Hungarian Economic Reform: Status and Prospects* (Budapest: United States Embassy, 1989), p. 10.

These plots produced most of Hungary's fruits, vegetables, and about half its chicken and pork. Another part of this sector is the black market, the extent of which has recently been estimated to have been about 10 percent of the total value of all goods and services produced. Such illegal activity was tolerated mainly for two reasons: the difficulty of preventing it, and the recognition that needed supplies were provided by those engaging in the black market. Artificially low wages and prices encourage entry into this sector.[45]

Agricultural cooperatives provided about half of Hungary's agricultural output. Industrial cooperatives, while dependent upon the state for financing and imported materials had control over their management, production process, and prices they can charge purchasers. While there are almost as many industrial cooperatives as state industrial enterprises, the average cooperative employed about 200 workers while its average state-owned counterpart employs over six times that number. However, the value of the output of state-owned industrial enterprises was only three times that of the industrial cooperatives. The difference was attributed to greater productivity and overall efficiency of the smaller, worker-managed enterprises.[46]

Hungary also had mixed enterprises, which included some combination of private, state, or cooperative enterprise or joint ventures between Hungarian and foreign enterprises. One example was a private merchant or producer hiring a few employees and establishing a place of business in part of a building controlled by an SOE. Throughout the 1980s the demand for such space exceeded the supply, and scarce building space was allocated by competitive auctioning. Another example occurred when workers from a state or collective enterprise worked as a team (e.g., computer programmers) for another enterprise.[47] These teams were small (from 2 to 30 members), self-managed, and free to contract with another enterprise for their services. When working for another enterprise the team could use machinery and equipment from their own enterprise, and consequently bore no financial risks. On an individual basis Hungarian workers were permitted to work in Western nations provided they were guaranteed a job before they left Hungary and they agreed to remit 25 percent of their hard currency earnings, which they were required to convert to forints through a state-controlled financial institution at the official exchange rate.[48] Cooperative ventures with foreign firms increased throughout the 1980s. As of 1981 there were

---

[45]Ease of entry was illustrated by the currency market. Anyone able and willing to acquire foreign exchange could earn income by selling hard currency to other Hungarians at exchange rates well in excess of the official rate set by state authorities. There is considerable demand for hard foreign currency (e.g., dollars), and due to state regulations most Hungarians are not able to obtain such currency at the official rate.

[46]Richet, *The Hungarian Model*, p. 172. Also see "Performance of the Hungarian Economy" section (pp. 515–520) for further discussion.

[47]For a detailed discussion of work teams, see Jan Adam, "Work-Teams: A New Phenomenon in Income Distribution in Hungary," *Comparative Economic Studies*, 31 (Spring 1989), 46–65.

[48]*East European Economic Handbook*, p. 151.

800 enterprises established as cooperative joint ventures with Western firms. One example involved Levi Strauss, which produced over 1 million pairs of blue jeans annually, 40 percent of which it was permitted to export.

After 1989 a debate arose regarding the nature of the inevitable privatization process. Two of Hungary's leading economists, Martin Tardos and Janos Kornai, favored a rapid pace for reforms overall, particularly the privatization of productive assets. They also argued for rapid reduction of subsidies and permitting bankruptcies partly in an effort to stimulate people to become part of the private sector. However, as discussed previously, a gradual transformation program was introduced in the early 1990s. A justification for the gradual pace of transformation, including privatization, was the number of problems and obstacles authorities realized Hungary faced.

First, it was recognized that there was an absence of entrepreneurial talent. Despite the extensive (for CEE) formal and informal private-sector activity prior to 1989, many participants had engaged in rent-seeking behavior and were very risk averse. In addition, most were involved in trading rather than producing goods, so obtaining existing production facilities was not appealing. Besides the lack of entrepreneurs there was also an absence of managerial talent with knowledge of accounting, finance, marketing, and management methods.

Second, there were fears of spontaneous (quiet and illegal) privatization. The new authorities anticipated resistance to privatization efforts by state-owned enterprise managers and bureaucrats who feared real changes in property rights and the emergence of a new, private managerial class and wished to preserve their privileged positions. These individuals learned under the pre-1989 economy that their income and social status depended upon interference and gaining some control over the wealth-creation and distribution process, not in creating wealth. Consequently, they continued to position themselves to extract benefits within an inefficient economy with state control. An example of such behavior since 1989 was the rise of interenterprise debt, as state-owned enterprises granted one another credit as a substitute means of payment in response to the new tight monetary policy designed to establish hard budget constraints on the enterprise level.

A third reason was fears that high interest rates, high taxes, the lack of financial infrastructure, and only modest foreign investment would inhibit privatization. High unemployment was anticipated if bankruptcies and sale of large enterprises became widespread, and there was a desire to moderate the inevitable increase in unemployment. Hungarian authorities realized they faced a problem concerning how to reabsorb unemployed workers into an economy characterized by heavy regional concentration of manufacturing. Many factory workers had developed firm-specific skills and were committed to remaining where they live. They feared a dramatic decline in the value of their homes if many of them were forced to sell and relocate simultaneously. In addition, they faced high housing prices should they have to relocate to an urban area for employment purposes.

Hungarian authorities defined new principal institutions with corresponding working rules regarding ownership and control.[49] The Law on Enterprise Councils specified new forms of business organization. State enterprises were categorized as either utilities or "strategic" and were to remain under state control; small enterprises with 500 or fewer workers to be governed by a council elected by employees; and medium and large enterprises. Enterprises in the second and third categories were to be controlled by a self-management system under which managers could select their own operating officer and could engage in mergers and joint ventures. In reality, workers had little influence.

The Law on Cooperatives provided new working rules for the cooperatives, all of which were required to transform into voluntary institutions. Members could dissolve, transform in a joint-stock or limited-liability company, or restructure the cooperative according to their preference. Working rules were also passed for new private firms and for foreign ownership. The Company Law defined working rules for partnerships, joint-stock, and limited-liability companies. As with other CEE nations, Hungary requires no special permission for foreigners to invest and guarantees remittance of profits and protection from confiscation. Foreigners do face restrictions should they wish to obtain majority ownership of a bank, and may only purchase land directly connected to the specific economic activity in which they are engaged.

Some basic principles Hungarian authorities adopted regarding the privatization process included that bankruptcy should only be permitted in "extraordinary" cases and that measures to privatize existing enterprises and to encourage creation of new private enterprises should be the focus. Despite general consensus for creating a "free market economy," some alternative means to privatize were criticized. It was feared that ex-Communist Party members and large enterprise managers would benefit from spontaneous privatization, and that foreigners would obtain the most profitable enterprises. In response Hungarian authorities created the State Property Agency. This institution, in turn, was criticized for exercising centralized "bureaucratic control" which led to further measures to decentralize the supervision and implementation of privatization as they pertained to establishing a value for the enterprises to be privatized and stimulating competition.[50] Given the public outcry against spontaneous privatization, it was decided to treat each enterprise on a case basis rather than establish "a strict set of rules applied to all of them."[51] The negotiation process has meant a gradual pace and, while reducing spontaneous privatization, has afforded enterprise managers time to resist privatization efforts. However, a policy of corporatization applicable to all enterprises by the end of 1992 was introduced.

The Hungarian privatization process has proceeded through a number of

---

[49]Much of the material for the rest of this section is from Roman Frydman, Andrzej Rapaczynski, John S. Earle, et al., *The Privatization Process in Central Europe* (London: Central European University Press, 1993), pp. 107–145.

[50]Frydman, Rapaczynski, Earle, et al., *The Privatization Process in Central Europe*, pp. 125, 128.

[51]Ibid.

methods. There was evidence that spontaneous privatization began to occur two years before the (what some Hungarians believed to be inevitable) collapse of the previous economy in 1989. New enterprises were created that were owned by enterprises (primarily managers and their friends), although the state may have retained some ownership and control rights. Managers initiate most privatization transactions, sometimes in an illegal manner. While such a process is the predominant means of privatization in Hungary (as opposed to vouchers, restitution, auction, employee or management buyouts, or distributing enterprise shares to workers), there is evidence of cases where the State Privatization Agency sold state-owned assets to coalitions of enterprise managers and bureaucrats on terms quite favorable to the buyers.

Hungary also has adopted a sales program after a "value" which served as the selling price had been established (often by foreign consultants). The program failed due to wide gaps between the value determined by analysts and the price the State Privatization Agency wished to receive (especially from foreign investors), and the demise of large enterprises beginning in 1990 with the collapse of trade accompanied by indifference and inability to maintain the facilities in the face of rising fuel prices. Many of these enterprises had obsolete equipment and were too energy intensive to be attractive to potential buyers. Finally, there was criticism from the radical wing of the Hungarian Democratic Forum that the State Privatization Agency was selling out to Western companies.[52] This led to the government extending its control over privatization further, while the State Privatization Agency became stricter in requiring Western investors to maintain certain employment levels after privatization.

Other methods that were more successful in terms of transferring ownership and control have included the mass-privatization program introduced in the spring of 1993 under which individuals were encouraged to become shareholders in privatized companies by first paying a fee to register, then obtaining an interest-free loan to purchase shares in (corporatized) firms slated to be privatized. Also successful were a "preprivatization" program pertaining to sale of municipal- and state-owned small retail, catering, and consumer service establishments under which most of the roughly 10,000 such firms have been sold; and corporatization.

Corporatization involves restructuring (i.e., changing the legal form of) an enterprise into a joint-stock or limited-liability company and transforming its management into a scheme similar to that of Western corporations before

---

[52]Hungary sought to sell some state-owned enterprises in their early 1990s' condition to foreigners either outright or through a joint venture with a Hungarian partner. There was a favorable tax break for joint ventures prior to mid-1993. In their first five years of operation, such firms (if they had "registration capital" of at least $520,000, a foreign partner had at least a 30 percent share, and at least half of the income generated was from production) were given 60 percent break, then a 40 percent break for the next five years. Given public pressure, this rule was revised in 1993 so that tax breaks only were applicable on the amount of dividends reinvested by the foreign partner in Hungary. See *The Economist: Business Eastern Europe*, July 19, 1993, p. 3.

attempting to privatize it. Of the CEE nations, only Hungary introduced such a process before 1989. In 1987 some "enterprising" state-owned enterprise managers "discovered that some pre-communist laws on commercial companies, dating back to the 19th century, had in fact never been revoked, and that the resulting legal loophole allowed the creation of subsidiaries capitalized with a portion of the assets of state enterprises."[53] As a result new corporate entities in the form of joint-stock or limited-liability companies began to be created. When managers began to abuse the law by acquiring shares in the new company, authorities changed to the working rules and reasserted state ownership.

In terms of effectiveness of its privatization efforts, it is estimated that about one third of Hungary's GDP was accounted for by the private sector in 1994. Corporatization has occurred throughout the economy. Transfer of ownership of large state-owned enterprises has moved slowly, although many have become joint-stock companies and some have been restructured. There has been rapid growth of private activity in small private retail trade and services, most private firms having been newly established. Cooperatives have been increasing in number, particularly in agriculture. There has also been considerable privatization throughout the agricultural sector, which should be expected given the absence of many monopolistic structures and ease of introducing viable price and incentive systems. Of all CEE nations, foreign investors (particularly from the United States, Germany, and Austria) have been most interested in Hungary. As early as 1989, almost 30 percent of incorporated firms in Hungary had some foreign ownership (either exclusive, majority, or minority).

Social Processes for Coordinating
Production and Distribution
Activities: From Gradual Reform
Schemes to Widespread
Transformation Measures

Between 1948 and the mid-1990s the relative importance of planning and markets in coordinating economic activity evolved during five identifiable time periods. Hungary was the first CEE nation to deviate from the Soviet model. (With the exception of Yugoslavia, which broke away from the Soviet bloc in 1948, Hungary was the first Eastern European nation to introduce most economic reforms.) The watershed year for reform was 1968 with the introduction of neoclassical liberal planning in the form of working rules to decentralize coordination of decision making. In 1980 a fourth period characterized by more extensive reforms began, and lasted until the radical reforms following the political revolution in 1989.

1948–1956.   The basic features of the "Stalinplan" process of coordination were discussed in Chapter 15. Planning as the formal process to coordinate economic activity began in 1950 when the first five-year plan was

---

[53]Frydman, Rapaczynski, Earle, et al., *The Privatization Process in Central Europe*, p. 141.

introduced. Its two primary objectives were rapid industrialization and a high rate of investment in capital. Household incomes, agriculture, and light industry were given low priority. Resource allocation occurred through the material-balances method. The planners sought to equate output targets with necessary supplies of scarce inputs. A balance was achieved through a bureaucratic iteration process (which, in reality, allocated inputs to higher-priority projects, with resources for other projects being allocated residually).

The state controlled foreign trade, and all import and export transactions were executed through state-controlled institutions specializing in such trade. Since Hungary was a small nation with few natural resources and sources of energy, it was heavily dependent upon foreign trade—especially with its COMECON partners. One working rule of this association required Hungary to export a fixed amount of specified products to the Soviet Union in return for credits with which Hungary had to purchase Soviet goods.

The state maintained financial control over the economy through the state bank (Hungarian National Bank), which issued all bank notes, allocated credit, and was in position to monitor all transactions between Hungarian enterprises. Transactions involving foreign trade were carried out through the Foreign Trade Bank, while the state budget was prepared and monitored by the Ministry of Finance. This ministry also allocated credit and cash to enterprises for investment and working capital purposes. All prices were established by the National Planning Office. These prices rarely changed, for their purpose was for measurement and control, not to reflect relative scarcities and facilitate efficient resource allocation. There was some flexibility of consumer goods prices, but since supplies were fixed these prices fluctuated according to changes in demand. State control over imports and exports made enterprises immune from world competition, and enterprises whose costs exceeded their revenues were given a state subsidy. In addition, heavy state subsidies enabled many consumer goods to be sold for very low prices.

1956–1967.   The first major reform of the Stalinplan process was in agriculture where mandatory production targets and deliveries to the state by cooperative farms were phased out by 1967, replaced by voluntary contracts offering farmers more favorable prices. In an effort to boost agricultural efficiency and output, state supervision of cooperatives was reduced as decentralized decision making was permitted for agricultural cooperatives. Peasants could select their manager, determine their own pension benefits, establish wages that reflected differentials in performance, and collectively decide what to produce (with the exception of grain production).[54] In addition, the state permitted some private activity that had been occurring, albeit illegally, such as production and sale of

---

[54]Michael Marrese, "Hungarian Agriculture: Lessons for the Soviet Union," *Comparative Economic Studies*, 32, 2 (Summer 1990), 159, 160.

produce and livestock from farmers' private plots at unregulated market prices. Farmers were free to purchase inputs such as fertilizer and seeds, receive credit, and acquire land. The state's rationale for such radical reform (for Eastern Europe) included the authorities' desire to promote output of farm products, the production of which was not characterized by economies of scale, and to increase the peasants' enthusiasm to participate in agricultural cooperatives. These cooperatives, in the interests of reinforcing the "socialist ownership" aspect of the Marxian philosophical basis, were being regulated in a manner similar to state farms.

1968–1978. Poor performance of Hungarian industrial and consumer goods enterprises throughout the 1960s, particularly the inability to satisfy domestic demand, stimulated the development of reform measures by economists. It was accepted by intellectuals and some high-ranking authorities that centralized planning was an ineffective, inefficient coordinating mechanism, and that agricultural performance had improved measurably due to the 1957–1967 reforms. Consequently, pressure began to mount on the Kadar regime to implement radical reforms. Memories of the 1956 popular uprising against Soviet influence influenced the Kadar regime to seek a compromise by adopting a new social process which suspended top-authority management through central planning. This process, contained in the New Economic Mechanism (NEM) introduced in 1968, "sought to integrate both central planning and market forces into one single system."[55] The primary objective of the NEM was to stimulate a market economy while retaining regulation as a means to control and coordinate economic activity, thereby avoiding the creation of a "real market."[56] Reforms pertained mainly to the nature of information received by enterprises and coordination of production and distribution activities.[57]

Instead of planners providing information to enterprises in the form of directives specifying production targets, the NEM sought to introduce "a combination of market forces and government-adjusted 'economic regulators' like prices, exchange rates, interest rates, taxes, and subsidies" according to which industrial and agricultural enterprise managers could make their production and distribution decisions.[58] It was optimistically, and perhaps naively, assumed by the central authorities that a decentralized form of planning, with "a homogeneous price system capable of function, as the reformers required, as a way of reflecting the wishes of the centre, costs and the level of demand," was an efficacious scheme for coordinating Hungary's production and distribution activities.[59]

[55]Jozsef Kobli, "The Status-Oriented Economy: Market Socialism in Hungary," *ISS*, 39 (1987), 367.

[56]Wim Swaan, "Price Regulation in Hungary: Indirect But Comprehensive Bureaucratic Control," *Comparative Economic Studies*, 31, 4 (Winter 1989), 41.

[57]For a more detailed discussion of these reform features, see Prybla, *Market and Plan Under Socialism*, pp. 214–243.

[58]Van Ness, *Market Reforms in Socialist Societies*, p. 54.

[59]Richet, *The Hungarian Model*, p. 65.

In practice, while the NEM appeared to place greater reliance upon markets and competitive prices, unregulated market forces had a minor role in coordinating Hungary's economic activity with the exception of agricultural produce grown on private plots and activity in the second economy. The contradiction of removing central planning but retaining the bureaucracy and a monopolistic industrial structure led to inefficient coordination of decision making. Among the problems with the reforms was the number of complicated price mechanisms which were not sensitive to changes in cost and demand factors; regulations pertaining to taxes, subsidies, and credit that changed too often to provide clear signals to the enterprise managers; and bureaucrats who sought to maintain their status by continuing to regulate economic activity through intervention by applying (often in an arbitrary, ad hoc manner) numerous guidance measures.[60]

For example, when certain enterprises suffered losses which threatened to increase unemployment bureaucrats could introduce regulations providing these enterprises subsidies, or when efficient enterprises sought to increase prices in the face of rising demand (thereby threatening inflation), bureaucrats could introduce measures to prevent price increases. Bureaucrats could respond to requests for a price increase from an efficient firm by reclassifying the product for which the price increase was requested into the "official product" category (which meant that the state was completely responsible for setting the price of the product), importing a similar product (to hold down the price of the Hungarian product for which the price increase was requested), giving the same firm a subsidy rather than permitting the price to increase, giving another enterprise incentive to produce a similar product, or by threatening to take one of these actions.[61] This type of bureaucratic reaction often occurred because authorities who accepted the Marxian philosophical basis were not sympathetic to more efficient, profit-oriented enterprises.

The existence of the bureaucratic bargaining process as a coordination mechanism meant that the ability of unregulated markets to improve enterprise productive efficiency was inhibited as the state continued to influence "regulators" such as prices, exchange rates, and interest rates by modifying these regulators if they did not promote those macroeconomic goals the state wished to achieve. Since regulations were not applied uniformly, managers would seek to identify the weakest link in the regulatory chain and bargain with bureaucrats for permission to raise prices, sell products abroad, or receive subsidies. Bureaucrats reacted to any perceived abuses by enterprises by increasing regulations, and a type of vicious cycle resulting in an ever increasing number of regulations was established.

---

[60]The failure of the NEM to improve coordination has been attributed to the absence of any reform in the "organizational and power stratification." See Kobli, "The Status-Oriented Economy," p. 369.

[61]For further discussion, see Swaan, "Price Regulation in Hungary," pp. 16–20.

1979–1989.   Measures toward greater decentralization and reliance upon market indicators (in lieu of the bureaucratization of economic life) were introduced during this period. Reforms were directed first at increasing domestic and foreign investment at the discretion of enterprise management; second, at developing capital markets so that investment funds were more easily obtainable and allocated more efficiently; and third, at making indicators such as prices and wages more reflective of market conditions. These will be discussed in turn.

Stimulating Investment.   In recognition of the inefficiency of large, SOEs and lack of flexibility in the economy, working rules to promote development of small and medium-sized enterprises were introduced. In the mid-1980s procedures were simplified for enabling individuals to establish small private business, known as "economic partnerships" if they consisted of no more than 30 people, and "petty cooperatives" if more than 30 people. Such enterprises were free to engage in any nonagricultural activity. By 1989 private enterprises were permitted to employ up to 500 people, to trade their stock on the Hungarian stock market (which opened in 1989), and (in the interest of attracting foreign investment) to be 100 percent foreign owned.

Enterprise management was freed of some bureaucratic intervention as much decision making was transferred to the enterprise level where investment decisions were to be made by a new decision-making body known as an enterprise council. At least half of the council's members had to be white-collar and blue-collar employees, while top management, other managers, and trade union representatives made up the rest of the council. The management structure of cooperatives was also reformed. Both enterprise and cooperative management structures were given the freedom to make decisions pertaining to methods of finance, mergers, as well as the determination (and dismissal) of the director of their respective enterprise. This reform had a broad application, for as of 1986 the percentage of industrial enterprises managed by enterprise councils, collective management, and ministry supervision (the SOEs) was 62 percent, 15 percent, and 23 percent, respectively.[62]

Linking the Hungarian economy to the international economy for the purpose of promoting productive efficiency and earning much-needed foreign currency was another priority of the 1980s' reforms. Trade controls were lessened, while joint ventures with foreign-owned firms were more aggressively pursued (i.e., application forms are processed more quickly, while construction workers apparently anxious to extend their nation's economic ties with Western nations take less time to complete joint-venture projects than projects solely managed by Hungarian firms). In addition, Hungary is seriously considering not only placing trade with the Soviet Union on a hard-currency basis, but has applied for an "Associate Member" relationship with the European Union as well.

---

[62]Jan Adam, "The Hungarian Economic Reform of the 1980s," *Soviet Studies*, 39, 4 (October 1987), 612.

Reform of Financial Institutions.   The 1980s witnessed the creation of new financial institutions and working rules for reorganizing existing institutions. On January 1, 1987 a dual banking system was introduced. The Hungarian National Bank would continue to function as a central bank, while new banks were created for the purpose of specializing in the allocation of commercial credit. These banks were permitted to accept deposits and had some discretion regarding the rates of interest they could pay depositors and charge borrowers. In addition, joint financial associations with Western banks were permitted (e.g., Citibank opened a Budapest branch in 1984).

As a result of these reforms central authorities no longer can allocate credit (except for SOEs) according to the conformity between the project for which funds were requested and planners' objectives. Enterprises could engage in self-financing, including selling stock in the new stock market. However, subsidies were still granted to SOEs (either through direct payments or in the form of price supports or tax concessions). One problem that remains is that calculating the profitability of an enterprise (for the purpose of awarding a subsidy) is difficult and ambiguous because costs and prices are still not a true reflection of relative scarcity.

Price and Wage Reform.   There were gradual changes aimed toward making prices and wages more reflective of market conditions. While authorities did not permit prices to be established according to demand and supply factors, which would not be possible until freer trade made Hungarian producers more sensitive to international prices, there was a complex price reform scheme introduced in 1980. The new scheme applied to enterprises exporting more than 5 percent of their output, which applied to over 70 percent of Hungary's industrial output, intending to make prices for these products more "competitive." What this meant was that prices for certain goods (e.g., energy, raw materials) were "set equal to Western world market prices (converted to forints at the prevailing exchange rates)."[63] Firms could increase their prices only to the level at which the new price equaled the world market price. On the other hand, if the enterprise's prices were already above world prices due to higher costs of production, they could still expect a subsidy. All other prices remained subject to the bureaucratic bargaining process and were established according to a complicated series of regulations, subject to frequent change. Meanwhile, prices of the other 30 percent of goods were set according to the markup over cost method that had been in effect since the late 1940s. Finally, the state reserved the right to intervene to set prices of any goods or services in the name of controlling inflation and reducing social tension.

Wage reform was introduced in 1985 to discourage upward wage drift (and thereby reduce inflationary pressure) in less efficient firms that had no incentives to hold down wages even if they were realizing losses due to the desire of the state to grant subsidies rather than permit enterprises to go bankrupt. The new rules permitted enterprise management to set wages according to "their own

---

[63]Van Ness, *Market Reforms in Socialist Societies*, p. 60.

consideration," although income earners would face a steep progressive income tax as well as a surtax if their wages grew by more than 3 percent annually.[64] However, by 1987 inflation caused authorities to introduce a wage freeze, and enterprises were required to have wage increases approved by state authorities.

1989–PRESENT.   Among the new authorities and economists there was a general consensus that Hungary needed to implement macroeconomic stabilization and transformation measures which included the following interrelated aspects: promoting growth and employment in the private sector, reducing inflation but softening the impact of necessary measures to do so, promoting private investment, establishing sources of credit for the private sector, making the forint convertible, upgrading infrastructure, reducing subsidies (particularly to state-owned enterprises), diversifying the nation's export market, improving the quality of goods produced, and simultaneously privatizing while reducing the state's role in economic matters. Disagreement over the nature and pace of the transformation program arose. This in part was due to ideological differences among authorities and advisors. Consequently, there was no widely shared view regarding what social processes for coordination of economic activity should be adopted.[65] In addition, there was widespread recognition that Hungary faced considerable problems and obstacles to transforming its economy.

Among the nation's most pressing problems in 1989 were macroeconomic instability and the absence of a business culture, an active second economy notwithstanding. Such problems aggravated faith in the nation's political problems, which included an absence of faith in authorities. Prior to 1990 there had been a long period of low economic growth, lack of credit, extensive foreign debt, and an industrial sector typified by energy-intensive, obsolete manufacturing facilities. It was understood that comprehensive reforms would be certain to exacerbate inflation, stimulate unemployment, adversely affect trade balances, and hinder the state's ability to provide social services and assistance to needy members of the population. In particular, considerable unemployment was (accurately) believed to be inevitable after any rapid privatization movement due to overstaffing of the state-owned enterprises and the difficulty many workers would face in being absorbed by the private sector. Such unemployment would be unpopular. Social unrest and hostility toward authorities in power were feared, since there likely would be inadequate funds to finance needed compensation.

Therefore, a strategy for introducing gradual reforms was adopted. This strategy was intended to be compatible with the goal of maintaining social peace by trying to ease burdens of the society only a step at a time. Among the gradual reforms was a plan to "demobilize" trade unions and "to get out of the hands of managers the

---

[64]Adam, "The Hungarian Economic Reform of the 1980s," pp. 615, 616.

[65]As mentioned earlier, there were blueprints for a "free market economy" provided by Janos Kornai and the Blue Ribbon Commission. However, these called for rapid transformation measures which Hungarian authorities found unacceptable.

control over the process of privatization, [and] economic decision-making."[66] These reforms were included in the March 1991 "five-year program of conversion and development of the Hungarian economy . . . [which included measures to] accelerate trade liberalization and rapid redirection of trade away from the former COMECON region to Western markets."[67] A stated goal was to emphasize privatization to the extent that by 1994 less than half of the economic enterprises would be state owned. The International Monetary Fund was instrumental in the initial formulation of policy measures, agreeing to provide credit in exchange for Hungary meeting targets pertaining to the size of its budget deficit as a percentage of GDP (it was to be no more than 5.3 percent of GDP in 1994) and specified rates of monetary growth.

Relative to promises and expectations, the 1991 economic program achieved success in the areas of short-term economic stabilization. Responding to pressure from the International Monetary Fund and other creditors, the authorities reduced subsidies to state-owned enterprises considerably, maintained a strict monetary policy, and quickly liberalized foreign trade. However, after the stabilization and transformation measures were introduced problems arose. Output fell much further than anticipated while unemployment and inflation performed worse than predicted as well (see "Performance of the Hungarian Economy," pp. 519–520). Pensioners suffered acutely since their incomes were indexed for only a 2 percent rate of inflation. It was difficult to reduce subsidies to state-owned enterprises dramatically due to fears of exacerbating the unemployment problem. There were inadequate funds to finance support of the unemployed. Double deficit problems arose, and the foreign debt problem remained serious. The end of COMECON resulted in a significant change in the flow of trade, with Hungary's exports to Western nations rising from less than half to almost three quarters of its exports from 1989 to 1991. The ability of export growth to contribute further to economic development was hindered, however, by trade restrictions—particularly from the European Union, which imposed limits on the quantity of Hungarian agricultural and textile products (among other goods) permitted into its market.

Foreign assistance to Hungary (and the rest of CEE) was provided by the newly created European Bank for Reconstruction and Development. Established by the World Bank, this organization was intended to provide a source of credit for enterprises and governments at all levels in the reconstruction and conversion of the economy. For example, in 1993 Budapest received a loan for over $75 million for the purpose of financing the purchase of housing (to be renovated), reconstructing the oldest underground railroad line, and providing much needed parking facilities.[68]

---

[66]Bruszt, "Workers, Managers, and State Bureaucrats," p. 20.

[67]Frydman, Rapaczynski, Earle, et al., *The Privatization Process in Central Europe*, p. 196.

[68]The European Bank for Reconstruction and Development has fallen short of its potential. During its first 18 months of existence, it spent almost half of its $1.2 billion budget on lavishly refurbishing its London headquarters. The bank also focuses on large-scale projects (such as restructuring obsolete state-owned enterprises) while neglecting to provide venture capital to many budding entrepreneurs much in need of credit.

Other social processes which have coordinated production and distribution activity in Hungary since 1989 are similar to those occurring in the rest of CEE, namely, a combination of unregulated markets (both legal and illegal), organized crime activity, negotiated agreements between interest groups, plus private Western influence in the form of foreign investors. By the mid-1990s the private sector was dominant in retail trade and services as well as agriculture. Foreign influence was felt in selected industries (travel, automobile manufacturing, electrical components, among others), and in infrastructure and banking. Unregulated or partially regulated markets are gradually becoming the primary means of coordination, but the influence of the state can be expected to remain strong for at least another decade.

EVOLUTION OF
ALTERNATIVE INSTITUTIONS

Hungary experienced more institutional changes from 1945 through 1988 than any other CEE nation for three reasons. First, the authorities were sensitive to public pressure (exemplified by the 1956 revolution) and willing to seek a compromise between the orthodox Marxian philosophical basis and the views of Hungarian reformers. Second, Hungary depends heavily on foreign trade, which requires that their products be competitive with world market prices. Third, and perhaps most importantly, the authorities openly recognized the limits of bureaucratic know-how and central planning as a coordinating mechanism, and were willing to decrease the state's role in decision making, ownership and control of the means of production, and coordination of economic activities. In addition, authorities were willing to sanction institutions engaging in private enterprise, albeit at a modest level.

Reform of the state organs responsible for controlling the economy began occurring in 1968. The National Planning Office's power was reduced somewhat, although the bureaucratic bargaining process that replaced central planning maintained significant bureaucratic influence. The Hungarian National Bank's monopoly over commercial banking activities ended in 1987 with the introduction of commercial banks where enterprises were free to seek credit. The liberalization of foreign trade regulations reduced the importance of the Foreign Trade Ministry and Bank of Foreign Trade, while the opening of a stock market (and commercial banking) had the same effect on the Ministry of Finance.

A new institution, the work team, was introduced in 1981 as another means for incomes of SOE workers to be supplemented (and to alleviate labor shortages and promote wage differentiation as well). The number of workers involved in such teams increased more than tenfold between 1982 and 1986 (from about 21,500 to over 260,000).[69] One problem with these teams was that while

---

[69] Adam, "Work Teams," p. 54.

higher wages were attractive to many workers, they could only engage in such activity (i.e., perform work for another enterprise) after completing their regular work at the SOE. Evidence indicates that work team members' productivity on the full-time job suffered, as did their health (from working too many extra hours).

By 1990 many of the working rules defining the boundaries for the principal institutions' activities had been modified or eliminated. The most significant change was the ending of the Communist Party's monopoly over political power. A parliamentary democracy took its place, and the ruling coalition Democratic Forum-Free Democratic Alliance was free to introduce economic reforms without having to legitimize the new working rules according to the Marxian philosophical basis. After the 1994 election a significant change occurred within the government as the Socialist Party, whose members were primarily ex-Communist Party members, rose to power as the leader of a new coalition.

There has been widespread change in economic institutions as a result of corporatization and other privatization programs, foreign investment, development of a stock market, the forint becoming convertible, and freedom of entry permitted to those wishing to form a new private business organization. In addition, Hungary has become an Associate Member of the European Union. This membership provides Hungary with a timetable for greater access to European Union markets as well as conditions Hungary must meet before it could be considered for full membership. Given the radical extent of institutional change, what is perhaps most noteworthy are the institutions which have either changed little or reemerged after seemingly having been eliminated. These include agricultural cooperatives (some of which have changed in legal form only), the uncivil economy (in which there are new participants while some individuals active before 1989 no longer are active),[70] and large state-owned manufacturing enterprises.

The large factories, although their legal form has most likely been transformed to a joint-stock or limited-liability company, continue to produce the same products using machinery and equipment that differs little from the pre-1989 era. Persistence of state-owned manufacturing enterprises is characteristic of all CEE nations due to the enormous task of modernizing these factories. When the magnitude of funds needed for a comprehensive effort is compared to the paucity of funds available from CEE governments, investors, and international organizations, one recognizes that many decades will be necessary for a substantive transformation to occur—unless a nation wishes to suddenly create

---

[70]An example is a friend who has worked as a waiter in one of Budapest's luxury hotels. Prior to 1989 he was one of very few Hungarians able to acquire hard currency (through tips he received). Using this currency, he was able to purchase consumer goods such as CB radios which (in a country with a serious shortage of telephones) he resold for seven times his purchase price. Since 1989 his ability to do "business" in such a manner has been eliminated given the easy access throughout Hungary to foreign-produced consumer goods. He has been replaced, however, by others looking to trade in contraband, avoid taxes, and take advantage of loopholes in the new commercial code.

huge increases in the number of its unemployed. There is not sufficient foreign investor interest to make up the difference, especially considering the obsolete, poorly equipped nature of many CEE factories.[71]

PERFORMANCE OF THE HUNGARIAN ECONOMY

Pre-1989

Hungary's performance, evaluated in terms of growth, productivity, inflation, unemployment, trade balance, debt, real wages, and selected standard of living indicators, was relatively good compared to the rest of CEE between the late 1950s and 1980. However, throughout the 1980s nearly all indicators became less favorable. Trends in these indicators will be presented, followed by a brief evaluation of the relative impact of the working rules and institutions on the overall performance as compared to the effect upon performance of changes in the world economic environment and macroeconomic policies pursued by Hungarian authorities.

GROWTH, PRODUCTIVITY, EFFICIENCY.   Figures for economic growth, measured in terms of net national product, national income, net material product, and real gross national product, are presented in Table 17-1. Growth of agricultural output was favorable from 1968 to 1989. It rose at an annual average rate of 3.5 percent during the 1970s, the highest rate of any Western or CEE nation.[72] This sector typically produced about 30 percent more than the nation consumes, so

TABLE 17-1 Hungarian Economic Growth, 1951–1988

	1951 -55	1956 -60	1961 -65	1966 -70	1971 -75	1976 -80	1981 -85	1986	1987	1988
NNP[1]	5.7%	5.9%	4.1%	6.8%						
NY[2]			3.3	6.2	4.5%	1.6%				
Net material product						2.8	2.5%			
Real GNP[3]								2.1%	0.9%	1.1%

[1]Net national product.
[2]National income.
[3]Real gross national product.

Sources: U.S. Department of State, *Hungarian Economic Reform: Status and Prospects* (Budapest: United States Embassy, 1989), p. 6; Janos Kornai, "The Hungarian Reform Process: Visions, Hopes, and Reality," *Journal of Economic Literature*, 24 (December 1986), 1721; Xavier Richet, *The Hungarian Model: Markets and Planning in a Socialist Economy* (Cambridge: Cambridge University Press, 1989), p. 151; Jan Prybla, *Market and Plan Under Socialism: The Bird in the Cage* (Stanford, CA: Hoover Institution Press, 1987), pp. 35, 239.

[71]In the following chapter, the Chinese policy for dealing with this problem is presented.
[72]Prybla, *Market and Plan Under Socialism*, p. 244.

agricultural exports were a primary source of hard currency. State policies contributing to this performance were, first, membership in cooperatives (the most prevalent agricultural institution) was voluntary; second, smaller enterprises were allowed to take advantage of market information and incentives; and third, prices and incentives effectively linked effort to reward, thereby stimulating output. Another major factor in Hungary's agricultural strength was that well over 50 percent of its land is suitable for agriculture, and the climate is quite favorable.

On the negative side, labor and capital productivity kept declining. The growth of labor productivity fell from an average annual rate of 3.7 percent between 1976 and 1980 to 2.2 percent between 1981 and 1985, while capital productivity declined, falling 3.1 percent and 2.8 percent for the same two periods.[73] Given these figures it is not surprising that the performance of Hungary's large state-owned industrial enterprises was poor. Almost half of them lost money, requiring large producer subsidies. As a percentage of state expenditures, producer subsidies accounted for about 18 percent of total state budget expenditures throughout the 1980s.[74] There was an inverse correlation between size (in terms of the value of capital plus the annual wage bill) of a state-owned industrial enterprise and average profitability. If the enterprises were divided into ten categories, average profitability of the smallest and second smallest enterprise categories was 26.1 percent and 21.3 percent in 1980, while the comparable figures for the second largest and largest enterprises were 9.9 percent and 6.9 percent, respectively.[75] The fact that enterprises in the two largest categories accounted for about 80 percent of Hungary's industrial output indicates the extent to which Hungary was unable to take advantage of economies of scale by having concentrated industrial output within large enterprises.

UNEMPLOYMENT AND INFLATION.   One positive feature of the pre-1989 Hungarian economic performance was the low rate of unemployment. Due to the philosophical basis committed to providing work for all job seekers and demographic factors which resulted in a relative shortage of adult males, there was considerable job security—the unemployment rate did not exceed 1 percent. However, inflation steadily worsened after 1960 (see Table 17-2), and accelerated in the late 1980s. This trend has been attributed to reforms which made some prices less rigid in the face of slow growth of supply, supply shocks (e.g., oil crises of 1970s), declining terms of trade and a worsening of Hungary's exchange rate, and the gradual removal of consumer subsidies. The state subsidized housing, food, heat, and transportation heavily, although the extent of subsidization declined. In 1983 consumer subsidies accounted for about 12 percent of state expenditures, but by 1988 this percentage had been reduced to less than 7 percent.[76]

---

[73]Richet, *The Hungarian Model*, p. 151.

[74]U.S. Department of State, *Hungarian Economic Reform*, p. 10.

[75]The profitability of the typical large state-owned state enterprise has been declining over the past decade, and many are now losing money. See Richet, *The Hungarian Model*, p. 171.

[76]U.S. Department of State, *Hungarian Economic Reform*, p. 10.

TABLE 17-2 Inflation[1]

1960–67	1967–73	1973–78	1978–84	1985	1986	1987	1988
1.0%	1.6%	3.9%	7.5%	6.9%	5.4%	8.5%	15.7%

[1]Average annual percent change in the consumer price index.

Sources: U.S. Department of State, *Hungarian Economic Reform: Status and Prospects* (Budapest: United States Embassy, 1989), p. 13; Janos Kornai, "The Hungarian Reform Process: Visions, Hopes, and Reality," *Journal of Economic Literature*, 24 (December 1986), p. 1720.

OTHER PERFORMANCE INDICATORS.   Foreign trade figures are significant for any small nation such as Hungary, and about 50 percent of all spending was related to the international economy. During the 1980s performance was particularly poor in this area. Between 1980 and 1986 the value of Hungary's trade (measured in dollars) declined over 12 percent while its hard-currency trade balance "swung from a $1.2 billion surplus in 1984 to a $540 million deficit in 1986."[77] The nation was borrowing heavily while pursuing an export promotion strategy (hoping that export growth would provide needed hard currency for technological imports). Due to bad management, productive inefficiency, and an inflexible economy the export boom did not materialize (in 1988 and 1989 the volume of hard-currency exports declined almost 10 percent each year).[78] As a result debt owed to foreigners increased so much that by 1990 Hungary had the highest debt per capita of any CEE nation.

Real wages declined from 1976 to 1989 after two quite favorable periods (1965–1970 and 1971–1975) during which real wages grew at an average annual rate of 4.5 percent and 5.8 percent, respectively.[79] During the 1980s there were only three years during which real wages increased, and in none of those years did they grow by as much as 2 percent. In 1988 real wages declined an estimated 6.5 percent. The fall in real wages, combined with the extra hours worked, helps to explain the decline in average life expectancy of males from about 66.5 to 65.0 between 1970 and 1985.[80]

In terms of the distribution of income prior to 1989, Hungary's was more equitable than that of most contemporary economies, albeit at lower levels of income. The 1968 reforms are credited with contributing to greater equability.[81] Those with higher incomes faced steep marginal income taxes (even by Western

[77]Ibid., p. 5; and Michael Marrese, "The Separability of Hungarian Foreign Trade with Respect to the Soviet Union, the Rest of the CMEA, and the West," *Comparative Economic Studies*, 31, 2 (Summer 1989), 32.

[78]*Hungary* (Budapest: American Embassy, 1989), p. 7.

[79]Pieter Boot, "Incentive Systems and Unemployment: The East European Experience," *Comparative Economic Studies*, 29, 1 (Spring 1987), 56.

[80]Ibid., p. 15.

[81]See Kornai, "The Hungarian Reform Process," p. 1725. Kornai says that in terms of the ratio of average income of individuals above the median to income of individuals below the median, the measure of Hungarian income inequality fell slightly from 1.92 in 1967 to 1.82 in 1982 (i.e., top 10 percent earn about 18 percent of all income, bottom 10 percent earn about 5 percent).

standards) on personal income as well as a value-added tax of about 25 percent on certain consumer goods. While Hungarians appeared to enjoy a higher material standard of living (indicated by measures of material goods and services and the rate of emigration to the West) than citizens of other CEE nations, there were shortages of housing, automobiles, and services such as medical care and telephone service. (The waiting time for a household to have a new telephone installed was about 15 years.)

SUMMARY OF PRE-1989 PERFORMANCE.   Some positive features of the economy's performance can be identified. In terms of availability and affordability of consumer goods, as well as the capacity to provide for its own agricultural needs and have a surplus for export, Hungary's economy outperformed all other CEE nations. Fewer shortages of goods occurred, and freedom to engage in entrepreneurial activity increased—especially for those working in a cooperative or a private enterprise. On the other hand, the 1980s featured an economic slowdown, followed by stagnation and decline. Real gross domestic product was only 12 percent higher in 1986 than in 1978, while both domestic consumption and real wages declined and exports sagged.[82] Productive capacity deteriorated, partly because existing machinery was not replaced quickly enough as investment in manufacturing as a percentage of all state investment fell. The technology problem was so acute that "the average age of manufactured product designs is now [1988] about 16 years, while the share of designs under three years old is less than 15 percent."[83] As a result, Hungarian exports became less competitive.

This problem was exacerbated by the state's policy of supporting the less productive enterprises, thereby preserving the existing manufacturing and incentive structure as well as inhibiting the mobility of workers from less to more productive enterprises. As state expenditures increased faster than receipts, so did the debt service burden. Meanwhile, more efficient enterprises faced uncertain bureaucratic regulation as well as high taxes on enterprise profits and worker incomes. Other causes of the declining performance included overemphasis on heavy industry, particularly in mining and metallurgy industries, and a neglected, decaying infrastructure—especially telecommunications.

The world economic environment was one factor contributing to the negative aspects of performance, especially the energy crises of the 1970s. In addition, authorities made some macroeconomic policy decisions that adversely affected the performance over the past decade. Most analysts of the Hungarian economy do not attribute the poor performance solely to the reforms introduced since 1968. However, nearly all agree that Hungarian authorities failed to introduce the type of institutions and working rules that would decentralize decision making and stimulate improved performance.

---

[82]Gabor Revesz, "How the Economic Reforms Were Distorted," *Eastern European Economics*, 27, 3 (Spring 1989), 65.

[83]U.S. Department of State, *Hungarian Economic Reforms*, p. 2.

1989–Present

As indicated in Chapter 16, Hungary's performance since 1989 has featured declining growth of GDP (with a positive 1 percent rate for 1994), rising levels of poverty and unemployment, declining real income, a more skewed distribution of income combined with greater concentration of wealth, rising crime, and persistent inflation (see Table 16-2). The nation's budget deficit was about 8.5 percent of GDP in 1994 (higher than the International Monetary Fund's target), due to the inability of many state-owned enterprises to make tax and social security payments combined with the inability of the state to collect revenue owed to it—a problem fueled by considerable tax evasion from those engaged in the social and uncivil economies.[84] Agricultural output has fallen each year since 1990, the decline exceeding 10 percent annually from 1991 to 1993. A risk survey conducted by *The Economist*, which rates nations according to their attractiveness for foreign investment, gave Hungary a worse rating in 1993 than in 1994. This was due to the nation's high budget deficit, declining exports, current account deficit, and continuing recession, making Hungary the only CEE nation whose risk rating worsened for that period. A spring 1994 survey indicated that only 18 percent of Hungarians believed "they were better off than before" 1989, a lower percentage than any CEE nation with the exception of Russia.[85] Favorable performance indicators include the positive growth of GDP following declines from 1989 to 1993, rising industrial output since 1993, more foreign investment ($7 billion) than the rest of CEE combined, and an estimated 60 percent of GDP produced by the private sector (if all illegal economic activity is included).

Overall, the performance through 1994 was not favorable as evaluated by the Hungarian voters. In addition to the factors discussed in Chapter 16, there are other reasons cited for Hungary's adverse indicators. The two most often cited (particularly for the 20 percent decline in GDP) have been the impact of bankruptcies and restructuring efforts on state-owned enterprises, and the collapse of COMECON trade. Hungarians look to their new authorities to introduce measures to ease the social costs of the transformation as well as to continue reform efforts to increase the influence of the private sector.

EVOLUTIONARY-INSTITUTIONAL CHANGE IN THE HUNGARIAN ECONOMY

Significant changes in the informal rules among citizens and intellectuals have been stimulated three times during the past 40 years (1956, 1968, 1989) by "[p]rolonged economic problems and/or the instability through disagreement

---

[84]*The Economist: Business Eastern Europe,* January 31, 1994, p. 5.
[85]"Bring Back the Goulash," *The Economist,* p. 7.

within the political leadership."[86] In 1956 the authorities did not heed popular demand for widespread reforms, for the rigidity and power of top authorities within the political structure enabled them to consolidate their power over the economy and to forestall radical reforms. The 1956 events illustrate the "political dilemma" of trying to reform a CSE, namely "that the very monopoly of political power that the party enjoys prevents the evolution of the political mechanisms required to successfully implement such fundamental economic reforms."[87]

Pressure continued to build, however, ultimately resulting in dramatic changes introduced by authorities in 1968. As one Hungarian scholar describes these reforms,

> [t]he idea of reforming the economic system was generated by dissatisfaction with the system's operation and performance . . . [e]conomic officials both in central control agencies and in firms as well as academics had become disappointed by the operation of the economic system, by the numerous irrationalities caused by it, and also by the deteriorating performance of the economy that could well be explained by, among other things, the malfunctioning of the planning and management systems.[88]

The continued monopoly over political power by the Communist Party enabled authorities to introduce only modest, piecemeal reforms (and to recentralize decision making if they believed it necessary) while continuing to exert bureaucratic control over the economy. The performance of the Hungarian economy deteriorated during the 1980s, partly as a result of these mutually contradictory rules.

A number of factors contributed to the radical upheaval in the late 1980s, culminating in the resignation of the Communist Party authorities and the election of new authorities. First, the credit crisis and failure of the export promotion policy plunged Hungary deeply into debt. Second, declining living standards created discontent among Hungarians who had become aware of their poor conditions relative to Western European nations. Finally, there was the "maverick of Hungarian national radicalism"[89] among intellectuals and some party members (e.g., Imre Pozsgay), which has manifested itself throughout the nation's history.

Since 1989 the Hungarian economy has been evolving, although the type of economy it wishes to establish and corresponding "beacon" to follow remain undetermined. While the "free market economy" was the first model proposed, subsequent events throughout CEE (particularly the worse than expected economic

[86]Laszlo Budavari, "Hesitating Steps Toward Self-Government in Hungary," *Economics of Planning,* 22, 1-2 (1988), 88. It remains to be seen if the change in political structure in 1994 will lead to a fourth shift in the direction toward which the Hungarian economy evolves.

[87]Van Ness, *Market Reforms in Socialist Societies,* p. 17.

[88]Bauer, "Reforming the Planned Economy," pp. 104, 105.

[89]Ignotus, *Hungary,* p. 299.

performance since 1989) combined with the public's fear of social and economic hardships from unregulated market forces led to institutional change within the political structure and a philosophical basis further removed from the initial proposals.[90] Economic and social uncertainties have arisen "as a result of the rapid growth of social burdens in the framework of [centralized] exclusionary policies."[91] Political support has shifted to the new coalition, which could lead to working rules more consistent with the philosophical basis which prevailed prior to 1989.

CONCLUDING REMARKS

Hungarian authorities need to articulate and justify a reform path that will receive widespread public support. Unlike their predecessors, the new authorities appear to have the willingness to evaluate if there are any relevant lessons from actual economies' development experiences that can provide useful insights as they develop a new transformation program for Hungary. Since there has been a shift in the informal rules favoring some variant of social democracy in both Poland and Hungary, this alternative is receiving consideration.

The case of Sweden may be useful, for it provides an example of economic reform in which macroeconomic stabilization and a higher standard of living were achieved while a safety net was provided and faith in authorities retained after reforms were introduced.[92] In order for Sweden's experience to be relevant for Hungary, the Swedish philosophical basis and measures to resolve similar problems must be both attainable and politically and economically appealing to Hungarians. As discussed in Chapter 13, there were four such problems faced by Sweden in 1932: reconciling cleavages within the political structure while adopting a philosophical basis that had broad political support and appealed to a majority of the electorate, achieving macroeconomic stability, increasing the competitiveness of a concentrated industrial structure, and improving the standard of living for families suffering from low incomes, a housing shortage, and inadequate health care.

Social Democratic ideals, which embody egalitarian and community concern, could appeal to those Hungarians who share these ideals. Having been imbued with Marxian ideals regarding an egalitarian income distribution and security for all citizens, Hungarians may wish to create a society in which social policy is assumed as a government responsibility. People would then receive social insurance and welfare benefits while enjoying economic and political

[90]This is discussed in Chapter 6 concerning Karl Polanyi's thesis.
[91]Bruszt, "Workers, Managers and State Bureaucrats," p. 30.
[92]Material for the remainder of this section is taken from James Angresano, "A Mixed Economy in Hungary? Lessons from the Swedish Experience," *Comparative Economic Studies,* 34, 1 (Spring 1992), 41–57.

freedoms. Income and wealth differentials would be minimized while social inequalities are reduced. Equal pay for equal work would be the rule, the state would commit to maintaining full employment, and individuals would be compensated for loss of income resulting from economic risks to which they are exposed. In addition, control over production would be concentrated in the private sector. On the other hand, some argue that given Hungarians' strong sense of individualism and dislike of regulation, the extent of Sweden's state paternalism would not be acceptable, nor would be the extent to which Sweden redistributes income.

The Swedish development experience, particularly the measures introduced between 1932 and 1960, offers Hungary the following lessons. First, reconciliation of political cleavages is necessary before a philosophical basis and reform measures with broad support can be adopted. Second, establishing political democracy does not mean rapid realization of economic prosperity. Sweden, facing conditions and obstacles less unfavorable than Hungary, took decades to achieve comprehensive economic reform. The third lesson is that achieving macroeconomic stability and improving competitiveness are both prerequisites for extensive state-funded social insurance and welfare measures. Fourth, cooperatives can be viable, attainable institutions for increasing the economy's competitiveness. Fifth, if a pay scheme which minimizes wage differentials and increases job security in return for modest wage demands is a desired means for promoting stabilization and competition, labor and management must acquiesce to its working rules. Finally, unless the Hungarian people demonstrate greater solidarity and faith in their authorities, Swedish-type stabilization policies and state-provided social insurance and welfare benefits will not be efficacious.

Hungarian reformers (as well as authorities in other CEE nations) would be well advised to evaluate the appeal and attainability of the philosophical basis and measures adopted not only by Sweden, but by France, Japan, and China, among other nations, to alleviate problems similar to those facing them today. The lessons provided by these experiences can provide the basis for decisions pertaining to the pace of transition, aims of macroeconomic policies during the early stages of transformation, achievement of competitiveness domestically and internationally, methods for expanding the private sector, and type and extent of social insurance and welfare programs to provide.

KEY TERMS AND CONCEPTS

Associate Member of the
European Union
Hungarian Democratic Forum
Joint Ventures

New Economic Mechanism
Second Economy
Socialist Party

QUESTIONS FOR DISCUSSION

1. What were the main features of Hungary's pre-1989 economic reforms?
2. Why did the pre-1989 reforms fail to result in a substantive transformation of the economy?
3. What obstacles did Hungary face to rapid transformation of its economy in 1989?
4. Using the evolutionary-institutional theory, explain why Hungarians voted for the Socialist Party in the 1994 elections.
5. What lessons can be learned from the Hungarian transformation experience concerning the efficacy of rapid transformation policies versus polices which seek a gradual transformation?

REFERENCES

Adam, Jan, "Work-Teams: A New Phenomenon in Income Distribution in Hungary," *Comparative Economic Studies,* 31, 1 (Spring 1989), 46–65.

————, "The Hungarian Economic Reform of the 1980s," *Soviet Studies,* 39, 4 (October 1987), 610–627.

Angresano, James, "A Myrdalian View of Evolving Socio-Economic Conditions in Central and East Europe," *Development Policy Review,* 12, 3 (September 1994), 251–275.

————, "A Mixed Economy for Hungary? Lessons from the Swedish Experience," *Comparative Economic Studies,* 34, 2 (Summer 1992), 41–57.

————, "Political and Economic Obstacles Inhibiting Comprehensive Reform in Hungary," *East European Quarterly,* 26, 1 (March 1992), 55–76.

Bauer, Tamas, "Reforming the Planned Economy: The Hungarian Experience," *The Annals of the American Academy of Political and Social Science: Privatizing and Marketizing Socialism,* 507 (January 1990), 103–112.

Blue Ribbon Commission, Project Hungary Action Program for "Hungary in Transformation to Freedom and Prosperity." Indianapolis: Hudson Institute, 1990.

Boot, Pieter, "Incentive Systems and Unemployment: The East European Experience," *Comparative Economic Studies,* 29, 1 (Spring 1987), 37–61.

Bornstein, Morris, ed., *Plan and Market: Economic Reform in Eastern Europe.* New Haven, CT: Yale University Press, 1973.

"Bring Back the Goulash: Hungary's Elections," *The Economist,* May 7, 1994, pp. 57–58.

Bruszt, Laszlo, "Workers, Managers and State Bureaucrats and the Economic Transformation in Hungary," Working paper prepared at Central European University, Prague, 1993.

Budavari, Laszlo, "Hesitating Steps Toward Self-Government in Hungary," *Economics of Planning,* 22, 1-2 (1988), 88–99.

Chapman, Bruce, "A Recipe for a Free-Market Hungary," *The Wall Street Journal,* April 6, 1990, p. A18.

East European Economic Handbook. London: Euromonitor Publications Limited, 1985.

The Economist: Business Eastern Europe, January 31, 1994, p. 5.

The Economist: Business Eastern Europe, July 19, 1993, p. 3.

Fischer, Tibour, "Hungary: The Self-Destruction of the Party." *The Wall Street Journal,* November 6, 1989, p. A17.

Frydman, Roman, Andrzej Rapaczynski, John S. Earle, et al., *The Privatization Process in Central Europe,* 1. London: Central European University Press, 1993.

Hungary. Budapest: American Embassy, September 1989.

Ignotus, Paul, *Hungary.* New York: Praeger Publishers, 1972.

Karacs, Imre, "Hungarian Panel Suggests Radical Economic Changes," *Washington Post,* April 22, 1989, p. D13.

Kobli, Jozsef, "The Status-Oriented Economy: Market Socialism in Hungary," *ISS,* 39 (1987), 365–375.

Kornai, Janos, "The Hungarian Reform Process: Visions, Hopes, and Reality," *Journal of Economic Literature,* 24 (December 1986), 1687–1737.

————, *The Road to a Free Economy: Shifting from a Socialist System—the Example of Hungary.* New York: W. W. Norton, 1991.

Lange, Oskar, and Fred M. Taylor, *On the Economic Theory of Socialism.* Minneapolis: University of Minnesota Press, 1964.

Lindblom, Charles E., *Politics and Markets.* New York: Basic Books, 1977.

Lovenduski, Joni, and Jean Woodall, *Politics and Society in Eastern Europe.* Bloomington, IN: Indiana University Press, 1987.

Marrese, Michael, "Hungarian Agriculture: Lessons for the Soviet Union," *Comparative Economic Studies,* 32, 2 (Summer 1990), 155–169.

————, "The Separability of Hungarian Foreign Trade with Respect to the Soviet Union, the Rest of the CMEA, and the West," *Comparative Economic Studies,* 31, 2 (Summer 1989), 1–41.

Prybla, Jan S., *Market and Plan Under Socialism: The Bird in the Cage.* Stanford, CA: Hoover Institution Press, 1987.

Revesz, Gabor, "How the Economic Reforms Were Distorted," *Eastern European Economics,* 27, 3 (Spring 1989), 61–84.

Richet, Xavier, translated by J. C. Whitehouse, *The Hungarian Model: Markets and Planning in a Socialist Economy.* Cambridge: Cambridge University Press, 1989.

Shangquan, Gao, Chen Uizi, and Wang Xiaoqiang, "Investigation of Reforms in Hungary and Yugoslavia," *Chinese Economic Studies,* 22, 3 (Spring 1989), 80–88.

Swaan, Wim, "Price Regulation in Hungary: Indirect But Comprehensive Bureaucratic Control," *Comparative Economic Studies,* 31, 4 (Winter 1989), 10–52.

Telesio, Piero, "Are East Europe's Executives Prepared for the 1990s?" *The Wall Street Journal,* January 15, 1990, p. A17.

U.S. Department of State, *Hungarian Economic Reform: Status and Prospects.* Budapest: United States Embassy, 1989.

Van Ness, Peter, ed., *Market Reforms in Socialist Societies: Comparing China and Hungary.* Boulder, CO: Lynne Rienner, 1989.

Zimbalist, Andrew, Howard J. Sherman, and Stuart Brown, *Comparing Economic Systems: A Political-EconomicApproach,* 2nd ed. San Diego: Harcourt Brace Jovanovich, 1989.

18

THE CHINESE ECONOMY SINCE 1976

In less than two decades since 1976,[1] China

has completed perhaps three-quarters of its transformation . . . What remains—in particular, institutionalizing factor markets in land, labor and capital—is a matter only of time, not of principle. Second, a decade and a half of double-digit economic growth, which shows no signs of abating, has media pundits and World Bank economists pondering: Will the "Japanese Miracle" of the post-war decades now be followed by an even more epochal "Chinese Miracle"?[2]

OBJECTIVES

1. Contrast the evolution of China's economy since 1976 from that of the previous three decades.
2. Analyze the change in philosophical basis and corresponding economic reforms introduced over the past 15 years.
3. Discuss specific economic reforms, and evaluate their impact on the economy's performance.
4. Distinguish the Chinese approach to transforming and developing its economy from that of Central and Eastern European (CEE) nations since 1989.
5. Identify the factors which have contributed to China having the world's fastest growing economy since the late 1980s.

INTRODUCTION

The Chinese economy has experienced a radical transformation over the past 45 years. This transformation was initiated by leaders (e.g., Mao Tse Tung) who held strong ideological convictions and had a blueprint for the new society they

---

[1]Note that the 1976–1978 period featured political transition after the death of Mao Tse Tung in 1976. This chapter focuses on China's economy since 1976, but often refers to 1978 as a benchmark year since, due to changes within the political structure and debate regarding a shift in philosophical basis, it took about two years to implement some substantive reforms.

[2]Bruce Reynolds, "Introduction" to Special Issue: "China's Transition to the Market," *China Economic Review*, 4, 2 (1993), 83.

wished for China to become. The path they planned for China was influenced by the pre-1949 economy—especially China's exploitation by foreign powers, and by these leaders' strong commitment to the teachings of Karl Marx and Vladimir Lenin.

The post-1976 Chinese economy can be evaluated from a number of perspectives. One is of an underdeveloped nation able to escape from the worst aspects of poverty. Another is of a nation which, while sympathetic to the philosophical basis for a command over a social economy (CSE), has been willing to take a pragmatic approach and experiment with alternatives (to the traditional CSE) institutional arrangements.[3] This has included the establishment of unique semiprivate forms of ownership and special economic zones (see pp. 537–539) with radically different working rules for these institutions than for the rest of the economy. Finally, China can be viewed as a transforming economy which, despite its willingness to experiment with economic reforms, retains a totalitarian political structure with considerable control by authorities over its citizens as well as over many economic activities in coexistence with a growing semiprivate and private sector. That China has been the world's fastest growing and most rapidly transforming economy for more than a decade qualifies it to be considered as the latest of the industrializing "Asian Tigers" and, therefore, as an important economy to analyze—especially regarding the lessons its evolution offers.

A HISTORY SHAPED BY FOREIGN INFLUENCE AND MAOIST IDEOLOGY

The pre-1978 philosophical basis, principal institutions, and state of the economy have been influenced considerably by the presence of foreign powers in China, the philosophy of Mao, and the working rules introduced by Mao and other high-ranking authorities in the industrial and agricultural sector. Prior to 1949 China was a semicolonial, feudal nation. Foreign powers owned and controlled about 40 percent of China's industrial assets,[4] the nation's transportation network, plus many of China's natural resources; dominated financial institutions; and dictated China's terms regarding foreign trade with the Western powers. This last factor was manifested by foreign control over working rules pertaining to tariffs, one example being the decision by foreign authorities not to permit China to establish tariffs to protect her fledging infant industries. The foreign presence created a dual society characterized on the one hand by modern treaty ports (e.g., Shanghai), and on the other hand by a traditional handicraft production sector plus a backward agricultural sector dominated by landlords and wealthy peasants. In addition,

---

[3]While pragmatic, Chinese leadership has held perceptions of industrialized society and industrialization which have been problematic (e.g., The Great Leap Forward).

[4]Carl Riskin, *China's Political Economy: The Quest For Development Since 1949* (Oxford: Oxford University Press, 1987), p. 19.

foreign presence inhibited the development of a unified political structure throughout China.

After the 1949 revolution led by Mao Tse Tung and Chou En Lai, an economic rehabilitation program was introduced. Although the Soviet influence was quite prominent during the early 1950s, after 1956 it gradually weakened. The philosophical basis for the economy's development program was provided by Mao. Two of the major tenets (all of which implied institutional change) were the primacy of class struggle and emphasis upon self-reliance. Self-reliance meant limiting foreign trade and foreign sources of investment funds (especially after the worsened relations between China and the Soviet Union), eliminating direct foreign investment in China, limiting state aid to economic units, and establishing "a cellular economy comprising . . . comprehensive sub-systems [e.g., a people's commune] where each and every production and administrative unit would be a complete, comprehensive, highly vertically and horizontally integrated and self-sufficient economy in its own right."[5] These cellular units were to be "autarchical" and "self-sufficient."[6] Another major tenet was the importance of developing people (rather than emphasizing production of goods and services), encouraging people to learn by doing and bringing everyone into the "socialist development effort," which would not only increase labor productivity but would also create "a society of truly free men."[7]

This last tenet is part of the reason that China's development strategy under Mao cannot be depicted by any macroeconomic model. The authorities were seeking the correct path to crude communism (see Chapter 15), and placed greater emphasis upon institutional reform and human development and less on technical factors. One Maoist view was that the "Will of the Red" (i.e., those with correct political consciousness) would prevail over technical experts. Politics came first, although there was willingness to experiment with non-CSE working rules. Mao did not believe strongly in central planning, but preferred to promote incentives to which groups of people on the local level (e.g., people's communes—see pp. 537–539), supervised by local authorities, would respond. Mao favored public ownership and control of the means of production and discouraged the profit motive. This ideology carried over into the principal institutions, especially the state planning commission, which had a modest staff (e.g., only a few dozen people during the Cultural Revolution which began in the mid-1960s), and into working rules which eliminated unregulated markets, thereby curbing the power of the "capitalist class" associated with foreign bourgeoisie interests.

[5]Cyril Z. Lin, "China's Distorted Economic Reform," *The Proceedings of the First Annual Conference of the Chinese Economic Association (UK)* (St. Antony's College, Oxford, December 18–19, 1989), p. 13.
[6]Ibid.
[7]Norman T. Uphoff and Warren F. Ilchman, eds., *The Political Economy of Development* (London: University of California Press, 1973), p. 149.

The Chinese development strategy in the early 1950s was similar to the strategy introduced in the Soviet Union by Stalin. Prior to 1957 there was emphasis upon collectivizing agriculture and developing heavy industry (especially steel) in urban areas through achieving economies of scale in state-owned enterprises (SOEs). There was a rapid shift toward social ownership of the means of production, so that the percentage of China's output provided by SOEs rose from 26 percent in 1949 to almost 80 percent by the late 1970s for industrial output, and from less than 7 percent to over 85 percent for agricultural output.[8] Between 1953 and 1976 heavy industry grew by a factor of 27, while light industry grew by a factor of nine.

A radical land reform program was implemented after 1949 as the state sought to redress the highly skewed distribution of land that characterized pre-1949 China, when about 10 percent of the population owned and controlled about 75 percent of the land.[9] Mao wanted an egalitarian social structure, and focused on the rural sector, where about 85 percent of the Chinese lived. Rules collectivizing agriculture were introduced so that an agrarian working class replaced the stratified society consisting of landlords, rich peasants, middle peasants (who owned enough land to support themselves but did not hire, and thereby "exploit," workers), and poor peasants. To achieve egalitarianism the Chinese authorities forced changes in the social relations of production through institutional changes such as people's communes. The ill-fated Great Leap Forward in 1958 and, to a degree, the Great Proletarian Cultural Revolution in 1966 were two attempts to find the correct "socialist" development path by decentralizing economic decision making, organization, and coordination. People's communes were established in place of villages, people were organized into production "brigades" and "teams."

Industrialization was part of Mao's rural development program. Production activities on the commune were diversified into areas such as forestry, fishing, light industry, and even heavy industry such as iron and steel during the Great Leap Forward. The commune mobilized and utilized surplus labor, facilitating rural development through development of light industry using local resources. This was deemed a more efficient use of resources than attempting to supply rural inhabitants with the output from large SOEs. The commune also was the level of administration which supplied essential services (e.g., health, education) to the rural population.

In terms of the economy's performance (e.g., growth, unemployment, and reducing income inequality), the Stalinist model served China well in the early 1950s. However, for ideological and efficiency reasons the Chinese did not continue to follow the Stalinist model strictly after 1957. As the Chinese economy became more complex, the inefficiencies inherent in a centrally planned social

[8]Xue Muqiao, ed., *Almanac of China's Economy 1981* (New York: Eurasia Press, 1982), p. 379.

[9]Dong Fureng, *Rural Reform, Nonfarm Development, and Rural Modernization in China* (Washington, DC: The World Bank, 1988), p. 4.

process for coordination became apparent. Both at the national and enterprise level, authorities were unwilling to adhere to the Soviet-style centralized (command from above) decision making both at the national and enterprise level. Mao preferred decentralization, especially in agriculture, as well as committee decisions in the management of industrial enterprises. The Chinese also departed from the Stalinist approach by placing more emphasis on the agricultural sector, stimulated by Mao's slogan "Agriculture as a Foundation, Industry as a Leading Factor."

The problem was that although they denounced the Soviet model, the Chinese only experimented with piecemeal economic reform and did not replace the Stalinist model's main features. This contributed to the development of a dual society. In the agricultural sector, where 80 percent of the population resided, living conditions were quite modest and many commune workers were underemployed. Labor productivity was low (grain output per laborer hardly increased between 1952 and 1977), as were household incomes relative to those earned by urban families employed in the industrial sector. The income differential between urban and rural families was about three to one when state subsidies were included (more benefits such as rent subsidies were received by urban families).

There were some favorable performance indicators. Inflation grew very slowly (about 1 percent annually between 1950 and 1979).[10] China attained economic and political independence. However, after the death of Mao in 1976 authorities realized they had inherited problems. Real wages had not grown for the previous two decades, and there was low growth of consumption and only modest improvements in the availability of food per person. Industrial growth fared better, but this was partly due to the high rate of savings and investment (about 30 percent), which came at the expense of household living standards. In response to this performance the philosophical basis of the new authorities changed, resulting in the willingness to experiment and introduce economic reforms.

A PRAGMATIC PHILOSOPHY
FOR DEVELOPMENT

After the death of Mao and the rise of Hua Guofeng to power, there was a change in China's philosophical basis. New authorities recognized that for the Communist Party to survive and retain control over the nation the best alternative was to promote economic reforms that were market oriented. While deciding to continue adhering to many aspects of the Marxisim-Leninism-Maoism philosophy, they sought to correct the errors of the Great Leap Forward and Great

---

[10]Xue Muqiao, ed., *Almanac of China's Economy 1981*, p. 983.

Proletarian Cultural Revolution movements. The new authorities sought to reduce the dominance of public ownership and commitment to a very egalitarian distribution of income. They recognized that the low agricultural and industrial productivity plaguing China were due to the Maoist emphasis upon egalitarianism. Authorities then reexamined the basic economic principles and corresponding working rules upon which the 1949–1975 development strategy had been based. They decided to dismiss "what there was in the way of egalitarian-communitarian socialism and replace it with a meritocratic socialism that includes capitalist features [e.g., giving individuals greater economic freedoms]."[11] One important view was that rewards should be more closely linked with effort and ability. Another view was to modify the "bone-deep phobia about foreign intervention," a strong legacy of Chinese history, and permit some foreign investment.[12]

Heavy emphasis upon ideology and idealism was replaced by pragmatism. With regard to the true path for China to follow, the new authorities believed that whatever works was the basis of truth. This was exemplified by Deng Xiaoping's statement that the color of a cat is not important as long as it catches mice. The authorities rejected the doctrinal politics of the Maoist era, especially the policies designed to stimulate continual class struggle, in favor of practical means to promote greater economic efficiency through modernization of the economy. The authorities' views were flexible, adapting to changing circumstances rather than adhering to a strict ideology or loyalty to past commitments. Their intention was not to transform their economy so that it would resemble that of Japan or South Korea, but to permit the establishment of some institutions and working rules similar to those of its Asian neighbors that would enhance the economy's performance while preserving their own security within the political structure.

Among the new beliefs (all of which broke from the Maoist principles) were that "to get rich is glorious"; that doing business was no longer a disgrace, and entrepreneurs are worthy, useful members of the community; that agriculture should be decollectivized; that markets and material incentives were necessary to stimulate output and efficiency; that foreign private direct investment should be encouraged; that value indicators such as prices, taxes, and interest rates should regulate output; that decentralization of decision making at the enterprise level was necessary; that the growth of light industry, including an expansion of small private firms, should be encouraged as a means to increase consumption levels; and that existing enterprises—particularly large SOEs, "constitute China's chief base of industrial modernization and should be the starting point of the new 'long

[11]Barrington Moore, Jr., *Authority and Inequality Under Capitalism and Socialism* (Oxford: Clarendon Press, 1987), p. 95.
[12]Mori Akira, "Capitalist Winds in Socialist China," *Japan Quarterly* (January-March 1993), p. 25. It is noteworthy that the Chinese remain hesitant concerning the extent of foreign investment to permit due to their "bitter historical experience."

march.'"[13] Therefore, the attitude toward the large SOEs was that implementing rapid privatization, introducing hard budget constraints, and permitting bankruptcies were not to be considered.

The philosophical basis did not contain a clear blueprint for economic development. The reforms were introduced on a trial-and-error basis, and much government control over economic activities was retained. The Chinese slogan "crossing the river by touching the stones at the bottom" reflected the authorities' commitment to adopt a pragmatic, flexible, less ideological philosophy and to become more sensitive to market-oriented reforms. Gradually, pragmatism came to mean "the willingness to adopt whatever works with little ideological constraint," so that authorities openly argued that "nothing prevents us from adopting in our socialist system anything that works well under a capitalist system."[14]

The first major set of reforms was introduced in 1978, and these were more radical than any reforms introduced prior to 1989 in any Central or Eastern European (CEE) nation. Chinese authorities recognized that the economic production level was too far behind the level necessary for "socialist reforms" to be achieved (e.g., all enterprises owned and controlled by the state, with narrow differentials in material incentives for workers). As a result they permitted what Leftist (pro-Mao) Chinese referred to as "capitalist road" measures. At the Third Plenum of the Eleventh Central Committee of the Chinese Communist Party in 1978, leftist views (e.g., continual class struggle) were replaced by a pragmatic philosophy emphasizing modernization and agricultural development to overcome backwardness and economic imbalances. The authorities were seeking to return to the 1953–1958 era during which the Chinese economy had performed favorably in terms of the rapid growth of industrial and agricultural output. They were determined to reverse the mistakes of seeking to introduce widespread institutional change too rapidly as was attempted in 1958 with the people's communes. They would endorse market-oriented reforms to address problematic aspects of the economy, but would seek to retain the dominance of publicly owned economic institutions and control over income distribution so as to minimize poverty.

During 1984 and 1985 there was a debate regarding a blueprint for future development. There were two viewpoints. The conservative reformers still had faith in the Stalinist-type planning scheme, and believed China should focus on central control over key industries while permitting some market-determined resource allocation. In other words, central planning should be primary while markets would be a secondary factor. The other viewpoint favored regulation of markets (similar to the Hungarian social process from 1968 to 1989—see Chapter

[13]Lin Ling, "A Good Start in Economic Structural Reform," *Chinese Economic Studies*, 26, 4 (Summer 1993), 7.
[14]Gregory C. Chow, "How and Why China Succeeded in Her Economic Reform," *China Economic Review*, 4, 2 (1993), 127.

17), and adopting whatever policies were conducive to favorable economic performance. Those holding the latter viewpoint also argued that the state only should retain central control over allocation of investment funds, and value indicators such as prices and interest rates (which were set by authorities) would be the means to regulate microeconomic activities. Ultimately the authorities reached a compromise, creating a hybrid model which combined central control by the state and some unregulated or partially regulated markets. There was agreement that the Soviet-type of central planning was not effective for China, and authorities were willing to experiment with more radical market-oriented reforms not unlike the indicative planning schemes introduced in some Asian countries including Japan. Subsequently, a pragmatic approach to economic development was adopted, including an export promotion program and emphasis upon modernizing existing enterprises while maximizing household incomes.

In 1989 and 1990, following student demonstrations and the violent response by the state, authorities became hostile to market reforms, believing that such reforms would threaten their power, as had occurred in CEE. Any major steps toward market-oriented reform were ruled out temporarily, and some authorities hinted that China should consider returning to heavy reliance upon central planning (similar to the Stalinist model including recollectivizing farms). Old slogans such as "Better Red Than Expert" were reintroduced by authorities, but they offered no coherent plan to improve the economy's performance. There was some discussion about a "managed private economy," but prices would not be permitted to fluctuate in response to market forces, and individuals would not be allowed to hold more property rights.

Having analyzed the CEE political revolutions and the subsequent performance of those economies, Chinese authorities were determined to continue following the path toward building socialism with Chinese characteristics while maintaining their complete control within the political structure. Marxist dogma was still given homage, but practical cooperative and market-oriented reforms continued to be introduced, particularly the encouragement of foreign investment. "Tribal consciousness" and the need for foreign funds, technology, and production and marketing expertise prevailed over ideology as China encouraged investments from their ethnic kin in Hong Kong and Taiwan.[15] Thus, while the "banner of socialism" was still being waved by authorities a "flexible approach . . . [was adopted for] dealing with economic realities."[16] This philosophy was exemplified by the adoption of the proposal to establish a "socialist market economy" at the 14th Community Party Congress in 1992.

Under such an economy public ownership would be integrated with cooperative and market ownership. The market mechanism would play a

[15]Akira, "Capitalist Winds in Socialist China," p. 26.
[16]Ibid., p. 19.

fundamental role in production and distribution activities, while the state would be responsible for macroeconomic stabilization and maintenance of equitable standards of living through a state-provided "social protection system." It was recognized that China, as have many OECD nations, could benefit from state guidance of the economy whereby the state would exercise indirect interference in economic activities by influencing relevant economic variables. Price controls would be gradually eliminated, and market adjustments should become the primary social process for economic coordination. Markets would be regulated rather than unfettered, but their ability to efficiently allocate resources and provide work incentives would be recognized.

Overall, the "socialist market economy" principles have become the basis for introduction of working rules pertaining first to localized economic reforms, which would be broadened in scope if the results of the reforms are deemed favorable. The human rights issue has not been dealt with by China's definition of such rights. To them they mean "the right to eat," so that maintenance of the authoritarian political structure is justified for purposes of promoting development, which is a similar condition that characterizes nearly all of the development experiences of Southeast Asian economies. To the typical Chinese the issues of ideology, totalitarian rule, and economic development may have been expressed by the reply of a Chinese farmer to the question of which economy he preferred, "capitalism" or "socialism." The lucid reply was "I like the way things are now. If it is called socialism, then I prefer socialism. If it is called capitalism, I prefer capitalism."[17]

EFFORTS TO ESTABLISH AN EGALITARIAN SOCIAL STRUCTURE WHILE MAINTAINING CENTRALIZED POLITICAL POWER

Social Structure

A prominent goal established after the 1949 revolution was to create an egalitarian social structure. Such a goal was consistent with the Marxian philosophical basis which emphasized that the highest stage of economic development would feature a classless society. Pursuit of egalitarianism was somewhat easier for the Chinese than their Soviet comrades, for the Chinese think of themselves as a homogeneous population. This is nearly the case, for about 95 percent of the Chinese are part of the Han ethnic group, while about 50 minorities comprise the remaining 5 percent of the population.

[17]Ibid., p. 22.

In reality there are social class differentials. Until the last few years the single most important factor distinguishing social classes was political power, and as a result the social structure closely mirrors the political structure. Listed according to declining status, there are the leading political authorities at the national ministerial level and above, plus governors of provinces; department directors; heads of departments under ministries or under provincial governments; several million officials at the county level plus students (often studying abroad) who are being groomed for high government positions; government officials below the county level; heads of certain institutions (health, education); and all other people, including intellectuals.

The 1978 (and subsequent) reforms have contributed to widening income differentials throughout society. Some Chinese entrepreneurs have been able to achieve higher status through private economic activity. One group that has recently done so is the "overseas Chinese" who left China before or since 1949 to work elsewhere in Asia, then returned after private investment was condoned. Some of these returning individuals, along with entrepreneurs who never left China, have been successful in business activity—particularly in the special economic zones located along the southern coast.

Political Structure

The Chinese political structure resembles that of the pre-1989 Soviet Union in terms of organization, functions particular authorities perform, and the "political and economic culture."[18] The values, priorities, and behavior of Chinese authorities at the national, local and enterprise levels—especially the Communist Party's exercise of power over principal institutions and working rules—remain similar to that of the pre-1978 period. This is not surprising, for China's authorities traditionally have been obsessed with preserving political stability, and the Chinese people's propensity toward harmonization, conformity, and respect for the elderly lends itself to the preservation of political stability. Deng Xiaoping has emphasized the importance of political stability and party unity, arguing that it was necessary for modernization of the economy. Having learned lessons from their own Great Proletarian Cultural Revolution and the 1989 political revolutions in CEE, and the replacement of some authorities in subsequent elections, Deng Xiaoping and other aging authorities remain determined to vanquish any challenges to their monopoly on political power, arguing it is necessary for successful reforms.[19] To some extent the Chinese population agrees. Being eager for political stability, they are willing to tolerate authoritarian rule as long as economic reforms continue and their living standards (currently at their highest level ever) continue to increase.

---

[18]Lin, "China's Distorted Economic Reform," p. 28.

[19]In a conversation with an American expert on the Russian economy, he stated that if he were Russia's economic advisor in 1990 and knew then what he knows today about Russian and Chinese transformation efforts, that he would have advised the Russians to retain a political monopoly in the interests of achieving a successful transformation.

Stability is achieved by the authorities' maintaining strict control over many economic activities (see "Social Process for Economic Coordination," pp. 549–559). In addition, authorities seek to "control and remold the day-to-day behavior and even the thoughts of the people."[20] Means of control include surveillance, campaigns with popular slogans (e.g., the Great Leap Forward), and what might euphemistically be called moral suasion (what Chinese dissidents and other observers describe as "enforced indoctrination").[21] The effectiveness of these measures to ensure political stability and control the economy declined during the 1980s as the public became disenchanted with the arbitrary exercise of power by bureaucrats, with authorities becoming wealthy through corruption, and with the growing realization of how poor China was compared to the rest of the world, especially Taiwan and Japan. Ultimately, the public's "enthusiasm . . . became increasingly synthetic"[22] in the face of campaigns and other means to retain political control. A student uprising in June 1989, however, was met with the use of force; thousands of young Chinese were killed and the leadership reasserted themselves—effectively prohibiting the introduction of rules that threatened to inhibit their power.

Although the 47 million member Communist Party is the dominant force in China's political structure, the chain of authority is not well defined in that there is an official and unofficial arrangement. The Communist Party, state government, and National People's Congress are three separate but interrelated institutions. Officially the highest-ranking official is the General Secretary of the Communist Party, who automatically is head of the party's political bureau and commander of all military forces. Below the Secretary is the Chairman of the Central Military Commission (the Communist Party's highest military organ); Deputy Chairman of the State Council (which consists of 12 vice premiers and about 30 ministers); the Premier (nominated by the State Council and then approved by the National People's Congress); Central Committee (which generally legitimizes State Council decisions); the State Council (authorities serving as liaisons between top party authorities and leaders of ministries); leaders of government ministries (one of which is the State Planning Commission); and the National People's Congress (the supreme legislative body, albeit in name only, for it ratifies higher authorities' decisions and initiates little legislation). It meets only two weeks each year, and its sessions serve to "provide a forum for ratifying and publicizing leadership decisions,"[23] thereby legitimizing higher authorities' decisions.

Recent concerns throughout the party are how to maintain its control over an economy characterized by the collapse of their control following the demise of

[20]Moore, *Authority and Inequality Under Capitalism and Socialism*, p. 81.

[21]Ibid.

[22]Ibid., p. 83.

[23]David Bachman, "China Hails the 'Socialist Market Economy,'" *The China Business Review* (July-August 1993), 34.

collective farming (and the subsequent massive rural urban migration) and expansion of market-oriented institutions and working rules. The top Chinese authority remains the ailing Deng Xiaoping, who many predict will die before the end of 1995. Although he has officially resigned from all official positions of authority and is said to be in poor health, he remains China's most powerful leader whose spiritual authority and authoritarian philosophy are respected. He is advised by retired leaders, many of whom are aged and lack a fresh vision and flexibility in the face of rising inflation and demands for greater subsidies to keep state-owned enterprises afloat. Observers predict that a core of technocrats will assume full control after Deng passes away, but that a political struggle will ensue over the issue of how to continue economic reforms without corresponding political reforms until a younger generation of authorities achieves legitimacy from the public.

EVOLUTION OF PRIVATE AND SEMIPRIVATE INSTITUTIONS THAT COEXIST WITH STATE INSTITUTIONS

Prior to the 1990s the institutions responsible for establishing and coordinating most of China's economic activity were the Communist Party; state organs such as the State Council, State Planning Commission, Price Bureau, ministries (e.g., agriculture, finance), People's Bank, and planning commissions on the provincial level; state-owned industrial enterprises, collectively owned urban and rural enterprises, and households involved with producing and distributing agricultural and nonagricultural products. The role of semiprivate and private, nonagricultural enterprises has been increasing quite rapidly in manufacturing, service, and merchant activities in both urban areas and rural areas.

The Communist Party's place in the economy remains similar to that of the monarch and Church during the medieval period. The party, mainly through the State Council (the supreme executive organ) provides the philosophical basis, establishes the working rules pertaining to the economy, and controls the People's Army, which enforces the rules if necessary. Many rules are implemented by the State Planning Commission, which focuses on long-term planning and the impact of investment projects, changes in macroeconomic variables (e.g., prices, wages) and new working rules on the economy. Despite decreased emphasis on national planning, the commission continues to direct "vestiges of the planned economy" and retains responsibility for approving major projects.[24]

Rising in importance due to transformation efforts have been the State Commission for Restructuring the Economy, and the State Economic and Trade

[24]Ibid., p. 42.

Commission. The former commission, established in 1982, formulates long-range plans in a manner not unlike those established by French indicative planners. It also provides a think tank for analysis of the dynamic interaction between the domestic and international economy (particularly the influence of foreign investment in China) and evaluates the impact of new political, social, and economic working rules and institutions. The Economic and Trade Commission was formed in 1992, and its tasks will include facilitating the reform of SOEs. Although their relative importance has been declining since 1977, SOEs still produce almost half of China's industrial output and receive about 15 percent of the state budget in the form of subsidies. Many of them operate according to centrally planned directives, although reforms providing more management autonomy and greater ability to respond to economic indicators (e.g., two-tiered pricing) have reduced the importance of national-level planners.

Collectively owned and managed enterprises, known as township and village enterprises (TVEs), are becoming more prominent throughout both rural and urban areas. They began to evolve in 1970, and by 1978 there were over 1.5 million TVEs and they employed about 20 percent of all industrial employees. Between 1978 and 1990 the number of TVEs grew to over 18 million, with more than 90 million workers. They currently account for more than half of China's industrial production.[25] In these enterprises, many of which are hybrid SOEs in the sense that local government authorities initially fund and closely control their major activities, the means of production are collectively owned (i.e., are the common property) and controlled by the workers in that unit, and workers determine how income is to be distributed among themselves. The collective is autonomous regarding production and distribution decisions. They serve to absorb some surplus labor while increasing output of goods and services that had been in short supply when the SOEs were responsible for most production. With the exception of the collective ownership, TVEs are similar to a private firm, and are "remarkably flexible, in that they are free to negotiate labor hiring terms, to fire labor, to go bankrupt, and to be set up and financed."[26]

The most prevalent institution throughout China in terms of number of people employed is in the agricultural sector. Large collectives called communes were the primary economic and governmental unit in rural China between 1958 and 1977. The typical commune had about 40,000 members. It was responsible for producing grain and other agricultural products; collecting taxes; formulating production plans; making decisions involving water resource management, construction of infrastructure; transportation; and development of rural industries. Commune authorities managed local industries which produced consumer and producer goods for local consumption. The commune members were divided into production

[25]Zhue Mei, "Non-agricultural Industrial Development in Chinese Rural Areas," *Development Policy Review*, 11, 3 (September 1993), p. 385.

[26]David M. Newberry, "Transformation in Mature Versus Emerging Economies: Why Has Hungary Been Less Successful Than China?" *China Economic Review*, 4, 2 (1993), 97.

brigades (about 15 per commune) and production teams (each with about 150 members). Following the introduction of the Household Responsibility System, a new working rule established in 1983, control over income rights to the land shifted from the commune to the production team and, gradually, to the individual household level. Communes have all but disappeared. The same functions performed by the commune are now performed by the village, while individual families make the key production and distribution decisions on their own plots of land.

The special economic zones, which began to be established in 1979 in coastal cities for the purposes of attracting direct foreign investment, are rapidly becoming a principal institution. Featuring plentiful and cheap labor, they are attractive to those Southeast Asian investors who share a common language and culture with the Chinese people. Stimulated by local authorities, some of whom are seeking to establish their special economic zone as a "socialist Hong Kong," these institutions are becoming prosperous industrial, financial, information, and even tourist centers. Within the special economic zones another institution that is evolving is the "locally based group enterprise." In the zones such enterprises do not face competition from "peer institutions" such as state-owned enterprises and, thus, entrepreneurs are able to develop them without having to overcome the obstacle of an "entrenched party-government hierarchy."[27]

Since China has adopted a policy of reducing its rural population from well over 80 percent to only 50 percent within the next half-century, the inability of existing cities to absorb such a population increase (estimated at 400 million people) requires that "new cities" develop. Within the special economic zones this process has begun, with foreign investors courted (with incentives such as little or no tax requirements or currency controls) to stimulate economic development so as to absorb workers currently in rural areas. An example is the new industrial city of Dongquan near Guangzhou, capital city of Guangdong Province (close to Hong Kong) whose population has swelled to over 2 million since 1984 with all development having been financed with foreign investment.[28]

BEHAVIOR OF THE NEW "SOCIALIST MARKET ECONOMY"

China's organization of decision making, working rules governing ownership and control of resources, and social processes for coordinating production and distribution decisions followed a similar pattern from about 1950 until the early

---

[27]T. Y. Shen, "An Institution for Entrepreneurship in Chinese Economic Reform," *The Journal of Socio-Economics*, 23, 3 (Fall 1994), 303–320. Examples of some prosperous special economic zones are presented in the "Social Processes" section, pp. 549–559.

[28]"Birth of the Instant City," *The Economist*, September 10, 1994, p. 34. Due to the breakdown of the commune system and rising wages in manufacturing, China is experiencing mass migration on an unprecedented level. It is estimated that within the next decade the population of Shanghai will exceed 20 million while that of Beijing will be over 15 million.

1990s. Centralization of control over the economy was established, followed by a decentralization program (e.g., the Great Leap Forward in 1957, the Great Proletarian Cultural Revolution in 1966, the economic reforms of 1978, and the second wave of economic reforms in 1984–1985). In each case the decentralization program either failed to achieve its lofty objectives, or was followed by public unrest which threatened political stability. The authorities then responded by following the "treadmill of reforms pattern," by introducing working rules to recentralize decision making, control, and coordination over economic activities. Unfortunately, centralized planning and control created the same problems faced throughout CEE prior to 1989, namely the absence of rational economic value indicators, inability to obtain enough information to make efficient resource allocation decisions, inflexibility and arbitrary exercise of power by bureaucrats, and lack of incentives to stimulate labor to be more productive.

Since the commitment to establish a "socialist market economy" in 1992, trends characterized by decentralized decision making, semiprivate (collective) and private ownership and control over productive resources, and much greater reliance upon market prices and freer trade to coordinate production and distribution activities have prevailed. Authorities appear more willing to refrain from reestablishing the "treadmill of reforms" pattern with the exception of finance where the People's Bank struggles to retain its control over financial resources against the growing financial power of local governments and new financial institutions.[29] The shift of priorities illustrates a unique feature of China's reforms, namely "the relaxation of control in the economic sphere" within a totalitarian political structure under which the state, until the early 1990s, had attempted to retain control over decision making, ownership, and activities of enterprises, and coordination of production and distribution activities.[30] The reduction of the state's role throughout the economy has coincided with China becoming the world's fastest growing economy for the past decade, experiencing significant transformation while standards of living continue to rise.

Spreading Decentralization of Resource Allocation Decision Making

Although working rules which decentralized decision making and reduced the extent of mandatory compliance with central planners' directives were introduced in the late 1970s, the extent of central and provincial authorities' influence over decisions remained considerable. The June 1989 political unrest was followed by the reassertion of Communist Party control over major segments of the economy.

---

[29]For a detailed analysis of centralization and decentralization of financial decision making, see Jin Lizuo, "Effects of Financial Decentralization on Industrial Growth in China (1952–88)," unpublished paper prepared at Oxford University, 1992; and "Monetary Policy and the Design of Financial Institutions in China (1978–90)," unpublished Ph.D. thesis, Oxford University.

[30]Yaozing Hu, "Market-Oriented Reforms in China," *Development Policy Review*, 11, 2 (June 1993), p. 197.

Some hard-line authorities argued that the pragmatic "do whatever works" philosophy espoused by Deng Xiaoping in the mid-1980s should be abandoned in favor of reestablishing the orthodox Marxist-Stalinist-Maoist philosophy. They called for a return to central planning and control over agricultural, trade, and industrial enterprise decisions. One authority argued that "[r]ecentralization is necessary . . . [because] if the central government has too little control, it will lose its ability to lead."[31] Although the events of 1992 dismissed reimposition of such a policy, this attitude illustrates that while there has been economic reform (the nature of which deviates significantly from the pre-1978 patterns of behavior and from those of CEE nations), China has yet to introduce meaningful political reform.

Prior to 1992, when high authorities received pressure from provincial and local authorities who feared the loss of power following market-oriented economic reforms, they either reversed the direction of decision-making organization or permitted new working rules on an ad hoc basis increasing the degree of indirect bureaucratic control over enterprises in all sectors. Continued expansion of collective and private institutions, the favorable performance of the economy, and top authorities recognizing the economic problems ensuing from emphasis on central planning led to the 1992 decision to reduce the influence of bureaucrats in favor of decentralized decision making.

In agriculture there has been a steady shift toward decentralization on the production unit level. Collective decision making was introduced in the late 1950s, but beginning in the mid-1970s the level of decision making shifted away from the people's commune to the production brigade and team level, and finally to the household level. By the mid-1990s all peasant households had adopted the responsibility system. Overall, the agricultural reforms introduced between 1979 and 1983 resulted in "a return to the pre-1956 or pre-cooperativisation regime of private household farming."[32] The manner in which centralized decision making has asserted itself has been through a dual-pricing scheme in which farmers contract to sell a certain quantity of their output to the state and then have been free to sell surplus above that quantity on an open market (pp. 551–553). Some corrupt state officials have been able to purchase grain and other produce from farmers at low prices (set by the state), and resell these goods on the open market for high prices, earning considerable profits. These same authorities resist plans to eliminate the dual-pricing scheme (in favor of a market price for all agricultural products), since it would mean farmers could decide where to sell their output and could choose not to sell to the state through public officials. However, the dual-pricing scheme is being phased out so that prices paid by the state for agricultural products that farmers are required to sell have been gradually rising to the level farmers can receive in the open market.

---

[31]Julia Leung, "Beijing Will Reassert Centralized Control," *The Wall Street Journal*, November 28, 1989, p. A10.
[32]Lin, "China's Distorted Economic Reform," p. 25.

There has been a shift from mandatory planning to a type of indicative planning, which places greater reliance on economic indicators such as prices and interest rates to guide enterprise decision making. Working rules granting SOEs more autonomy also have been introduced, giving them freedom to invest, purchase inputs, and produce and market their output as they choose after meeting planning quotas. The expanded power for SOE managers to make decisions has led to conflicts between them and ministry authorities. However, given the performance of the economy following reforms that have granted greater autonomy to farmers and industry managers since the late 1970s, further reforms providing more managerial freedoms have been introduced.

As with other Chinese reforms, an incremental, bottom-up approach was selected instead of a top-down reform scheme. Thus, reforms first were introduced on a small-scale, experimental basis. One such experiment in expanded enterprise decision-making authority occurred in Sichuan. Enterprise managers were permitted to purchase raw materials on the open market, produce what they wished for sale on the market after they had met their state-assigned production quotas, and retain some profits with which they could make investment decisions. The intent was to stimulate "distinct material interest" among managers through granting them greater autonomy and encouraging them to pursue profits by attempting to meet demand as it existed on Chinese markets.[33] Authorities (especially those on the provincial and municipal level) still retain the power to approve the decisions of most industrial enterprises, especially when the acquisition of scarce inputs or attempts to market output in local markets which are subject to state-determined protective measures are involved. As in other sectors the administrative power is being reduced in favor of collective and individual decision making—particularly in township and village enterprises and throughout special economic zones where foreign investors are the key decision makers.

Private, Collective, Hybrid, Experimental, and State Forms of Ownership and Control of Resources

Since 1978 the right to possess, use, dispose of, and make use of the goods or services produced has been gradually shifting away from state ownership and control toward more control through other types of institutions, some uniquely Chinese. The purpose of the shift towards more collective and private control over resources, according to the central authorities, was to alleviate rising unemployment, reduce the state budget deficit, stimulate improved factor productivity, and promote output of a better quality and greater variety of consumer goods and services. China's enterprises have experienced dramatic changes in their ownership structure, as the rapid growth of collective and private

---

[33]Joseph Fewsmith, "Editor's Introduction to Lin Ling on Sichuan's Economic Reform," *Chinese Economic Studies*, 26, 4 (Summer 1993), 4.

enterprises has resulted in about three quarters of the value of China's retail goods being produced by these enterprises. The Chinese continue to experiment with different forms of ownership, albeit without clearly defining property rights. Four examples are the auctioning of SOEs to Hong Kong investors by local authorities seeking a source of public revenue; converting SOEs to joint ventures with the intent of attracting foreign managerial expertise and technology in return for tax breaks; converting SOEs to limited-liability companies; and creating joint-stock companies by attempting to sell shares of stock on Chinese or foreign stock markets to Chinese workers, Chinese citizens, or foreigners.[34]

While the extent of state ownership is being gradually reduced, state control has declined considerably as Chinese authorities implement their "market supplanting" policies.[35] By the mid-1990s the number of products whose production and distribution remained under strict central control was about 20 versus hundreds a few years earlier. If reformed SOEs are considered to be operating in the interest of making a profit, then by the mid-1990s almost three quarters of China's output is being produced by profit-oriented firms. In terms of industrial output, the nonstate sector is becoming more important. By 1993 just over half of the industrial output was produced by SOEs (many of which had been or are being converted to joint-stock or limited companies), more than one third by collectively-owned enterprises, and over 10 percent by either privately owned firms or joint ventures with foreign investors. All indications are that output by SOEs would continue declining relative to these other enterprises.[36] On the other hand, if government expenditures as a percentage of gross domestic product are used to indicate the extent of central and local authority control and if both budgetary and off-budgetary expenditures are included, evidence indicates that the decline in government control over total spending in China has been modest.

The shift has not been simply a transfer of control from the public to the private sector, for the change in income and property rights affects collective and private enterprises as well as the public sector. The production and distribution process still involves relations between authorities at different levels of government and between all types of public, collective, and private enterprise because a collective or private institution "is still merely an appendage of an administrative and political organ."[37] The state's power to control resources (e.g., allocate electricity, chemical fertilizers, credit, and business licenses) has been significant, and alleged abuses of this control by provincial and lower-level municipal authorities have been the focus of charges of corruption leveled against these officials.

[34]Gary H. Jefferson, "Summary of Panel Discussion on Enterprise Reform: International Symposium on Economic Transition in China, Hainan Province," *China Economic Review*, 4, 2 (1993), 145.

[35]Yan Wang and Vinod Thomas, "Market Supplanting versus Market Fostering Interventions: China, East Asia and Other Developing Countries," *China Economic Review*, 4, 2 (1993), 252.

[36]Gao Shangquan, "Taking a Market-Oriented Direction and Pushing Forward in a Gradual Way—the Basic Experience of China's Economic Reform," *China Economic Review*, 4, 2 (1993), 130.

[37]Lin, "China's Distorted Economic Reform," p. 26.

In cities and municipalities outside the special economic zones, some claim that business licenses are strictly limited to those with connections to Communist Party authorities, and that both the individual receiving the license and the authorities granting the license may profit from a virtual monopoly (e.g., the sole right to import a certain product for sale in a given city or province) if competition is restricted. Many Chinese have been skeptical of economic reforms involving decentralization of control, fearing a wave of public corruption not uncommon throughout Chinese history. According to one expert

> those who enjoy political prerogatives, such as governmental organs and senior party officials and their relatives, have exploited market transactions to their own full advantage. In a partly reformed system where two systems (plan and market) coexist side-by-side and two sets of prices reign, influence means access to scarce materials distributed through the state allocation system at low controlled prices which could then be sold on free markets at grossly inflated prices. It is no coincidence that corruption has grown proportionately to marketization in China.[38]

Some particular features of ownership and control pertaining to national versus local control, SOEs, urban and rural collectives (TVEs), joint ventures and individually owned (private) enterprise, experimental institutions or regions (e.g., a stock market, special economic zones), and authority control over population and public administration are discussed next. In most urban areas there are state factories and stores; collective factories (particularly TVEs) and retail firms (both large and small), and collective repair services; small and medium-sized private firms, and self-employed craftspeople, service workers, and vendors. The "new cities" in special economic zones feature joint ventures and foreign-owned enterprises alongside local Chinese private firms. In rural areas there are collective farms, individually controlled farms, and nonfarm enterprises controlled collectively (TVEs) and individually.

NATIONAL VERSUS LOCAL CONTROL.   Local authorities, especially in coastal areas designated as special economic zones, have been seeking to enhance their control over their source of revenue while attracting foreign investment. They have established working rules pertaining to taxation conducive to attracting private investment, particularly from abroad. There also has been a shift in control over land. First, Chinese entrepreneurs, seeking to lure foreigners interested in building luxury villas or golf courses and in other ventures that would cater to the wealthier Chinese, speculated heavily in real estate. Central authorities responded, seeking to end speculation and promote long-term investment that would require foreigners to pay what central authorities believed should be their fair share of taxes. In 1993 central authorities attempted to close

---

[38]Ibid., p. 26.

1,000 of China's 1,200 economic development zones, many of which had been established by local authorities. Central authorities have passed working rules limiting the ability of foreign firms to recruit their own staff, and imposing high tax rates on profits the firm seeks to remit. A struggle for control ensued, and while the central government did not approve any new investment projects in the first four months of 1994, its control obviously has weakened. This is indicated by local authorities having approved over 90,000 new investment projects during the same period, resulting in over $200 billion of new investment which (central authorities fear) will fuel inflation.[39]

Another example of a struggle for control concerned attempts by local authorities whose jurisdiction was outside of the rapidly developing coastal cities to engage in rent-seeking behavior and protect local markets and industry. In the 1980s such authorities sought to block exports of scarce commodities produced within their own region since other regional enterprises needed those inputs. The local authorities lobbied for, and received, import protection—arguing that coastal areas were being given priority regarding the allocation of investment funds, more autonomy over their finances, and were becoming dominant over other regions. The central authorities responded in 1990 by ordering the "dismantling" of regional trade blockades.[40]

STATE-OWNED ENTERPRISES.   Beginning in 1979 a gradual process giving more autonomy to SOEs corresponding with reduced central control over production of many goods has been operative. SOEs have not been required to transfer their entire surplus to the central authorities. Instead, they have been permitted to retain some of their profit to finance investment and pay bonuses. New experimental methods were introduced in the 1980s which allowed SOEs "to organize extra-plan production after completing the state plan, to sell their products (including the means of production) that had not been purchased without going through the material bureau or the commercial departments, [and] to use their own funds to increase expanded reproduction, . . . [among other freedoms.]"[41]

After 1984 the contract management responsibility system was introduced in nearly all state-owned enterprises. One provision of this scheme was to permit firms to retain profits (a higher percentage of profits than the earlier reforms permitted), enabling these enterprises to use any surplus earned to invest, purchase goods for collective consumption (by all workers), or award bonuses. The enterprises could also secure a bank loan for investment purposes, and had more autonomy regarding what they could produce. Until the early 1990s nonprofitable state-owned enterprises had not been held accountable for their

[39]"China's Pig of a Problem," *The Economist*, September 17, 1994, p. 35.
[40]Andrew H. Wedeman, "Editor's Introduction," *Chinese Economic Studies*, 26, 5 (Fall 1993), 3.
[41]Lin Ling, "A Good Start in Economic Structural Reform," pp. 9, 10.

inability to cover all costs incurred, as the state has been committed to subsidizing such enterprises. Despite a working rule permitting bankruptcies that was introduced in late 1988 for political reasons (i.e., fear of unrest due to rising unemployment in a nation where people expect lifetime employment security), only three of the many losing SOEs were permitted to go bankrupt in 1989 among many losing enterprises.

By the mid-1990s SOEs (structured either as traditional SOEs, joint-stock, or limited-liability companies) account for about half of China's industrial output, and employ over half of all urban workers. Those SOEs remaining under tight central control produce about 20 products considered of strategic importance (e.g., energy, transport). They are controlled by authorities who issue mandatory output targets and make other major production and distribution decisions. The remaining SOEs are in a gradual process of becoming either joint-stock or limited-liability companies with greater management control, responding to resource and product prices that increasingly reflect market forces.[42] There is no intention to privatize rapidly all SOEs. Having learned from the CEE experience where higher unemployment ensued from dramatic reduction in SOE subsidies, Chinese authorities realize a long, gradual process is required to reform its SOEs into firms able to survive without state support. Part of the nation's privatization strategy is to encourage growth of TVEs and private firms, which will gradually become dominant over SOEs, recognizing the intractable problem of converting SOEs into efficient enterprises capable of generating sufficient revenue to perpetuate their existence.

While there is a commitment to turn most SOEs into joint-stock or limited-liability companies, it is understood that ownership by private individuals of a majority of shares is unlikely given the average family income, availability of attractive investments in the growing private and semiprivate sectors, and the desire of most Chinese families to purchase consumer goods previously unavailable to them. Consequently, most shares in reformed SOEs would be held by public institutions, with a new form of public ownership required. Unlike CEE nations, China's SOEs, while in principle owned by the entire population, have been treated as "the exclusive property either of a particular central government ministry, or of a particular local government."[43] Chinese authorities are seeking to rearrange "effective ownership" so that a number of public institutions "own" each enterprise, and that it would be in the interest of these institutions that their enterprise earn a profit. Such reform is consistent with the Chinese desire to transfer ownership and control over

---

[42]In 1993 the central authorities announced plans to transform about one third of SOEs into limited-liability companies responsible for their own profits and losses, and the possibility of bankruptcy if they could not cover their costs.

[43]Adrian Wood, "Joint Stock Companies with Rearranged Public Ownership: What Can We learn from Recent Chinese and East European Experience with State Enterprises?" *China Economic Review*, 4, 2 (1993), 182

management to agents who "are primarily interested in profitability, and . . . can control the behavior of managers."[44]

      COLLECTIVES.   Urban collectives including TVEs account for about one third of the value of industrial output, while collectively owned rural industries account for another 5 percent. Urban collectives employ over 20 percent of all urban workers. The impact of reforms on collectives and private institutions in terms of employment has been considerable. The number of workers employed in urban collectives almost doubled between 1975 and 1984 (from 17.7 million to over 32 million), while the number of private-sector workers in urban areas grew from less than 250,000 in 1975 to almost 3.5 million by 1984.[45] This growth corresponded with the value of retail sales accounted for by state enterprises falling from 80 percent in 1981 to about 45 percent in 1984. Meanwhile, the increase in collective units, private units, and peasant sales to the nonfarm population increased from about 14 percent to 39 percent, 2 percent to 10 percent, and 4 percent to 5 percent, respectively, over the 1981–1984 period.[46] By 1989 the weakening of restrictions on rural industry had made collectives so important that the value of rural nonagricultural output increased from less than one third to almost two thirds of total rural output.[47]

      INDIVIDUALLY OWNED ENTERPRISES.   On individual land holdings farmers have income but not property rights to the land they work, for the state remains owner of all land. Farmers can sign leases for 15 to 30 years, which they can sell to other farmers. In essence, privatization of agriculture began in 1979 with the personal responsibility which has enabled people to keep profits they earned. In urban areas about 1 percent of the work force are self-employed. They primarily engage in craft, repair, domestic service, and merchant activities.

      EXPERIMENTAL INSTITUTIONS: STOCK MARKET AND SPECIAL ECONOMIC ZONES.   In 1986 an experiment was made as the state opened a small "stock market," and for the first time since the 1949 revolution the public could purchase bonds secured by earnings of a Chinese enterprise. The stock market is state controlled, and its function is to serve as a secondary market for bonds. Collective enterprises could sell bonds through the stock market to raise funds for investment, while the state could sell bonds to finance special needs (e.g., a construction project).

      The Special Economic Zones, many of which were located in 14 coastal cities were established in 1979 to attract foreign investment, foreign exchange, and

---

[44]Ibid., p. 183.

[45]Riskin, *China's Political Economy*, p. 355.

[46]Ibid., p. 359.

[47]Denise Hare, "Rural Nonagricultural Activities and Their Impact on the Distribution of Income: Evidence from Farm Households in Southern China," *China Economic Review*, 4, 1 (1994), 60.

technology using tax preferences and other privileges. The objective was to permit China to improve its ability to export goods and to provide an area in which redundant rural workers might obtain employment. In an experiment of new economic policies, enterprise managers were permitted to fire unsatisfactory workers. The most prominent example is in Shenzhen, located near Hong Kong. It has been transformed into a modern urban area whose population is about 1 million, and whose inhabitants enjoy a standard of living that is "the highest in the country."[48] This experiment aroused critics who argue that Shenzhen's high crime rates and (suspected) high incidence of corruption are due to the "decadent" influence of Western values following the rapid increase in foreign investment and technology.[49] However, the rapid growth and development of these zones have encouraged authorities on the national and local levels to favor further private ownership and control of new enterprises.

Taking all institutions together, there has been a steady shift concerning the relative importance of public versus collective and private ownership and control over resources. Diminished central state control is indicated by the dramatic increase in private-sector employment in retail sales, the decline in state revenue as a proportion of national income, and the decline in central control of investment. Although the stock market and special economic zones encountered resistance from authorities and workers, both have prospered. China has a history of reversing policy and periodically recentralizing control over the economy. However, the success of reforms since 1979 and recognition that economic performance would be adversely affected if SOEs and planned directives dominated the economy give reason to believe that the shift in ownership and control in favor of collectives and private individuals will continue for the remainder of this century.

POPULATION AND PUBLIC ADMINISTRATION.   Two other issues pertaining to control over resources is China's population policy and rules pertaining to public administration. In a nation with over 80 percent of its population in rural areas and where the mode of production is very labor intensive, the number of workers an agricultural unit is able to employ is important. While the commune and production brigade were the primary agricultural unit, households did not suffer the effects of a labor shortage. However, as the level of control has become the household plot the official government policy of "one couple-one child" confronts families with a brutal economic reality. There is no pension program for rural inhabitants; in addition, when they are elderly a couple can expect no help from a daughter, who becomes bound to her husband's family after marriage. Consequently, not having a son not

---

[48]William A. Joseph, "China's Special Economic Zones" *China*, 2nd ed. (Guilford, CT: Dushkin, 1987), p. 22.
[49]Ibid.

only results in an opportunity cost in terms of work not performed and income not generated, but in the likelihood that a couple will suffer from poverty in their later years.

The state at various levels exercises considerable control over families, seeking to enforce the one child per couple policy. There is a "Tragedy of the Commons" problem—a paradox between individual actions and the nation's needs.[50] Unless they or another family member can obtain employment in a TVE or "new city," farmers need sons to work on their land. However, with China's population of over 1 billion people and a population density about 25 times that of the United States on the arable land area, the state has been taking strong measures to reduce the rate of population growth. In addition to strong moral suasion, other methods include incentives such as bonuses to couples who pledge to have only one child, generous maternity leave for the first child, preferential treatment for one-child families regarding day care, housing assignments, school placement, fines, and loss of promotion opportunities at work for the parents of the second (and other) children. Some observers claim that pregnant women have been forced to have abortions. Finally, reports of female infanticide have been made as families seek to have the one child permitted to them be a son.

Finally, China relies heavily on quotas to control the behavior of its public servants. There are quotas which "extend to virtually every aspect of Chinese life . . . The fixation with quotas reflects the Chinese passion for numbers and the bureaucratic need to quantify everything in the management of a country as large as China."[51] For example, traffic authorities are given a quota for the number of traffic fatalities "permitted" in the area under their jurisdiction. If the number exceeds this, managers suffer loss of bonuses and the units responsible may be fined. Other examples where quotas are used as performance indicators and the criteria for remuneration include deaths from carbon monoxide poisoning, drowning, food poisoning, and fires.

Social Processes for Economic Coordination:
A Willingness to Experiment with Schemes
to Replace or Supplement Planning

Since 1978, China's social process for coordinating production and distribution activities has been a mixture of policies introduced in a step-by-step, ad hoc, trial-and-error basis rather than as part of a coherent reform program. No policy would be introduced nationally until it had been experimented with on the micro (local) level and lessons from the experiences determined. The reform strategy has favored a gradual approach, reflecting central authorities' desires to move in a market-oriented direction by increasing the proportion of activities coordinated

[50]For a complete description of this theory, see Garrett Hardin, "The Tragedy of the Commons," *Science*, 168 (November 8, 1968), 1243–1248.
[51]Lena Sun, "Quotas Rule China as Residents Live Fill-in-the-Numbers Lives," *Austin American-Statesman*, December 26, 1993, p. A21.

by markets, and in the process causing SOEs to react to competitive pressures. The policy also has been designed to retain "political cohesion," which means preserving the central authorities' position within the political structure.[52] Reforms intended to serve as partial substitutes for central planning have been introduced, grafted onto the existing (i.e., late 1970s) economy. The reforms have included expanded material incentives and wage differentials; greater freedom for enterprise managers to engage in foreign trade; fewer regulated prices; rules permitting bankruptcies; and taxation of enterprises. Authorities are committed to transforming the planning institutions while encouraging the evolution of collective and private institutions. The ability to coordinate production and distribution activities has been shifting, albeit with an occasional reversal, from the central authorities to those on the municipal and local levels

In the late 1970s authorities introduced "market supplanting" reforms where some market forces were permitted as a social process. However, the signals from the market were distorted considerably by irrational pricing and other policies subject to the influence of bureaucrats and other authorities who encouraged graft and caused inefficient economic outcomes. However, the interventions of the state increasingly became "market fostering" in nature which emphasized growth and economic efficiency. According to the economy's performance, the reforms have fostered economic growth, improvement in productivity, and higher living standards.[53] Periodic bursts of inflation stimulated authorities to slow (or attempt to slow) the pace of reforms, then "release the brakes" if inflation seemed to be under control.

Reforms were first introduced in rural areas from 1978 to 1984, with the household responsibility system and encouragement of rural markets and collective enterprises. Due to the success of these experiments, further experimental reforms were conducted in selected cities, including reforms of SOEs and pricing rules. From 1984 to 1988 reforms focused on urban areas, and some were introduced nationwide, particularly decontrol of consumer goods production. The key elements of the mid-1980s' reforms were granting more autonomy to SOE managers (the "contract responsibility system"); introducing a type of indicative planning while reducing the scope of central planning; permitting more prices to be determined by market forces; seeking to achieve macroeconomic stabilization through greater reliance upon changes in taxes and interest rates; fostering collective enterprise development; and permitting an expansion of foreign trade and investment activity.[54]

After the 1989 political protests, many reform programs (e.g., further decontrol of prices, and sales of SOEs through selling shares in these enterprises

[52]Gao Shanghuan, "Taking a Market-Oriented Direction and Pushing Forward in a Gradual Way—the Basic Experience of China's Economic Reform," p. 129. It is noteworthy that examples of authoritarian governments promoting economic development are common to Southeast Asia—including the Occupation Authority's reform efforts in Japan from 1946 to 1952 (see Chapters 9 and 10).

[53]Wang and Thomas, "Market Supplanting versus Market Fostering Interventions," p. 243.

[54]Chow, "How and Why China Succeeded in Her Economic Reform," pp. 122–123.

to the workers) were postponed, while individuals engaged in private enterprise were harassed by authorities. However, beginning in 1992 after authorities believed their position was secure, and in the face of rising unemployment, they resumed encouraging reform measures that had been introduced and openly committed to build a socialist market economy. Thereafter, existing reforms were expanded, new reforms introduced, the role of the central government in coordinating economic activities was further curtailed, and an open door policy focusing on foreign investment was endorsed.

AGRICULTURE.   There have been three periods during which rural development reforms have been introduced: 1979–1985, 1986–1991, and since 1992. In 1978 a "new leap forward" set of reforms was introduced, which emphasized decollectivization of agriculture and a "household responsibility system." During this period the state wanted to increase agricultural production, so it provided material incentives such as increases in procurement prices (about 20 percent to over 30 percent), and froze the quota for mandatory delivery of output to the state. Nonagricultural activities (e.g., transport, commercial, and service) through formation of collective economic associations or individual enterprises were encouraged in rural areas, while unregulated rural markets, which had existed unofficially, were encouraged. The key working rule was the household responsibility system. This scheme was a type of land reform shifting more income and property rights to the household level which, in effect, encouraged private farming. Families were assigned plots by their collective, required to pay a fixed rent, and given the authority to sign a lease granting them income rights and leasing rights for a 15- to 30-year period. The household would sign a contract with the state to produce a given level of output and sell it to the state at a procurement price. The household was free to sell any surplus above this level to the state for a higher above-quota price, or could sell the output in the open market in what amounted to a three-tiered pricing scheme.

There were some problems with the reforms. The state was committed to purchase all surplus grain production, and when too much grain was produced the budget deficit increased because the state has to fulfill its promise to purchase above-quota output at the agreed-upon price. In response, the grain contracting system changed the state's policy regarding the role of planning and prices in 1985. Farmers, who could voluntarily choose to participate, were paid the above-quota price for 70 percent of their output, but only the lower procurement price for the remainder of the output. This rule served to shift output to alternative products and services as well as to induce farmers to sell more of what they produced on the open market. The state did, however, continue to purchase the last 30 percent at the procurement price if the market price fell below this level— a form of subsidy which protected farmers who chose not to diversify. Overall, the grain contracting system is a hybrid scheme between central planning and free market for the agricultural sector. The state is only required to purchase a limited amount of grain, and farmers are given price incentives to grow the type of grain the state wants. Farmers can seek to increase their income by diversifying production, producing other products which they can sell on the open market, if they choose to face the uncertainties of the market.

Since 1992 the price paid to farmers by the state has been rising almost to the level of the market price. Incentives to produce for the market led to growth rates of grain production which have exceeded that of population growth, thereby contributing to a more diversified Chinese diet as excess grain used for livestock feed has permitted more beef and poultry to be raised. Authorities also continue to emphasize rural development of nonagricultural enterprises. This development policy is necessary because as agricultural productivity increases and the need for agricultural labor is reduced, excess farm labor will need alternative types of employment. China wishes to avoid the significant urban problems faced by nearly all developing countries which have permitted rural-urban migration, particularly shortages of housing, infrastructure, and inability to absorb all the migrant labor into the labor force. The Chinese policy of developing rural areas (as well as encouraging establishment of new cities) has thus been adopted for cost and social unrest reasons. The new policy is to encourage people to "leave the land but not the countryside, enter the factory but not the city."[55] Authorities recognized that given the fragmented nature of China's rural sector, introducing reforms there posed less of a threat to their control should unrest ensue.

Reform measures included encouragement of collectives (TVEs) where enterprises would be collectively owned at the village, township, or country level and thus would provide employment opportunities for local labor as well as a source of revenue for local government. These industries can easily focus on providing some seasonal employment opportunities to supplement agricultural activities. Thus, many jobs could be created in rural areas with redundant workers without any central government investment required. Specific policy mixes for rural development have been the subject of experiments, two of which have been the Southern Jiangsu model and Wenzhou model.

The former model was introduced as a model for rural development in areas close to a large city. Public ownership of firms was encouraged, with management by local government. It was believed that such a model would enable local authorities to retain control over development and able to introduce measures to lessen income inequalities if they arose. The Wenzhou model was experimented with in remote areas. Private and collective ownership of firms was encouraged, with management either by the household or collective. The intent was to develop rural entrepreneurs and to introduce rural inhabitants to aspects of market activity. The result in Wenzhou was that from 1978 to 1988 the number of agricultural workers fell from about 80 percent to 40 percent of the labor force. There was a type of putting out system with over 100,000 household enterprises engaged in cottage industries complemented by considerable private trader

[55]Zhu Mei, "Non-agricultural Industrial Development in Chinese Rural Areas," p. 384.

activity and specialized markets. When this success was publicized nationally, it enhanced the reputation of this particular rural development model.[56] What perhaps has not been as widely publicized is that rapid rural growth has been accompanied by greater disparities in income distribution primarily due to differentials households earn from nonagricultural activities.

ENTERPRISES. There were limited reforms pertaining to enterprises introduced between 1979 and 1984, although it was recognized that a lack of individual and enterprise autonomy, absence of work incentives, and excessive central control by the authorities over SOEs were inhibiting the economy's performance. In response, authorities decided to change the structure of management by giving them greater autonomy while reducing the state's role. Central planners since have reduced the number of goods subject to mandatory targets to about 20 (it had been over 500 during the 1970s). There was experimentation with SOEs concerning self-management and an indicative type of planning, which began in Sichuan in 1978. Six enterprises were allowed to make decisions concerning sale of their output on the market and were permitted to retain some of their profits for reinvestment purposes. The success of this experiment led to an expansion to include first 100, then about 6,000 SOEs, which then were responsible collectively for about 60 percent of all SOE output.

Enterprises filled quotas according to contracts, then could sell above-quota output on the market. Enterprises were also permitted to purchase certain inputs on wholesale markets. However, bureaucrats continued to have influence over product mix and size of labor force, and appointed enterprise managers. Finally, enterprises were permitted to award bonuses based upon profits they earned. This, however, resulted in three problems. The first pertained to the lack of meaningful price and cost indicators from which profits were computed (see pp. 555–556). The second problem was that the retained profits have not been used according to the working rules established. Most profits have been awarded as bonuses and allocated for fixed investment, with too little used for working capital. The third problem is that the flow of revenue to the state became less certain.

To alleviate the third problem, the profit remittance system was replaced by the contract system for SOEs after 1986. Enterprises were required to pay a tax to the state (about 50 percent of profits), thereby assuring a more consistent inflow of revenue for the budget. Enterprise managers were given greater autonomy over investment and production decisions as long as they fulfilled contractual tax and profit obligations. Turnover taxes were imposed by the state on these enterprises' output. Work units within the enterprise were paid according to their productivity (the factory responsibility system). Central authorities also began to encourage the establishment of collectively owned enterprises.

[56]Claude Aubert, Review of Dong Fureng and Peter Noland, eds., *Market Forces in China* (London: Zed Books, 1990), in *Journal of Comparative Economics*, 16, 1 (1992), 179–181.

The effect of these reforms, combined with encouraging competition through the growth of a private sector (partly through encouraging direct foreign investment) and the breaking up of monopoly firms into smaller enterprises, was improved factor productivity and rapid growth of industrial output. Foreign direct investment has been a significant factor in coastal cities, the outstanding example being in the Guangdong Province located just north of Hong Kong and Macao. Its capital, Guangzhou was designated an open coastal city in 1984, and "aggressive economic development" was encouraged there by central authorities. The result has been the transformation of villages into cities, construction of superhighways, factories, and office buildings in what was agricultural land, and considerable managerial expertise introduced by Hong Kong investors.[57] In this region, and in other special economic zones, the central authorities have taken steps to stimulate further development of Chinese industries For example, they announced in 1994 that no more joint ventures would be permitted in certain industries (e.g., automobiles), and that future joint ventures would be permitted under the condition that at least 40 percent (then rising to 60 percent within a few years) of the auto's components would have to be produced within China—an industrial policy not unlike that practiced by Japan beyond.[58] On the other hand, central authorities are eager to attract foreign investors to the chemical industry, particularly to produce plastics of which China imports about half its needs. Central authorities prefer that China become a net exporter of plastics, but more than $10 billion in investment in new chemical factories will be required to achieve this goal.

PRICE REFORM.   Reforms began in 1979, when price increases for agricultural products were announced as part of the household responsibility system. The favorable performance of the agricultural sector after the reforms (see pp. 561–562) stimulated authorities' desire to introduce further price reforms. There have been three phases of price reform. From 1979 to 1984 there was a period of price adjustment during which prices were raised or reduced (e.g., prices of staple farm products were increased by the state). The objective was to replace gradually the state's irrational working rules pertaining to prices. After authorities had learned from the experiences of agricultural price reform, it was decided to introduce the three-tiered pricing scheme (state procurement prices, prices for above-plan output, and free market prices) during 1983 to 1985 to many enterprise activities. After 1987, in the face of rising inflation and a desire to reassert central control, price reforms were reversed as the state resumed control over more prices. In the early 1990s greater emphasis again was placed by authorities on permitting unregulated prices to coordinate production and distribution activities.

[57]Akira, "Capitalist Winds in China," p. 20.
[58]"Slow Car to China," *The Economist*, April 16, 1994, pp. 71–72.

The three-tiered pricing system enabled farmers to receive higher prices for above-plan goods produced. There was a strong incentive to increase output, for above-plan prices were sometimes two or three times greater than procurement prices. However, there were problems with a coordinating scheme that featured the coexistence of goods at planned prices and goods at market prices. The main problem was that enterprises managers and state authorities higher in rank then negotiated the procurement and above-plan prices. Unfortunately in China, these negotiations in conjunction with the tiered pricing scheme resulted in bribery, corruption, and crime becoming a common process for coordinating production and distribution activities.

Enterprises would obtain lower-priced products as inputs (acquiring them via negotiations with superiors), have these products classified as above-plan output, and then sell the products at higher (above-plan) prices. With the large profits enterprises could bribe authorities for favors and supplement their own incomes. For example, assume steel was in short supply. A firm hoarding steel (which it acquired as an input) could have it transferred from an in-plan to an above-quota classification through negotiation with planning authorities. The above-quota steel would sell for very high prices to users who needed it. Bureaucrats engaged in such activity themselves, acquiring scarce products at the lower price and then reselling them at above-plan prices. Such situations were relevant, for prior to the 1990s about 40 percent of China's steel consumption was purchased on "free markets."[59]

A dual-pricing scheme has some advantages for a transforming economy. Markets could be encouraged to evolve gradually rather than be expected to emerge following the introduction of a laissez-faire policy toward prices in an effort to "get the prices right." Output quotas stayed constant while private output increased, and when the latter reached a desired level, quotas could be reduced. In the process people unaccustomed to market activity could learn about the type of decision making that was required when dealing with market institutions. On the other hand, the disadvantages of dual prices were that if large price differentials existed between state-administered and market prices corruption was invited, and that the profitability of SOEs depended upon quota inputs and output, which led to much lobbying by SOE managers for favorable allocation of inputs (and for high prices to be set by authorities for their output).

By 1992 many price distortions had been corrected in a gradual manner by merging the state-administered and market prices into one price. Other price reforms designed to liberalize prices that were introduced during the early 1990s included a large reduction of goods allocated by central planning, and setting prices approximating market levels for grain sold in urban areas. Some argue that rationing of goods and services (such as housing, fuel, and grain) had the effect of

[59]For further discussion, see Wu Jinglian and Zhao Renwei, "The Dual Pricing System in China's Industry," in Bruce L. Reynolds, ed., *Chinese Economic Reform* (Boston: Academic Press, 1988), pp. 19–28.

distorting consumer behavior in favor of greater demand for unrationed goods and services and, thus, inflation. For example, rent accounts for only about 1 percent of the typical family's expenditures (representing a type of in-kind subsidy), and the cost of fuel is also kept low. Some fear that maintenance of rationed goods at very low prices ultimately may lead to either very high prices or shortages of such goods, and that rent and fuel costs should be permitted to increase toward a market price level (as grain prices have been permitted to do).[60]

TRADE POLICY.   Authorities have moved away from administered control over trade in favor of economic incentives and permitting virtually free trade in the special economic zones. They have also taken steps to integrate China's economy with the other Chinese communities in Southeast Asia by fostering establishment of what is essentially a "Chinese Common Market," featuring close links between China, Hong Kong, and Taiwan. The wealthier economies complement that of China, for while Hong Kong and Taiwan provide financial strength and managerial expertise, China provides labor that is relatively cheap, natural resources (particularly land), and some technical expertise as well as industrial capacity. Entering this informal regional trade bloc is a type of industrial policy for China, for designated areas on the mainland are opened to investment from its two wealthier neighbors. In addition, the trade bloc provides China and these neighbors greater power when negotiating trade matters with the rest of the world.

There has been considerable trade and investment between members and guarantees for intermember investment, which has been conducive to regional corporations being established. From 1979 to 1989 trade between China and Hong Kong grew about 35 percent per year. China has become the island's largest supplier of imports, and its second largest market for exports, while Hong Kong is China's main source of foreign investment. There are over 2 million Chinese workers in Guangdong Province employed by Hong Kong-based enterprises.[61]

China is one of 18 nations which has declared the intention of establishment of an Asian-Pacific Free Trade Area (APEC). The objective is to remove all trade barriers among Pacific Rim nations and the United States by the year 2020. Should such an agreement become a formal working rule, China would become part of the world's largest economically integrated group of nations, for APEC accounts for over 40 percent of the world's population, over 40 percent of global trade, and more than half the value of world output.

CHINA'S TRANSFORMATION POLICIES VERSUS CEE TRANSFORMATION POLICIES.   If performance of the economy is the main criteria for evaluating

[60]Evidence indicates that the rapid increase in demand for higher-quality food and consumer durables, which exceeds the rise in per capita income, is due to low prices of rationed goods.

[61]For further discussion, see Chu-Yuan Cheng, "Concept and Practice of a 'Greater Chinese Common Market,'" *Chinese Economic Studies*, 26, 6 (Winter 1993–94), 5–12.

economic and political policies, then China's transformation policies have been considerably more successful than those of CEE (see Chapter 16, pp. 464–476). There have been a number of significant differences between political and economic aspects of the respective transformation programs. First, democracy in CEE seems to limit the extent of reforms, while Chinese authorities can introduce pragmatic reforms gradually without much opposition. Since the CEE political parties needed broad support for their policies, they needed an ideology as a rallying point. On the other hand, China's authorities sought to remain in power and economic success rather than ideology was more important. Political stability enabled gradual reforms to be introduced, whereas in CEE the public demanded a rapid reallocation of economic power away from previous authorities, necessitating radical, rapid reforms. Unfortunately for CEE authorities, the absence of economic success has witnessed the reelection of former Communist Party authorities in some nations.

Third, the Chinese strategy was to introduce reforms that would improve overall well-being from the beginning, while in CEE the welfare implications of dramatic reforms were ignored with ideological concerns taking precedence. One analyst argues there is an irony to the CEE "shock" approach designed to "rush the process of reforms . . . [because doing so] may well have hurt and slowed it [the reform process] by sacrificing too much of the present."[62] On the other hand, China's gradual, incremental reform process which consistently followed an experimental approach enabled it to build market-oriented principal institutions and stimulate market-oriented behavior throughout areas of the economy—particularly new enterprises (including TVEs) and special economic zones. The new principal institutions were not implanted from some foreign model, but were "hybrid and home grown."[63] Authorities permitted time and experience to determine the efficacy of experimental reforms (e.g., special economic zones). Pragmatism and gradual reforms which provided time for "learning and adapting" prevailed over ideology, "the inevitable result of compromises among a myriad of conflicting proposals, through a long process of trial and error—versus in CEE where new authorities responded to a sense of urgency and selected 'imported' solutions instead of developing their own working rules and principal institutions."[64]

Chinese reformers may have recognized that their policies required time to overcome institutional resistance and gain broad support, and that favorable economic performance needed to be associated with the reforms. They also understood that in a large, densely populated nation with wide differentials in level of development throughout the nation it was neither possible nor advisable

[62]Uijang Wang, "Eastern Europe and China: Institutional Development as a Resource Allocation Problem," *China Economic Review*, 4, 1 (1993), 37.

[63]Bruce L. Reynolds, "Introduction" to Special Issue: "China's Transition to the Market," p. 83.

[64]Ping Chen, "China's Challenge to Economic Orthodoxy: Asian Reform as an Evolutionary, Self-Organizing Process," *China Economic Review*, 4, 2 (1993), 138–140.

to introduce reforms nationwide without any experimentation. Finally, the reform strategy "accommodates the needs of politics," for success of Chinese reforms required political and social stability—both of which would have been threatened by radical reforms which "inevitably surpass the social endurance and cause social turmoil, thus hindering the reform [as has occurred in CEE]."[65]

SUMMARY OF REFORMS.   The willingness of Chinese authorities to reduce the role of planning with indirect bureaucratic control, tiered pricing scheme, and other reforms intended to retain elements of the pre-1979 economy in a pragmatic manner while promoting market-oriented measures and developing some unique principal institutions make the transformation program unique. The decision to subsidize losing SOEs and gradually reform them, stimulated by the authorities' fear of unemployment and social unrest if too many SOEs were permitted to go bankrupt, appears to have been fortuitous.

One analyst identified the necessary ingredients for successful transformation of an economy.[66] These included the ability to establish macroeconomic stability at the beginning of the reform process through monetary and fiscal policy measures, while introducing modest reforms that were successful in terms of promoting the well-being of the entire population. A subsequent round of reforms common to successful transformation programs would include promoting competition, requiring hard budget constraints, creating market-oriented institutions and working rules, and reducing the bureaucratic nature of state-owned enterprises and state regulatory institutions. Finally, after the first two rounds have been completed, comprehensive transformation of state-owned enterprises needs to be achieved. The same analyst concludes that "by accident or design, China appears to be following this virtuous sequence and enjoying rapid growth . . . [whereas] CEE countries were unable or unwilling to follow this sequence, and have found reform far more painful."[67]

INSTITUTIONAL CHANGE:
ECONOMIC REFORM WITHOUT
POLITICAL REFORM

There have been two general features of institutional change throughout the post-1976 period. One is the absence of political reform, with virtually no change occurring in the Communist Party leadership and ability to establish the basis for working rules. When these authorities introduced decentralization measures,

[65]Gao Shangquan, "Taking a Market-Oriented Direction and Pushing Forward in a Gradual Way—the Basic Experience of China's Economic Reform," pp. 132–133.
[66]Newberry, "Transformation in Mature Versus Emerging Economies: Why Has Hungary Been Less Successful Than China?" pp. 91–92.
[67]Ibid., p. 91.

there has been a decrease in power of central planners, but with a corresponding increase in provincial and municipal authorities' power.

The other feature pertains to the extent of hybrid, market-oriented institutions which have evolved gradually. Being unsure as to which economic institutions to create or support, the Chinese have relied upon an approach exemplified by the saying that the best way to cross over a river is by "touching the rocks as you cross the river—deciding on the next step only after have completed the previous step." Chinese authorities recognize that "[e]conomic institutions require time to change and people to operate modern enterprises and financial institutions require time to acquire the necessary human capital."[68] Semiprivate and private institutions have developed and increased in importance while SOEs are being transformed in joint-stock companies at a very modest rate. Meanwhile, planning and regulatory institutions, including some ministries, have had their influence curtailed significantly as the direct influence over economic activity by state authorities is being replaced gradually by indirect means of control, which rely upon economic incentives and changes in economic variables. Reform of the economic planning institutions was necessary to promote economic efficiency and growth, and change occurred not only in the Economic Planning Commission but in industrial ministries, as well as state banking and foreign trade institutions. In some cases ministries were transformed into "nonministerial organizations," such as restructuring the Ministry of Foreign Economic Relations and Trade, which had a monopoly over trade activities, into the Ministry of Foreign Trade and Economic Cooperation responsible for promoting trade through economic incentives and attracting foreign investment.

SOE reform has been gradual and difficult, partly because of the complex, dynamic types of complementary changes required. These include reforms to financial and tax institutions, as well as new regulatory and accounting working rules—all of which must overcome bureaucratic and managerial resistance to loss of power and control. Markets for inputs must be present for complete reform of SOEs to occur. Changes which have occurred within SOEs include permitting their managers to make decisions pertaining to pricing, being paid bonuses that reflect the performance of their enterprise, paying wages that reflect changes in labor productivity, purchasing inputs whose prices (as well as the prices for nearly all enterprise outputs) are gradually rising to reflect market forces, and making investment decisions using profits earned by the enterprise. The structure of ownership has changed dramatically away from state ownership and control with the growth of TVEs, private enterprises, and restructuring of SOEs into joint-stock companies. New research units have also developed, some located in new technology development zones. Their projects increasingly are stimulated by SOE managers' desires to determine customer needs as indicated by market forces.[69]

[68]Chow, "How and Why China Succeeded in Her Economic Reform," p. 127.
[69]Yaozing Hu, "Market-Oriented Reforms in China," p. 195.

The growth of special enterprise zones, which initially were an island of virtually free enterprise in a sea of a regulated economy, has been significant. These zones have attracted considerable foreign investment, and these funds, new advanced technology, and managerial expertise "have become an indispensable part in driving China towards modernization."[70] They also have aroused bureaucratic resentment. Policy reversals and the government's austerity program initiated in 1988 caused the cancellation of some ambitious programs involving purchases from foreigners, and more recently the central authorities have sought to reassert their control over decision making by authorities in the zones concerning attracting foreign investment and rules pertaining to the investment.

Two stock markets have been established. One is located in the traditional setting of Shanghai, while the other has been established in Shenzhen where economic activity features special economic zones. The state-controlled exchanges have offered shares in some SOEs to the Chinese people, while a secondary market offers foreigners the opportunity to purchase shares as well. When Chinese households exhibited "strong demand" for such shares, the state responded by offering shares of stock in additional SOEs.[71] Authorities permit some Chinese firms, including Shanghai Petrochemical, to offer their shares for sale on the Hong Kong and New York stock exchanges.

In the late 1970s and 1980s there was a decline in importance of what had been China's most prominent institution (in terms of number of people directly involved)—the people's commune. In the process of agricultural reform (e.g., the household responsibility system), the village (collectives) and households emerged as the basic agrarian institutions. In addition, TVEs grew in importance as indicated by the fact that while in 1978 the TVE influence accounted for about 9 percent of China's industrial production, by the late 1980s they accounted for over 33 percent (and exceed 40 percent by the mid-1990s).[72]

PERFORMANCE: THE WORLD'S FASTEST GROWING ECONOMY

Based upon indicators of performance such as economic growth, inflation, unemployment, trade deficit, productivity, income distribution, standard of living, and crime China's economic performance was favorable between 1978 and 1984, then experienced a number of adverse trends for the next five years. This was partly due to extensive centralization of economic control and coordination. Then a period of very favorable performance in growth, unemployment, and

---

[70]Gao Shangquan, "Taking a Market-Oriented Direction and Pushing Forward in a Gradual Way—the Basic Experience of China's Economic Reform," pp. 130–131.

[71]Wood, "Joint Stock Companies with Rearranged Public Ownership," p. 184.

[72]Jan Svejnar, "Productive Efficiency and Employment in China's Township, Village, and Private Enterprise," paper presented at the Allied Social Sciences Meetings, Atlanta, December 28–30, 1989, p. 2.

standard of living followed during the 1990s. Overall, since 1978 there has been a dramatic increase in living standards, particularly among rural and special economic zone households, rising productivity in agricultural and semiprivate and private enterprises, and transformation to the extent that profit-oriented firms account for over two thirds of China's production.

*Economic Growth, Unemployment, and
Inflation*

From 1979 to 1988 the growth of China's gross national product (GNP) was very high, well above that of CEE, increasing at an annual rate of 9.6 percent—the highest of any Asian nation during that period.[73] The gross output value of industry increased 12.8 percent annually.[74] During 1989 and 1990, however, growth declined considerably (to 5 percent in 1990) due to the reduction in investment. (Credit had been restricted as part of an austerity program to combat rapid inflation.) Agricultural output increased on an annual average of 6.2 percent between 1979 and 1988 (but an average of only 3.9 percent between 1985 and 1988).[75] After the 1979 reforms more acreage was planted for cash crops, yields per *mu* (about one sixth of an acre) increased, and labor productivity grew (about 5.8 percent annually).[76]

Due to the interrelationship between inputs, output, and consumption, the increase in nonagricultural output has grown even faster than agricultural output. During the 1990s China's economy has grown faster than any nation in the world. After growth rates of about 5 percent and 7 percent in 1990 and 1991, respectively, growth exceeded 12 percent the next two years, and was over 10 percent in 1994. This rapid growth is primarily due to expansion of TVEs, enterprises in the special economic zones, and other private activity. Overall, gross domestic product per capita has grown about 6 percent annually since 1965, while the nation's gross national product increased about 275 percent from 1978 to 1993 (versus less than 40 percent for the U.S. economy during the same period).

Concerning unemployment, the rate of urban unemployment fell from 5.3 percent in 1978 to about 2 percent between 1986 and 1988. However, it rose to over 3 percent in 1989[77] and is expected to exceed 5 percent in the mid-1990s. Some

---

[73]State Statistical Bureau of the People's Republic of China, *China Statistical Abstract 1989* (New York: Praeger, 1989), p. 5.

[74]Ibid.

[75]Ibid. The post-1978 reforms have been credited with having "helped to release deep-rooted entrepreneurial impulses among China's peasants that have long been suppressed." See A. Doak Barnett, "China's Modernization: Development and Reform in the 1980s," p. 134, in Joint Economic Committee of the Congress, *China's Economy Looks Toward the Year 2000*, 1 (Washington, DC: U.S. Government Printing Office, 1986). The quote is taken from Bruce F. Johnston, "The Political Economy of Agricultural Development in the Soviet Union and China," *Food Research Institute Studies*, 21, 2 (1989), 132.

[76]Riskin, *China's Political Economy*, p. 297.

[77]State Statistical Bureau of the People's Republic of China, *China Statistical Abstract 1989*, p. 21. While these figures are low by OECD standards, unemployment is not consistent with the Marxian-Stalinist-Maoist philosophical basis, and consequently unacceptable to the Chinese people.

argue that these percentages understate the employment situation. There is an underemployment problem in SOEs (perhaps as much as a third to half of the work force) where layoffs are not permitted and many workers are redundant.[78] In addition, there are estimates that combined unemployment and underemployment equals about 20 percent of the urban labor force. For rural areas, indications are that well over 20 percent of the labor force is not fully employed.

During the 1979–1990 period, inflation averaged about 5.4 percent a year. However, it was about 18 percent in 1988 and 1989 before falling below 3 percent in 1990 and 1991.[79] Since 1992 inflation has been a problem, exceeding 10 percent in that year and rising to over 22 percent in 1994. Prices of goods sold in unregulated markets have been rising even faster, perhaps over 30 percent on an annual basis. What is interesting in China is that while nominal growth of the money supply (M_2) averaged over 23 percent annually during the 1979–1990 period and growth of real GNP was 8.8 percent, inflation was not much greater.[80] This has been attributed to both repressed and disguised inflation given the prevalence of administered prices (especially for rent) and increases in state subsidies. However, during the 1990s inflation accelerated and has persisted.

Why has there been a recent acceleration of inflation? Wage increases exceed productivity increases; input shortages result in above-plan prices having to be paid; the incentive system is defective (e.g., not only are bankruptcies of inefficient SOEs not permitted for fear of high unemployment and subsequent social unrest, but losing enterprises receive subsidies). If there is an excess supply of an SOE product, there is no decrease in the prices to "clear the market." (This results in unsold output being stored at state expense. One estimate puts the number of unsold bicycles in state inventory at over 30 million, while another estimate states that unsold inventories produced by SOEs—if their value is equivalent to the price that approximates market value for similar products— equal over 5 percent of gross domestic product.) The economy overheated after reforms were introduced and investment rose rapidly. Rapid increases in money supply (estimated to exceed 30 percent during the early and mid-1990s) have contributed significantly to inflationary pressure. Reasons for the rapid increase include the need to support unprofitable SOEs whose debts grew over 50 percent in the first half of 1994 alone; and authorities' desire to stimulate priority investment. Due to the absence of capital markets and authorities' desire to maintain control over the allocation of credit (some argue they did not trust alternative financial institutions beyond their control), as well as not to engage in significant deficit spending, bank loans were expanded.[81] Some fear that in an effort to curtail inflation, authorities will slow the pace of SOE structural reforms.

---

[78]It is estimated the Sinopec Yanshan chemical factory's work force of 47,000 is about ten times the number of workers employed by a comparable chemical factory in a Western industrialized nation.

[79]State Statistical Bureau of the People's Republic of China, *China Statistical Abstract 1989*, p. 86.

[80]Jin Lizuo, "Monetary Policy and the Design of Financial Institutions in China," pp. 1–5.

[81]Ibid., pp. 5–10, 238–242.

Investment and Productivity

For industrial SOEs there is evidence that the factor productivity growth throughout the 1980s (which some argue was about 2 percent to 4 percent annually, while others claim it was "only negligible")[82] was due to extensive use of resources (i.e., mobilizing the labor force and increasing other inputs through a high rate of investment), and to increased foreign investment. While factor productivity in TVEs has been favorable (growing approximately 2 percent to 4 percent annually), there has been a lack of dynamic efficiency in SOEs whose technology generally is backward and management too bureaucratic. Low productivity of SOEs is reflected by the increase in subsidies as a percentage of total payments to these enterprises. Subsidies accounted for 6.5 percent of enterprise payments in 1978, 15.2 percent in 1986, and 21.4 percent in 1988 (and indications are that state subsidies to losing SOEs have been greater during the 1990s than in 1989).[83] Overall, subsidies for SOEs rose from less than 10 percent of the state budget in 1978 to almost 30 percent in 1990.

Analysts claim that much of China's industrial SOE investment has been inefficiently and irrationally allocated. There has been until recently extensive indirect and direct bureaucratic control and an absence of capital markets. The real rate of interest borne by enterprises was negative, for throughout much of the 1980s inflation has averaged 9 percent while interest rates remained about 5 percent. Another problem was due to bureaucratic allocation of resources without meaningful value indicators. An enterprise's success depended more upon the influence managers could wield over the authorities than upon the efficiency and hard work of managers and workers.

On the other hand, China's rate of gross domestic private investment as a percentage of GDP exceeded 34 percent in the 1970s and 1980s, and has been well over 35 percent in the 1990s. Nearly 80 percent of foreign investment comes from Hong Kong and Taiwan, although some argue that some of these funds are really domestic investment that is "round tripping" from investors in the mainland through a Hong Kong bank, and then back into China. Studies do indicate that the high level of investment, with the new technology, managerial skills, and competition pressure on other Chinese firms, is responsible for improved labor productivity and technical progress—especially in private firms located in special economic zones.

Foreign Trade

China's volume of trade increased considerably during the late Mao and post-Mao era. From 1973 to 1985 China's export volume rose from twentieth to fifteenth among all nations, while its import volume in 1985 ranked eleventh compared to twenty-

---

[82]Wing Thye Woo, Gang Fan, Wen Hai, and Yibiao Jin, "The Efficiency and Macroeconomic Consequences of Chinese Enterprise Reform," *China Economic Review*, 4, 2 (1993), 153.
[83]State Statistical Bureau, *China Statistical Abstract 1989*, p. 92.

third in 1973.[84] Since then China's trade volume has grown more rapidly, especially with Hong Kong and Taiwan, which account for about three quarters of China's exports and imports. As a percentage of national income, trade has grown from about 10 percent of national income in the late 1970s to about 40 percent in the mid-1990s. The special economic zones have contributed significantly, and it is estimated that over 40 percent of China's foreign trade occurs in the Guangdong province.

China continually has been experiencing a trade deficit, which should be expected. Imports are over 85 percent manufactured goods and less than 15 percent primary goods, while exports are about 70 percent manufactured goods (e.g., textiles) and 30 percent primary goods. Since income elasticity of demand for manufactured goods is above that of primary goods, and since income elasticity of China's manufactured goods is lower than for the industrial goods and luxury and high-quality consumer goods it imports, over time a trade deficit is inevitable. The size of the deficit was modest between 1978 and 1988 as the average annual rate of export growth (17.2 percent) was only slightly below that of imports (17.6 percent).[85] During the 1990s the deficit has been about 8 percent to 10 percent. It is estimated that the overall impact of trade has been to create jobs in China, especially in urban areas.[86]

Distribution of Income and Standard of Living

China's income distribution has become more unequal following the economic reforms, both within and between urban and rural areas. Income from nonagricultural activities in rural areas is less equally distributed than agricultural income, which until the mid-1990s tended to be equalized due to state grain procurement policies. Those Chinese residing either in or close to the rapidly growing coastal regions have experienced greater increases in income than the rest of the population—especially some entrepreneurs and stock investors. Government employees—well-educated officials in particular—not only have realized little gain in real income, but in recent years have suffered a decrease in real income in the face of high inflation. Overall, however, by international standards China's "inequality [of income distribution] is clearly one of the lowest in the world."[87] Reforms have favored industrious peasants, those working for a TVE, special economic zone residents, and to a lesser extent SOE workers. There are, however, many peasants worse off than they were when the commune system

[84]Peter Van Ness, ed., *Market Reforms in Socialist Societies: Comparing China and Hungary.* (Boulder, CO: Lynne Rienner, 1989), p. 119.

[85]State Statistical Bureau, *China Statistical Abstract 1989*, p. 5.

[86]See Bruce Reynolds, "Trade, Employment, and Inequality," in Reynolds, ed., *Chinese Economic Reform: How Far, How Fast?* (Boston: Academic Press, 1988), pp. 189–199.

[87]Reynolds, ed., *Chinese Economic Reform*, p. 170. Personal incomes of commune members grew much more rapidly than SOE workers between 1979 and 1983. For further discussion, see Nicholas R. Lardy, "Consumption and Living Standards in China, 1979–83," *The China Quarterly* (December 1984), pp. 849–865.

was in effect due to the reduction or loss of entitlements such as subsidized health care and free education.

In terms of the growth of peasant real incomes, the increase was over 35 percent between 1978 and 1981, and for households with small individually managed plots it more than doubled.[88] Between 1978 and 1988 per capita consumption of staple and durable consumer goods increased considerably. For products such as grain, pork, fresh eggs, and cloth, the increases were 27 percent, 94 percent, 290 percent, and 53 percent, respectively.[89] Between 1980 and 1988 the average number of bicycles, television sets, refrigerators, and washing machines sold per day rose from 32,000 to 113,000, 1,000 to 73,000, 151 to 20,096, and 600 to 4,700, respectively, and these favorable trends continued into the 1990s.[90] Meanwhile, demand for higher-quality food such as better cuts of meat, milk, and eggs has increased. Chinese urban consumers, aided by subsidies for rent and fuel, consume a higher-quality diet than residents of countries with more than double China's per capita GNP.

According to one study, China's physical quality of life index (PQLI) compares favorably to that of other nations.[91] As of the late 1970s not only was China's PQLI 15 points above the average of underdeveloped countries (i.e., nations whose per capita income is below $400), but was comparable to that of nations whose gross national product was five to six times that of China's.[92] The average adult life expectancy at birth is over 70 years, higher than other nations with comparable per capita incomes. One important indicator of health, infant mortality, has fallen from about 90 per 1,000 to less than 30 since the mid-1960s. One standard of living indicator that worsened during the 1980s was crime and corruption, which increased considerably. Reasons for rising crime ("serious and violent" crimes are estimated to have increased 20 percent in the first half of 1994 alone) include more peasants migrating to newly developing urban areas where their struggle to survive has meant rising rates of theft and burglary. Many analysts blame the tiered pricing scheme for stimulating rampant corruption among agricultural bureaucrats. There is evidence that corruption and bribery are spreading throughout urban areas due to China having the most corrupt authorities since the 1949 revolution. In response, the state announced a major crackdown on corruption, such as outlawing the practice of authorities setting up their own side business to benefit from their position, and requiring bribes for fees

[88]Lee Travers, "Post-1978 Economic Policy and Peasant Income in China," *The China Quarterly* (June 1984), pp. 244, 245.

[89]State Statistical Bureau, *China Statistical Abstract 1989*, p. 90.

[90]Ibid., p. 13.

[91]See Morris D. Morris, *Measuring the Condition of the World's Poor: The Physical Quality of Life Index* (New York: Pergamon Press, 1979), cited in Van Ness, *Market Reforms in Socialist Societies*, p. 178. The PQLI is a weighted index which uses the following criteria: per capita GNP, per capita real growth of GNP, population growth, life expectancy at birth, infant mortality rate, literacy, and per capita public education spending.

[92]Ibid.

that should be free (e.g., to obtain an apartment, enroll children into the better schools, or to see a physician).

Summary

The performance of the Chinese economy is particularly noteworthy, especially when compared to that of CEE. Using comparable performance indicators, trends in China, except for inflation and political democracy, are either similar to or more positive than corresponding results in CEE.[93] In nearly every year since 1978, China's actual performance has exceeded that planned or anticipated by authorities, while in CEE the decline in economic activity following the implementation of transformation measures has consistently exceeded the most pessimistic forecasts of policymakers and their foreign advisors. In consequence, the social and economic costs borne by the Chinese during their transformation have been much less than in CEE. The percentage of households living below the poverty line in China fell from about 44 percent (rural) and 11 percent (urban) in 1981 to about 13 percent (rural) and 3 percent (urban) by 1990.[94] Given the rapid economic growth since 1990, these percentages have declined further, while the comparable figures in CEE have risen dramatically (see Chapter 16, pp. 466–472).

Why has China's economy outperformed those of CEE nations during their respective transformation periods? First, China chose not to rush transformation, but to gradually reform SOEs while encouraging growth of the semiprivate and private sectors (especially in the agricultural sector). Therefore, SOEs were exposed slowly to competitive forces while maintaining social insurance for its citizens during the transformation. In CEE too much emphasis was placed upon privatization and reforming SOEs and too little on fostering development of entrepreneurial activity. Second, while there is corruption in China there appears to be an absence of the national crime syndicates common throughout CEE, with a corresponding deterrent to foreign investment in those nations. Third, the collapse of the trading bloc throughout CEE damaged those economies while China has been expanding trade with rapidly growing Asian neighbors.

Another reason is that China's growth rates have steadily increased, while those of CEE collapsed after 1989. Only from 1993 to 1994 were some CEE nations experiencing positive growth, albeit from a smaller base than in 1989. Therefore,

---

[93]See James Angresano, "A Myrdalian View of Change in Central and Eastern Europe," *Development Policy Review*, 12, 3 (September 1994), 251–275; Joseph C. H. Chai, "Consumption and Living Standards in China," *The China Quarterly*, 131 (September 1992), 721–749; Chow, "How and Why China Succeeded in Her Economic Reform;" Robert Michael Field, "China's Industrial Performance Since 1978," *The China Quarterly*, 131 (September 1992), 577–607; Peter Harrold; "The Future of China's Economic Reforms," *The China Business Review* (July-August 1993), pp. 8–9; Newberry, "Transformation in Mature Versus Emerging Economies: Why Has Hungary Been Less Successful Than China?" and K. C. Yeh, "Macroeconomic Issues in China in the 1990s," *The China Quarterly*, 131 (September 1992), 501–544.

[94]Chai, "Consumption and Living Standards in China," p. 741.

China has been able to receive strong support from its population, experience high rates of investment (especially by attracting Chinese people living in Hong Kong or Taiwan to invest in the mainland), and maintain social spending levels without increasing taxes dramatically, unlike in CEE where absence of growth has meant declining investment and either raising taxes or cutting social services. Fifth, China developed its own transformation program without foreign advice or financial aid, thereby avoiding the "coercive isomorphism" CEE nations felt to comply with the wishes of Western donors and advisors. Related to this has been China's willingness to be pragmatic and experiment with unique, hybrid institutions, while in CEE a blueprint approach to transformation with ideological constraints was favored to establish a "free market economy." Sixth, China selected a sequence of reforms in which initial increases in output provided "strong positive feedbacks amplifying the positive . . . features of reform . . . [whereas in CEE] initial pain . . . worsen[ed] the problem" as those nations focused too much on speed and did not introduce reforms in the proper sequence.[95] Finally, China has maintained political stability and could adopt a long-run perspective to its transformation efforts. In CEE the lack of political stability and loss of central control contributed to the declining output and distribution problems.

As an underdeveloped country, China has been successful regarding the ability to lower its population growth rate (since the 1950s), increase health care and education coverage especially throughout the rural areas, raise material standards of living for many, reduce poverty, keep unemployment low, increase average life expectancy, and dramatically reduce foreign domination of its economy and political structure. Relative to all nations China has experienced enormous progress over the last decade, except for its industrial SOEs. Some believe that China's favorable performance will decline due to the burden of maintaining and restructuring these large firms.

There have been significant leadership mistakes since the 1970s. Authorities believed China's agricultural problems were solved by the mid-1980s and were naive by planning to reform the urban economy within five years. Since 1949 China has had a propensity for such overenthusiasm, resulting in the decentralization-recentralization cycle. Too much overheating of the economy was initiated by high rates of investment in industry, while the agricultural sector, infrastructure, and education were ignored. Corruption was widespread among authorities and their families. The post-1984 price reforms not only contributed to a highly unbalanced industrial structure, but also triggered a nationwide panic buying spree, leading to more inflation. This was followed in 1988 by a declaration that no more price reform would occur, and in 1990 by the recentralization movement to secure political control. Finally, the household responsibility system stimulated population growth. Following the adoption of this system by most farmers, a need for more family labor was created. In response, birth

[95]Newberry, "Transformation in Mature Versus Emerging Economies: Why Has Hungary Been Less Successful Than China?" p. 90.

rates increased (from 17.5 per 1,000 in 1984 to 20.8 per 1,000 in 1988) while the population growth rate increased from 1.08 percent in 1984 to 1.42 percent in 1988.[96]

CHINA'S COMPLEX, UNPREDICTABLE DEVELOPMENT AS AN ILLUSTRATION OF THE EVOLUTIONARY-INSTITUTIONAL THEORY

"The [shock] approach, which assumes a high degree of transferability of institutions from one society to another, reflects the underlying paradigm of modern economics—an equilibrium-oriented approach which says, 'Get the prices right, and the rest will follow.' But in reality, social change is a complex, path-dependent, and unpredictable process."[97]

In 1949, 1958, 1966, 1978, and 1989 China's authorities have reacted against corruption and unfavorable performance of the economy (especially relative to its Asian neighbors and Western industrial powers) by introducing new working rules which first (early 1950s) established a command over a social economy but later deviated from the Stalinist model. Pragmatic reforms have not been consistent with an internally coherent philosophical basis, but favorable performance has been experienced throughout the past decade. Economic reforms have moved in a very political direction. Authorities who desire to maintain their position within the social structure have not been willing to allow significant competition in the political arena. However, Chinese authorities have been willing to introduce pragmatic, experimental economic reforms that have proven to be self-reinforcing and successful. The authorities perhaps recognize that economies are complex, and their path is unpredictable. They were willing to learn from the experimental, micro-level reforms before implementing them on a broader basis. Reforms and experiments such as the family responsibility system, TVEs, and special economic zones "all interact[ed] with each other through waves of positive feedback: communication, learning imitation."[98] Since an overwhelming majority of the Chinese population benefited from the reforms, there was a greater desire among authorities to widen and deepen the reforms, or reverse them if experience demonstrated they were not effective. The result was what the evolutionary-institutional theory predicts, namely positive performance creates "a virtuous circle of 'reforming–benefiting–deepening the reforms.' Each round of [successful] reforms makes the next round inevitable and indispensable."[99]

[96]State Statistical Bureau, *China Statistical Abstract 1989*, p. 16. This increase is not consistent with China's best interests, as defined by the authorities.

[97]Ping Chen, "China's Challenge to Economic Orthodoxy: Asian Reform as an Evolutionary, Self-Organizing Process," p. 140.

[98]Ibid.

[99]Wang and Thomas, "Market Supplanting versus Market Fostering Interventions: China, East Asia and Other Developing Countries," p. 254.

SOME THOUGHT REGARDING CHINA'S FUTURE

Prior to the late 1970s, by adopting planning as a social process for coordination, China was able to avoid many problems that plague those underdeveloped nations which have relied heavily upon a predominantly market process to coordinate production and distribution activities. Since then it has developed a transformation strategy that has succeeded in the development of some unique principal institutions and corresponding working rules in an economy that has been the world's fastest growing in the 1990s. What remains to be seen is if this pace can continue, or if the task of reforming SOEs that are a drain on the economy and the maintenance of an authoritarian political structure will outweigh the positive impact of expanding semiprivate and private economic activity and reverse the economy's favorable performance.

KEY TERMS AND CONCEPTS

Contract Management Responsibility System
Household Responsibility System
Pragmatic Reforms

Special Economic Zones
Three-Tiered Pricing System
Township-Village Enterprise

QUESTIONS FOR DISCUSSION

1. What were the people's communes, and how were they consistent with the Maoist philosophical basis?
2. Outline the main features of the three-tiered pricing system.
3. Compare the working rules applying to a typical rural household for both the commune system and the household responsibility system.
4. Compare the Chinese transformation program since 1979 with that adopted in most CEE nations (see Chapter 16).
5. How does the philosophical basis introduced by Hua Guofeng in the late 1970s differ from that introduced by Mao Tse Tung after the 1949 revolution?
6. Compare the performance of the Chinese economy since 1978 with that of CEE nations since 1989. Identify what you believe are reasons the Chinese economy has performed better (in terms of the performance indicators presented in Chapter 16) than the CEE nations.
7. Outline the pragmatic, experimental nature of China's transformation program. What are its strengths and weaknesses?

REFERENCES

Akira, Mori, "Capitalist Winds in Socialist China," *Japan Quarterly* (January-March 1993), pp. 19–27.

Angresano, James, "A Myrdalian View of Change in Central and Eastern Europe," *Development Policy Review*, 12, 3 (September 1994), 251–275.

Aubert, Claude, Review of Dong Fureng and Peter Nolan, eds., *Market Forces in China* (London: Zed Books, 1990), in *Journal of Comparative Economics*, 16, 1 (1992), 179–181.

Bachman, David, "China Hails the 'Socialist Market Economy,'" *The China Business Review* (July-August 1993), pp. 34–43.

Bell, Michael W., Hoe E. Khor, and Kalapana Kochhar, *China at the Threshold of a Market Economy*. Washington, DC: International Monetary Fund, 1993.

"Birth of the Instant City," *The Economist*, September 10, 1994, pp. 34–35.

Chai, Joseph C. H., "Consumption and Living Standards in China," *The China Quarterly*, no. 131 (September 1992), pp. 721–749.

Chen, Ping, "China's Challenge to Economic Orthodoxy: Asian Reform as an Evolutionary, Self-Organizing Process," *China Economic Review*, 4, 2 (1993), 137–142.

Chen, Shenshen, "Editor's Introduction to Price Reform in China," *Chinese Economic Studies* 22, 3 (Spring 1989), 3–13.

Chern, Wen S., and Terry Sicular, "Introduction." *China Economic Review*, 5, 1 (1994), v–viii.

"China's Pig of a Problem," *The Economist*, September 17, 1994, pp. 35–36.

Chow, Gregory C., "How and Why China Succeeded in Her Economic Reform," *China Economic Review*, 4, 2 (1993), 117–128.

_____, *The Chinese Economy*. New York: Harper & Row, 1985.

Chu-Yuan Cheng, "Concept and Practice of a 'Greater Chinese Common Market,'" *Chinese Economic Studies* 26, 6 (Winter 1993–94), 5–12.

Economic and Social Commission for Asia and the Pacific, *Economic Bulletin For Asia and the Pacific*, 36, 2. New York: United Nations, December 1985.

The Economist: Business China. April 4, 1994, pp. 1–3; May 2, 1994, p. 6; and August 8, 1994, pp. 45, 11.

Fewsmith, Joseph, "Editor's Introduction to Lin Ling on Sichuan's Economic Reform," *Chinese Economic Studies*, 26, 4 (Summer 1993), 3–6.

Field, Robert Michael, "China's Industrial Performance Since 1978," *The China Quarterly*, 131 (September 1992), 577–607.

Fureng, Dong, *Rural Reform, Nonfarm Development, and Rural Modernization in China*. Washington, DC: The World Bank, 1988.

Hardin, Garrett, "The Tragedy of the Commons," *Science*, 168 (November 8, 1968), 1243–1248.

Hare, Denise, "Rural Nonagricultural Activities and Their Impact on the Distribution of Income: Evidence from Farm Households in Southern China," *China Economic Review*, 4, 1 (1994), 59–82.

Harrold, Peter, "The Future of China's Economic Reforms," *The China Business Review* (July-August 1993), pp. 8–9.

Hsiung, Bingyuang, and Louis Putterman, "Pre- and Post-Reform Income Distribution in a Chinese Commune: The Case of Dahe Township in Hebei Province," *Journal of Comparative Economics*, 13, 3 (September 1989), 406–445.

Hu, Yaozing, "Market-Oriented Reforms in China," *Development Policy Review*, 11, 2 (June 1993), 195–204.

Ignatius, Adi, "China's Economic Reform Program Stalls," *The Wall Street Journal*, September 26, 1989, p. A22.

Ishikawa, Shigeru, "China's Economic System Reform: Underlying Factors and Prospects," *World Development*, 11, 8 (1983), 647–658.

Jefferson, Gary H., "Summary of Panel Discussion on Enterprise Reform: International Symposium on Economic Transition in China, Hainan Province," *China Economic Review*, 4, 2 (1993), 143–148.

Johnson, D. Gale, "Does China Have a Grain Problem?" *China Economic Review*, 4, 1 (1994), 1–14.

Johnston, Bruce F., "The Political Economy of Agricultural Development in the Soviet Union and China," *Food Research Institute Studies*, 21, 2 (1989), 97–138.

Joseph, William A., ed., "China's Special Economic Zones," *China*, 2nd ed. Guilford, CT: Dushkin, 1987.

Khan, Azizur Rahman, Keith Griffin, Carl Riskin, and Zhao Renwei, "Household Income and Its Distribution in China," *The China Quarterly*, 132 (December 1992), 1029–1061.

Kristof, Nicholas D., "China to Crack Down on Corruption," *Austin American-Statesman*, August 22, 1993, p. A6.

Lardy, Nicholas R., *China in the World Economy*. Washington, DC: Institute for International Economics, 1994.

_____, "Consumption and Living Standards in China, 1979–83," *The China Quarterly* (December 1984), 849–865.

Leung, Julia, "Beijing Will Reassert Centralized Control," *The Wall Street Journal*, November 28, 1989, p. A10.

Lim, David, "Explaining the Growth Performances of Asian Developing Economies," *Economic Development and Cultural Change*, 42, 4 (July 1994), 829–844.

Lin, Cyril Z., "China's Distorted Economic Reform," *The Proceedings of the First Annual Conference of the Chinese Economic Association (UK)*. St. Antony's College, Oxford, December 18–19, 1989, pp. 12–30.

Lindblom, Charles, *Politics and Markets*. New York: Basic Books, 1977.

Ling, Lin, "A Good Start in Economic Structural Reform," *Chinese Economic Studies*, 26, 4 (Summer 1993), 7–16.

_____, "Some Problems in Economic Reform—Preliminary Views on Sichuan's Enterprise Reform Experiments," *Chinese Economic Studies*, 26, 4 (Summer 1993), 45–62.

Lizuo, Jin, "Monetary Policy and the Design of Financial Institutions in China" (1978–90). Unpublished Ph.D. thesis, Oxford University, 1993.

_____, "Effects of Financial Decentralization on Industrial Growth in China

(1952–88)," unpublished paper prepared at Oxford University, 1992.

Lord, Winston, "China and America: Beyond the Big Chill," *Foreign Affairs*, 68, 4 (Fall 1989), 1–26.

McGregor, James, "Jobless Peasants Swarm Through China," *The Wall Street Journal*, May 2, 1991, p. A12.

_____, "Premier Describes Economic Woes Afflicting China," *The Wall Street Journal*, March 26, 1991, p. A19.

Mei, Zhu, "Non-agricultural Industrial Development in Chinese Rural Areas," *Development Policy Review*, 11, 3 (September 1993), 383–392.

Moore, Jr., Barrington, *Authority and Inequality Under Capitalism and Socialism.* Oxford: Clarendon Press, 1987.

Muqiao, Xue, ed., *Almanac of China's Economy 1981.* New York: Eurasia Press, 1982.

Myers, Ramon H., *The Chinese Economy Past and Present.* Belmont, CA: Wadsworth, 1980.

Newberry, David M., "Transformation in Mature Versus Emerging Economies: Why Has Hungary Been Less Successful Than China?" *China Economic Review,* 4, 2 (1993), 89–116.

Oi, Jean C., "Peasant Grain Marketing and State Procurement: China's Grain Contracting System," *The China Quarterly* (June 1986), pp. 272–290.

Park, Albert, Scott Rozelle, and Fang Cai, "China's Grain Policy Reforms: Implications for Equity, Stabilization, and Efficiency," *China Economic Review*, 4, 1 (1994), 15–33.

Perkins, Dwight H., "Summary: Why Is Reforming State-Owned Enterprises So Difficult?" *China Economic Review*, 4, 2 (1993), 149–151.

Prybla, Jan, Review of George T. Crane *The Political Economy of China's Special Economic Zones*, in *Journal of Comparative Economics*, 16, 1 (1992), 172–173.

Putterman, Louis, "Effort, Productivity, and Incentives in a 1970s Chinese People's Commune," *Journal of Comparative Economics*, 14, 1 (March 1990), 88–104.

Reynolds, Bruce L., "Introduction" to Special Issue: "China's Transition to the Market," *China Economic Review*, 4, 2 (1993), 83–84.

_____, ed., *Chinese Economic Reform: How Far, How Fast?* Boston: Academic Press, 1988.

Riskin, Carl, *China's Political Economy: The Quest For Development Since 1949.* Oxford: Oxford University Press, 1987.

Schmidt, Marlis, *Economic Reforms in the People's Republic of China Since 1979.* West Cornwall, CT: Locust Hill Press, 1987.

Shangquan, Gao, "Taking a Market-Oriented Direction and Pushing Forward in a Gradual Way—the Basic Experience of China's Economic Reform," *China Economic Review*, 4, 2 (1993), 129–136.

Shen, T. Y., "An Institution for Entrepreneurship in Chinese Economic Reform," *The Journal of Socio-Economics*, 23, 3 (Fall 1994), 303–320.

"Slow Car to China," *The Economist*, April 16, 1994, pp. 71–72.

State Statistical Bureau of the People's Republic of China, *China Statistical*

Abstract 1989. New York: Praeger, 1989.

Sun, Lena H., "Quotas Rule China as Residents Live Fill-in-the-Numbers Lives," *Austin American-Statesman,* December 26, 1993, p. A21.

Svejnar, Jan, "Productive Efficiency and Employment in China's Township, Village, and Private Enterprise," Paper presented at the Allied Social Science Meetings, Atlanta, December 28–30, 1989.

Todaro, Michael P., *Economic Development in the Third World,* 3rd ed. New York: Longman, 1985.

Travers, Lee, "Post-1978 Economic Policy and Peasant Income in China," *The China Quarterly* (June 1984), pp. 241–259.

Uphoff, Norman T., and Warren F. Ilchman, eds., *The Political Economy of Development.* London: University of California Press, 1972.

Van Ness, Peter, ed., *Market Reforms in Socialist Societies: Comparing China and Hungary.* Boulder, CO: Lynne Rienner, 1989.

Walder, Andrew G., "Wage Reform and the Web of Factory Interests," *The China Quarterly,* 109 (March 1987), 22–41.

Wang, Uijiang, "Eastern Europe and China: Institutional Development as a Resource Allocation Problem," *China Economic Review,* 4, 1 (1993), 37–47.

Wang, Zhi, and Wen S. Chern, "Effects of Rationing on the Consumption Behavior of Chinese Urban Households During 1981–1987," *Journal of Comparative Economics,* 16, 1 (March 1992), 1–26.

Wang, Yan, and Vinod Thomas, "Market Supplanting versus Market Fostering Interventions: China, East Asia and Other Developing Countries," *China Economic Review,* 4, 2 (1993), 243–258.

Wedeman, Andrew H., "Editor's Introduction," *Chinese Economic Studies,* 26, 5 (Fall 1993), 3–7.

Woo, Wing Thye, Gang Fan, Wen Hai, and Yibiao Jin, "The Efficiency and Macroeconomic Consequences of Chinese Enterprise Reform," *China Economic Review,* 4, 2 (1993), 153–168.

Wood, Adrian, "Joint Stock Companies with Rearranged Public Ownership: What Can We Learn from Recent Chinese and East European Experience with State Enterprises?" *China Economic Review,* 4, 2 (1993), 181–193.

Xue Muqiao, ed., *Almanac of China's Economy 1981.* New York: Eurasia Press, 1982.

Yeh, K. C., "Macroeconomic Issues in China in the 1990s," *The China Quarterly,* 131 (September 1992), 501–544.

19

SUMMARY AND CONCLUSIONS: LESSONS FROM AN EVOLUTIONARY-INSTITUTIONAL ANALYSIS OF ECONOMIES

INTRODUCTION

A stone taken from another mountain can be used to sharpen tools.[1]

The first chapter introduced a hypothetical committee established to select essential elements for transforming the economy of a Central American nation whose performance was unsatisfactory and whose political regime had been deposed. The following questions were posed:

1. What should be the philosophical basis upon which the new economy will be based?
2. What institutions and corresponding working rules should be adopted for production and distribution activities so that a favorable performance is achieved?

Subsequent chapters analyzed actual economies from an evolutionary-institutional perspective. While the development experience of each economy was characterized by unique features, some common features can be identified. Taken together, these features provide lessons, and thereby a basis for answering the preceding questions.

---

[1]Tzong-shian Yu, "The Price Paid for Accelerating Economic Growth—The Case of Taiwan," *China Economic Review,* 4, 2 (1993), 261. This Chinese saying means that the lessons which can be observed through the experience of others is important.

574

THE EVOLUTIONARY-INSTITUTIONAL
NATURE OF ECONOMIES RESTATED

The previous examples of actual experiences demonstrated that economies are characterized by an ongoing process of institutional change. Authorities respond to fluid informal rules by modifying, replacing, or introducing new institutions and corresponding formal working rules. These rules define the economy's legal structure and delimit "who is able to define the terms under which commodity transactions will occur."[2] In turn, the informal rules generally are influenced by a new technology or by the economy's performance—particularly if society's goals as reflected in the philosophical basis in the form of some ethical consensus are not satisfied. Institutions and attitudes are not exogenous factors nor do they remain static. They are an evolutionary "changing configuration" which is endogenous to the economy.[3]

The broad, interdisciplinary analyses of economies presented in earlier chapters identify tendencies and indicate possible directions toward which the economy in question may evolve. The evolutionary-institutional theory holds that it is not possible to reach determinate conclusions regarding an economy's behavior or anticipated performance. Some macroeconomic models based almost exclusively on formal mathematical equations purport to identify a precise development path for an economy under a particular policy while assuming a particular set of institutions. However, experience indicates that such models have failed to predict the behavior of an economy consistently or with any degree of precision. The models tend to be based upon simplistic assumptions—including the belief that "human beings behave as uniformly as hydrogen molecules."[4] They focus on quantifiable economic variables—with "free market economy" institutions and philosophy assumed given—in the name of scientific precision. Among the significant nonquantifiable factors formal economic models fail to account for are a nation's historical legacy, informal rules regarding economic activity, and shifting political structure. That exogenous factors (e.g., a rapid decrease in the value of a nation's currency such as the Mexican peso, or the earthquake in Kobe, Japan—both in early 1995) are inevitable is omitted by these models as well. However, all of these factors and other noneconomic variables continually affect an economy's performance.

[2]Daniel Bromley, "Reconstituting Economic Systems: Institutions in National Economic Development," *Development Policy Review,* 11 (1993), 134.

[3]T. Y. Shen, "An Institution for Entrepreneurship in Chinese Economic Reform," *The Journal of Socio-Economics,* 23, 3 (Fall 1994), 303.

[4]Jude Wanniski, "Macroeconomics: The Enemy Within," *The Wall Street Journal,* June 27, 1991, p. A14. He argues that "[t]he economics curriculum has become as mathematical as the physics department [and that t]he further away economics strays from reality, the better it can be sold as 'scientifically precise.'"

HISTORICAL LEGACY: LEARNING
FROM THE PAST TO UNDERSTAND
THE PRESENT ECONOMY AND TO
AVOID POLICY MISTAKES
FOR THE FUTURE

Each economy analyzed revealed that there were unique historical and exogenous factors that influenced its evolution, behavior, and performance. Therefore, a comprehensive understanding of a nation's historical legacy is essential before a philosophical basis and working rules consistent with that philosophy should be proposed. State guidance was acceptable to the French after World War II partly because of their favorable experience with this process for coordinating economic activity. The distribution of income according to the outcome of production through unregulated markets was favored by the English in the 1830s, but was not acceptable to the Swedes a century later.

The Japanese economy, while rooted in a philosophy and working rules consistent with those of a guided market economy, is heavily influenced by the Japanese culture and the Japanese-style of economic management. The same can be said for France. China's fear of foreign influence contributed to its choosing to develop unique, hybrid principal institutions (such as the township-village enterprises which have had a favorable impact on the nation's rapid economic growth and transformation) in lieu of foreign market-oriented institutions.

Ignoring the importance of historical legacy and not studying the lessons provided by different economies' development experiences can have undesirable consequences. For example, the absence of an historical perspective contributed to some policymakers believing that a relatively simple recipe for transforming Central and Eastern European (CEE) economies could be implemented and yield favorable results within a short period of time. However, throughout most of the CEE region "substantial retrogression . . . occurred after the first momentous changes promised a more rewarding outcome. [At that time analysts realized that t]he transition tasks ahead therefore remain utterly daunting in more than a trivial sense."[5]

PHILOSOPHICAL BASIS: THE NEED
TO UNDERSTAND SOCIETAL VALUES
AND IDENTIFY THE CONSENSUS VIEW

We must start [analysis of an economy] with some sense of an ethical consensus . . . across the polity. This then leads to some sense of the purposes of the state and therefore its pertinent policy interests. One then

---

[5]Jozef M. Van Brabant, "Lessons from the Wholesale Transformations in the East," *Comparative Economic Studies*, 35, 4 (Winter 1993), 84.

gets what we may call operating institutions—rules—that will frame individual domains of choice.[6]

A philosophical basis with a corresponding political structure, principal institutions, and working rules that are consistent and acceptable to a majority of the population is essential for an economy to perform favorably over an extended period. Such a philosophical basis is woven into the fabric of a nation's tradition, as in the English and Swedish examples. The nineteenth-century English society accepted rules which rewarded people according to their market-determined contributions, while the Swedes strongly preferred a more egalitarian redistribution process featuring broad social insurance and welfare programs. In the case of medieval England, there was clarity of the philosophical basis due to widespread acceptance of the teachings of the Church and views of the monarch regarding rules coordinating economic activity.

The major economic philosophers, Adam Smith, John Stuart Mill, Karl Marx, and John Maynard Keynes were influential because their philosophy was acceptable to authorities (and many of their fellow citizens) who believed the working rules were appropriate for the prevailing economic and political conditions. Keynes's views in particular were adopted sooner after he proposed them than were those of the other philosophers because of the negative economic performance experienced by many economies during the 1930s. The acceptance of Adolph Hitler's leadership principle was consistent with the perceived needs of Germany during this same period.

On the other hand, the attempt to develop the Chinese economy through the Great Leap Forward, when the nation was not prepared for such a radical departure from the prevailing philosophy and working rules, has been recognized as a disastrous policy in terms of economic performance. Since the death of Mao, the Chinese authorities recognized the dynamic, complex nature of transforming an economy and chose not to rely upon any philosophical basis common to other nations. Instead, they developed their own pragmatic, experimental, "crossing the river by feeling the stones" approach that has generated favorable performance since the late 1970s. This "determined pragmatism"[7] approach differs markedly from that taken in most CEE nations where ideological positions of policymakers led to an abstract model of a "free market economy" being proposed for economies unprepared for such a dramatic transformation.

In the case of Japan, an abrupt change in the philosophical basis in 1946 was accepted by the population. This was partly because the working rules permitted the social structure, which is based upon Confucian philosophy, to remain relatively intact. An advantage for Japan, as well as Sweden, China, and to a lesser extent France, is that in nations with a relatively homogeneous culture and unified sense of national purpose, harmony between the goal of policymakers and

---

[6]Bromley, "Reconstituting Economic Systems: Institutions in National Economic Development," p. 136.
[7]Van Brabant, "Lessons from the Wholesale Transformations in the East," p. 98.

the performance of the economy is much more easily achieved than in more heterogeneous societies (e.g., the former Soviet Union).

SOCIAL STRUCTURE:
A WIDENING GAP CREATES
SOCIAL AND POLITICAL UNREST

The many contemporary reformers (e.g., the Blue Ribbon Commission which proposed reforms for Hungary) who were quick to suggest unregulated markets as *the* alternative for CEE economies ignored some essential lessons of history. Many would agree that an economy in which unregulated markets are dominant permits individuals to improve their material standard of living through hard, enterprising effort. However, others recognize that such sudden changes in the social structure and the long-standing philosophical basis stimulate serious resistance from citizens in nations where dramatic changes in principal institutions and working rules were introduced. Such was the case throughout CEE, especially in response to increased poverty levels and a more skewed distribution of income. The double movement discussed in Chapter 6 addressed this matter, and the absence of laissez-faire market economies among contemporary major nations illustrates that throughout history economies whose main social process has been unregulated markets are the exception, not the rule.

It is noteworthy that in all societies in which markets are an important social process for coordination, the public demands measures to protect themselves from market forces (e.g., social insurance and welfare schemes, tariffs and quotas, subsidies). In some cases it is a form of rent-seeking behavior, in others a matter of preserving material standard of living and position within the social structure. The recommendation that state-owned enterprises be privatized or permitted to go bankrupt is sound from an economic efficiency viewpoint, but must account for the inevitable public backlash from those who expect lifetime employment security and suddenly find themselves unemployed. This is one reason that Chinese reformers have chosen a gradual reform process away from state ownership and control so as to lessen the hardships endured by those who lose their jobs— focusing on developing the semiprivate and private sector instead.

Another lesson that has been ignored since 1989 is that throughout history few economies have made a relatively painless transition (i.e., without altering the social structure while adversely affecting a large proportion of society) to an alternative economy unless they received considerable outside assistance (e.g., Japan, aided by the United States after World War II). Even with that assistance it was decades before a majority of the Japanese people realized a higher material standard of living. As with their rapidly growing East Asian neighbors, Japan's economic performance included egalitarian growth with nearly all segments of society benefiting. This has had the effect of maintaining social stability, and in the process has promoted political stability as well.

POLITICAL STRUCTURE: IS DEMOCRACY A PREREQUISITE FOR SUCCESSFUL PERFORMANCE BY AN ECONOMY?

A stable political structure is important as the primary means to unify a nation and to provide leadership in which citizens have faith. A lesson from CEE is that transformation measures may have been more effective if the political structure featured a political party to which an overwhelming majority of authorities belonged and which a majority of citizens recognized as legitimate. Willingness to abide by the rules and accept some hardships of a transformation program will not occur without faith in central authorities. The absence of such faith facilitates moral decay and illegal activities becoming widespread (e.g., public corruption, black market activities). Public discontent with the new authorities also has resulted in the election of parties led by former Communist Party officials in about 90 percent of the CEE nations.

In establishing and interpreting working rules, authorities play the key role in any economy that is not heavily dependent on unregulated markets. Honest, efficient, and knowledgeable policymakers can introduce institutions and rules that propel an economy's development, as have the Japanese, French, and Swedish authorities. A democratic political structure is not, however, always necessary for either market-oriented institutions and rules to dominate the economy or for a favorable economic performance. This has been demonstrated by some East Asian nations. They lack "pluralistic political decision making,"[8] but have adopted many market-oriented features while achieving very favorable levels of economic growth and, in the process, improving the well-being of the poorest segments of their societies.

On the other hand, when authorities have a monopoly over political power as well as over the information received by the general public, the potential for adverse effects upon the economy's performance is increased. Poor performances can be ignored while policies designed to perpetuate the same authorities' hold on power are introduced. Such was the case throughout CEE prior to the late 1980s and China until the late 1970s. One particular problem faced by these economies was the incompatibility of market reforms with political structures whose authorities have a strong propensity to control economic activity. As a result, reforms designed to decentralize decision making and control were ineffective as some form of indirect bureaucratic control (and perhaps corruption) replaced central control. The experience of Hungary illustrates the extremely close link between the political structure, reforms, and the economy's performance. Due to the unwillingness of Communist Party authorities to relinquish control over the economy, reforms introduced prior to 1989 were piecemeal, and indirect

[8]Ibid., p. 101.

control replaced direct control. The bureaucratization of economic life continued, and ultimately the unfavorable performance of the economy led to the downfall of the Communist Party and the emergence of a new political structure.

PRINCIPAL INSTITUTIONS AND
THEIR WORKING RULES

> The problem in economic development "is not one of getting prices right. Rather, the problem is to get the [institutions and their] rules right."[9]

Institutions and corresponding working rules, both of which are fluid and endogenous, reflect the philosophical basis of an economy and its performance, for better or worse. China's hybrid institutions such as the township and village enterprises evolved from a pragmatic view toward rural reform. They were able to overcome the constraints on their evolution posed by the "entrenched party-government hierarchy," and were encouraged to expand after the initial experiments establishing these enterprises were deemed successful.[10]

The institutions adopted by Germany in the 1930s were consistent with Adolph Hitler's "leadership principle," with highly centralized decision making and control over economic activity. When reforms were introduced in China and throughout CEE prior to 1989, while principal institutions remained unchanged and political whims dictated resource allocation decisions, the effect of the reforms upon the economy's performance were negligible, if not negative. The evolution of radically different principal institutions in these same nations has contributed to considerable transformation of the economies, albeit with different degrees of favorable performance.

INSTITUTIONAL CHANGE:
THE OUTCOME OF AN
EVOLUTIONARY PROCESS

Since 1989 many economies have been undergoing radical transformation. These economies include not only those in CEE and China, but the European Union with the enlargement to 15 nations, with at least six other nations waiting to join. While the extent and pace of such reform are unlikely to be duplicated in the near future, the continual evolution of economies is to be expected—through an ongoing process of modification (or replacement) of existing principal institutions and the emergence of new principal institutions—with their corresponding working rules.

[9]Bromley, "Reconstituting Economic Systems: Institutions in National Economic Development," p. 150.
[10]Shen, "An Institution for Entrepreneurship in Chinese Economic Reform," p. 306.

The examples included in previous chapters illustrate that whether such change is gradual or dramatic depends upon the nature of the political structure and the performance of the economy in question. Evolution, however, is certain since an economy at any point in time that is experiencing favorable performance will not be able to maintain that performance indefinitely by relying upon the same principal institutions and working rules. Change likely will become more frequent as linkages between nations (particularly regional trading blocs) deepen and new nations join existing organizations (such as CEE nations becoming European Union members)—thereby forcing all members to adapt to new competitive pressures.

BEHAVIOR AND PERFORMANCE OF THE ECONOMY

> When evaluating how an economy's performance influences the well-being of society's members, "[m]uch depends on the indicator[s] used to measure their welfare."[11]

Behavior and performance are linked together. The ultimate concern of political authorities and economic policymakers, besides maintaining their positions within the social and political structure, is to establish institutions and working rules which improve performance. A number of points are indicated by the examples included in the previous chapters.

One is that similar working rules have coincided with divergent results in different economies. Private or state commitments to provide employment security do not seem to have had the same detrimental effect in Japan or Sweden as they did pre-1989 CEE or as they continue to have in China's state-owned industrial enterprises. Whereas income redistribution and employment security did not appear to hinder Sweden's economic performance (until recently), such has not been the case in economies where bankruptcy of losing enterprises and layoffs were not permitted (or are "permitted," depending upon which working rules are ignored). In the case of Japan, such security may have contributed to improved labor productivity. Analysis indicates that for the seven "Asian Tigers" (Hong Kong, Indonesia, Malaysia, Singapore, South Korea, Taiwan, and Thailand) and Japan, all of which have experienced rapid improvement in many performance indicators since 1965, there is no single model and set of policies which contributed to their success. Rather, these countries "pursued a diverse mix of policies with varying degrees of intervention."[12]

Another point concerns state ownership, control, and guidance. Nationalization of industries and a high degree of government spending as a

---

[11]"How Poor are the Poor?" *The Economist,* October 1, 1994, p. 106.
[12]"Economic Miracle or Myth?" *The Economist,* October 2, 1993, pp. 41–42.

percentage of gross national product were consistent with favorable economic performance in France, but were inconsistent with favorable economic performance throughout CEE in the 1970s and 1980s. There are many examples where active state guidance has received credit for stimulating the economy's performance. Such was the case in Germany in the early 1930s, France and Japan after World War II, Sweden throughout the 1932–1990 period, and the "Asian Tigers" since the mid-1960s. The Asian nations all engaged in state intervention in the form of export promotion, direct credit guarantees, subsidies, barriers protecting domestic industry, and high levels of investment in primary and secondary education.[13] As with other economies which have developed rapidly, Asian states have provided adequate infrastructure and established conditions for domestic and foreign investment. Some pursued active industrial policies, albeit with less success.

As discussed in Chapter 2, the term *success* applied to an economy's performance should be used cautiously. The relative success or failure of different economies in generating progress for their citizens is subject to the values of an analyst (including a definition of *success* or *favorable development*). For example, different conclusions can be drawn regarding the performance of Latin American and sub-Sahara African nations since the mid-1970s. Standard indicators of performance indicate that people in most of these nations are worse off. However, if social indicators such as average life expectancy and the incidence of literacy, infant mortality, and malnutrition are included in the measure of performance most people in those nations may be better off today.

CONCLUDING REMARKS— TRANSFORMING AN ECONOMY

> Finally, there are transformations that cannot be accomplished quickly. Examples are privatization [and] restructuring the state-owned enterprises . . . Most advocates of shock therapy appear to believe that a radical transformation in attitudes, expectations, and behavior in economic agents can conceivably be accomplished in a comparatively brief period of time. Neither logic nor history favors such a thesis![14]

There is no recipe in the form of an answer or set of answers that will guarantee that a new economy will perform successfully. There is no "correct" economy for all societies, arguments by diehard advocates of free market economies/capitalism, communism, or other "isms" notwithstanding. Favorable and poor performance

---

[13]Those seeking to identify factors contributing to the Asian economies' performance should note that the economic environment these nations faced was characterized by relatively stable currencies; worldwide promotion of freer trade, investment, and migration; and political stability.

[14]Van Brabant, "Lessons from the Wholesale Transformations in the East," p. 81.

have been realized by the same types of economies, while different nations have realized favorable economic performance under completely different economies. Although the laissez-faire market economy may have been efficacious in the late nineteenth and early twentieth centuries, all Western nations decided to abandon this economy by the mid-1930s.

There are common institutions and working rules present in nearly every twentieth-century economy that has experienced above-average rates of economic growth, modest inflation, and unemployment, while witnessing improved material standards of living for nearly all segments of their respective societies. These include the presence of effective competition both domestically and internationally; the ability to enforce the economy's working rules; sound fiscal and monetary policy; high levels of savings and investment; ability and willingness to absorb foreign investment and technology; and a willingness of political authorities to experiment with and adapt new working rules for institutions.[15] Nearly all of these features are found in economies which differ in terms of their political structure, historical legacy, culture, and philosophy toward the economy.

The examples of actual economies have illustrated how economies change over time in response to changing performance indicators and exogenous events (e.g., Hungary in 1989). Therefore, reformers should expect that the economy they introduce eventually will be modified and perhaps replaced. A changing world environment affects the range of options open to reformers. As natural environmental concerns increase in importance and working rules with a global impact are introduced by supranational bodies, constraints on economic growth will be introduced. This has implications for unregulated markets (remember that Adam Smith's model of a market economy was a growth model) due to the problem of external costs (e.g., pollution) imposed by industrial production.

Another point to remember is that there is a cost borne by most citizens any time an economy undergoes reforms or is replaced, as demonstrated in Chapter 16. The process generally begins with political reform and new working rules, and affects the social structure as well as the performance of the economy. This was illustrated vividly by the reforms introduced in the Soviet Union by Stalin in 1928. This concern, as well as some similarities in philosophical basis, has induced some CEE reformers (especially those in Poland and Hungary during the mid-1990s) to seek to learn from the Scandinavian democratically controlled social economies for guidance as they seek to reform their economies. The appeal of relative freedom for producers with a strong role played by the state in redistributing benefits (so as to protect citizens from economic forces beyond their control) is gaining strength.

---

[15]For further discussion, see Tony Killick, "East Asian Miracles and Development Ideology," *Development Policy Review,* 12 (1994), 69–79; and Lawrence J. Lau, *Executive Summary—Models of Development: A Comparative Study of Economic Growth in South Korea and Taiwan* (San Francisco: ICS Press, 1990).

As a closing comment, while your committee proposes a philosophical basis, principal institutions, and working rules that are consistent with the Latin American nation's historical legacy and context, bear in mind that these institutions and rules are likely to evolve in an unknown direction depending upon the influence of the economy's performance (as well as exogenous factors initiated by other economies or by nature) on the authorities who ultimately establish and interpret an economy's working rules.

REFERENCES

Bromley, Daniel W., "Reconstituting Economic Systems: Institutions in National Economic Development," *Development Policy Review,* 11 (1993), 131–151.

"Economic Miracle or Myth?" *The Economist,* October 2, 1993, pp. 41–42.

"How Poor are the Poor?" *The Economist,* October 1, 1994, p. 106.

Killick, Tony, "East Asian Miracles and Development Ideology," *Development Policy Review,* 12 (1994), 69–79.

Lau, Lawrence J., *Executive Summary—Models of Development: A Comparative Study of Economic Growth in South Korea and Taiwan.* San Francisco: ICS Press, 1990.

Pedersen, Ove, "Private Property Reforms in West and East," *The Journal of Socio-Economics,* 22, 1 (Spring 1993), 395–415.

Shen, T. Y., "An Institution for Entrepreneurship in Chinese Economic Reform," *The Journal of Socio-Economics,* 23, 3 (Fall 1994), 303–320.

"Treating with Tigers," *The Economist,* April 16, 1994, pp. 21–22.

Van Brabant, Jozef M., "Lessons from the Wholesale Transformations in the East," *Comparative Economic Studies,* 35, 4 (Winter 1993), 73–102.

Wanniski, Jude, "Macroeconomics: The Enemy Within," *The Wall Street Journal,* June 27, 1991, p. A14.

Yu, Tzong-shian, "The Price Paid for Accelerating Economic Growth—The Case of Taiwan," *China Economic Review,* 4, 2 (1993), 259–265.

GLOSSARY OF KEY TERMS
AND CONCEPTS

Alienation	A Marxian term for the condition resulting from capitalism due to class conflict between the property-owning (bourgeoisie) and working (proletariat) classes.
Associate Member of the European Union	Status offered Hungary and other CEE nations by the EU. Associate members are offered more favorable terms concerning exporting to and investing in the EU than nonmember nations.
Barter	Moneyless market exchange where the goods or services traded are considered to be of equal value by those engaged in the exchange.
Biased Conclusions	Outcome resulting from analysis which is systematically twisted in the one direction best fitting the analyst's purposes of rationalizing a particular view.
Capitalism	Marx's description of England's industrial, laissez-faire market economy (LFME) in the early nineteenth century. This economy was characterized by a highly concentrated ownership and control of productive resources by a small bourgeoisie class.
Central Planning	The major social process for economic coordination adopted throughout Central and Eastern Europe prior to 1989 under which most production and distribution activities were guided by central authorities' preferences.
Church	The Catholic Church, significant for its basic tenets of the medieval period—especially as they pertained to the philosophical basis for economic activity.
Collective Wage Bargaining	Swedish practice prior to the 1990s involving leaders from each of the three major trade union confederations bargaining with leaders of the employer's confederation to establish wage rates for comparable work on a national basis.

585

Common Agricultural Policy	A European Union (EU) measure under which the supranational institutions of the EU make major price and production decisions for many agricultural products produced in member nations.
Conceptualized Reality	A philosopher's conception of history, human behavior, and the economic order (principal institutions, working rules, and behavior of the economy).
Confucian Beliefs	The teachings which provide the basis for the informal rules regarding the Japanese ethic toward social, political, and economic behavior, especially before 1946.
Contract Management Responsibility System	A reform introduced in China in the late 1970s. It permitted most state-owned enterprises to retain a higher percentage of profits than previously permitted, and allowed managers to make decisions pertaining to the investment of profits, purchase of goods that could be consumed collectively, or awarding of bonuses to workers.
Cooperatives	An institution (quite prevalent in Sweden) that is organized on the basis of joint action and self-help. Cooperatives typically feature open membership, no political affiliation, and one member/one vote.
Corn Laws	Late eighteenth- and nineteenth- century trade restrictions (sliding tariffs) in England which regulated the price of corn (i.e., wheat) so as to maintain a minimum price for domestically produced grain.
Corporative State	The German authorities' organization of society during the 1930s. This organization was hierarchical, with the elite at the pinnacle, with a system of corporations established to control most economic activities.
Corporatization	This is a process being adopted throughout CEE which converts state-owned enterprises into joint-stock companies owned by the state, but with a management structure and working rules not unlike private corporations. This conversion is intended as an interim stage before the enterprise ownership and control can be transferred into private hands.
Crude Communism	A Marxian term (which he also referred to as socialism) for the stage of society that evolves after capitalism's demise.
Democratically Controlled Social Economy	A social economy that does not rely heavily on laissez-faire policies for coordinating economic activity. Instead there is a preference for collective control with authorities introducing working rules intended to complement market forces and protect society from the adverse effects of such forces.
Double Bluff	According to Keynes's interpretation of history, this was the basis for a large share of income generated to be retained by the capitalist class, who were supposed to reinvest most of it in capital equipment—with the laboring class accepting a modest return for their efforts.
Double Movement	The conflict between the desire of English authorities in the mid-nineteenth century to introduce the working rules of an LFME and people seeking working rules which protected them from adverse effects of unregulated market forces.

Economic Base	A Marxian term for the forces of production (main instruments of production) and relations of production (social and working relations between people) in an economy. The economic base and superstructure are essential component's of the Marxian conception of an economy.
Economic Integration	Process whereby participating economies merge economic and political rules and decision-making institutions into one of a number of forms (e.g., free trade area, common market), depending upon the degree of integration desired.
Economic Planning	Activities by state authorities to modify, control, or supplement unregulated market activity.
Economy	An instituted process composed of the aggregate of institutions which perform economic functions and determine economic conditions. These institutions behave according to working rules.
Economy's Performance	This can be defined in many ways, depending upon the performance criteria selected, methods of measurement, and weights attached to each criterion when overall performance (in the form of an index) is calculated. It is an analyst's evaluation of the degree to which an economy satisfies a society's wants and needs.
Enclosure Movement	The enclosure of land which had been small, scattered plots previously farmed by tenant farmers into larger units, normally enclosed by hedges or ditches in response to greater commercialization of agriculture.
European Coal and Steel Community	Multinational organization formed in 1951 by six nations with the objective of ensuring efficient output and distribution of coal and steel through coordination from supranational institutions comprised of authorities from each member nation.
European Community	As of 1992, the 12 European nations striving to establish a common market level of integration. Due to the decision to strive toward establishing an economic and monetary union level of integration, it is now referred to as the European Union.
European Currency Unit	The ECU serves as the numeraire for EU financial statements and the exchange-rate mechanism applicable to member nations, as well as the denominator for credit operations and the unit for settling accounts between member nations' monetary authorities.
European Monetary System	Established by the European Community in 1979 as an exchange-rate mechanism. Its main objectives have been to minimize exchange-rate instability, fight inflation, and provide closer monetary cooperation among member nations.
European Union	Name given to the European Community after the early 1990s' commitment to work towards establishing the economic and monetary union level of integration.
Exploitation	A Marxian term describing the condition under which laborers did not receive the full value of what they produce, the surplus being retained by the property owner.
Factory	One of the principal institutions in nineteenth-century England, characterized by heavy machinery and equipment and poor working conditions.

Feudal Attitudes	Medieval informal rules regarding economic behavior, especially the belief that the social and political structure should be strict, rigid, and shaped like a pyramid with many peasants supporting a few nobles and clergy.
Feudal Order	Social structure which characterized medieval England and pre-World War II Japan. Society was divided into strata of differing status and authority, with respect for authority expected of everyone.
Folkhem	In Swedish this means "people's home." It was a slogan which contains the Swedish ideal of equality, embodying the belief that all citizens should be treated equally as if they were part of one family.
Free Market Economy	Idealized, textbook version of an LFME advocated for the transforming CEE nations by their authorities and Western advisors.
Freer Trade	Condition where trade among nations is subject to fewer trade restrictions than generally exist.
Free Trade	Condition where trade among nations would not be subject to any tariffs, quotas, or other restrictions. Such a situation has almost never occurred.
Gini Coefficient	A Gini coefficient is the ratio of the area between the Lorenz curve and the line of equality to the entire area under the line of equality. It ranges in value from slightly greater than 0 to 1.0.
Gold Standard	An international monetary mechanism established to automatically coordinate international trade and finance transactions among nations in response to trade deficits or trade surpluses. Two features of this standard were that the currency of each member nation was fixed relative to a certain quantity of gold, and a nation's money supply was directly related to the quantity of gold in that country.
Gosplan	The state planning commission in the former Soviet Union which was responsible for formulating a plan capable of satisfying the goals and priorities established by leading Communist Party authorities.
Grain Dole	A redistribution scheme established by Roman authorities which required state-funded acquisition, transport and storage, and distribution of grain to urban citizens and members of the army.
Great Industrialization Debate	A debate which began in the former Soviet Union in 1924, focusing on what type of political structure, principal institutions, and working rules the nation should adopt to promote economic development.
Guild	A medieval association of skilled members of the same occupation (e.g., weavers), all subject to similar working rules.
Historical Legacy	An economy's institutions and economic, political, and social conditions at the beginning of the period being analyzed.

Household Responsibility System	Working rule introduced by Chinese authorities in 1983 to reform rules governing the people's communes. Control over income rights to the land shifted away from collective control to the individual household level. Peasants signed a contract to deliver a fixed quota of output to the state for a state-determined price, then were free to sell any surplus on the open market or to the state (for a higher price than paid for the quota).
Hungarian Democratic Forum	A new political party which emerged in Hungary after the 1989 revolution. The party received the most votes (42 percent) in the 1990 election.
Import Penetration	The size of the domestic market accounted for by foreign producers. Presence of tariff and nontariff barriers can inhibit foreign penetration, something Japan often is accused of doing.
Indicative Planning	A French brand of planning intended to complement market forces by influencing (to the extent possible) the macroeconomic and microeconomic environment and guiding the private sector. The goal is to facilitate more rational decision making among leaders of the private and public sectors in the interests of pursuing agreed-upon national goals.
Industrial Revolution	Beginning in the early to mid-eighteenth century in England, this revolution consisted of three interrelated revolutions: technological, social, and economic. Together they transformed England from an agrarian to the world's first industrialized society.
Institution	Normative patterns of social organization and behavior which define modes of action or social relationships that society believes are expected and proper in particular situations. The patterns of these and other institutions are regularized by common informal and formal working rules.
Involuntary Unemployment	A condition where the demand for labor is less than the supply of labor at a prevailing wage, so that some individuals willing to accept either the prevailing wage or less than this wage are unable to find employment.
Jamlikhet	A Swedish slogan signifying the ideal of social justice. It is the belief that incomes should be equalized to minimize the differential between groups within the social structure.
Joint Venture	An activity in which two or more firms (which may be from different nations) pool their funds and management expertise to purchase an existing firm or establish a new firm.
Keiretsu	A principal institution of the Japanese economy. It is a closely affiliated confederation of heterogeneous firms which combines vertical and horizontal integration while seeking benefits of specialization.
Keynesian Revolution	Mid-1930s period during which time the policy prescriptions contained in the philosophical basis of Keynes, proposed during a period of adverse economic performance, were implemented in many industrial economies.

Keynes's Model of an LFME	Behavioral assumptions and theories developed by Keynes to depict the behavior of an LFME. He used it to demonstrate that such an economy tended towards an equilibrium level of output in which high unemployment was likely.
Laissez-faire	This French terminology literally means "let people do what they want." It was coined by Adam Smith and represented his preferred social process for economic coordination of the LFME he advocated.
Leadership Principle	The elevation of the Nazi Party leader as the supreme authority of a glorious, strong, superior state with power to exert control over the economy.
Liquidity Trap	Keynes's scenario in which there were low interest rates and the demand to hold money became insensitive to changes in the money supply. If such a condition prevailed, monetary policy would become impotent for stimulating investment.
Lorenz Curve	A curve which plots the percentage of income received by specific segments of the population, such as each decile or quintile. It is plotted against a line of perfect equality whereby each segment would receive an equal proportion of income. For example, the upper 20 percent of the population would receive 20 percent of the income, and so on.
Maastricht Treaty	The treaty drafted in 1991 by the EU members that established the provisions for both an economic and monetary union (EMU) and a political union. The EMU treaty designated that there should be a common currency, a central bank (EuroFed), single monetary policy, close coordination of fiscal and monetary policies, prohibition of monetizing public deficits, and avoidance of large fiscal deficits for all members.
Macroeconomic Stabilization Policies	A set of macroeconomic policies recommended for CEE transformation in the early 1990s. They included strict monetary and fiscal policies, rapidly privatizing state property, eliminating subsidies to enterprises and households, reforming the tax system and rules for accounting, liberalizing prices, making the currency internally convertible while stabilizing the exchange rate, holding down wage increases, and opening up the domestic market by eliminating tariffs and subsidies.
Malthus's Population Theory	A theory which stated that the rate of population growth would exceed the rate of agricultural output. It was instrumental in the radical reform of England's Poor Laws in 1834.
Manor	The manor was the primary administrative and fiscal unit for the village. It held jurisdictional powers over nearly all property rights, resource allocation, and criminal matters.
Market Economy	This term is used synonymously with the laissez-faire market economy, the prime example of which evolved in England during the nineteenth century.
Means Test	A method of establishing if an individual meets the eligibility requirements for a social insurance or welfare program. In some countries no such tests are required, in the interests of a more cooperative, harmonious society.

Meidner Plan   A Swedish plan to gradually transfer ownership and control of the means of production to trade union workers, using some profits earned by the enterprise as well as some funds generated from a payroll tax.

Mercantile Policies   Policies introduced in sixteenth-century England (and in some other European nations) which gave the state an active role in regulating economic matters for the purpose of enhancing the monarch's wealth and power.

Ministry of International Trade and Industry   Japanese institution responsible for giving order and direction to the business community. Included among its methods are regulating production and distribution activities of manufacturers, and regulating foreign trade.

Monarch   The king or queen of England, powerful in economic affairs during the medieval and mercantile periods.

Nationalization   Process by which the state assumes control over what had been privately owned property. It is generally associated with the establishment of state-owned enterprises.

Negotiated Economy   An economy in which emphasis is placed upon developing social cooperation through gaining a consensus among the interest-group representatives of the main economic actors. The objective is to build consensus for economic policies and recognizing state involvement in the transformation—especially in regard to industrial policy. Some use this term to describe the Scandinavian economies, particularly Denmark.

New Economic Mechanism   A series of reform measures introduced by Hungarian authorities in 1968 designed to decentralize decision making, giving greater autonomy to enterprise managers regarding investment, production, and sales decisions.

New Economic Policy   Introduced in the former Soviet Union in 1921 under Vladimir Lenin to promote rapid industrialization. It permitted some unregulated market activity and private ownership, and the experience with this policy served as the basis for Stalin establishing central planning and strict state ownership and control over the economy.

Occupation Authority   Authorities representing the allied powers which governed Japan from 1946 to 1952. They were responsible for imposing institutional reform while democratizing the nation's political and economic institutions as well as demilitarizing the nation.

Patterned Pluralism   The process through which Japanese state authorities and private-sector leaders interact. It is a cooperative decision-making process with bureaucratic authorities coordinating the effort in the attempt to reach a consensus so that voluntary compliance by all parties will ensue.

Perestroika   Mikhail Gorbachev's slogan, introduced in 1985, for restructuring the Soviet economy.

Performance Criteria	Indicators such as economic growth, inflation, and poverty which, taken together, will comprise the analyst's definition of performance.
Performance Index	A value determined by adding the quantitative performance measure of each criterion weighted according to its relative importance.
Philosophical Basis	A viewpoint which specifies the place of an individual within society, an ideal state of political, social, and economic reality to serve as a set of ultimate goals for society, and a general program suggesting broad policy measures that will guide society from its actual conditions towards the ideal reality.
Poor Laws	Informal and formal rules prevailing from the early sixteenth to nineteenth centuries which governed income support and activities of England's impoverished citizens.
Pragmatic Reforms	Term used to describe the nonideological, experimental methods of transforming their economy introduced by Chinese authorities since 1976.
Preceptorial System	A mechanism for controlling the 1930s' German society, using education to mobilize support for goals and working rules determined by the leading Nazi Party authorities.
Premodern Economy	A general term for the hundreds of diverse economies that existed before the late eighteenth century.
Primacy of Politics	The view in Nazi Germany that working rules for the economy were secondary to political goals, and that the party leader could make all significant political and economic decisions.
Privatization	The process of changing property rights so that ownership and control over a resource or enterprise formerly owned and controlled by the state is transferred to private ownership and control.
Propensity to Consume	A behavioral assumption of Keynes which refers to the proportion of income spent on consumption.
Public Enterprises	Enterprises owned and controlled by the state. Also known as state-owned enterprises.
Religious Attitude	Philosophical bases of the Catholic Church and those of Martin Luther and John Calvin towards economic behavior and activity.
Restitution	In CEE the process of returning state-owned and controlled property (or giving a financial settlement) to previous owners from whom it had been confiscated or nationalized without payment.
Ricardo's Theory of Comparative Advantage	Theory which states that free trade between nations, with each nation specializing in the production of that good for which it has a comparative advantage, will lead to greater world output and lower prices than if barriers to trade are erected.

Ringi-sei Decision Making	Process used in Japan to achieve cooperation and persuasion. Continual consultation among members of a group occur until a consensus agreement is reached, with emphasis placed upon the best interest of the organization over that of an individual or one group.
Say's Law of Markets	To Jean Baptiste Say it meant that supply creates its own demand, which means that in an LFME, the process of production will create incomes sufficient to purchase all goods and services produced. As a result, that economy automatically would tend to a full-employment level of output.
Second Economy	The illegal economy, or black market, which serves as an alternative social process for coordinating production and distribution in many economies— particularly in Central and Eastern Europe.
Self-regulating Markets	A social process for coordinating production and distribution decisions in which prices are established by unregulated market forces, and production and distribution decisions are made by individual producers, consumers, and investors in response to changes in prices—with a minimum of state regulation.
Single European Act	Signed in 1986 by European Community members, amending the 1957 Treaty of Rome for the purpose of formally establishing the common market level of integration by 1992.
Smith's Laws of the Market	Four laws which identify the informal working rules of Adam Smith's LFME model.
Social and Political Structures	Identification of status and political ranks within an economy that explain which authorities have the power to establish and interpret the working rules.
Social Economy	In broad terms, an economy established by authorities so that a greater degree of control over economic activity will be exerted by social forces, usually through the political structure, rather than unregulated market forces being permitted to have extensve influence over economic activity.
Socialism	The tendency inherent in society to subordinate unregulated market forces so as to direct production and distribution to achieve results deemed in the best interest of society.
Socialist Party	The political party dominant in most CEE nations as of the mid-1990s. Many of its leaders were authorities in the pre-1989 Communist Party.
Sogo Shosha	The ten great trading companies responsible for transactions involving a majority of Japan's imports and exports.
Solidaristic Wage Policy	Swedish labor-management negotiation process under which wage restraint was exercised by labor, wage differentials narrowed by employers, and active labor market measures provided by the state to minimize unemployment.

Special Economic Zones	Geographical regions established by Chinese authorities on an experimental basis to attract foreign investment and technology. The working rules of these zones were considerably freer from authority control than rules pertaining to the rest of the economy.
State's Agenda	Keynes's policy prescriptions for alleviating the problems of an LFME included an expanded role for the state to guide economic activity.
State Guidance	State-directed measures to promote economic growth, reform, and coordinate economic activity.
State Intervention	Conscious efforts by state authorities to influence decision making, ownership and control, or coordination of production and distribution activities.
State Paternalism	Activities by the state to provide extensive social insurance and welfare benefits to all citizens, with a corresponding reduction in some personal freedom (e.g., due to high tax rates and extensive measures to redistribute income).
Superstructure	Marx's description for the system of education, literature, and property rights which bind together society's informal and formal working rules. Together, the economic base and superstructure are central to the Marxian conception of an economy.
Supranational Institutions	Institutions composed of authorities from many nations to which member nations have relinquished some of their national sovereignty.
Three-Tiered Pricing System	Remuneration scheme associated with the Chinese household responsibility system. It involves a modest fixed price paid by the state for the quota required, a higher price offered by the state for any surplus, and the option given to the peasant of selling the surplus either to the state or on an open market at the prevailing market price.
Town	In the medieval period towns were permanent settlements in which a large proportion of the population was occupied in nonagricultural pursuits. The town's social, political, and economic institutions and working rules were distinct from feudal institutions.
Township-Village Enterprises	Semiprivate, collectively owned and managed industrial enterprises that began to evolve throughout China in 1970. Many of them were funded by local government authorities. The enterprise is autonomous regarding production, distribution, and hiring decisions, and workers determine how income is to be distributed among themselves.
Trade Creation	Occurs after a trade agreement such as the formation of a customs union when an increased volume of imports from lower-cost member nations (or nations involved in the agreement) ensues.
Trade Diversion	Opposite of trade creation in that the trade agreement results in trade being diverted away from a lower-cost nation not a party to the agreement (or member of the customs union) to a higher-cost party or member nation.

Treadmill of Reforms Process common to pre-1989 CEE when modest reforms were introduced to improve economic performance through reduction of central control, followed by the reassertion of control by central authorities due to either fear of losing power or following the absence of noticeable improvement in the economy's performance.

Treaty of Rome Treaty signed in 1957 by the six original members of the European Coal and Steel Community establishing the European Economic Community, committing members to accept the working rules of a customs union.

True Communism Karl Marx's vision of the highest stage of society which would evolve after the demise of what he referred to as capitalism and crude communism. At this highest stage people's consciousnesses would be such that the prevailing informal working rule would be "from each according to [their] ability, to each according to [their] needs."

Uncivil Economy Unofficial economic activity within an economy characterized by smuggling, taking bribes, exchanging currency, and any other economic activity that is monetized and illegal.

Villeinage The servile, unfree status of medieval peasants, who generally are referred to as villeins or serfs.

Vision The ideal set of economic and social conditions an economic philosopher envisions for society.

Working Rules The economy is comprised of a number of interrelated institutions whose boundaries for permissible and forbidden activity are established by working rules.

Zaibatsu Large conglomerates which dominated the Japanese economy before 1946. They were owned and controlled by a single family.

INDEX

A

Act of Settlement (1662)   94
Agriculture:
   in ancient Rome,   45, 50, 51, 52
   in China,   529, 530, 532, 537, 538-39, 541-42,
      551-53
   in Hungary,   484, 486, 495-96, 497, 501, 503,
      506-7, 508, 519
   in medieval England, 64, 67-69, 70-72, 73-76,
      78-80, 82-84
   in Soviet Union,   401, 402, 403
      and collectivization,   404, 408, 412, 418, 421
Augustus, Caesar 42-44, 47, 55

B

Bank of Japan   170, 184
Behavior of the economy:
   in ancient Rome,   49-57
   in CEE,   448-63
   in China,   539-559
   components of,   17-18
   defined,   15, 16
   and economic transformation,   582-83
   in England (LFME),   119-23
   in European Union,   344-61
   in France,   245-54
   in Germany,   143-47
   in Hungary,   496-513
   in Japan,   197-212
   in medieval England,   72-80
   in Soviet Union,   408-13
   in Sweden,   297-314
Beveridge, William   261, 262, 273-76
   reforms proposed,   273-74
   vision,   274
Beveridge Report   263, 273-76
   impact of,   275-76
   reasons for establishment,   273-74
   reforms proposed,   274-75
Black market (*see* Second economy)
Brezhnev, Leonid,   414

C

CAP (*see* Common Agricultural Policy)
Capitalism (Marxian),   386-87, 389, 390-91
Cecchini Report (EU),   374
Central and East European transformation:
   in Bulgaria,   9, 26, 444, 453-55, 466-73
   consequences of policies,   466-73
   critique of policies,   473-76
   in Czech Republic,   444, 455-56, 466-73
   lessons from 1990-1994 experience,   434-39
   performance and policies—compared to China,
      566-68
   in Poland,   444, 456-57, 466-73
   policies,   458-63
   privatization,   451-57
      in Bulgaria,   453-55
      in Czech Republic,   455-56
      in Poland,   456-57
   social and uncivil economies,   447-48
Church (Catholic) in medieval England:
   and code of economic behavior,   63-65
   effect upon production and distribution,   80
Churchill, Winston,   331
Cicero,   44, 45
Civic patrimony, in ancient Rome   43-44
Collective enterprises, in China,   547

COMECON (see Council for Mutual Economic Assistance)
Common Agricultural Policy, in EU,   175, 244, 247, 335, 340, 346, 351-54, 358, 365
European Agricultural Guarantee and Guidance Fund,   353
Common external policy, in EU,   351
Communism, crude,   387, 394-96, 399, 400, 528
Communism, true,   386, 387, 389, 394, 396-97
Communist Party:
in China,   532, 535, 536, 537, 541, 544, 559
in Hungary,   485, 486, 487, 488, 492-93, 494, 514, 520, 521
in Soviet Union,   404, 405, 406, 407, 408, 409, 410, 416, 422, 425, 426
Competition policy, in EU, 354-56
Contract responsibility system, in China,   550
Cooperatives:
and DCSE philosophy,   262, 268
in Sweden,   282, 294, 295-97, 299, 302, 315
Corn Laws,   112, 113, 123
Council for Mutual Economic Assistance (COMECON),   433, 454, 506, 512, 520
Council of Europe (European Council),   246, 343, 345, 368-70
Council of Ministers, in EU,   332, 342-43, 363, 368-70
Court of Justice, in EU,   332, 339, 340, 343-44

D

Delors, Jacques,   337
Deng Xaioping,   398, 531, 535, 537, 541
Dodge, Joseph,   174, 208
Double bluff,   156, 157
Double movement,   338
in nineteenth-century England,   122-23, 128

E

Economic and Monetary Union (EMU),   334, 349-50, 363-64, 374, 376, 379
Economic growth (see Growth, economic)
Economic planning:
in China,   529-30, 532-34, 536, 537, 540-42, 550, 559
in France,   236, 237-38, 239, 244-45, 246, 251-52, 253, 254
in Hungary,   484, 485, 486, 487, 492, 493-95, 505-8
in Japan,   206-7
in Soviet Union,   403, 407, 409, 410-12, 415-16, 424, 425
Economic system (see Economy)
Economy:
definition of,   4, 5
modern,   39
performance of (see Performance of the economy)
premodern,   41

ECU (see European Currency Unit)
Enclosure movement,   90-91
effect of,   91
Engels, Friedrich,   386-87, 395, 397
Enlargement (EU),   333, 341, 362, 364-68, 376
and Hungary,   366-68, 509, 514
EU (see European Union)
European Atomic Energy Commission (Euratom),   330
European Bank for Reconstruction and Development (EBRD),   512
European Coal and Steel Community (ECSC),   239, 330, 332, 346, 358
European Commission,   8, 334, 340, 341, 342, 345, 354, 355, 359, 363, 369, 370
European Community (see European Union)
European Council (see Council of Europe)
European Currency Unit (ECU),   347-48
European Economic Community (EEC),   330, 333
European Free Trade Association (EFTA),   333, 378
European integration,   331
advantages of,   379-80
common market,   333, 351, 357, 358, 379
customs union,   333, 379, 380
Economic and Monetary Union (EMU),   334, 349, 350, 363-64, 376-77, 379
free trade area,   339, 378-79
European Monetary System (EMS),   334, 347-49, 374
European Fund for Monetary Cooperation, 347-48
"snake in the tunnel,"   347
European Parliament,   334, 340, 341, 342, 343, 369, 370
European Union (EU),   164, 325, 316-56
budget,   346-47
competition from Japan and U.S.A.,   371, 372
decision-making reform,   368-70
definition of,   330
and Hungary,   366-68, 509, 514
as an illustration of evolutionary-institutional theory,   19
Evaluating and comparing economies:
basic issues,   24-27
comparing economies,   32
criteria for,   28-30
evaluation procedure,   27-28
examples of,   32-36
and objectivity,   26-27
performance index, compilation of,   31-32
Evolutionary-institutional approach, five themes of,   7-11
Evolutionary-institutional framework:
outline of,   15-16
six interrelated factors,   13-16
Evolutionary-institutional theory:
alternative to orthodox approach,   12-14
in ancient Rome,   59

and CEE transformation, 476-77
in China, 568-69
contributions of, 11-12
in England (LFME), 128
in European Union, 19
and evolution of economies, 13, 14
in France, 257-58
in Germany, 151-52
in Hungary 520-21
in Japan, 228-29
main features, 7-15
in medieval England, 84-85
in Soviet Union, 425
in Sweden, 323-25
Exploitation of labor, and Karl Marx, 390-92

F

Fabian Society, 261, 262, 263, 270-73, 274,
    276, 335
  goals of, 271
  impact of, 272-73
  means for reform, 272
  philosophy of, 271
  reforms proposed, 271-72
Factory productivity:
  in China, 529-30, 561-64
  in England (LFME), 117
  in European Union, 371, 372
  in Germany, 150
  in Hungary, 515, 516
  in Soviet Union, 419, 421
Fiscal policy, 18
  in England (LFME), 121-22
  in European Union, 333-34, 336, 363-64, 376
  in Germany, 145-46
  in France, 244-45
  in Hungary, 472, 480
  in Japan, 174-75, 206-12
  in medieval England, 64
  in Sweden, 304-14
Formal working rules, as related to informal
    rules, 4, 5
Free trade policy, nineteenth-century debate,
    112-14

G

George, Henry 270
German unification, 362-63
Glasnost, 416
Gold standard, in nineteenth-century England,
    118, 121-22, 124
Gorbachev, Mikhail, 19, 398, 406, 416-18, 421-24,
    424, 426
Government expenditures, percentage of GDP:
  in France, 218, 294
  in Japan, 218, 294
  in Sweden, 218, 303, 319
  in United States, 218

Grain contracting system, in China, 551
Grain dole, in ancient Rome, 42, 55-56, 57
Great Industrialization Debate, 400, 401-3
Great Leap Forward, 429, 578
Great Proletarian Cultural Revolution, 529,
    530-31
Growth, economic:
  in ancient Rome, 58-59
  in China, 527, 529, 561-63, 566-68
  criterion for evaluating and comparing
    economies, 28-29
  in England (LFME), 125
  in European Union, 215, 217
  in France, 215, 217
  in Germany, 148, 149, 150
  in Hungary, 470, 473
  in Japan, 170, 171, 173, 210, 211, 212, 215-17,
    223, 281, 317, 371
  in medieval England, 83
  in OECD, 419
  in Soviet Union, 418-19, 421, 423
  in Sweden, 215, 217, 281, 282, 316, 318, 320, 322
  in United States, 215, 217, 281, 317, 371, 419
Guilds in medieval England:
  craft, 76-77, 78, 84
  merchant, 76, 78, 84

H

High Authority, in EU, 332
Historical legacy and context:
  in ancient Rome, 42-43
  in China, 527-30, 577
  defined, 14-15
  in England (LFME), 88-91, 111-12
  in European Union, 331-34
  in France, 234-36, 577
  in Germany, 132-35
  in Hungary, 484-87
  in Japan, 168-74, 577
  and lessons from analysis of economies, 577
  in medieval England, 62-63
  place within evolutionary-institutional theory,
    15
  as related to an economy, 13, 15
  in Soviet Union, 398-403
  in Sweden, 280-82
Hitler, Adolph, 135, 136, 137, 141, 142, 143, 145,
    147, 148, 151
Hong Kong, 25, 123, 209, 560
Household Responsibility System, in China,
    541, 551
Hua Gofeng, 530

I

Income distribution:
  in China, 529, 530, 565-66
  criterion for evaluating and comparing
    economies, 30-31

Income distribution (*cont.*)
  in England (LFME),   114, 127
  in France,   240-41, 258
  in Germany,   150
  in Hungary,   487, 518
  in Japan,   220, 222
  in Marx's evaluation of capitalism,   387, 390-91
  in Soviet Union,   405
  in Sweden,   280, 288-89
Indicative planning:
  in China,   533, 542
  and European Union,   357
  in France,   18, 233, 237-38, 244-45, 247, 251-53, 254
Industrial policy:
  in France,   251-53
  in Japan,   208-11, 224
  in Sweden,   312
Industrial Revolution:
  in England,   94-95
  in Japan,   171-72
  Marx's interpretation of,   389-90
  in Soviet Union,   399
  in Sweden,   281-82
Inflation:
  in China,   530, 561-63
  in England (LFME),   125
  in European Union,   216, 372
  in France,   216, 255
  in Germany,   133, 134, 149
  in Hungary,   506, 510-11, 512, 516-17
  in Japan,   173, 215-16
  in medieval England,   83
  in Soviet Union,   419, 422
  in Sweden,   216, 282, 318, 319
  in United States,   216
Informal rules, as related to formal working rules,   4, 5
Institution:
  characteristics of,   4, 5, 13
  defined,   3-5
  and working rules,   4, 5
Institutional change:
  in ancient Rome,   58
  in CEE,   463-64
  in China,   559-61
  defined,   16
  in England (LFME),   124
  in European Union,   362-68
  in France,   254-55
  in Germany,   151-52
  in Hungary,   513-15
  in Japan,   212-14
  in medieval England,   80-82
  as outcome of evolutionary process,   581-82
  place within evolutionary-institutional framework,   14, 16, 17, 18
  in Soviet Union,   413-16
  in Sweden,   314-15

Institutions, principal   (*see* Principal institutions)
International Monetary Fund (IMF),   9, 26, 436, 444, 448, 463, 489
Investment:
  in ancient Rome,   53
  in China,   530, 539, 548, 563-64
  in England (LFME),   121, 125
  in European Union,   217, 349, 351
  in France,   217, 235, 254
  in Germany,   149, 150
  in Hungary,   511, 512, 519
  in Japan,   208-9, 216-17, 223-24
  and Keynesian revolution,   155, 156, 157, 158, 159-62, 163-64
  in medieval England,   83
  in Soviet Union,   404, 407, 410-11, 414
  in Sweden,   217, 300-301
  in United States,   217

J

Japan,   172, 174-232
  attitudes toward big business,   172
  average life expectancy,   167, 219
  economy, state of in 1946,   172-74
  enterprise unions,   193
  as a feudal economy,   168-69
  industrial relations,   170-71, 194
  labor management relations,   176, 177, 214, 224-25
  lifetime employment practices,   173, 177
  modernization of,   169-72
  parliament (Diet),   179, 180, 181, 199, 200
  performance of economy:
    evaluation of,   32-36
    factors contributing to,   223-27
  seniority wage system,   173, 177
  trade policies,   176, 203, 208-9, 221
Just price doctrine,   65

K

Kadar, Janos,   486, 492, 507
Keiretsu,   185-87, 189-90, 194, 201, 205, 213, 228, 449
Keynes, John Maynard,   10, 105, 154, 155-64
  analytical framework,   159
  and Beveridge Report,   275
  career,   155-56
  conclusions and policy prescriptions,   163-64
  interpretation of history,   156-58
  model of LFME,   159-62
Kosygin, Alexei,   414, 415
Khrushchev, Nikita,   414

L

Labor:
  in England's LFME,   118-19, 124
  in medieval England,   74-77, 82-83

Labor (*cont.*)
    unit costs in manufacturing:
        in France,   218
        in Japan,   218
        in Sweden,   218
        in United States,   218
Labor market policies, in Sweden,   302-3, 306,
        308, 309-10, 311, 312-13
Labor Party, British,   269, 273, 276
Laissez-faire market economy (LFME):
    as a "market system,"   118-19
    and Protestant ethic,   91-93
Laissez-faire policies:
    in France,   234, 235
    in United States,   11
Land reform:
    in China,   528
    in Hungary,   484, 495-96
    in Japan,   174, 211-12, 219
    in Soviet Union,   399, 402, 403, 418
Leadership principle, in Germany,   139
Lenin, Vladimir,   398, 399-400, 401, 402, 527
LFME (*see* Laissez-fair market economy)
Liberal Democratic Party, in Japan,   179, 194
Liquidity trap,   161-62
List, Frederic,   175

M

Malthus, Thomas,   102-4, 112, 159, 267
    and Poor Laws,   104
    population theory,   102-4
Mao Tse Tung,   398, 526, 527, 528, 529, 530, 531
Markets:
    and premodern economies,   40
    unregulated trade:
        in ancient Rome,   52-53
        in England (LFME),   111-14, 118-19, 120,
            121, 125-26
        in France,   234-35, 251, 252
        in Germany,   145
        in Japan,   205
        in medieval England,   78-80, 81, 83
        in Sweden,   304, 305
Marx, Karl,   270, 291, 385-98, 399, 400, 403,
        404, 530
    and alienation of proletariat,   390-93
    conception of society,   387-88
    and DCSE philosophy,   261, 270
    and exploitation of proletariat,   390-91
    factors influencing philosophy,   385-87
    and medieval England,   82
    mission of,   386
    model of capitalism's demise,   390-94
    model of crude communism,   394-96
    theory of history,   388-90
    vision of true communism,   396-97
Meiji regime,   168, 169, 170
Mercantile era,   88-90

Mercantile policies:
    and Adam Smith,   97-98
    effect of,   90
    state regulation of economy,   88-89
Mercantilists,   234
Mill, John Stuart,   10, 261, 262, 266-69, 270, 274,
        277, 335, 578
    criticism of LFME,   267
    reforms proposed,   268-69
    vision,   267
Ministry of Finance, Japan,   180, 181, 182-83,
        199, 200, 206-7, 228
Ministry of International Trade and Industry
        (MITI), Japan,   180, 181, 183, 187, 194
Mitterand, Francois,   239, 241, 252, 254
Mixed economies, defined,   25
Mixed enterprises, in Hungary,   501
Mixed price mechanism, in Hungary,   508
Monetary policy:
    in ancient Rome,   57
    in China,   540
    in England (LFME),   121-22
    in European Union,   333, 338, 347-50, 375
    in France,   244
    in Japan,   174, 208
    in Keynes's model,   160, 161-62
    in medieval England,   64
Monetary Union (*see* Economic and Monetary
        Union)
Monnett, Jean,   237, 244, 335, 337, 341
Myrdal, Gunnar and Alva,   284, 285, 307

N

Nationalization;
    and a DCSE,   262, 268, 272
    in France,   238, 242, 243, 245, 246, 247-51
    in Sweden   307
National Socialist German Workers (Nazi) Party,
        · 134, 135, 136, 137, 138, 139, 140, 142, 147,
        148, 151, 152
New Economic Mechanism (NEM), in Hungary,
        486-87, 496, 500, 507-8
New economic policy:
    and scissors crisis,   401
    in Soviet Union,   14, 400-401, 402, 403
North American Free Trade Area (NAFTA),   378

O

Occupation Authority (Supreme Commander for
        the Allied Powers), in Japan,   174, 178-79,
        181, 183, 184-85, 194, 201-2, 208, 211, 212
Organization for Economic Cooperation and
        Development (OECD),   200, 202, 203,
        211, 222, 299-300, 303, 304, 313, 316,
        318, 321
Organization for Petroleum Exporting Countries
        (OPEC),   4

Organization of resource allocation decision
        making:
    alternatives for,   16, 17
    in ancient Rome,   49-50
    in CEE,   448-49
    in China,   540-42
    in England (LFME),   119-20
    in European Union,   345-50
    in France,   246
    in Germany,   143-44
    in Hungary,   496-99
    in Japan,   198-201
    in medieval England,   72-74
    in Soviet Union,   409
    in Sweden,   297-99
Owen, Robert,   261, 263-66, 268, 269, 274, 275
    criticism of LFME,   264
    impact of,   266
    philosophy,   263-65
    reforms proposed,   265-66
Ownershp and control of resources:
    alternatives for,   16, 18
    in ancient Rome,   50-52
    in CEE,   449-57
    in China,   542-49
    in England (LFME),   120
    in European Union,   351-57
    in France,   246-51
    in Germany,   144-45
    in Hungary,   499-505
    in Japan,   201-4
    in medieval England,   74-77
    in Soviet Union,   409-10
    in Sweden,   299-304

P

Peasant Revolt of 1381,   82
Peel's Act of 1844,   124, 128
People's Communes, in China,   529, 538-39, 541
Perestroika,   409, 416
Performance of the economy:
    in ancient Rome,   58-59
    in China,   561-68
    defined,   16, 17-19
    in England (LFME),   125-27
    in European Union,   368-75
    evaluation method,   27-32
    and evolutionary-institutional theory,   16,
        17-19
    and evolution of economies,   582
    factors influencing,   25
    in France,   255-57
    in Germany,   148-51
    in Hungary,   515-20
    in Japan,   215-27
    in medieval England,   82-83
    in Soviet Union,   418-24
        1928-1984,   418-20

        1985-1989,   421-24
    in Sweden,   316-23
Philosophical basis:
    in ancient Rome,   43-44
    in CEE,   440-42
    in China,   520-34
    for CSE,   385-98
    for DCSE,   261-77
    definition of,   6, 15-16
    in England (LFME),   112-14
    in European Union,   335-39
    in France,   236-39
    in Germany,   135-39
    for GME,   154-64
    in Hungary,   487-90
    in Japan,   174-76
    for LFME,   95-109
    in medieval England,   63-65
    as related to an economy,   10-11
    in Soviet Union,   403-4
    in Sweden,   282-87
Poor Law Reform Act (1834),   104, 112, 116, 118
Poor Laws,   93-94, 104-5
Pricing policy in China:
    dual-pricing scheme (two-tiered system),
        541, 544, 551-52, 555
    three-tiered system,   555
Principal institutions:
    in ancient Rome,   46-49
    in CEE,   445-48
    characteristics of,   5, 8-9, 13, 15, 17
    in China,   537-39
    in England's LFME,   116-19
    in European Union,   342-45
    and evolutionary-institutional theory,   11, 15
    in France,   243-45
    in Germany,   141-43
    in Hungary,   494-96
    in Japan,   180-93
    in medieval England,   69-72
    as related to an economy,   8, 9, 15
    in Soviet Union,   406-8
    in Sweden,   294-97
Privatization:
    in CEE,   449-57
    in France,   249-50
    in Hungary,   502-5
    in Soviet Union,   417-18

R

Redistribution schemes, in ancient Rome,   54-56
Regional policy (EU),   357
Religious attitude, change in,   91-93
    Protestant ethic,   93
    Protestant Reformation,   92
Ricardo, David,   95, 107-9, 112, 175, 267, 380
    and Corn Laws,   107-9
    and free trade theory,   107-109
Ringi-sei decision method (Japan),   178, 198, 237

S

Say, Jean Baptiste,   95, 102, 104-7
  and Keynesian philosophy,   156, 161
  law of markets,   104-7
  and macroeconomic stabilization policy,   104
Schuman, Robert,   332
Schumpeterian entrepreneurs,   235
Second economy (black market—uncivil
   economy):
  in CEE,   447, 471
  in Hungary,   494, 500, 501
  in Soviet Union,   410, 413
Shaw, George Bernard,   261-62, 270
Shock therapy,   458, 460-61
Single European Act of 1986,   334, 343, 345,
   358, 360
Slave labor, in ancient Rome,   47-48, 51, 58
Smith, Adam,   6, 10, 91, 95, 96-102
  conceptualized reality,   97-98
  and economic growth,   100-101
  model of an LFME economy,   98-102
  role of the state,   102
  vision,   96-97
Smoot-Hawley Tariff,   133
Social and political structures:
  in ancient Rome,   44-46
  in CEE,   443-48
  in China,   534-37
  defined,   15, 16
  in England (LFME),   114-16
  in European Union,   339-42
  and evolutionary-institutional theory,   16
  in France,   240-43
  in Germany,   139-41
  in Hungary,   490-94
  in Japan,   176-80
  in medieval England,   66-69
  as related to an economy,   15, 16
  in Soviet Union,   404-6
  in Sweden,   287-94
Social Democratic Party, in Sweden,   281, 283,
   284, 285, 286, 291, 292, 293, 305-18, 323, 324
Socialism, defined,   263
Socialist government, in France,   239, 243, 255,
   258
Social policy, in EU,   356-57
Social process for economic coordination:
  alternatives for,   16, 18
  in ancient Rome,   52-57
  in CEE,   458-63
  in China,   549-59
  in England (LFME),   120-23
  in European Union,   357-61
  in France,   251-54
  in Germany,   145-47
  in Hungary,   505-13
  in Japan,   204-12
  in medieval England,   77-80

  in Soviet Union,   410-13
  in Sweden,   304-14
SOEs (*see* State-owned enterprises)
Sogo Shosha,   191-92, 213
Solidaristic wage policy (Sweden),   298, 299,
   306, 308, 311, 312
Special economic zones, in China,   539, 547-48,
   557, 560, 561, 562, 569
Stalin, Joseph, and Stalinist principles,   398, 400,
   402, 403, 414, 425, 529
Standard of living:
  in CEE,   464, 473
  in China,   561, 565-56
  in England (LFME),   127
  in Japan,   219-23
  in Soviet Union,   423
State-owned enterprises (SOEs):
  in CEE,   446, 455, 456, 457, 459
  in China,   529, 538, 543, 545, 546, 548, 550,
   551, 553, 554, 556, 558, 559, 560, 563,
   567, 569
  in France,   243, 246-51, 252, 254-55,
   257-58, 437
  in Hungary,   495, 496, 497, 499-505, 513-14
  in Soviet Union,   407-8, 410, 417-18, 425
  in Sweden,   299-300
Statute of Artificers,   94
Stockholm school of economics,   307
Supranational institutions,   342-44
Supreme Commander for the Allied Powers
   (*see* Occupation Authority)
Swedish Employer's Confederation (SAF),   295

T

Taxes:
  in ancient Rome,   42-43, 49-50, 59
  Corn Laws,   107-9, 112, 113
  in England (LFME),   112, 114, 123
  in European Union,   346, 350, 353, 358, 359,
   360, 361
  in Germany,   133
  in Hungary,   463, 464, 465, 468, 473
  in Japan,   200, 202, 203, 211, 218
  in medieval England,   72, 73, 74, 75, 77, 81
  in mercantile era,   88-90
  in Sweden,   301, 303-4, 310, 311, 319, 320, 321,
   322, 324
Thatcher, Margaret, and EU,   334
Township and village enterprises (TVEs), China,
   528, 544, 546, 547, 549, 552, 557, 560, 569
Trade, state regulation of:
  in ancient Rome,   52, 53-56
  in China,   533, 556-57
  in England (LFME),   118-19
  in France,   234, 235, 236-39, 244-45, 247, 250-51
  in Germany,   134, 142-43, 144-47, 151-52
  in Hungary   484, 487-88, 505-8, 511
  in Japan,   168-69, 204-12

Trade, state regulation of (*cont.*)
  in medieval England,   77-78
  in Sweden,   280-81, 304-5
Trade creation, and EU,   333, 373, 380
Trade diversion, and EU,   380
Trade policy in EU,   356
Trade unions:
  and DCSE philosophy,   268
  in European Union,   339
  in France,   242
  in Germany,   138, 144
  in Sweden,   294-95, 306, 308, 312, 313, 324
Transport policy, in EU,   356
Treadmill of reforms,   415
Treaty of Rome,   331, 332-34
  provisions of,   332

U

Underground economy (*see* Second economy)
Unemployment:
  in CEE,   468, 561-62
  in China,   529, 562
  in European Union,   215-16, 371, 375
  in France,   215-16, 248, 252
  in Germany,   138, 148, 149, 154, 155
  in Hungary,   484, 516-17, 519
  in Japan,   170, 172, 210, 215-16
  and Keynes's philosophy,   155-56, 158, 159-61, 163-64
  in Marx's evaluation of capitalism,   391-93
  in Soviet Union,   154, 155, 421, 422, 423
  in Sweden,   215-16, 282, 307, 308, 309, 310, 311, 312, 313, 316, 320, 321
  in United States,   215-16
United States, evaluation of economy's performance:

1965-1988,   33-34
1993,   35
1983-1995,   36

W

Wage earner funds, in Sweden,   301
Wages:
  in China,   561, 565
  in England (LFME),   127
  in Germany,   146, 150
  in Hungary,   509, 517-18
  in medieval England,   83
  in Soviet Union,   412
  in Sweden,   318
War Communism,   400
Webb, Sydney and Beatrice,   262, 270, 276
Working rules:
  defined,   4, 5
  and evolutionary-institutional theory, 13, 14, 15-17
  as related to economy and institutions,   5, 8-10
Workweek, average:
  in Japan,   222-23
  in United States,   222-23
  in West Germany,   222-23
World Bank,   9, 26, 436, 448, 489, 512, 526

Y

Yeltsin, Boris,   416-17

Z

Zaibatsu,   170, 171, 172, 174, 179, 185, 186, 212
Zaikai,   178, 180, 181, 193, 199, 201, 227